ESSENTIAL PAPERS IN PSYCHOANALYSIS

ESSENTIAL PAPERS ON TRANSFERENCE

Aaron H. Esman, M.D.
Editor

NEW YORK UNIVERSITY PRESS
NEW YORK AND LONDON

Library of Congress Cataloging-in-Publication Data

Essential papers on transference / Aaron H. Esman, editor.
    p.   cm. — (Essential papers in psychoanalysis)
    Includes bibliographical references.
    ISBN 0–8147–2176–1 (alk. paper) — ISBN 0–8147–2177–X
    1. Transference (Psychology)   I. Esman, Aaron H.   II. Series.
RC489.T73E77   1990
616.89'17—dc20   90–30186
                                                                CIP

New York University Press books are printed on acid-free paper, and their
binding materials are chosen for strength and durability.

p   10   9   8   7   6   5   4   3   2

Contents

Introduction

Amidst the welter of competing or complementary theories that have characterized psychoanalysis over the century of its existence, the concept of transference and the conviction of its central importance in the therapeutic process appears to be a unifying theme. None of Freud's epochal discoveries —the power of the dynamic unconscious; the meaningfulness of the dream; the universality of intrapsychic conflict; the critical role of repression; the phenomena of infantile sexuality—has proved to be more heuristically productive or more clinically valuable than his demonstration that humans regularly and inevitably repeat with the analyst and with other important figures in their current lives patterns of relationship, of fantasy, and of conflict with the crucial figures in their childhood—primarily their parents.

Even for Freud, however, the awareness of this phenomenon and the understanding of its specific significance in the analytic situation itself came only gradually. The flamboyant transference events in Breuer's case of Anna O and the unfortunate outcome in the case of Dora served to consolidate in Freud's mind a view of transference as a resistance phenomenon, as an obstacle to the recollection of early traumatic events that, in his view at the time, constituted the true essence of the psychoanalytic process. Emphasis in this early period, thus, was on the "management" of the transference, on finding ways to prevent its interference with the proper business of the analysis—recognizing, always, the inevitability of its occurrence. Indeed, Freud was most concerned about the interference generated by the "negative" (i.e., hostile) and the erotized transference; the "positive" transference he considered "unobjectionable," "the vehicle of success in psycho-analysis" (33).

Freud was also concerned to distinguish the analytic transference from the effects of suggestion in the hypnotic treatment he had learned in France and that had been the forerunner of his own psychoanalytic technique. He, as well as his early followers and students, was at great pains to define the transference as a spontaneous product of the analytic situation, emerging from the patient rather than imposed by the analyst. Ultimately, Freud came to view as essential for analytic cure the development of a new mental structure, the "transference neurosis"—a re-creation of the original neurosis in the analytic situation itself, with the patient experiencing the analyst as the object of his or her infantile wishes and the focus of his or her pathogenic conflicts. The crucial importance of the transference neurosis—indeed, its very reality as a clinical phenomenon—has been and continues to be a matter of debate among psychoanalysts to this day.

Over the ensuing decades several themes appear and reappear. One to which Freud alluded is that of the uniqueness versus the ubiquity of transference; is it a special creation of the analytic situation or is it an inevitable and universal aspect of all human relations? Further, are transference phenomena always based on a repetition of past experiences or may they be newly generated by the special conditions of the analysis? More central and perhaps more heated is the continuing debate about the primacy of transference interpretation in what Strachey called the "mutative" effects of analysis—for example, whether such interpretations are simply more convincing than others or are the only kind that are truly effective therapeutically. Echoes of this debate resound through the years and are to be heard in some of the most recent literature. And finally, Are all of the patient's reactions to the analyst in the analytic situation to be construed as transference or do some partake of the "real," "non-neurotic" relationship or of the "working alliance?"

This volume seeks to present what in its editor's view are some of the central papers on the subject of transference from Freud's time to our own. Although most reflect viewpoints within the psychoanalytic mainstream, efforts have been made to be as inclusive as possible; thus neo-Freudian, Kohutian, and Lacanian statements are represented. It will become clear to the reader that the meaning, the therapeutic use, and even the theoretical explanation of transference and transference phenomena have undergone significant changes over the years. The transference has become a sort of projective device, a vessel into which each commentator pours the essence of his or her approach to the clinical situation and to the understanding of that unique interactional process that constitutes the analytic situation.

The papers reprinted here are arranged more or less chronologically. An attempt at a rigorous thematic arrangement has proved unsuccessful, since certain themes appear and reappear over time, while several authors deal with several or all in individual essays. The initial group (ca. 1909–36), that of the pioneers, demonstrates the efforts of Freud and his early followers to grasp and to deal with the powerful phenomenon they were only beginning to recognize and to attempt to understand. The middle period (ca. 1936–60) reflects the consolidation of therapeutic technique and the attempts of both

European and American analysts to bring the concept of transference into consonance with the increasingly important constructs of ego psychology. In the latest period (ca. 1960–87), we find a balance between reassertion of traditional views and various revisionist statements and reconsiderations of some of the classical positions.

THE PIONEERS (CA. 1909–1936)

As noted earlier, Freud's awareness of the actuality of transference phenomena—that is, of the development in the patient of powerful feelings and wishes toward the therapist in the "talking cure"—began when he first learned from Joseph Breuer of the events that occurred in his treatment of Anna O. It was not, however, until the debacle with Dora that the full force of this phenomenon was brought home to him—if not of his own countertransference feelings as well. Transferences are, Freud said, "new editions or facsimiles of the impulses and fantasies that are aroused and made conscious during the progress of the analysis; but they have this peculiarity . . . that they replace some earlier person by the person of the physician" (Freud 1905, 116). "Psychoanalytic treatment does not *create* transferences, it merely brings them to light like so many other hidden psychical factors" (ibid., 117, emphasis in original).

Freud did not again deal in detail with the subject of transference until 1912, in "The Dynamics of Transference." In fact, the first paper devoted specifically to the subject was Ferenczi's "Introjection and Transference," published in 1909. Ferenczi offered an exposition on the topic, drawing his stimulus from Freud's reference to "transferences" in *The Interpretation of Dreams* and the Dora case. Transference, he states, is a special case of the mechanism of displacement, is ubiquitous in life but especially pronounced in neurotics, and makes its most explicit appearance in the relationship of patient to physician — in or outside of psychoanalysis. He relates the transference to other psychic mechanisms, most particularly projection and introjection, and defends psychoanalysis against accusations of improperly generating transference reactions in its patients. "The critics who look on these transferences as dangerous should," he says, "condemn the non-analytic modes of treatment more severely than the psycho-analytic method, since the former really intensify the transferences, while the latter strives to uncover and to resolve them as soon as possible" (26).

It was not until 1912, in "The Dynamics of Transference," that Freud returned to the subject. Here he explains in terms of libido economy and in the context of the topographic model of the mind the inevitable emergence of the transference in the analytic situation and its role as a primary mode of resistance. "The transference-idea has penetrated into consciousness in front of any other possible associations *because* it satisfies the resistance" (31, emphasis on original) — but only if it is a negative or erotic transference. The analyst's role is to "control" or "remove" the transference resistance. "It is," Freud says, "on that field that the victory must be won" (35).

The problems posed by the erotic transference are further explored in "Observations on Transference-Love." Here Freud speaks systematically about the dangers of unregulated countertransference, and he admonishes his colleagues on the need to maintain analytic neutrality in the face of the patient's importunate demand for fulfillment of her erotic longings. Here he coins the much-debated aphorism, "the treatment must be carried out in abstinence" (42). He makes it clear that "transference love" is not to be dismissed as insignificant or deviant; it draws on the same infantile well-springs as the love of everyday life. It is the analyst's business to deal with it analytically rather than by gratifying or rejecting it.

Freud's illumination of the phenomenon of transference notwithstanding, little appeared in the literature bearing specifically on the topic for a number of years. It would seem that, as Strachey points out, this was due to the preoccupation of most analysts, particularly in the context of the rise of ego psychology, with the analysis of resistances and of character traits. It was, therefore, not until 1934 that the most important and, to this day, the most influential post-Freudian contribution to the analysis of transference appeared — Strachey's "Nature of the Therapeutic Action of Psycho-Analysis." Strongly reflecting the influence of Melanie Klein, Strachey outlines the notion that the central analytic task is the resolution of archaic superego elements in the structure of the mind, and that the definitive instrument for effecting this is what he terms "mutative interpretation." Such an interpretation must, he says, "be emotionally 'immediate' " and "directed to the 'point of urgency' " (69); "the point of urgency is nearly always to be found in the transference" (73). Therefore, only transference interpretations are likely to be mutative. As will be seen, the reverberations of this shot are still being heard today.

Freud's early view of the transference as a resistance to the analytic work was echoed and exemplified by Sterba, in his report of a case that obviously derived from his European experiences (for example, the description of goose stuffing). Here he spells out technical measures for the dissolution of such resistances, which include explanations along the lines that "the hostility towards his father . . . could not be analyzed if he developed the unconscious hostility and consequent anxiety towards the analyst that he formerly had for his father" (86). In other words, the transference was essentially enjoined, rather than analyzed, by appealing to what Sterba came to call the "observing ego," as opposed to the "experiencing ego."

Among the first to apply psychoanalytic principles outside the consulting room was August Aichhorn. Trained as an educator, Aichhorn undertook to work with delinquent adolescents in Vienna and established the first therapeutic school based on psychoanalytic principles; in this setting, he became the mentor for a generation of child analysts, including Erikson, Blos, Ekstein, Redl, and others. In his classic text, *Wayward Youth,* Aichhorn demonstrated some of the extraordinary techniques he devised for treating dissocial adolescents — in particular, ways of manipulating the transference in order to establish a positive relationship at the outset of treatment (in his view, a *sine qua non* for such work).

The appearance in 1936 of Anna Freud's *The Ego and the Mechanisms of Defense* represented a landmark in the evolution of psychoanalytic theory and technique. Ms. Freud's detailed codification of the defensive apparatus and her emphasis on the necessity of analyzing not merely the *id* elements but also the *ego* elements of the mind signaled major changes in the way analysts thought about and carried on their clinical work. Nonetheless, her observations on the role of transference analysis, trenchant as they were, remain within the framework of the traditional view of transference phenomena as "repetitions and not new creations." The function of the analysis of transference is to put the "transferred affective impulse . . . back into its place in the past" (111). Ms. Freud drew the valuable distinction among the transference of "libidinal" impulses, the transference of defense, and acting in the transference. Her contribution emphasized the critical value of the analysis of defense transference, which, as she explained, is far more difficult than that of transferred drive impulses because the patient experiences it as ego-syntonic.

The dominant trend in early discussions was the presumption that the transference is an "autogenous" product of the patient induced, no doubt, by the special character of the analytic situation but emerging out of the patient's own needs and unfulfilled infantile wishes. Bibring-Lehner (later in the United States, simply Bibring) was one of the first to suggest that particular characteristics of the analyst or of his or her behavior can so shape the emerging transference as to create an impenetrable resistance that might necessitate a change of analyst. In particular, Bibring-Lehner addressed the matter of the sex of the analyst, but clearly other factors might suffice to blur the patient's distinction between transference and reality and thus to create an unanalyzable stalemate. She spoke, too, of the necessity of a "predominantly positive transference based on confidence, without whose help we cannot overcome the transference-neurosis" (121); this clearly prefigures the concept of the "therapeutic" or "working" alliance that later becomes a focus on controversy.

THE MIDDLE PERIOD (CA. 1936–1960)

The concerns of those who contributed to the ongoing discussion of transference and its place in analytic theory and technique during this period were to relate its phenomenology to the growing understanding of the ego, both in its defensive and (in Hartmann's terms) "autonomous" aspects, to new theories of early development and to a growing concern in some quarters with "interpersonal" as opposed to purely "intrapsychic" aspects of personality function. A further stimulus was Alexander's (1946) advocacy of active role playing by the analyst in order to provide the patient with a "corrective emotional experience," at least in psychoanalytic psychotherapy if not in analysis proper.

In her very practically oriented paper, Greenacre emphasizes the distinction, first stated by Freud, between the analytic transference and that which characterizes other modes of therapy. All manipulation, exploitation, all use of transference for "corrective emotional experience" is excluded from the psychoanalytic situation, which relies exclusively on interpretation to achieve its therapeutic goal. Greenacre's view of the analyst's role in analysis as well as in the world outside is a relatively austere one; she would preclude the analyst from publicly participating in social or political activities that might tend to reveal aspects of the analyst's person that would contaminate the transference. Like Freud, Stone, and others she distinguishes between a "basic," essentially nonconflictual transference derived from the early mother-child relationship and the analytic transference proper, which involves projection onto the analyst of unconscious conflictual material. As will be seen, others (for example, Brenner) challenge this distinction.

It is, however, echoed in Elizabeth Zetzel's masterful review of what were, at the time of writing, the dominant trends in the field. She proposed, following the usage of Edward Bibring, the concept of the "therapeutic alliance," derived, as was Greenacre's "basic transference," from the positive aspects of the mother-child relationship. Like virtually all other commentators she asserted the centrality of transference interpretation in the analytic process, but she outlines in sharp detail some of the differences in form and content of such interpretations between Freudian and Kleinian analysts—that is, between those who are concerned with the role of the ego and the analysis of defense and those who emphasize the importance of early object relations and primitive instinctual fantasy.

Like Greenacre and Zetzel, Greenson distinguishes between what he calls the "working alliance" and the "transference neurosis." He contends that without the development of the former the latter cannot be analyzed effectively. The "working alliance" depends not only on the patient's capacity to establish adequate object ties and to assess reality but also on the analyst's assumption of an attitude that permits such an alliance to emerge. Thus, Greenson advocates an analytic stance that, while adhering to the rule of abstinence, allows for more "realistic" gratifications and a less austere stance than Greenacre would encourage. Greenson's definition of transference—that it always represents a repetition of past experience and that it is always "inappropriate to the present"—will later be challenged by Gill, who contends that transference reactions may well be appropriate responses to aspects of the psychoanalytic situation of which both patient and analyst are not necessarily aware.

In striking contrast to these views, Brenner categorically rejects the notions of "therapeutic" and "working" alliances as distinct from the analytic transference, and with them the admonition to the analyst to be "human" or "empathic" in order to encourage such states. In his view, "both refer to aspects of the transference that neither deserve a special name nor require special treatment" (156). "In analysis," he says, "it is best for the patient if one approaches *everything* analytically. It is as important to understand why a patient is closely 'allied' with his analyst . . . as it is to understand why there seems to be no 'alliance' at all" (182, emphasis in original).

In an extremely thoughtful, systematic exploration of the topic, Macalpine argues that transference is induced in patients by the infantile situation in which the analysis, by its very nature, places them. As do hypnotic subjects, analysands adapt by regression and, if they are predisposed to do so, will experience the present in terms of their infantile past. What distinguishes analysis from hypnosis is the nonparticipation of the analyst in the process—

that is, the analyst's avoidance, by the management of his or her counter-transference, of active suggestion. "The analytic transference relationship ought, strictly speaking, not to be referred to as a relationship between analysand and analyst, but more precisely as the analysand's relation to his analyst" (216). In this Macalpine stands apart from more recent object relations theorists who stress the mutual dyadic aspect of the analytic situation.

Nunberg, too, analogizes the analytic situation to that of hypnosis, in its induction of a regressive state in which the patient submits to the analyst's implicit parental power and authority. The patient then projects onto the analyst his or her unconscious representation of the parent, seeking to achieve an "identity of perception" between the two images. Primarily it is the superego, he contends, that is thus projected, and it is through the analysis of these projections that the patient is enabled to deal more effectively with reality. (One must note in passing the androcentric note in Nunberg's tendency to denote the source of the superego as exclusively "the father" and the transference projection as that of the "father image.")

Melanie Klein's approach to the transference is rooted, of course, in her conception of the developmental process and the role of early object relations, which, she maintains, exist from the beginning of life. The transference represents a displacement not only of actual aspects of parents but also of split-off projected and introjected part-object representations from early infancy — persecutory "bad" objects or benevolent "good" ones. Like Gill, Klein both emphasizes the importance of attending to and interpreting subtle or disguised references to the analyst and maintains the therapeutic necessity of relating all associative content to transference fantasies and wishes, with special emphasis on the negative transference. (Another lucid exposition of the Kleinian approach to the transference is that of Paula Heimann [1956].)

Under the influence of Mrs. Klein many British analysts, D. W. Winnicott among them, have undertaken to analyze patients with what Americans would speak of as severe ego disturbances — borderline and psychotic in nature. Winnicott's approach to the handling of transferences in such patients emerged from his developmental concepts — in particular, his stress on the crucial significance of "good enough mothering" and his constructs of "true" and "false" self (Winnicott 1960). He contends that, in work with such patients, "the setting [of the analysis] becomes more important than the interpretation" (248) and that the analyst must provide a "good enough adaptation" to the patient's needs. These ideas appear to be closely related to Kohut's emphasis on the role of "empathy" in the treatment of narcissistic disorders and to Zetzel's ideas about the "therapeutic alliance." (It should be noted that Zetzel underwent a period of training in the British school.)

The "Sullivanian," or "interpersonal," school of analysis is represented in the paper of Janet Rioch. It is of interest to note that, written in 1943, this essay anticipates a number of themes that will emerge later in "mainstream" analytic thought. In particular Rioch observes that, just as the person's characteristic modes of relating to others develop in interaction with parents, transference phenomena will emerge in large part in reaction to the characteristics of the analyst, rather than as automatic and internally driven repetitions. In her emphasis on the role of the analyst in evoking transference responses, she prefigures the views of Merton Gill. Similarly, in her statement that in analysis the patient "discovers that part of himself which had to be repressed at the time of the original experience" (258) she appears to anticipate Winnicott's ideas about "true" and "false" selves.

Freud distinguished between the "transference neuroses" and the "narcissistic neuroses," which included schizophrenia. He contended that patients in the latter group did not establish transferences and thus were inaccessible to psychoanalytic therapy. Like Winnicott, Fromm-Reichmann, from her experience with schizophrenics at Chestnut Lodge, challenges this dictum. Though clearly not adaptable to the conventional analytic situation, such patients do, she contends, form intense transference reactions and are susceptible to analytically informed, though often unorthodox, therapeutic interventions. Though many would question the ultimate effectiveness of such therapy today (McGlashan 1984), Fromm-Reichmann's descriptions of her special techniques for establishing contact with persons in profound states of narcissistic regression and for understanding their transference reactions are impressive and are still of value.

THE MODERN PERIOD (CA. 1960–1987)

Recent decades have witnessed a resurgence of interest in the transference in all its aspects—theoretical and technical. Stimulated by new analytic perspectives both in Europe and in the United States and by influences stemming from linguistics and philosophy, a number of commentators have sought to reconsider traditional viewpoints and to accommodate new observational data.

In his long, densely written paper Stone undertakes a comprehensive statement of his views on the varied aspects of the transference from developmental and clinical perspectives. In particular, he sets forth a distinction between the "primordial" and the "mature" transference "from which", he says, "the various clinical and demonstrable forms are derived." Where the "primordial" transference is "derived from the effort to master the series of crucial separations from the mother" (284), the mature transference "encompasses . . . the wish to understand, and to be understood" and "in its peak development . . . the wish for increasingly accurate interpretations" (297–98). The "mature" transference draws then on autonomous ego functions and is a "dynamic and integral part of the 'therapeutic alliance' " (299). Stone also deals *in extenso* with the Stracheyan question of the special "mutative" value of transference interpretation. While not devaluing these, he argues persuasively for the importance of the patient's real life experiences and the analytic value of interpretations related to them.

One of the most forceful statements of the centrality of the transference to the analytic experience is that of Brian Bird. In his view, there is something unique about the analytic transference; indeed, for him, everything that occurs in the analysis on the part of both patient and analyst partakes of transference elements. But for Bird, what is essential for the therapeutic effect is not merely the analysis of transference "feeling" but the evolution and analysis of a full-blown transference neurosis. And, he asserts, the quintessence of the transference neurosis is an analytic stalemate, in which an intrapsychic conflict has been replaced by an interpersonal one involving the patient and a split-off aspect of his or her neurosis that has been assigned to the analyst. It is in the interpretation and resolution of such stalemates—including a rigorous analysis of the patient's hostile, destructive wishes—that the true work and the "hardest part" of analysis goes on.

Gill, in basic agreement, carries the argument even further. He distinguishes between the patient's resistance to awareness of transference and the resistance to the resolution of the transference. It is the former, where transference experiences are largely unconscious and ego-syntonic, that is the more difficult; and it is the analyst's task to allow the transference to evolve and flourish so that the patient can be made aware of it. In order to do so, the analyst must be alert to and interpret indirect and veiled allusions to the transference and, further, seek out those elements of the analytic situation, including the analyst's own behaviors, that serve as the "day-residue" for such transference responses. Gill strongly advocates a focus on the here-and-now factors, allowing genetic determinants to emerge on their own rather than interpreting them.

As noted earlier, the distinction between what has been called the "basic" transference, or the "therapeutic alliance" or the "working alliance," on the one hand and the analytic transference or transference neurosis on the other has been a staple of controversy. Stein, reflecting on Freud's term "the unobjectionable part of the transference," takes issue with this distinction, insisting, like Brenner, that there is no difference in principle among all these aspects of the totality of transference phenomena. He cautions against the practice of leaving the "unobjectionable" or "basic" transferences unanalyzed; they are, he says, "the manifest resultant of a complex web of unconscious conflicts which must be, and are capable of being, sought for and described" (399). The assumption that they are to be understood as rooted merely in early infant development is, he believes, unwarranted.

In the context of his reassessment of basic psychoanalytic concepts, Schafer, influenced by British analytic philosophy, provides a revised view of transference and transference interpretation — in particular, of the character of transference as "repetition." As Schafer sees it, transference experiences are new ones, created by the analytic situation; and it is the act of analytic interpretation that constitutes them as repetitions. More properly they can be seen as metaphoric communications; thus, "they represent movement forward, not backward" (419). Interpretation does not merely recover or uncover old meanings; it creates new meanings that help the patient to make sense — *psychoanalytic* sense — of his or her life and modes of relating to others. Transference, Schafer says, is "the emotional experiencing of the past *as it is now remembered*" (418–19, emphasis in original), not as it "really" happened.

Loewald considers the status of the transference neurosis in the setting of contemporary practice, in which the modal patient suffers from a character neurosis rather than from the "classical" symptom neuroses of an earlier era. Given the more diffuse developmental etiology of the character disturbances, transference manifestations tend to be less defined and less focused; indeed, a transference neurosis in the classical sense may not appear at all. Thus, "transference neurosis is not so much an entity to be found in the patient, but an operational concept . . . a creature of the analytic situation (429). Even where a full-blown transference neurosis does not develop, however, much can be accomplished. "The repercussions of what has occurred,'' Loewald states, ''may turn out to be deeper and more far-reaching than anticipated'' (433).

Strachey's pivotal advocacy of the exclusively ''mutative'' value of trans- ference interpretation has led to one of the major controversies in the litera- ture. In its extreme form, the position taken was not only that transference interpretations were crucial but that interpretations addressed to extratransfer- ential experiences were in principle ineffective and useless. Leites, a noncli- nician, surveys the literature in order to argue strongly for the other side— for the view, that is, that the analysis of current and past experiences with others can be as effective and meaningful as can the unifocal address to the transference. Without minimizing the special impact of transference interpre- tations, Leites seeks to undo the dogmatism and rigidity he sees inherent in what he refers to as ''Strachey's Law.''

In the evolution of what came to be his ''psychology of the self,'' Heinz Kohut demarcated a typology of transference reactions that were, in his view, characteristic of patients with narcissistic personality disorders. These, the ''idealizing'' and ''mirror'' transferences, reflected specific types of depri- vation in early parent-child interactions that generated a persistent need for special types of what he came to call ''self-object'' attachments—in and out of the analytic situation. Kohut's meticulous descriptions of these transfer- ence phenomena and of their analytic management were a source of stimula- tion and instruction to many analysts, even to those who were unwilling to follow some of the later developments in his theoretical and technical think- ing. (Readers will note a significant relationship between some of Kohut's ideas and those of Winnicott and other members of the British school.)

Of recent commentators, perhaps the most gnomic, the least penetrable, and certainly the most devoted to paradox was Jacques Lacan. His discus- sions of the transference, like much of his theoretical commentaries, are scattered through his writings and the recorded text of his lectures; the one more or less organized statement on the subject is reproduced here. In it, he takes exception to what he regards as the ''American'' concept of appealing, through the therapeutic alliance, to the ''mature'' portion of the ego or (anathema to him) the ''autonomous functions.'' Lacan does share the gen- eral view that the transference is central to the analytic experience and seems to echo Freud in conceiving it primarily as a resistance—as a ''closing up'' of the unconscious. His discussion is characterized by obscurity and linguistic play and leaves one uncertain as to his actual technical approach, but the central thread of his focus on language as the basic element in the structure

of mental life—"the unconscious is structured like a language"—is e
itly maintained in this text (Lacan 1978, 20).

Kernberg's reflections on the transference are couched in the content¹ ⸜
his "ego psychological–object relations" theoretical framework. Though
sharing the recent emphasis on here-and-now aspects of transference interpretation, he regards the links with infantile precursors, conceived in terms of
early internalized object relations, as essential. He urges openness of mind
and tolerance of uncertainty, however, rather than imposing on the patient
preconceived ideas about etiology and pathogenesis. In particular, he dis-
tances himself from what he regards as the restrictive concepts of "self-
psychology," especially regarding the role of aggression. Further, while
attending closely to all aspects of communication in the session, Kernberg
aligns himself with those who regard both extra-analytic and intra-analytic
experience as valid material for interpretation.

It should be evident that the alternative views of transference as a repetition of infantile experience and as a new creation in the setting of the analytic
situation have formed the basis of a continuing debate from the earliest years.
In his assessment of current ideas of transference interpretation, Cooper
refers to these respectively as the "historical" and the "modernist" views,
attributing recent interest in the latter position to changing philosophical
concepts of reality and the rise to prominence of object relations theories in
analysis. Cooper comes down squarely for the "modernist" view, maintaining, like Gill, that the actuality of the analyst's person and behavior are
powerful determinants of the patient's transference reactions and must be
accorded attention at least equal to that given to recalled or reconstructed
infantile determinants. He opts, that is, for a "synchronic" rather than a
"diachronic" view of the transference and like Spence (1982), Schafer
(1983), and others questions the possibility of re-creating from the analysis
of the transference or from anything else a "true" version of the life history.

REFERENCES

Alexander, F., and French. T. 1946. *Psychoanalytic therapy.* New York: Norton.
Freud, S. 1905. Fragment of the analysis of a case of hysteria. *Std. Edn.* 7:3–124.
Heimann, P. 1956. Dynamics of transference interpretations. *Int. J. Psycho-Anal.* 37:303–10.
Lacan, J. 1978. *The four fundamental concepts of psychoanalysis.* Edited by J. A. Miller. New York: Norton.
McGlashan, T. 1984. The Chestnut Lodge follow-up study. Part 2. Long-term outcome of schizophrenia and the affective disorders. *Arch. Gen. Psychiat.* 41:586–601.

Schafer, R. 1983. "Psychoanalytic reconstruction." In *The analytic attitude*, 193–203. New York: Basic Books.

Spence, D. 1982. *Narrative truth and historical truth: Meaning and interpretation in psychoanalysis*. New York: Norton.

Winnicott, D. 1960. "Ego distortion in terms of true and false self." In *The maturational processes and the facilitating environment*, 140–52. New York: International Universities Press.

1. Introjection and Transference

Sandor Ferenczi

I. INTROJECTION IN THE NEUROSES

The productivity of the neurosis (during a course of psycho-analytic treatment) is far from being extinguished, but exercises itself in the creation of a peculiar sort of thought-formation, mostly unconscious, to which the name 'transferences' may be given.

"These transferences are re-impressions and reproductions of the emotions and phantasies that have to be awakened and brought into consciousness during the progress of the analysis, and are characterised by the replacement of a former person by the physician."

In these sentences Freud announced, in the masterly description of a hysterical case,[1] one of his most significant discoveries.

Whoever since then, following Freud's indications, has tried to investigate psycho-analytically the mental life of neurotics, must have become convinced of the truth of this observation. The greatest difficulties of such an analysis, indeed, proceed from the remarkable peculiarity of neurotics that "in order to avoid insight into their own unconscious, they transfer to the physician treating them all their affects (hate, love) that have been reinforced from the unconscious."[2]

When, however, one becomes more familiar with the workings of the neurotic mind, one recognises that the psychoneurotic's inclination to transference expresses itself not only in the special case of a psycho-analytic treatment, and not only in regard to the physician, but that *transference is a psychical mechanism that is characteristic of the neurosis altogether, one that is evidenced in all situations of life, and which underlies most of the pathological manifestations.*

With increasing experience one becomes convinced that the apparently motiveless extravagance of affect, the excessive hate, love and sympathy of neurotics, are also nothing else than transferences, by means of which long

Reprinted from Sandor Ferenczi, *Sex in Psychoanalysis* (New York: Basic Books, 1909), 35–57.

forgotten psychical experiences are (in the unconscious phantasy) brought into connection with the current occasion, and the current reaction exaggerated by the affect of unconscious ideational complexes. The tendency of hysterical patients to use exaggeration in the expression of their emotions has long been known, and often ridiculed. Freud has shown us that it is rather we physicians who deserve the ridicule, because failing to understand the symbolism of hysterical symptoms—the language of hysteria, so to speak—we have either looked upon these symptoms as implying simulation, or fancied we had settled them by the use of abstruse physiological terms. It was Freud's *psychological* conception of hysterical symptoms and character traits that first really disclosed the neurotic mind. Thus he found that the inclination of psychoneurotics to *imitation,* and the *"psychical infection"* so frequent among hysterics, are not simple automatisms, but find their explanation in unconscious pretensions and wishes, which the patient does not confess even to himself, and which are incapable of becoming conscious. The patient copies the symptoms or character traits of a person when "on the basis of an identical aetiological claim" he *identifies* himself in his unconscious with him.[3] The well-known impressionability also of many neurotics, their capacity to feel in the most intense way for the experiences of others, to put themselves in the place of a third person, finds its explanation in hysterical identification; and their impulsive philanthropic and magnanimous deeds are only reactions to these unconscious instigations—are therefore in the last analysis egoistic actions governed by the "unpleasantness (*Unlust*) principle." The fact that every sort of humanitarian or reform movement, the propaganda of abstinence (vegetarianism, anti-alcoholism, abolitionism), revolutionary organisations and sects, conspiracies for or against the religious, political, or moral order, teem with neuropaths is similarly to be explained by the transference of interest from censored egoistic (erotic or violent) tendencies of the unconscious on to fields where they can work themselves out without any self-reproach. The daily occurrences of a simple civic life also, however, offer neurotics the richest opportunity for the displacement on to permissible fields of impulses that are incapable of being conscious. An example of this is the unconscious identification of grossly sexual genital functions with those of the oral organs (eating, kissing), as was first established by Freud. In a number of analyses I have been able to prove that the partiality of hysterics for dainty feeding, their inclination to eat indigestible material (chalk, unripe fruit, etc.), their peculiar search for exotic dishes, their preference or idiosyncrasy in regard to food of a certain form or consistency, that all this was concerned with the displacement of interest from repressed erotic (genital or coprophilic) inclinations, and was an indication of a lack of sexual satisfaction. (The well-known manias of pregnant women also, which, by the way, I have observed with non-pregnant women as well at the menstrual time, I have many times been able to trace to insufficient satisfactions, relative to the increased ''sexual hunger.'') Otto Gross and Stekel found a similar cause with hysterical kleptomania.

I am aware that in the examples brought forward I have confounded the expressions *Displacement* and *Transference*. Transference, however, is only a special case of the neurotic's inclination to displacement; in order to escape from complexes that are unpleasant, and hence have become unconscious, he is forced to meet the persons and things of the outer world with exaggerated interest (love, hate, passionate manias, idiosyncrasy) on the basis of the most superficial ''aetiological pretensions'' and analogies.

A course of psycho-analytic treatment offers the most favourable conditions for the occurrence of such a transference. The impulses that have been repressed, and are gradually becoming conscious, first meet *''in statu nascendi''* the person of the physician, and seek to link their unsatisfied valencies to his personality. If we pursued this comparison taken from chemistry we might conceive of psycho-analysis, so far as the transference is concerned, as a kind of *catalysis*. The person of the physician has here the effect of a catalytic ferment that temporarily attracts to itself the affects split off by the dissection. In a technically correct psycho-analysis, however, the bond thus formed is only a loose one, the interest of the patient being led back as soon as possible to its original, covered-over sources and brought into permanent connection with them.

What slight and trivial motives suffice with neurotics for the transference of affects is indicated in the quoted work of Freud. We may add a few characteristic examples. A hysterical patient with very strong sexual repression betrayed first in a dream the transference to the physician. (I, the physician, am operating on her nose, and she is wearing a frisure à la Cléo de Mérode.) Whoever has already analytically interpreted dreams will readily believe that in this dream, as well also as in the unconscious waking thought, I have taken the place of the rhinologist who once made improper advances to the patient; the frisure of the well-known demi-mondaine is too plain a hint of this. Whenever the physician appears in the patient's dreams the analysis discovers with certainty signs of transference. Stekel's book on anxiety states[4] has many pretty examples of this. The case just mentioned, however, is also typical in another way. Patients very often use the opportunity to revive all the sexual excitations they have previously noticed and repressed during medical examinations (in unconscious phantasies about undressing and being percussed, palpated, and "operated on"), and to replace in the unconscious the previous physicians in question by the person of the present one. One need only be a physician to become the object of this kind of transference; the mystical part played in the sexual phantasy of the child by the doctor, who knows all forbidden things, who may look at and touch everything that is concealed, is an obvious determining factor in unconscious fancying, and therefore also in the transference occurring in a subsequent neurosis.[5]

With the extraordinary significance that attaches (according to Freud's conclusion which is confirmed daily) to the repressed "Oedipus-complex" (hate and love towards the parents) in every case of neurosis, one is not surprised that the "paternal" air, the friendly and indulgent manner, with which the physician has to meet the patient in psycho-analysis gets so frequently used as a bridge to the transference of conscious feelings of sympathy and unconscious erotic phantasies, the original objects of which were the parents. The physician is always one of the "revenants" (Freud) in whom the neurotic patient hopes to find again the vanished figures of childhood. Nevertheless, one less friendly remark, reminding him of a duty or of punctuality, or a tone that is only a *nuance* sharper than usual, on the part of the analysing physician is sufficient to make him incur all the patient's hate and anger that is directed against moralising persons who demand respect (parent, husband).

The ascertaining of such transferences of positive and negative effects is exceedingly important for the analysis, for neurotics are mostly persons who believe themselves incapable either of loving or of hating (often denying to themselves even the most primitive knowledge about sexuality); they are therefore either anaesthetic or else good to a fault, and nothing is more suited to shatter their erroneous belief in their own lack of feeling and angelic goodness than having their contrary feeling-currents detected and exposed *in flagranti*. The transferences are still more important as points of departure for the continuation of the analysis in the direction of the more deeply repressed thought-complexes.

Ridiculously slight resemblances also: the colour of the hair, facial traits, a gesture of the physician, the way in which he holds a cigarette or a pen, the identity or the similarity in sound of the Christian name with that of some person who has been significant to the patient; even such distant analogies as these are sufficient to establish the transference. The fact that a transference on the ground of such petty analogies strikes us as ridiculous reminds me that Freud in a category of wit showed the "presentation by means of a detail" to be the agent that sets free the pleasure, *i.e.* reinforces it from the unconscious; in all dreams also we find similar allusions to things, persons, and events by the help of minimal details. The poetical figure "pars pro toto" is thus quite current in the language of the unconscious.

The sex of the physician is in itself a much-used bridge for the transference. Female patients very often attach their unconscious heterosexual phantasies to the fact that the physician is a man; this gives them the possibility of reviving the repressed complexes that are associated with the idea of masculinity. Still the homosexual component that is hidden in everyone sees to it that men also seek to transfer to the physician their "sympathy" and friendship—or the contrary. It is enough, however, that something in the physician seems to the patient to be "feminine" for women to bring their homosexual, and men their heterosexual interests, or their aversion that is related to this, into connection with the person of the physician.

In a number of cases I succeeded in demonstrating that the relaxation of the ethical censor in the physician's consulting room was partly determined by the lessened feeling of responsibility on the patient's part. The consciousness that the physician is responsible for everything that happens (in his own room) favours the emergence of day-dreams, first unconscious, later becoming conscious, which very often have as their subject a violent sexual assault on the part of the physician and then mostly end with the exemplary punishment of such a villain (his being sentenced, publicly degraded through newspaper articles, shot in a duel, etc.). It is just in this sort of moral disguise that the repressed wishes of people can become conscious. As another motive lessening the feeling of responsibility I recognised in a patient the idea that "the doctor can do everything," by which she understood the operative removal of any possible consequences of a *liaison*.

In the analysis the patients have to communicate all these lewd plans, just as everything else that occurs to them. In the non-analytic treatment of neurotics all this remains unknown to the physician, and as a result the phantasies sometimes attain an almost hallucinatory character and may end in a public or legal calumny.

The circumstance that other persons also are being treated psychotherapeutically allows the patients to indulge without any, or with very little, self-reproach the affects of jealousy, envy, hate, and violence that are hidden in their unconscious. Naturally the patient has then in the analysis to detach these "inadequate"[6] feeling-impulses also from the current inciting cause, and associate them with much more significant personalities and situations. The same holds good for the more or less conscious thought-processes and feeling-impulses that have their starting-point in the financial contract between the patient and physician. In this way many "magnanimous," "generous" people have to see and admit in the analysis that the feelings of avarice, of ruthless selfishness, and of ignoble covetousness are not quite so foreign to them as they had previously liked to believe. (Freud is accustomed to say, "People treat money questions with the same mendacity as they do sexual ones. In the analysis both have to be discussed with the same frankness.") That the money complex, transferred to the treatment, is often only the cover for much more deeply hidden impulses Freud has established in a masterly characterological study ("Charakter und Analerotik").

When we bear in mind these different varieties of the transference to the physician, we become decidedly strengthened in our assumption that this is only one manifestation, although in a practical way the most important one, of the general neurotic *passion for transference*. This passion, or mania, we may regard as the most fundamental peculiarity of the neuroses, and also that which goes most to explain their conversion and substitution symptoms. All neurotics suffer from *flight from their complexes;* they take flight into illness, as Freud says, from the pleasure that has become disagreeable; that is to say, they withdraw the "sexual hunger" from certain ideational complexes that were formerly charged with pleasantness. When the withdrawal of "sexual hunger" is less complete, the interest for what formerly was loved or hated disappears, being succeeded by indifference; if the detachment of the "sexual hunger" is more complete, then the censor does not let pass even the slight degree of interest necessary for the exercising of attention—the complex becomes "repressed," "forgotten," and incapable of being conscious. It would seem, however, as though the mind did not easily tolerate "sexual hunger" that has been released from its complex, and is thus "free-floating." In the anxiety neurosis, as Freud has shown, the deviation of the somatic sexual excitation from the psychical field converts the pleasure into anxiety. In the psychoneuroses we have to presuppose a similar alteration; here *the deviation of the psychosexual hunger from certain ideational complexes causes a sort of lasting unrest,* which the patient tries to mitigate as much as possible. He manages also to neutralise a greater or less part by the way of conversion (hysteria) or of substitution (obsessional neurosis). It seems, however, as if this bond were scarcely ever an absolute one, so that a variable amount of free-floating and complex-escaping excitation remains over, which seeks satisfaction from external objects. The idea of this excitation could be used to explain the neurotic passion for transference, and be made responsible for the "manias" of the neurotic. (In the *petite hystérie* these manias seem to constitute the essence of the disease.)

To understand better the fundamental character of neurotics one has to compare their behaviour with that of patients suffering from dementia praecox and paranoia. The dement completely detaches his interest from the outer world and becomes auto-erotic (Jung,[7] Abraham[8]). The paranoiac, as Freud has pointed out, would like to do the same, but cannot, and so projects on to the outer world the interest that has become a burden to him. The neurosis stands in this respect in a diametrical contrast to paranoia. Whereas the paranoiac expels from his ego the impulses that have become unpleasant, the neurotic helps himself by taking into the ego as large as possible a part of the outer world, making it the object of unconscious phantasies. This is a kind of diluting process, by means of which he tries to mitigate the poignancy of free-floating, unsatisfied, and unsatisfiable, unconscious wish-impulses. One might give to this process, in contrast to projection, the name of *Introjection*.

The neurotic is constantly seeking for objects with whom he can identify himself, to whom he can transfer feelings, whom he can thus draw into his circle of interest, *i.e.* introject. We see the paranoiac on a similar search for objects who might be suitable for the projection of "sexual hunger" that is creating unpleasant feeling. So finally there appear the opposite characters of the large-hearted, impressionable, excitable neurotic, easily flaming up with love of all the world or provoked to hate of all the world, and that of the narrow-souled, suspicious paranoiac, who thinks he is being observed, persecuted, or loved by the whole world. The psychoneurotic suffers from a widening, the paranoic from a shrinking of his ego.

When we revise the ontogenesis of the ego-consciousness on the basis of the new knowledge, we come to the conclusion that the paranoiac projection and the neurotic introjection are merely extreme cases of psychical processes the primary forms of which are to be demonstrated in every normal being.

We may suppose that to the new-born child everything perceived by the senses appears unitary, so to speak monistic. Only later does he learn to distinguish from his ego the malicious things, forming an outer world, that do not obey his will. That would be the first projection process, the primordial projection, and the later paranoiac probably makes use of the path thus traced out, in order to expel still more of his ego into the outer world.

A part of the outer world, however, greater or less, is not so easily cast off from the ego, but continually obtrudes itself again on the latter, challenging it, so to speak; "Fight with me or be my friend" (Wagner, Götterdämmerung, Act I). If the individual has unsettled affects at his disposal, and these he soon has, he accepts this challenge by extending his "interest" from the ego on to the part of the outer world. The first loving and hating is a transference of auto-erotic pleasant and unpleasant feelings on to the objects that evoke those feelings. The first "object-love" and the first "object-hate" are, so to speak, the primordial transferences, the roots of every future introjection.

Freud's discoveries in the field of psychopathology of everyday life convince us that the capacity for projection and displacement is present also in normal human beings, and often overshoots the mark. Further, the way in which civilised man adjusts his ego to the world, his philosophic and religious metaphysics, is according to Freud only metapsychology, for the most part a projection of feeling-impulses into the outer world. Probably, however, besides projection introjection is significant for man's view of the world. The extensive part played in mythology by the anthropomorphising of lifeless objects seems to speaks in favour of this idea. Kleinpaul's able work on the development of speech,[9] to the psychological significance of which Abraham[10] has called attention, shows convincingly how man succeeds in representing the whole audible and inaudible environment by means of the ego, no form of projection and introjection remaining untried thereby. The way in which in the formation of speech a series of human sounds and noises gets identified with an object on the ground of the most superficial acoustic analogy, and of the slightest "aetiological claim," reminds one strongly of the neurotic transference-bridges mentioned above.

The neurotic thus makes use of a path that is much frequented by the normal as well when he seeks to mollify the free-floating affects by extension of his circle of interest, i.e. by introjection, and when, so as to be able to keep unconscious various affective connections with certain objects that concern him nearly, he lavishes his affects on all possible objects that do not concern him.

In analysing a neurotic one often succeeds in tracing out historically this extension of the circle of interest. Thus I had a patient who was reminded of sexual events of childhood by reading a novel and thereupon produced a phobia of novels, which later extended to books altogether, and finally to everything in print. The flight from a tendency to masturbate caused in one of my obsessional patients a phobia of privies (where he used to indulge this tendency); later there developed from this a claustrophobia, fear of being alone in any closed space. I have been able to show that psychical impotence in very many cases is conditioned by the transference to all women of the respect for the mother or sister. With a painter the pleasure of gazing at objects, and with this the choice of his profession, proved to be a "replacement" for objects that as a child he might not look at.

In the association investigations carried out by Jung[11] we can find the experimental confirmation of this inclination of neurotics to introjection. What is characteristic for the neurosis Jung designates as the relatively high number of "complex-reactions": the stimulus-words are interpreted by the neurotic "in terms of his complex." The healthy person responds quickly with an indifferent reaction-word that is associated by either the content or the sound. With the neurotic the unsatisfied affects seize on the stimulus-word and seek to exploit it in their own sense, for which the most indirect association is good enough. *Thus it is not that the stimulus-words evoke the complicated reaction, but that the stimulus-hungry affects of neurotics come to meet them.* Applying the newly coined word, one may say that *the neurotic "introjects" the stimulus-words of the experiment.*

The objection will be raised that extension of the circle of interest, identifying of oneself with many people—indeed with the whole human race—, and sensitiveness for the stimuli of the outer world, are attributes with which normal persons also, and especially the most distinguished representatives of the race, are endowed; that one cannot, therefore, designate introjection as the psychical mechanism that is typical and characteristic of the neuroses. Against this objection must be brought the knowledge that the fundamental differences, assumed before Freud's time, between normal and psychoneurotic do not exist. Freud showed us that "the neuroses have no special psychical content that is peculiar to them and occurs only in them," and according to Jung's statement, neurotics suffer from complexes with which we all fight. The difference between the two is only quantitative and of practical import. The healthy person transfers his affects and identifies himself on the basis of "aetiological claims" that have a much better motive than in the case of the neurotic, and thus does not dissipate his psychical energies so foolishly as the latter does.

Another difference, to the cardinal importance of which Freud has called attention, is that the healthy person is conscious of the greater part of his introjection, whereas with the neurotic this remains for the most part repressed, finds expression in *unconscious* phantasies, and becomes manifest to the expert only indirectly, symbolically. It very often appears in the form of "reaction-formations," as an excessive accentuation in consciousness of a current of feeling that is the opposite of the unconscious one.

The fact that the pre-Freudian literature contained nothing of all these matters, of transferences to the physician, of introjections—*ça ne les empê-chait pas d'exister*. With this remark I consider answered also those critics who repudiate the positive results of psycho-analysis as not even worthy of being re-examined, but who readily accept our estimate, on which we insist, of the difficulties of this method of investigation, and use it as a weapon against the new movement. Thus I have come across among others the curious objection that psycho-analysis is dangerous because it brings about transferences to the physician, where significantly enough there was never any talk of the negative transferences,[12] but always of the erotic ones.

If, however, transference is dangerous, then, to be consistent, all neurologists, including the opponents of Freud, must give up having anything to do with neurotics, for we get more and more convinced that in the non-analytic and non-psycho-therapeutic methods of treating the neuroses also transference plays the greatest, and probably the sole important part, only that in these methods of treatment—as Freud rightly points out—merely the positive feelings towards the physician come to expression, for when unfriendly transferences make their appearance the patient leaves the "antipathetic doctor." The positive transferences, however, are overlooked by the physician, who surmises nothing, and the curative effect is attributed to the physical measures or to an obscurely conceived idea of "suggestion."

The transference shews itself most clearly in the treatment by *hypnotism* and *suggestion,* as I shall try to demonstrate in detail in the following chapter of this work.[13]

Since I have known something about transferences, the behaviour of the hysteric who after the end of a suggestion treatment asked for my photograph, in order—so she said—to be reminded of my words by looking at it, appears to me in its true light. She simply wanted to have a memento of me, as I had given so many pleasant quarters of an hour to her conflict-tortured soul by stroking her forehead, by friendly, gentle talk, and by letting her fancies have free rein in a darkened room. Another patient, with a washing mania, even confessed to me once that to please a sympathetic doctor she could often suppress her obsessive act.

These are not exceptional cases, but are typical, and they help to explain not only the hypnotism and suggestion "cures" of psychoneurotics, but also all the others by means of electrotherapy, mechanotherapy, hydrotherapy and massage.

It is not intended to deny that more reasonable conditions of living improve the nutrition and the general sense of well-being, and in this way can to some extent help to subdue psychoneurotic symptoms, but the main curative agency with all these methods of treatment is the unconscious transference, in which the disguised satisfaction of libidinous tendencies (in mechanotherapy the vibration, in hydrotherapy and massage the rubbing of the skin) certainly plays a part.

Freud summarises these considerations in the saying that *we may treat a neurotic any way we like, he always treats himself psychotherapeutically, that is to say, with transferences.* What we describe as introjections and other symptoms of the disease are really—in Freud's opinion, with which I fully agree—self-taught attempts on the patient's part to cure himself. He lets the same mechanism function, however, when he meets a physician that wants to cure him: he tries—as a rule quite unconsciously—to "transfer," and when this is successful the improvement of the condition is the result.

The plea may be raised that when the non-analytic methods of treatment follow—although unconsciously—the path automatically laid down by the sick mind they are in the right. The transference therapy would thus be, so to speak, a natural way of healing, psycho-analysis on the other hand something artificial, imposed on nature. This objection might be irrefutable. The patient does in fact "heal" his mental conflicts through repression, displacement, and transference of disagreeable complexes; unfortunately what is repressed compensates itself by creating "costly replacement-formations" (Freud), so that we have to regard neuroses as "healing attempts that have miscarried" (Freud), where really "medicina pejor morbo." It would be very wrong to want to imitate Nature slavishly even here, and to follow her along a road where in the case in question she has shewn her incapacity. Psycho-analysis wishes to individualise, while Nature disdains this; analysis aims at making capable for life and action persons who have been ruined by the summary repression-procedure of that Nature who does not concern herself with the weakly individual being. It is not enough here to displace the repressed complexes a little further by the help of transference to the physician, to discharge a little of their affective tension, and so to achieve a temporary improvement. If one wants seriously to help the patient one must lead him by means of analysis to overcome—opposing the unpleasantness-principle —the *resistances* (Freud) that hinder him from gazing at his own naked mental physiognomy.

Present-day neurology, however, will not hear of complexes, resistances, and introjections, and quite unconsciously makes use of a psychotherapeutic measure that in many cases is really effective, namely transference; it cures, so to speak, "unconsciously," and even designates as dangerous the really effective principle of all methods of healing the psycho-neuroses.

The critics who look on these transferences as dangerous should condemn the non-analytic modes of treatment more severely than the psycho-analytic method, since the former really intensify the transferences, while the latter strives to uncover and to resolve them as soon as possible.

I deny, however, that transference is harmful, and surmise rather that—at least in the pathology of the neuroses—the ancient belief, which strikes its roots deep in the mind of the people, will be confirmed, that diseases are to be cured by "sympathy." Those who scornfully reproach us with explaining and wanting to cure "everything from one point" are still far too much influenced by that ascetic-religious view of life, with its depreciation of everything sexual, which for nearly two thousand years has prevented the attainment of insight into the great significance that "sexual hunger" has for the mental life of the normal and pathological.

NOTES

1. "Bruchstück einer Hysterie-analyse," in Sammlung Kleiner Schriften zur Neurosenlehre, Bd. II.
2. Ferenczi, "Ueber Aktual-und Psychoneurosen im Sinne Freuds," Wiener klin. Rundschau, 1908, Nr. 48 to 51.
3. Freud. Die Traumdeutung. 2e Aufl., S. 107.
4. Stekel, Nervöse Angstzustände, 1908.
5. Compare the remark about the "doctor game" in Freud's article on "Infantile Sexualtheorien," Kleine Schriften, 2e Folge, S. 171.
6. (*I. e.* disproportionate, misplaced, or inappropriate. Transl.)
7. Jung, Zur Psychologie der Dementia Praecox, 1907. ("Lack of pleasant *rapport* in dementia praecox.")
8. Abraham, "Die psychosexuellen Differenzen der Hysterie und der Dementia praecox," Zentralbl. f. Nervenheilk. u. Psych., 1908. ("The contrast between dementia praecox and

hysteria lies in the auto-erotism of the former. Turning away of 'sexual hunger' in the former, excessive investment of the object in the latter.")

9. Kleinpaul, Das Stromgebiet der Sprache, 1893.
10. Abraham, Traum und Mythos, 1909.
11. Jung, Diagnostische Assoziationsstudien, 1906.
12. The practical significance and the exceptional position of the kind of introjections that have as their object the person of the physician, and which are discovered in analysis, make it desirable that the term "transferences" given to them by Freud be retained. The designation "introjection" would be applicable for all other cases of the same psychical mechanism.
13. Ferenczi, Sex in Psychoanalysis, Chap. III.

2. The Dynamics of Transference

Sigmund Freud

The almost inexhaustible topic of transference has recenbly been dealt with by Wilhelm Stekel [1911*b*] in this journal[1] on descriptive lines. I should like in the following pages to add a few remarks to explain how it is that transference is necessarily brought about during a psycho-analytic treatment, and how it comes to play its familiar part in it.

It must be understood that each individual, through the combined operation of his innate disposition and the influences brought to bear on him during his early years, has acquired a specific method of his own in his conduct of his erotic life—that is, in the preconditions to falling in love which he lays down, in the instincts he satisfies and the aims he sets himself in the course of it.[2] This produces what might be described as a stereotype plate (or several such), which is constantly repeated—constantly reprinted afresh—in the course of the person's life, so far as external circumstances and the nature of the love-objects accessible to him permit, and which is certainly not entirely insusceptible to change in the face of recent experiences. Now, our observations have shown that only a portion of these impulses which determine the course of erotic life have passed through the full process of psychical development. That portion is directed towards reality, is at the disposal of the conscious personality, and forms a part of it. Another portion of the libidinal impulses has been held up in the course of development; it has been kept away from the conscious personality and from reality, and has either been prevented from further expansion except in phantasy or has remained wholly in the unconscious so that it is unknown to the personality's consciousness. If someone's need for love is not entirely satisfied by reality, he is bound to approach every new person whom he meets with libidinal anticipatory ideas; and it is highly probable that both portions of his libido, the portion that is

Reprinted from James Strachey, ed., *The Standard Edition of the Complete Psychological Works of Sigmund Freud* by permission of Sigmund Freud Copyrights Ltd, The Institute of Psycho-Analysis, The Hogarth Press, and Basic Books, Inc.

capable of becoming conscious as well as the unconscious one, have a share in forming that attitude.

Thus it is a perfectly normal and intelligible thing that the libidinal cathexis of someone who is partly unsatisfied, a cathexis which is held ready in anticipation, should be directed as well to the figure of the doctor. It follows from our earlier hypothesis that this cathexis will have recourse to prototypes, will attach itself to one of the stereotype plates which are present in the subject; or, to put the position in another way, the cathexis will introduce the doctor into one of the psychical 'series' which the patient has already formed. If the 'father-imago', to use the apt term introduced by Jung (1911, 164), is the decisive factor in bringing this about, the outcome will tally with the real relations of the subject to his doctor. But the transference is not tied to this particular prototype: it may also come about on the lines of the mother-imago or brother-imago. The peculiarities of the transference to the doctor, thanks to which it exceeds, both in amount and nature, anything that could be justified on sensible or rational grounds, are made intelligible if we bear in mind that this transference has precisely been set up not only by the *conscious* anticipatory ideas but also by those that have been held back or are unconscious.

There would be nothing more to discuss or worry about in this behaviour of transference, if it were not that two points remain unexplained about it which are of particular interest to psycho-analysis. Firstly, we do not understand why transference is so much more intense with neurotic subjects in analysis than it is with other such people who are not being analysed; and secondly, it remains a puzzle why in analysis transference emerges as *the most powerful resistance* to the treatment, whereas outside analysis it must be regarded as the vehicle of cure and the condition of success. For our experience has shown us—and the fact can be confirmed as often as we please—that if a patient's free associations fail[3] the stoppage can invariably be removed by an assurance that he is being dominated at the moment by an association which is concerned with the doctor himself or with something connected with him. As soon as this explanation is given, the stoppage is removed, or the situation is changed from one in which the associations fail into one in which they are being kept back. At first sight it appears to be an immense disadvantage in psycho-analysis as a method that what is elsewhere the strongest factor towards success is changed in it into the most powerful medium of resistance. If, however, we examine the situation more closely, we can at least clear away the first of our two problems. It is not a fact that transference emerges with greater intensity and lack of restraint during psycho-analysis than outside it. In institutions in which nerve patients are treated non-analytically, we can observe transference occurring with the greatest intensity and in the most unworthy forms, extending to nothing less than mental bondage, and moreover showing the plainest erotic colouring. Gabriele Reuter, with her sharp powers of observation, described this at a time when there was no such thing as psycho-analysis, in a remarkable book which betrays in every respect the clearest insight into the nature and genesis of neuroses.[4] These characteristics of transference are therefore to be attributed not to psycho-analysis but to neurosis itself.

Our second problem—the problem of why transference appears in psycho-analysis as resistance—has been left for the moment untouched; and we must now approach it more closely. Let us picture the psychological situation during the treatment. An invariable and indispensable precondition of *every* onset of a psychoneurosis is the process to which Jung has given the appropriate name of 'introversion'.[5] That is to say: the portion of libido which is capable of becoming conscious and is directed towards reality is diminished, and the portion which is directed *away* from reality and is unconscious, and which, though it may still feed the subject's phantasies, nevertheless belongs to the unconscious, is proportionately increased. The libido (whether wholly or in part) has entered on a regressive course and has revived the subject's infantile imagos.[6] The analytic treatment now proceeds to follow it; it seeks to track down the libido, to make it accessible to consciousness and, in the end, serviceable for reality. Where the investigations of analysis come upon the libido withdrawn into its hiding-place, a struggle is bound to break out; all the forces which have caused the libido to regress will rise up as 'resistances' against the work of analysis, in order to conserve the new state of things. For if the libido's introversion or regression had not been justified by a particular relation between the subject and the external world—stated in the most general terms, by the frustration of satisfaction[7]—and if it had not for the moment even become expedient, it could never have taken place at all. But the resistances from this source are not the only ones or indeed the most powerful. The libido at the disposal of the subject's personality had always been under the influence of the attraction of his unconscious complexes (or, more correctly, of the portions of those complexes belonging to the unconscious),[8] and it entered on a regressive course because the attraction of reality had diminished. In order to liberate it, this attraction of the unconscious has to be overcome; that is, the repression of the unconscious instincts and of their productions, which has meanwhile been set up in the subject, must be removed. This is responsible for by far the largest part of the resistance, which so often causes the illness to persist even after the turning away from reality has lost its temporary justification. The analysis has to struggle against the resistances from both these sources. The resistance accompanies the treatment step by step. Every single association, every act of the person under treatment must reckon with the resistance and represents a compromise between the forces that are striving towards recovery and the opposing ones which I have described.

If now we follow a pathogenic complex from its representation in the conscious (whether this is an obvious one in the form of a symptom or something quite inconspicuous) to its root in the unconscious, we shall soon enter a region in which the resistance makes itself felt so clearly that the next association must take account of it and appear as a compromise between its demands and those of the work of investigation. It is at this point, on the evidence of our experience, that transference enters on the scene. When anything in the complexive material (in the subject-matter of the complex) is suitable for being transferred on to the figure of the doctor, that transference is carried out; it produces the next association, and announces itself by indications of a resistance—by a stoppage, for instance. We infer from this experience that the transference-idea has penetrated into consciousness in front of any other possible associations *because* it satisfies the resistance. An event of this sort is repeated on countless occasions in the course of an analysis. Over and over again, when we come near to a pathogenic complex, the portion of that complex which is capable of transference is first pushed forward into consciousness and defended with the greatest obstinacy.[9]

After it has been overcome, the overcoming of the other portions of the complex raises few further difficulties. The longer an analytic treatment lasts and the more clearly the patient realizes that distortions of the pathogenic material cannot by themselves offer any protection against its being uncovered, the more consistently does he make use of the one sort of distortion which obviously affords him the greatest advantages—distortion through transference. These circumstances tend towards a situation in which finally every conflict has to be fought out in the sphere of transference.

Thus transference in the analytic treatment invariably appears to us in the first instance as the strongest weapon of the resistance, and we may conclude that the intensity and persistence of the transference are an effect and an expression of the resistance. The *mechanism* of transference is, it is true, dealt with when we have traced it back to the state of readiness of the libido, which has remained in possession of infantile imagos; but the part transference plays in the treatment can only be explained if we enter into its relations with resistance.

How does it come about that transference is so admirably suited to be a means of resistance? It might be thought that the answer can be given without difficulty. For it is evident that it becomes particularly hard to admit to any proscribed wishful impulse if it has to be revealed in front of the very person to whom the impulse relates. Such a necessity gives rise to situations which in the real world seem scarcely possible. But it is precisely this that the patient is aiming at when he makes the object of his emotional impulses coincide with the doctor. Further consideration, however, shows that this apparent gain cannot provide the solution of the problem. Indeed, a relation of affectionate and devoted dependence can, on the contrary, help a person over all the difficulties of making an admission. In analogous real situations people will usually say: 'I feel no shame in front of you: I can say anything to you.' Thus the transference to the doctor might just as easily serve to *facilitate* admissions, and it is not clear why it should make things more difficult.

The answer to the question which has been repeated so often in these pages is not to be reached by further reflection but by what we discover when we examine individual transference-resistances occurring during treatment. We find in the end that we cannot understand the employment of transference as resistance so long as we think simply of 'transference'. We must make up our minds to distinguish a 'positive' transference from a 'negative' one, the transference of affectionate feelings from that of hostile ones, and to treat the two sorts of transference to the doctor separately. Positive transference is then further divisible into transference of friendly or affectionate feelings which are admissible to consciousness and transference of prolongations of those feelings into the unconscious. As regards the latter, analysis shows that they invariably go back to erotic sources. And we are thus led to the discovery that all the emotional relations of sympathy, friendship, trust, and the like, which can be turned to good account in our lives, are genetically linked with sexuality and have developed from purely sexual desires through a softening of their sexual aim, however pure and unsensual they may appear to our conscious self-perception. Originally we knew only sexual objects;

and psycho-analysis shows us that people who in our real life are merely admired or respected may still be sexual objects for our unconscious.

Thus the solution of the puzzle is that transference to the doctor is suitable for resistance to the treatment only in so far as it is a negative transference or a positive transference of repressed erotic impulses. If we 'remove' the transference by making it conscious, we are detaching only these two components of the emotional act from the person of the doctor; the other component, which is admissible to consciousness and unobjectionable, persists and is the vehicle of success in psycho-analysis exactly as it is in other methods of treatment. To this extent we readily admit that the results of psychoanalysis rest upon suggestion; by suggestion, however, we must understand, as Ferenczi (1909) does, the influencing of a person by means of the transference phenomena which are possible in his case. We take care of the patient's final independence by employing suggestion in order to get him to accomplish a piece of psychical work which has as its necessary result a permanent improvement in his psychical situation.

The further question may be raised of why it is that the resistance phenomena of transference only appear in psycho-analysis and not in indifferent forms of treatment (e.g. in institutions) as well. The reply is that they do show themselves in these other situations too, but they have to be recognized as such. The breaking out of a negative transference is actually quite a common event in institutions. As soon as a patient comes under the dominance of the negative transference he leaves the institution in an unchanged or relapsed condition. The erotic transference does not have such an inhibiting effect in institutions, since in them, just as in ordinary life, it is glossed over instead of being uncovered. But it is manifested quite clearly as a resistance to recovery, not, it is true, by driving the patient out of the institution—on the contrary, it holds him back in it—but by keeping him at a distance from life. For, from the point of view of recovery, it is a matter of complete indifference whether the patient overcomes this or that anxiety or inhibition in the institution; what matters is that he shall be free of it in his real life as well.

The negative transference deserves a detailed examination, which it cannot be given within the limits of the present paper. In the curable forms of psychoneurosis it is found side by side with the affectionate transference, often directed simultaneously towards the same person. Bleuler has coined the excellent term 'ambivalence' to describe this phenomenon.[10] Up to a point, ambivalence of feeling of this sort seems to be normal; but a high degree of it is certainly a special peculiarity of neurotic people. In obsessional neurotics an early separation of the 'pairs of opposites'[11] seems to be characteristic of their instinctual life and to be one of their constitutional preconditions. Ambivalence in the emotional trends of neurotics is the best explanation of their ability to enlist their transferences in the service of resistance. Where the capacity for transference has become essentially limited to a negative one, as is the case with paranoics, there ceases to be any possibility of influence or cure.

In all these reflections, however, we have hitherto dealt only with one side of the phenomenon of transference; we must turn our attention to another aspect of the same subject. Anyone who forms a correct appreciation of the way in which a person in analysis, as soon as he comes under the dominance of any considerable transference-resistance, is flung out of his real relation to the doctor, how he feels at liberty then to disregard the fundamental rule of psycho-analysis[12] which lays it down that whatever comes into one's head must be reported without criticizing it, how he forgets the intentions with which he started the treatment, and how he regards with indifference logical arguments and conclusions which only a short time before had made a great impression on him—anyone who has observed all this will feel it necessary to look for an explanation of his impression in other factors besides those that have already been adduced. Nor are such factors far to seek: they arise once again from the psychological situation in which the treatment places the patient.

In the process of seeking out the libido which has escaped from the patient's conscious, we have penetrated into the realm of the unconscious. The reactions which we bring about reveal at the same time some of the characteristics which we have come to know from the study of dreams. The unconscious impulses do not want to be remembered in the way the treatment desires them to be, but endeavour to reproduce themselves in accordance with the timelessness of the unconscious and its capacity for hallucination.[13] Just as happens in dreams, the patient regards the products of the awakening of his unconscious impulses as contemporaneous and real; he seeks to put his passions into action without taking any account of the real situation. The doctor tries to compel him to fit these emotional impulses into the nexus of the treatment and of his life-history, to submit them to intellectual consideration and to understand them in the light of their psychical value. This struggle between the doctor and the patient, between intellect and instinctual life, between understanding and seeking to act, is played out almost exclusively in the phenomena of transference. It is on that field that the victory must be won—the victory whose expression is the permanent cure of the neurosis. It cannot be disputed that controlling the phenomena of transference presents the psycho-analyst with the greatest difficulties. But it should not be forgotten that it is precisely they that do us the inestimable service of making the patient's hidden and forgotten erotic impulses immediate and manifest. For when all is said and done, it is impossible to destroy anyone *in absentia* or *in effigie*.[14]

NOTES

1. [The *Zentralblatt für Psychoanalyse*, in which the present paper first appeared.]
2. I take this opportunity of defending myself against the mistaken charge of having denied the importance of innate (constitutional) factors because I have stressed that of infantile impressions. A charge such as this arises from the restricted nature of what men look for in the field of causation: in contrast to what ordinarily holds good in the real world, people prefer to be satisfied with a single causative factor. Psycho-analysis has talked a lot about the accidental factors in aetiology and little about the constitutional ones; but that is only because it was able to contribute something fresh to the former, while, to begin with, it knew no more than was commonly known about the latter. We refuse to posit any contrast in principle between the two sets of aetiological factors; on the contrary, we assume that the two sets regularly act jointly in bringing about the observed result. Δαίμων καὶ Τύχη [Endowment and Chance] determine a man's fate—rarely or never one of these powers alone. The amount of aetiological effectiveness to be attributed to each of them can only be arrived at in every individual case separately. These cases may be arranged in a series according to the varying proportion in which the two factors are present, and this series will no doubt have its extreme cases. We shall estimate the share taken by constitution or experience differently in individual cases according to the stage reached by our knowledge; and we shall retain the right to modify our judgement along with changes in our understanding. Incidentally, one might venture to regard constitution itself as a precipitate from the accidental effects produced on the endlessly long chain of our ancestors.
3. I mean when they really cease, and not when, for instance, the patient keeps them back owing to ordinary feelings of unpleasure.
4. *Aus guter Familie*, Berlin, 1895.
5. Even though some of Jung's remarks give the impression that he regards this introversion as something which is characteristic of dementia praecox and does not come into account in the same way in other neuroses.—[This seems to be the first published occasion of Freud's use of 'introversion'. The term was first introduced in June, 1910b, 38; but Freud is probably criticizing Jung, 1911, 135–6 n. (English translation, 1916, 487). Some further comment on Jung's use of the term will be found in a footnote to a later technical paper (1913c, p. 125 below) as well as in Freud's paper on narcissism (1914c, *Standard Ed.*, **14**, 74) and in a passage towards the end of Lecture XXIII of the *Introductory Lectures* (1916–17). Freud used the term extremely seldom in his later writings.]
6. It would be convenient if we could say 'it has recathected his infantile complexes'. But this

would be incorrect: the only justifiable way of putting it would be 'the unconscious portions of those complexes'.—The topics dealt with in this paper are so extraordinarily involved that it is tempting to embark on a number of contiguous problems whose clarification would in point of fact be necessary before it would be possible to speak in unambiguous terms of the psychical processes that are to be described here. These problems include the drawing of a line of distinction between introversion and regression, the fitting of the theory of complexes into the libido theory, the relations of phantasying to the conscious and the unconscious as well as to reality—and others besides. I need not apologize for having resisted this temptation in the present paper.

7. [See the full discussion of this in the paper on 'Types of Onset of Neurosis' (1912c), *Standard Ed.*, **12**, 231 ff.]

8. [Cf. the beginning of footnote 6, on the previous page.]

9. This, however, should not lead us to conclude in general that the element selected for transference-resistance is of peculiar pathogenic importance. If in the course of a battle there is a particularly embittered struggle over the possession of some little church or some individual farm, there is no need to suppose that the church is a national shrine, perhaps, or that the house shelters the army's pay-chest. The value of the object may be a purely tactical one and may perhaps emerge only in this one battle.

10. Bleuler, 1911, 43–4 and 305–6.—Cf. a lecture on ambivalence delivered by him in Berne in 1910, reported in the *Zentralblatt für Psychoanalyse*, **1**, 266.—Stekel has proposed the term 'bipolarity' for the same phenomenon.—[This appears to have been Freud's first mention of the word 'ambivalence'. He occasionally used it in a sense other than Bleuler's, to describe the simultaneous presence of active and passive impulses. See an Editor's footnote, *Standard Ed.*, **14**, 131.]

11. [The pairs of opposite instincts were first described by Freud in his *Three Essays* (1905d), *Standard Ed.*, **7**, 160 and 166–7, and later on in 'Instincts and their Vicissitudes' (1915c), *Standard Ed.*, **14**, 127 ff. Their importance in obsessional neurosis was discussed in the 'Rat Man' case history (1909d), *Standard Ed.*, **10**, 237 ff.]

12. [This seems to be the first use of what was henceforward to become the regular description of the essential technical rule. A very similar phrase ('the main rule of psycho-analysis') had, however, been used already in the third of Freud's Clark University Lectures (1910a), *Standard Ed.*, **11**, 33. The idea itself, of course, goes back a long way; it is expressed, for instance, in Chapter II of *The Interpretation of Dreams* (1900a), *Standard Ed.*, **4**, 101, in essentially the same terms as in the paper 'On Beginning the Treatment' (1913c), *Standard Ed.*, **12**, 134, where, incidentally, the subject will be found discussed in a long footnote.]

13. [This is elaborated in a later technical paper 'Recollecting, Repeating and Working-Through' (1914g), *Standard Ed.*, **12**, 150.

14. [Cf. the similar remark near the bottom of *Standard Ed.*, **12**, 152.

3. Observations on Transference-Love (Further Recommendations on the Technique of Psycho-Analysis III)

Sigmund Freud

Every beginner in psycho-analysis probably feels alarmed at first at the difficulties in store for him when he comes to interpret the patient's associations and to deal with the reproduction of the repressed. When the time comes, however, he soon learns to look upon these difficulties as insignificant, and instead becomes convinced that the only really serious difficulties he has to meet lie in the management of the transference.

Among the situations which arise in this connection I shall select one which is very sharply circumscribed; and I shall select it, partly because it occurs so often and is so important in its real aspects and partly because of its theoretical interest. What I have in mind is the case in which a woman patient shows by unmistakable indications, or openly declares, that she has fallen in love, as any other mortal woman might, with the doctor who is analysing her. This situation has its distressing and comical aspects, as well as its serious ones. It is also determined by so many and such complicated factors, it is so unavoidable and so difficult to clear up, that a discussion of it to meet a vital need of analytic technique has long been overdue. But since we who laugh at other people's failings are not always free from them ourselves, we have not so far been precisely in a hurry to fulfil this task. We are constantly coming up against the obligation to professional discretion—a discretion which cannot be dispensed with in real life, but which is of no service in our science. In so far as psycho-analytic publications are a part of real life, too, we have here an insoluble contradiction. I have recently disregarded this matter of discretion at one point,[1] and shown how this same transference situation held back the development of psycho-analytic therapy during its first decade.

Reprinted from James Strachey, ed., *The Standard Edition of the Complete Psychological Works of Sigmund Freud* by permission of Sigmund Freud Copyrights Ltd, The Institute of Psycho-Analysis, The Hogarth Press, and Basic Books, Inc.

To a well-educated layman (for that is what the ideal civilized person is in regard to psycho-analysis) things that have to do with love are incommensurable with everything else; they are, as it were, written on a special page on which no other writing is tolerated. If a woman patient has fallen in love with her doctor it seems to such a layman that only two outcomes are possible. One, which happens comparatively rarely, is that all the circumstances allow of a permanent legal union between them; the other, which is more frequent, is that the doctor and the patient part and give up the work they have begun which was to have led to her recovery, as though it had been interrupted by some elemental phenomenon. There is, to be sure, a third conceivable outcome, which even seems compatible with a continuation of the treatment. This is that they should enter into a love-relationship which is illicit and which is not intended to last for ever. But such a course is made impossible by conventional morality and professional standards. Nevertheless, our layman will beg the analyst to reassure him as unambiguously as possible that this third alternative is excluded.

It is clear that a psycho-analyst must look at things from a different point of view.

Let us take the case of the second outcome of the situation we are considering. After the patient has fallen in love with her doctor, they part; the treatment is given up. But soon the patient's condition necessitates her making a second attempt at analysis, with another doctor. The next thing that happens is that she feels she has fallen in love with this second doctor too; and if she breaks off with him and begins yet again, the same thing will happen with the third doctor, and so on. This phenomenon, which occurs without fail and which is, as we know, one of the foundations of the psycho-analytic theory, may be evaluated from two points of view, that of the doctor who is carrying out the analysis and that of the patient who is in need of it.

For the doctor the phenomenon signifies a valuable piece of enlightenment and a useful warning against any tendency to a counter-transference which may be present in his own mind.[2] He must recognize that the patient's falling in love is induced by the analytic situation and is not to be attributed to the charms of his own person; so that he has no grounds whatever for being proud of such a 'conquest', as it would be called outside analysis. And it is always well to be reminded of this. For the patient, however, there are two alternatives: either she must relinquish psycho-analytic treatment or she must accept falling in love with her doctor as an inescapable fate.[3]

I have no doubt that the patient's relatives and friends will decide as emphatically for the first of these two alternatives as the analyst will for the second. But I think that here is a case in which the decision cannot be left to the tender—or rather, the egoistic and jealous—concern of her relatives. The welfare of the patient alone should be the touchstone; her relatives' love cannot cure her neurosis. The analyst need not push himself forward, but he may insist that he is indispensable for the achievement of certain ends. Any relative who adopts Tolstoy's attitude to this problem can remain in undisturbed possession of his wife or daughter; but he will have to try to put up with the fact that she, for her part, retains her neurosis and the interference with her capacity for love which it involves. The situation, after all, is similar to that in a gynaecological treatment. Moreover, the jealous father or husband is greatly mistaken if he thinks that the patient will escape falling in love with her doctor if he hands her over to some kind of treatment other than analysis for combating her neurosis. The difference, on the contrary, will only be that a love of this kind, which is bound to remain unexpressed and unanalysed, can never make the contribution to the patient's recovery which analysis would have extracted from it.

It has come to my knowledge that some doctors who practise analysis frequently[4] prepare their patients for the emergence of the erotic transference or even urge them to 'go ahead and fall in love with the doctor so that the treatment may make progress'. I can hardly imagine a more senseless proceeding. In doing so, an analyst robs the phenomenon of the element of spontaneity which is so convincing and lays up obstacles for himself in the future which are hard to overcome.[5]

At a first glance it certainly does not look as if the patient's falling in love in the transference could result in any advantage to the treatment. No matter how amenable she has been up till then, she suddenly loses all understanding of the treatment and all interest in it, and will not speak or hear about anything but her love, which she demands to have returned. She gives up her symptoms or pays no attention to them; indeed, she declares that she is well. There is a complete change of scene; it is as though some piece of make-believe had been stopped by the sudden irruption of reality—as when, for instance, a cry of fire is raised during a theatrical performance. No doctor who experiences this for the first time will find it easy to retain his grasp on the analytic situation and to keep clear of the illusion that the treatment is really at an end.

A little reflection enables one to find one's bearings. First and foremost, one keeps in mind the suspicion that anything that interferes with the continuation of the treatment may be an expression of resistance.[6] There can be no doubt that the outbreak of a passionate demand for love is largely the work of resistance. One will have long since noticed in the patient the signs of an affectionate transference, and one will have been able to feel certain that her docility, her acceptance of the analytic explanations, her remarkable comprehension and the high degree of intelligence she showed were to be attributed to this attitude towards her doctor. Now all this is swept away. She has become quite without insight and seems to be swallowed up in her love. Moreover, this change quite regularly occurs precisely at a point of time when one is having to try to bring her to admit or remember some particularly distressing and heavily repressed piece of her life-history. She has been in love, therefore, for a long time; but now the resistance is beginning to make use of her love in order to hinder the continuation of the treatment, to deflect all her interest from the work and to put the analyst in an awkward position.

If one looks into the situation more closely one recognizes the influence of motives which further complicate things—of which some are connected with being in love and others are particular expressions of resistance. Of the first kind are the patient's endeavour to assure herself of her irresistibility, to destroy the doctor's authority by bringing him down to the level of a lover and to gain all the other promised advantages incidental to the satisfaction of love. As regards the resistance, we may suspect that on occasion it makes use of a declaration of love on the patient's part as a means of putting her analyst's severity to the test, so that, if he should show signs of compliance, he may expect to be taken to task for it. But above all, one gets an impression that the resistance is acting as an *agent provocateur;* it heightens the patient's state of being in love and exaggerates her readiness for sexual surrender in order to justify the workings of repression all the more emphatically, by pointing to the dangers of such licentiousness.[7] All these accessory motives, which in simpler cases may not be present, have, as we know, been regarded by Adler as the essential part of the whole process.[8]

But how is the analyst to behave in order not to come to grief over this situation, supposing he is convinced that the treatment should be carried on in spite of this erotic transference and should take it in its stride?

It would be easy for me to lay stress on the universally accepted standards of morality and to insist that the analyst must never under any circumstances accept or return the tender feelings that are offered him: that, instead, he must consider that the time has come for him to put before the woman who is in love with him the demands of social morality and the necessity for renunciation, and to succeed in making her give up her desires, and, having surmounted the animal side of her self, go on with the work of analysis.

I shall not, however, fulfil these expectations—neither the first nor the second of them. Not the first, because I am writing not for patients but for doctors who have serious difficulties to contend with, and also because in this instance I am able to trace the moral prescription back to its source, namely to expediency. I am on this occasion in the happy position of being able to replace the moral embargo by considerations of analytic technique, without any alteration in the outcome.

Even more decidedly, however, do I decline to fulfil the second of the expectations I have mentioned. To urge the patient to suppress, renounce or sublimate her instincts the moment she had admitted her erotic transference would be, not an analytic way of dealing with them, but a senseless one. It would be just as though, after summoning up a spirit from the underworld by cunning spells, one were to send him down again without having asked him a single question. One would have brought the repressed into consciousness, only to repress it once more in a fright. Nor should we deceive ourselves about the success of any such proceeding. As we know, the passions are little affected by sublime speeches. The patient will feel only the humiliation, and she will not fail to take her revenge for it.

Just as little can I advocate a middle course, which would recommend itself to some people as being specially ingenious. This would consist in declaring that one returns the patient's fond feelings but at the same time in avoiding any physical implementation of this fondness until one is able to guide the relationship into calmer channels and raise it to a higher level. My objection to this expedient is that psycho-analytic treatment is founded on truthfulness. In this fact lies a great part of its educative effect and its ethical value. It is dangerous to depart from this foundation. Anyone who has become saturated in the analytic technique will no longer be able to make use of the lies and pretences which the doctor normally finds unavoidable; and if, with the best intentions, he does attempt to do so, he is very likely to betray himself. Since we demand strict truthfulness from our patients, we jeopardize our whole authority if we let ourselves be caught out by them in a departure from the truth. Besides, the experiment of letting oneself go a little way in tender feelings for the patient is not altogether without danger. Our control over ourselves is not so complete that we may not suddenly one day go further than we had intended. In my opinion, therefore, we ought not to give up the neutrality towards the patient, which we have acquired through keeping the counter-transference in check.

I have already let it be understood that analytic technique requires of the physician that he should deny to the patient who is craving for love the satisfaction she demands. The treatment must be carried out in abstinence. By this I do not mean physical abstinence alone, nor yet the deprivation of everything that the patient desires, for perhaps no sick person could tolerate this. Instead, I shall state it as a fundamental principle that the patient's need and longing should be allowed to persist in her, in order that they may serve as forces impelling her to do work and to make changes, and that we must beware of appeasing those forces by means of surrogates. And what we could offer would never be anything else than a surrogate, for the patient's condition is such that, until her repressions are removed, she is incapable of getting real satisfaction.

Let us admit that this fundamental principle of the treatment being carried out in abstinence extends far beyond the single case we are considering here, and that it needs to be thoroughly discussed in order that we may define the limits of its possible application.[9] We will not enter into this now, however, but will keep as close as possible to the situation from which we started out. What would happen if the doctor were to behave differently and, supposing both parties were free, if he were to avail himself of that freedom in order to return the patient's love and to still her need for affection?

If he has been guided by the calculation that this compliance on his part will ensure his domination over his patient and thus enable him to influence her to perform the tasks required by the treatment, and in this way to liberate herself permanently from her neurosis—then experience would inevitably show him that his calculation was wrong. The patient would achieve *her* aim, but he would never achieve *his*. What would happen to the doctor and the patient would only be what happened, according to the amusing anecdote, to the pastor and the insurance agent. The insurance agent, a free-thinker, lay at the point of death and his relatives insisted on bringing in a man of God to convert him before he died. The interview lasted so long that those who were waiting outside began to have hopes. At last the door of the sick-chamber opened. The free-thinker had not been converted; but the pastor went away insured.

If the patient's advances were returned it would be a great triumph for her, but a complete defeat for the treatment. She would have succeeded in what all patients strive for in analysis—she would have succeeded in acting out, in repeating in real life, what she ought only to have remembered, to have reproduced as psychical material and to have kept within the sphere of psychical events.[10] In the further course of the love-relationship she would bring out all the inhibitions and pathological reactions of her erotic life, without there being any possibility of correcting them; and the distressing episode would end in remorse and a great strengthening of her propensity to repression. The love-relationship in fact destroys the patient's susceptibility to influence from analytic treatment. A combination of the two would be an impossibility.

It is, therefore, just as disastrous for the analysis if the patient's craving for love is gratified as if it is suppressed. The course the analyst must pursue is neither of these; it is one for which there is no model in real life. He must take care not to steer away from the transference-love, or to repulse it or to make it distasteful to the patient; but he must just as resolutely withhold any response to it. He must keep firm hold of the transference-love, but treat it as something unreal, as a situation which has to be gone through in the treatment and traced back to its unconscious origins and which must assist in bringing all that is most deeply hidden in the patient's erotic life into her consciousness and therefore under her control. The more plainly the analyst lets it be seen that he is proof against every temptation, the more readily will he be able to extract from the situation its analytic content. The patient, whose sexual repression is of course not yet removed but merely pushed into the background, will then feel safe enough to allow all her preconditions for loving, all the phantasies springing from her sexual desires, all the detailed characteristics of her state of being in love, to come to light; and from these she will herself open the way to the infantile roots of her love.

There is, it is true, one class of women with whom this attempt to preserve the erotic transference for the purposes of analytic work without satisfying it will not succeed. These are women of elemental passionateness who tolerate no surrogates. They are children of nature who refuse to accept the psychical in place of the material, who, in the poet's words, are accessible only to 'the logic of soup, with dumplings for arguments'. With such people one has the choice between returning their love or else bringing down upon oneself the full enmity of a woman scorned. In neither case can one safeguard the interests of the treatment. One has to withdraw, unsuccessful; and all one can do is to turn the problem over in one's mind of how it is that a capacity for neurosis is joined with such an intractable need for love.

Many analysts will no doubt be agreed on the method by which other women, who are less violent in their love, can be gradually made to adopt the analytic attitude. What we do, above all, is to stress to the patient the unmistakable element of resistance in this 'love'. Genuine love, we say, would make her docile and intensify her readiness to solve the problems of her case, simply because the man she was in love with expected it of her. In such a case she would gladly choose the road to completion of the treatment, in order to acquire value in the doctor's eyes and to prepare herself for real life, where this feeling of love could find a proper place. Instead of this, we point out, she is showing a stubborn and rebellious spirit, she has thrown up all interest in her treatment, and clearly feels no respect for the doctor's well-founded convictions. She is thus bringing out a resistance under the guise of being in love with him; and in addition to this she has no compunction in placing him in a cleft stick. For if he refuses her love, as his duty and his understanding compel him to do, she can play the part of a woman scorned, and then withdraw from his therapeutic efforts out of revenge and resentment, exactly as she is now doing out of her ostensible love.

As a second argument against the genuineness of this love we advance the fact that it exhibits not a single new feature arising from the present situation, but is entirely composed of repetitions and copies of earlier reactions, including infantile ones. We undertake to prove this by a detailed analysis of the patient's behaviour in love.

If the necessary amount of patience is added to these arguments, it is usually possible to overcome the difficult situation and to continue the work with a love which has been moderated or transformed; the work then aims at uncovering the patient's infantile object-choice and the phantasies woven round it.

I should now like, however, to examine these arguments with a critical eye and to raise the question whether, in putting them forward to the patient, we are really telling the truth, or whether we are not resorting in our desperation to concealments and misrepresentations. In other words: can we truly say that the state of being in love which becomes manifest in analytic treatment is not a real one?

I think we have told the patient the truth, but not the whole truth regardless of the consequences. Of our two arguments the first is the stronger. The part played by resistance in transference-love is unquestionable and very considerable. Nevertheless the resistance did not, after all, *create* this love; it finds it ready to hand, makes use of it and aggravates its manifestations. Nor is the genuineness of the phenomenon disproved by the resistance. The second argument is far weaker. It is true that the love consists of new editions of old traits and that it repeats infantile reactions. But this is the essential character of every state of being in love. There is no such state which does not reproduce infantile prototypes. It is precisely from this infantile determination that it receives its compulsive character, verging as it does on the pathological. Transference-love has perhaps a degree less of freedom than the love which appears in ordinary life and is called normal; it displays its dependence on the infantile pattern more clearly and is less adaptable and capable of modification; but that is all, and not what is essential.

By what other signs can the genuineness of a love be recognized? By its efficacy, its serviceability in achieving the aim of love? In this respect transference-love seems to be second to none; one has the impression that one could obtain anything from it.

Let us sum up, therefore. We have no right to dispute that the state of being in love which makes its appearance in the course of analytic treatment had the character of a 'genuine' love. If it seems so lacking in normality, this is sufficiently explained by the fact that being in love in ordinary life, outside analysis, is also more similar to abnormal than to normal mental phenomena. Nevertheless, transference-love is characterized by certain features which ensure it a special position. In the first place, it is provoked by the analytic situation; secondly, it is greatly intensified by the resistance, which dominates the situation; and thirdly, it is lacking to a high degree in a regard for reality, is less sensible, less concerned about consequences and more blind in its valuation of the loved person than we are prepared to admit in the case of normal love. We should not forget, however, that these departures from the norm constitute precisely what is essential about being in love.

As regards the analyst's line of action, it is the first of these three features of transference-love which is the decisive factor. He has evoked this love by instituting analytic treatment in order to cure the neurosis. For him, it is an unavoidable consequence of a medical situation, like the exposure of a patient's body or the imparting of a vital secret. It is therefore plain to him that he must not derive any personal advantage from it. The patient's willingness makes no difference; it merely throws the whole responsibility on the analyst himself. Indeed, as he must know, the patient had been prepared for no other mechanism of cure. After all the difficulties have been successfully overcome, she will often confess to having had an anticipatory phantasy at the time when she entered the treatment, to the effect that if she behaved well she would be rewarded at the end by the doctor's affection.

For the doctor, ethical motives unite with the technical ones to restrain him from giving the patient his love. The aim he has to keep in view is that this woman, whose capacity for love is impaired by infantile fixations, should gain free command over a function which is of such inestimable importance to her; that she should not, however, dissipate it in the treatment, but keep it ready for the time when, after her treatment, the demands of real life make themselves felt. He must not stage the scene of a dog-race in which the prize was to be a garland of sausages but which some humorist spoilt by throwing a single sausage on to the track. The result was, of course, that the dogs threw themselves upon it and forgot all about the race and about the garland that was luring them to victory in the far distance. I do not mean to say that it is always easy for the doctor to keep within the limits prescribed by ethics and technique. Those who are still youngish and not yet bound by strong ties may in particular find it a hard task. Sexual love is undoubtedly one of the chief things in life, and the union of mental and bodily satisfaction in the enjoyment of love is one of its culminating peaks. Apart from a few queer fanatics, all the world knows this and conducts its life accordingly; science alone is too delicate to admit it. Again, when a woman sues for love, to reject and refuse is a distressing part for a man to play; and, in spite of neurosis and resistance, there is an incomparable fascination in a woman of high principles who confesses her passion. It is not a patient's crudely sensual desires which constitute the temptation. These are more likely to repel, and it will call for all the doctor's tolerance if he is to regard them as a natural phenomenon. It is rather, perhaps, a woman's subtler and aim-inhibited wishes which bring with them the danger of making a man forget his technique and his medical task for the sake of a fine experience.

And yet it is quite out of the question for the analyst to give way. However highly he may prize love he must prize even more highly the opportunity for helping his patient over a decisive stage in her life. She has to learn from him to overcome the pleasure principle, to give up a satisfaction which lies to hand but is socially not acceptable, in favour of a more distant one, which is perhaps altogether uncertain, but which is both psychologically and socially unimpeachable. To achieve this overcoming, she has to be led through the primal period of her mental development and on that path she has to acquire the extra piece of mental freedom which distinguishes conscious mental activity—in the systematic sense—from unconscious.[11]

The analytic psychotherapist thus has a threefold battle to wage—in his own mind against the forces which seek to drag him down from the analytic level; outside the analysis, against opponents who dispute the importance he attaches to the sexual instinctual forces and hinder him from making use of them in his scientific technique; and inside the analysis, against his patients, who at first behave like opponents but later on reveal the overvaluation of sexual life which dominates them, and who try to make him captive to their socially untamed passion.

The lay public, about whose attitude to psycho-analysis I spoke at the outset, will doubtless seize upon this discussion of transference-love as another opportunity for directing the attention of the world to the serious danger of this therapeutic method. The psycho-analyst knows that he is working with highly explosive forces and that he needs to proceed with as much caution and conscientiousness as a chemist. But when have chemists ever been forbidden, because of the danger, from handling explosive substances, which are indispensable, on account of their effects? It is remarkable that psycho-analysis has to win for itself afresh all the liberties which have long since been accorded to other medical activities. I am certainly not in favour of giving up the harmless methods of treatment. For many cases they are sufficient, and, when all is said, human society has no more use for the *furor sanandi*[12] than for any other fanaticism. But to believe that the psychoneuroses are to be conquered by operating with harmless little remedies is grossly to under-estimate those disorders both as to their origin and their practical importance. No; in medical practice there will always be room for the *'ferrum'* and the *'ignis'* side by side with the *'medicina'*;[13] and in the same way we shall never be able to do without a strictly regular, undiluted psycho-analysis which is not afraid to handle the most dangerous mental impulses and to obtain mastery over them for the benefit of the patient.

NOTES

1. In the first section of my contribution to the history of the psycho-analytic movement (1914*d*). [This refers to Breuer's difficulties over the transference in the case of Anna O. (*Standard Ed.*, **14**, 12).]
2. [The question of the 'counter-transference' had already been raised by Freud in his Nurem-

berg Congress paper (1910*d*), *Standard Ed.*, **11**, 144–5. He returns to it below, on pp. 42 f. and 46 f. Apart from these passages, it is hard to find any other explicit discussions of the subject in Freud's published works.]

3. We know that the transference can manifest itself in other, less tender feelings, but I do not propose to go into that side of the matter here. [See the paper on 'The Dynamics of Transference' (1912*b*), *Standard Ed.*, **12**, 105.]

4. [*'Häufig.'* In the first edition only, the word here is *'frühzeitig'* ('early').]

5. [In the first edition only, this paragraph (which is in the nature of a parenthesis) was printed in small type.]

6. [Freud had already stated this still more categorically in the first edition of *The Interpretation of Dreams* (1900*a*), *Standard Ed.*, **5**, 517. But in 1925 he added a long footnote to the passage, explaining its sense and qualifying the terms in which he had expressed himself.]

7. [Cf. *Standard Ed.*, **12**, 152–3.]

8. [Cf. Adler, 1911, 219.]

9. [Freud took this subject up again in his Budapest Congress paper (1919*a*), *Standard Ed.*, **17**, 162–3.]

10. See the preceding paper [*Standard Ed.*, **12**, 150].

11. [This distinction is explained in *Standard Ed.*, **12**, 266.]

12. ['Passion for curing people.']

13. [An allusion to a saying attributed to Hippocrates: 'Those diseases which medicines do not cure, iron (the knife?) cures; those which iron cannot cure, fire cures; and those which fire cannot cure are to be reckoned wholly incurable.' *Aphorisms*, VII, 87 (*trans.* 1849).]

4. The Nature of the Therapeutic Action of Psycho-Analysis

James Strachey

INTRODUCTORY

It was as a therapeutic procedure that psycho-analysis originated. It is in the main as a therapeutic agency that it exists to-day. We may well be surprised, therefore, at the relatively small proportion of psycho-analytical literature which has been concerned with the mechanisms by which its therapeutic effects are achieved. A very considerable quantity of data have been accumulated in the course of the last thirty or forty years which throw light upon the nature and workings of the human mind; perceptible progress has been made in the task of classifying and subsuming such data into a body of generalized hypotheses or scientific laws. But there has been a remarkable hesitation in applying these findings in any great detail to the therapeutic process itself. I cannot help feeling that this hesitation has been responsible for the fact that so many discussions upon the practical details of analytic technique seem to leave us at cross-purposes and at an inconclusive end. How, for instance, can we expect to agree upon the vexed question of whether and when we should give a 'deep interpretation', while we have no clear idea of what we *mean* by a 'deep interpretation', while, indeed, we have no exactly formulated view of the concept of 'interpretation' itself, no precise knowledge of what 'interpretation' is and what effect it has upon our patients? We should gain much, I think, from a clearer grasp of problems such as this. If we could arrive at a more detailed understanding of the workings of the therapeutic process we should be less prone to those occasional feelings of utter disorientation which few analysts are fortunate enough to escape; and the analytic movement itself might be less at the mercy of proposals for abrupt alterations in the ordinary technical procedure—proposals which derive much of their strength from the prevailing uncertainty as to

Reprinted by permission from the *International Journal of Psycho-Analysis* 15 (1934): 126–59. Copyright © Institute of Psycho-Analysis.

the exact nature of the analytic therapy. My present paper is a tentative attack upon this problem; and even though it should turn out that its very doubtful conclusions cannot be maintained, I shall be satisfied if I have drawn attention to the urgency of the problem itself. I am most anxious, however, to make it clear that what follows is not a practical discussion upon psycho-analytic technique. Its immediate bearings are merely theoretical. I have taken as my raw material the various sorts of procedures which (in spite of very considerable individual deviations) would be generally regarded as within the limits of 'orthodox' psycho-analysis and the various sorts of effects which observation shows that the application of such procedures tends to bring about; I have set up a hypothesis which endeavours to explain more or less coherently why these particular procedures bring about these particular effects; and I have tried to show that, if my hypothesis about the nature of the therapeutic action of psycho-analysis is valid, certain implications follow from it which might perhaps serve as criteria in forming a judgment of the probable effectiveness of any particular type of procedure.

RETROSPECT

It will be objected, no doubt, that I have exaggerated the novelty of my topic.[1] 'After all', it will be said, 'we *do* understand and have long understood the main principles that govern the therapeutic action of analysis'. And to this, of course, I entirely agree; indeed I propose to begin what I have to say by summarizing as shortly as possible the accepted views upon the subject. For this purpose I must go back to the period between the years 1912 and 1917 during which Freud gave us the greater part of what he has written directly on the therapeutic side of psycho-analysis, namely the series of papers on technique[2] and the twenty-seventh and twenty-eighth chapters of the *Introductory Lectures*.

'RESISTANCE ANALYSIS'

This period was characterized by the systematic application of the method known as 'resistance analysis'. The method in question was by no means a new one even at that time, and it was based upon ideas which had long been implicit in analytical theory, and in particular upon one of the earliest of Freud's views of the function of neurotic symptoms. According to that view (which was derived essentially from the study of hysteria) the function of the neurotic symptom was to defend the patient's personality against an unconscious trend of thought that was unacceptable to it, while at the same time gratifying the trend up to a certain point. It seemed to follow, therefore, that if the analyst were to investigate and discover the unconscious trend and make the patient aware of it—if he were to make what was unconscious conscious—the whole *raison d'être* of the symptom would cease and it must automatically disappear. Two difficulties arose, however. In the first place some part of the patient's mind was found to raise obstacles to the process, to offer resistance to the analyst when he tried to discover the unconscious trend; and it was easy to conclude that this was the same part of the patient's mind as had originally repudiated the unconscious trend and had thus necessitated the creation of the symptom. But, in the second place, even when this obstacle seemed to be surmounted, even when the analyst had succeeded in guessing or deducing the nature of the unconscious trend, had drawn the patient's attention to it and had apparently made him fully aware of it—even then it would often happen that the symptom persisted unshaken. The realization of these difficulties led to important results both theoretically and practically. *Theoretically,* it became evident that there were two senses in which a patient could become conscious of an unconscious trend; he could be made aware of it by the analyst in some intellectual sense without becoming 'really' conscious of it. To make this state of things more intelligible, Freud devised a kind of pictorial allegory. He imagined the mind as a kind of map. The original objectionable trend was pictured as being located in one region of this map and the newly discovered information about it, communicated to the patient by the analyst, in another. It was only if these two impressions could be 'brought together' (whatever exactly that might mean) that the unconscious trend would be 'really' made conscious. What prevented this from happening was a force within the patient, a barrier—once again, evidently, the same 'resistance' which had opposed the analyst's attempts at investigating the unconscious trend and which had contributed to the original production of the symptom. The removal of this resistance was the essential preliminary to the patient's becoming 'really' conscious of the unconscious trend. And it was at this point that the *practical* lesson emerged: as analysts our main task is not so much to investigate the objectionable unconscious trend as to get rid of the patient's resistance to it.

But how are we to set about this task of demolishing the resistance? Once again by the same process of investigation and explanation which we have already applied to the unconscious trend. But this time we are not faced by such difficulties as before, for the forces that are keeping up the repression, although they are to some extent unconscious, do not belong to the unconscious in the systematic sense; they are a part of the patient's ego, which is co-operating with us, and are thus more accessible. Nevertheless the existing state of equilibrium will not be upset, the ego will not be induced to do the work of re-adjustment that is required of it, unless we are able by our analytic procedure to mobilize some fresh force upon our side.

What forces can we count upon? The patient's will to recovery, in the first place, which led him to embark upon the analysis. And, again, a number of intellectual considerations which we can bring to his notice. We can make him understand the structure of his symptom and the motives for his repudiation of the objectionable trend. We can point out the fact that these motives are out-of-date and no longer valid; that they may have been reasonable when he was a baby, but are no longer so now that he is grown up. And finally we can insist that his original solution of the difficulty has only led to illness, while the new one that we propose holds out a prospect of health. Such motives as these may play a part in inducing the patient to abandon his resistances; nevertheless it is from an entirely different quarter that the decisive factor emerges. This factor, I need hardly say, is the transference. And I must now recall, very briefly, the main ideas held by Freud on that subject during the period with which I am dealing.

TRANSFERENCE

I should like to remark first that, although from very early times Freud had called attention to the fact that transference manifested itself in two ways— negatively as well as positively, a good deal less was said or known about the negative transference than about the positive. This of course corresponds to the circumstance that interest in the destructive and aggressive impulses in general is only a comparatively recent development. Transference was regarded predominantly as a *libidinal* phenomenon. It was suggested that in everyone there existed a certain number of unsatisfied libidinal impulses, and that whenever some new person came upon the scene these impulses were ready to attach themselves to him. This was the account of transference as a universal phenomenon. In neurotics, owing to the abnormally large quantities of unattached libido present in them, the tendency to transference would be correspondingly greater; and the peculiar circumstances of the analytic situation would further increase it. It was evidently the existence of these feelings of love, thrown by the patient upon the analyst, that provided the necessary extra force to induce his ego to give up its resistances, undo the repressions and adopt a fresh solution of its ancient problems. This instrument, without which no therapeutic result could be obtained, was at once seen to be no stranger; it was in fact the familiar power of suggestion, which had ostensibly been abandoned long before. Now, however, it was being employed in a very different way, in fact in a contrary direction. In pre-analytic days it had aimed at bringing about an increase in the degree of repression; now it was used to overcome the resistance of the ego, that is to say, to allow the repression to be removed.

But the situation became more and more complicated as more facts about transference came to light. In the first place, the feelings transferred turned out to be of various sorts; besides the loving ones there were the hostile ones, which were naturally far from assisting the analyst's efforts. But, even apart from the hostile transference, the libidinal feelings themselves fell into two groups: friendly and affectionate feelings which were capable of being conscious, and purely erotic ones which had usually to remain unconscious. And these latter feelings, when they became too powerful, stirred up the repressive forces of the ego and thus increased its resistances instead of diminishing them, and in fact produced a state of things that was not easily distinguishable from a negative transference. And beyond all this there arose the whole question of the lack of permanence of all suggestive treatments. Did not the existence of the transference threaten to leave the analytic patient in the same unending dependence upon the analyst?

All of these difficulties were got over by the discovery that the transference itself could be analysed. Its analysis, indeed, was soon found to be the most important part of the whole treatment. It was possible to make conscious its roots in the repressed unconscious just as it was possible to make conscious any other repressed material—that is, by inducing the ego to abandon its resistances—and there was nothing self-contradictory in the fact that the force used for resolving the transference was the transference itself. And once it had been made conscious, its unmanageable, infantile, permanent characteristics disappeared; what was left was like any other 'real' human relationship. But the necessity for constantly analysing the transference became still more apparent from another discovery. It was found that as work proceeded the transference tended, as it were, to eat up the entire analysis. More and more of the patient's libido became concentrated upon his relation to the analyst, the patient's original symptoms were drained of their cathexis, and there appeared instead an artificial neurosis to which Freud gave the name of the 'transference neurosis'. The original conflicts, which had led to the onset of neurosis, began to be re-enacted in the relation to the analyst. Now this unexpected event is far from being the misfortune that at first sight it might seem to be. In fact it gives us our great opportunity. Instead of having to deal as best we may with conflicts of the remote past, which are concerned with dead circumstances and mummified personalities, and whose outcome is already determined, we find ourselves involved in an actual and immediate situation, in which we and the patient are the principal characters and the development of which is to some extent at least under our control. But if we bring it about that in this revivified transference conflict the patient chooses a new solution instead of the old one, a solution in which the primitive and unadaptable method of repression is replaced by behaviour more in contact with reality, then, even after his detachment from the analysis, he will never be able to fall back into his former neurosis. The solution of the transference conflict implies the simultaneous solution of the infantile conflict of which it is a new edition. 'The change', says Freud in his *Introductory Lectures*, 'is made possible by alterations in the ego occurring as a consequence of the analyst's suggestions. At the expense of the unconscious, the ego becomes wider by the work of interpretation which brings the unconscious material into consciousness; through education it becomes reconciled to the libido and is made willing to grant it a certain degree of satisfaction; and its horror of the claims of its libido is lessened by the new capacity it acquires to expend a certain amount of the libido in sublimation. The more nearly the course of the treatment corresponds with this ideal description the greater will be the success of the psycho-analytic therapy'.[3] I quote these words of Freud's to make it quite clear that at the time he wrote them he held that the ultimate factor in the therapeutic action of psychoanalysis was suggestion on the part of the analyst acting upon the patient's ego in such a way as to make it more tolerant of the libidinal trends.

THE SUPER-EGO

In the years that have passed since he wrote this passage Freud has produced extremely little that bears directly on the subject; and that little goes to show that he has not altered his views of the main principles involved. Indeed, in the additional lectures which were published last year, he explicitly states that he has nothing to add to the theoretical discussion upon therapy given in the original lectures fifteen years earlier.[4] At the same time there has in the interval been a considerable further development of his theoretical opinions, and especially in the region of ego-psychology. He has, in particular, formulated the concept of the super-ego. The re-statement in super-ego terms of the principles of therapeutics which he laid down in the period of resistance analysis may not involve many changes. But it is reasonable to expect that information about the super-ego will be of special interest from our point of view; and in two ways. In the first place, it would at first sight seem highly probable that the super-ego should play an important part, direct or indirect, in the setting-up and maintaining of the repressions and resistances the demolition of which has been the chief aim of analysis. And this is confirmed by an examination of the classification of the various kinds of resistance made by Freud in *Hemmung Symptom und Angst* (1926).[5] Of the five sorts of resistance there mentioned it is true that only one is attributed to the direct intervention of the super-ego, but two of the ego-resistances—the repression-resistance and the transference-resistance—although actually originating from the ego, are as a rule set up by it out of fear of the super-ego. It seems likely enough therefore that when Freud wrote the words which I have just quoted, to the effect that the favourable change in the patient 'is made possible by alterations in the ego' he was thinking, in part at all events, of that portion of the ego which he subsequently separated off into the super-ego. Quite apart from this, moreover, in another of Freud's more recent works, the *Group Psychology* (1921), there are passages which suggest a different point— namely, that it may be largely through the patient's super-ego that the analyst is able to influence him. These passages occur in the course of his discussion on the nature of hypnosis and suggestion.[6] He definitely rejects Bernheim's view that all hypnotic phenomena are traceable to the factor of suggestion, and adopts the alternative theory that suggestion is a partial manifestation of the state of hypnosis. The state of hypnosis, again, is found in certain respects to resemble the state of being in love. There is 'the same humble subjection, the same compliance, the same absence of criticism towards the hypnotist as towards the loved object'; in particular, there can be no doubt that the hypnotist, like the loved object, 'has stepped into the place of the subject's ego-ideal'. Now since suggestion is a partial form of hypnosis and since the analyst brings about his changes in the patient's attitude by means of suggestion, it seems to follow that the analyst owes his effectiveness, at all events in some respects, to his having stepped into the place of the patient's super-ego. Thus there are two convergent lines of argument which point to the patient's super-ego as occupying a key position in analytic therapy: it is a part of the patient's mind in which a favourable alteration would be likely to lead to general improvement, and it is a part of the patient's mind which is especially subject to the analyst's influence.

Such plausible notions as these were followed up almost immediately after the super-ego made its first *début*.[7] They were developed by Ernest Jones, for instance, in his paper on 'The Nature of Auto-Suggestion'.[8] Soon afterwards[9] Alexander launched his theory that the principal aim of all psycho-analytic therapy must be the complete demolition of the super-ego and the assumption of its functions by the ego. According to his account, the treatment falls into two phases. In the first phase the functions of the patient's super-ego are handed over to the analyst, and in the second phase they are passed back again to the patient, but this time to his ego. The super-ego, according to this view of Alexander's (though he explicitly limits his use of the word to the *unconscious* parts of the ego-ideal), is a portion of the fundamental apparatus which is essentially primitive, out of date and out of touch with reality, which is incapable of adapting itself, and which operates automatically, with the monotonous uniformity of a reflex. Any useful functions that it performs can be carried out by the ego, and there is therefore nothing to be done with it but to scrap it. This wholesale attack upon the super-ego seems to be of questionable validity. It seems probable that its abolition, even if that were practical politics, would involve the abolition of a large number of highly desirable mental activities. But the idea that the analyst temporarily takes over the functions of the patient's super-ego during the treatment and by so doing in some way alters it agrees with the tentative remarks which I have already made.

So, too, do some passages in a paper by Radó upon 'The Economic Principle in Psycho-Analytic Technique'.[10] The second part of this paper, which was to have dealt with psycho-analysis, has unfortunately never been published; but the first one, on hypnotism and catharsis,[11] contains much that is of interest. It includes a theory that the hypnotic subject introjects the hypnotist in the form of what Radó calls a 'parasitic super-ego', which draws off the energy and takes over the functions of the subject's original super-ego. One feature of the situation brought out by Radó is the unstable and temporary nature of this whole arrangement. If, for instance, the hypnotist gives a command which is too much in opposition to the subject's original super-ego, the parasite is promptly extruded. And, in any case, when the state of hypnosis comes to an end, the sway of the parasite super-ego also terminates and the original super-ego resumes its functions.

However debatable may be the details of Radó's description, it not only emphasizes once again the notion of the super-ego as the fulcrum of psychotherapy, but it draws attention to the important distinction between the effects of hypnosis and analysis in the matter of permanence. Hypnosis acts essentially in a temporary way, and Radó's theory of the parasitic super-ego, which does not really replace the original one but merely throws it out of action, gives a very good picture of its apparent workings. Analysis, on the other hand, in so so far as it seeks to affect the patient's super-ego, aims at something much more far-reaching and permanent—namely, at an integral change in the nature of the patient's super-ego itself.[12] Some even more recent developments in psycho-analytic theory give a hint, so it seems to me, of the kind of lines along which a clearer understanding of the question may perhaps be reached.

INTROJECTION AND PROJECTION

This latest growth of theory has been very much occupied with the destructive impulses and has brought them for the first time into the centre of interest; and attention has at the same time been concentrated on the correlated problems of guilt and anxiety. What I have in mind especially are the ideas upon the formation of the super-ego recently developed by Melanie Klein and the importance which she attributes to the processes of introjection and projection in the development of the personality. I will re-state what I believe to be her views in an exceedingly schematic outline.[13] The individual, she holds, is perpetually introjecting and projecting the objects of its id-impulses, and the character of the introjected objects depends on the character of the id-impulses directed towards the external objects. Thus, for instance, during the stage of a child's libidinal development in which it is dominated by feelings of oral aggression, its feelings towards its external object will be orally aggressive; it will then introject the object, and the introjected object will now act (in the manner of a super-ego) in an orally aggressive way towards the child's ego. The next event will be the projection of this orally aggressive introjected object back on to the external object, which will now in its turn appear to be orally aggressive. The fact of the external object being thus felt as dangerous and destructive once more causes the id-impulses to adopt an even more aggressive and destructive attitude towards the object in self-defence. A vicious circle is thus established. This process seeks to account for the extreme severity of the super-ego in small children, as well as for their unreasonable fear of outside objects. In the course of the development of the normal individual, his libido eventually reaches the genital stage, at which the positive impulses predominate. His attitude towards his external objects will thus become more friendly, and accordingly his introjected object (or super-ego) will become less severe and his ego's contact with reality will be less distorted. In the case of the neurotic, however, for various reasons—whether on account of frustration or of an incapacity of the ego to tolerate id-impulses, or of an inherent excess of the destructive components—development to the genital stage does not occur, but the individual remains fixated at a pre-genital level. His ego is thus left exposed to the pressure of a savage id on the one hand and a correspondingly savage super-ego on the other, and the vicious circle I have just described is perpetuated.

THE NEUROTIC VICIOUS CIRCLE

I should like to suggest that the hypothesis which I have stated in this bald fashion may be useful in helping us to form a picture not only of the mechanism of a *neurosis* but also of the mechanism of its *cure*. There is, after all, nothing new in regarding a neurosis as essentially an obstacle or deflecting force in the path of normal development; nor is there anything new in the belief that psycho-analysis (owing to the peculiarities of the analytic situation) is able to remove the obstacle and so allow the normal development to proceed. I am only trying to make our conceptions a little more precise by supposing that the pathological obstacle to the neurotic individual's further growth is in the nature of a vicious circle of the kind I have described. If a breach could somehow or other be made in the vicious circle, the processes of development would proceed upon their normal course. If, for instance, the patient could be made less frightened of his super-ego or introjected object, he would project less terrifying imagos on to the outer object and would therefore have less need to feel hostility towards it; the object which he then introjected would in turn be less savage in its pressure upon the id-impulses, which would be able to lose something of their primitive ferocity. In short, a *benign* circle would be set up instead of the vicious one, and ultimately the patient's libidinal development would proceed to the genital level, when, as in the case of a normal adult, his super-ego will be comparatively mild and his ego will have a relatively undistorted contact with reality.[14]

But at what point in the vicious circle is the breach to be made and how is it actually to be effected? It is obvious that to alter the character of a person's super-ego is easier said than done. Nevertheless, the quotations that I have already made from earlier discussions of the subject strongly suggest that the super-ego will be found to play an important part in the solution of our problem. Before we go further, however, it will be necessary to consider a little more closely the nature of what is described as the analytic situation. The relation between the two persons concerned in it is a highly complex one, and for our present purposes I am going to isolate two elements in it. In the first place, the patient in analysis tends to centre the whole of his id-impulses upon the analyst. I shall not comment further upon this fact or its implications, since they are so immensely familiar. I will only emphasize their vital importance to all that follows and proceed at once to the second element of the analytic situation which I wish to isolate. The patient in analysis tends to accept the analyst in some way or other as a substitute for his own super-ego. I propose at this point to imitate with a slight difference the convenient phrase which was used by Radó in his account of hypnosis and to say that in analysis the patient tends to make the analyst into an 'auxiliary super-ego'. This phrase and the relation described by it evidently require some explanation.

THE ANALYST AS 'AUXILIARY SUPER-EGO'

When a neurotic patient meets a new object in ordinary life, according to our underlying hypothesis he will tend to project on to it his introjected archaic objects and the new object will become to that extent a phantasy object. It is to be presumed that his introjected objects are more or less separated out into two groups, which function as a 'good' introjected object (or mild super-ego) and a 'bad' introjected object (or harsh super-ego). According to the degree to which his ego maintains contacts with reality, the 'good' introjected object will be projected on to benevolent real outside objects and the 'bad' one on to malignant real outside objects. Since, however, he is by hypothesis neurotic, the 'bad' introjected object will predominate, and will tend to be projected more than the 'good' one; and there will further be a tendency, even where to begin with the 'good' object was projected, for the 'bad' one after a time to take its place. Consequently, it will be true to say that in

general the neurotic's phantasy objects in the outer world will be predominantly dangerous and hostile. Moreover, since even his 'good' introjected
objects will be 'good' according to an archaic and infantile standard, and will
be to some extent maintained simply for the purpose of counteracting the
'bad' objects, even his 'good' phantasy objects in the outer world will be
very much out of touch with reality. Going back now to the moment when
our neurotic patient meets a new object in real life and supposing (as will be
the more usual case) that he projects his 'bad' introjected object on to it—
the phantasy external object will then seem to him to be dangerous; he will
be frightened of it and, to defend himself against it, will become more angry.
Thus when he introjects this new object in turn, it will merely be adding one
more terrifying imago to those he has already introjected. The new introjected imago will in fact simply be a duplicate of the original archaic ones,
and his super-ego will remain almost exactly as it was. The same will be also
true *mutatis mutandis* where he begins by projecting his 'good' introjected
object on to the new external object he has met with. No doubt, as a result,
there will be a slight strengthening of his kind super-ego at the expense of
his harsh one, and to that extent his condition will be improved. But there
will be no *qualitative* change in his super-ego, for the new 'good' object
introjected will only be a duplicate of an archaic original and will only reinforce the archaic 'good' super-ego already present.

The effect when this neurotic patient comes in contact with a new object
in analysis is from the first moment to create a different situation. His super-
ego is in any case neither homogeneous nor well-organised; the account we
have given of it hitherto has been over-simplified and schematic. Actually
the introjected imagos which go to make it up are derived from a variety of
different stages of his history and function to some extent independently.
Now, owing to the peculiarities of the analytic circumstances and of the
analyst's behaviour, the introjected imago of the analyst tends in part to be
rather definitely separated off from the rest of the patient's super-ego. (This,
of course, presupposes a certain degree of contact with reality on his part.
Here we have one of the fundamental criteria of accessibility to analytic
treatment; another, which we have already implicitly noticed, is the patient's
ability to attach his id-impulses to the analyst.) This separation between the
imago of the introjected analyst and the rest of the patient's super-ego
becomes evident at quite an early stage of the treatment; for instance in
connection with the fundamental rule of free association. The new bit of
super-ego tells the patient that he is allowed to say anything that may come

into his head. This works satisfactorily for a little; but soon there comes a conflict between the new bit and the rest, for the original super-ego says: 'You must *not* say this, for, if you do, you will be using an obscene word or betraying so-and-so's confidences'. The separation off of the new bit—what I have called the 'auxiliary' super-ego—tends to persist for the very reason that it usually operates in a different direction from the rest of the super-ego. And this is true not only of the 'harsh' super-ego but also of the 'mild' one. For, though the auxiliary super-ego is in fact kindly, it is not kindly in the same archaic way as the patient's introjected 'good' imagos. The most important characteristic of the auxiliary super-ego is that its advice to the ego is consistently based upon *real* and *contemporary* considerations and this in itself serves to differentiate it from the greater part of the original super-ego.

In spite of this, however, the situation is extremely insecure. There is a constant tendency for the whole distinction to break down. The patient is liable at any moment to project his terrifying imago on to the analyst just as though he were anyone else he might have met in the course of his life. If this happens, the introjected imago of the analyst will be wholly incorporated into the rest of the patient's harsh super-ego, and the auxiliary super-ego will disappear. And even when the *content* of the auxiliary super-ego's advice is realised as being different from or contrary to that of the original super-ego, very often its *quality* will be felt as being the same. For instance, the patient may feel that the analyst has said to him: 'If you don't say whatever comes into your head, I shall give you a good hiding', or, 'If you don't become conscious of this piece of the unconscious I shall turn you out of the room'. Nevertheless, labile though it is, and limited as is its authority, this peculiar relation between the analyst and the patient's ego seems to put into the analyst's grasp his main instrument in assisting the development of the therapeutic process. What is this main weapon in the analyst's armoury? Its name springs at once to our lips. The weapon is, of course, interpretation. And here we reach the core of the problem that I want to discuss in the present paper.

INTERPRETATION

What, then, *is* interpretation? and how does it work? Extremely little seems to be known about it, but this does not prevent an almost universal belief in its remarkable efficacy as a weapon: interpretation has, it must be confessed, many of the qualities of a *magic* weapon. It is, of course, felt as such by many patients. Some of them spend hours at a time in providing interpretations of their own—often ingenious, illuminating, correct. Others, again, derive a direct libidinal gratification from being given interpretations and may even develop something parallel to a drug-addiction to them. In non-analytical circles interpretation is usually either scoffed at as something ludicrous, or dreaded as a frightful danger. This last attitude is shared, I think, more than is often realized, by a certain number of analysts. This was particularly revealed by the reactions shown in many quarters when the idea of giving interpretations to small children was first mooted by Melanie Klein. But I believe it would be true in general to say that analysts are inclined to feel interpretation as something extremely powerful whether for good or ill. I am speaking now of our *feelings* about interpretation as distinguished from our reasoned beliefs. And there might seem to be a good many grounds for thinking that our feelings on the subject tend to distort our beliefs. At all events, many of these beliefs seem superficially to be contradictory; and the contradictions do not always spring from different schools of thought, but are apparently sometimes held simultaneously by one individual. Thus, we are told that if we interpret too soon or too rashly, we run the risk of losing a patient; that unless we interpret promptly and deeply we run the risk of losing a patient; that interpretation may give rise to intolerable and unmanageable outbreaks of anxiety by 'liberating' it; that interpretation is the only way of enabling a patient to cope with an unmanageable outbreak of anxiety by 'resolving' it; that interpretations must always refer to material on the very point of emerging into consciousness; that the most useful interpretations are really deep ones; 'Be cautious with your interpretations!' says one voice; 'When in doubt, interpret!' says another. Nevertheless, although there is evidently a good deal of confusion in all of this, I do not think these views are necessarily incompatible; the various pieces of advice may turn out to refer to different circumstances and different cases and to imply different uses of the word 'interpretation'.

For the word is evidently used in more than one sense. It is, after all, perhaps only a synonym for the old phrase we have already come across— 'making what is unconscious conscious', and it shares all of that phrase's ambiguities. For in one sense, if you give a German-English dictionary to someone who knows no German, you will be giving him a collection of interpretations, and this, I think, is the kind of sense in which the nature of interpretation has been discussed in a recent paper by Bernfeld.[15] Such descriptive interpretations have evidently no relevance to our present topic, and I shall proceed without more ado to define as clearly as I can one particular sort of interpretation, which seems to me to be actually the ultimate instrument of psycho-analytic therapy and to which for convenience I shall give the name of 'mutative' interpretation.

I shall first of all give a schematized outline of what I understand by a mutative interpretation, leaving the details to be filled in afterwards; and, with a view to clarity of exposition, I shall take as an instance the interpretation of a hostile impulse. By virtue of his power (his strictly limited power) as auxiliary super-ego, the analyst gives permission for a certain small quantity of the patient's id-energy (in our instance, in the form of an aggressive impulse) to become conscious.[16] Since the analyst is also, from the nature of things, the *object* of the patient's id-impulses, the quantity of these impulses which is now released into consciousness will become consciously directed towards the analyst. This is the critical point. If all goes well, the patient's ego will become aware of the contrast between the aggressive character of his feelings and the real nature of the analyst, who does not behave like the patient's 'good' or 'bad' archaic objects. The patient, that is to say, will become aware of a distinction between his archaic phantasy object and the real external object. The interpretation has now become a mutative one, since it has produced a breach in the neurotic vicious circle. For the patient, having become aware of the lack of aggressiveness in the real external object, will be able to diminish his own aggressiveness; the new object which he introjects will be less aggressive, and consequently the aggressiveness of his super-ego will also be diminished. As a further corollary to these events, and simultaneously with them, the patient will obtain access to the infantile material which is being re-experienced by him in his relation to the analyst.

Such is the general scheme of the mutative interpretation. You will notice that in my account the process appears to fall into two phases. I am anxious not to pre-judge the question of whether these two phases are in temporal sequence or whether they may not really be two simultaneous aspects of a single event. But for descriptive purposes it is easier to deal with them as though they were successive. First, then, there is the phase in which the patient becomes conscious of a particular quantity of id-energy as being directed towards the analyst; and secondly there is the phase in which the patient becomes aware that this id-energy is directed towards an archaic phantasy object and not towards a real one.

THE FIRST PHASE OF INTERPRETATION

The first phase of a mutative interpretation—that in which a portion of the patient's id-relation to the analyst is made conscious in virtue of the latter's position as auxiliary super-ego—is in itself complex. In the classical model of an interpretation, the patient will first be made aware of a state of tension in his ego, will next be made aware that there is a repressive factor at work (that his super-ego is threatening him with punishment), and will only then be made aware of the id-impulse which has stirred up the protests of his super-ego and so given rise to the anxiety in his ego. This is the classical scheme. In actual practice, the analyst finds himself working from all three sides at once, or in irregular succession. At one moment a small portion of the patient's super-ego may be revealed to him in all its savagery, at another the shrinking defencelessness of his ego, at yet another his attention may be directed to the attempts which he is making at restitution—at compensating for his hostility; on some occasions a fraction of id-energy may even be directly encouraged to break its way through the last remains of an already weakened resistance. There is, however, one characteristic which all of these various operations have in common; they are essentially upon a small scale. For the mutative interpretation is inevitably governed by the principle of minimal doses. It is, I think, a commonly agreed clinical fact that alterations in a patient under analysis appear almost always to be extremely gradual: we are inclined to suspect sudden and large changes as an indication that suggestive rather than psycho-analytic processes are at work. The gradual nature of the changes brought about in psycho-analysis will be explained if, as I am suggesting, those changes are the result of the summation of an immense number of minute steps, each of which corresponds to a mutative interpretation. And the smallness of each step is in turn imposed by the very nature of the analytic situation. For each interpretation involves the release of a certain quantity of id-energy, and, as we shall see in a moment, if the quantity released is too large, the highly unstable state of equilibrium which enables the analyst to function as the patient's auxiliary super-ego is bound to be upset. The whole analytic situation will thus be imperilled, since it is only in virtue of the analyst's acting as auxiliary super-ego that these releases of id-energy can occur at all.

Let us examine in greater detail the effects which follow from the analyst attempting to bring too great a quantity of id-energy into the patient's consciousness all at once.[17] On the one hand, nothing whatever may happen, or on the other hand there may be an unmanageable result; but in neither event will a mutative interpretation have been effected. In the former case (in which there is apparently no effect) the analyst's power as auxiliary super-ego will not have been strong enough for the job he has set himself. But this again may be for two very different reasons. It may be that the id-impulses he was trying to bring out were not in fact sufficiently urgent at the moment: for, after all, the emergence of an id-impulse depends on two factors—not only on the permission of the super-ego, but also on the urgency (the degree of cathexis) of the id-impulse itself. This, then, may be one cause of an apparently negative response to an interpretation, and evidently a fairly harmless one. But the same apparent result may also be due to something else; in spite of the id-impulse being really urgent, the strength of the patient's own repressive forces (the degree of repression) may have been too great to allow his ego to listen to the persuasive voice of the auxiliary super-ego. Now here we have a situation dynamically identical with the next one we have to consider, though economically different. This next situation is one in which the patient accepts the interpretation, that is, allows the id-impulse into his consciousness, but is immediately overwhelmed with anxiety. This may show itself in a number of ways: for instance, the patient may produce a manifest anxiety-attack, or he may exhibit signs of 'real' anger with the analyst with complete lack of insight, or he may break off the analysis. In any of these cases the analytic situation will, for the moment at least, have broken down. The patient will be behaving just as the hypnotic subject behaves when, having been ordered by the hypnotist to perform an action too much at variance with his own conscience, he breaks off the hypnotic relation and wakes up from his trance. This state of things, which is *manifest* where the patient responds to an interpretation with an actual outbreak of anxiety or one of its equivalents, may be *latent* where the patient shews no response. And this latter case may be the more awkward of the two, since it is masked, and it may sometimes, I think, be the effect of a greater overdose of interpretation than where manifest anxiety arises (though obviously other factors will be of determining importance here and in partic-ular the nature of the patient's neurosis). I have ascribed this threatened collapse of the analytic situation to an overdose of interpretation: but it might be more accurate in some ways to ascribe it to an *insufficient* dose. For what has happened is that the second phase of the interpretative process has not occurred: the phase in which the patient becomes aware that his impulse is directed towards an archaic phantasy object and not towards a real one.

THE SECOND PHASE OF INTERPRETATION

In the second phase of a complete interpretation, therefore, a crucial part is played by the patient's sense of reality: for the successful outcome of that phase depends upon his ability, at the critical moment of the emergence into consciousness of the released quantity of id-energy, to distinguish between his phantasy object and the real analyst. The problem here is closely related to one that I have already discussed, namely that of the extreme liability of the analyst's position as auxiliary super-ego. The analytic situation is all the time threatening to degenerate into a 'real' situation. But this actually means the opposite of what it appears to. It means that the patient is all the time on the brink of turning the real external object (the analyst) into the archaic one; that is to say, he is on the brink of projecting his primitive introjected imagos on to him. In so far as the patient actually does this, the analyst becomes like anyone else that he meets in real life—a phantasy object. The analyst then ceases to possess the peculiar advantages derived from the analytic situation; he will be introjected like all other phantasy objects into the patient's super-ego, and will no longer be able to function in the peculiar ways which are essential to the effecting of a mutative interpretation. In this difficulty the patient's sense of reality is an essential but a very feeble ally; indeed, an improvement in it is one of the things that we hope the analysis will bring about. It is important, therefore, not to submit it to any unnecessary strain; and that is the fundamental reason why the analyst must avoid any real behaviour that is likely to confirm the patient's view of him as a 'bad' or a 'good' phantasy object. This is perhaps more obvious as regards the 'bad' object. If, for instance, the analyst were to shew that he was really shocked or frightened by one of the patient's id-impulses, the patient would immediately treat him in that respect as a dangerous object and introject him into his archaic severe super-ego. Thereafter, on the one hand, there would be a diminution in the analyst's power to function as an auxiliary super-ego and to allow the patient's ego to become conscious of his id-impulses—that is to say, in his power to bring about the *first* phase of a mutative interpretation; and, on the other hand, he would, as a real object, become sensibly less distinguishable from the patient's 'bad' phantasy object and to that extent the carrying through of the *second* phase of a mutative interpretation would also be made more difficult. Or again, there is another case. Supposing the analyst behaves in an opposite way and actively urges the patient to give free rein to his id-impulses. There is then a possibility of the patient confusing the analyst with the imago of a treacherous parent who first encourages him to seek gratification, and then suddenly turns and punishes him. In such a case, the patient's ego may look for defence by itself suddenly turning upon the analyst as though he were his own id, and treating him with all the severity of which his super-ego is capable. Here again, the analyst is running a risk of losing his privileged position. But it may be equally unwise for the analyst to act really in such a way as to encourage the patient to project his 'good' introjected object on to him. For the patient will then tend to regard him as a good object in an archaic sense and will incorporate him with his archaic 'good' imagos and will use him as a protection against his 'bad' ones. In that way, his infantile positive impulses as well as his negative ones may escape analysis, for there may no longer be a possibility for his ego to make a comparison between the phantasy external object and the real one. It will perhaps be argued that, with the best will in the world, the analyst, however careful he may be, will be unable to prevent the patient from projecting these various imagos on to him. This is of course indisputable, and, indeed, the whole effectiveness of analysis depends upon its being so. The lesson of these difficulties is merely to remind us that the patient's sense of reality has the narrowest limits. It is a paradoxical fact that the best way of ensuring that his ego shall be able to distinguish between phantasy and reality is to withhold reality from him as much as possible. But it is true. His ego is so weak—so much at the mercy of his id and super-ego—that he can only cope with reality if it is administered in minimal doses. And these doses are in fact what the analyst gives him, in the form of interpretations.

INTERPRETATION AND REASSURANCE

It seems to me possible that an approach to the twin practical problems of interpretation and reassurance may be facilitated by this distinction between the two phases of interpretation. Both procedures may, it would appear, be useful or even essential in certain circumstances and inadvisable or even dangerous in others. In the case of interpretation,[18] the first of our hypothetical phases may be said to 'liberate' anxiety, and the second to 'resolve' it. Where a quantity of anxiety is already present or on the point of breaking out, an interpretation, owing to the efficacy of its second phase, may enable the patient to recognize the unreality of his terrifying phantasy object and so to reduce his own hostility and consequently his anxiety. On the other hand, to induce the ego to allow a quantity of id-energy into consciousness is obviously to court an outbreak of anxiety in a personality with a harsh super-ego. And this is precisely what the analyst does in the first phase of an interpretation. As regards 'reassurance', I can only allude briefly here to some of the problems it raises.[19] I believe, incidentally, that the term needs to be defined almost as urgently as 'interpretation', and that it covers a number of different mechanisms. But in the present connection reassurance may be regarded as behaviour on the part of the analyst calculated to make the patient regard him as a 'good' phantasy object rather than as a real one. I have already given some reasons for doubting the expediency of this, though it seems to be generally felt that the procedure may sometimes be of great value, especially in psychotic cases. It might, moreover, be supposed at first sight that the adoption of such an attitude by the analyst might actually directly favour the prospect of making a mutative interpretation. But I believe that it will be seen on reflection that this is not in fact the case: for precisely in so far as the patient regards the analyst as his phantasy object, the second phase of the interpretation does not occur—since it is of the essence of that phase that in it the patient should make a distinction between his phantasy object and the real one. It is true that his anxiety may be reduced; but this result will not have been achieved by a method that involves a permanent qualitative change in his super-ego. Thus, whatever tactical importance reassurance may possess, it cannot, I think, claim to be regarded as an ultimate operative factor in psycho-analytic therapy.

It must here be noticed that certain other sorts of behaviour on the part of the analyst may be dynamically equivalent to the giving of a mutative interpretation, or to one or other of the two phases of that process. For instance, an 'active' injunction of the kind contemplated by Ferenczi may amount to an example of the first phase of an interpretation; the analyst is making use of his peculiar position in order to induce the patient to become conscious in a particularly vigorous fashion of certain of his id-impulses. One of the objections to this form of procedure may be expressed by saying that the analyst has very little control over the dosage of the id-energy that is thus released, and very little guarantee that the second phase of the interpretation will follow. He may therefore be unwittingly precipitating one of those critical situations which are always liable to arise in the case of an incomplete interpretation. Incidentally, the same dynamic pattern may arise when the analyst requires the patient to produce a 'forced' phantasy or even (especially at an early stage in an analysis) when the analyst asks the patient a question; here again, the analyst is in effect giving a blindfold interpretation, which it may prove impossible to carry beyond its first phase. On the other hand, situations are fairly constantly arising in the course of an analysis in which the patient becomes conscious of small quantities of id-energy without any direct provocation on the part of the analyst. An anxiety situation might then develop, if it were not that the analyst, by his behaviour or, one might say, absence of behaviour, enables the patient to mobilize his sense of reality and make the necessary distinction between an archaic object and a real one. What the analyst is doing here is equivalent to bringing about the second phase of an interpretation, and the whole episode may amount to the making of a mutative interpretation. It is difficult to estimate what proportion of the therapeutic changes which occur during analysis may not be due to *implicit* mutative interpretations of this kind. Incidentally, this type of situation seems sometimes to be regarded, incorrectly as I think, as an example of reassurance.

'IMMEDIACY' OF MUTATIVE INTERPRETATIONS

But it is now time to turn to two other characteristics which appear to be essential properties of every mutative interpretation. There is in the first place one already touched upon in considering the apparent or real absence of effect which sometimes follows upon the giving of an interpretation. A mutative interpretation can only be applied to an id-impulse which is actually in a state of cathexis. This seems self-evident; for the dynamic changes in the patient's mind implied by a mutative interpretation can only be brought about by the operation of a charge of energy originating in the patient himself: the function of the analyst is merely to ensure that the energy shall flow along one channel rather than along another. It follows from this that the purely informative 'dictionary' type of interpretation will be non-mutative, however useful it may be as a prelude to mutative interpretations. And this leads to a number of practical inferences. Every mutative interpretation must be emotionally 'immediate'; the patient must experience it as something actual. This requirment, that the interpretation must be 'immediate', may be expressed in another way by saying that interpretations must always be directed to the 'point of urgency'. At any given moment some particular id-impulse will be in activity; *this* is the impulse that is susceptible of mutative interpretation at that time, and no other one. It is, no doubt, neither possible nor desirable to be giving mutative interpretations all the time; but, as Melanie Klein has pointed out, it is a most precious quality in an analyst to be able at any moment to pick out the point of urgency.[20]

'DEEP' INTERPRETATION

But the fact that every mutative interpretation must deal with an 'urgent' impulse takes us back one more to the commonly felt fear of the explosive possibilities of interpretation, and particularly of what is vaguely referred to as 'deep' interpretation. The ambiguity of the term, however, need not bother us. It describes, no doubt, the interpretation of material which is either genetically early and historically distant from the patient's actual experience or which is under an especially heavy weight of repression—material, in any case, which is in the normal course of things exceedingly inaccessible to his ego and remote from it. There seems reason to believe, moreover, that the anxiety which is liable to be aroused by the approach of such material to consciousness may be of peculiar severity.[21] The question whether it is 'safe' to interpret such material will, as usual, mainly depend upon whether the second phase of the interpretation can be carried through. In the ordinary run of case the material which is urgent during the earlier stages of the analysis is not deep. We have to deal at first only with more or less far-going displacements of the deep impulses, and the deep material itself is only reached later and by degrees, so that no sudden appearance of unmanageable quantities of anxiety is to be anticipated. In exceptional cases, however, owing to some peculiarity in the structure of the neurosis, deep impulses may be urgent at a very early stage of the analysis. We are then faced by a dilemma. If we give an interpretation of this deep material, the amount of anxiety produced in the patient may be so great that his sense of reality may not be sufficient to permit of the second phase being accomplished, and the whole analysis may be jeopardised. But it must not be thought that, in such critical cases as we are now considering, the difficulty can necessarily be avoided simply by not giving any interpretation or by giving more superficial interpretations of non-urgent material or by attempting reassurances. It seems probable, in fact, that these alternative procedures may do little or nothing to obviate the trouble; on the contrary, they may even exacerbate the tension created by the urgency of the deep impulses which are the actual cause of the threatening anxiety. Thus the anxiety may break out in spite of these palliative efforts and, if so, it will be doing so under the most unfavourable conditions, that is to say, outside the mitigating influences afforded by the mechanism of interpretation. It is possible, therefore, that, of the two alternative procedures which are open to the analyst faced by such a difficulty, the interpretation of the urgent id-impulses, deep though they may be, will actually be the safer.

'SPECIFICITY' OF MUTATIVE INTERPRETATIONS

I shall have occasion to return to this point for a moment later on, but I must now proceed to the mention of one further quality which it seems necessary for an interpretation to possess before it can be mutative, a quality which is perhaps only another aspect of the one we have been describing. A mutative interpretation must be *'specific'*: that is to say, detailed and concrete. This is, in practice, a matter of degree. When the analyst embarks upon a given theme, his interpretations cannot always avoid being vague and general to begin with; but it will be necessary eventually to work out and interpret all the details of the patient's phantasy system. In proportion as this is done the interpretations will be mutative, and much of the necessity for apparent repetitions of interpretations already made is really to be explained by the need for filling in the details. I think it possible that some of the delays which despairing analysts attribute to the patient's id-resistance could be traced to this source. It seems as though vagueness in interpretation gives the defensive forces of the patient's ego the opportunity, for which they are always on the lookout, of baffling the analyst's attempt at coaxing an urgent id-impulse into consciousness. A similarly blunting effect can be produced by certain forms of reassurance, such as the tacking on to an interpretation of an ethnological parallel or of a theoretical explanation: a procedure which may at the last moment turn a mutative interpretation into a non-mutative one. The apparent effect may be highly gratifying to the analyst; but later experience may show that nothing of permanent use has been achieved or even that the patient has been given an opportunity for increasing the strength of his defences. Here we have evidently reached a topic discussed not long ago by Edward Glover in one of the very few papers in the whole literature which seriously attacks the problem of interpretation.[22] Glover argues that, whereas a *blatantly* inexact interpretation is likely to have no effect at all, a *slightly* inexact one may have a therapeutic effect of a non-analytic, or rather anti-analytic, kind by enabling the patient to make a deeper and more efficient repression. He uses this as a possible explanation of a fact that has always seemed mysterious, namely, that in the earlier days of analysis, when much that we now know of the characteristics of the unconscious was still undiscovered, and when interpretation must therefore often have been inexact, therapeutic results were nevertheless obtained.

ABREACTION

The possibility which Glover here discusses serves to remind us more generally of the difficulty of being certain that the effects that follow any given interpretation are genuinely the effects of interpretation and not transference phenomena of one kind or another. I have already remarked that many patients derive direct libidinal gratification from interpretation as such; and I think that some of the striking signs of abreaction which occasionally follow an interpretation ought not necessarily to be accepted by the analyst as evidence of anything more than that the interpretation has gone home in a libidinal sense.

The whole problem, however, of the relation of abreaction to psychanalysis is a disputed one. Its therapeutic results seem, up to a point, undeniable. It was from them, indeed, that analysis was born; and even today there are psycho-therapists who rely on it almost exclusively. During the War [World War I], in particular, its effectiveness was widely confirmed in cases of 'shell-shock'. It has also been argued often enough that it plays a leading part in bringing about the results of psycho-analysis. Rank and Ferenczi, for instance, declared that in spite of all advances in our knowledge abreaction remained the essential agent in analytic therapy.[23] More recently, Reik has supported a somewhat similar view in maintaining that 'the element of surprise is the most important part of analytic technique'.[24] A much less extreme attitude is taken by Nunberg in the chapter upon therapeutics in his text-book of psycho-analysis.[25] But he, too, regards abreaction as one of the component factors in analysis, and in two ways. In the first place, he mentions the improvement brought about by abreaction in the usual sense of the word, which he plausibly attributes to a relief of endo-psychic tension due to a discharge of accumulated affect. And in the second place, he points to a similar relief of tension upon a small scale arising from the actual process of becoming conscious of something hitherto unconscious, basing himself upon a statement of Freud's that the act of becoming conscious involves a discharge of energy.[26] On the other hand, Radó appears to regard abreaction as opposed in its function to analysis. He asserts that the therapeutic effect of catharsis is to be attributed to the fact that (together with other forms of non-analytic psycho-therapy) it offers the patient an artificial neurosis in exchange for his original one, and that the phenomena observable when abreaction occurs are akin to those of an hysterical attack.[27] A consideration of the views of these various authorities suggests that what we describe as 'abreaction' may cover two different processes: one a discharge of affect and the other a libidinal gratification. If so, the first of these might be regarded (like various other procedures) as an occasional adjunct to analysis, sometimes, no doubt, a useful one, and possibly even as an inevitable accompaniment of mutative interpretations; whereas the second process might be viewed with more suspicion, as an event likely to impede analysis—especially if its true nature were unrecognised. But with either form there would seem good reason to believe that the effects of abreaction are permanent only in cases in which the predominant ætiological factor is an external event: that is to say, that it does not in itself bring about any radical qualitative alteration in the patient's mind. Whatever part it may play in analysis is thus unlikely to be of anything more than an ancillary nature.

EXTRA-TRANSFERENCE INTERPRETATIONS

If we now turn back and consider for a little the picture I have given of a mutative interpretation with its various characteristics, we shall notice that my description appears to exclude every kind of interpretation except those of a single class—the class, namely, of *transference* interpretations. Is it to be understood that no extra-transference interpretation can set in motion the chain of events which I have suggested as being the essence of psycho-analytical therapy? That is indeed my opinion, and it is one of my main objects in writing this paper to throw into relief—what has, of course, already been observed, but never, I believe, with enough explicitness—the dynamic distinctions between transference and extra-transference interpretations. These distinctions may be grouped under two heads. In the first place, extra-transference interpretations are far less likely to be given at the point of urgency. This must necessarily be so, since in the case of an extra-transference interpretation the object of the id-impulse which is brought into consciousness is not the analyst and is not immediately present, whereas, apart from the earliest stages of an analysis and other exceptional circumstances, the point of urgency is nearly always to be found in the transference. It follows that extra-transference interpretations tend to be concerned with impulses which are distant both in time and space and are thus likely to be devoid of immediate energy. In extreme instances, indeed, they may approach very closely to what I have already described as the handing-over to the patient of a German-English dictionary. But in the second place, once more owing to the fact that the object of the id-impulse is not actually present, it is less easy for the patient, in the case of an extra-transference interpretation, to become directly aware of the distinction between the real object and the phantasy object. Thus it would appear that, with extra-transference interpretations, on the one hand what I have described as the first phase of a mutative interpretation is less likely to occur, and on the other hand, if the first phase *does* occur, the second phase is less likely to follow. In other words, an extra-transference interpretation is liable to be both less effective and more risky than a transference one.[28] Each of these points deserves a few words of separate examination.

It is, of course, a matter of common experience among analysts that it is possible with certain patients to continue indefinitely giving interpretations without producing any apparent effect whatever. There is an amusing criticism of this kind of 'interpretation-fanaticism' in the excellent historical chapter of Rank and Ferenczi.[29] But it is clear from their words that what they have in mind are essentially extra-transference interpretations, for the burden of their criticism is that such a procedure implies neglect of the analytic situation. This is the simplest case, where a waste of time and energy is the main result. But there are other occasions, on which a policy of giving strings of extra-transference interpretations is apt to lead the analyst into more positive difficulties. Attention was drawn by Reich[30] a few years ago in the course of some technical discussions in Vienna to a tendency among inexperienced analysts to get into trouble by eliciting from the patient great quantities of material in a disordered and unrelated fashion: this may, he maintained, be carried to such lengths that the analysis is brought to an irremediable state of chaos. He pointed out very truly that the material we have to deal with is stratified and that it is highly important in digging it out not to interfere more than we can help with the arrangement of the strata. He had in mind, of course, the analogy of an incompetent archæologist, whose clumsiness may obliterate for all time the possibility of reconstructing the history of an important site. I do not myself feel so pessimistic about the results in the case of a clumsy analysis, since there is the essential difference that our material is alive and will, as it were, re-stratify itself of its own accord if it is given the opportunity: that is to say, in the analytic situation. At the same time, I agree as to the presence of the risk, and it seems to me to be particularly likely to occur where extra-transference interpretation is excessively or exclusively resorted to. The means of preventing it, and the remedy if it has occurred, lie in returning to transference interpretation at the point of urgency. For if we can discover which of the material is 'immediate' in the sense I have described, the problem of stratification is automatically solved; and it is a characteristic of most extra-transference material that it has no immediacy and that consequently its stratification is far more difficult to decipher. The measures suggested by Reich himself for preventing the occurrence of this state of chaos are not inconsistent with mine; for he stresses the importance of interpreting *resistances* as opposed to the primary id-impulses themselves—and this, indeed, was a policy that was laid down at an early stage in the history of analysis. But it is, of course, one of the characteristics of a resistance that it arises in relation to the analyst; and thus the interpretation of a resistance will almost inevitably be a transference interpretation.

But the most serious risks that arise from the making of extra-transference interpretations are due to the inherent difficulty in completing their second phase or in knowing whether their second phase has been completed or not. They are from their nature unpredictable in their effects. There seems, indeed, to be a special risk of the patient not carrying through the second phase of the interpretation but of projecting the id-impulse that has been made conscious on to the analyst. This risk, no doubt, applies to some extent also to transference interpretations. But the situation is less likely to arise when the object of the id-impulse is actually present and is moreover the same person as the maker of the interpretation.[31] (We may here once more recall the problem of 'deep' interpretation, and point out that its dangers, even in the most unfavorable circumstances, seem to be greatly diminished if the interpretation in question is a transference interpretation.) Moreover, there appears to be more chance of this whole process occurring silently and so being overlooked in the case of an extra-transference interpretation, particularly in the earlier stages of an analysis. For this reason, it would seem to be important after giving an extra-transference interpretation to be specially on the *qui vive* for transference complications. This last peculiarity of extra-transference interpretations is actually one of their most important from a practical point of view. For on account of it they can be made to act as 'feeders' for the transference situation, and so to pave the way for mutative interpretations. In other words, by giving an extra-transference interpretation, the analyst can often provoke a situation in the transference of which he can then give a mutative interpretation.

It must not be supposed that because I am attributing these special qualities to transference interpretations, I am therefore maintaining that no others should be made. On the contrary, it is probable that a large majority of our interpretations are outside the transference—though it should be added that it often happens that when one is ostensibly giving an extra-transference interpretation one is implicitly giving a transference one. A cake cannot be made of nothing but currants; and, though it is true that extra-transference interpretations are not for the most part mutative, and do not themselves bring about the crucial results that involve a permanent change in the patient's mind, they are none the less essential. If I may take an analogy from trench warfare, the acceptance of a transference interpretation corresponds to the capture of a key position, while the extra-transference interpretations correspond to the general advance and to the consolidation of a fresh line which are made possible by the capture of the key position. But when this general advance goes beyond a certain point, there will be another check, and the capture of a further key position will be necessary before progress can be resumed. An oscillation of this kind between transference and extra-transference interpretations will represent the normal course of events in an analysis.

MUTATIVE INTERPRETATIONS AND THE ANALYST

Although the giving of mutative interpretations may thus only occupy a small portion of psycho-analytic treatment, it will, upon my hypothesis, be the most important part from the point of view of deeply influencing the patient's mind. It may be of interest to consider in conclusion how a moment which is of such importance to the patient affects the analyst himself. Mrs. Klein has suggested to me that there must be some quite special internal difficulty to be overcome by the analyst in giving interpretations. And this, I am sure, applies particularly to the giving of mutative interpretations. This is shown in their avoidance by psycho-therapists of non-analytic schools; but many psycho-analysts will be aware of traces of the same tendency in themselves. It may be rationalized into the difficulty of deciding whether or not the particular moment has come for making an interpretation. But behind this there is sometimes a lurking difficulty in the actual *giving* of the interpretation, for there seems to be a constant temptation for the analyst to do something else instead. He may ask questions, or he may give reassurances or advice or discourses upon theory, or he may give interpretations—but interpretations that are not mutative, extra-transference interpretations, interpretations that are non-immediate, or ambiguous, or inexact—or he may give two or more alternative interpretations simultaneously, or he may give interpretations and at the same time show his own scepticism about them. All of this strongly suggests that the giving of a mutative interpretation is a crucial act for the analyst as well as for the patient, and that he is exposing himself to some great danger in doing so. And this in turn will become intelligible when we reflect that at the moment of interpretation the analyst is in fact deliberately evoking a quantity of the patient's id-energy while it is alive and actual and unambiguous and aimed directly at himself. Such a moment must above all others put to the test his relations with his own unconscious impulses.

SUMMARY

I will end by summarizing the four main points of the hypothesis I have put forward:

(1) The final result of psycho-analytic therapy is to enable the neurotic patient's whole mental organization, which is held in check at an infantile stage of development, to continue its progress towards a normal adult state.

(2) The principle effective alteration consists in a profound qualitative modification of the patient's super-ego, from which the other alterations follow in the main automatically.

(3) This modification of the patient's super-ego is brought about in a series of innumerable small steps by the agency of mutative interpretations, which are effected by the analyst in virtue of his position as object of the patient's id-impulses and as auxiliary super-ego.

(4) The fact that the mutative interpretation is the ultimate operative factor in the therapeutic action of psycho-analysis does not imply the exclusion of many other procedures (such as suggestion, reassurance, abreaction, etc.) as elements in the treatment of any particular patient.

NOTES

1. I have not attempted to compile a full bibliography of the subject, though a number of the more important contributions to it are referred to in the following pages.
2. *Collected Papers*, Vol. II.
3. P. 381.
4. *New Introductory Lectures* (1933), p. 194.

5. Pp. 117–118.

6. P. 77.

7. In Freud's paper at the Berlin Congress in 1922, subsequently expanded into *The Ego and the Id* (1923).

8. *Int. J. Psycho-Anal.*, Vol. IV, 1923.

9. At the Salzburg Congress in 1924: 'A Metapsychological Description of the Process of Cure', *Int. J. Psycho-Anal.*, Vol. VI, 1925.

10. Also first read at Salzburg in 1924.

11. *Int. J. Psycho-Anal.*, Vol. VI, 1925; in a revised form in German, *Zeitschrift*, Bd. XII, 1926.

12. This hypothesis seems to imply a contradiction of some authoritative pronouncements, according to which the structure of the super-ego is finally laid down and fixed at a very early age. Thus Freud appears in several passages to hold that the super-ego (or at all events its central core) is formed once and for all at the period at which the child emerges from its Oedipus complex. (See, for instance, *The Ego and the Id*, pp. 68–69.) So, too, Melanie Klein speaks of the development of the super-ego 'ceasing' and of its formation 'having reached completion' at the onset of the latency period (*The Psycho-Analysis of Children*, pp. 250 and 252), though in many other passages (e.g., p. 369) she implies that the super-ego can be altered at a later age under analysis. I do not know how far the contradiction is a real one. My theory does not in the least dispute the fact that in the normal course of events the super-ego becomes fixed at an early age and subsequently remains essentially unaltered. Indeed, it is a part of my view that in practice nothing except the process of psycho-analysis *can* alter it. It is of course a familiar fact that in many respects the analytic situation re-constitutes an infantile condition in the patient, so that the fact of being analysed may, as it were, throw the patient's super-ego once more into the melting pot. Or, again, perhaps it is another mark of the non-adult nature of the neurotic that his super-ego remains in a malleable state.

13. See *The Psycho-Analysis of Children* (1932), passim, especially Chapters VIII and IX.

14. A similar view has often been suggested by Melanie Klein. See, for instance, *The Psycho-Analysis of Children*, p. 369. It has been developed more explicitly and at greater length by Melitta Schmideberg: 'Zur Psychoanalyse asozialer Kinder und Jugendlicher' (*Zeitschrift*, Bd. XVIII, 1932).

15. 'Der Begriff der Deutung in der Psychoanalyse', *Zeitschrift für angewandte Psychologie*, Bd. 42, 1932. A critical summary of this by Gerö will be found in *Imago*, Bd. XIX, 1933.

16. I am making no attempt at describing the process in correct meta-psychological terms. For instance, in Freud's view, the antithesis between conscious and unconscious is not, strictly speaking, applicable to instinctual impulses themselves, but only to the ideas which repre-sent them in the mind. ('The Unconscious', *Collected Papers*, Vol. IV, p. 109.) Neverthe-less, for the sake of simplicity, I speak throughout this paper of 'making id-impulses conscious'.

17. Incidentally, it seems as though a *qualitative* factor may be concerned as well: that is, some *kinds* of id-impulses may be more repugnant to the ego than others.

18. For the necessity for 'continuous and deep-going interpretations' in order to diminish or prevent anxiety-attacks, see Melanie Klein's *Psycho-Analysis of Children*, pp. 58–59. On the other hand: 'The anxiety belonging to the deep levels is far greater, both in amount and intensity, and it is therefore imperative that its liberation should be duly regulated'. (*Ibid.*, p. 139.)

19. Its uses were discussed by Melitta Schmideberg in a paper read to the British Psycho-Analytical Society on February 7, 1934.

20. *The Psycho-Analysis of Children*, pp. 58–59.
21. *Ibid.*, p. 139.
22. 'The Therapeutic Effect of Inexact Interpretation', *J. Int. Psycho-Anal.*, Vol. XII, 1931.
23. *Entwicklungsziele der Psychoanalyse* (1924), p. 27.
24. 'New Ways in Psycho-Analytic Technique', *Int. J. Psycho-Anal.*, Vol. XIV, 1933.
25. *Allgemeine Neurosenlehre auf psychoanalytischer Grundlage* (1932), pp. 303–304. This chapter appears in English in an abbreviated version as a contribution to Lorand's *Psycho-Analysis To-day* (1933). There is very little, I think, in Nunberg's comprehensive catalogue of the factors at work in analytic therapy that conflicts with the views expressed in the present paper, though I have given a different account of the inter-relation between those factors.
26. *Beyond the Pleasure Principle*, p. 28.
27. 'The Economic Principle in Psycho-Analytic Technique', *Int. J. Psycho-Anal.*, Vol. VI, 1925.
28. This corresponds to the fact that the pseudo-analysts and 'wild' analysts limit themselves as a rule to extra-transference interpretations. It will be remembered that this was true of Freud's original 'wild' analyst ('Observations on "Wild" Psycho-Analysis' (1910), *Collected Papers*, Vol. II).
29. *Entwicklungsziele der Psychoanalyse*, p. 31.
30. 'Bericht über das "Seminar für psychoanalytische Therapie" in Wien', *Zeitschrift*, Bd. XIII, 1927. This has recently been re-published as a chapter in Reich's volume upon *Charakteranalyse* (1933), which contains a quantity of other material with an interesting bearing on the subject of the present paper.
31. It even seems likely that the whole possibility of effecting mutative interpretations may depend upon this fact that in the analytic situation the giver of the interpretation and the object of the id-impulse interpreted are one and the same person. I am not thinking here of the argument mentioned above—that it is easier under that condition for the patient to distinguish between his phantasy object and the real object—but of a deeper consideration. The patient's original super-ego is, as I have argued, a product of the introjection of his archaic objects distorted by the projection of his infantile id-impulses. I have also suggested that our only means of altering the character of this harsh original super-ego is through the mediation of an auxiliary super-ego which is the product of the patient's introjection of the analyst as an object. The process of analysis may from this point of view be regarded as an infiltration of the rigid and unadaptable original super-ego by the auxiliary super-ego with its greater contact with the ego and with reality. This infiltration is the work of the mutative interpretations; and it consists in a repeated process of introjection of imagos of the analyst —imagos, that is to say, of a real figure and not of an archaic and distorted projection—so that the quality of the original super-ego becomes gradually changed. And since the aim of the mutative interpretations is thus to cause the introjection of the analyst, it follows that the id-impulses which they interpret must have the analyst as their object. If this is so, the views expressed in the present paper will require some emendation. For in that case, the first criterion of a mutative interpretation would be that it must be a transference interpretation. Nevertheless, the quality of urgency would still remain important; for, of all the possible transference interpretations which could be made at any particular moment, only the one which dealt with an urgent id-impulse would be mutative. On the other hand, an extra-transference interpretation even of an extremely urgent id-impulse could never be mutative—though it might, of course, produce temporary relief along the lines of abreaction or reassurance.

5. The Dynamics of the Dissolution of the Transference Resistance

Richard Sterba

In addition to the interpretation of the content of the unconscious, a considerable amount of the work in therapeutic analysis is required for the interpretation and dissolution of the resistances. Only through the dissolution of the resistances is it possible to interpret the content of the unconscious and to reconstruct the past.

We seek here to investigate the dynamics of the dissolution of a specific group of resistances called transference resistances. Transference resistances are of a peculiar importance, as they can be observed throughout the course of analysis and are very often the common ground on which other types of resistances find the possibility of expressing themselves.

Before we can approach the dynamics of the dissolution of these resistances, it will be necessary to acquaint ourselves with the dynamics of the development of these resistances. Let us repeat what Freud wrote about the origin of the transference resistance in his paper, The Dynamics of the Transference:

'Now as we follow a pathogenic complex from its representative in consciousness (whether this be a conspicuous symptom or something apparently quite insignificant) back to its root in the unconscious, we soon come to a place where the resistance makes itself felt so strongly that it affects the next association, which has to appear as a compromise between the demands of this resistance and those of the work of exploration. Experience shows that this is where the transference enters on the scene. When there is anything in the complex-material (the content of the complex), which can be at all suitably transferred to the person of the physician, such a transference will be effected and from it will arise the next association; it will then manifest itself by the signs of resistance—for instance, a cessation in the flow of associations. We conclude from such experiences that this transferred idea is able to force itself through to consciousness in preference to all other associations, just *because* it also satisfies resistance. This type of incident is repeated innumerable times during an analysis. Over and over again, when one draws near to a pathogenic complex, that part of it

Reprinted by permission from the *Psychoanalytic Quarterly* 9 (1940):363–79.

which is first thrust forward into consciousness will be some aspect of it which can be transferred; having been so, it will then be defended with the utmost obstinacy by the patient.'[1]

The development of the transference resistance occurs, according to Freud's description, in this way: out of the material lying near to the preconscious, that part which is suitable for transference pushes itself forward into the consciousness and takes possession of the analyst. However, whether the analyst becomes a hated, a loved or a feared person in a particular situation, depends upon which relationship is favorable for the resistance, that is, for the prevention of the appearance of unconscious material.

In order to facilitate an understanding of what follows, it may be advisable to illustrate with a case history how the transference is established as a *resistance* against the investigating work of the analysis. The case I am now going to report is especially adapted to our investigation because a particular transference resistance formed the main obstacle to the progress of the treatment for a long period of the analysis. The patient was dismissed, free of his symptoms and with his character favorably changed after a two-year analysis.

This patient was a twenty-seven-year-old bank employee. When the analysis began he was out of work. He wanted to be treated for depression, general inactivity and headaches which were very painful at times. The principal symptoms were, however, difficulties with eating which had led to a considerable loss of weight. He had to chew every mouthful of food for a long time; fibrous meat and the skins of fruit he had to spit out, for when he tried to swallow them he became terrified that he would choke. For a long time after this symptom had made its appearance—fifteen months before the beginning of the analysis—he had lived only on milk and chocolates. At the same time, he developed a sexual disturbance in the form of ejaculatio præcox. The patient was often constipated and had suffered from pruritus ani since his neurosis had broken out.

Characterologically the patient belonged to the group of passive feminine personalities; he was very submissive, very obedient to everyone and very fearful that he might injure somebody. He was extremely cowardly; sometimes however, though not very often, he would display an outbreak of blind hatred against persons of whom he was afraid, particularly against his superiors, but only when these persons were not present. In these attacks of rage and hatred, at a safe distance from the person causing his displeasure, he would express his emotions in the most violent manner, but the next time he encountered the person, he would behave as submissively and humbly as ever.

His symptoms were developing gradually when the patient's father became ill with angina pectoris two years before the analysis started; he died seven months before the beginning of the analysis. Following this event the symptoms became greatly intensified. The patient began to suffer from painful thoughts about death; he would imagine himself lying in his grave and every person he saw, even those sitting opposite him in the street cars, made him conjecture how long this person still had to live. The headaches and the depression increased greatly.

Subsequent to his father's death, he had lost large sums of money through bad speculations and loans. It was plain that he had an instinctual tendency to lose money and that money played a central role in his life. His every thought was directed towards making money and his fantasies were largely built around this theme. Money was also the central theme of a series of symptomatic acts which occurred in the latter part of his puberty. These consisted in stealing money from his mother in order to visit houses of prostitution. This money, however, his mother had secretly taken from his father who was very miserly, and who sometimes did not give her sufficient for household expenses. This act of stealing money with its attendant symbolism very soon came into the centre of the analytic situation.

The patient showed towards me the same servile and submissive attitude that he expressed towards everyone. He always said when talking about the analysis, 'I let myself be analyzed because . . .' This description was the direct opposite of one used by a woman patient who was very masculine and narcissistic. When she spoke about her analysis, she always said, 'I am doing an analysis because . . .'

The patient was extremely anxious to follow the basic rule of analysis, but after a few weeks thoughts occurred to him which were tormenting. He tried very carefully to avoid them because they could have been considered as gibes and taunts at the analyst. For instance, when he saw my hat hanging in the hall, he thought, involuntarily, 'H'm, I don't like this hat', but he became very frightened by this thought because he knew the hat belonged to me and he felt he ought not to think anything bad about me or my things. Such associations occurred rarely at the beginning of the analysis, but later they occurred frequently. He became frightened of them and of the analysis, that is, of the analyst. This anxiety became so intense that his associations began to be blocked and the progress of the analysis was stopped, as he developed almost a prohibition of thinking. He had to avoid very carefully all references to me and my surroundings. When sitting in the waiting room, for example, he did not trust himself to look around as he was afraid that something in the room might strike him unpleasantly and this might be followed by a hostile thought about me.

This period was initiated by the following dream: he was being hunted by the police because he had embezzled money; he was very frightened. This was to be interpreted as a transference dream, the analyst being represented by the police. It soon became clear that he developed this anxiety due to a transference from the father to the analyst. The anxiety made it impossible for him to obey the fundamental rule because it blocked all associations which were directed against me. It hindered bringing into consciousness one of the most powerful emotions of his psyche—his hatred of his father. One can easily observe how the transference serves the resistance. This resistance is composed of the repression resistance, the resistance caused by the unconscious guilt feeling, and the resistance from the repetition compulsion. His fear of his father was the center of his neurosis. The fear of being choked while eating was closely connected with his fear of his father, for in this symptom the patient experienced an identification with the dying father as a punishment for the death wishes directed towards him. The father's fatal illness was an angina pectoris with attacks of choking, particularly during eating. Deeper down, however, the oral symptom was found to be an expression of defense against a libidinal relationship with the father, in which the patient was identified with his mother on a passive masochistic basis.

The analysis of the libidinal part of the symptom led us back to a childhood observation from his fourth year. The father, personally, used forcefully to stuff food into the geese which were owned by the family. Once the little boy was present when a goose choked in his father's hands during this cruel process. In the anxiety of being choked while eating solid foods, it is apparent that his castration fear was displaced to the oral zone as a result of putting himself in the passive feminine position, an identification with the choking goose (mother).

This patient's strong anxiety was thus brought into the analysis from the very beginning. The result of the development of this anxiety in which the analyst was made the father surrogate was to prevent the confession of just those emotional impulses as a result of which the anxiety originally developed. In many instances the result of a psychic action must also be considered as its motive. It becomes evident that fear of the analyst transferred from the father has been developed for the purpose of resistance. Moreover, we find a very similar reliving of an infantile fear during the transference, such as is described by Freud in the History of an Infantile Neurosis. There he writes:

'The first "transitory symptom" which the patient produced during the treatment went back to the wolf-phobia and to the fairy tale of "The Seven Little Goats". In the room in which the first sittings were held, there was a large grandfather clock opposite the patient who lay upon a sofa facing away from me. I was struck by the fact that from time to time he turned his face towards me, looked at me in a very friendly way as though to propitiate me, and then turned his glance from me to the clock. I thought at the time that, in this way, he was showing his eagerness for the end of the hour. A long time afterwards, the patient reminded me of this piece of dumb show and gave me an explanation of it; for he recalled that the youngest of the seven little goats hid himself in the case of the grandfather's clock while his six brothers and sisters were eaten up by the wolf. So what he meant was: "Be kind to me! Must I be frightened of you? Are you going to eat me up? Shall I hide myself from you in the clock-case like the youngest little goat?" '[2]

The fact that the recollection and reconstruction of this pantomime in the wolf-man's analysis took place only 'a long time after' it had been acted out indicates, although Freud does not point it out directly, that the transference of Freud's patient was at that time of a resistance character. We know from the duration of the analysis and from the supplement to the analysis by Ruth Mack Brunswick that the resistances of this patient were unusually strong and that they yielded finally only to the pressure of a fixed time limit. It is understandable from the ubiquity of the castration fear that anxiety often plays a most important role in the transference resistance.

Every infantile attitude against which the ego has necessarily to defend itself, may appear in the transference to serve the resistance. This is particularly true of the erotic tendencies of the positive and the negative oedipus complex, sadistic aggression, the pregenital instincts, and so on. Because the transference serves the resistance, the patient acts out infantile experiences to avoid conscious remembrance of them. This leads on the part of the ego to a defense which is directed against the analysis because the analyst has become, in the transference, the representative of the emotional tendency against which the ego has to defend itself. The transference thus serves the repression which the analysis aims to abolish. When our patient makes a father image of the analyst—acts towards him as he would towards his father —he has created the relationship in order to avoid remembering forbidden emotional trends towards the father. Freud writes in Recollection, Repetition and Working Through, 'The greater the resistance, the more extensively will expressing in action (repetition) be substituted for recollecting'.[3] By acting them out in the analysis, resistances, no matter from what source, become transference resistances.

The analyst's task is to overcome this transference resistance which hinders the progress of the psychoanalytic process. The analyst thereby finds himself in a difficult situation, for he is the object of the emotional repetition operating in the patient in order to hinder the recollections for which the analyst asks. So the analyst has to contend with a vicious circle into which it is necessary for him to break. The analyst's only weapon is the interpretation of the resistance. An understanding of this acting out has necessarily to precede the interpretation of the resistance. The fact that the acting out, since it forms the transference resistance, contains the material against which the resistance arises, makes it possible for us to gain the understanding of the resistance which is necessary for the interpretation. In the manner of expression of the acted out psychic tendencies, in their temporal connection with certain accessory circumstances reported innocently by the patient, possibilities of understanding and recognition lie open to the analyst. Often transference dreams shed light on the particular infantile object and on what will be repeated in the analysis to serve the purpose of the resistance.

In this case, the transference became comprehensible very early. The symptomatic act which was reported in the fourth analytic hour—of stealing during puberty his father's money from his mother in order to visit prostitutes—and the dream of a few weeks later of the police wanting him on a charge of embezzlement, made the transference situation and the defense against which it was developed immediately clear. This was so much clearer because the hatred which the patient directed against capitalists extended also to the police whose protection of the capitalists made him furious. His ego was defending itself against making the discovery of his own hostile wish to castrate his father. This defense took the form of anxiety because following the dream of embezzlement, the patient developed the fear that some hostile thought about the analyst might occur to him. He repeatedly found himself thinking he could steal some merchandise from a wholesale merchant who had befriended him by giving him large sums of money. He became greatly frightened over this thought because it was exceedingly painful to him to confess it in the analysis. He had frequently in his associations linked the analyst with this merchant in various dreams.

Soon after these connections were recognized, an interpretation of his transference resistance was made to the patient. It consisted of explaining to him, illustrated by the corresponding material, that he was acting towards the analyst as he had towards his father and that he was doing it, although unconsciously, in order to hinder the further progress of the analysis. The analyst tried to make it clear to him that the hostility towards his father, which to some extent was still not conscious, could not be analyzed if he developed the unconscious hostility and consequent anxiety towards the analyst that he formerly had for his father. His attention was drawn to the fact that his fear of hostile thoughts towards the analyst was a result of his inner inclination to such thoughts and proof of unconscious hostility to the analyst.

When an analyst interprets the transference resistance, he opposes the ego of the patient, as the organ controlling reality, to the instinctual activity reenacted in the transference. During the transference, the patient's ego is influenced by instinctual strivings of the id to which, in our case, it reacts with anxiety. The analyst assists the ego, attacked by the id, offering it the possibility of an identification which satisfies the reality testing needs of the ego. This identification of the reality testing parts of the patient's ego is made possible by the fact that the analyst continuously observes and interprets to the patient the psychological situation without prejudice.

The invitation to this identification comes from the analyst. From the beginning of treatment, comments are made by the analyst about the work they will have to accomplish in common during the cure. Many phrases such as, 'Let us recall what you dreamed, or thought, or did there', used by the analyst contain this invitation to identification with him as it is implied every time the analyst uses 'we' to refer to the patient and himself. This identification with the analyst is based first on the patient's wish for recovery and second on the positive transference. The latter plays the most important part. On the other hand, however, unconscious parts of this libidinal factor can interfere with the therapeutic process.

In our patient, acceptance of the father's authority contributed much to the readiness for the identification, but the unconscious passive feminine attitude with the resulting danger of castration increased anxiety to a point where the positive transference operated in the direction of the transference resistance. This identification is based finally on a narcissistic satisfaction resulting from the participation in the intellectual work of gaining insight during the analysis.

The analyst therefore tries by means of interpretation to separate those parts of the patient's ego that face and assess reality, from another part which functions in carrying out the unconscious instinctual wishes, or works to suppress those wishes which create the anxiety reaction. By interpretation, the analyst keeps the reality testing parts of the ego from being flooded by the material reenacted from the past in the transference situation. The dynamics for this purpose are obtained by the analyst from the identification of the patient with himself. Through the interpretation the analyst tries to strengthen the ego, even if temporarily, against the instinctual acting out. The possibility of identification with the analyst—so necessary for the interpretation—is a *conditio sine qua non* for analytic treatment.

Separating the part of the ego occupied by the unconscious from its reality testing function cannot be accomplished with one interpretation but by long repetition. The interpretation may be strengthened in the meantime by the convincing power of newly emerging material. The identification grows through stronger support from the intellect, or becomes more efficacious through a libidinal reinforcement of the identification. Often the separation of the ego from instinctual activity in the beginning of analysis lasts only a short time—perhaps only one analytic hour or a portion of an analytic hour—and acting out of instinctual drives immediately afterwards reasserts its dominance over the ego. In these short phases however in which acting out is interrupted with the aid of identification with the analyst, to this brief dynamic effect of temporary identification, a topographical change may be added: to the acted out material some recollection may rise to consciousness. With this topographical change the temporary strengthening of the ego through identification with the analyst becomes a permanent strengthening owing to the enlargement of the ego's control over hitherto inaccessible parts of the unconscious.

Comprehension of the analysis of the transference was not very great in the beginning with our patient. His ego was too greatly occupied with the defenses against the instincts and with the defense against anxiety. Interpretation, however carefully made, increased his anxiety and his submissiveness. Later he came to recognize the parallel between the feared father and the analyst and to recollect instances of fear of his father which to a great extent he had forgotten.

First he remembered the anxiety he had felt immediately after his father's death. He failed to arrive in time for the funeral—the father died abroad—although he could easily have been present, since he had known beforehand of the father's serious illness and approaching death. Next he remembered the first night he spent at home after his father's death and how, because of his fear, it was impossible for him to sleep alone. Finally, he recalled the terrible attack of anxiety he had when in going through his father's clothes he held in his hands the trousers which his mother told him his father had last worn. In horror he threw the trousers into a corner of the room and for twenty-four hours did not dare to reenter the room. He then related a strange event which had occurred during his puberty. He had masturbated since his fifteenth year, often with conscious fantasies about his mother. One day, when he was seventeen, he had a headache, went to bed and masturbated to get rid of it, but the headache grew worse and he felt miserable, dizzy and numb. He became feverish during the night, and the doctor called in the morning and declared the illness to be influenza.

The father was greatly distressed about this illness of his son whom he so much loved, and on the following day had a fainting attack with convulsions and foamed at the mouth. This was the first of a short series of attacks which the doctor diagnosed as epilepsy related to cerebral arteriosclerosis. Our patient attributed his own illness to the masturbation and had been afraid that the doctor in examining him would make the discovery. His reaction to the father's attacks was one of intense anxiety and a bad feeling of guilt, for unconsciously he connected the father's attacks too with his own masturbation through which he considered he had become ill, thus causing his father's excitation and worry. The temporal connection between his masturbation and the father's first epileptic attacks was taken as a manifestation of magic and owing to his constant death wishes, he identified the epileptic with the cardiac attacks. After this he refrained to a great extent from masturbating and also from stealing money. The father's attacks of angina pectoris he identified with the epileptic ones, thus connecting the death of his father with masturbation. Subsequent to the father's attacks of angina pectoris he ceased entirely to masturbate and it was then that the first neurotic symptoms appeared in the form of depression, fear of suffocation when eating, constipation and pruritus ani.

Through the repeated interpretations of the transference resistance, a first step was taken towards bringing the unconscious to consciousness, for the patient remembered his fear of his father. He did not however lose his fear of the analyst, but the process of controlling this anxiety was initiated by the fact that, through the interpretation, a part of the acted out material was transformed into recollection and thus the original object of the anxiety became distinctly recognized as such. Simultaneously the patient's feeling of hatred increased, not against the analyst towards whom he had become on the contrary more servile, but against capitalists and against the Christian race to which the analyst belonged and towards which the Jewish patient always felt hostile and at the same time fearful. It was not difficult to show him that he had displaced his hatred from the analyst to capitalists, partly satisfied it by his racial hatred.

One day after he had had another outbreak against capitalism and in his rage had expressed the opinion that things could not be better until two hundred company directors had been hanged, he had the following dream: the analyst is standing beside his desk. He hurriedly sees and dismisses one patient after the other, talking to them in Czech. He earns a great deal of money.

The writing desk the patient recognized as that of his former director. He had always hated the Czech nation and my name is of Czech origin. The capitalist is to him a substitute for his own father, for the latter possessed the money the patient was obliged to steal in order to go to prostitutes (mother). The money in this case has the typical significance of the penis—the potency of the father.

A dream he had much later in his analysis confirmed this symbolic significance of money and merchandise in a most striking fashion. Following an outbreak in which he dared to insult the analyst quite openly, he dreamed that a police officer was handling him very roughly. The following day in the dream, he went to the same place to deliver some merchandise and as he handed over the goods from his sample case, he saw that they were all male sexual organs. This dream represents the development of his passive feminine character. It was possible for the patient to take the servile attitude which enabled him to eliminate every direct manifestation of hate because this attitude gave him a libidinous satisfaction which in the past he had obtained by the passive feminine surrender to his father and which was relived in the transference.

In comparison with the dream in which the patient is wanted by the police for embezzlement, the other dream in which the analyst standing at his writing desk is earning a great deal of money, shows the progress from anxiety to manifest hatred that is only hinted at first in dreams. This inner change caused by the continuous influence of the interpretation became much clearer in a symptomatic act which occurred in the sixth month of the analysis.

One day as the patient was leaving the analytic hour, he was accosted in the street by a man who wanted to sell him silk stockings at a very low price. The patient was sure that they were stolen goods, but despite or rather because of this, he went into a doorway with the man and bought six pairs of the stockings from him. Immediately afterwards he was afraid that I might have seen him from my window. In his unconscious, stealing and receiving stolen goods were identical; the neighborhood of my house and the time the incident had occurred which was just after the analytic hour, made the action appear to him as though it had been committed against me. On the same day he imposed on himself a punishment, a kind of symbolic castration. Then he discovered that the man had only given him three pairs of stockings instead of six, and that they were of very inferior material. Soon after he had given the stockings to his fiancée for whom he had bought them, he broke an object which he liked very much. He avoided for weeks afterwards going through the street where the incident had occurred—my apartment being also accessible from another street—because he was afraid the police might have seen him and arrest him for receiving stolen goods.

The patient repeats in the transference a symptomatic act of his puberty, the symbolic castration of the father, followed by anxiety and self-punishment. The progress from development of anxiety to acted-out manifestations of hatred and the active castrative wish corresponds to a dissolution of anxiety accomplished by two factors. First, the interpretation of the anxiety in the analytic transference serving the resistance. Consciousness of his fear of his father and the strengthening of the ego connected with it, made possible the dissolution of anxiety through recognition of the difference between reality and infantile fantasy. Second, the absence of any affective reaction on the part of the analyst is of important significance for the dissipation of the anxiety. The reaction of increased anxiety and passivity to the initial interpretation is related to the patient's expectation that the analyst would react with anger and retaliation to the discovery of the hatred which the patient felt for him. When this did not occur and when his increasing hatred against capitalists and the revelation of the fact that this hatred too was directed against the analyst and had merely been displaced, was also not followed by any rebuke or withdrawal of interest from the psychological situation—the objective observation and explanation still being carried on by the analyst—the patient was able to recognize that some of his anxiety was irrational. The interpretation was now able to be effective because infantile material was recollected and recognized as belonging to the suppressed and displaced hatred. The very lack of emotional reaction on the part of the analyst made it easier for the patient's ego to observe the transference in identification with the analyst on a reality basis. The analyst's objectivity showed that he considered the patient's hostility belonged not to the actual situation, but to the forgotten infantile past. We know however that just this lack of emotional reaction on the part of the analyst may afford an opportunity for the development of severe transference resistances. It serves excellently to establish a continuous reaction of disappointment in a patient. If this kind of disappointment had been experienced in childhood by the patient, it would often be repeated in the analysis, with the analyst as object, to serve the purpose of the resistance. It could only be overcome through the interpretation of the resistance character of the repetition by strengthening the ego through identification with the analyst.

The time required for the dissolution of resistances was discussed by Freud in his paper, Recollection, Repetition and Working Through.[4] 'There Freud speaks about the slight effect of a single interpretation of the resistance and about the necessity for repetition over a long period of time. This repetition is the 'working through' of resistances and is compared with the 'abreaction of quantities of affects'. When the analyst draws the patient's attention to his repetitive acting-out in the transference, the effort has often only a very momentary effect; the quantitative effect is a very slight one in comparison with the powerful mass of resistance. If we imagine the quantity of energy involved in a single interpretation in comparison with the enormous quantity of transference resistance, we can apply to the situation the physical principle of energy in the following formula: work = energy × distance. According to this formula the work of the dissolution of the resistance by means of the slight effect of our interpretation can only be accomplished when the distance is correspondingly great; therefore the distance, in our case expressed in time, for the 'working through' of the transference resistance is necessarily a long one.

The quantity of the transference resistance is to a great extent dependent on the quantity of other resistances. Resistances have the tendency to accumulate wherever there is a favorable opportunity to withstand the analysis. In most cases the transference offers the best opportunity. In the case used for illustration, for example, we see that the resistance coming from the compulsive repetition, from the unconscious feeling of guilt and from the resistance by repression, takes part in building up the transference resistance. Freud speaks of the transformation of resistances into negative, hostile transferences;[5] it is on account of this transformation that the dissolution of the transference resistance so often becomes the chief task of the therapeutic work. In the case of our patient, the analysis finally showed the development of anxiety in the transference to be castration anxiety which had arisen from infantile masturbation with accompanying incestuous wishes towards the mother and the hatred and castration wishes towards the father. In the analytic situation, the same castration anxiety developed which had been the reason for the repression of the infantile masturbation. Thus this infantile masturbation is the last determining factor in the development of anxiety in the analysis. If the resistance resulting from this anxiety is augmented by the addition of other resistances, then the final resistance in the analysis cannot be considered as an index to the amount of the genuine infantile anxiety; for the anxiety resulting from infantile masturbation, on account of its particular capacity for being used as a resistance in analysis, becomes the nucleus of crystallization or the basis for the addition of all the other resistances. In a footnote to his paper The Dynamics of the Transference, this idea was alluded to by Freud. The footnote I shall quote belongs to the following sentence in the text: 'Over and over again, when one draws near to a pathogenic complex, that part of it which is first thrust forward into consciousness will be some aspect of it which can be transferred; having been so, it will then be defended with the utmost obstinacy by the patient.' The footnote says: 'From which however one need not infer in general any very particular pathogenic importance in the point selected for resistance by transference. In warfare, when a bitter fight is raging over the possession of some little chapel or a single farmhouse, we do not necessarily assume that the church is a national monument, or that the barns contain the military funds. Their value may be merely tactical; in the next onslaught they will very likely be of no importance.'[6]

The dissolution of the transference resistance means then not only the dissolution of the resistance resulting from the genuine infantile castration anxiety but also a liberation of the supporting resistances which often can only later be separately dissolved, because during the phase of the violent acting-out in the transference these resistances are not accessible to interpretation and dissolution. I have the impression that the supporting resistances do not cause an increase of the anxiety, though they do make it more refractory to dissolution in the analysis. The problem of quality will have to be the subject of a further examination.

NOTES

1. Frued: Coll. Papers, II, p. 316.
2. Freud: Coll. Papers, III, p. 511.
3. Coll. Papers, II, p. 370.
4. Freud: Coll. Papers, II, p. 366.
5. Freud: *Introductory Lectures on Psycho-Analysis*. London: Allen & Unwin, 1922, p. 379.
6. Coll. Papers, II, p. 317.

6. The Transference

August Aichhorn

We have used the term "transference" several times, and in the last case we attributed the therapeutic results to the transference without further definition of the word. We shall now consider more closely the emotional relationship which is thus designated. During a psychoanalytic treatment, the patient allows the analyst to play a predominating role in his emotional life. This is of great importance in the analytic process. After the treatment is over, this situation is changed. The patient builds up feelings of affection for and resistance to his analyst which, in their ebb and flow, so exceed the normal degree of feeling that the phenomenon has long attracted the theoretical interest of the analyst. Freud studied this phenomenon thoroughly, explained it, and gave it the name "transference." We shall understand later why he chose exactly this term.

I cannot reproduce for you all of Freud's research about the transference, but must limit myself to essentials. When we speak of the transference in connexion with social re-education, we mean the emotional response of the pupil toward the educator or counsellor or therapist, as the case may be, without meaning that it takes place in exactly the same way as in an analysis. The "counter-transference" is the emotional attitude of the teacher toward the pupil, the counsellor toward his charge, the therapist toward the patient. The feeling which the child develops for the mentor is conditioned by a much earlier relationship to someone else. We must take cognizance of this fact in order to understand these relationships. The tender relationships which go to make up the child's love life are no longer strange to us. Many of these have already been touched upon in the foregoing chapters.[1] We have learned how the small boy takes the father and mother as love objects. We have followed the strivings which arise out of this relationship, the Oedipus situation; we have seen how this runs its course and terminates in an identification with the parents. We have also had opportunity to consider the relationships between brothers and sisters, how their original rivalry is transformed into affection through the pressure of their feeling for the parents. We know that the boy at puberty must give up his first love objects within the family and transfer his libido to individuals outside the family.

Our present purpose is to consider the effects of these first experiences from a certain angle. The child's attachment to the family, the continuance and the subsequent dissolution of these love relationships within the family, not only leave a deep effect on the child through the resulting identifications; they determine at the same time the actual form of his love relationships in the future. Freud compares these forms, without implying too great a rigidity, to copper plates for engraving. He has shown that in the emotional relationships of our later life we can do nothing but make an imprint from one or another of these patterns which we have established in early childhood.

Why Freud chose the term "transference" for the emotional relationship between patient and analyst is easy to understand. The feelings which arose long ago in another situation are transferred to the analyst. To the counsellor of the child, the knowledge of the transference mechanism is indispensable. In order to influence the dissocial behaviour, he must bring his charge into the transference situation. The study of the transference in the dissocial child shows regularly a love life that has been disturbed in early childhood by a lack of affection or an undue amount of affection. A satisfactory social adjustment depends on certain conditions, among them an adequate constitutional endowment and early love relationships which have been confined within certain limits. Society determines these limits just as definitely as the later love life of an individual is determined by the early form of his libidinal development. The child develops normally and assumes his proper place in society if he can cultivate in the nursery such relationships as can favourably be carried over into the school and from there into the ever-broadening world around him. His attitude toward his parents must be such that it can be carried over to the teacher, and that toward his brothers and sisters must be transferred to his schoolmates. Every new contact, according to the degree of authority or maturity which the person represents, repeats a previous relationship with very little deviation. People whose early adjustments follow such a normal course have no difficulties in their emotional relationships with others; they are able to form new ties, to deepen them, or to break them off without conflict when the situation demands it.

We can easily see why an attempt to change the present order of society always meets with resistance and where the radical reformer will have to use the greatest leverage. Our attitude to society and its members has a certain standard form. It gets its imprint from the structure of the family and the emotional relationships set up within the family. Therefore the parents, especially the father, assume overwhelming responsibility for the social orientation of the child. The persistent, ineradicable libidinal relationships carried over from childhood are facts with which social reformers must reckon. If the family represents the best preparation for the present social order, which seems to be the case, then the introduction of a new order means that the family must be uprooted and replaced by a different personal world for the child. It is beyond our scope to attempt a solution of this question, which concerns those who strive to build up a new order of society. We are remedial educators and must recognize these sociological relationships. We can ally ourselves with whatever social system we will, but we have the path of our present activity well marked out for us, to bring dissocial youth into line with present-day society.

If the child is harmed through too great disappointment or too great indulgence in his early love life, he builds up reaction patterns which are damaged, incomplete, or too delicate to support the wear and tear of life. He is incapable of forming libidinal object relationships which are considered normal by society. His unpreparedness for life, his inability to regulate his conscious and unconscious libidinal strivings and to confine his libidinal expectations within normal bounds, create an insecurity in relation to his fellow men and constitute one of the first and most important conditions for the development of delinquency. Following this point of view, we look for the primary causes of dissocial behaviour in early childhood, where the abnormal libidinal ties are established. The word "delinquency" is an expression used to describe a relationship to people and things which is at variance with what society approves in the individual.

It is not immediately clear from the particular form of the delinquency just what libidinal disturbance in childhood had given rise to the dissocial expression. Until we have a psychoanalytically constructed scheme for the diagnosis of delinquency, we may content ourselves by separating these forms into two groups: (1) border-line neurotic cases with dissocial symptoms, and (2) dissocial cases in which that part of the ego giving rise to the dissocial behaviour shows no trace of neurosis. In the first type, the individual finds himself in an inner conflict because of the nature of his love relationships; a part of his own personality forbids the indulgence of libidinal desires and strivings. The dissocial behaviour results from this conflict. In the second type, the individual finds himself in open conflict with his environment, because the outer world has frustrated his childish libidinal desires.

The differences in the forms of dissocial behaviour are important for many reasons. At present, they are significant to us because of the various ways in which the transference is established in these two types. We know that with a normal child the transference takes place of itself through the kindly efforts of the responsible adult. The teacher in his attitude repeats the situations long familiar to the child, and thereby evokes a parental relationship. He does not maintain this relationship at the same level, but continually deepens it as long as he is the parental substitute.

When a neurotic child with symptoms of delinquency comes into the institution, the tendency to transfer his attitude toward his parents to the persons in authority is immediately noticeable. The worker will adopt the same attitude toward the dissocial child as to the normal child, and bring him into a positive transference, if he acts toward him in such a way as to prevent a repetition with the worker of the situation with the parents which led to the conflict. In psychoanalysis, on the other hand, it is of greatest importance to let this situation repeat itself. In a sense the worker becomes the father or the mother but still not wholly so; he represents their claims, but in the right moment he must let the dissocial child know that he has insight into his difficulties and that he will not interpret the behaviour in the same way as do the parents. He will respond to the child's feeling of a need for punishment, but he will not completely satisfy it.

He will conduct himself entirely differently in the case of the child who is in open conflict with society. In this instance he must take the child's part, be in agreement with his behaviour, and in the severest cases even give the child to understand that in his place he would behave just the same way. The guilt feelings found so clearly in the neurotic cases with dissocial behaviour are present in these cases also. These feelings do not arise, however, from the dissocial ego, but have another source.

Why does the educator conduct himself differently in dealing with this second type? These children, too, he must draw into a positive transference to him, but what is applicable and appropriate for a normal or a neurotic child would here achieve the opposite result. Otherwise the worker would bring onto himself all the hate and aggression which the child bears toward society, thus leading the child into a negative instead of a positive transference, and creating a situation in which the child is not amenable to training.

What I have said about psychoanalytic theory is only a bare outline. A much deeper study of the transference is necessary to anyone interested in re-educational work from the psychoanalytic point of view. The practical application of this theory is not easy, since we deal mostly with mixed types. The attitude of the counsellor cannot be as uniform as I have pictured it for you. We do not have enough description of individual forms of dissocial behaviour to enable us to offer detailed instructions about how to deal with them. At present our psychoanalytic knowledge is such that a correct procedure cannot be stated specifically for each and every dissocial individual.

The necessity for bringing the child into a good relationship to his mentor is of prime importance. The worker cannot leave this to chance; he must deliberately achieve it and he must face the fact that no effective work is possible without it. It is important for him to grasp the psychic situation of the dissocial child in the very first contact he makes with him, because only thus can he know what attitude to adopt. There is a further difficulty in that the dissocial child takes pains to hide his real nature; he misrepresents himself and lies. This is to be taken for granted; it should not surprise or upset us. Dissocial children do not come to us of their own free will but are brought to us, very often with the threat, "You'll soon find out what's going to happen to you." Generally parents resort to our help only after every other means, including corporal punishment, has failed. To the child, we are only another form of punishment, an enemy against whom he must be on his guard, not a source of help to him. There is a great difference between this and the psychoanalytic situation, where the patient comes voluntarily for help. To the dissocial child, we are a menace because we represent society, with which he is in conflict. He must protect himself against this terrible danger and be careful what he says in order not to give himself away. It is hard to make some of these delinquent children talk; they remain unresponsive and stubborn. One thing they all have in common; they do not tell the truth. Some lie stupidly, pitiably; others, especially the older ones, show great skill and sophistication. The extremely submissive child, the "dandy," the very jovial, or the exaggeratedly sincere, are especially hard to reach. This behaviour is so much to be expected that we are not surprised or disarmed by it. The inexperienced teacher or adviser is easily irritated, especially when the lies are transparent, but he must not let the child be aware of this. He must deal with the situation immediately without telling the child that he sees through his behaviour.

There is nothing remarkable in the behaviour of the dissocial; it differs only quantitatively from normal behaviour. We all hide our real selves and use a great deal of psychic energy to mislead our neighbours. We masquerade more or less, according to necessity. Most of us learn in the nursery the necessity of presenting ourselves in accordance with the environmental demands, and thus we consciously or unconsciously build up a shell around ourselves. Anyone who has had experience with young children must have noticed how they immediately begin to dissimulate when a grown-up comes into the room. Most children succeed in behaving in the manner which they think is expected of them. Thus they lessen the danger to themselves and at the same time they are casting the permanent moulds of their mannerisms and their behaviour. How many parents really bother themselves about the inner life of their children? Is this mask a necessity for life? I do not know, but it often seems that the person on whom childhood experiences have forced the cleverest mask is best able to cope with reality. It is not surprising that the dissocial individual masquerades to a greater extent, and more consciously, than the normal. He is only drawing logical deductions from his unfortunate experiences. Why should he be sincere with those people who represent disagreeable authority? This is an unfair demand!

We must look further into the differences between the situation of social retraining and the analytic situation. The analyst expects to meet in his patient unconscious resistances which prevent him from being honest or make him silent; but the treatment is in vain when the patient lies persistently. Those who work with dissocial children expect to be lied to. To send the child away because he lies is only giving in to him. We must wait and hope to penetrate the mask which covers the real psychic situation. In the institution it does not matter if this is not achieved immediately; it means merely that the establishment of the transference is postponed. In the clinic, however, we must work more quickly. Talking with the patient does not always suffice; we must introduce other remedial measures. Generally we see the delinquent child only a few times; we are forced to take some steps after the first few interviews, to formulate some tentative conception of the difficulty and to establish a positive transference as quickly as possible. This means we must get at least a peep behind the mask. If the child is not put in an institution, he remains in the old situation under the same influences which caused the trouble. In such cases we wish to establish the transference as quickly as possible, to intensify the child's positive feelings for us that are aroused while the child is with us, and to bring them rapidly to such a pitch that they can no longer be easily disturbed by the old influences. To carry on such work successfully presupposes a long experience.

Let us interrupt our theoretical consideration here and see how the worker tries to grasp the situation, to establish the transference and to lift the mask. How others work, I do not know; I can only try to show you what I usually do. A youth comes into the consulting room. At first glance he seems to be the bully type. If we take a stern tone with him, he rejects us immediately and we can never get a transference established. If we are cordial and friendly, he becomes distrustful and rejects us or he takes this for weakness on our part and reacts with increased roughness. If we approach a boy who is intellectually superior with a severe air, he feels himself immediately on sure ground and master of the situation because he meets that attitude often in life. He looks with suspicion on people who are nice to him and is more than ever on his guard. The timid ones, who come in frightened, are easily reduced to tears by a stern demeanour and fall into a state which may be confused with sulkiness. How shall we conduct ourselves in order to establish a good contact with the child? I usually begin with a friendly look or attitude, sometimes I say, ''How do you do,'' or I may only shake hands in silence. I say that there is nothing here to be afraid of, that this is neither a police station nor a court. Sometimes I tell a joke by way of introduction. This gives me an opportunity to size up the situation. We sit down opposite each other. Just how I proceed toward the establishment of the transference in an individual case depends on the impression I have of the youth as he first enters the room.

I consider this first moment of our coming together of the utmost importance. It is more than a ''feeling out'' of the situation; it must have the appearance of certainty and sureness and must be put through as quickly as possible because in most cases it forms the foundation for our later relationship. The adolescent does the same thing when he comes into contact with me. He wants to know right away what kind of person he is dealing with. Children usually try to orient themselves quickly, but for the most part they are not clever about it. The adolescent, however, often develops an amazing ability at this. We can observe a momentary gleam in the eye, a hardly perceptible movement of the lips, an involuntary gesture, a ''watchful waiting'' attitude, although he may be in a state of conflict. The older he is, the harder it is to know whether he will prove stubborn, or openly scornful and resistant. It is especially difficult when he assumes an air of sincerity or unctuous submissiveness. If I accept this as genuine, he immediately feels superior although he may sense that I have the upper hand.

After this sizing up of each other is over, a struggle begins for the mastery of the situation. This may be brief or it may be prolonged, and I must confess that I do not always come out victorious. You must not think of this struggle, however, as a mutual show of conscious strength. There are many unconscious factors in it; we feel rather than know what actually takes place. My attitude from the very beginning lets the boy feel that I have a power over him. He is justified when he senses this as a danger. He does not feel this as an entirely new situation; he has experienced it often before. I am thus no different from his mother, father, or teacher. If he is a border-line case of neurosis with dissocial features, or a mixed form where the dissocial features are predominant, I remain in the position of the parents but, as our association progresses, I act somewhat differently. If the child is in open conflict and expecting an attack, he is disappointed. I do not ask him what he has done, I do not press him to tell me what has happened, and, in contrast to the police or Juvenile Court, I do not try to pry out of him information which he is unwilling to give. In many cases where I feel the child wants to be questioned so that he can come into opposition to me, I say that he may hold back whatever information he wishes, that I understand that one does not want to tell everything to a person he has met for the first time. When I add that I would do likewise, he is usually willing to fall into conversation with me about something remote from his difficulties but in line with his interests. To describe my attitude from the moment when I let the boy feel some activity in me, I would say that I become progressively passive the more he expects an attack from me. This astonishes him, he feels uncertain, he does not know where he stands. He feels, rather than understands, that I am not an authority with whom he must fight, but an understanding ally. I avoid the word "friend" intentionally since he has no friends; he allies himself with others only because he needs them to achieve some end.

In a natural fashion, I begin to speak of things which interest most boys but are in no way connected with their dissocial behaviour. Eight out of ten are interested in football. One must know the teams, the best players, the last match, the scores, etc. Less often one finds a contact through books, mostly through adventure and detective stories. It is often easy to talk about movies and in this way make the child lose his caution.

With little girls I talk about fairy tales and games. Often one does not need to go far afield. A remark about the clothes or jewellery they wear may start the ball rolling. I let the half-grown girls tell me about styles in clothes, in haircuts, or the price of toilet articles. I ask the youngest children who are afraid to talk what they like to eat; we discuss desserts and candies. Thus I reach topics which the child carries on in the conversation. Sometimes it is difficult, sometimes easy, but as a rule it is possible to arrive unobtrusively at what I wish to know. In the first interview I usually get the positive transference well enough under way to secure some explanations and to gain some influence.

It is also necessary to get some idea of the child's relationship to the members of the family and other people in the environment. Adolescent children usually answer such questions directly; with younger children this is more difficult. Either they do not answer questions at all or they answer in a way which is worthless for our purpose. We must learn their attitudes through various makeshifts, such as talking about games and stories.

I asked a ten-year-old girl if she liked to read. When she said "Yes," I asked what she liked best.

"Fairy tales."

"Without stopping to think, tell me the name of a fairy tale you like."

"Snow-White."

"What part in it?"

"Where the old witch sold Snow-White the poisoned apple."

"Were there pictures in your book?"

"Yes."

"One of the witch, too?"

"Yes."

"Describe the witch for me, not exactly as she is in the picture, but how you think of her."

She described the witch in detail, her size, her hair, her facial expression, mouth, teeth, and clothes. When I asked where she got these various characteristics, it turned out that they were a collection from people whom the child disliked. This does not always turn out so propitiously. Sometimes the figure described does not fit the disliked people in the environment.

Another little girl told me that she liked to play with dolls. I asked her to describe in detail a doll she would like to have. This again resulted in a composite figure, but this time it had the features of the people she loved.

A twelve-year-old girl once sat opposite me giving no sign through her facial expression, movement, or speech what kind of emotional situation she was in. I asked what colour she liked best.

"Red."

I continued, "When I think of a colour, I always think of something which has that colour. On what do you see red?"

"On the front car of the grotto-train in the amusement park."

"Now tell me what colour you like least."

"Black."

"Where do you see black?"

"Your shoes and tie."

"But surely something else black occurs to you, too?"

"The hole where the grotto-train goes in is black, too."

What all this may symbolize need not concern us at the moment. We need only consider how the anxiety connected with the ride in the grotto-train has been displaced onto me. She sat in front of me in the same anxious tension that she sat in the train in the amusement park. Perhaps she wanted to ask, "What's coming next?" How do we know this? My shoes and my cravat (which was really grey) had for the child the same colour as the grotto which she did not like. You can see how we get material from which we draw conclusions about the psychological situation of the child. I certainly would not have received a satisfactory answer to a direct question, for even if she had been ready to tell the truth she would not have known how to describe how she felt.

In such a tense situation we can accomplish nothing. I let her tell me about the trip through the grotto. Brightly lighted pictures appeared suddenly in the dark, devils roasting poor souls on hellish fires, dwarfs digging in the bowels of the earth for treasure, and such things. Something uncanny was always appearing and nothing cheerful or happy ever happened. We went from this to the shooting galleries, from one stand to another, and to the merry-go-round. Then laughing, she told me about a funny fortune teller who could tell what was going to happen to you. When I asked what amusing experiences she could remember, she told of another trip to the amusement park at the time she was confirmed. With this her mood changed completely, making it possible for the transference to begin. She was now accessible to questions which came to the point. I do not need to mention the fact that the child had no conception of my intention.

Sometimes a deep distrust shows itself. Perhaps I have acted clumsily, perhaps I am dealing with a special type of personality. Then I must resort to some other method. I will report such a case where in a brief time I succeeded not only in overcoming the distrust but also in discovering how it arose.

A sixteen-year-old girl, who had been suspected of being a prostitute because of her behaviour and appearance, had suddenly shown a complete change. Her bold manner had disappeared and in her dress and behaviour she had become a conventional, respectable girl. The social worker wanted to know what had happened. Naturally I did not know, but asked to see the girl. We sat down together and she showed very evident distrust of me. I asked how things were at home but got no answer. Did she like to read? What did she think about? No answer. Would she tell me a dream? Continued silence. Thereupon I laughed and said, "You think it's dangerous to talk to me. I can understand that, but certainly it can't be dangerous to tell me the story of a movie you've seen." She laughed and started to tell about a circus acrobat who had to dive from a high place through a burning ring. Two girls were in love with him. One of the girls, out of jealousy, cut the wire and made him fall into the fire-ring. Thee second girl saved him but sacrificed her life to do so. As you can guess from this summary, the story did not tally exactly with what she had seen, but showed her own version of it. I asked her what pleased her best in it and got the answer I expected, namely, that the girl sacrificed herself for her lover. I then asked if she could remember how the hero looked. When she answered the affirmative, I asked her to describe what he must look like to please her. She described him as a strong, young, slender, dark-haired, clean-shaven man with bright eyes. Now I said, "Tell me, what does Franz look like?" She understood immediately that I meant her boy friend, was a little embarrassed, and then described him to look just like the movie hero. She went on without further effort on my part to say that he was studying chemistry but her mother refused to let her go with him. It was clear that the change in the girl was to be ascribed to her affection for the man. By attacking her distrust, I soon succeeded in overcoming her resistance.

I shall now present a case to show you how the transference can help one to find the deeper-lying causes of dissocial behaviour.

A city school reported that for several months a thirteen-year-old boy had been absent on Tuesdays and Fridays. The history stated that instead of going to school he went to the horse market, not out of any special interest or because of the tips he may have got for small chores, but only to be in the neighbourhood of the horse-dealers. I do not regard every unusual bit of behaviour as springing from some obscure motive, but try first to find a simple explanation. Since I have always found that, after the transference is established, the child will go to school regularly if I show him that it pleases me, I tried it in this case. We must realize that in many cases no one troubles himself about a child's going to school and that he therefore has no incentive to endure the unpleasantness of school life. In such truancy cases, I have the boy come to me first every week, then every two weeks, and later less often. When he knows that I am interested in all the pleasant and unpleasant happenings in the previous school week, he enters into the school life, and the truancy subsides. With this boy who went to the horse market, the transference was established in the first interview. He came for the next two weeks and reported that he had been in school. The third week the mother came to say that he was going to school regularly, but twice a week he did not come home until late in the evening and she thought from the way he smelled that he must have been in the horse market again.

We see in this case how the transference blocked the outlet for a symptom. The force behind the symptom, however, was still effective and produced a new symptom. The boy could not stay away from school because of his feeling for me. Now we see that this was not a case of ordinary truancy. Something attracted him to the horses and it was only a coincidence that the time for school and the horses was the same. Through the transference, I could see that we were dealing with a deeper mechanism. One needs psycho-analytic methods in the treatment of such a case. I do not want you to conclude from what I have said that I have any hard and fast rules which enable me to establish the transference in all cases. I only want to protect you from making the crudest mistakes in your practice by giving you some hints from my own experience.

When the child comes to us in the institution, we do not feel obliged to hurry the establishment of the transference. Unless it is a case of neurosis with dissocial features, we are friendly, but show no extraordinary interest in him or his fate and do not force ourselves upon him. We ignore his distrust, his secret or open opposition, his condescension, scorn, or whatever he may show against us. The preparation for the transference he gets from his companions. He usually makes quick contacts with the other boys not because he shows his real self to them or because he needs friendship, but because he must have an audience to whom he can relate an exaggerated account of his adventures, for whom he even improvises new escapades when reality offers nothing impressive enough. According to his custom, he begins to collect information about the details of organization and the people with whom he comes in contact. Is the counsellor a "good fellow," can he be annoyed or teased, and how? He hears a great deal from the boys who are about ready to leave the institution. He learns the characteristics of the people on the staff, what the real life of the institution is like. Through this contact with the other boys, he saves himself from the disillusionment which often follows first impressions, and comes in touch with an authority from which he does not need to turn distrustfully away, or which he tolerates, with clenched teeth, until such time as he attains his freedom and attempts a revenge.

If the *milieu* has done its part, the transference begins to develop as the counsellor gradually lets himself be drawn out of his passive role and responds to the newcomer in a neutral but friendly manner. Sometimes he pays more attention to the boy, sometimes less. This fluctuation of interest is not a matter of indifference to the youth. If he is distrustful because the counsellor seems to pay undue attention to him today, tomorrow he will be reassured if no notice is taken of him. He betrays a definite excitement the next day, however, if he thinks the counsellor has observed his unpolished shoes with displeasure. The shoes will be more highly polished or dirtier according to the positive or negative feeling aroused in him, or they will remain the same if no transference is under way. In this case we must wait. What I have said about the shoes is true for a host of other small details which the educator must be quick to recognize and to evaluate. He must sense the ambivalence or changes from affection to distrust in the relationship of his charge to him. There are no general directions for this. We must observe at first-hand how the experienced counsellor directs these waves of feeling and strives deliberately to raise the crests to a higher point. It is easy to recognize when the positive relationship reaches a climax. Often the feelings of affection break out with such vehemence and strength that the child waits in great tension for his counsellor to appear, does something to attract his attention, runs after him, or find something to do which brings him into his counsellor's vicinity. The unskilled worker will not recognize the importance of this moment, will be on the defensive and not realize that the affection of the boy can thus be changed into hate. On the contrary, when the hate reaction sets in, he will flatter himself that he has always seen through the hypocrite. If we try to show him how he misinterprets the situation, he turns a deaf ear. He does not understand that he is interpreting as cause what is really effect.

I would like to show you how hard it often is to establish a transference with individuals of the highly narcissistic type—that is, those who are in love with themselves. I cite the case of a seventeen-year-old boy who had gambled and speculated on the stock exchange and had made a lot of money.

He had begun at fifteen as a cashier for a street money-changer, who entrusted him with orders on the exchange and made it possible for him to speculate on his own. He accumulated a small fortune for a boy, and made himself independent. He travelled to other countries and imported things which he sold as a bootlegger. This business paid well. He led a free and easy life in night clubs, gambled, and associated with the demi-monde. When his money gave out, he began pawning his mother's clothes. His mother, who had been left a widow after an unhappy marriage, had repeatedly tried to reform the boy. Since she could do nothing with him, she appealed for help to a social agency which brought him to us.

He was one of those boys who give no apparent trouble in an institution. Such youths are polite and obliging, handy and useful in simple office work. They know how to get along with others and soon achieve the role of gang leader. When one works more intensively with them, one learns to see their difficulties. Inwardly demoralized but outwardly as smooth as glass, they offer no point of attack. Their behaviour is a mask, but a very good one. They show no interest in the personnel, and ward off every attempt to establish a real relationship to them. Thus the transference, which must of necessity be very strongly positive if one is to accomplish anything with them educationally, is almost impossible to establish. In the institution they give the impression of being cured very speedily but when at large again they revert to their old behaviour. We must use the greatest caution with them.

Our man of the world knew how to withdraw from every effort to influence him. He was with us several months without any transference having been established in the psychoanalytic sense. We could see, however, that he had been influenced by the environment. I thought it a good idea to get him away from it for a time so that he could compare the discomforts of another environment with those which he enjoyed with us, feeling that this realization might make him accessible to therapy. For this purpose, however, he must not be sent away; he must go of his own accord. I had to avoid letting him know of my intention. The best way to achieve my purpose was to influence his feeling about the institution. Occasionally, running away from the institution takes place as the result of a sudden emotional state or because of a dream, and then it is hard to prevent. In most cases, however, it requires long preparation and should not escape the sharp eye of the counsellor. Aside from our position against punishment in general in a reform school, we regard it as a complete lack of understanding to punish returned runaways. The running away takes place only when the "outside" is a more attractive place than the "inside." If we can induce the boy to talk to us while he is in this conflict, we can often make the "inside" seem more attractive without mentioning his intention of running away. We can accomplish the opposite effect if we recall the outer world to his memory as more attractive than the life in the institution.

A short talk was sufficient to put our gambler in the right mood. A half hour after he left me, I got the report that he had run away. The first part of my treatment had worked. The counsellor did not know that I had provoked this. I confide such things to the personnel only when I need their co-operation, since it is extremely difficult when one lives among the boys to conceal such things. If such a plan does not succeed, it gives rise to unending differences of opinion. With our young gambler, this successful provocation to run away was a prologue to the establishment of the transference. I expected his return on the second day. When he had not turned up after a week, I feared that I had made a mistake.

At nine o'clock in the evening ten days later, someone knocked on my door. It was the runaway. He was so exhausted physically and under such psychological tension that I felt I could accomplish much more with him than I had planned. I did not reproach him for going away, as he evidently expected. I only looked at him seriously and said, "How long has it been since you had something to eat?" "Yesterday evening." I took him into the dining room of my apartment where my family was at supper and had a place set for him. This boy, who was usually the complete master of a situation, was so upset that he could not eat. Although I was quite aware of this, I said, "Why don't you eat?" "I can't. Couldn't I eat outside?" "Yes, go into the kitchen." His plate was refilled until he was satisfied. When he had finished eating, it was ten o'clock. I went out and said to him, "It's too late for you to go into your group tonight. You can sleep here." A bed was fixed for him in the hall. I patted him on the head and said good-night to him.

The next morning the transference was in effect. How strongly positive it was I learned from a mistake which I made later. Without realizing it I gave him grounds for jealousy, in that I let one of his comrades check up on his bookkeeping, in which he often made errors. The counsellor to whom he was entrusted succeeded, however, in making good the mistake in this especially difficult case. Soon after this he was allowed to bring the supplies from the city. He never let himself be led astray after that. He left the institution to become a salesman and for years has had a satisfactory record as a clerk in a business establishment.

The establishment of the transference seldom necessitates such an artifice. Generally the ordinary course of events is enough. I reported this case merely to show you how impossible it is to lay down general rules.

NOTES

1. [see Aichhorn, *Wayward Youth.*]

7. Transference

Anna Freud

The same theoretical distinction between observation of the id on the one hand and observation of the ego on the other may be drawn in the case of that which is perhaps the most powerful instrument in the analyst's hand: the interpretation of the transference. By transference we mean all those impulses experienced by the patient in his relation with the analyst which are not newly created by the objective analytic situation but have their source in early—indeed, the very earliest—object-relations and are now merely revived under the influence of the repetition-compulsion. Because these impulses are repetitions and not new creations they are of incomparable value as a means of information about the patient's past affective experiences. We shall see that we can distinguish different types of transference-phenomena according to the degree of their complexity.

(*a*) Transference of libidinal impulses.—The first type of transference is extremely simple. The patient finds himself disturbed in his relation to the analyst by passionate emotions, e.g. love, hate, jealousy and anxiety, which do not seem to be justified by the facts of the actual situation. The patient himself resists these emotions and feels ashamed, humiliated and so forth, when they manifest themselves against his will. Often it is only by insisting on the fundamental rule of analysis that we succeed in forcing a passage for them to conscious expression. Further investigation reveals the true character of these affects—they are irruptions of the id. They have their source in old affective constellations, such as the Oedipus and the castration-complex, and they become comprehensible and indeed are justified if we disengage them from the analytic situation and insert them into some infantile affective situation. When thus put back into their proper place, they help us to fill up an amnestic gap in the patient's past and provide us with fresh information about his infantile instinctual and affective life. Generally he is quite willing

Excerpted from Anna Freud, *The Ego and the Mechanisms of Defense* (New York: International Universities Press, 1936), 18–25. Reprinted by permission of the Estate of Anna Freud by arrangement with Mark Paterson & Associates, Colchester, England, and International Universities Press.

to co-operate with us in our interpretation, for he himself feels that the transferred affective impulse is an intrusive foreign body. By putting it back into its place in the past we release him from an impulse in the present which is alien to his ego, thus enabling him to carry on the work of analysis. It should be noted that the interpretation of this first type of transference assists in the observation of the id only.

(*b*) Transference of defence.—The case alters when we come to the second type of transference. The repetition-compulsion, which dominates the patient in the analytic situation, extends not only to former id-impulses but equally to former defensive measures against the instincts. Thus he not only transfers undistorted infantile id-impulses, which become subject to a censorship on the part of the adult ego secondarily and not until they force their way to conscious expression; he transfers also id-impulses in all those forms of distortion which took shape while he was still in infancy. It may happen in extreme cases that the instinctual impulse itself never enters into the transference at all but only the specific defence adopted by the ego against some positive or negative attitude of the libido, as, for instance, the reaction of flight from a positive love-fixation in latent female homosexuality of the submissive, feminine-masochistic attitude, to which Wilhelm Reich has called attention in male patients whose relations to their fathers were once characterized by aggression. In my opinion we do our patients a great injustice if we describe these transferred defence-reactions as 'camouflage' or say that the patients are 'pulling the analyst's leg' or purposely deceiving him in some other way. And indeed we shall find it hard to induce them by an iron insistence on the fundamental rule, that is to say, by putting pressure upon them to be candid, to expose the id-impulse which lies hidden under the defence as manifested in the transference. The patient *is* in fact candid when he gives expression to the impulse or affect in the only way still open to him, namely, in the distorted defensive measure. I think that in such a case the analyst ought not to omit all the intermediate stages in the transformation which the instinct has undergone and endeavour at all costs to arrive directly at the primitive instinctual impulse against which the ego has set up its defence and to introduce it into the patient's consciousness. The more correct method is to change the focus of attention in the analysis, shifting it in the first place from the instinct to the specific mechanism of defence, i.e. from the id to the ego. If we succeed in retracing the path followed by the instinct in its various transformations, the gain in the analysis is twofold. The transference-phenomenon which we have interpreted falls into two parts, both of which have their origin in the past: a libidinal or aggressive element, which belongs to the id, and a defence-mechanism, which we must attribute to the ego—in the most instructive cases to the ego of the same infantile period in which the id-impulse first arose. Not only do we fill in a gap in the patient's memory of his instinctual life, as we may also do when interpreting the first, simple type of transference, but we acquire information which completes and fills in the gaps in the history of his ego-development or, to put it another way, the history of the transformations through which his instincts have passed.

The interpretation of the second type of transference is more fruitful than that of the first type but it is responsible for most of the technical difficulties which arise between analyst and patient. The latter does not feel the second kind of transference-reaction to be a foreign body, and this is not surprising when we reflect how great a part the ego plays—even though it be the ego of earlier years—in its production. It is not easy to convince him of the repetitive nature of these phenomena. The form in which they emerge in his consciousness is ego-syntonic. The distortions demanded by the censorship were accomplished long ago and the adult ego sees no reason for being on its guard against their making their appearance in his free associations. By means of rationalization he easily shuts his eyes to the discrepancies between cause and effect which are so noticeable to the observer and make it evident that the transference has no objective justification. When the transference-reactions take this form, we cannot count on the patient's willing co-operation, as we can when they are of the type first described. Whenever the interpretation touches on the unknown elements of the ego, its activities in the past, that ego is wholly opposed to the work of analysis. Here evidently we have the situation which we commonly describe by the not very felicitous term, 'character-analysis.'

From the theoretical standpoint, the phenomena revealed by interpretation of the transference fall into two groups: that of id-contents and that of ego-activities, which in each case have been brought into consciousness. The results of interpretation during the patient's free association may be similarly classified: the uninterrupted flow of associations throws light on the contents of the id, the occurrence of a resistance on the defence-mechanisms employed by the ego. The only difference is that interpretations of the transference relate exclusively to the past and may light up in a moment whole periods of the patient's past life, while the id-contents revealed in free association are not connected with any particular period and the ego's defensive operations, manifested during the analytic hour in the form of resistance to free association, may belong to his present life also.

(c) Acting in the transference.—Yet another important contribution to our knowledge of the patient is made by a third form of transference. In dream-interpretation, free association, the interpretation of resistance and in the forms of transference hitherto described, the patient as we see him is always inside the analytic situation, i.e. in an unnatural endopsychical state. The relation of the two institutions in respect of strength has been upset: the balance is weighted in favour of the id, in the one case through the influence of sleep and in the other, through the observance of the fundamental rule of analysis. The strength of the ego-factors when we encounter them—whether in the form of the dream-censorship or in that of resistance to free associations—has always been impaired and their influence diminished, and often it is extremely difficult for us to picture them in their natural magnitude and vigour. We are all familiar with the accusation not infrequently made against analysts—that they may have a good knowledge of a patient's unconscious but are bad judges of his ego. There is probably a certain amount of justification in this criticism, for the analyst lacks opportunities of observing the patient's whole ego in action.

Now an intensification of the transference may occur, during which for the time being the patient ceases to observe the strict rules of analytic treatment and begins to act out in the behaviour of his daily life both the instinctual impulses and the defensive reactions which are embodied in his transferred affects. This is what is known as *acting* in the transference—a process in which, strictly speaking, the bounds of analysis have already been overstepped. It is instructive from the analyst's standpoint, in that the patient's psychic structure is thus automatically revealed in its natural proportions. Whenever we succeed in interpreting this 'acting,' we can divide the transference-activities into their component parts and so discover the actual quantity of energy supplied at that particular moment by the different institutions. In contrast to the observations that we made during the patient's free associations this situation shows us the absolute and the relative amount naturally contributed by each institution.

Although in this respect the interpretation of 'acting' in the transference affords us some valuable insight, the therapeutic gain is generally small. The bringing of the unconscious into consciousness and the exercise of therapeutic influence upon the relations between id, ego and super-ego clearly depend upon the analytic situation, which is artificially produced and still resembles hypnosis in that the activity of the ego-institutions is curtailed. As long as the ego continues to function freely or if it makes common cause with the id and simply carries out its behests, there is but little opportunity for endopsychical displacements and the bringing to bear of influence from without. Hence this third form of transference, which we call *acting,* is even more difficult for the analyst to deal with than the transference of the various modes of defence. It is natural that he should try to restrict it as far as possible by means of the analytical interpretations which he gives and the non-analytical prohibitions which he imposes.

8. A Contribution to the Subject of Transference-Resistance

Grete Bibring-Lehner

Ladies and Gentlemen,—Those of you who can look back to a long record of analytical experience will have perhaps been able to observe that in a certain, well-nigh typical class of case, which need not necessarily be characterized by special difficulties in structure, your therapeutic efforts have been of little or no avail. It was this circumstance which first led me to state the problems now to be discussed.

In the second place we find that an analysis which has threatened to break down, among other reasons, because even painstaking analytical work has proved incapable of overcoming the patient's transference-resistance (positive or negative) often undergoes a remarkable change in the further course of its development so soon as the patient is obliged, whether for external or internal reasons, to find another analyst. This fact can be observed most often and most clearly when the sex of the second analyst differs from that of the first. We then find, after a comparatively short time has elapsed, that certain resistances, which it had been impossible for month after month to overcome, now become accessible to analysis, but above everything, that the transference situation assumes a different complexion. No doubt, even in cases where a patient simply breaks off analysis and later resumes it with the same analyst, we often observe what appear to be favourable changes occurring in the analytical work accomplished by the patient, as a consequence of this proceeding. They are conditioned for the most part by the circumstance that the interruption has the effect of a warning and increases the patient's willingness to satisfy the analyst by more energetic co-operation. So far as it rests with the patient, his ego-resistances are thereby reduced and he takes greater pains over the analysis. Nevertheless these changes scarcely ever produce effects such as those that arise in the circumstances mentioned

Reprinted by permission from the *International Journal of Psycho-Analysis* 17 (1936): 181–89. Copyright © Institute of Psycho-Analysis.

above, nor are they so long maintained; and, above all, they do not affect the transference relationship to an equal extent.

We are accustomed to attribute the responsibility for a neurosis to a combination of two factors, namely the instinctual structure and the influences of reality in childhood. On the other hand, we conceive the transference-neurosis (i.e. the infantile attitude in the patient's relation to the analyst which is artificially revived by the analytic situation) as an expression of unsatisfied and repressed instinctual wishes, which are now in turn directed to the analyst as an imaginary object and remain on the whole unaffected by the analytical environment in which they flourish. The transference-neurosis is not a reactive, but an active manifestation; it is regulated not by reality, but by the spontaneous pressure of the id. The influence which analysis exerts on the formation of the transference is rather more general in its implications; our uncovering of the Ucs promotes in an especial degree the tendencies to transference already present in the neurotic, and the progress of analysis brings about a deployment of those aspects of the transference which are appropriate to each stage of the analysis.

I will now give an account of two cases in which this conception of the spontaneous nature of the transference-neurosis and of its independence requires, as I think, some qualification, and which rather suggest that under well-defined conditions a part of reality, represented in the person of the analyst, may exercise a not inconsiderable influence on the course and shape assumed by the transference. In this way I hope to find a link with the two problems from which I started, why with certain cases failure occurs as an almost typical experience in analytic practice, and why a change of analyst will often have such beneficial effects on the analysis.

A patient who had been treated over a long period by a very experienced analyst—the analysis had to be given up mainly for external reasons—suffered from severe anxiety- and punishment-phantasies, elaborated with the most uncompromising detail, in connection with ideas of the Last Judgement. The single elements in this impending settlement of accounts with God centred, as appeared from the abundant analytic material, round his childhood relation to a father who had in fact been very sadistic, and had committed daily excesses in punishing the little boy. His associations on the subject made a thorough discussion possible of his homosexuality, his masochism, his active and passive castration-wishes in relation to his father, and his sense of guilt originating in anxieties over masturbation. His relation to the analyst was on a basis of father-transference and was consequently expressed in a violently aggressive and provocative demeanour, coupled with a paralysing fear that the analyst would fall upon him, strike him and throw him out. But in spite of the many interpretations offered and detailed analysis of the patient's behaviour and attitude, no change at all took place either in the form or content of this transference, which had developed into a violent resistance. An unproductive period continued in this way for months; the patient repeated the same material which yielded nothing fresh. During this phase the treatment was broken off owing to the intervention of external factors and the patient was sent to me for treatment, not because any hope was entertained that the analysis would benefit greatly (the analyst in question took a very pessimistic view of the case), but because an attempt had to be made to free the patient from the transference, which was a source of torment to him. After a relatively short time had elapsed, the patient established a mother-transference, without at first giving up his attitude of aggression and anxiety. Nevertheless he now shewed himself willing to discuss the transference-situation belonging to the previous analysis. We then discovered that throughout the whole period occupied by the earlier analysis the patient had been under the impression, never revised, that his analyst had in fact the same dangerous personality as his father. I must here insist that this impression remained wholly unmodified in spite of every effort on the part of the analyst to make clear its transference significance. The roots of this idea were to be found first and foremost in the strict and somewhat uncompromising attitude which our colleague had decided to adopt in the present case, a procedure readily suggested by the imperious and childishly exacting character of the patient's transference. In addition to this the analyst happened to make use of certain expressions which the boy's father had similarly applied to him as a child. But the result of this was that the real differences between these two figures ceased to exist in the patient's mind. His reactions in this situation formed an exact counterpart to those of his childhood, with its anxieties and rages, and were regarded by the patient as a legitimate, indeed a natural, form of behaviour. Only when a transference to the second analyst had been established in its turn and the other relationship had then assumed a more normal degree of intensity and perspective, was it possible for the patient to introduce the necessary corrections. Withal, our efforts were principally directed to examining every reproach levelled against the first analyst from the point of view of reality and, in appropriate instances, establishing connections with the corresponding experiences of the patient's childhood, which formed the basis of those reproaches. There was nothing surprising in the developments which now occurred. The patient's transference-manifestations and resistances underwent a change, fresh mental content emerged into the foreground, and in the light of the material we were able to extend our insight and acquire the needful further understanding of his symptoms which had so long remained absent. It was now possible for the analysis, which had at first seemed hopeless, to make successful progress along normal lines.

The point of most interest to us here is the fact that processes which ordinarily occur within the limits of a single analysis were, in the present case, sharply divided and apportioned between two separate analyses. We may sum up as follows: the first analysis really foundered on the powerful resistances of the patient's transference, which derived their peculiar accent from the circumstance that the analyst both by reason of his sex and of certain elements in his behaviour, indeed even by his use of certain expressions, forfeited as it were the phantom-like qualities of his existence and so became a kind of re-incarnation in reality of the most significant figure in the patient's childhood and neurosis, his father. This led to so great an increase in the patient's reactions of anxiety, hate and deep distrust that in spite of persistent interpretation in connection with his central problem, his relation to his father, the analysis was unable to penetrate to deeper levels. In the second analysis, a mother-transference was early established. This enabled the patient at last to put himself at a certain distance from his conflict with his father and subsequently to resolve the infantile relationship. When at a later stage the patient produced a fresh father-transference, it was in a substantially milder form. There are two factors which appear to me important in this connection: first, the aggressive and anxiety-ridden relation to the father was more readily capable of being transferred to a male analyst; and secondly, a cognate factor on which I would like to lay special stress, the similarity noted in relation to the real behaviour of father and analyst had decisively strengthened the patient's resistances.

The same experience could be made in another case which proceeded in the reverse direction, from myself to a male analyst. The case in question was that of a patient twenty-three years old, suffering from impotence, which was only temporarily relieved with prostitutes after he had carried out certain oral perversions. In addition, he had a particularly disturbed relation to his mother, a stern, energetic and masterful woman. This was essentially due, on the one hand, to his utterly childish dependence on her, which obliged him in everything to conform strictly to her views, and on the other, to the hatred which led him to oppose her and hurt her by playing the part of a backward and helpless child, an attitude which had a profoundly disturbing effect both on his love-life and on his career (he was employed in his mother's business). Already after a short period of analysis the unconscious determinants of his symptoms were revealed in his strong oral demands, which went back to painful disappointments experienced at the hands of his mother. The patient's whole youth consisted in a series of exceptionally severe frustrations; for example, from earliest childhood advantage was taken of every opportunity which offered to send the child away for months to be looked after by strangers; when he did stay at home with his parents, his education was taken in hand by governesses, of whom his mother demanded severity; while she herself, much absorbed as she was by her business interests, treated him for the most part only to punishments, blows and derision. The father, who as compared with his wife occupied a subordinate position in the household, displayed a somewhat more friendly and under-standing attitude towards the patient until his sixth year, and turned away from the child in disappointment and anger only when his severe difficulties in learning became apparent, which was already the case during his first year at school. The transference soon set in in its full force and led to the most violent scenes in the analysis. It presented the same picture as his relation to his mother; in this connection the fact of my profession specially contributed to make a profound impression on the patient and played a very important part. In accordance both with the outlook of the petit-bourgeois milieu in which the patient lived and, more especially, with his own neurotic inhibition in intellectual fields, a woman engaged in an intellectual profession repre-sented for him a masculine woman, in exactly the same way as his mother did, who, apart from her qualities already mentioned, also held the chief position in her firm. The main difficulty in this analysis consisted in the patient's violent acting-out of the transference-relationship in all its aspects. He made vehement demands on me to take him on my lap, carry him about and feed him, because his mother, wicked woman that she was, had never done so herself. He wanted to strike me, he heaped abuse on his mother and on myself, and would no longer address me except by the familiar 'Du'—all this to the accompaniment of severe outbreaks of anxiety and sweating, and with such intense emotion that he would cling to the sofa to avoid putting his impulses into action. In this way he reproduced his infantile wishes and the furious disappointment which he had experienced in his relations with his mother. There was, however, a further aspect of this acting-out in which his neurotic reactions to frustration expressed themselves in a special form. It was just this aspect which was responsible for the real difficulty in the analysis and ultimately led to its being broken off. For his inability to work and to learn, a symptom which implied a defiant refusal to fulfil his mother's ambitions or to accept her meagre proofs of love or the interest (infused, it is true, with aggression) which she vouchsafed him, resulted in analysis in his being unwilling and unable to hear what I said or to understand what I meant. He gave direct expression to this in the following formula: 'I don't understand! I don't understand! It would suit you very well if I understood you, and that is just the reason why I don't.' His anxiety and bewilderment over these experiences gave rise to suicidal ideas, and, running parallel with the processes occurring during treatment, his behaviour outside analysis assumed a singular aspect. He began to display a violently threatening attitude towards his mother, together with an unusual excitability, so that his family and their medical advisers wished to prohibit analysis and have the patient placed in an institution. I decided to break off the treatment. The same considerations which furnished the occasion for this paper led me to advise the patient not to abandon his efforts to get well, but to continue analysis with a colleague. The patient acted on my suggestion. After a certain interval, the anticipated relief was in fact forthcoming and it became possible for the analysis to resume its course, at first in the shape of a father-transference. This was all the more possible, seeing that the patient's childhood relationship to his father had been far less intense and involved far less conflict.[1]

I think that the material here adduced in a summary form allows us to infer that the extremely violent transference to myself, characterized mainly by action, was contributed to by the two following facts: (1) in analysis with a woman analyst the patient's mother-transference was the first to come into play; and (2) my professional occupation caused him to reproduce in his relation to me, as a 'masculine woman', and in an unmodified and unmitigated form, just those elements of his transference which held dangers for the analysis, those namely arising from his conflict with a bad, unloving and masculine mother. It was only in the analysis which followed that he was able, as happened in the earlier case mentioned, to regain insight to a sufficient extent to avoid being completely submerged by a repetition of these conflicts and was able instead to overcome by the help of reflection and deliberation the experiences of his childhood and the transference.

It seems, then, that under certain conditions, it may have a very unfavourable effect on the work of analysis if we make a breach in the illusory quality proper to the transference, of which mention was made at the beginning of this paper. And this is specially the case if the real person of the analyst, by reason, principally, of his sex, in conjunction with certain features of his personality, reveals extensive similarities to those real objects from the patient's childhood whose influence was paramount. The effects liable to be produced by the analyst's real personality can naturally, in principle, refer to any of his qualities, as well to general ones, such as a friendly or reserved attitude, a disposition to severity or kindliness, as to those of a more personal kind, especially e.g. the form of his counter-transference, where chance plays a considerable part. The psychic importance which these attributes possess for the patient's transference dispositions may determine the role which those attributes are destined to play in an analysis. I have put the question of the analyst's sex in the foreground because its effects are particularly apparent and because they were so powerful in the cases mentioned. Now in certain analyses it is by no means a matter of indifference whether they begin with one or another form of transference. In the case of women with powerful masculine strivings and an intense wish for identification on a basis of masculinity, analysis with a man will create a situation other than would analysis with a woman, where the resistances would perhaps be principally formed out of projected self-contempt. An elderly, kindly analyst may stimulate fewer difficulties in this type of woman patient than a younger man who will at once attract to himself the resistances based upon rivalry. We find a profuse variety of relations which are not readily reduced to order.[2] In addition, the real attitude of the analyst's personality, as we have used the phrase, may in many cases result in an intensification of the patient's symptoms and affective modes of reaction in a *desirable* sense and may thus create a situation favourable to analysis. If, however, the influence of this reality is such that their intensification exceeds a certain maximum, the situation which ensues—one impossible to control by purely analytical means—may be described as follows. (1) The patient's conflicts emerge in the transference in all their intensity and quite without warning instead of by gradual degrees, so that the ego's resistances are heightened as a defence against this onslaught. (2) There results a kind of fixation to this transference-conflict, a rigid transference system, which now prevents the patient bringing out associations and affects not comprised in its scheme, just as it paralyses the further expansion of transference-attitudes essential to the progress of the analysis. (3) The formation of a predominantly positive transference based on confidence, without whose help we cannot overcome the transference-neurosis in its constantly changing manifestations, fails to materialize. The patient's ego is so overwhelmed by affects that that part of his personality which has remained healthy is unable to make proper headway. Notwithstanding that we confront the adult elements in the ego with the infantile ones, i.e. with the totality of those infantile reactions which still remain operative, this is unable to make a sufficiently profound impression, so as to lead to a gradual mastering of resistances. The sequel leads either, as in the first case, to complete inhibition, owing to the constant struggle to put up a defence against this form of transference, or, as with the second patient, to a violent eruption of the unconscious impulses and to acting-out on a scale calculated to imperil the whole analysis.

The practical consequences of these remarks are comparatively simple and already apparent. Whenever we obtain the impression that a particular form of transference is not regulated mainly by the patient's unconscious, but also, and in a more considerable measure, by the realities of the analytical milieu and the special character of the analyst's personality, and when the difficulties which we have just described make their appearance, we shall consider it desirable not to continue the treatment ourselves. But there is also no reason why it should be abandoned as hopeless; on the contrary, we have to some extent to sacrifice our therapeutic ambitions in the interests of therapeutic responsibility, and arrange after mature deliberation for a change of analyst. This change is to be effected under conditions which, in conformity with the insight we have already acquired into the structure of the case, will allow the repetition of infantile relationships in the transference to assume the most favourable form possible.

Finally, reference should here be made to a particular factor which often exercises a decisive influence on the course of the second analysis. It frequently happens that the patient, motivated by feelings of disappointment, defiance or revenge, tries to keep the negative aspects of the transference permanently fastened on to the first analyst, accentuating a contrast between him and the second analyst, in order to conceal thereby the negative attitudes emerging in the second analysis. Needless to say, it will be an important task for the second analyst to pay full attention to this fact and so prevent the earlier resistances from reproducing themselves in a displaced and latent form.

NOTES

1. The case here described is discussed in much greater detail in Bergler's paper, 'Zur Problematik der Pseudodebilität'. *Internationale Zeitschrift für Psychoanalyse,* Bd. XVIII, 1932.
2. I shall have to reserve for a later paper any attempt to pass beyond these tentative formulations and to describe various typical situations of this kind which would then furnish points of view for the decisions that one might on occasion be compelled to take in allotting analysts to such patients. Similarly, within the limits of this paper, I can only point out that our theme provides an approach to the problem of 'Transference and Love' as well as to the interesting questions connected with the whole subject of second analyses.

9. The Role of Transference: Practical Considerations in Relation to Psychoanalytic Therapy

Phyllis Greenacre

It is my intention to discuss some of the practical considerations in psychoanalytic treatment in their relationship to the role of the transference. I shall not enter into any extensive technical or historical survey but shall confine myself to a few problems expressed in nontechnical terms, and without benefit of quotation. I shall deal with these problems in the following order: (1) a discussion of the essentials of the transference relationship; (2) a brief outline of two different points of view regarding the utilization of the transference in therapy; and (3) a discussion of practical arrangements as they are determined by the transference.

I

First as to the nature of the transference relationship itself: If two people are repeatedly alone together some sort of emotional bond will develop between them. Even though they may be strangers engaged in relatively neutral occupations, not directed by one or the other for or against the "other one," it will probably not be long before a predominantly friendly or predominantly unfriendly tone will develop between them. The speed and the intensity of this development will be enhanced by the frequency of the periods in each other's company.

Human beings do not thrive well in isolation, being sustained then mostly by memories and hopes, even to the point of hallucination, or by reaching out to nonhuman living things (like Mendel and the beans). This need for sensory contact, basically the contact of warm touch of another body but secondarily experienced in the other senses as well (even the word "contact"

Reprinted from the *Journal of the American Psychoanalytic Association* 2 (1954): 671–84, by permission of International Universities Press, Inc.

is significant), probably comes from the long period of care which the human infant must have before he is able to sustain himself. Lonely infants fed and cared for regularly and with sterile impersonal efficiency do not live to childhood.

Even if the periods of repeated contact between two individuals do not comprise a major part of their time, still such an emotional bond develops and does so more quickly and more sensitively if the two persons are *alone* together; i.e., the more the spontaneous currents and emanations of feeling must be concentrated the one upon the other and not shared, divided, or reflected among members of a group. I have already indicated that I believe the matrix of this *is* a veritable matrix; i.e., comes largely from the original mother-infant quasi-union of the first months of life. This I consider the basic transference; or one might call it the primary transference, or some part of primitive social instinct.

Now if both people are adults but one is troubled and the other is versed in the ways of trouble and will endeavor to put the torchlight of his understanding at the disposal of the troubled one, to lend it to him that he may find his way more expeditiously, the situation more nearly approximates that of the analytic relationship. The analyst acts then like an extra function, or set of functions, which is lent to the analysand for the latter's temporary use and benefit.

Since this relationship may, in its most primitive aspects, be based on the mother-child relationship and since the patient is a troubled person seeking help, one can see at once that the relationship will not be one of equal mutual warming, but that there will be a tendency for the patient to develop an attitude of expectant dependent receptiveness toward the physician. It is the aim of treatment, however, to increase the patient's maturity, to realize his capacity for self-direction, his "self-possession" (in the deeper sense of the word); and *not* to augment his state of helplessness and dependence, with which he in his neurotic suffering is already burdened.

How then is the patient's autonomy to be safeguarded and strengthened, in the very situation which might seem to favor its depletion? The chief safeguard is the analyst's sticking to the work of actually analyzing, and not serving as guide, model, or teacher, no matter how luring these roles may be. He must therefore genuinely leave matters of decision in the patient's own hands without guiding interference. We all know that the work of analysis consists very largely in helping the patient to rid himself of the tensions, patterned attitudes, and expectations which have arisen in the vicissitudes of the past and are impinging unhelpfully upon current situations, so much so that they actually distort his appreciation of and his reactive possibilities to the present problems of his life; and that this help of riddance is carried out through a mutual exploration of the forgotten past, using mainly the special techniques of free association and dream analysis.

The analytic relationship is used entirely for the benefit of the patient. Analysis is the profession of the therapist and he sets his fee and makes his time arrangements with his patient in advance; and thereafter attempts to keep these constant except when extraordinary reality conditions intrude to force a dislocation of these elements of the reality framework. The analyst does not intrude his life, his point of view—moral, political or religious or any other—into his responses to his patient. His aim rather is to listen, to clarify and to communicate step by step an understanding of the patient's current dilemmas in relation to the intrusion into them of inappropriate emotional attitudes and action tendencies having their origin in the past. This sounds too mechanistic and too simple, but will be considered again in dealing further with the transference development. In the very neutrality and constancy of the physical arrangements of treatment, in their noncontamination by contributions from the analyst's own life, and in the essentially research and nondirective attitude of the analyst, many forces which might diminish the patient's autonomy are avoided.

It is quite apparent that in nonanalytic relationships, in just everyday give-and-take contacts, we react not merely on the basis of the realistic current elements of the situation but as these influence us additionally in accordance with their stirring memories of past experiences, whether or not these are available to direct recall. Indeed we seem to be more influenced when the memory is not available, and we mistake the feeling aroused by the past for one belonging intrinsically to the present. In each life situation, whole series of memory reactions of more or less related situations are re-evoked, and it is certainly not merely the present but a composite of past experiences which is influencing the attitudes and actions of the individual at any given time.

Now in the artificial situation of the analytic relationship, there develops early a firm basic transference, derived from the mother-child relationship but expressed in the confidence in the knowledge and integrity of the analyst and the helpfulness of the method; but in addition the nonparticipation of the analyst in a personal way in the relationship creates a "tilted" emotional relationship, a kind of psychic suction in which many of the past attitudes, specific experiences and fantasies of the patient are re-enacted in fragments or sometimes in surprisingly well-organized dramas with the analyst as the main figure of significance to the patient. This revival of past experiences with their full emotional accompaniment focused upon the analyst, is not only more possible but can be more easily seen, understood, and interpreted if the psychic field is not already cluttered with personal bits from the analyst's life. This of course is the work with the neurotic symptoms and patterns as they occur in the transference; i.e., projected directly upon the analyst. Many times it is the most convincing medium of demonstration and interpretation to the patient and permits a greater degree of relief, probably because the memories are thus being actually experienced with their *full* emotional resonance, and not merely being reported and talked about with a *partial* reliving. One should recall that even in the matter of a confession, more relief is obtained if the events are specifically told, than if simply the recognition of wrongdoing is admitted in general terms.

So much time has been spent on these very elementary conditions for analysis because recently there has been a tendency to disregard them somewhat, and sometimes to ignore—on the basis that they are unnecessary, cumbersome or just so much rigid ritual anyway—the restrictions and to resent the deprivations which, admittedly artificial, are designed to promote the development of the full display of neurotic manifestations in the transference.

II

In regard to the role of the transference development, it seems that two fundamental and divergent points of view are represented more and more clearly among us. The one sees the transference relationship in its full development (permitting and even emphasizing the repetition in the transference of older, nuclear experiences) as the most delicate, subtle, and precious medium of work and considers that its development should be furthered, its existence safeguarded, and its content analyzed. The other (with which I am less familiar) regards the basic positive transference in the form of mutual respect and confidence as essential for the best progress of the work, very much as it is in any other therapeutic or co-operative working relationship, but considers intensity of transference relationship beyond this as largely a dependency reaction which should be diluted or dispersed as expeditiously as possible, by indicating to the patient that his reactions *are* those of different varieties of dependency, belonging to his childhood rather than to adulthood, and by encouraging him as quickly as possible to change his actions in the outer world, to undertake new experiences which will then, with the emotional support of the analyst, be of a different nature and configuration than those which he has experienced in the past. It is even said that transference reactions needing specific interpretation should be avoided, and the relationship with the analyst is used for its emotional leverage in the enticement, direction or persuasion of the patient to his new undertakings. Thus hopefully, the patient will not remain dependent on the analyst because he will be throughout engaging himself in new and beneficial experiences in reality, although he is at the same time depending on the analyst's explanatory encouragement. Guided and suggested or at least supported by the analyst, he enters the "corrective experience," and is supposed to break the habitual neurotic constellation which has previously held him. This appears to be little more than the old-fashioned habit training with especially strong suggestive influencing. Or it might be compared to the re-conditioning experiences in which the approval of the analyst is the reward for running the new maze.

The contrast of these two points of view is summarized as, first, one which encourages, develops and utilizes the full transference reaction as a medium of re-experience and interpretation; and second, one which utilizes only the basic transference, avoids the intensity of the full transference development, directs by interpreting dynamic lines and relationships rather than eliciting and interpreting specific past experiences, and encourages and promotes new experiences *per se* during the analytic work, often as quickly as possible. In the former there is a considerable reliance on the "working through" process, utilizing the analyst as an essential focus; in the latter a considerable reliance on the "working out" process, carrying into reality activity new behavior patterns under the suggestion and support of the analyst, and sometimes even with his stage management. The aim in the "working through" is a loosening of the neurotic tendencies at their source, since deepest emotional tensions are invested in the specific experiences; while in the "working out," counteracting, neutralizing or freshly coating experiences are relied upon to coerce the emotions into new patterns without paying too much specific attention to the old. One is a method of detailed analysis; the other of survey, and forward propulsion with the aid of the strong suggestion of personal attachment which will, however, presumably and paradoxically be without increased dependency. If we keep in mind these two divergent points of view, I think we may understand different emphases in technique and even in the maintenance of practical arrangements.

III

Much has been said in the recent past concerning the rules and rituals of analysis, the worshipful obedience which our organization is said to exact of its devotees. The magic numbers three, four and five seem to recur. But rules are the implementation of principles; i.e., the forms of their specific application, and no rule is very significant except as it represents the general practice of a desirable principle. In addition, there is no rule which may not have to be modified. It is from this angle of principles that practical procedures will be discussed here.

In the sort of psychoanalysis with which I am dealing, *the full transference relationship is accepted,* its establishment promoted and safeguarded, and its content examined and selectively interpreted. To the end of its speedy establishment, it is well to have analytic sessions spaced sufficiently close together that a sense of continuity of relationship (between analyst and analysand) and of content of material produced may be sustained. It would seem then that as nearly as possible a daily contact avoiding frequent or long gaps in treatment is desirable. In the setting of the organization of most lives, the analysis takes its place in the work of the week and accordingly five or six sessions are allocated to it. Later in many analyses it may be desirable to reduce the number of sessions, after the relationship between analyst and analysand has been consolidated, and the analyst has been able to determine the analysand's reactions to interruptions, first apparent in the reactions to week ends. If the analysand carries over a day's interruption well, without the relationship cooling off too much or the content being lost sight of, then it may be possible to carry the analysis of a three- or four-session-a-week basis, keeping a good rhythm of work with the patient. The desirability of this, however, can only be determined after the analyst has had a chance to gauge the patient's natural tempo and needs and the character of his important defenses; and this must vary from patient to patient. This initial period is generally at least a year, and more often longer.

There are three additional unfavorable factors here, however, which are seldom mentioned: (1) The actual prolongation of the treatment by spreading or infrequent spacing of sessions, in analytic work as well as in other psychotherapeutic approaches. If this prolongation is great, there is that much longer impact on other arrangements of the patient's life. ''Brief psychotherapies'' are sometimes paradoxically extended over very long times indeed, being repeatedly ended and reopened, because little was consolidated in treatment and all sorts of extraneous and unnecessary interferences entered. (2) The larger the number of analytic patients possible at any given time when sessions per patient are less frequent, the greater the tax on the analyst in keeping at his mental fingertips the full range of facts and reactions belonging to each patient. The monetary recompense may, however, be greatly increased. Here again the feasibility of spacing must depend on some factors belonging to the analyst's special equipment and demands, combined with the patient's ability to "carry over," and there will inevitably be considerable variability in these. (3) The less frequent the therapeutic sessions the greater may be the risk of inadequate analysis of the negative transference. Especially with those patients where hours are made less frequent because the patient is thought by the analyst to be "wasting the hour" by what appears as unproductive talk or by silence, or where the analyst fears that the patient is feeling guilty over his silences, it has sometimes been recommended that the patient be given a vacation from treatment or that sessions be made less frequent. From my experience in the reanalysis of a number of patients, it has seemed to me rather that many of these periods are due to the patient's difficulty in expressing hostile or erotic feelings. It is about these feelings, rather than about his silence, that he feels guilty. Too often if he is given a rest or hours are made infrequent, these emotional attitudes are never brought out to be analyzed, and appear later on in disturbing forms. I am further impressed with the fact that those analysts who talk most about the dangers of dependence seem rarely to consider the reciprocal relationship between tenacious dependency and unanalyzed negative transference. In so far as negative attitudes toward the analyst are not analyzed or even expressed, the need of the patient to be reassured of the love and protection of the analyst becomes enormously increased and demanding. The analyst may see only this side of the picture and erroneously attempt to deal with it by greater spacing of contacts.

The length of the hour is, as a matter of practice, generally maintained at forty-five to sixty minutes. Certainly it is desirable that a sufficient span of time be permitted for a kind of natural organic pattern of productivity to occur during many of the sessions. The hour is our time unit in general use, perhaps because it does involve some kind of natural span of this kind, and is a feasible unit fitting into the working day. While there have been many experiments of speeding up analytic sessions to two a day or increasing the length to two hours at one session, no such practice has generally taken hold. It is my belief, however, that a regular allotment of time—the same duration and so far as possible on a prearranged and constant week-by-week schedule (in contrast to varying spans of time in sessions at irregular periods not expected in advance)—generally aids in the rhythm and continuity of the work and minimizes utilization of external situations as resistance by the patients.

The idea has been advanced by some that it would be wiser, when feasible, to have so flexible a schedule that it would be possible to see patients according to their sense of need, a kind of on-demand feeding programme; or such resiliency that hours could be lengthened or shortened according to the seeming current emotional state of the patient. While I have little doubt that this may be desirable in some open psychotic conditions, I do doubt its benefit in other conditions. I believe that in neurotic and even in many borderline states, patients gain a sense of strength in relation to reality and growing inner capacity in the ability to carry on regular work, tolerating some discomforts and anxieties, knowing that these will be worked with at a regular time, and have actually a lesser degree of (oral) dependency than where appointments are made on demand. This does not mean, however, that in situations of crisis from inner or outer reasons, extra appointments should necessarily be denied.

No discussion of practical arrangements for psychoanalytic therapy would be complete without paying one's respects to the question of whether the couch or the chair is to be used by the analysand during his treatment session. Indeed to many lay people and to some psychiatrists the use of the couch became sometimes the main or only index of whether the treatment was psychoanalytic or a discussion method. Couch meant psychoanalysis; chair meant no psychoanalysis. With the increased popularity of psychoanalysis, unfortunately some young psychiatrists became analysts through the purchase of a couch and the reading of the dream-book; and with the increased interest in recent years in the hypnotic and drug and electroshock therapies, the couch is more or less routine equipment and no longer a mark of distinction. Although its use was originally probably derived from the hypnotic therapy with which analysis originated, it was retained—not as a residual organ— but because it was of service in inducing a state of mild relaxation and limiting gross movement in the analysand, a condition favorable for attention to the flow of associative thought so necessary for the exploration of unconscious connections. Furthermore with the analyst sitting at the head of the couch, the patient is not distracted by watching the analyst's facial expression and attempting to read it and accommodate to it, while the analyst can rest his face the more by not having to be looked at all day long and to inhibit or control the unconscious blend of reaction and reflection in his facial expression. As every analyst knows, there are some patients in marginal relationship with reality who find it very difficult to talk unless communication is maintained through visual as well as through spoken contact. Such patients naturally require to be treated vis-à-vis, but generally require other marked changes in analytic technique as well. Many analysts make a considerable distinction between what is said before the patient gets on the couch and immediately after he arises from it, from that which is couch born. Certainly there may be considerable significance in the difference in his postural relationship to the analyst and its connection with his utterances. One notices these things rather naturally with each patient and quite as naturally determines what importance to put upon them. Only a very compulsive analyst will want to determine an inexorable precision of rule of interpretation about these matters, or to prescribe every detail of the analyst's office. The general principle is to keep the physical arrangements of the office substantially the same throughout the treatment. Certainly this aids in limiting diverting influences and intrusions.

The safeguarding of the transference relationship is of prime importance. The relationship is an artificial one, arranged and maintained for the definite purpose of drawing the neurotic reactions into a sharp focus and reflecting them upon the analyst and the analytic situation. It is therefore just as necessary to keep the field pure for the clear reflection of the memories emerging from the past, as it is not to contaminate a field of surgical operation, or to avoid getting extraneous dirt onto a microscopic slide, which will blur or obscure the important findings, create artifacts and confuse interpretative understanding.

The two sets of considerations in safeguarding the transference field of work which seem most important to me are the strict maintenance of the confidences of the patient and, second, the elimination of other avenues of relationship with the patient than that of analysis. Both of these are difficult to maintain, but only by keeping the principles continually in mind, training oneself to respect safeguarding rules and closely examining any times in which violations occur, can an analyst really do justice to his work; and only if he is willing to maintain this degree of respect for his patient, himself, and his work, is he genuinely up to the job in hand. I cannot in the least agree with the remark of a quite eminent analyst, repeated to me several times, that so many analysts overstep the boundaries of the transference—even in grossly sexual ways—that therefore the best thing to do is to say nothing about these incidents. It is only by discussing these possibilities (rather than by punishing the offenders) and by emphasizing their dangers to students and among ourselves that we can really develop our science to the research precision which must be aimed at in each clinical case.

In regard to maintaining the confidence of the patient, all would probably agree on the unwisdom of gossiping about patients, although even here, where should a person draw the line? It is not always easy to say where professional discussion ends and anecdotal interest starts. Further than this, seemingly less hazardous but in my opinion even more seriously endangering analytic work, is the giving and receiving of information directly about the patient to and from relatives, sincerely interested friends and even physicians. Here there is the danger not only of the breach of the patient's confidence, but the breakdown of the analyst's own integrity of work with the patient, his tendency to become prejudiced, seemingly paradoxically, by the supposed objective facts obtained from other sources. While it is undoubtedly true that an analyst's vision of the total situation may at certain points be seriously impaired by his need to stick to the microscopy of his work or by an overidentification with the patient, still it seems that this is in the long run less distorting—in that it leaves the autonomy of the patient intact and "objectivity" is obtained through the patient's changing activities and reality testing in the world—than if the analyst succumbs to the pressure of outside information, which is sometimes not in the least objective, and begins insidiously to exert "corrective" influential pressure in the analysis, sometimes without even being aware that he is doing so. Therefore it is a better principle to seek or to give specific information about a patient only with the patient's definite knowledge, understanding and wish.

It is almost self-evident that the same problems of breach of confidence, of insidious therapeutic pressure, and of the enormous complication of the changing transference identity of the analyst militate against sound analytic work in the simultaneous analysis of married couples or of those in close emotional relationships. While this may occasionally seem necessary under very extraordinary circumstances, it is at best a precarious proceeding. It has recently been sometimes justified on the basis of the wealth of factual background available to the analyst and the greater skill possible in handling the situation. That greater skill is demanded is evident; that that degree of skill is frequently possible seems dubious. In the reanalysis of analysts in my own practice, I have sometimes found that such a strong wish on the part of the analyst represented rather an unusual degree of unresolved primal-scene scoptophilia in the analyst himself.

The need to avoid violation of the transference field by the establishment of other avenues of relationship with the patient demands a high degree of restraint and sacrifice on the part of the analyst. It demands, among other things the sacrifice on the part of the analyst of conspicuous public participation even in very worthy social and political "causes" to which he may lend his name or his activities. For in so far as the analyst is thrown into so active, even though general, a pressure role outside the analysis, his situation is the more complicated inside the analysis. It may be impossible for him to detect this if it means then that the patient just automatically does not dare to think of certain things which he unconsciously feels would cause him to be unacceptable to this particular analyst. Such deletions from the analysis only turn up on reanalysis or in the negative transference reactions which crop up after the termination of an analysis. The analyst must forego the privilege of eliciting the patient's admiration for his personal exploits.

Another form of contamination of the transference occurs when the analyst asks special favors, even seemingly minor ones, from his patient. This is frequently done and justified on the basis that the request is only a minor one; or, on the opposite basis, that the external situation is so important as to warrant breaking the rule; or that the analyst's skill is so great and his knowledge of his patient's inner situation so nearly perfect that he can afford to do so with impunity; or even that he is really doing it for the benefit of the patient; yet it may be followed by really severe disturbance. This rule about not entering into other relationships with the analysand is one which deserves always our most careful and respectful scrutiny.

This leads back again to consideration of that grosser overstepping of the transference limits in the establishment of a sexual relationship between analyst and analysand either during the analysis or relatively soon after it is officially terminated. That this is not so infrequent as one would wish to think becomes apparent to anyone who does many reanalyses. That its occurrence is often denied and the situation rather quickly explained by involved analysts as due to a hysterical fantasy on the part of the patient (indeed one knows how universal and necessary such fantasies are) is an indication of how great is the temptation. It would seem that there is a factor in this which is one of the not immediately observable implications of the setup of the analytic consulting room, with the patient in a passive-receptive position, and the whole situation one of intimacy and shutting out of the external world. Certainly such a situation is most provocative to a male analyst and a female patient.

It is my contention, however, that an equally distorting but not so obvious invasion of the transference relationship may occur with the female analyst, who may be drawn unconsciously into an overly protective, essentially maternal nursing attitude toward the suffering patient, whether man or woman. One must remember in considering the effects of such transgressions that the analytic situation *is* an artificial, tilted one; that there is none other in life that it really reproduces. In this very fact is its enormous force and capacity for utilization as a medium of establishing new integration. It is one which more nearly reproduces the demand of the child for a perfectly understanding parent, than any parent-child relationship can possibly approach, and it is the only one in life in which no emotional counterdemand is to be expected. It is produced for the purpose of drawing these infantile and childish reactions into a new life for the sake of their being understood and newly assimilated by the suffering adult whom the child has become. For this very reason, the carrying through into a relationship in life of the incestuous fantasy of the patient may be more grave in its subsequent distortion of the patient's life than any actual incestuous seduction in childhood has been.

Psychoanalysis is a hard taskmaster. Even in its practice it demands the accuracy, the fidelity, and the devotion of the true research worker. It is not something to be played with or even to be too lightly experimented with. The power of the unconscious is such that it "gets back" at those who work with it and treat it too lightly. There are some unfortunate sides to the markedly increased popularity of psychoanalysis since the last World War. Perhaps chief among these is the fact that because its importance, in its derived forms, was seen clearly under war conditions and attracted the attention of physicians and psychiatrists rather generally, the demand for training became so great that a growing temptation arose for the substitution of some of the therapies derived from psychoanalysis for psychoanalysis itself, at the risk of expediency being rationalized as tested theory.

10. Current Concepts of Transference

Elizabeth R. Zetzel

There are few current problems concerning the problem of transference that Freud did not recognize either implicitly or explicitly in the development of his theoretical and clinical framework. For all essential purposes, moreover, his formulations, in spite of certain shifts in emphasis, remain integral to contemporary psycho-analytic theory and practice. Recent developments mainly concern the impact of an ego-psychological approach; the significance of object relations, both current and infantile, external and internal; the role of aggression in mental life, and the part played by regression and the repetition compulsion in the transference. Nevertheless, analysis of the infantile oedipal situation in the setting of a genuine transference neurosis is still considered a primary goal of psycho-analytic procedure.

Originally, transference was ascribed to displacement on to the analyst of repressed wishes and fantasies derived from early childhood. The transference neurosis was viewed as a compromise formation similar to dreams and other neurotic symptoms. Resistance, defined as the clinical manifestation of repression, could be diminished or abolished by interpretation mainly directed towards the content of the repressed. Transference resistance, both positive and negative, was ascribed to the threatened emergence of repressed unconscious material in the analytic situation. Soon, with the development of a structural approach, the superego described as the heir to the genital oedipal situation was also recognized as playing a leading part in the transference situation. The analyst was subsequently viewed not only as the object by displacement of infantile incestuous fantasies, but also as the substitute by projection for the prohibiting parental figures which had been internalized as the definitive superego. The effect of transference interpretation in mitigating undue severity of the superego has, therefore, been emphasized in many discussions of the concept of transference.

Certain expansions in the structural approach related to increased recogni-

Reprinted by permission from the *International Journal of Psycho-Analysis* 37 (1956): 367–76. Copyright © Institute of Psycho-Analysis.

tion of the role of early object relations in the development of both ego and superego have affected current concepts of transference. In this connection, the significance of the analytic situation as a repetition of the early mother-child relationship has been stressed from different points of view. An equally important development relates to Freud's revised concept of anxiety which not only led to theoretical developments in the field of ego psychology, but also brought about related clinical changes in the work of many analysts. As a result, attention was no longer mainly focused on the content of the unconscious. In addition, increasing importance was attributed to the defensive processes by means of which the anxiety which would be engendered if repression and other related mechanisms were broken down, was avoided in the analytic situation. Differences in the interpretation of the role of the analyst and the nature of transference developed from emphasis, on the one hand, on the importance of early object relations, and on the other, from primary attention to the role of the ego and its defences. These defences first emerged clearly in discussion of the technique of child analysis, in which Melanie Klein (1) and Anna Freud (2), the pioneers in this field, played leading roles.

From a theoretical point of view, discussion foreshadowing the problems which face us today was presented in 1934 in well-known papers by Richard Sterba (3) and James Strachey (4), and further elaborated at the Marienbad Symposium at which Edward Bibring (5) made an important contribution. The importance of identification with, or introjection of, the analyst in the transference situation was clearly indicated. Therapeutic results were attributed to the effect of this process in mitigating the need for pathological defences. Strachey, however, considerably influenced by the work of Melanie Klein, regarded transference as essentially a projection on to the analyst of the patient's own superego. The therapeutic process was attributed to subsequent introjection of a modified superego as a result of 'mutative' transference interpretation. Sterba and Bibring, on the other hand, intimately involved with development of the ego-psychological approach, emphasized the central role of the ego, postulating a therapeutic split and identification with the analyst as an essential feature of transference. To some extent, this difference of opinion may be regarded as semantic. If the superego is explicitly defined as the heir of the genital Oedipus conflict, then earlier intrasystemic conflicts within the ego, although they may be related retrospectively to the definitive superego, must, nevertheless, be defined as contained within the ego. Later divisions within the ego of the type indicated by Sterba and very much expanded by Edward Bibring in his concept of therapeutic alliance between the analyst and the healthy part of the patient's ego, must also be excluded from superego significance. In contrast, those who attribute pregenital intrasystemic conflicts within the ego primarily to the introjection of objects, consider that the resultant state of internal conflict resembles in all dynamic respects the situation seen in later conflicts between ego and superego. They, therefore, believe that these structures develop simultaneously and suggest that no sharp distinction should be made between pre-oedipal, oedipal, and post-oedipal superego.

The differences, however, are not entirely verbal, since those who attribute superego formation to the early months of life tend to attribute a significance to early object relations which differs from the conception of those who stress control and neutralization of instinctual energy as primary functions of the ego. This theoretical difference necessarily implies some disagreement as to the dynamic situation both in childhood and in adult life, inevitably reflected in the concept of transference and in hypotheses as to the nature of the therapeutic process. From one point of view, the role of the ego is central and crucial at every phase of analysis. A differentiation is made between transference as therapeutic alliance and the transference neurosis, which, on the whole, is considered a manifestation of resistance. Effective analysis depends on a sound therapeutic alliance, a prerequisite for which is the existence, before analysis, of a degree of mature ego functions, the absence of which in certain severely disturbed patients and in young children may preclude traditional psycho-analytic procedure. Whenever indicated, interpretation must deal with transference manifestations, which means, in effect, that the transference must be analysed. The process of analysis, however, is not exclusively ascribed to transference interpretation. Other interpretations of unconscious material, whether related to defence or to early fantasy, will be equally effective provided they are accurately timed and provided a satisfactory therapeutic alliance has been made. Those, in contrast, who stress the importance of early object relations emphasize the crucial role of transference as an object relationship, distorted though this may be by a variety of defences against primitive unresolved conflicts. The central role of the ego, both in the early stages of development and in the analytic process, is definitely accepted. The nature of the ego is, however, considered at all times to be determined by its external and internal objects. Therapeutic progress indicated by changes in ego function results, therefore, primarily from a change in object relations through interpretation of the transference situation. Less differentiation is made between transference as therapeutic alliance and the transference neurosis as a manifestation of resistance. Therapeutic progress depends almost exclusively on transference interpretation. Other interpretations, although indicated at times, are not, in general, considered an essential feature of the analytic process. From this point of view, the preanalytic maturity of the patient's ego is not stressed as a prerequisite for analysis; children and relatively disturbed patients are considered potentially suitable for traditional psycho-analytic procedure.

These differences in theoretical orientation are not only reflected in the approach to children and disturbed patients. They may also be recognized in significant variations of technique in respect to all clinical groups, which inevitably affect the opening phases, understanding of the inevitable regressive features of the transference neurosis, and handling of the terminal phases of analysis. I shall try to underline the main problems by emphasizing contrast, rather than similarity. I shall also try to avoid too detailed discussion of controversial theory regarding the nature of early ego development by a somewhat arbitrary differentiation between those who relate ego analysis to the analysis of defences and those who stress the primary significance of object relations both in the transference, and in the development and definitive structure of the ego. Needless to say, this involves some over-simplification. I hope, however, that it may, at the same time, clarify certain important issues. To take up first the analysis of patients generally agreed to be suitable for classical analytic procedure, the transference neuroses. Those who emphasize the role of the ego and the analysis of defences, not only maintain Freud's conviction that analysis should proceed from surface to depth, but also consider that early material in the analytic situation derives, in general, from defensive processes rather than from displacement on to the analyst of early instinctual fantasies. Deep transference interpretation in the early phases of analysis will, therefore, either be meaningless to the patient since its unconscious significance is so inaccessible, or, if the defences are precarious, will lead to premature and possibly intolerable anxiety. Premature interpretation of the equally unconscious automatic defensive processes by means of which instinctual fantasy has been kept unconscious is also ineffective and undesirable. There are, however, differences of opinion within this group, as to how far analysis of defence can be separated from analysis of content. Waelder (6), for example, has stressed the impossibility of such separation. Fenichel (7), however, considered that at least theoretical separation should be made and indicated that, as far as possible, analysis of defence should precede analysis of unconscious fantasy. It is, nevertheless, generally agreed that the transference neurosis develops, as a rule, after ego defences have been sufficiently undermined to mobilize previously hidden instinctual conflict. During both the early stages of analysis, and at frequent points after the development of the transference neurosis, defence against the transference will become a main feature of the analytic situation.

This approach, as already indicated, is based on certain definite premises regarding the nature and function of the ego in respect to the control and neutralization of instinctual energy and unconscious fantasy. While the importance of early object relations is not neglected, the conviction that early transference interpretation is ineffective and potentially dangerous is related to the hypothesis that the instinctual energy available to the mature ego has been neutralized and is, for all effective purposes, relatively or absolutely divorced from its unconscious fantasy meaning at the beginning of analysis. In contrast, there are a number of analysts of differing theoretical orientation who do not view the development of the mature ego as a relative separation of ego functions from unconscious sources, but consider that unconscious fantasy continues to operate in all conscious mental activity. These analysts also tend on the whole to emphasize the crucial significance of primitive fantasy in respect to the development of the transference situation. The individual entering analysis will inevitably have unconscious fantasies concerning the analyst derived from primitive sources. This material, although deep in one sense, is, nevertheless, strongly current and accessible to interpretation. Mrs. Klein (8, 9), in addition, relates the development and definitive structure of both ego and superego to unconscious fantasy determined by the earliest phases of object relationship. She emphasizes the role of early introjective and projective processes in relation to primitive anxiety ascribed to the death instinct and related aggressive fantasies. The unresolved difficulties and conflicts of the earliest period continue to colour object relations throughout life. Failure to achieve an essentially satisfactory object relationship in this early period, and failure to master relative loss of that object without retaining its good internal representative, will not only affect all object relations and definitive ego function, but more specifically determine the nature of anxiety-provoking fantasies on entering the analytic situation. According to this point of view, therefore, early transference interpretation, even thought it may relate to fantasies derived from an early period of life, should result not in an increase, but a decrease of anxiety.

In considering next problems of transference in relation to analysis of the transference neurosis, two main points must be kept in mind. First, as already indicated, those who emphasize the analysis of defence tend to make a definite differentiation between transference as therapeutic alliance and the transference neurosis as a compromise formation which serves the purposes of resistance. In contrast, those who emphasize the importance of early object relations view the transference primarily as a revival or repetition, sometimes attributed to symbolic processes of early struggles in respect to objects. Here, no sharp differentiation is made between the early manifestations of transference and the transference neurosis. In view, moreover, of the weight given to the role of unconscious fantasy and internal objects in every phase of mental life, healthy and pathological functions, though differing in essential respects, do not differ with regard to their direct dependence on unconscious sources.

In the second place, the role of regression in the transference situation is subject to wide differences of opinion. It was, of course, one of Freud's earliest discoveries that regression to earlier points of fixation is a cardinal feature, not only in the development of neurosis and psychosis, but also in the revival of earlier conflicts in the transference situation. With the development of psycho-analysis and its application to an ever increasing range of disturbed personalities, the role of regression in the analytic situation has received increased attention. The significance of the analytic situation as a means of fostering regression as a prerequisite for the therapeutic work has been emphasized by Ida Macalpine (10) in a recent paper. Differing opinions as to the significance, value, and technical handling of regressive manifestations form the basis of important modifications of analytic technique which will be considered presently. In respect, however, to the transference neuroses, the view recently expressed by Phyllis Greenacre (11) that regression, an indispensable feature of the transference situation, is to be resolved by traditional technique would be generally accepted. It is also a matter of general agreement that a prerequisite for successful analysis is revival and repetition in the analytic situation of the struggles of primitive stages of development. Those who emphasize defence analysis, however, tend to view regression as a manifestation of resistance; as a primitive mechanism of defence employed by the ego in the setting of the transference neurosis. Analysis of these regressive manifestations with their potential dangers depends on the existing and continued functioning of adequate ego strength to maintain therapeutic alliance at an adult level. Those, in contrast, who stress the significance of transference as a revival of the early mother-child relationship do not emphasize regression as an indication of resistance or defence. The revival of these primitive experiences in the transference situation is, in fact, regarded as an essential prerequisite for satisfactory psychological maturation and true genitality. The Kleinian school, as already indicated, stress the continued activity of primitive conflicts in determining essential features of the transference at every stage of analysis. Their increasingly overt revival in the analytic situation, therefore, signifies a deepening of the analysis, and in general, is regarded as an indication of diminution rather than increase of resistance. The dangers involved according to this point of view are determined more by failure to mitigate primitive anxiety by suitable transference interpretation, than by failure to achieve, in the early phases of analysis, a sound therapeutic alliance based on the maturity of the patient's essential ego characteristics.

In considering, briefly, the terminal phases of analysis, many unresolved problems concerning the goal of therapy and definition of a completed psycho-analysis must be kept in mind. Distinction must also be made between the technical problems of the terminal phase and evaluation of transference resolution after the analysis has been terminated. There is widespread agreement as to the frequent revival in the terminal phases of primitive transference manifestations apparently resolved during the early phase of analysis. Balint (12), and those who accept Ferenczi's concept of primary passive love, suggest that some gratification of primitive passive needs may be essential for successful termination. To Mrs. Klein (13) the terminal phases of analysis also represent a repetition of important features of the early mother-child relationship. According to her point of view, this period represents, in essence, a revival of the early weaning situation. Completion depends on a mastery of early depressive struggles culminating in successful introjection of the analyst as a good object. Although, in this connection, emphasis differs considerably, it should be noted that those who stress the importance of identification with the analyst as a basis for therapeutic alliance, also accept the inevitability of some permanent modifications of a similar nature. Those, however, who make a definite differentiation between transference and the transference neurosis stress the importance of analysis and resolution of the transference neurosis as a main prerequisite for successful termination. The identification based on therapeutic alliance must be interpreted and understood, particularly with reference to the reality aspects of the analyst's personality. In spite, therefore, of significant important differences, there are, as already indicated in connection with the earlier papers of Sterba and Strachey, important points of agreement in respect to the goal of psycho-analysis.

The differences already considered indicate some basic current problems of transference. So far, however, discussion has been limited to variations within the framework of a traditional technique. We must now consider problems related to overt modifications. Here it is essential to distinguish between variations introduced in respect to certain clinical conditions, often as a preliminary to classical psycho-analysis, and modifications based on changes in basic approach which lead to significant alterations with regard both to the method and to the aim of therapy. It is generally agreed that some variations of technique are indicated in the treatment of certain character neuroses, borderline patients, and the psychoses. The nature and meaning of such changes is, however, viewed differently according to the relative emphasis placed on the ego and its defences, on underlying unconscious conflicts, and on the significance and handling of regression in the therapeutic situation. In 'Analysis Terminable and Interminable' (14), Freud suggested that certain ego attributes may be inborn or constitutional and, therefore, probably inaccessible to psychoanalytic procedure. Hartmann (15, 16, 17) has suggested that in addition to these primary attributes, other ego characteristics, originally developed for defensive purposes, and the related neutralized instinctual energy at the disposal of the ego, may be relatively or absolutely divorced from unconscious fantasy. This not only explains the relative inefficacy of early transference interpretation, but also hints at possible limitations in the potentialities of analysis attributable to secondary autonomy of the ego which is considered to be relatively irreversible. In certain cases, moreover, it is suggested that analysis of precarious or seriously pathological defences—particularly those concerned with the control of aggressive impulses—may be not only ineffective, but dangerous. The relative failure of ego development in such cases not only precludes the development of a genuine therapeutic alliance, but also raises the risk of a serious regressive, often predominantly hostile transference situation. In certain cases, therefore, a preliminary period of psycho-therapy is recommended in order to explore the capacities of the patient to tolerate traditional psycho-analysis. In others, as Robert Knight (18) in his paper on borderline states, and as many analysts working with psychotic patients have suggested, psycho-analytic procedure is not considered applicable. Instead, a therapeutic approach based on analytic understanding which, in essence, utilizes an essentially implicit positive transference as a means of reinforcing, rather than analysing the precarious defences of the individual, is advocated. In contrast, Herbert Rosenfeld (19) has approached even severely disturbed psychotic patients with minimal modifications of psycho-analytic technique. Only changes which the severity of the patient's condition enforces are introduced. Here, the dangers of regression in therapy are not emphasized since primitive fantasy is considered to be active under all circumstances. The most primitive period is viewed in terms of early object relations with special stress on persecutory anxiety related to the death instinct. Interpretation of this primitive fantasy in the transference situation, as already indicated, is considered to diminish rather than to increase psychotic anxiety and to offer the best opportunity of strengthening the severely threatened psychotic ego. Other analysts, Dr. Winnicott (20), for example, attribute psychosis mainly to severe traumatic experiences, particularly of deprivation in early infancy. According to this point of view, profound regression offers an opportunity to fulfil, in the transference situation, primitive needs which had not been met at the appropriate level of development. Similar suggestions have been proposed by Margolin (21) and others, in the concept of anaclitic treatment of serious psychosomatic disease. This approach is also based on the premise that the inevitable regression shown by certain patients should be utilized in therapy, as a means of gratifying, in an extremely permissive transference situation, demands which had not been met in infancy. It must, in this connection, be noted that the gratifications recommended in the treatment of severely disturbed patients are determined by the conviction that these patients are incapable of developing transference as we understand it in connection with neuroses and must therefore be handled by a modified technique.

The opinions so far considered, however much they may differ in certain respects, are nonetheless all based on the fundamental premise that an essential difference between analysis and other methods of therapy depends on whether or not interpretation of transference is an integral feature of technical procedure. Results based on the effects of suggestion are to be avoided, as far as possible, whenever traditional technique is employed. This goal has, however, proved more difficult to achieve than Freud expected when he first discerned the significance of symptomatic recovery based on positive transference. The importance of suggestion, even in the most strict analytic methods, has been repeatedly stressed by Edward Glover and others (22, 23). Widespread and increasing emphasis as to the part played by the analyst's personality in determining the nature of the individual transference also implies recognition of unavoidable suggestive tendencies in the therapeutic process. Many analysts to-day believe that the classical conception of analytic objectivity and anonymity cannot be maintained. Instead, thorough analysis of reality aspects of the therapist's personality and point of view is advocated as an essential feature of transference analysis and an indispensable prerequisite for the dynamic changes already discussed in relation to the termination of analysis. It thus remains the ultimate goal of psycho-analysts, whatever their theoretical orientation, to avoid, as far as is humanly possible, results based on the unrecognized or unanalysed action of suggestion, and to maintain, as a primary goal, the resolution of such results through consistent and careful interpretation.

There are, however, a number of therapists, both within and outside the field of psycho-analysis, who consider that the transference situation should not be handled only or mainly as a setting for interpretation even in the treatment or analysis of neurotic patients. Instead, they advocate utilization of the transference relationship for the manipulation of corrective emotional experience. The theoretical orientation of those utilizing this concept of transference may be closer to, or more distant from, a Freudian point of view according to the degree to which current relationships are seen as determined by past events. At one extreme, current aspects and cultural factors are considered of predominant importance; at the other, mental development is viewed in essentially Freudian terms and modifications of technique are ascribed to inherent limitations of the analytic method rather than to essentially changed conceptions of the early phases of mental development. Of this group, Alexander (24) is perhaps the best example. It is thirty years since, in his Salzburg paper, he indicated the tendency for patients to regress, even after apparently successful transference analysis of the oedipal situation to narcissistic dependent pregenital levels which prove stubborn and refractory to transference interpretation. In his more recent work, the role of regression in the transference situation has been increasingly stressed. The emergence and persistence of dependent, pregenital demands in a very wide range of clinical conditions, it is argued, indicates that the encouragement of a regressive transference situation is undesirable and therapeutically ineffective. The analyst, therefore, should when this threatens adopt a definite role explicitly differing from the behaviour of the parents in early childhood in order to bring about therapeutic results through a corrective emotional experience in the transference situation. This, it is suggested, will obviate the tendency to regression, thus curtailing the length of treatment and improving therapeutic results. Limitation of regressive manifestations by active steps modifying traditional analytic procedure in a variety of ways is also frequently indicated, according to this point of view.

It will be clear that to those who maintain the conviction that interpretation of all transference manifestations remains an essential feature of psychoanalysis, the type of modification here described, even though based on a Freudian reconstruction of the early phases of mental development, represents a major modification. It is determined by a conviction that psychoanalysis, as a therapeutic method, has limitations related to the tendency to regression, which cannot be resolved by traditional technique. Moreover, the fundamental premise on which the conception of corrective emotional experience is based minimizes the significance of insight and recall. It is, essentially, suggested that corrective emotional experience alone may bring about qualitative dynamic alterations in mental structure, which can lead to a satisfactory therapeutic goal. This implies a definite modification of the analytic hypothesis that current problems are determined by the defences against instinctual impulses and/or internalized objects which had been set up during the decisive periods of early development. An analytic result therefore depends on the revival, repetition and mastery of earlier conflicts in the current experience of the transference situation with insight an indispensable feature of an analytic goal.

Since certain important modifications are related to the concept of regression in the transference situation, I should like briefly to consider this concept in relation to the repetition compulsion. That transference, essentially a revival of earlier emotional experience, must be regarded as a manifestation of the repetition compulsion is generally accepted. It is, however, necessary to distinguish between repetition compulsion as an attempt to master traumatic experience and repetition compulsion as an attempt to return to a real or fantasied earlier state of rest or gratification. Lagache (25), in a recent paper, has related the repetition compulsion to an inherent need to return to any problem previously left unsolved. From this point of view, the regressive aspects of the transference situation are to be regarded as a necessary preliminary to the mastery of unresolved conflict. From the second point of view, however, the regressive aspects of transference are mainly attributed to a wish to return to an earlier state of rest or narcissistic gratification, to the maintenance of the *status quo* in preference to any progressive action, and finally, to Freud's original conception of the death instinct. There is a good deal to suggest that both aspects of the repetition compulsion may be seen in the regressive aspects of every analysis. To those who feel that regressive self-destructive forces tend to be stronger than progressive libidinal impulses, the potentialities of the analytic approach will inevitably appear to be limited. Those, in contrast, who regard the reappearance in the transference situation of earlier conflicts as an indication of tendencies to master and progress will continue to feel that the classical analytic method remains the optimal approach to psychological illness wherever it is applicable.

To conclude: I have tried in this paper to outline some current problems of transference both in relation to the history of psycho-analytic thought and in relation to the theoretical premises on which they are based. With regard to contemporary views which advocate serious modification of analytic technique, I cannot improve on the remarks made by Ernest Jones (26) in his Introduction to the Salzburg Symposium thirty years ago. 'Depreciation of the Freudian (infantile) factors at the expense of the pre-Freudian (pre-infantile and post-infantile) is a highly characteristic manifestation of the general human resistance against the former, being usually a flight from the Oedipus conflict which is the centre of infantile factors. We also note that the practice of psycho-analysis does not always insure immunity from this reaction.' With regard, finally, to the important problems which arise from genuine scientific differences within the framework of traditional technique, I have tried to focus the issues for discussion by emphasizing as objectively as possible divergence rather than agreement. I should like, however, to close on a more personal note. I have had the unusual opportunity over the past ten years to observe at close quarters impressive achievements by analysts of widely divergent theoretical orientation. All of them are in complete agreement as to the primary importance of transference analysis. None have accepted any significant modifications of traditional technique as a means of either shortening analysis or accepting a modified analytic goal. All finally agree as to the basic importance of understanding the significance and possible dangers of counter-transference manifestations. Unfortunately, however, this vitally important unconscious reaction is not limited to the individual analytic situation. It may also be aroused in respect to scientific theories both within and outside our special field of knowledge. Just as, therefore, resolution of the individual transference situation depends on the analyst's understanding of his own counter-transference, so too, similar insight and objectivity on a wider scale may determine resolution of the problems I have outlined to-day.

BIBLIOGRAPHY

1. Klein, M. 'Symposium on Child Analysis' (1927). Published in *Contributions to Psycho-analysis, 1941–45*. (London: Hogarth, 1948.)
2. Freud, A. (1926). 'Introduction to the Technique in the Analysis of Children' (Vienna): *The Psychoanalytic Treatment of Children*. (Imago Publishing Co., 1945.)
3. Sterba, R. 'The Fate of the Ego in Analytic Therapy', *Int. J. Psycho-Anal.*, 1934, 15, 117–126.
4. Strachey, J. 'The Nature of the Therapeutic Action of Psycho-Analysis', *Int. J. Psycho-Anal.*, 1934, 15, 130–137.
5. Bibring, E. 'Therapeutic Results of Psycho-Analysis', *Int. J. Psycho-Anal.*, 1937, 18, 170–189.
6. Waelder, R. Contribution to Panel on Defence Mechanisms and Psychoanalytic Technique. Mid-Winter meeting of the American Psychoanalytic Association 1953. (Report published in the *Journal of the American Psychoanalytic Association*, April 1954.)
7. Fenichel, O. 'Problems of Psychoanalytic Technique', *Psychoanal. Quart.*, 1941.
8. Klein, M. *Contribution to Psychoanalysis, 1941–45*. (London: Hogarth, 1948.)
9. Klein, M., *et al.* (1950). *Developments in Psychoanalysis*. (London: Hogarth.)
10. Macalpine, I. 'The Development of the Transference', *Psychoanal. Quart.*, 1959, 19, 501–519.
11. Greenacre, P. 'The Role of Transference. Practical Considerations in Relation to Psycho-analytic Therapy', *J. Amer. Psychoanal. Assoc.*, 1954, 2, 671–684.
12. Balint, M. *Primary Love and Psycho-Analytic Technique*. (London: Hogarth, 1952.)
13. Klein, M. 'On the Criteria for the Termination of an Analysis', *Int. J. Psycho-Anal.*, 1950, 31, Part 3.
14. Freud, S. (1937). 'Analysis Terminable and Interminable', *Collected Papers*, V. (London: Hogarth, 1950.)
15. Hartmann, H. (1950). 'Psychoanalysis and Developmental Psychology', *Psychoanal. Study of the Child*, V. (New York: International Universities Press.)
16. ———(1952). 'The Mutual Influences in the Development of Ego and Id', *Psychoanal. Study of the Child*, VII. (New York: International Universities Press.)
17. ———, Kris, E., and Loewenstein, R. (1946). 'Comments on the Formation of Psychic Structure', *Psychoanal. Study of the Child*, II. (New York: International Universities Press.)
18. Knight, R. 'Borderline States', *Psychoanalytic Psychiatry and Psychology*, 1954, 1, 97–109.
19. Rosenfeld, H. 'Transference-phenomena and Transference-analysis in an Acute Catatonic Schizophrenic Patient', *Int. J. Psycho-Anal.*, 1952, 33, 457–464.
20. Winnicott, D. W. 'Metapsychological and Clinical Aspects of Regression within the Psychoanalytical Set-up', *Int. J. Psycho-Anal.*, 1955, 36, 16–26.
21. Margolin, S. 'Genetic and Dynamic Psycho-physiological Determinants of Pathophysiological Processes'. *The Psychosomatic Concept in Psychoanalysis*, ed. Felix Deutsch. (New York: International Universities Press, 1953, pp.8–36.)

22. Glover, E. *The Technique of Psychoanalysis.* (New York: International Universities Press, 1955.)

23. ———'Therapeutic Criteria of Psychoanalysis', *Int. J. Psycho-Anal.*, 1954.

24. Alexander, F. Contribution to the Symposium held at the Eighth International Psycho-Analytic Congress, Salzburg, April 21, 1924. Published in *Int. J. Psycho-Anal.*, 1925, 6, 13–34.

25. Lagache, D. 'Quelques Aspects du Transfert' (Some Aspects of Transference)', *Revue Française de Psychanalyse,* 15, 407–424.

26. Jones, E. 'Introduction to the Symposium on Theories of Therapeutic Results.' Published in *Int. J. Psycho-Anal.*, 1925, 6, 1–4.

11. The Working Alliance and the Transference Neurosis

Ralph R. Greenson

The clinical material on which this presentation is based is derived from patients who developed unexpected difficulties in the course of psychoanalytic therapy. Some of these patients had undergone one or more analyses with other analysts; other were patients of mine who returned for further analysis. In this group there were patients who were unable to get beyond the preliminary phases of analysis. Even after several years of analysis they were not really 'in analysis'. Others seemed interminable; there was a marked discrepancy between the copiousness of insight and the paucity of change. The clinical syndromes these cases manifested were heterogeneous in diagnostic category, ego functions, or dynamics of personality. The key to understanding the essential pathology as well as the therapeutic stalemate was in the failure of the patient to develop a reliable working relation with the analyst. In each case the patient was either unable to establish or maintain a durable working alliance with the analyst and the analyst neglected this fact, pursuing instead the analysis of other transference phenomena. This error in technique was observable in psychoanalysts with a wide range of clinical experience and I recognized the same shortcoming in myself when I resumed analysis with patients previously treated.

In working with these seemingly unanalyzable or interminable patients I became impressed by the importance of separating the patient's reactions to the analyst into two distinct categories: the transference neurosis and the working alliance. Actually this classification is neither complete nor precise. However, this differentiation helps make it possible to give equal attention to two essentially different transference reactions.

My clinical experiences in regard to the working alliance were enhanced and clarified by Elizabeth Zetzel in Current Concepts of Transference *(32)*. In that essay she introduced the term 'therapeutic alliance' and indicated how

Reprinted by permission from the *Psychoanalytic Quarterly* 34(1965): 155–81.

important she considered it by demonstrating that one could differentiate between the classical psychoanalysts and the British school by whether they handled or ignored this aspect of the transference. Leo Stone *(31)* gave further insight and fresh impetus in my attempts to clarify and formulate the problem of the working alliance and its relation to other transference phenomena.

The concept of a working alliance is an old one in both psychiatric and psychoanalytic literature. It has been described under a variety of labels but, except for Zetzel and Stone, it either has been considered of secondary importance or has not been clearly separated from other transference reactions. It is the contention of this paper that the working alliance is as essential for psychoanalytic therapy as the transference neurosis. For successful psychoanalytic treatment a patient must be able to develop a full-blown transference neurosis and also to establish and maintain a reliable working alliance. The working alliance deserves to be recognized as a full and equal partner in the patient-therapist relationship.

DEFINITION OF TERMS

Transference is the experiencing of feelings, drives, attitudes, fantasies, and defenses toward a person in the present which are inappropriate to that person and are a repetition, a displacement of reactions originating in regard to significant persons of early childhood *(4, 6, 11)*. I emphasize that for a reaction to be considered transference it must have two characteristics: it must be a repetition of the past and it must be inappropriate to the present.

During analysis several transference phenomena can be distinguished. In the early phases we see usually sporadic, transient reactions, aptly called 'floating' transference reactions by Glover *(17)*. Freud described more enduring transference phenomena which develop when the transference situation is properly handled. Then all the patient's neurotic symptoms are replaced by a neurosis in the transference relation of which he can be cured by therapeutic work. 'It is a new edition of the old disease' *(9, 11)*. I would modify this concept and say that the transference neurosis is in effect when the analyst and the analysis become the central concern in the patient's life. The transference neurosis includes more than the infantile neurosis; the patient also relives the later editions and variations of his original neurosis. The 'floating' transference phenomena ordinarily do not belong to the transference neurosis.

However, for simplification, the phrase, transference neurosis, here refers to the more regressive and inappropriate transference reactions.

The term 'working alliance' is used in preference to diverse terms others have employed for designating the relatively non-neurotic, rational rapport which the patient has with his analyst. It is this reasonable and purposeful part of the feelings the patient has for the analyst that makes for the working alliance. The label 'working alliance' was selected because it emphasizes its outstanding function: it centers on the patient's ability to work in the analytic situation. Terms like the 'therapeutic alliance' *(32)*, the 'rational transference' *(2)*, and the 'mature transference' *(31)* refer to similar concepts. The designation 'working alliance', however, has the advantage of stressing the vital elements: the patient's capacity to work purposefully in the treatment situation. It can be seen at its clearest when a patient, in the throes of an intense transference neurosis, can yet maintain an effective working relationship with the analyst.

The reliable core of the working alliance is formed by the patient's motivation to overcome his illness, his conscious and rational willingness to cooperate, and his ability to follow the instructions and insights of his analyst. The actual alliance is formed essentially between the patient's reasonable ego and the analyst's analyzing ego *(29)*. The medium that makes this possible is the patient's partial identification with the analyst's approach as he attempts to understand the patient's behavior.

The working alliance comes to the fore in the analytic situation in the same way as the patient's reasonable ego: the observing, analyzing ego is split off from his experiencing ego *(30)*. The analyst's interventions separate the working attitudes from the neurotic transference phenomena just as his interventions split off the reasonable ego from the irrational one. These two sets of phenomena are parallel and express analogous psychic events from different points of reference. Patients who cannot split off a reasonable, observing ego will not be able to maintain a working relation and vice versa.

This differentiation between transference neurosis and working alliance, however, is not absolute since the working alliance may contain elements of the infantile neurosis which eventually will require analysis. For example, the patient may work well temporarily in order to gain the analyst's love, and this ultimately will lead to strong resistances; or the overvaluation of the analyst's character and ability may also serve the working alliance well in the beginning of the analysis, only to become a source of strong resistance later. Not only can the transference neurosis invade the working alliance but the working alliance itself can be misused defensively to ward off the more regressive transference phenomena. Despite these intermixtures, the separation of the patient's reactions to the analyst into these two groupings, transference neurosis and working alliance, seems to have clinical and technical value.

SURVEY OF THE LITERATURE

Freud spoke of the friendly and affectionate aspects of the transference which are admissible to consciousness and which are 'the vehicle of success in psychoanalysis . . .' (6, p.105). Of rapport he wrote: 'It remains the first aim of the treatment to attach him [the patient] to it and to the person of the doctor. To ensure this, nothing need be done but to give him time. If one exhibits a serious interest in him, carefully clears away the resistances that crop up at the beginning and avoids making certain mistakes, he will of himself form such at attachment. . . . It is certainly possible to forfeit this first success if from the start one takes up any standpoint other than one of sympathetic understanding' (8, pp.139–140).

Sterba (30) wrote about the patient's identification with the analyst which leads to the patient's concern with the work they have to accomplish in common—but he gave this aspect of the transference no special designation. Fenichel (2, p. 27) described the 'rational transference' as an aim-inhibited positive transference which is necessary for analysis. Elizabeth Zetzel's emphasis on the importance of the 'therapeutic alliance' was discussed above. Loewald's paper on the therapeutic action of psychoanalysis is a penetrating and sensitive study of the different kinds of relations the patient develops toward the analyst during psychoanalysis (23). Some of his ideas are directly concerned with what I call the working alliance. Leo Stone devotes himself to the complexities in the relation between analyst and patient. He refers to the 'mature transference' which he believed to be: (a) in opposition to the 'primordial transference' reactions and (b) essential for a successful analysis (31, p. 106).

The Symposium on Curative Factors in Psychoanalysis presented before the Twenty-second Congress of the International Psychoanalytical Association (1962) contained many references to the special transference reactions that make for a therapeutic alliance and also some discussion of the analyst's contribution to the 'good' analytic situation. Gitelson (16) spoke of the rapport on which we depend in the beginning of analysis and which eventuates in transference. He stressed the necessity for the analyst to present himself as a good object and as an auxiliary ego. Myerson *(25)*, Nacht *(26)*, Segal *(27)*, Kuiper *(22)*, Garma *(13)*, King *(21)*, and Heimann *(20)* took issue with him on one or another aspect of his approach. In some measure the disagreement seems to be due to failure to distinguish clearly between the working alliance and the more regressive transference phenomena.

This brief and incomplete survey reveals that many analysts, including Freud, recognized that in psychoanalytic treatment another kind of relation to the analyst is necessary besides the more regressive transference reactions.

DEVELOPMENT OF THE WORKING ALLIANCE

Aberrations

The first clinical examples show how the course of development of the working alliance deviated markedly from that of the usual psychoanalytic patient. The reason for proceeding this way stems from the fact that in the classical analytic patient the working alliance develops almost imperceptibly, relatively silently, and seemingly independently of any special activity on the part of the analyst. The irregular cases highlight different processes and procedures which take place almost invisibly in the usual analytic patient.

Some years ago an analyst from another city referred an intelligent middle-aged man who had had more than six years of previous analysis. Certain general conditions had improved but his original analyst believed the patient needed additional analysis because he was still unable to marry and was very lonely. From the beginning of the therapy I was struck by the fact that he was absolutely passive about recognizing and working with his resistances. It turned out that he expected them to be pointed out continuously as his previous analyst had done. It also impressed me that the moment I made some intervention he had an immediate response, although often incomprehensible. I discovered that he thought it his duty to reply immediately to every intervention since he believed it would be a sign of resistance, and therefore bad, to keep silent for a moment or so to mull over what had been said. Apparently his previous analyst had never recognized his fear of being silent as a resistance. In free association the patient searched actively for things to talk about and, if more than one idea occurred to him, he chose what seemed to be the item he thought I was looking for without mentioning the multiple choices. When I requested information, he often answered by free association so that the result was bizarre. For example, when I asked him what his middle name was he answered: 'Raskolnikov', the first name that occurred to him. When I recovered my composure and questioned this he defended himself by saying that he thought he was supposed to free associate. I soon gained the impression that this man had never really established a working relation with his first analyst. He did not know what he was supposed to do in the analytic situation. He had been lying down in front of an analyst for many years, meekly submitting to what he imagined the previous analyst had demanded, constant and instant free association. Patient and analyst had been indulging in a caricature of psychoanalysis. True, the patient had developed some regressive transference reactions, some of which had been interpreted, but the lack of a consistent working alliance left the whole procedure amorphous, confused, and ineffectual.

Although I realized that the magnitude of the patient's problems could not be due solely or even mainly to the first analyst's technical shortcomings, I thought the patient ought to be given a fair opportunity to see whether he could work in an analytic situation. Besides, this clarification would also expose the patient's pathology more vividly. Therefore, in the first months of our work together, I carefully explained, whenever it seemed appropriate, the different tasks that psychoanalytic therapy requires of the patient. He reacted to this information as though it were all new to him and seemed eager to try to work in the way I described. However, it soon became clear that he could not just say what came to his mind, he felt compelled to find out what I was looking for. He could not keep silent and mull over what I said; he was afraid of the blank spaces, they signified some awful danger. If he were silent he might think; if he thought he might disagree with me, and to disagree was tantamount to killing me. His striking passivity and compliance were revealed as a form of ingratiation, covering up an inner emptiness, an insatiable infantile hunger, and a terrible rage. In a period of six months it became clear that this man was a schizoid 'as if' character who could not bear the deprivations of classical psychoanalysis (1). I therefore helped him obtain supportive psychotherapy with a woman therapist.

A woman I had previously analyzed for some four years resumed analysis after an interval of six years. We both knew when she had interrupted treatment that there was a great deal of unfinished analysis, but we agreed that an interval without analysis might clarify the unusual obscurities and difficulties we encountered in trying to achieve a better resolution of her highly ambivalent, complaining, clinging, sadomasochistic transference. I had suggested her going to another analyst, since, in general, I have found a change in analysts is more productive than a return to the old one. It usually offers new insights into the old transference reactions and adds new transference possibilities. However, for external reasons this was not feasible and I undertook the resumption of her analysis, although with some reservations.

In her first hours on the couch I was struck by the strange way the patient worked in the analysis. Then I quickly recalled that this had often happened in the past; it appeared more striking now since I was no longer accustomed to it; it seemed almost bizarre. After a certain moment in the hour the patient would speak almost incessantly; there would be disconnected sentences, part of a recital of a recent event, an occasional obscene phrase with no mention of its strangeness or that it was an obsessive thought, and then back to the recital of a past event. The patient seemed to be completely oblivious to her odd way of speaking and never spontaneously mentioned it. When I confronted her with this she at first seemed unknowing and then felt attacked.

I realized that in the previous analysis there had been many such hours or parts of hours whenever the patient was very anxious and tried to ward off her awareness of anxiety as well as analysis of it. I recalled that we had uncovered some of the meanings and historical determinants of such behavior. For example, her mother had been a great chatterer, had talked to the child as a grownup before she could understand. Her incomprehensible talking to me was an identification with her mother and an acting out in the analytic situation. Furthermore, the mother had used a stream of talk to express both anxiety and hostility to her husband, an essentially quiet man. The patient took over this pattern from her mother and re-enacted it in the analytic hour whenever she was anxious and hostile and when she was torn between hurting me and holding onto me.

We came to understand that this mode of behavior also denoted a regression in ego functions from secondary process toward primary process, a kind of 'sleep-talking' with me, a reenactment of sleeping with the parents. This peculiar way of talking had recurred many times during the first analysis and although various determinants had been analyzed it still persisted to some degree up to the interruption of that analysis. Whenever I tried to confront the patient with a misuse of one of the analytic procedures, we would be sidetracked by her reactions to my confrontation or by new material that came up. She might recall some past event which seemed relevant or, in the next hours, dreams or new memories would appear and we never really returned to the subject of why she was unable to do some part of the psychoanalytic work. In her second analysis, I would not be put off. Whenever the merest trace of the same disconnected manner of talking appeared, or whenever it seemed relevant, I confronted her with the problem and kept her to this subject until she at least acknowledged what was under discussion. The patient attempted to use all her old methods of defense against confrontations of her resistances. I listened only for a short time to her protestations and evasions and repeatedly pointed out their resistive function. I did not work with any new material until convinced the patient was in a good working alliance with me.

Slowly the patient began to face her misuse of the basic rule. She herself became aware of how she at times consciously, at other preconsciously, and, at still other times, unconsciously, blurred the real purpose of free association. It became clear that when the patient felt anxious in her relation to me she would let herself slip into this regressive 'sleep-talking' manner of speech. It was a kind of 'spiteful obedience'—spiteful in so far as she knew it was an evasion of true free association. It was obedience inasmuch as she submitted to this regressive or, one might say, incontinent way of talking. This arose whenever she felt a certain kind of hostility toward me. She felt this as an urge to pour out a stream of poison upon me that led her to feel I would be destroyed and lost to her and she would feel alone and frightened. Then she would quickly dive into sleep-talking as though saying: 'I am a little child who is partly asleep and is not responsible for what is coming out of me. Don't leave me; let me sleep on with you; it is just harmless urine that is coming out of me.' Other determinants will not be discussed since they would lead too far afield.

It was fascinating to see how differently this analysis proceeded from the previous one. I do not mean to imply that this patient's tendency to misuse her ability to regress in ego functioning completely disappeared. However, my vigorous pursuit of the analysis of the defective working alliance, my constant attention to the maintenance of a good working relation, my refusal to be misled into analyzing other aspects of her transference neurosis had their effects. The second analysis had a completely different flavor and atmosphere. In the first analysis I had an interesting and whimsical patient who was frustrating because I was so often lost by her capricious wanderings.

In the second, though still a whimsical patient she also was an ally who not only helped me when I was lost but pointed out that I was being led astray even before I realized it.

The third patient, a young man, entered analysis with me after he had spent two and one half years with an analyst in another city, which had left him almost completely untouched. He had obtained certain insights but had the distinct impression that his former analyst really disapproved of infantile sexuality even though the young man realized that analysts were not supposed to be contemptuous of it. In the preliminary interviews the patient told me that he had the greatest difficulty in talking about masturbation and previously often consciously withheld this information. He had informed the former analyst about the existence of many conscious secrets but nevertheless stubbornly refused to divulge them. He had never wholeheartedly given himself up to free association and reported many hours of long silence. However, the patient's manner of relating his history to me and my general clinical impression led me to believe that he was analyzable despite the fact that he had not been able to form a working alliance with his first analyst.

I undertook the analysis and learned a great deal about this patient's negative reactions to his previous analyst, some of which stemmed from his way of conducting that analysis. For example, in one of the first hours on the couch the patient took out a cigarette and lit it. I asked him what he was feeling when he decided to light the cigarette. He answered petulantly that he knew he was not supposed to smoke in his previous analysis and now he supposed that I too would forbid it. I told him that I wanted to know what feelings, ideas, and sensations were going on in him at the moment that he decided to light the cigarette. He then revealed that he had become somewhat frightened in the hour and to hide this anxiety from me he decided to light the cigarette. I replied that it was preferable for such feelings and ideas to be expressed in words instead of actions because then I would understand more precisely what was going on in him. He realized then that I was not forbidding him to smoke but only pointing out that it was more helpful to the process of being analyzed if he expressed himself in words and feelings. He contrasted this with his first analyst who told him before he went to the couch that it was customary not to smoke during sessions. There was no explanation for this and the patient felt that his first analyst was being arbitrary.

In a later hour the patient asked me whether I was married. I countered by asking him what he imagined about that. He hesitantly revealed that he was torn between two sets of fantasies, one that I was a bachelor who loved his work and lived only for his patients; the other that I was a happily married man with many children. He went on spontaneously to tell me that he hoped I was happily married because then I would be in a better position to help him with his sexual problems. Then he corrected himself and said it was painful to think of me as having sexual relations with my wife because that was embarrassing and none of his business. I then pointed out to him how, by not answering his question and by asking him instead to tell his fantasies about the answer, he revealed the cause of his curiosity. I told him I would not answer questions when I felt that more was to be gained by keeping silent and letting him associate to his own question. At this point the patient became somewhat tearful and, after a short pause, told me that in the beginning of his previous analysis he had asked many questions. His former analyst never answered nor did he explain why he was silent. He felt his analyst's silence as a degradation and humiliation and now realized that his own later silences were a retaliation for this imagined injustice. Somewhat later he saw that he had identified himself with his first analyst's supposed contempt. He, the patient, felt disdain for his analyst's prudishness and at the same time was full of severe self-reproach for his own sexual practices which he then projected onto the analyst.

It was instructive to me to see how an identification with the previous analyst based on fear and hostility led to a distortion of the working relationship instead of an effective working alliance. The whole atmosphere of the first analysis was contaminated by hostile, mistrustful, retaliative feelings and attitudes. This turned out to be a repetition of the patient's behavior toward his father, a point the first analyst had recognized and interpreted. The analysis of this transference resistance, however, was ineffectual, partly because the first analyst worked in such a way as to justify constantly the patient's infantile neurotic behavior and so furthered the invasion of the working alliance by the transference neurosis.

I worked with this patient for approximately four years and almost from the beginning a relatively effective working alliance was established. However, my manner of conducting analysis, which seemed to him to indicate some genuine human concern for his welfare and respect for his position as a patient also mobilized important transference resistances in a later phase of the analysis. In the third year I began to realize that, despite what appeared to be a good working alliance and a strong transference neurosis, there were many areas of the patient's outside life that did not seem to change commensurately with the analytic work. Eventually I discovered that the patient had developed a subtle but specific inhibition in doing analytic work outside the analytic hour. If he became upset outside he would ask himself what upset him. Usually he succeeded in recalling the situation in question. Sometimes he even recalled the meaning of that event that he had learned from me at some previous time, but this insight would be relatively meaningless to him; it felt foreign, artificial, and remembered by rote. It was not his insight; it was mine, and therefore had no living significance for him. Hence, he was relatively blank about the meaning of the upsetting events.

Apparently, although he seemed to have established a working alliance with me in the analytic situation, this did not continue outside. Analysis revealed that the patient did not allow himself to assume any attitude, approach, or point of view that was like mine outside the analytic hour. He felt that to permit himself to do so would be tantamount to admitting that I had entered into him. This was intolerable because he felt this to be a homosexual assault, a repetition of several childhood and adolescent traumas. Slowly we uncovered how the patient had sexualized and aggressivized the process of introjection.

This new insight was the starting point for the patient to learn to discriminate among the different varieties of 'taking in'. Gradually he was able to re-establish a nonhomosexual identification with me in adapting an analytic point of view. Thus a working relation that had been invaded by the transference neurosis was once again relatively free of infantile neurotic features. The previous insights that had remained ineffectual eventually led to significant and lasting changes.[1]

Those patients who cling tenaciously to the working alliance because they are terrified of the regressive features of the transference neurosis should be briefly mentioned. They develop a reasonable relation to the analyst and do not allow themselves to feel anything irrational, be it sexual, aggressive, or both. Prolonged reasonableness in an analysis is a pseudo-reasonableness for a variety of unconscious neurotic motives.

For about two years a young social scientist who had an intellectual knowledge of psychoanalysis maintained a positive and reasonable attitude toward me, his analyst. If his dreams indicated hostility or homosexuality he acknowledged this but claimed that he knew he was supposed to feel such things toward his analyst but he 'really' did not. If he came late or forgot to pay his bill he again admitted that it might seem that he did not want to come or pay his bill but 'actually' it was not so. He had violent anger reactions to other psychiatrists he knew, but insisted they deserved it and I was different. He became infatuated with another male analyst for a period of time and 'guessed' he must remind him of me, but this was said playfully. All of my attempts to get the patient to recognize his persistent reasonableness as a means of avoiding or belittling his deeper feelings and impulses failed. Even my attempts to trace the historical origins of this mode of behavior were unproductive. He had adopted the role of 'odd ball', clown, harmless non-conformist in his high school years and was repeating this in the analysis. Since I could not get the patient to work further or consistently on this problem, I finally told him that we had to face the fact that we were getting nowhere and we ought to consider some alternative besides continuing psychoanalysis with me. The patient was silent for a few moments and said 'frankly' he was disappointed. He sighed and then went on to make a free associationlike remark. I stopped him and asked him what in the world he was doing. He replied that he 'guessed' I sounded somewhat annoyed. I assured him it was no guess. Then slowly he looked at me and asked if he might sit up. I nodded and he did. He was quite shaken, sober, pale, and in obvious distress. After some moments of silence he said that maybe he would be able to work better if he could look at me. He had to be sure I was not laughing at him, or angry, or getting sexually excited. I asked him about the last point. He told me that he often fantasied that perhaps I was being sexually excited by what he said but hid it from him. This he had never brought up before, it was just a 'fleeting idea'. But this fleeting idea led quickly to many memories of his father repeatedly and unnecessarily taking his temperature rectally. He proceeded to a host of homosexual and sadomasochistic fantasies. The persistent reasonableness was a defense against these as well as a playful attempt to tease me into acting out with him. My behavior, in the hour described above, was not well controlled, but it led to awareness that the patient's working alliance was being used to ward off the transference neurosis.

The working alliance had become the façade for the transference neurosis. It was his neurotic character structure hiding as well as expressing his underlying neurosis. Only when the patient's acting out was interrupted and he realized he was about to lose the transference object did his rigidly reasonable behavior become ego-alien and accessible to therapy. He needed several weeks of being able to look at me, to test out whether my reactions could be trusted. Then he became able to distinguish between genuine reasonableness and the teasing, spiteful reasonableness of his character neurosis and the analysis began to move.

The Classical Analytic Patient

The term classical in this connection refers to a heterogeneous group of patients who are analyzable by the classical psychoanalytic technique without major modifications. They suffer from some form of transference neurosis, a symptom or character neurosis, without any appreciable defect in ego functions. In such patients the working transference develops almost imperceptibly, relatively silently, and seemingly independently of any special activity or intervention on the part of the analyst. Usually signs of the working alliance appear in about the third to sixth month of analysis. Most frequently the first indications of this development are: the patient becomes silent and then, instead of waiting for the analyst to intervene, he himself ventures the opinion that he seems to be avoiding something. Or he interrupts a rather desultory report of some event and comments that he must be running away from something. If the analyst remains silent the patient spontaneously asks himself what it can be that is making him so evasive and he will let his thoughts drift into free associations.

It is obvious that the patient has made a partial and temporary identification with me and now is working with himself in the same manner as I have been working on his resistances. If I review the situation I usually find that prior to this development the patient has experienced some sporadic sexual or hostile transference reaction which has temporarily caused a strong resistance. I patiently and tactfully demonstrate this resistance, then clarify how it operated, what its purpose was, and eventually interpret and reconstruct its probably historical source. Only after effective transference-resistance analysis is the patient able to develop a partial working alliance. However, it is necessary to go back to the beginning of the analysis to get a detailed view of its development.

There is great variety in the manner in which a patient enters into the preliminary interviews. In part this is determined by his past history in regard to psychoanalysts, physicians, and authority figures and strangers, as well as his reactions to such conditions as being sick or needing and asking for help (15). Furthermore, his knowledge or lack of it about procedures of psychoanalysis and the reputation of the psychoanalyst also influence his initial responses. Thus the patient comes to the initial interview with a preformed relationship to me, partly transference and partly based on reality, depending on how much he fills in the unknowns inappropriately out of his own past.

The preliminary interviews heavily color the patient's reactions to the analyst. This is determined mainly by the patient's feelings about exposing himself as well as his responses to my method of approach and my personality. Here too I believe we see a mixture of transference and realistic reactions. Exposure of one's self is apt to stir up reverberations of past denudings in front of parents, doctors, or others, and is therefore likely to produce transference reactions. My technique of conducting the interviews will do the same the more it seems strange, painful, or incomprehensible to the patient. Only those methods of approach that seem understandable to him may lead to realistic reactions. My 'analyst' personality as it is manifested in the first interviews may also stir up both transference and realistic reactions. It is my impression that those qualities that seem strange, threatening, or nonprofessional evoke strong transference reactions along with anxiety. Traits the patient believes indicate a therapeutic intent, compassion, and expertness may produce realistic response as well as positive transference reactions. The clinical material from the third case indicates how the manner, attitude, and technique of the analyst in the beginning of both analyses decisively colored the analytic situation.

By the time I have decided that psychoanalysis is the treatment of choice, I shall have gained the impression that the patient in question seems to have the potential for forming a working alliance with me along with his transference neurosis. My discussion with the patient of why I believe psychoanalysis is the best method of therapy for him, the explanations of the frequency of visits, duration, fee, and similar matters, and the patient's own appraisal of his capacity to meet these requirements will be of additional value in revealing the patient's ability to form a working alliance.

The first few months of analysis with the patient lying on the couch attempting to free associate can best be epitomized as a combination of testing and confessing. The patient tests his ability to free associate and to expose his guilt and anxiety-producing experiences. Simultaneously he is probing his analyst's reactions to these productions *(10, 18)*. There is a good deal of history telling and reporting of everyday events. My interventions are aimed at pointing out and exploring fairly obvious resistances and inappropriate affects. When the material is quite clear I try to make connections between past and present behavior patterns. As a consequence, the patient usually begins to feel that perhaps I understand him. Then he dares to regress, to let himself experience some transient aspect of his neurosis in the transference in regard to my person. When I succeed in analyzing this effectively then I have at least temporarily succeeded in establishing a reasonable ego and a working alliance alongside of the experiencing ego and the transference neurosis. Once the patient has experienced this oscillation between transference neurosis and working alliance in regard to one area, he becomes more willing to risk future regressions in that same area of the transference neurosis. However every new aspect of the transference neurosis may bring about an impairment of the working alliance and temporary loss of it.

ORIGINS OF THE WORKING ALLIANCE

Contributions of the Patient

For a working alliance to take place, the patient must have the capacity to form object relations since all transference reactions are a special variety of them. People who are essentially narcissistic will not be able to achieve consistent transferences. Furthermore, the working alliance is a relatively rational, desexualized, and deaggressivized transference phenomenon. Patients must have been able to form such sublimated, aim-inhibited relations in their outside life. In the course of analysis the patient is expected to be able to regress to the more primitive and irrational transference reactions that are under the influence of the primary process. To achieve a working alliance, however, the patient must be able to re-establish the secondary process, to split off a relatively reasonable object relationship to the analyst from the more regressive transference reactions. Individuals who suffer from a severe lack of or impairment in ego functions may well be able to experience regressive transference reactions but will have difficulty in maintaining a working alliance. On the other hand, those who dare not give up their reality testing even temporarily and partially, and those who must cling to a fixed form of object relationship are also poor subjects for psychoanalysis. This is confirmed by the clinical findings that psychotics, borderline cases, impulse ridden characters, and young children usually require modifications in the classical psychoanalytic technique (13, 14, 17). Freud had this in mind when he distinguished transference neuroses which are readily analyzable from narcissistic neuroses which are not.

The patient's susceptibility to transference reactions stems from his state of instinctual dissatisfaction and his resultant need for opportunities for discharge. This creates a hunger for objects and a proneness for transference reactions in general (3). Satisfied or apathetic people have fewer transference reactions. The awareness of neurotic suffering also compels the patient to establish a relationship to the analyst. On a conscious and rational level the therapist offers realistic hope of alleviating the neurotic misery. However, the patient's helplessness in regard to his suffering mobilizes early longings for an omnipotent parent. The working alliance has both a rational and irrational component. The above indicates that the analyzable patient must have the need for transference reactions, the capacity to regress and permit neurotic transference reactions, and have the ego strength or that particular form of ego resilience that enables him to interrupt his regression in order to reinstate the reasonable and purposeful working alliance (cf. 23). The patient's ego functions play an important part in the implementation of the working alliance in addition to a role in object relations. In order to do the analytic work the patient must be able to communicate in a variety of ways; in words, with feelings, and yet restrain his actions. He must be able to express himself in words, intelligibly with order and logic, give information when indicated and also be able to regress partially and do some amount of free association. He must be able to listen to the analyst, comprehend, reflect, mull over, and introspect. To some degree he also must remember, observe himself, fantasy, and report. This is only a partial list of ego functions that play a role in the patient's capacity to establish and maintain a working alliance; we also expect the patient simultaneously to develop a transference neurosis. Thus his contribution to the working alliance depends on two antithetical properties: his capacity to maintain contact with the reality of the analytic situation and also his willingness to risk regressing into his fantasy world. It is the oscillation between these two positions that is essential for analytic work.

Contributions of the Analytic Situation

Greenacre (18), Macalpine (24), and Spitz (28) all have pointed out how different elements of the analytic setting and procedures promote regression and the transference neurosis. Some of these same elements also aid in forming the working alliance. The high frequency of visits and long duration of the treatment not only encourage regression but also indicate the long-range objectives and the importance of detailed, intimate communication. The couch and the silence give opportunity for introspection and reflection as well as production of fantasy. The fact that the patient is troubled, unknowing, and being looked after by someone relatively untroubled and expert stirs up the wish to learn and to emulate. Above all the analyst's constant emphasis on attempting to gain understanding of all that goes on in the patient, the fact that nothing is too small, obscure, ugly, or beautiful to escape the analyst's search for comprehension—all this tends to evoke in the patient the wish to know, to find answers, to find causes. This does not deny that the analyst's probings stir up resistances: it merely asserts that it also stirs up the patient's curiosity and his search for causality.

Freud stated that in order to establish rapport one needs time and an attitude of sympathetic understanding (8). Sterba (29) stressed the identificatory processes. The fact that the analyst continuously observes and interprets reality to the patient leads the patient to identify partially with this aspect of the analyst. The invitation to this identification comes from the analyst. From the beginning of treatment, the analyst comments about the work they have to accomplish together. The use of such terms as 'let us look at this', or 'we can see', promotes this. Loewald stressed how the analyst's concern for the patient's potentials stimulates growth and new developments (23).

Fenichel (2) believed it is the analytic atmosphere that is the most important factor in persuading the patient to accept on trial something formerly rejected. Stone (31) emphasized the analyst's willingness to offer the patient certain legitimate, controlled gratifications. I would add that the constant scrutiny of how the patient and the analyst seem to be working together, the mutual concern with the working alliance, in itself serves to enhance it.

Contributions of the Analyst

It is interesting to observe how some analysts take theoretical positions apparently in accord with their manifest personality and other subscribe to theories that seem to contradict their character traits. Some use technique to project, others to protect, their personality. This finding is not meant as a criticism of either group, since happy and unhappy unions can be observed in both. Some rigid analysts advocate strictest adherence to the 'rule of abstinence' and I have seen the same type of analyst attempt to practice the most crass manipulative, gratifying 'corrective emotional experience' psychotherapy. Many apparently care-free and easy-going analysts practice a strict 'rule of abstinence' type of therapy while some of this same character provoke their patients to act out or indulge them in some kind of mutual gratification therapy. Some analysts practice analysis that suits their personality; some use their patients to discharge repressed desires. Be that as it may, these considerations are relevant to the problems inherent in the establishment of the working alliance. Here, however, only a brief outline of the problems can be attempted. The basic issue is: what characteristics of personality and what theoretical orientation in the analyst will insure the development of a working alliance as well as the development of a full-blown transference neurosis?

I have already briefly indicated how certain aspects of the analytic situation facilitate production of a transference neurosis. This can be condensed to the following: we induce the patient to regress and to develop a transference neurosis by providing a situation that consists of a mixture of deprivation, a sleeplike condition, and constancy. Patients develop a transference neurosis from a variety of different analysts as long as the analytic situation provides a goodly amount of deprivation administered in a predictable manner over a suitable length of time. For a good therapeutic result, however, one must also achieve a good working relationship.

What attitudes of the analyst are most likely to produce a good working alliance? My third case indicates how the patient identified himself with his previous analyst on the basis of identification with the aggressor, on a hostile basis. This identification did not produce a therapeutic alliance; it produced a combination of spite and defiance, and interfered with the psychoanalytic work. The reason for this was that the personality of the first analyst seemed cold and aloof, traits which resembled the patient's father, and he was not able to differentiate his first analyst from his regressive transference feelings. How differently he reacted to me in the beginning. He was clearly able to differentiate me from his parent and therefore he was able to make a temporary and partial identification with me, and thus to do the analytic work.

The most important contribution of the psychoanalyst to a good working relationship comes from his daily work with the patient. His consistent and unwavering pursuit of insight in dealing with any and all of the patient's material and behavior is the crucial factor. Other inconsistencies may cause the patient pain, but they do not interfere significantly with the establishment of a working alliance. Yet there are analysts who work consistently and analytically and still seem to have difficulty in inducing their patients to develop a working alliance. I believe this may be due to the kind of atmosphere they create. In part, the disturbance may be the result of too literal acceptance of two suggestions made by Freud: the concept of the analyst as a mirror and the rule of abstinence *(7, 10, 12)*. These two rules have led many analysts to adopt an austere, aloof, and even authoritarian attitude toward their patients. I believe this to be a misunderstanding of Freud's intention; at best, an attitude incompatible with the formation of an effective working alliance.

The reference to the mirror and the rule of abstinence were suggested to help the analyst safeguard the transference from contamination, a point Greenacre *(18)* has amplified. The mirror refers to the notion that the analyst should be 'opaque' to the patient, nonintrusive in terms of imposing his values and standards upon the patient. It does not mean that the analyst shall be inanimate, cold, and unresponsive. The rule of abstinence refers to the importance of not gratifying the patient's infantile and neurotic wishes. It does not mean that all the patient's wishes are to be frustrated. Sometimes one may have to gratify a neurotic wish temporarily. Even the frustration of the neurotic wishes has to be carried on in such a way as not to demean or traumatize the patient.

While it is true that Freud stressed the deprivational aspects of the analytic situation, I believe he did so because at that time (1912–1919) the danger was that analysts would permit themselves to overreact and to act out with their patients. Incidentally, if one reads Freud's case histories, one does not get the impression that the analytic atmosphere of his analyses was one of coldness or austerity. For example, in the original record of the case of the Rat man, Freud appended a note, dated December 28, to the published paper *(5)*, 'He was hungry and was fed'. Then on January 2, 'Besides this he apparently only had trivialities to report and I was able to say a great deal to him today'.

It is obvious that if we want the patient to develop a relatively realistic and reasonable working alliance, we have to work in a manner that is both realistic and reasonable despite the fact that the procedures and processes of psychoanalysis are strange, unique, and even artificial. Smugness, ritualism, timidity, authoritarianism, aloofness, and indulgence have no place in the analytic situation.

The patient will not only be influenced by the content of our work but by how we work, the attitude, the manner, the mood, and the atmosphere in which we work. He will react to and identify himself particularly with those aspects that need not necessarily be conscious to us. Glover *(17)* stressed the need of the analyst to be natural and straightforward, decrying the pretense, for example, that all arrangements about time and fee are made exclusively for the patient's benefit. Fenichel (2) emphasized that above all the analyst should be human and was appalled that so many of his patients were surprised by his naturalness and freedom. Sterba (30), stressing the 'let us look, we shall see' approach, hints at his way of working. Stone (31) goes even further in emphasizing legitimate gratifications and the therapeutic attitude and intention of the psychoanalyst that are necessary for the patient.

All analysts recognize the need for deprivations in psychoanalysis; they would also agree in principle on the analyst's need to be human. The problem arises, however, in determining what is meant by humanness in the analytic situation and how does one reconcile this with the principle of deprivation. Essentially the humanness of the analyst is expressed in his compassion, concern, and therapeutic intent toward his patient. It matters to him how the patient fares, he is not just an observer or a research worker. He is a physician or a therapist, and his aim is to help the patient get well. He keeps his eye on the long-range goal, sacrificing temporary and quick results for later and lasting changes. Humanness is also expressed in the attitude that the patient is to be respected as an individual. We cannot repeatedly demean a patient by imposing rules and regulations upon him without explanation and then expect him to work with us as an adult. For a working alliance it is imperative that the analyst show consistent concern for the rights of the patient throughout the analysis. Though I let my patient see that I am involved with him and concerned, my reactions have to be non-intrusive. I try not to take sides in any of his conflicts except that I am working against his resistances, his damaging neurotic behavior, and his self-destructiveness. Basically, however, humanness consists of understanding and insight conveyed in an atmosphere of serious work, straightforwardness, compassion, and restraint (19).

The above outline is my personal point of view on how to resolve the conflict between the maintenance of distance and the closeness necessary for analytic work and is not offered as a prescription for all analysts. However, despite great variation in analysts' personalities, these two antithetical elements must be taken into account and handled if good analytic results are to be obtained. The transference neurosis and the working alliance are parallel antithetical forces in transference phenomena; each is of equal importance.

SUMMARY

Some analyses are impeded or totally thwarted by failure of patient and analyst to form a working alliance. Clinical examples of such failure are examined, showing how they were corrected. Formation of the working alliance, its characteristics, and its relation to transference are discussed. It is contended that the working alliance is equally as important as the transference neurosis.

NOTES

1. This case is described in greater detail in a paper entitled The Problem of Working Through. In *Tribute to Marie Bonaparte*. Edited by Max Schur. (New York: International Universities Press, 1965).

REFERENCES

1. Deutsch, Helene: *Some Forms of Emotional Disturbance and Their Relationship to Schizophrenia*. Psychoanal. Q., XI, 1942, pp. 301–321.
2. Fenichel, Otto: *Problems of Psychoanalytic Technique*. New York: The Psychoanalytic Quarterly, Inc., 1941.
3. Ferenczi, Sandor: *Introjection and Transference* (1909). In *Sex in Psychoanalysis*. New York: Basic Books, Inc., 1950.
4. Freud: *Fragment of an Analysis of a Case of Hysteria* (1905 [1901]). Standard Edition, VII, pp. 116–117.
5. ———: *Notes upon a Case of Obsessional Neurosis* (1909). Standard Edition, X, p. 303.
6. ———: *The Dynamics of Transference* (1912). Standard Edition, XII.
7. ———: *Recommendations to Physicians Practicing Psychoanalysis*. (1912). *Ibid.*
8. ———: *On Beginning the Treatment* (1913). *Ibid.*
9. ———: *Remembering, Repeating and Working Through* (1914). *Ibid.*
10. ———: *Observations on Transference Love* (1915 [1914]). *Ibid.*
11. ———: *Introductory Lectures on Psychoanalysis* (1916–1917 [1915–1917]). Standard Edition, XV, XVI.
12. ———: *Lines of Advance in Psychoanalytic Therapy* (1919 [1918]). Standard Edition, XVII.
13. Garma, Angel: Contribution to Discussion on *The Curative Factors in Psychoanalysis*, Int. J. Psa., XLIII, 1962, pp. 221–224.
14. Gill, Merton M.: *Psychoanalysis and Exploratory Psychotherapy*. J. Amer. Psa. Assn., II, 1954, pp. 771–797.
15. ———: Newman, Richard; and Redlich, Frederick C.: *The Initial Interview in Psychiatric Practice*. New York: International Universities Press, Inc., 1954.
16. Gitelson, Maxwell: *The Curative Factors in Psychoanalysis. The First Phase of Psychoanalysis*. Int. J. Psa., XLIII, 1962, pp. 194–205.

17. Glover, Edward: *The Technique of Psychoanalysis.* (Chapters I–III, VII–VIII.) New York: International Universities Press, Inc., 1955.

18. Greenacre, Phyllis: *The Role of Transference, Practical Considerations in Relation to Psychoanalytic Therapy.* J. Amer. Psa. Assn., II, 1954, pp. 671–684.

19. Greenson, Ralph R.: *Variations in Classical Psychoanalytic Technique: An Introduction.* Int. J. Psa., XXXIX, 1958, pp. 200–201.

20. Heimann, Paula: Contribution to Discussion on *The Curative Factors in Psychoanalysis,* Int. J. Psa., XLIII, 1962, pp. 228–231.

21. King, Pearl: Contribution to Discussion on *The Curative Factors in Psychoanalysis. Op. cit.,* pp. 225–227.

22. Kuiper, Pieter: Contribution to Discussion on *The Curative Factors in Psychoanalysis. Op. cit.,* pp. 218–220.

23. Loewald, Hans: *On the Therapeutic Action of Psychoanalysis.* Int. J. Psa., XLI, 1960, pp. 16–33.

24. Macalpine, Ida: *The Development of Transference.* Psychoanal. Q., XIX, 1950, pp. 501–539.

25. Myerson, Paul G.: Footnote in Gitelson, Maxwell: *The Curative Factors in Psychoanalysis. Op. cit.,* p. 202.

26. Nacht, Sacha: *The Curative Factors in Psychoanalysis. Op. cit.,* pp. 206–211.

27. Segal, Hanna: *The Curative Factors in Psychoanalysis. Op. cit.,* pp. 212–217.

28. Spitz, René A.: *Transference: The Analytical Setting and Its Prototype.* Int. J. Psa., XXXVII, 1956, pp. 380–385.

29. Sterba, Richard: *The Fate of the Ego in Analytic Therapy.* Int. J. Psa., XV, 1934, pp. 117–126.

30. ———: *The Dynamics of the Dissolution of the Transference Resistance.* Psychoanal. Q., IX, 1940, pp. 363–379.

31. Stone, Leo: *The Psychoanalytic Situation.* New York: International Universities Press, Inc., 1961.

32. Zetzel, Elizabeth R.: *Current Concepts of Transference.* Int. J. Psa., XXXVII, 1956, pp. 369–376.

12. Working Alliance, Therapeutic Alliance, and Transference

Charles Brenner

Interest in the therapeutic or working alliance dates from a paper by Zetzel (1956) on transference. The idea of an alliance between analyst and the reasonable part of the patient's ego had been referred to earlier by Bibring (1937), but it attracted little interest in discussions of psychoanalytic technique. Since Zetzel's paper and a later one by Greenson (1965), interest in the subject has been much more widespread. For example, Modell (1972, p. 263), in a review of Zetzel's collected papers, wrote that "much of what Zetzel described concerning the capacity for the development of the therapeutic alliance . . . is noncontroversial." Similarly, Lampl-de Groot (1975, p. 668) wrote that "most authors" distinguish between transference and working alliance.

There are analysts, however, who question the validity of the distinction just referred to. Arlow and I (1966) raised questions concerning the theoretical assumption on which Zetzel based her idea of a therapeutic alliance, namely, that the analytic situation is necessarily a repetition of the relationship between mother and infant. More recently, Kanzer (1975) and Arlow (1975) each expressed reservations about the concepts of therapeutic and working alliance, emphasizing the technical difficulties to which they are likely to give rise. I share their misgivings (Brenner, 1976, p. 120) and join with them, if Lampl-de Groot is right, as members of an unconvinced minority. I believe that it is neither correct nor useful to distinguish between transference and therapeutic or working alliance. In order to support my opinion I shall, in this paper, review the meaning of therapeutic and working alliance as I understand it, as well as the data on which the concepts were originally based. Because I believe there is a close relation between these concepts and the question of gratification versus frustration of transference wishes in analysis, I shall spend some time discussing the latter topic as well.

Reprinted from the *Journal of the American Psychoanalytic Association* 27, suppl. (1979): 137–57, by permission of International Universities Press, Inc.

Zetzel's concept of therapeutic alliance can be summarized as follows. According to her, when a patient enters analysis he "is asked to relinquish crucial inner defenses and controls against ego-alien impulses and fantasies previously motivated by signals of internal danger" (1966, p. 100). Still according to Zetzel, "The patient, however, will only be capable of tolerating the added stress roused by specific fantasies which emerge in his transference neurosis, if his basic needs and anxieties have been acknowledged in the opening stages of treatment" (1966, p. 100). Acknowledging a patient's basic needs and anxieties, said Zetzel, is what an analyst must do at the start of analysis in order to make possible what is analysis proper, namely, the interpretation of the patient's instinctual conflicts, especially as they become manifest in the transference neurosis. Therapeutic alliance, according to Zetzel, precedes analysis. It is different and distinct from the transference neurosis. It is essentially, in her view, a recapitulation of the very early relation between mother and infant. As an infant turns with expectant faith to its mother for help, so does a patient turn to his analyst. An analyst, therefore, must be like a good mother, with "intuitive adaptive responses" (1966, p. 97) to each patient's needs and anxieties. Thus, "the initial stage [of analysis] involves achievement of a special object relationship leading to a new ego identification" (1966, p. 92), i.e., an identification (= alliance) with the analyst. As already noted, this ego identification "is to be regarded as an essential prerequisite . . . to the analytic process itself" (1966, p. 99).

In her 1956 paper Zetzel gave no clinical illustrations. In the paper just quoted, she gave two illustrative clinical excerpts, one from an analysis she had supervised, the other, apparently, from an analysis she had conducted herself. This case material will be discussed below.

Greenson's concept of therapeutic alliance—he prefers the term working alliance—essentially corresponds with Zetzel's. His first extensive presentation was in 1965, though it was by no means his only one (see Greenson, 1966, 1967). Like Zetzel, Greenson (1965) separated working alliance from transference neurosis. The latter, he said, must be analyzed for analysis to be successful, while the former must be established for the latter to be analyzable. According to Greenson, a good working alliance is essential throughout an analysis. He believes it can be best established—or, perhaps, only established—if an analyst, in addition to showing by his day-to-day behavior a "consistent and unwavering pursuit of insight in dealing with any and all of the patient's material and behavior" (1965, p. 221) also creates a proper working atmosphere (1965, p. 223). In other words, according to Greenson, in addition to being analytic, which is crucial, an analyst must also be human. "Essentially the humanness of the analyst is expressed in his compassion, concern, and therapeutic intent toward his patient. . . . Humanness is also expressed in the attitude that the patient is to be respected as an individual. . . . Basically . . . humanness consists of understanding and insight conveyed in an atmosphere of serious work, straightforwardness, compassion, and restraint" (1965, pp. 223–224). Greenson included in his paper illustrative material from the analyses of four of his own patients. This material will be discussed below.

In trying to reach a decision about the validity of the concept of therapeutic alliance as something distinct from transference neurosis, one is faced first of all with the question of the basis on which to test it. It seems to me that a pragmatic test is likely to be the most useful. To marshal arguments for and against the concept of therapeutic alliance that rest on its compatibility or incompatibility with psychoanalytic theories of transference, or of conflict, or of the relative importance of oedipal and preoedipal factors in later mental functioning runs the risk of engaging in a logomachy—a mere war of words. If it were possible, the most useful test of the validity of the concept of therapeutic alliance would probably be via clinical conferences—perhaps a continuous case seminar—over an extended period. Since that is rarely feasible, one can at least examine the illustrative case material offered to support the validity of the concept in question. After all, both Zetzel and Greenson have said, in effect, that their clinical experience has convinced them that analysts must be more than merely analytical in their behavior with their patients. They must have "intuitive adaptive responses" (Zetzel); they must create the right "kind of atmosphere" (Greenson). What is the clinical material that illustrates the soundness of these claims?

Zetzel (1966, pp. 94–97) presented material from the beginning of an analysis she supervised. It was the candidate-analysts's first case. The patient was a 25-year-old "girl [who] suffered from serious inhibitions in respect to her heterosexual relationships." "In the initial interview, after careful consideration, the fee set had been somewhat higher than the patient anticipated. The patient had agreed that she could pay this moderate fee but had clearly felt disappointed." From the very start of her first hour the patient showed evidence that she was disappointed and angry at having to pay more than she had expected (or hoped) to. (1) "She . . . commented that analysis is a luxury." (2) She classified "herself as a receptive character." (3) "She . . . speculated about her mother. She was probably a hoarder. This was not fair to her mother who would be horrified.'' (4) '' . . . she referred to some recent dealing with a printer in connection with some work he was to do for her employer. He agreed to do a job for $35; the patient asked her employer for $60 just to be sure. The printer then sent a bill for $120. In a very angry voice the patient said: 'I told him I didn't think much of his way of doing business. I'm glad I told him.' '' In her report, Zetzel called attention to the patient's anger at her analyst as well as to indications, in this and other things she said during her first analytic hour, that an analyst might despise and laugh at ''crackpots'' like her.

The analyst himself made no comment about all of this to his patient. It was, after all, his very first analytic patient. ''In subsequent hours during the first week of analysis, there was considerable additional material of a similar nature, with an increasing tendency to view the rather silent analyst as an unreal, omnipotent figure. The patient felt threatened by feelings of helplessness against which she defended herself through denial and some displacement. The candidate concerned, discussing the situation in his supervisory session, became aware of his rigidity and concern lest any activity on his part should be regarded an unanalytic in respect to this, his first analytic patient. He adopted, subsequently, a slightly more active and human attitude, indicating to the patient his recognition of her anxiety'' (p. 96). This resulted, we are told, in an immediate improvement of the analytic situation. The patient became more comfortable, and her reality testing improved in the sense that she realized (and said) that her analyst was not a special Olympian figure, as she had imagined him to be, but an ordinary person like herself.

According to Zetzel, this vignette illustrates the bad effect of excessive rigidity on the part of an analyst and the good effect of a more relaxed and human attitude with a patient in whom the unfamiliar analytic situation stirred up basic anxieties that derived from her very early relationship with her mother, with ''related changes in the perception of reality which, unchecked, might have hindered the development of a satisfactory analytic situation'' (p. 97). When the analyst became more human, the patient became more secure in her relationship with him, with the result that ''she could not only reintegrate previously achieved ego capacities but could also initiate the added ego maturation which would later become achieved through the analytic process'' (p. 97).

The reader will note that we have not been told just what it was that the analyst did after the supervisory hour that he had not done before—information that seems to me too important to have been omitted. Some details concerning just what the analyst did and how the patient responded should help in deciding how instrumental the change in his attitude and activity really were.

Equally important, it would seem, is Zetzel's failure to pay any attention to the fact, which she recognized, that the patient was disappointed and angry about the fee she had to pay. It seems likely that the patient was not only disappointed and angry, but ashamed and frightened as well. At least she called herself greedy and fancied she was being laughed at. Should none of this have been interpreted to the patient? Was it best that nothing was said to her about being angry at her analyst and afraid to say so for fear of being laughed at and thought greedy? Zetzel did not even discuss the possibility of making such an interpretation. She did raise the possibility of making an immediate deep (i.e., genetically oriented) interpretation of the "type . . . described by Mrs. Klein and her followers" (pp. 95–96), and dismissed the idea as unwise. Such an interpretation, according to Zetzel, should have dealt with features of the patient's early relationship to her mother as demonstrated in transference to her analyst. In Zetzel's opinion it would have been premature to make such a reconstructive interpretation in the first hour. I agree with that opinion, but I am not persuaded that the patient's reaction to her fee was of so little importance as a determinant of her view of her analyst as an "unreal, omnipotent figure" and of the fact that for several days she "felt threatened by feelings of helplessness" (p. 96). Apparently something the analyst said or did after his first supervisory hour reassured her. Perhaps he smiled at her as he greeted or dismissed her. Whatever it was, it helped her to feel more positively toward him and relieved her distress. But would it not have been as effective symptomatically, and more useful analytically, to have dealt with the patient's initial difficulty by interpretation rather than by being more "human" and "relaxed"? What Zetzel recommended worked in the case she reported, but it is hardly a convincing illustration of her general thesis, I think.

One can see also how difficult it is to discuss the matter away from the clinical material, so to speak. The questions one wants answered about the analyst's actual behavior, for example, could be answered only in the setting of a seminar or a dialogue, and in such a setting, with discussion back and forth, one might also expect much more to emerge in the way of clinical material that would be pertinent to the task of deciding on the validity of Zetzel's generalizations about therapeutic alliance as distinct from transference in analysis.

Her second illustration is less useful for discussion than her first, for it contains no analytic material but merely a summary statement that the patient "had experienced unusual difficulty in accepting the passive components of the analytic situation. It had been hard for her to lie down, hard for her to free associate, and particularly hard to accept the slow, often mysterious nature of the analytic process. She wanted to be active, to work hard, and to make things happen. Though a positive therapeutic alliance had been established with ease, she was anxiously aware of her need to remain in control" (p. 102). All of this, according to Zetzel, was related to the patient's oedipal wishes and conflicts, which were abundantly demonstrated in the course of her analysis. This is neither new nor unusual, nor did Zetzel consider it to be so. Her point was that interpretation alone would not have been enough. What she called a dual approach is necessary, and she described it as follows. "In the initial stages of analysis it had been necessary to give due recognition to her fear of passivity and loss of control. As the analysis progressed, however, her anxiety diminished, not only through interpretation of the transference neurosis, but also through her increased capacity to tolerate passivity, frustration and delay. This, in turn, initiated a more mature positive ego identification with the analyst and qualitative changes in the analytic situation itself" (p. 103), which led to analytic progress. One is left without more information than that regarding what factors in the analytic situation other than interpretation increased her capacity to tolerate passivity, frustration, and delay.

Here again, therefore, one cannot judge from the printed record what data persuaded Zetzel that more than correct transference interpretations are necessary for analytic progress, that therapeutic alliance is distinct from transference neurosis, and that it is no less important to foster the alliance than to interpret the transference.

Greenson's (1965) illustrative case material was drawn from the analyses of four of his own patients: Three of the four had been in analysis previously, two with other analysts, one with Greenson himself. Each patient had been or seemed to be "unanalyzable or interminable" (p. 200). This was due to previously unrecognized difficulty in the working alliance (= therapeutic alliance) between patient and analyst.

The first patient was a middle-aged man who had had more than six years of analysis with a previous analyst. "Certain general conditions had improved, but his original analyst believed the patient needed additional analysis because he was still unable to marry and was very lonely" (p. 205).

When he began analysis with Greenson, Greenson promptly recognized evidence of an extremely compliant attitude that was expressed by his behavior during the analytic sessions. The patient never took the initiative "about recognizing and working with his resistances." He waited for Greenson to point them out, but he always responded immediately when Greenson did intervene, since not to do so would have been a "sign of resistance," which the patient thought was bad (p. 205). In the course of Greenson's attempts to deal with his patient's resistance, which Greenson formulated as an inability to establish a satisfactory working alliance, it became clear that the patient's "striking passivity and compliance were . . . a form of ingratiation, covering up an inner emptiness, an insatiable infantile hunger, and a terrible rage" (p. 206). After six months Greenson concluded that he was attempting to analyze an unanalyzable patient and referred him to a colleague for psychotherapy.

Here again it is difficult to see what relevance the illustrative material has to the thesis that there is a working alliance that is distinguishable from the transference neurosis and that must be fostered by being tactful and human with analytic patients. Greenson himself made clear that this was a patient who was unanalyzable and who could accomplish nothing of value in analysis despite Greenson's strenuous efforts to enlist his cooperation in the analytic work. Greenson made equally clear his opinion that the first analyst's failure to recognize that, despite his compliance, the patient was unanalyzable had resulted in more than six years of therapy that was a mere "caricature of analysis" (p. 206). If this case material illustrates anything about the working alliance, it illustrates that serious transference resistances are not successfully resolved by being human and making efforts to enlist a patient's cooperation. In may well be that the patient was, as Greenson believed him to be, wholly unsuitable for analysis from the start and that interpretation of his emptiness, hunger, rage, and defensive compliance would have been no more successful than was Greenson's humanness in mitigating the patient's resistance to analysis; but, certainly, interpretation couldn't have been less successful than being human was. This illustration hardly serves to recommend the value of Greenson's (and Zetzel's) technical maneuvers.

The second patient was a woman who had been in analysis with Greenson for four years and returned for further analysis after an interval of six years. The second time, Greenson, older and more experienced, recognized more clearly than he had done during the patient's first period of analysis that her way of talking during sessions—her way of "associating"—must be analyzed if she was to work to capacity in analysis. Only by bending every effort to analyze her transference behavior—her "misuse" of the procedure of analysis (p. 208)—was Greenson able to ensure that his patient's second analysis was more fruitful than her first had been.

Interesting and convincing as is this clinical material in many respects, I do not see that it supports Greenson's thesis. It is always enjoyable to read—or listen to—clinical material. It is instructive and delightful to do so when it gives one a chance to observe a master like Greenson at work. But here again is case material that seems to illustrate something quite at odds with Greenson's generalizations about working alliance. It is material illustrating very well that, when a patient's ability to cooperate in the work of analysis is compromised, it is often a consequence or manifestation of transference and that it is dealt with best by correct understanding and consistent interpretation.

Greenson's third patient was a young man who had previously been in analysis with another (male) analyst for two and a half years. This analysis "had left him almost completely untouched" (p. 209). The patient consciously withheld embarrassing thoughts, refused to divulge "many conscious secrets" (p. 210), and was silent for long periods during many sessions.

Greenson attributed the patient's resistance during his first analysis to the analyst's behavior. It was for this reason, he believed, that the patient "had not been able to form a working alliance." In contrast to the patient's first analyst, Greenson was tactful and explained why he behaved as he did on some occasions. Instead of telling the patient "that it was customary not to smoke during sessions," as the first analyst had done, Greenson explained that what was important was to know "what feelings, ideas, and sensations were going on in him at the moment that he decided to light the cigarette . . . that it was preferable for such feelings and ideas to be expressed in words instead of actions" (p. 210), since in that way they could be understood. Greenson followed a similar course in a later hour when the patient asked if Greenson was married: "I then pointed out to him how, by not answering his question and by asking him instead to tell his fantasies about the answer, he revealed the cause of his curiosity. I told him I would not answer questions when I felt that more was to be gained by keeping silent and letting him associate to his own question. At this point the patient became somewhat tearful and . . . told me that in the beginning of his previous analysis he had asked many questions. His former analyst never answered nor did he explain why he was silent. He felt his analyst's silence as a degradation and humiliation and now realized that his own later silences were a retaliation for this imagined injustice'' (p. 211).

Here, then, is some case material that illustrates the point about a working or therapeutic alliance that Greenson and Zetzel make. Being intuitive and tactfully human fosters a patient's ability to work analytically. Failing to be so interferes with the development of that ability and may make analysis impossible. But would it not be equally correct to say that the first analyst did not recognize that certain aspects of the analytic situation—his own lack of response to questions, his advice not to smoke, and his failure to offer explanations for his conduct—angered the patient and resolved him to get even in kind? And is this not transference? Not every patient gets angry at his analyst's behavior. Not every angry patient is unable to complain, nor is every one spitefully stubborn even at his own expense. Was it the first analyst's behavior that stalemated the first analysis, or was it, more importantly, the first analyst's failure to understand and interpret his patient's transference resistance?

I do not raise these objections to Greenson's (and, I suspect, Zetzel's) explanation because I am in favor of rudeness or aloofness on the part of an analyst toward his patients. I raise them because I am convinced that it is important to every analyst's technical proficiency to understand his patients as fully and as correctly as possible. To modify merely by one's behavior, as Greenson did, a transference reaction so intense that it stalemated analytic progress for two years, without even raising the question why the patient reacted as he did—to proceed as though it is natural (human?) to be angry with someone who tries to be helpful in a way that one doesn't understand the reasons for—seems to me to be of doubtful value in analysis. No two analysts behave exactly the same. Some explain why they discourage smoking and don't answer questions; some don't explain. Experience indicates that either course of behavior is compatible with technical proficiency. What is not compatible with it is failure to recognize a patient's anger if one doesn't explain, and consequent failure to bring it into the analysis. And it can, in some circumstances, be equally damaging to fail to recognize a patient's unexpressed reaction when one *does* explain. In my opinion, it is not being more or less ''human'' that is most important. What is most important, I believe, is to understand correctly the nature and origin of one's patients' transference reactions however one behaves.

Greenson's fourth patient was also a young man. After two years of analysis during which the patient was superficially cooperative but took nothing seriously, Greenson told the patient they were getting nowhere and suggested interrupting treatment. The patient expressed some disappointment, but obviously didn't take Greenson's suggestion for interruption of treatment any more seriously than he had taken whatever else Greenson had said during the previous two years. Instead, he went on talking as though nothing of consequence had been said. Greenson interrupted angrily to ask him what he thought he was doing. The patient responded that Greenson sounded annoyed with him, to which Greenson replied that he certainly was. This really shook the patient. He sat up and soon confessed that he often thought of Greenson laughing at him, being angry, and being sexually excited. It turned out that the patient's father had frequently taken the patient's temperature rectally when he was a boy. The patient then "proceeded to [tell] a host of homosexual and sadomasochistic fantasies. The persistent reasonableness [had been] a defense against these as well as a playful attempt to tease me into acting out with him" (p. 214). After this confrontation, analytic progress became possible. According to Greenson, this material is illustrative of a pseudo or false working alliance that had to be changed into a true working alliance before analysis could progress.

Once again, I believe, we have been presented with interesting and instructive clinical material that does not support or illustrate Greenson's main thesis: that working alliance is different from transference neurosis. This was a patient who for two years acted out in analysis his unconscious wish to provoke his analyst to attack him. Only when this was understood and analyzed could analytic progress be made. If the material illustrates anything, it illustrates that when a patient is so uncooperative and resistant as to cause the analysis to reach an impasse, correct understanding of unconscious transference wishes, and correct interpretation to the patient based on that understanding, may resolve the seeming impasse and make cooperation and further progress possible.

In short, I am convinced by all the available evidence that the concepts of therapeutic alliance and working alliance that have been current in psychoanalytic literature since 1956 are neither valid nor useful. In analysis, resistances are best analyzed, not overcome by suggestion or by some corrective emotional experience. That is to say, their nature and origin are to be understood and, when understood, interpreted to the patient.

This is not to say that one can always analyze resistance successfully. In the first place, it is not always possible to understand the nature and origin of resistance. And even when an analyst believes he does understand a resistance, at least to considerable degree, interpretation does not always lead to constructive change. Analysis is not a panacea, nor is it universally applicable. Sometimes a patient who seemed eminently suited for analysis before analysis began turns out not to be so when analysis has got under way. However, when a patient *is* in analysis, the better one understands his resistances and the more knowledgeably one is able to interpret their determinants to him, the better the chance that the patient can cooperate constructively. Whether at the beginning, in the midst, or in the final stages of analysis, timely, accurate interpretations that are based on correct understanding are far more useful in promoting a patient's ability to do his part than is any behavior, however well intentioned, humane, and intuitively compassionate, that is intended to make him feel less withdrawn, uncomfortable, or antagonistic. In analysis, it is best for the patient if one approaches *everything* analytically. It is as important to understand why a patient is closely "allied" with his analyst in the analytic work as it is to understand why there seems to be no "alliance" at all. As Friedman (1969) remarked, any idea that, apart from wanting help and gratification from his analyst, a "patient wishes to, or should wish to, engage in a process *per se* [i.e., wishes to engage in analysis for its own sake] is supported by neither analytic theory nor commonsense" (p. 152).

As we have seen, the practical importance of the concept of a therapeutic or working alliance between patient and analyst, according to Zetzel and Greenson, lies in the recommendation that if analysts are more relaxed, more human, more giving to their patients, the analytic process will profit thereby. Clearly, one of the problems involved in following their recommendation is the question of frustration versus gratification of transference wishes. We all agree that abstinence (= frustration of wishes of instinctual origin) is a necessary part of the analytic situation. However, since *some* degree of gratification of *some* unconscious infantile wishes is inescapably part of every relationship with another person, including one's analyst, the questions that naturally arise are "How much frustration? How much gratification? When? and what kind(s)?"

The most thoughtful, penetrating, and thorough discussion of the whole problem of frustration versus gratification of patients' wishes in analysis is to be found in Stone's *The Psychoanalytic Situation* (1961). Stone emphasized repeatedly something to which, I believe, neither Zetzel nor Greenson paid sufficient attention, namely, that one cannot make generalizations that cover every case. Whenever one must decide whether to gratify a patient's wishes, whether by answering a question or by giving information about oneself or by a schedule change or in any other way, the decision should rest on the analyst's understanding of the patient's conflicts, on his understanding of that patient's transference at that time and, thus, on the analyst's prediction, based on his best clinical judgment, of the likely effect on the course of the analysis of gratifying or frustrating the patient's wish(es) at that moment. In addition, Stone emphasized how difficult it often is to be sure that one *does* understand correctly and that one is making the correct decision.

Thus, Stone was both cautious and circumspect in his technical recommendations, which may be summarized as follows. Rules—e.g., the rule of abstinence—are recommendations with a purpose, not orders to be followed blindly and without exception. Stone believes that an analyst should be guided in his behavior by the recognition of what Stone insists is fundamental to the analytic situation, namely, that the patient is there for help and that he views his analyst as his doctor (by which Stone means therapist, not necessarily an M.D.) on whose professional commitment he can count (p. 42). Thus, "There are occasions when, for example, it is insufficient to interpret why a patient does not go for physical examination, or for contraceptive advice" (p. 32), times when his analyst should advise him or her to go. More than that, according to Stone, the psychoanalytic method as such "imposes certain severe restrictions" (p. 42) on analytic patients, and he deems it neither humane nor wise for an analyst to be unnecessarily frustrating: ". . . the intrinsic formal stringencies of the situation are sufficient to contraindicate superfluous deprivations in the analyst's personal attitude" (p. 22). Specifically, Stone can see more potential good than harm for analysis if a patient knows a few simple facts, not too intimate, about his analyst and his personal life.

I thoroughly agree with Stone's major emphases: that analysis is a form of therapy, that a patient should be able to count on his analyst's professional commitment to him as a "doctor," that the business of analysis is to analyze *that* case, that technical rules are not commandments, and that in every instance one should be guided by one's analytic understanding of the entire analytic situation. Moreover, the examples of analytic reserve that Stone cites with disapproval seem as unwarranted to me as they do to Stone. It seems to me, however, that what Stone recommends with respect to what wishes are permissibly and usefully gratified in analysis is likely not to be in the best interests of analytic progress. Nor do I agree that it is in the nature of things that patients will suffer from what Stone calls the severe restrictions of the analytic situation, and that analysts, as good doctors, should aim at keeping to an irreducible minimum the suffering they must impose on their patients by subjecting them to analysis. I have no doubt that it is as possible to pervert analysis as it is to pervert anything else and that an unconsciously cruel or sadistic analyst can misuse analysis to gratify his unconscious wishes under the guise of authoritarian analytic "correctness." I can believe, too, that patients who stay long in such a situation are all the things Stone says they are encouraged by their unconsciously sadistic analysts to be: passive, submissive, awestruck, worshipful and masochistic (p. 66). But to agree that a sadistic analyst and a masochistic patient can unconsciously pervert analysis is not to say that the analytic situation is a source of suffering to patients in and of itself.

I believe, in fact, that the truth is quite otherwise. Provided his analyst is competent (= adequately trained and himself sufficiently well analyzed), it is a patient's own illness that determines whether he experiences the analytic situation in and of itself as a source of pain, as essentially neutral, as a welcome anodyne, or as a positive source of pleasure. Every experienced analyst has had patients who felt analysis to be each of these at the start. Every patient has times during his analysis when he feels analysis to be each of them in turn. Whatever an analytic patient feels about the analytic situation, whether it be suffering, indifference, or gratification, is analytic material. It should, in principle, be treated like any other material: understood if possible and interpreted if appropriate. It is neither inhumane nor inhuman for an analyst to be guided by this principle in his attitude and behavior toward his patients.

If, for example, a patient suffers a catastrophe or a success in life, it is not the best for him and his analysis for his analyst to express sympathy or congratulations before "going on to analyze." It is true enough that it often does no harm for an analyst to be thus conventionally "human." Still, there are times when his being "human" under such circumstances can be harmful, and one cannot always know in advance when those times will be. As an example, for his analyst to express sympathy for a patient who has just lost a close relative may make it more difficult than it would otherwise be for the patient to express pleasure or spite or exhibitionistic satisfaction over the loss. As another example, it is difficult for me to imagine instructing an adult patient to have a physical examination or to go for contraceptive information. I can easily imagine saying to a patient that there must be a reason why he is neglecting his health and that I wonder what his thoughts are about it, or to another that there must be some reason why she is inviting or risking pregnancy and that I wonder what she thinks about it. Either such statement, however phrased, is perfectly in keeping with an analytic attitude on the part of an analyst. Either is quite as analytic, i.e., quite as appropriate to an analytic situation, as it would be to point out to a patient that he invariably tells his dreams at the end of an hour or that he is consistently late in paying his bill—to choose two everyday examples. I cannot imagine circumstances that would justify telling an analytic patient to get a physical examination or to be fitted for a diaphragm any more than I can imagine telling an analytic patient to please tell his dreams early in the hour and to be prompt in paying his bill.

As I have written elsewhere (1976), I believe that an analyst's human responsibility to his patients is to understand them as best he can and to convey to them what he understands for their benefit. An analyst's behavior and attitude are unique, to be sure, but they are none the less human and humane for being unique. When analysis is applicable and effective, it offers the best method that is now available for reducing neurotic suffering. For an analyst to be consistently analytic with his patients may hurt more at the moment than for him to be other than analytic, but it is not cruel. It is the best way we have of helping those who come to us for relief of pain not to continue to suffer in the future as they have in the past. When any doctor *cannot* cure, he is reduced to doing his best to relieve pain. *"Sine opio nulla medicina,"* was good medicine when nothing but palliatives were known. I believe it was in that sense that Freud (1912) compared psychoanalysis to surgery, namely, that both look to cure patients rather than merely to make them comfortable. When a doctor believes he can *cure* a patient, however, neither he nor his patient will be dissuaded from making the attempt because some suffering is unavoidably involved.

I cannot believe that any analyst who deserves the name thinks of analysis as something other than therapy. I am sure that every analyst feels a professional commitment to his patients of the sort that both Stone (1961) and Greenson (1967) have rightly emphasized. I agree, as well, that analysts should be alert to whatever difficulties a patient may have in cooperating in analysis, however covert and subtle those difficulties are. I do not believe, though, that therapeutic alliance or working alliance are useful concepts. I do not agree with Zetzel than an alliance is distinct from the remainder of a patient's transference nor with Greenson's less sweeping formula that working alliance and transference neurosis are to be distinguished from one another even though they are closely related. A patient's resistances in analysis are analytic material. Whatever may be their intensity and however they show themselves—in the transference or in some other way—they are best understood and dealt with when the analyst views them as analytical material and attempts to analyze them. These are conclusions I have reached pragmatically, though I believe them to be consonant with psychoanalytic theory as well. They are conclusions based on experience with my own analytic patients as well as with cases brought to me for consultation and supervision by colleagues, and on a careful, sympathetic study of the reasons advanced to support the usefulness or necessity of distinguishing between alliance and the rest of the transference by those colleagues, led by Zetzel and Greenson, who have argued for doing so. I believe that the distinction they propose is a specious one and that its consequences for analytic practice are, generally speaking, undesirable.

SUMMARY

Examination of the clinical evidence offered by proponents for the concepts of therapeutic and working alliance leads the author to conclude that neither concept is justifiable. Both refer to aspects of the transference that neither deserve a special name nor require special treatment. The related topic of frustration/gratification as necessarily inherent in the analytic situation is also considered.

REFERENCES

Arlow, J. A. (1975), Discussion of Kanzer's paper. *Internat. J. Psychoanal. Psychother.*, 4:69–73.
———— & Brenner, C. (1966), The psychoanalytic situation. In *Psychoanalysis in the Americas*, ed. R. E. Litman. New York: International Universities Press, pp. 23–43; 133–138.
Bibring, E. (1937), Symposium on the theory of the therapeutic results of psychoanalysis. *Internat. J. Psycho-Anal.*, 18:170–189.
Brenner, C. (1976), *Psychoanalytic Technique and Psychic Conflict.* New York: International Universities Press.
Freud, S. (1912), Recommendations to physicians practising psychoanalysis. *Standard Edition*, 12:109–120.
Friedman, L. (1969), The therapeutic alliance. *Internat. J. Psycho-Anal.*, 50:139–153.
Greenson, R. R. (1965), The working alliance and the transference neurosis. In *Explorations in Psychoanalysis.* New York: International Universities Press, 1978, pp. 199–224.
———— (1966), Contribution to discussion of *The Psychoanalytic Situation.* In *Psychoanalysis*

in the Americas, ed. R. E. Litman. New York: International Universities Press, pp. 131–132.

———— (1967), *The Technique and Practice of Psychoanalysis.* New York: International Universities Press.

Kanzer, M. (1975), The therapeutic and working alliances. *Internat. J. Psychoanal. Psychother.,* 4:48–68.

Lampl-de Groot, J. (1975), Vicissitudes of narcissism and problems of civilization. *The Psychoanalytic Study of the Child,* 30:663–681. New Haven: Yale University Press.

Modell, A. H. (1972), Review of *The Capacity for Emotional Growth* by E. R. Zetzel. *Psychoanal. Quart.,* 41:261–265.

Stone, L. (1961), *The Psychoanalytic Situation.* New York: International Universities Press.

Zetzel, E. R. (1956), Current concepts of transference. *Internat. J. Psycho-Anal.,* 37:369–378.

———— (1966), The analytic situation. In *Psychoanalysis in the Americas,* ed. R. E. Litman. New York: International Universities Press, pp. 86–106.

13. The Development of the Transference

Ida Macalpine

INTRODUCTION

Transference is an integral part of psychoanalysis. A vast, widely scattered literature exists on the subject. In most contributions on any psychoanalytic theme there is to be found, often tucked away from easy access, some reference to it. It forms of necessity the main topic of papers and treatises on psychoanalytic technique; but '. . . it is amazing how small a proportion of the very extensive psychoanalytic literature is devoted to psychoanalytic technique', states Fenichel *(1)*, 'and how much less to the theory of technique'. There is no single contribution which comprehends all the facts known and the various opinions. This is all the more remarkable as differing opinions are held about the mechanism of transference, and its mode of production seems particularly little understood. In the absence of a comprehensive critical evaluation, the student may well be bewildered at finding that most authors, before getting to their subject matter, deem it necessary to give their personal interpretations of what they mean by the 'transference' and 'transference neurosis'. This is well illustrated by Fenichel's book on the theory of the neuroses *(3)* which, containing more than one thousand six hundred and forty references, quotes only one reference in the section on Transference.

The lack of knowledge of the causation of transference appears largely to have gone unnoticed. It seems tacitly to be assumed that the subject is fully understood. Fenichel, for instance, writes *(3):* 'Freud was at first surprised when he met with the phenomenon of transference; today, Freud's discoveries make it easy to understand it theoretically. The analytic situation induces the development of derivatives of the repressed, and at the same time a resistance is operative against it . . . the patient misunderstands the present in terms of the past.' If one scrutinizes this frequently quoted reference, one realizes that it gives no theoretical explanation of the factors which produce

Reprinted by permission from the *Psychoanalytic Quarterly* 19(1950):501–39.

transference. However illuminating and pointed this and other similes may be, they are descriptive rather than explanatory.

The causes of the limited understanding of transference are historical, inherent in the subject matter, and psychological.

REASONS FOR THE LACK OF RESEARCH

Historical

As psychoanalysis developed, there was a natural striving to differentiate it from hypnosis, its precursor, similarities between the two tending to be overlooked. The mode of production and the emergence of the transference (positive, negative, and the transference neurosis) were considered an entirely new phenomenon peculiar to psychoanalysis, and altogether distinct from what occurred in hypnosis.

In this differentiation from hypnosis, psychoanalysis had to come to terms with the concept of 'suggestion'. Many psychoanalytic writers, and more particularly others, have complained about the inaccurate and inexact use of this term. The great impetus toward research into 'suggestion' came from the study of hypnosis. With the appearance (1886) of Bernheim's book *(4)*, hypnosis ceased to be considered a symptom of hysteria, the nucleus of hypnosis was established as the effect of suggestion, and it is Bernheim's merit that he showed that all people are subject to the influence of suggestion and that the hysteric differs chiefly in his abnormal susceptibility to it. This seemed to Freud a great advance in recognizing the importance of a mental mechanism in the production of disease. In the introduction he wrote (1888) to his translation into German of Bernheim's book *(5)*, which is of historical interest because it is believed to be Freud's first publication on a psychological subject, Freud stresses the great importance of Bernheim's '. . . insistence upon the fact that hypnosis and hypnotic suggestion can be applied, not only to hysterics and to seriously neuropathic patients, but also to the majority of healthy persons', and his belief that this 'is calculated to extend the interest of physicians in this therapeutic method far beyond the narrow circle of neuropathologists' *(6)*. The significance of suggestion was thus established, but its meaning had yet to be clarified. Freud tried to find a link between the physiological (somatic) and mental (psychological) phenomena in hypnosis: 'In my opinion', he stated, 'the shifting and ambiguous use of the word "suggestion" lends to this antithesis a deceptive sharpness which it does not in reality possess'. He then set out to give a definition of suggestion to embrace both its physiological and mental manifestations: 'It is worth while considering what it is we can legitimately call a "suggestion". No doubt some kind of mental influence is implied by the term; and I should like to put forward the view that what distinguishes a suggestion from other kinds of mental influence, such as a command or the giving of a piece of information or instruction, is that in the case of a suggestion an idea is aroused in another person's brain which is not examined in regard to its origin but is accepted just as though it had arisen spontaneously in that brain.' Freud did not succeed in giving the term a clear and unequivocal definition.

The physiological phenomena (vascular, muscular, etc.) had yet to be brought under the roof of suggestion, if hypnosis and hysteria were to be claimed for psychopathology. Physiological functions not subject to conscious control, and Freud's earlier definition of suggestion, did not cover them; hence, in this preanalytic paper, Freud widens the meaning of suggestion by introducing 'indirect suggestion.' He says, 'Indirect suggestions, in which a series of intermediate links out of the subject's own activity are inserted between the external stimulus and the result, are none the less mental processes; but they are no longer exposed to the full light of consciousness which falls upon direct suggestions'. It is important to note that the factor of an unconscious operation of suggestion is now introduced for the first time in Freud's writing. If, for example, it be suggested to a patient that he close his eyes, and if thereupon he fall asleep, he has added his own association (sleep follows closing of the eyes) to the initial stimulus. The patient is then said to be subject to 'indirect suggestion' because the suggestive stimulus opened the door for a chain of associations in the patient's mind; in other words, the patient reacts to the suggestive stimulus by a series of autosuggestions. Freud in this paper, and later, uses the 'indirect suggestion' as synonymous with 'autosuggestion'.

When suggestion was found by Bernheim to be the basis of hypnosis, it remained to be explained why most but not all persons could be hypnotized, or were susceptible to suggestion, and why some were more readily hypnotizable than others; thus, beside the activity of the hypnotist, a factor inherent in the patient was established and had to be examined. This factor was referred to as the patient's suggestibility. The nature of what went on in the patient's mind during hypnosis was soon made the subject of extensive investigations, and interest was progressively concentrated on the subjective psychological process. Ferenczi (7) showed that the hypnotist when giving a command is replacing the subject's parental imagos and, more important, is so accepted by the patient. Freud *(8)* concluded that hypnosis constitutes a mutual libidinal tie. He found that the mechanism by which the patient becomes suggestible is a splitting from the ego of the ego-ideal which is transferred to the suggester. As the ego-ideal normally has the function of testing reality,[1] this faculty is greatly diminished in hypnosis, and this accounts both for the patient's credulity and his further regression from reality toward the pleasure principle. According to Freud, the degree of a person's suggestibility depends on the degree of maturity. The less distinction between ego and ego-ideal, the more ready the identification with authority. Thus we find that in the understanding of hypnosis and suggestion the subject's suggestibility came to outweigh the suggester's activities. Ernest Jones *(12)* shows that there is no fundamental difference between autosuggestion and allosuggestion; both constitute libidinal regression to narcissism. Abraham *(13),* in his paper on Coué, shows that the subjects of this form of autosuggestion regressed to states of obsessional neurosis. McDougall *(14)* speaks of 'the subject's attitude of submissiveness as "suggestibility" '. As the common factor brought out by all these investigations is regression, it would seem justifiable to define suggestibility as adaptability by regression.

In the investigations of hypnosis, the stress has been placed at different times on extrinsic factors (the implanting of an idea or the hypnotist's activities); or on intrinsic factors (the patient's suggestibility). In fact, whereas the 'implantation' of a foreign idea, independent of any factors operative within the patient, was first considered to constitute the whole process of suggestion, the pendulum soon swung to the other extreme, and the endopsychic process (capacity to regress) was considered the essence of hypnosis. Through this historical development 'suggestion' and 'suggestibility' came to be confused, although it is quite clear that suggestibility distinctly implies a state or readiness as opposed to the actual process of suggestion. Unfortunately, however, these two terms have crept into psychoanalytic literature as having the same meaning. It is in part due to this fact that transference came to be considered a spontaneous manifestation to the neglect of precipitating factors. These ambiguities have never been overcome; moreover, they are to some extent responsible for the lack of understanding of the genesis and nature of transference.

To differentiate the new psychoanalytic technique from hypnosis there was a repudiation of suggestion in psychoanalysis. Later, however, this was questioned, and the term, suggestion, was reintroduced into psychoanalytic terminology. Freud *(15)* makes the arresting statements: '. . . and we have to admit that we have only abandoned hypnosis in our methods in order to discover suggestion again in the shape of transference'; and, in another paper *(21)*, 'Transference is equivalent to the force which is called "suggestion" '; still later *(23)*: 'It is quite true that psychoanalysis, like other psychotherapeutic methods, works *by means of suggestion,* the difference being, however, that it (transference or suggestion) is not the decisive factor'. While Freud equates here transference and suggestion, he says a little earlier in the same paper *(23)*: 'One easily recognizes in transference the same factor which the hypnotists have called *"suggestibility",* and which is the carrier of the hypnotic rapport'. In his Introductory Lectures *(18)* Freud also uses transference and suggestion interchangeably, but specifies the meaning of suggestion in psychoanalysis by stating that 'direct suggestion' was abandoned in psychoanalysis, and that it is used only to uncover instead of covering up. Ernest Jones *(25)* states that suggestion covers two processes: '. . . "verbal suggestion" and "affective suggestion", of which the latter is the more primary and is necessary for the action of the former. "Affective suggestion" is a rapport which depends on the transference *(Übertragung)* of certain positive affective processes in the unconscious region of the subject's mind. . . . suggestion plays a part in all methods of treatment of the psychoneuroses except the psychoanalytic one.' This new terminology does not seem clear. 'Affective suggestion' obviously represents 'suggestibility'. In the way it is expressed it plainly contradicts Freud's statement with regard to the role of 'suggestion' in psychoanalysis, although Freud and Jones were probably in full agreement about what they meant. But this confusing and haphazard use of terms could not but influence adversely the full understanding of analytic transference. One might even take it as proof that transference is not fully understood; if it were, it could be stated simply and clearly.

That Freud was dissatisfied about the definition of transference and suggestion is confirmed by his statement *(9)*: 'Having kept away from the riddle of suggestion for some thirty years, I find on approaching it again that there is no change in the situation. . . . The word is acquiring a more and more extended use, and a looser and looser meaning.' He introduces yet another differentiation of suggestion 'as used in psychoanalysis' from suggestion in all other psychotherapies. As used in psychoanalysis, argue Freud—and one is tempted to say by way of special pleading—suggestion is distinct from its use in other therapies through the fact that transference is continually ana-

lyzed in psychoanalysis and so resolved, implying that the effects of suggestion are thereby undone. This statement found its way into psychoanalytic
literature in many places, and gained acceptance as a standard valid argument: the factor of suggestion is held to be eliminated by the resolution of
the transference, and this is regarded as the essential difference between
psychoanalysis and all other psychotherapies. But it is dubiously scientific to
include in the definition of suggestion the subsequent relation between therapist and patient; neither is it scientifically precise to qualify 'suggestion' by
its function: whether the aim of suggestion be that of covering up or uncovering, it is either suggestion or it is not. Little methodological advantage
could be gained by using 'suggestion' to fit the occasion, and then to treat
the terms 'suggestion', 'suggestibility', and 'transference' as synonymous. It
is therefore not surprising that the understanding of analytic transference has
suffered from this persisting inexact and unscientific formulation.

One must agree with Dalbiez *(26)* when he says, 'The freudians' deplora-
ble habit (which they owe, indeed, to Freud himself) of identifying transference with suggestion has largely contributed to discrediting psychoanalytic
interpretations. The truth is that positive transference brings about the most
favorable conditions for the intervention of suggestion, but it is by no means
identical with it.' Dalbiez defines suggestion as '. . . unconscious and involuntary realization of the content of a representation'. This neatly condenses
the factors which Freud postulated, namely, autosuggestion, direct and indirect suggestion, and their unconscious operation.

To summarize this historical review, it may be stated that, despite ambiguities, it may be generally accepted that in the classical technique of psycho-
analysis, suggestion so defined is used only to induce the analysand to realize
that he can be helped and that he can remember.

The Subject Matter

An important factor responsible for the neglect of the theory of transference
was the early preoccupation of analysts with demonstrating the various mechanisms involved in transference. Interest in the genesis of transference was
sidetracked by focusing research on the manifestations of resistance and the
mechanisms of defense. These mechanisms were often given as explanations
of the phenomenon of transference, and their operation was taken to explain
its nature and occurrence.

Psychological (Countertransference)

The neglect of this subject may in part be the result of the personal anxieties of analysts. Edward Glover *(27)* comments on the absence of open discussion about psychoanalytic technique, and considers the possibility of subjective anxieties: '. . . this seems all the more likely in that so much technical discussion centers round the phenomena of transference and countertransference, both positive and negative'. There may in addition enter into it an unconscious endeavor to steer clear of any active 'interference' or, more exactly, to remove any suspicion of methods reminiscent of the hypnotist.

GENERAL SURVEY OF THE LITERATURE

A survey of the literature within the strict limits of the scope of this paper would simply summarize what has been said about the causation of psychoanalytic transference. But although this can be done easily, it is of doubtful value without a survey first of the literature about transference manifestations in general, and without a survey of what transference is held to be and to mean. It would then be obvious that many differences of opinion coexist and many differing interpretations have been given; but unfortunately, in the absence of a comprehensive critical survey of the subject, such a task is, in fact, impossible because there are no clear-cut definitions and many differences of opinion as to what transference is. This is in part attributable to the state of a growing science and to the fact that most authors approach the subject from one angle only.

To begin with, there is no consensus of opinion about the use of the term 'transference' which is referred to variously as 'the transference', 'a transference', 'transferences', 'transference state', and sometimes as 'analytical rapport'.

Does transference embrace the whole affective relationship between analyst and analysand, or the more restricted 'neurotic transference' manifestations? Freud used the term in both senses. To this fact Silverberg *(28)* recently drew attention, and argued that transference should be limited to 'irrational' manifestations, maintaining that if the analysand says 'good morning' to his analyst it is unreasonable to include such behavior under the term transference. The contrary view is also expressed: that transference, after the opening stage, is everywhere, and the analysand's every action can be given a transference interpretation *(30)*.

Can transference be adjusted to reality, or are transference and reality mutually exclusive, so that some action can only be either the one or the other; or can they coexist so that behavior in accord with reality can be given a transference meaning as in forced transference interpretations? Alexander *(31)* comes to the conclusion that they are '. . . truly mutually exclusive, just as the more general concept 'neurosis'' is quite incompatible with that of reality adjusted behavior'.

Freud *(34)* divided transference into positive and negative. Fenichel *(2)* queries this subdivision, arguing that, 'Transference forms in neurotics are mostly ambivalent, or positive and negative simultaneously'. Fenichel *(2)* states further that manifestations of transference ought to be valued by their 'resistance value', noting that '. . . positive transference, although acting as a welcome motive for overcoming resistances, must be looked upon as a resistance in so far as it is *transference*'. Ferenczi *(37)*, on the contrary, after stating that a violent positive transference, especially in the early stages of analysis, is often nothing but resistance, emphasizes that in other cases, and particularly in the later stages of analysis, it is essentially the vehicle by which unconscious strivings can reach the surface. Most often the inherent ambivalence of transference manifestations is stressed and looked upon as a typical exhibition of the neurotic personality.

The next query arises from one special aspect of transference: 'acting out' in analysis. Freud *(38)* introduced the term 'repetition compulsion' and he says: 'In the case of a patient in analysis . . . it is plain that the compulsion to repeat in analysis the occurrences of his infantile life disregards *in every way* the pleasure principle'. In a comprehensive critical survey of the subject, Kubie *(39)* comes to the conclusion that the whole conception of a compulsion to repeat for the sake of repetition is of questionable value as a scientific concept, and were better eliminated. He believes the conception of a 'repetition compulsion' involves the disputed death instinct, and that the term is used in psychoanalytic literature with such widely differing connotations that it has lost most, if not all, of its original meaning. Freud introduced the term for the one variety of transference reaction called acting out, but it is, in fact, applied to all transference manifestations. Anna Freud *(40)* defines transference as: '. . . all those impulses experienced by the patient in his relation with the analyst which are not newly created by the objective analytic situation but have their source in early . . . object relations and are now merely revived under the influence of the repetition compulsion'. Ought, then, the term 'repetition compulsion' be rejected or retained and, if retained, is it applicable to all transference reactions, or to acting out only?

This leads to the question of whether transference manifestations are essentially neurotic, as Freud *(22)* most often maintains: 'The striking peculiarity of neurotics to develop affectionate as well as hostile feelings toward their analyst is called "transference" '. Other authors, however, treat transference as an example of the mechanism of displacement, and hold it to be a 'normal' mechanism. Abraham *(42)* considers a capacity for transference identical with a capacity for adaptation which is 'sublimited sexual transference', and he believes that the sexual impulse in the neurotic is distinguishable from the normal only by its excessive strength. Glover *(44)* states: 'Accessibility to human influence depends on the patient's capacity to establish *transferences,* i.e., to repeat in current situations . . . attitudes developed in early family life'. Is transference, then, consequent to trauma, conflict, and repression, and so exclusively neurotic, or is it normal?

In answer to the question, is transference rational or irrational, Silverberg *(28)* maintains that transference should be defined as something having the two essential qualities: that it be 'irrational and disagreeable to the patient'. Fenichel *(2)* agrees that 'transference is bound up with the fact that a person does not react rationally to the influence of the outer world'. It is evident that no advantage or clarification of the term 'transference' has followed its assessment as 'rational' or otherwise. It is particularly unfortunate that the antithesis, 'rational' versus 'irrational', was introduced, as it was precisely psychoanalysis which demonstrated that rational behavior can be traced to 'irrational' roots. What is transferred: affects, emotions, ideas, conflicts, attitudes, experiences? Freud says only affects of love and hate are included; but Glover *(45)* finds that 'Up to that date [1937] discussion of transference was influenced for the most part by the understanding of one unconscious mechanism only, that of displacement', and he concludes 'that an adequate conception of transference must reflect *the totality* of the individual's development . . . he displaces onto the analyst, not merely affects and ideas but *all* he has ever learned or forgotten throughout his mental development.' Are these transferred to the person of the analyst, or also to the analytic situation; is extra-analytic behavior to be classed as transference?

Are positive and negative transferences felt by the analysand to be an 'intrusive foreign body', as Anna Freud states *(41)* in discussing the transfer-

ence of libidinal impulses, or are they agreeable to the analysand, a gratification so great that they serve as resistances? Alexander *(32)* concludes that
transference gratifications are the greatest source of unduly prolonging analysis; he reminds his readers that whereas Freud *(46)* initially had the greatest
difficulty in persuading his patients to continue analysis, he soon had equally
great difficulty in persuading them to give it up.

Freud *(36)* divides positive transference into sympathetic and positive
transference. The relation between the two is not clearly defined, and sympathetic transference is sometimes referred to as analytic rapport. Do the two
merge, or remain district; is sympathetic transference resolved with positive
and negative transference? Discussion of the importance of positive transference at the beginning of analysis and as carrier of the whole analysis has
lately been revived among child analysts *(49, 50)*. This has extended to the
question of whether or not a transference neurosis in children is desirable or
even possible. While this dispute touches on the fundaments of psychoanalytic theory, the definitions offered as a basis for the discussion are not very
precise.

The contradictions in the literature about transference could be multiplied,
but as exemplifying the conspicuous absence of a unified conception they
will suffice. Alexander *(33)* states: 'Although it is agreed that the central
dynamic problem in psychoanalytic therapy is the handling of transference,
there is a good deal of confusion as to what transference really means'. He
comes to the conclusion that the transference relationship becomes identical
with a transference neurosis, except that the transient neurotic transference
reactions are not usually dignified with the name of 'transference neurosis'.
He thus questions the need for the term transference neurosis altogether. As
to the transference neurosis itself, there is a similar haziness of the conception. Definitions usually begin with 'When symptoms loosen up . . .', or
'When the level of conflict is reached . . .', or 'When the neurotic conflict is
shifted to the analytic situation . . .', or 'When the productivity of illness
becomes centered round one place only, the relation to the analyst . . .'; yet,
strictly speaking, such pronouncements are descriptions, not definitions.
Freud's *(16)* definition of transference neurosis implicitly and explicitly refers
only to the neurotic person, so that one is left with the impression that only
neurotics form a transference neurosis. Sachs *(51)*, on the contrary, '. . .
found the difference between the analyses of training candidates and of
neurotic patients negligible'.

HISTORICAL SUMMARY OF THE LITERATURE

It may be held that many of the contradictions in the literature are largely semantic, that in enumerating them haphazardly, discrepancies are brought into false relief. A truer picture, it may be argued, would have been given if historical periods had been made the guiding principle. Developmental stages in psychoanalysis were of course reflected in current concepts of transference.

In the very first allusion (1895) to what later developed into the concept of transference *(70)*, Freud says that the patient made 'a false connection' to the person of the analyst, when an affect became conscious which related to memories which were still unconscious. This connection Freud thought to be due to 'the associative force prevailing in the conscious mind'. It is interesting to note that with this first observation Freud had already noted that the affect precedes the factual material emerging from repression. He adds that there is nothing disquieting in this because '. . . the patients gradually come to appreciate that in these transferences onto the person of the physician they are subject to a compulsion and a deception, which vanishes with the termination of analysis'.

In 1905 Freud stresses the sexual nature of these impulses which are felt toward the physician. 'What', he asks, 'are transferences? They are new editions or facsimiles of the tendencies and fantasies which are aroused and made conscious during the progress of the analysis . . .' *(71)*. Fantasies are now added to affects. 'If one goes into the theory of analytic technique', he continues, 'it becomes evident that transference is an inevitable necessity'. At this historic point Freud established the fundamental importance of transference in psychoanalysis with its specific technical meaning. The importance of this passage is confirmed by a footnote added in 1923. It is noteworthy that Freud mentions in this passage that transferred impulses are not only sympathetic or affectionate, but that they can also be hostile.

About 1906 transference was regarded as a displacement of affect. Analysis was largely interested in unearthing forgotten traumata and in searching for complexes. Much of the theory was still influenced by the cathartic method. Psychoanalysis was then, says Freud, '. . . above all an art of interpretation' *(69)*. Freud stated later that '. . . the next aim was to compel the patient to confirm the reconstruction through his own memory. In this endeavor the chief emphasis was on the resistances of the patient; the art now lay in unveiling these as soon as possible, in calling the patient's attention to them . . . and teaching him to abandon these resistances. It then became increasingly clear, however, that the bringing into consciousness of unconscious material was not fully attainable by this method either. The patient cannot recall all that lies repressed . . . and so gains no conviction that the reconstruction is correct. He is obliged, rather, to repeat as a current experience what is repressed instead of recollecting it as a part of the past.' The importance of resistance in the form of acting out is now introduced (repetition compulsion).

Beyond the Pleasure Principle (1920) was followed by Group Psychology and the Analysis of the Ego (1921) and The Ego and the Id (1923). The new concepts introduced were the superego, the more specific function of the ego, and the conception of the id as containing not only repressed material (formerly Ucs) but also as a reservoir of instincts. Resistance was extended to ego and superego and id resistance. This gave rise to some confusion, because it can be used as meaning the resistance of one psychic instance to analysis, or the resistance of one psychic instance, say the ego, to another psychic instance, say the id; but the term resistance has been used chiefly as resistance to the progress of analysis generally. The id was shown to offer no resistance, but to lead to acting out, which in turn, however, is a resistance to recollection. At times, the unconscious can only be recovered in action, and while it is therefore 'material' in the strict sense of the word, it is still resistance to verbalized recollection.

The mechanisms considered to be operative in transference were displacement, projection and introjection, identification, compulsion to repeat. The importance of 'working through' was stressed. In 1924 discussion took place about the relative values of intellectual insight versus affective re-experiencing as the essence of analytic experience, an issue of vital importance in interpreting the transference to the patient.

In the period following, this added knowledge was gradually integrated, but with overemphasis on some of the new aspects as they first arose. In the absence of a comprehensive critical survey of the subject, authors found it necessary to explain what they meant when they used the term 'transference'.

With this integration new factors of confusion arose. Viewed arbitrarily from, let us say 1946, the conception of transference has been influenced by (1), child analysis; (2), attempts at treating psychotics; (3), psychosomatic medicine; (4), the disproportion between the number of analysts and the growing number of patients seeking analysis, leading to attempts to shorten the process of analysis.

Direct interpretation of unconscious content is again being stressed by some analysts of children in such a way that the methods are reminiscent of the beginnings of psychoanalysis. But on closer examination, there seems to be a difference in principle: unconscious material which presents itself in play is given a direct transference meaning from the beginning. The therapist interprets forward, as it were. The interpretation is not from current material backward to Ucs content, but from the allegedly presented unconscious material to an alleged immediate transference significance. This, it should be noted, is a mental process of the therapist and not of the patient; hence in the strict scientific sense, it is a matter of countertransference rather than of transference. Something similar takes place in the classical technique when forced transference interpretations are given, the important difference being that these are used in the classical method only sparingly and never until the transference neurosis is well established, and analysis has become a compulsion. It is precisely at this theoretical point, in the writer's opinion, that the dispute is centered among child analysts about the possibility or existence of a transference neurosis among children.

In the treatment of psychotics the concept of transference is developing a new orientation. In some of these techniques the therapist interprets to himself the meaning of the psychotic fantasy and joins the patient in acting out. Strictly speaking, this is active countertransference.

In psychosomatic medicine, particularly in 'short therapy', transference is either disregarded or actively manipulated in a way which, from a theoretical point of view, amounts to an abandonment of Freud's 'spontaneous' manifestations.

All in all, changes in the concept of transference are not constructively progressive. Critical attention needs to be drawn to the fact that not only is there no consensus of opinion about the concept of transference, but there cannot be until transference is comprehensively studied as a dynamic process. The lack of precision is to some extent due to a disregard of its historical development. Nor can there be a consensus of opinion so long as the relation of transference manifestations to the three stages of analysis is neglected. It is to the detriment of scientific exactitude that divergent groups do not sharply define but rather gloss over fundamental differences. There is a tendency to claim orthodoxy, and to hide the deviations behind one tendentiously and arbitrarily selected quotation from Freud.

LITERATURE ON PRODUCTION OF TRANSFERENCE

In the face of such divergent opinions on the nature and manifestations of transference, one might well expect a multitude of hypotheses and opinions as to how these manifestations come about. But this is not the case. On the contrary, there is the nearest approach to full unanimity and accord throughout the psychoanalytic literature on this point. Transference manifestations are held to arise within the analysand spontaneously. 'This peculiarity of the transference is not, therefore', says Freud, 'to be placed to the account of psychoanalytic treatment, but is to be ascribed to the patient's neurosis itself' *(35)*. Elsewhere *(24)* he states: 'In every analytic treatment, the patient develops, without any activity on the part of the analyst, an intense affective relation to him. . . . It must not be assumed that analysis produces the transference. . . . The psychoanalytic treatment does not produce the transference, it only unmasks it.' Ferenczi, in discussing the positive and negative transference says: '. . . and it has particularly to be stressed that this process is the patient's own work and is hardly ever produced by the analyst' *(52)*. 'Analytical transference appears spontaneously; the analyst need only take care not to disturb this process' *(53)*. Rado states, 'The analyst did not deliberately set out to effect this new artificial formation [the transference neurosis]; he merely observed that such a process took place and forthwith made use of it for his own purposes' *(54)*. And Freud further states: 'The fact of the transference appearing, although neither desired nor induced by either physician or patient, in every neurotic who comes under treatment . . . has always seemed to me . . . proof that the source of the propelling forces of neurosis lies in the sexual life' *(57)*.

There is, however, a reference by Freud from which one has to infer that he had in mind some other factor in the genesis of transference apart from spontaneity—in fact, some outside influence: the analyst 'must recognize that the patient's falling in love is induced by the analytic situation . . .' *(58)*. 'He [the analyst] has evoked this love by undertaking analytic treatment in order to cure the neurosis; for him, it is an unavoidable consequence of a medical situation . . .' *(59)*. Freud did not amplify or specify what importance he attached to this casual remark.

Anna Freud *(48)* states that the child analyst has to woo the little patient to gain its love and affection before analysis can proceed, and she says, parenthetically, that something similar takes place in the analysis of adults.

Another reference to the effect that transference phenomena are not completely spontaneous is found in a statement by Glover *(60)*, summarizing the effects of inexact interpretation. He says that the artificial phobic and hysterical formations resulting from incomplete or inexact interpretations are not an entirely new conception. Hypnotic manifestations had long been considered 'an induced hysteria' and Abraham considered that states of autosuggestion were induced obsessional systems. He proceeds, '. . . and of course the induction or development of a transference neurosis during analysis is regarded as an integral part of the process'. One is entitled from the context to assume that Glover commits himself to the view that some outside factors are operative which induce the transference neurosis. But it is hardly a coincidence that it is no more than a hint.

The impression gained from the literature on the whole is that the spontaneity of transference is considered established and generally accepted; in fact, this opinion seems jealously guarded for reasons referred to.

EXPOSITION OF PROBLEM

Psychoanalysis developed from hypnosis. A study of the older psychotherapeutic methods, therefore, may still yield data which are applicable to the understanding of psychoanalysis: 'One cannot overestimate the significance of hypnotism in the development of psychoanalysis. Theoretically and therapeutically, psychoanalysis is the trustee of hypnotism' *(61)*. It is in comparing hypnotic and analytic transference that the writer believes the clue to the phenomenon and the production of transference may be found. It was only after hypnosis had been practiced empirically for a long time that its mechanism was given explanations by Bernheim, Freud, and Ferenczi. Freud demonstrated that the hypnotist suddenly assumed a role of authority which instantly transformed the relationship for the patient (by way of traumata) into a parent-child relationship. Rado *(55)*, investigating hypnosis, came to the conclusion that '. . . the hypnotist is promoted from being an object of the ego to the position of a "parasitic superego" '. Freud *(10)* stated, 'No one can doubt that the hypnotist has stepped into the place of the ego-ideal'. Later he says that '. . . the hypnotic relation is the devotion of someone in love to an unlimited degree but with sexual satisfaction excluded'*(11)*. In other places Freud stressed repeatedly and with great emphasis that in hypnosis factors of a 'coarsely sexual nature' were at work, and that the quantities of libido mobilized were focused on the hypnotist.

Psychoanalysis like hypnosis began empirically. One may speculate that analytic transference is a derivative of hypnosis, motivated by instinctual (libidinal) drives and, *mutatis mutandis,* produced in a way comparable to the hypnotic trance.

When one compares hypnosis and transference it appears that hypnotic 'rapport' contains the elements of transference condensed or superimposed. If what makes the patient go to the hypnotist is called sympathetic transference, hypnosis can be said to embrace positive transference and the transference neurosis,[2] and when the hypnotic 'rapport' is broken, the manifestations of negative transference. The analogy of course ends when transference is not resolved in hypnosis as it is in analysis, but is allowed to persist. To look upon it from another angle, analytic transference manifestations are a slow motion picture of hypnotic transference manifestions; they take some time to develop, unfold slowly and gradually, and not all at once as in hypnosis. If the hypnotist becomes the patient's 'parasitic superego', similarly, the modification of the analysand's superego has for some time been considered a standard feature of psychoanalysis.

Strachey *(63)* sees in the analyst 'an auxiliary superego'. Discussing this and examining projection and introjection of archaic superego formations to the analyst, he says *(62):* the analyst '. . . hopes, in short, that he himself will be introjected by the patient as a superego, introjected, however, not at a single gulp and as an archaic object, whether good or bad, but little by little, and as a real person'. Another possible similarity between the modes of action of hypnosis and analytic transference is to be found in the state of hysterical dissociation in hypnosis; in psychoanalysis a splitting of the ego into an experiencing and an observing part (which follows the projection of the superego to the analyst) also takes place. Sterba *(64, 65),* stressing the usefulness of interpretation of transference resistances, shows that this takes place through a kind of dissociation of the ego at the precise moment when these transferences are interpreted. Both in hypnosis and psychoanalysis libido is mobilized and concentrated in the hypnotic and analytic situations, in hypnosis again condensed in one short experience, while in psychoanalysis a constant flow of libido in the analytic situation is aimed at. Ferenczi's 'active therapy' was intended to increase or keep steady this libidinal flow. Freud first encountered positive transference (love), and only later discovered the negative transference. This sequence is the rule in analysis, and in this there is another analogy to hypnosis. Finally, it is generally recognized that the same type of patient responds to hypnosis as to psychoanalysis; in fact, the hypnotizability of hysterics gave Freud the impetus to develop the psychoanalytic technique, and hysterics are still the paradigm for classical psychoanalytic technique.

It is comparatively easy today to get a bird's-eye view of the development of analytic transference from hypnotic reactions, and make a comparison between the two. Freud, who had to find his way gradually toward the creation of a new technique, was completely taken by surprise when he first encountered transference in his new technique. He stressed repeatedly and emphatically that these demonstrations of love and hate emanate from the patient unaided, that they are part and parcel of the 'neurotic', and that they have to be considered a 'new edition' of the patient's neurosis. He maintained that these manifestations appear without the analyst's endeavor, indeed, in spite of him (as they represent resistances), and that nothing will prevent their occurrence. Freud's view is still undisputed in psychoanalytic literature; thus arose the conception that the analyst did nothing to evoke these reactions, in marked contradistinction to the hypnotist's direct activities; the analyst offered himself tacitly as a superego in contrast to the noisy machinations of the hypnotist.

Transference was, in the early days of psychoanalysis, believed to be a characteristic and pathognomonic sign of hysteria. This was a heritage from hypnosis. Later, these same manifestations were found in other neurotic conditions, in the psychoneuroses, or the transference neuroses. When in the course of time psychoanalysis was applied to an ever-widening circle of cases, it was found that students in psychoanalytic training, who did not openly fall into any of these categories, formed transferences in exactly the same way. This was explained by the fact that between 'normal' and 'neurotic' there is a gradual transition, that in point of fact we are all potentially neurotic. In this way, historically, the onus of responsibility for the appearance of transference was shifted imperceptibly from the hysteric to the psychoneurotic, and then to the normal personality. When this stage was reached, transference was held to be one of the many ways in which the universal mental mechanism of displacement was at work. The capacity to 'transfer' or 'displace' was demonstrated to operate in everybody to a greater or lesser degree; its use came to be looked upon as a normal, in fact, an indispensable mechanism. The significance of this shift of emphasis from a hysterical trait to a universal mechanism as the source of transference has, however, not received due attention. It has not aroused much comment nor an attempt to revise the fundamental principles underlying psychoanalytic procedure and understanding.

Transference is still held to arise spontaneously from within the analysand, just as when psychoanalytic experience embraced only hysterics. It is generally taught that the duty of the analyst is, at best, to allow sufficient time for transference to develop, and not to disturb this 'natural' process by early interpretation *(47)*. This role of the analyst is well illustrated in the similes of the analyst as 'catalyst' (Ferenczi), or as a 'mirror' (Fenichel).

DISCUSSION

If transference is an example of a universal mental mechanism (displacement), or if, in Abraham's sense, it is equated with a capacity for adaptation of which everybody is capable and which everybody employs at times in varying degrees, why does it invariably occur with such great intensity in every analysis? The answer to this question appears to be that transference is induced from without in a manner comparable to the production of hypnosis. The analysand brings, in varying degrees, an inherent capacity, a readiness to form transferences, and this readiness is met by something which converts it into an actuality. In hypnosis the patient's inherent capacity to be hypnotized is induced by the command of the hypnotist, and the patient submits instantly. In psychoanalysis it is neither achieved in one session nor is it a matter of obeying. Psychoanalytic technique creates an infantile setting, of which the 'neutrality' of the analyst is but one feature among others. To this infantile setting the analysand—if he is analyzable—has to adapt, albeit by regression. In their aggregate, these factors, which go to constitute this infantile setting, amount to a reduction of the analysand's object world and denial of object relations in the analytic room. To this deprivation of object relation he responds by curtailing conscious ego functions and giving himself over to the pleasure principle; and following his free associations, he is thereby sent along the trek into infantile reactions and attitudes.

Before discussing in detail the factors which constitute this infantile analytic setting to which the analysand is exposed, it is necessary to appreciate the fact that it is common in psychoanalytic literature to find the analytic situation referred to as one to which the analysand reacts as if it were an infantile one. But it is generally understood that the analysand is alone responsible for this attitude. As an explanation of why he should regard it always as an infantile situation, one mostly finds the explanation that the security, the absence of adverse criticism, the encouragement derived from the analyst's neutrality, the allaying of fears and anxieties, create an atmosphere which is conducive to regression. Yet it is well established in the literature that it is far from being the rule that the analytic couch allays anxieties, nor is the analytic situation always felt as a place of security: the projection of a more or less severe superego onto the analyst is not conducive to allaying fears. Many patients first react with increased anxieties, and analysis is frequently felt by the analysand as fraught with danger both from within and without. Many patients from the start have mutilation and castration anxieties, and at times analysis is equated in the analysand's mind with a sexual attack. The analyst's task is to overcome these resistances, but the analytic situation per se does not bring it about. In point of fact, the security of analysis as an explanation of the regression is paradoxical: as in life, security makes for stability, whereas stress, frustration, and insecurity initiate regressions. This trend of thought does not run counter to accepted and current psychoanalytic teaching; it is rather an exposition of Freud's established principles about the conception of neurosis. The self-contradictory statement, that the security of analysis induces the analysand to regress, is carried uncritically from one psychoanalytic publication to another.

The factors which constitute this infantile setting are manifold. They have been described singly by various authors at various times. It is not pretended that this thesis has anything new to add to them except in so far as the aggregate has never been described as amounting to a decisive outside influence on the patient. These factors are given here in outline, this description attempting only to establish the features of the standard psychoanalytic technique:

1. *Curtailment of object world.* External stimuli are reduced to a minimum (Freud at first asked his patients even to keep their eyes shut). Relaxation on the couch has also to be valued as a reduction of inner stimuli, and as an elimination of any gratification from looking or being looked at. The position on the couch approximates the infantile posture.
2. *The constancy of environment,* which stimulates fantasy.
3. *The fixed routine* of the analytic 'ceremonial'; the 'discipline' to which the analysand has to conform and which is reminiscent of a strict infantile routine.
4. The single factor of *not receiving a reply* from the analyst is likely to be felt by the analysand as a repetition of infantile situations. The analysand —uninitiated in the technique—will not only expect answers to his

questions but he will expect conversation, help, encouragement, and criticism.

5. The *timelessness* of the unconscious.[3]
6. *Interpretations* on an infantile level stimulate infantile behavior.
7. *Ego function* is reduced to a state intermediate between sleeping and waking.
8. *Diminished personal responsibility* in analytic sessions.
9. The analysand will approach the analyst in the first place much in the same way as the patient with an organic disease consults his physician; this relationship in itself contains a strong *element of magic (67)*, a strong infantile element.
10. *Free association,* liberating unconscious fantasy from conscious control.
11. *Authority of the analyst* (parent): this projection is a loss, or severe restriction of object relations to the analyst, and the analysand is thus forced to fall back on fantasy.
12. In this setting, and having *the full sympathetic attention of another being,* the analysand will be led to expect, which according to the reality principle he is entitled to do, that he is dependent on and loved by the analyst. Disillusionment is quickly followed by regression.
13. The analysand at first gains an illusion of complete freedom; that he will be unable to select or guide his thoughts at will is one facet of infantile frustration.
14. *Frustration of every gratification* repeatedly mobilizes libido and initiates further regressions to deeper levels. The continual denial of all gratification and object relations mobilizes libido for the recovery of memories, but its significance lies also in the fact that frustration as such is a repetition of infantile situations, and most likely the most important single factor. It would be true to say that we grow up by frustration.
15. Under these influences, the analysand becomes more and more divorced from the reality principle, and falls under the sway of the pleasure principle.

These features illustrate sufficiently that the analysand is exposed to an infantile setting in which he is led to believe that he has perfect freedom, that he is loved, and that he will be helped in a way he expects. The immutability of a constant passive environment forces him to adapt, i.e., to regress to infantile levels. The reality value to the analytic session lies precisely in its unchanging unreality, and in its unyielding passivity lies the 'activity', the influence which the analytic atmosphere exerts. With this unexpected environment, the patient—if he has any adaptability—has to come to terms, and he can do so only by regression. Frustration of all gratification pervades the analytic work. Freud *(68)* says: 'As far as his relations with the physician are concerned, the patient must have unfulfilled wishes in abundance. It is expedient to deny him precisely those satisfactions which he desires most intensely and expresses most importunately.' This is a description of the denial of object relation in the analytic room. The present thesis stresses the significance not only of the loss of object relation, but, as a factor of at least equal importance, the loss of object world in the analytic room, the various factors of which are set out above.

It is evident that all these factors working together constitute a definite environmental and emotional influence on the analysand. He is subjected to a rigid environment, not by any direct activity of the analyst, but by the analytic technique. This conception is far removed from the current teaching of complete passivity on the part of the analyst. One may legitimately go one step further and call to mind what Freud *(20)* said about the etiology of the neuroses: '. . . people fall ill of a neurosis when the possibility of satisfaction for their libido is denied them — they fall ill in consequence of a ''frustration'' — and that their symptoms are actually substitutes for the missing satisfaction'.

Regression in the analysand is initiated and kept up by this selfsame mechanism and if, in actual life, a person falls ill of a neurosis because 'reality frustrates all gratification', the analysand likewise responds to the frustrating infantile setting by regressing and by developing a transference neurosis. In hypnosis the patient is suddenly confronted with a parent figure to which he instantly submits. Psychoanalysis places and keeps the analysand in an infantile setting, both environmental and emotional, and the analysand adapts to it gradually by regression.

The same may be said to be true of all psychotherapy; yet it appears peculiar to psychoanalysis that such an infantile setting is systematically created and its influence exerted on the analysand throughout the treatment. Unlike any other therapist, the analyst remains outside the play which the analysand is enacting; he watches and observes the analysand's reactions and attitudes in isolation. To have created such an instrument of investigation may well be looked upon as the most important stroke of Freud's genius.

It can no longer be maintained that the analysand's reactions in analysis occur spontaneously. His behavior is a response to the rigid infantile setting to which he is exposed. This poses many problems for further investigation. One of these is, how does it react on the patient? He must know it, consciously or unconsciously. It would be interesting to follow up whether perhaps the frequent feeling of being in danger, of losing something, of being coerced, or of being attacked, is a feeling provoked in the analysand in response to the emotional and environmental pressure exerted on him. It would be feasible to assume that this creates a negative transference, and as positive transference must exist as well (otherwise treatment would be discontinued), a subsequent state of ambivalence must ensue. Here one might look for an explanation why ambivalent attitudes are prevalent in analysis. These are generally looked upon as spontaneous manifestations of the analysand's neurosis. Following the argument of this thesis, this double attitude of the analysand, the positive feelings toward the analyst and analysis, and a negative response to the pressure exerted on him by continual frustration and loss of object world and object relation, could be looked upon as the normal sequitur of analytic technique. It would not constitute ambivalence in its strict sense, because the patient is reacting to two different objects simultaneously and has not as in true ambivalence two attitudes to one and the same object. The common appearance of this pseudo ambivalence can then no longer be adduced as evidence of the existence or part of a preanalytic neurosis.

The patient comes to analysis with the hope and expectation of being helped. He thus expects gratification of some kind, but none of his expectations are fulfilled. He gives confidence and gets none in return; he works hard and expects praise in vain. He confesses his sins without absolution given or punishment proffered.He expects analysis to become a partnership, but he is left alone. He projects onto the analyst his superego and expects from him guidance and control of his instinctual drives in exchange, but he finds this hope, too, is illusory and that he himself has to learn to exercise these powers. It is quite true, assessing the process as a whole, that the analysand is misled and hoodwinked as analysis proceeds. The only safeguard he is given against rebelling and discontinuing treatment is the absolute certainty and continual proof that this procedure, with all the pressure and frustration it imposes, is necessary for his own good, and that it is an objective method with the sole aim of benefiting him and for no other purpose than his own. In particular, the disinterestedness of the analyst must assure the patient that no subjective factors enter into it. In this light, the moral integrity of the analyst, so often stressed, becomes a safeguard for the patient to proceed with analysis; it is a technical device and not a moral precept.

A word might be added about the driving force of analysis in the light of this thesis. The libido necessary for continual regression and memory work is looked upon by Freud *(19)* as being derived from the relinquished symptoms. He says that the therapeutic task has two phases: 'In the first, libido is forced away from the symptoms into the transference and there concentrated; and in the second phase the battle rages round this new object and the libido is again disengaged from the transference object'. As so often in Freud's statements, this description applies to clinical neuroses; but psychoanalysis takes the same course in nonneurotics. The main driving force may be considered to be derived in every analysis from such libido as is continually freed by the denial of object world and by the frustration of libidinal impulses.

CONCLUSIONS

If the conception be accepted that analytic transference is actively induced in a 'transference-ready' analysand by exposing him to an infantile setting to which he has gradually to adapt by regression, certain conclusions follow.

Stages in Analysis

Analysis can then be divided into stages, the first stage being the initial period in which the analysand gradually adapts to an infantile setting. Regressive, infantile reactions and attitudes manifest themselves with gathering momentum during what might be described as the induction of the transference neurosis. This stage corresponds to what Glover *(29)* has called the stage of 'floating transferences'. In the second stage his regression is well established and the analysand represents the infant at various stages of development with such intensity that all his actions—in and out of analysis —are imbued with reactivated infantile reactions, consciously or unconsciously. During this stage, under constant pressure of analytic frustration, he withdraws progressively to earlier, 'safer' infantile patterns of behavior, and the level of his conflict is sooner or later reached. Reaching the level of his conflict is not, however, the touchstone of the existence of a transference neurosis. Further, the analysand transfers not only onto the analyst, but onto the situation as a whole; and he transfers not only affects, although these may be the most conspicuous, but in fact his whole mental development. This conception makes it easier to understand with what alacrity analysands fasten their love and hate drives onto the analyst regardless of sex and irrespective of suitability as an object.

The transference neurosis may be defined as the stage in analysis when the analysand has so far adapted to the infantile analytic setting—the main features of which are the denial of object relations and continual libidinal frustration—that his regressive trend is well established, and the various developmental levels reached, relived, and worked through.

A third, or terminal, stage represents the gradual retracing of the way back into adulthood toward newly won independence, freed from an archaic super-ego and weaned from the analytic superego. However great the distance from maturity back into childhood at the commencement of analysis, the duration of the first and second stages of analysis is as long and takes as much time as the return journey back into maturity and independence. Only part of this way back from infantile levels to maturity falls within the time limit of analysis in its third stage; the rest and the full adaptation to adulthood are most often completed by the analysand after termination of analysis. In this last postanalytic stage great improvements often occur. In this conception the answer may be found to the often discussed and not fully explained problem of improvements after termination of analysis.

It is superfluous to point out that these stages are theoretical, as in reality they never occur neatly separated but always overlap.

Resistance

The initial aim of analysis is to induce a regression; whatever impedes it is a resistance. If instead of such a movement there occurs a standstill (whether in the form of acting out or of direct transference gratifications), or if the movement instead of being regressive turns in the direction of apparent maturity (flight into health), one can speak of a resistance. Theoretically, acting out is a formidable variety of resistance because the analysand mistakes the unreality of the analytic relationship for reality and attempts to establish reality relations with the analyst. In this attitude he stultifies the analytic procedure for the time being, as he throws the motor force of analysis—the denial of all object relations in the analytic room and of the gratification of libido derived therefrom—out of action. In cases in which early 'transference successes' are won and the patient quickly relinquishes his symptoms, the analysis is in danger of terminating at this point. The mechanism of these transference successes is in a way the counterpart of acting out. The patient regresses rapidly to the level of childhood, and forms an unconscious fantasy of a mutual child-parent relationship. He mistakes such reality and object relation as exists as a basis in the analytic relationship wholly for an infantile one and unconsciously obeys (spites or obliges) the parent imago. What happens in these cases is in fact that the analysand has in fantasy formed a mutual hypnotic transference relation with the analyst; analytic interpretation was either not quick enough to prevent it, or the analysand's transference readiness was too strong. He could not be made to adapt gradually to the infantile setting. In other words, the analysand faced with the stimulus of an infantile situation proceeds by way of autosuggestion (or indirect suggestion) to rid himself of a symptom.

Transference has resistance value in so far as it impedes the recovery of memories and so stops the regressive orientation. Per se it is the only possible vehicle for unconscious content to come to consciousness. Transference should therefore not be indiscriminately equated with resistance as Fenichel did.

Countertransference

The analyst himself is also subjected to the infantile setting of which he is a part. In fact, the infantile setting to which he is exposed contains one more important infantile factor, the regressing analysand. The analyst's ego is also split into an observing and experiencing one. The analyst has had his own thorough analysis and knows what to expect, and furthermore, unlike the analysand, is in an authoritative position. Whereas it is the analysand's task to adapt actively to the infantile setting by regression, it is incumbent on the analyst to remain resistant to such adaptation. While the analysand has to experience the past and observe the present, the analyst has to experience the present and observe the past; he must resist any regressive trend within himself. If he fall victim to his own technique, and experience the past instead of observing it, he is subject to counterresistance. The phenomenon of countertransference may be best described by paraphrasing Fenichel's simile: the analyst misunderstands the past in terms of the present.

Accessibility to Psychoanalytic Treatment

If the thesis of this paper prove correct, a clue could be found to the accessibility of various types of patients to psychoanalytic treatment. To respond to the classical analytic technique, analysands must have some object relations intact, and must have at their disposal enough adaptability to meet the infantile analytic setting by further regression. For both hypnosis and psychoanalysis there is a sliding scale from the hysteric to the schizophrenic. Abraham (43) said: 'The negativism of dementia præcox is the most complete antithesis of transference. In contrast to hysteria these patients are only to a very slight degree accessible to hypnosis. In attempting to psychoanalyze them we notice the absence of transference again.' The high degree of suggestibility, i.e., the capacity to form transferences, is well known as a leading feature of hysteria. Hysteria, and the whole group belonging to the transference neuroses are distinguished by an impaired and immature adjustment to reality; their reactions are intermingled with infantile attitudes and mechanisms. Hence under pressure from the infantile analytic milieu they respond freely and relatively quickly with increased infantile behavior to the loss of object world and object relations. The neurotic character responds less easily and less freely because its object relations are relatively firmly established (for instance, well-functioning sublimations), and hence are harder to resolve analytically. The denial of object relations and libidinal gratification in analysis is frequently parried by reinforced sublimations; but before analysis can proceed this 'sublimated object relationship' must first be reversed.

Psychotics are refractory to the classical technique, according to this thesis, because their object relations are deficient and slender, and nothing therefore remains of which the analytic pressure of the classical technique could deprive these patients; or their object relations are too slight for their denial to make any difference. Freud (17) says: '. . . on the basis of our clinical observations of these patients we stated that they must have abandoned the investment of objects with libido, and transformed the object libido into ego libido'. As the core of the classical technique is the denial of object relations of the patient through his exposure to an infantile milieu, the narcissistic regressives must consequently prove inaccessible to the classical approach. This does not, of course, exclude them from analytical methods which deviate from the classical form. The main change of approach for them will have to be an adjustment of the technique in the early stages of analytic treatment. This aspect has a bearing also on the problems of transference and particularly on the transference neurosis that are in dispute among child analysts.

Definition of Analytic Transference

If a person with a certain degree of inherent suggestibility is subjected to a suggestive stimulus and reacts to it, he can be said to be under the influence of suggestion. To arrive at a definition of analytic transference, it is necessary first to introduce an analogous term for suggestibility in hypnosis and speak of a person's inherent capacity or readiness to form transferences. This readiness is precisely the same factor and may be defined in the same way as suggestibility, namely, a capacity to adapt by regression. Whereas in hypnosis the precipitating factor is the suggestive stimulus, followed by suggestion, in psychoanalysis the person's adaptability by regression is met by the outside stimulus (or precipitating factor) of the infantile analytic setting. In psychoanalysis it is not followed by suggestion from the analyst, but by continued pressure to further regression through the exposure to the infantile analytic setting. If the person reacts to it he will form a transference relationship, i.e., he will regress and form relations to early imagos. Analytic transference may thus be defined as a person's gradual adaptation by regression to the infantile analytic setting.

Spontaneity of Transference

Transference cannot be regarded as a spontaneous neurotic reaction. It can be said to be the resultant of two sets of forces: the analysand's inherent readiness for transference, and the external stimulus of the infantile setting. There are, then, to be distinguished in the mechanism of analytic transference intrinsic and extrinsic factors: the response to the analytic situation will vary in intensity with different types of analysands. The capacity to form a transference neurosis was found to be inherent—varying only in quantity—in all analysands who could be anlayzed at all, whether they were neurotic or not. To account for this, the term 'neurotic' was extended until it lost most of its meaning because the precipitating factor, the infantile setting, was not perceived.

It is interesting historically to observe that in the heyday of hypnosis, hypnotizability was considered to be a characteristic trait of hysteria; hypnosis in fact was considered an 'artificial hysteria' (Charcot). Precisely the same situation has arisen in psychoanalysis with respect to the transference neurosis. When, to his amazement, Freud first encountered transference in his new technique, which he applied to neurotic patients only, he attributed 'this strange phenomenon of transference' to the patient's neurosis, and he saw in it 'a characteristic peculiar to neurotics'. When he coined for the acute manifestations of transference the designation 'transference neurosis', it was explicitly affirmed that these manifestations were a 'new edition' of an old neurosis revealing itself within the framework of psychoanalytic treatment. Once the concept of transference neurosis had become a tenet in psychoanalytic teaching, the acute manifestations were without further questioning accepted as inseparably linked with the neurotic.

Thus historically the linkage of transference with neurosis is an exact replica of the early linkage of hypnosis with the hysteric. Freud, in his preanalytic period, hailed with enthusiasm Bernheim's demonstration that most people were hypnotizable and that hypnosis was no longer to be regarded as inseparable from hysteria. In the introduction to Bernheim's book, Freud *(6)* said: 'The achievement of Bernheim . . . consists precisely in having stripped the manifestations of hypnotism of their strangeness by linking them up with familiar phenomena of normal psychological life and of sleep'. In the face of this statement, it is extraordinary that psychoanalysis has never officially divorced transference from clinical neurosis.

Resolution of Transference

The resolution of transference has been considered the safeguard against and proof of the fact that suggestion plays no part in psychoanalysis. The validity of this argument was questioned earlier on the grounds that the meaning and definition of 'suggestion' is in itself vague and shifting and used with varying connotations. Additional weight is given to this caution when it is realized that the resolution itself of psychoanalytic transference is not understood in all its aspects. True enough, its manifestations are continually analyzed in psychoanalysis and an attempt is made to reduce them, but its ultimate resolution or even its ultimate fate is not clearly understood. Whenever it is finally resolved, it is during an ill-defined period after termination of analysis. By this feature alone it escapes strict scientific observation. It might even be argued that analytic transference in some of its aspects must in the last resort resolve itself. In hypnosis, of course, no attempt is ever made to resolve the transference; but this should not be thought of as if it were bound to persist. More correctly it is left to look after itself. This trend of thought is followed here not in any way to distract from the essential difference in the resolution of hypnotic and analytic transferences respectively, but in order to emphasize that from the standpoint of theory the conception is not exact enough and hence likely to create confusion of fundamental issues instead of clarifying them. It seems important to stress this point as, by sheer weight of habit and repetition, ambiguous conceptions tend to assume the character and dignity of clear scientific concepts.

There is, however, another difference between hypnotic and analytic transference which is free from all ambiguity, and which may well be considered of more cardinal significance in demarcating psychoanalysis from all other psychotherapies. The hypothesis has been presented here that both hypnosis and psychoanalysis exploit infantile situations which they both create. But in hypnosis the transference is really and truly a mutual relationship existing between the hypnotist and the hypnotized. The hypnotic subject certainly transfers, but he is also transferred to. One is tempted to say that countertransference is obligatory in and an essential part of hypnosis (and for that matter of all psychotherapies in which the patient is helped, encouraged, advised or criticized). This interaction between hypnotist and hypnotized made Freud describe hypnosis as a 'group formation of two'. The patient is subjected to direct suggestion against the symptom. In psychoanalytic therapy alone the analysand is not transferred to. The analyst has to resist all temptation to regress, he remains neutral, aloof, a spectator, and he is never a coactor. The analysand is induced to regress and to 'transfer' alone in response to the infantile analytic setting. The analytic transference relationship ought, strictly speaking, not to be referred to as a relationship between analysand and analyst, but more precisely as the analysand's relation to his analyst. Analysis keeps the analysand in isolation. By its essential nature analysis, in contradistinction to hypnosis, is not a group formation of two. It is thereby not denied that analysis is a 'team work'; in so far as it is, an 'objective' relation exists between the analyst and the analysand. Because the analyst remains outside the regressive movement, because it is his duty to prove resistant to countertransference by virtue of his own analysis, suggestion can inherently play no part in the classical procedure of psychoanalytic technique.

It is of historical interest to look back upon the development of psychoanalysis and find that, although the theoretical basis as shown in this paper has never been advanced, the subject of countertransference was unconsciously felt to be the most vulnerable point and the most significant issue in psychoanalysis. The literature regarding the 'handling of transference' easily verifies this statement. Through this postulated immunity to regression the concept of the analyst's passivity rightly arose, but was wrongly allowed to be extended to a concept of passivity governing the whole of psychoanalytic technique.

To make transference and its development the essential difference between psychoanalysis and all other psychotherapies, psychoanalytic technique may be defined as the only psychotherapeutic method in which a one-sided, infantile regression—analytic transference—is induced in a patient (analysand), analyzed, worked through, and finally resolved.

SUMMARY

1. Attention is drawn to the absence of a clear understanding of the fundamental concept of analytic transference, and the reasons for this deficiency are outlined. 2. The discrepancies and uncertainties about the term are demonstrated. 3. Despite fundamental differences of opinion about the nature of transference there is a surprising unanimity and full accord about the causation of transference manifestations. These are held to arise spontaneously from within the analysand (the neurotic). 4. A hypothesis is presented disputing the spontaneous emergence of transference. 5. From a close analogy drawn between hypnotic and analytic transferences it is inferred that the analogy extends to the production of these phenomena: that analytic transference is induced in a 'transference-ready' analysand actively, and from the analytic environment. 6. The analysand is exposed to a rigid infantile setting to which he has gradually to adapt by regression. 7. The factors which constitute this infantile setting are described and discussed; the problems arising out of this 'activity' and their influence on the patient are approached. 8. Conclusions are drawn from this conception regarding states in analysis, and a definition of 'transference neurosis' is advanced. Resistance, countertransference, and accessibility to psychoanalytic treatment are discussed. Psychoanalytic transference is defined and its resolution critically surveyed.

NOTES

1. Freud later contradicted this statement in *The Ego and the Id,* Chapter III, p. 34, fn.
2. Rado *(56)* says: 'It would not constitute, one imagines, a departure from customary analytical modes of expression to suggest that this transference of libido from the symptoms to the hypnotic experience represents the formation of a hypnotic transference neurosis'.
3. Nunberg *(66)* says: 'The patient's sense of time seems to be put out of action, the past becomes the present and the present becomes the past'.

REFERENCES

1. Fenichel, Otto: *Problems of Psychoanalytic Technique.* New York: The Psychoanalytic Quarterly, Inc., 1941, p. 98.
2. ———: *Ibid.,* pp. 27, 28.
3. ———: *The Psychoanalytic Theory of Neurosis.* New York: W. W. Norton & Co., 1945, p. 29.
4. Bernheim, H.: *De la suggestion et de ses applications à la thérapeutique.* Paris: Octave Doin, 1886.
5. Freud: *Hypnotism and Suggestion.* Int. J. Psa., XXVII, 1946, pp. 59–64.
6. ———: *Ibid.,* p. 60.
7. Ferenczi, Sandor: Introjection and Transference. In *Contributions to Psychoanalysis.* Boston: Richard G. Badger, 1916.
8. Freud: *Group Psychology and the Analysis of the Ego.* London: Hogarth Press, 1940, p. 78.
9. ———: *Ibid.,* p. 36.
10. ———: *Ibid.,* p. 77.
11. ———: *Ibid.,* p. 77.
12. Jones, Ernest: The Nature of Autosuggestion. In *Papers on Psychoanalysis.* London: Baillière, Tindall and Cox, 1948, p. 289.
13. Abraham, Karl: *Psychoanalytic Notes on Coué's Method of Self-Mastery.* Int. J. Psa., VII, 1926, pp. 190–213.
14. McDougall, William: *A Note on Suggestion.* J. Neurology and Psychopathology, I, 1920–1921, p. 1.
15. Freud: Transference and Suggestion. In *Introductory Lectures on Psychoanalysis.* London: Allen and Unwin, 1933, p. 373.
16. ———: *Ibid.,* p. 371.
17. ———: *Ibid.,* p. 374.
18. ———: The Analytic Therapy. In *ibid.,* p. 377.
19. ———: *Ibid.,* pp. 380, 381.
20. ———: Aspects of Development and Regression. In *ibid.,* p. 289.
21. ———: *Selbstdarstellung.* Ges. Werke, XIV, p. 68.
22. ———: *Ibid.,* p. 67.
23. ———: *An Autobiographical Study.* London: Hogarth Press, 1946, pp. 76, 77.
24. ———: *Ibid.,* p. 75.
25. Jones, Ernest: Action of Suggestion in Psychotherapy. In *Papers on Psychoanalysis.* London: Baillière, Tindall & Cox, 1918, p. 359.

26. Dalbiez, Roland: *Psychoanalytical Method and the Doctrine of Freud.* New York: Long-mans, Green & Co., 1941. Vol. II, pp. 114, 115.
27. Glover, Edward, Editor: *An Investigation of the Technique of Psychoanalysis.* London: Baillière, Tindall and Cox, 1940, pp. 1–2.
28. Silverberg, William V.: *The Concept of Transference.* Psychoanal. Q., XVII, 1948, p. 303.
29. Glover, Edward: *The Technique of Psychoanalysis.* London: Baillière, Tindall & Cox, 1928, p. 24.
30. ———: *Ibid.,* p. 79.
31. Alexander, Franz, and French, Thomas M.: *Psychoanalytic Therapy.* New York: The Ronald Press Co., 1946, p. 72.
32. ———: *Ibid.,* p. 34.
33. ———: *Ibid.,* p. 73.
34. Freud: *The Dynamics of Transference.* Coll. Papers, II, p. 319.
35. ———: *Ibid.,* p. 315.
36. ———: *Ibid.,* p. 319.
37. Ferenczi, Sandor: *Bausteine zur Psychoanalyse.* Bern: Verlag Hans Huber, 1939. Vol. III, p. 237.
38. Freud: *Beyond the Pleasure Principle.* London: Int. Psa. Press [1920] 1922, p. 44.
39. Kubie, Lawrence S.: *A Critical Analysis of the Concept of the Repetition Compulsion.* Int. J. Psa., XX, 1939, p. 390.
40. Freud, Anna: *The Ego and the Mechanisms of Defense.* London: Hogarth Press, 1947, p. 18.
41. ———: *Ibid.,* p. 19.
42. Abraham, Karl: The Psycho-Sexual Differences between Hysteria and Dementia Præcox. In *Selected Papers.* London: Hogarth Press, 1948, p. 66.
43. ———: *Ibid.,* p. 71.
44. Glover, Edward: *Psychoanalysis.* London: Staples Press, 1949, p. 309.
45. ———: *Therapeutic Results of Psychoanalysis.* Int. J. Psa., XVIII, 1937, p. 127.
46. Freud: *On Beginning the Treatment.* Coll. Papers, II, p. 350.
47. ———: *Ibid.,* p. 360.
48. Freud, Anna: *The Psychoanalytical Treatment of Children.* London: Imago Publishing Co., Ltd., 1946, p. 16.
49. ———: *Ibid.,* p. 34.
50. Klein, Melanie: Symposium on Child-Analysis. In *Contributions to Psychoanalysis.* London: Hogarth Press, 1948, pp. 165, 166.
51. Sachs, Hanns: *Observations of a Training Analyst.* Psychoanal. Q., XVI, 1947, pp. 157–168.
52. Ferenczi, Sandor: Glaube, Unglaube und Überzeugung. In *Populäre Vorträge über Psychoanalyse.* Leipzig and Vienna: Int. Psa. Verlag, 1922, p. 187.
53. ———: *Bausteine zur Psychoanalyse.* Leipzig and Vienna: Int. Psa. Verlag, 1927. Vol. II, pp. 64–65.
54. Rado, Sandor: *The Economic Principle in Psychoanalytic Technique.* Int. J. Psa., VI, 1925, p. 36.
55. ———: *Ibid.,* p. 40.
56. ———: *Ibid.,* pp. 36, 37.
57. Freud: *On the History of the Psychoanalytic Movement.* Coll. Papers, I, p. 293.
58. ———: *Observations on Transference Love.* Coll. Papers, II, p. 379.
59. ———: *Ibid.,* p. 388.

60. Glover, Edward: *The Therapeutic Effect of Inexact Interpretation.* Int. J. Psa., XII, 1931, p. 411.
61. Freud: *Kurzer Abriss der Psychoanalyse.* Ges. Werke, XIII, p. 407.
62. Strachey, James: *On Therapeutic Results of Psychoanalysis.* Int. J. Psa., XVIII, 1937, p. 144.
63. ———: *The Nature of Therapeutic Action of Psychoanalysis.* Int. J. Psa., XV, 1934, p. 139.
64. Sterba, Richard: *The Fate of the Ego in Analytic Therapy.* Int. J. Psa., XV, 1934, pp. 119, 120.
65. ———: *The Dynamics of the Dissolution of the Transference Resistance.* Psychoanal. Q., IX, 1940, pp. 363–379.
66. Nunberg, Herman: The Theory of the Therapeutic Results in Psychoanalysis. In *Practice and Theory of Psychoanalysis.* New York: Nervous and Mental Disease Monographs, 1948, p. 170.
67. ———: Psychological Interrelations between Physician and Patient. In *ibid.,* p. 178.
68. Freud: *The Ways of Psychoanalytic Therapy.* Coll. Papers, II, p. 398.
69. ———: *Beyond the Pleasure Principle. Op. cit.,* p. 17.
70. Breuer, Josef, and Freud: Psychotherapy of Hysteria (1895). In *Studies in Hysteria.* New York: Nervous and Mental Disease Monographs, 1936, pp. 230, 231.
71. Freud: *Fragment of an Analysis of a Case of Hysteria* (1905). Coll. Papers, III, p. 139.

14. Transference and Reality

Herman Nunberg

A patient of mine was from the beginning of treatment very critical of me; whatever I did or said was wrong. She found fault with everything. She corrected me constantly, trying to teach me what to do, how to behave, what to think and what to say—not only what to say, but also how to say it. Because I could not give in to her attempts to re-educate me, she felt hurt and angry. Although she soon recognized that she expected literally to find her father in me, she did not change her attitude. The more conscious the attachment to her father became to her, the more she demanded that I change to the likeness of his image within her.

What did this attitude express? Certainly, it did not reflect the phenomenon that we call transference. It revealed merely her *readiness* for transference. This readiness obviously produced two attitudes in her: first, an expectation of finding her *real* father in the analyst; secondly, the wish to change the *real* person of the analyst into her father as she imagined him. As this desire could not be realized, she suffered constantly from disappointments, frustrations and anger. This situation led to conflicts with her analyst on a *quasi-real basis*. Thus it is evident that she did not 'transfer' her emotions from her father to her analyst, but rather that she *attempted* to transform her analyst into her father. The particular fixation to her father created the wish to find his reincarnation in the person of the analyst, and, since her desire to transform the latter into a person *identical* with her father could not be fulfilled, the attempts to establish a working transference were futile. Thus transference often breaks down not because of primary aggression, which is the driving force of the so-called negative transference, but because of disappointments and frustrated efforts at establishing an identity of present images with past ones.

What is transference? In spite of disagreement on the part of some of my colleagues, I still agree with Dr. de Saussure that transference is a projection.

Reprinted by permission from the *International Journal of Psycho-Analysis* 32 (1951):1–9. Copyright © Institute of Psycho-Analysis.

The term 'projection' means that the patient's inner and unconscious relations with his first libidinal objects are externalized. In the transference situation the analyst tries to unmask the projections or externalizations whenever they appear during the treatment. What part identification plays in transference will be seen later.

As a matter of fact, the word 'transference' is self-explanatory. It says that the patient displaces emotions belonging to an unconscious representation of a repressed object to a mental representation of an object of the external world. This object represented within the ego is the analyst, on whom emotions and ideas belonging to the repressed unconscious objects are projected. The repressed objects belong to the past, mostly to the patient's early childhood, and are thus unreal. Trying to substitute a real object (for example the analyst) for the unreal one, the patient is bound to run into misunderstandings, to become confused and to suffer frustrations. The split of the personality and the resulting incongruity of the drives is obvious: the essential repressed wish is unconscious and belongs to the past, its preconscious derivatives having undergone certain rationalizations are projected on external objects and, when perceived, become conscious. If, for instance, a grown boy is excessively attached to his mother, he is not satisfied with the kind of gratification her substitute offers him in reality, but expects unconsciously those gratifications that he has experienced in the past.[1]

If in transference, projection of internal and unconscious images onto real objects is taking place, then the first patient's attitude can hardly be called transference. She did not project the image of her father on to the analyst: she tried to change her analyst according to the image of her father.

The next example is different. A patient was unable to understand me when she was lying on the couch with her eyes *open*. When she closed her eyes she could understand me; it then seemed to her as if she were hearing a ghost talking, and my voice sounded like the voice of her dead father. This illusion had almost the intensity of a hallucination.

The difference in respect to transference between this patient and the first one is striking: the first patient only *tried* to transform her analyst into her father, she tried to change a real person into an image of the past, she attempted to make the analyst conform with her memories of her father, to establish an identical picture of both; the second patient *succeeded* in getting an identical picture of her father through the medium of a real person, the analyst, to such an extent that the analyst's voice became her father's voice; she almost had a hallucination of her father. In the first case the effort to effect a transference failed, in the second it was successful. The second patient's feelings for the analyst in the psycho-analytic situation revived the repressed image of her father which she projected on the analyst, so that the two became almost identical. In fact, at times father and analyst became confused in her mind. The first patient tried unsuccessfully to transform the person of the present into the person of the past, whereas the second patient experienced the person of the past in the person of the present. Present objects and past images became identical in her mind.

The tendency to establish 'identical pictures' is perhaps better illustrated by a fragment of the second patient's dream: water was pouring out through a hole in her refrigerator. *She held her hand under the hole in order to stop the flow but the hole sucked her hand in so that it hurt.*

The day-residue consisted of the fact that the refrigerator was out of order and that the patient feared an overflow of water in her kitchen. The evening preceding this dream she had a visitor with whom she talked about sex education. The visitor told her that she forbade her little daughter to put her hand into her nose or mouth because a disease might enter her body. The patient was shocked and thought that this little girl later in life would think that a disease would enter her body when she had sexual intercourse. She herself suffered from severe phobias of touching, among them a fear of infection through the vagina during her pregnancy. Long before her marriage she was afraid of the pain during intercourse and at childbirth. She asserted that the pain in the dream was very *real*. In the same session she told me that on her way to my office she had thought she would even agree to my cutting off her arm if only I could help her to get well. At this point two childhood recollections came to her mind; first, that when she used to stuff her finger into her nose she felt pain, and secondly, that *a woman once told her of another little girl who put her hand in a toilet bowl and had her arm caught in the pipe of the bowl* because of the strong suction when the toilet upstairs flushed. The patient stressed that the pain in her arm felt in the dream persisted when she was awake.

What happened here? The real and conscious fear of her kitchen being flooded by the leaking refrigerator, and the preconscious ideas and fears of her masturbatory activities stimulated by the conversation with her visitor revived a picture of her childhood which she dreaded because it reminded her of masturbation and the fears connected with it. In other words, a real expectation produced a regression and revived a picture from childhood which, in the dream, acquired qualities of reality. Freud calls this phenomenon the 'identity of perceptions' *(Wahrnehmungsidentität)*. This means that an actual perception of an idea revives old, unconscious, repressed ideas or emotions to such an extent that they are perceived as actual images although their meaning is not recognized by the conscious psychic apparatus; thus present and old ideas and emotions become identical for a while. This tendency to revive old ideas and perceptions and to make the present coincide with the past, forms the basis of the phenomenon which is called 'acting out'.

Another example may perhaps be even more instructive. About eight months after the conclusion of his analysis, a patient asked me to see him immediately because of sudden panic and insomnia. I do not wish to go into the details of this complicated symptom. I wish only to say that the cause of this sudden panic and insomnia was his newborn son. When his wife came home with the infant from the hospital, she put it, as arranged in advance, in the room adjoining the parents' bedroom. For the night she wanted to close the door between the two rooms, but he wanted it open in order to hear every sound in the child's room. Since she, nevertheless, closed the door, he became frantic, overwhelmed by panic, and unable to sleep, trying to listen to all the sounds that seemed to him to emanate from the baby's room. This condition, which had lasted for several days by the time he came to see me, gave me the opportunity to remind him that he had had quite a number of fears in different periods of his life. I drew his attention to one particular fear of his childhood: frequently, when his parents were not home at night, he was seized by the idea that his rabbits out in the yard were being killed, and he insisted that his nurse go and find out whether they were still alive. When I mentioned this, he remembered another fear of his early childhood whose importance he could only now fully comprehend. This fear concerned the door of his room which faced his mother's room across the hallway. When his door stood open he could see whether his mother was at home: then he felt secure and could go to sleep. But when the door was closed, he felt alone, deserted by his mother, and therefore could not sleep and became panicky. Throughout his childhood he feared that his mother would leave him. About the age of five, he tried repeatedly to run away from home, pretending to leave his mother, thus reversing his fear of being deserted by her.

The panic caused by the closing of his child's door thus betrayed his infantile fear of being left alone by his mother. The urgent desire to keep the door open reflected the ritual of his childhood to keep his own door open.

The difference between the actual and the infantile situation lies only in the fact that the subject is changed: instead of himself as a child being anxious about his mother's love, he was now as a mature man anxious about his son's safety and well-being. The situation was thus reversed; the insomnia and anxiety were, however, unchanged. It is obvious that the patient projected one part of his ego on to his son and that he identified another part with his mother. His son incarnated himself, and he incarnated his mother. Both these representations were, of course, unconscious. It is probable that his infantile wish to see what was going on in his mother's room was overdetermined: the actual panic might also reflect the one felt while overhearing the noises of the primal scene. This, however, would not change the meaning of our patient's reaction to his son; on the contrary, it would only broaden our interpretation.

For the purpose of our discussion the bare fact that our patient attempted to re-establish in the present a situation as it existed in childhood is more significant than is the meaning of the panic. What he wanted was simple enough: he wished to have the door open. The fulfilment of this wish would have repeated in actuality the infantile situation of the open door, and would have spared him anxiety.

This example shows—as do many cases—that the tendency to 'transfer' infantile experiences into reality and to act them out can be observed not only in the transference situation but also independently of it. *An urge to establish identity of perceptions through repetition of past experiences is thus, in conformity with Freud's ideas, undeniable.*

Now we can see that the establishment of identical perceptions is an act of projection as well as identification. Identification, as we know, has several meanings. One of them expresses a community of feelings and thoughts in a group formation. The analysis is a group formation of two persons. The common goal of analyst and patient is helping, i.e. curing the patient. This alone could suffice to establish an identification. Identification, however, is also a regressive substitute for love, if the love object in the external world becomes a part of the ego. In analysis the common goal of analyst and patient leads first to identification of the patient with the analyst and further to the revival of the deeper identifications with the parents. Hardly has this identification taken place when the patient tries to lodge with the analyst the reactivated residues of the infantile relationship with the parents. This can be accomplished only by means of projection. It seems thus as if projection helped to find the lost object in the outside world, as if the analyst were a screen on which the patient projected his unconscious pictures. In fact, when we reach certain depths in analysis, it is difficult to discern between identification and projection. It seems as if the boundaries of the ego were removed, as Federn would say, in which state the subject feels as if he were a part of the external world and the external world a part of himself. This corresponds to states of transitivism which Freud, in *Totem and Taboo,* ascribed to the animistic phase of human development. Later he referred to similar states as 'oceanic feelings'. States of this kind can, not too infrequently, be observed in those psycho-analytical sessions during which the patient is very deeply immersed in his unconscious id.

Although transference makes use of both mechanisms, identification and projection, one fact remains unchanged: the *tendency* to establish identity of old and new perceptions.

The tendency to bring about 'identity of perceptions' seems to satisfy the repetition compulsion which, as is well known, is the driving force of many a psychic phenomenon. Compelling the individual to preserve the past, it is a conservative principle. And yet, as soon as it is coupled with the phenomenon of transference, it becomes a progressive element, in the sense, of course, of psychic topography. This statement may require some amplification. An actual event reactivates an old repressed one which, on its part, tries to replace the new experience; this can best be observed in dreams. The attempt to re-live repressed experiences in actual ones is only in part successful, as the censorship of the dream or the resistance of the ego tries to disguise them. According to our theoretical conception of the psychic apparatus, this fact can be expressed also in the following way: certain perceptions and sensations produced by stimuli of daily life undergo historical and topical regressions to corresponding old, repressed, unconscious experiences. As soon as the cathexis of the actual experience (i.e., the charge of psychic energy) reaches the psychic representations of the repressed and fixated experiences in the unconscious id, it strengthens and re-activates them. These reactivated unconscious representations now manifest a tendency to 'progression', i.e a tendency to reach the perceptual and motor end of the psychic apparatus. Here they give the perceptions of actual events and the sensations produced by them an unconscious tinge; the ego behaves as if it were the id. Through this process the analyst, in the transference situation, becomes the representative of the objects of the unconscious strivings.

The readiness for transference exists, as indicated before, independently of the psycho-analytic situation. The mere fact that a patient decides to seek help from an analyst (or other therapist) furthers this phenomenon. Furthermore, the analyst's request for free associations stimulates reproduction of old memories, i.e. of mental repetition of repressed experiences. In addition, the repetition of old images stirs up emotions which once accompanied them. These old and yet new, actual, emotions try to attach themselves to the only real object available, the psycho-analyst, and to find an outlet in wishes, fantasies and actions directed towards him. It seems as if a new experience could not be assimilated—in the sense of the synthetic function of the ego— unless it found its way to the old patterns. Therefore it is not surprising that transference occurs also in other than psycho-analytic therapies. The psycho-analyst and the non-psycho-analyst differ in their treatment and understanding of this phenomenon, in that the former treats the transference symptoms as illusions while the latter takes them at their face value, i.e. as realities.

The transference proceeds according to the need to assimilate actual experiences in such a way that their perception either conforms to or becomes identical with repressed unconscious ideas. What has been once experienced —particularly in childhood—seems to form an indelible imprint in the unconscious from which patterns develop. These patterns may be dormant for a long time and become active only under certain circumstances. The latency of these patterns, or their state of unconsciousness, is responsible for the fact that the meaning of the present experiences following these patterns remains unconscious. However, it must be added that complete gratification of the need for 'identity of perceptions' is not achieved as a rule, except in dreams, delusions and hallucinations. In the transference situation the unconscious pattern overshadows the conscious perception of an actual event and produces an illusion, while in dreams or psychoses the same pattern or image forms hallucinations. Hence illusions can be reality-tested, hallucinations can not, or can only in part.

It might appear as if the concept of transference and the concept of repetition compulsion had been confused here, but this is certainly not the case. In so far as a repetition of previous states takes place in the transference situation, transference is a manifestation of the repetition compulsion. In so far, however, as in transference the wishes and drives are directed towards the objects of the external world, though through the repetition of old experiences, transference is independent of the repetition compulsion. Repetition compulsion points to the past, transference to actuality (reality) and thus, in a sense, to the future. Repetition compulsion tries to fixate, to 'freeze', the old psychic reality, hence it becomes a regressive force; transference attempts to re-animate these 'frozen' psychic formations, to discharge their energy and to satisfy them in a new and present reality, and thus becomes a progressive force.

I would say that transference is like Janus, two-faced, with one face turned to the past, the other to the present. Through transference the patient lives the present in the past and the past in the present. In his speech he betrays a lack of feeling for the sequence of events, which is conceived as time. This lack, however, is not characteristic only of the transference to the analyst. Almost all neurotics are confused in relation to the element of time, whether they are in treatment or not. Many patients in analysis can identify recent events only after elucidation of childhood experiences; others condense experiences from different periods of their life into one event and can keep them apart only after thorough analysis, etc. The fact that the patient loses the sense of time in the transference situation is not surprising, as it corresponds to the phenomenon that repressed unconscious events, events of the past, are experienced in the present as if no time had elapsed. Indeed, we know from Freud that the unconscious is timeless.

That past and present flow together may seem an obstacle to recognizing the past in the present. But closer examination shows that through re-animation of the representations of repressed objects in the transference situation, the ego gains direct access to its childhood experiences; not the entire ego, of course, but only that part which has not been altered by the repression and has remained intact. This intact ego now has an opportunity to confront its feelings for and expectations from the analyst with the situation in the past, in childhood, and to compare them with one another as if the whole life were spread in front of the inner eye on a single plane. As soon as the patient becomes conscious of his transference, he gains the ability to assess his actual feelings in relation to the infantile situation. This helps him to distinguish between the images returning from the past and the perceptions of external, actual objects, and thus to *test reality* better than before. Some patients accept reality then as it is, others do not. The first patient discussed here did not accept reality; she could not give up the peculiar attachment to her father. She would rather have changed the world than change herself by accepting the analyst as an object of the outside world. The second patient was able to see that the analyst represented a new edition of her father, an edition which she herself created. The third patient became aware that his son represented himself as a child. It is evident that divesting the actual experiences in the transference of the influence of repressed images enhances reality testing. If, as often happens, in the course of free associations the patient produces images which have the intensity of real perceptions, or are hallucinations, the analyst may almost always be sure that he is dealing with actual memories. When the patient accepts such 'hallucinations' as memories, he loses the incentive to project the memories (unconscious images) into the external world and then to perceive them as realities.

As indicated before, patients try to 'act out' their repressed unconscious in the transference, by repeating certain patterns of their life. They bend reality, so to speak, in the transference situation. Sometimes the repetitions are helpful for the analysis, sometimes they make the analysis difficult. Then they form certain types of resistances. Freud said once that in the resistances the patient reveals his character. A very simple example may illustrate this fact. A patient showed from the very beginning an astonishing willingness for and understanding of the analysis. His associations flowed easily, he produced important recollections, and so on. He continued in this way for a fairly long period, yet the analysis did not make any progress, until we found that his mother used to ask him to tell her everything he thought and did during the day. Our patient confided all his thoughts to her until late in adolescence. It gave him great pleasure when she was talking with him at night while sitting on his bed, and he could see, through her thin nightgown, the contours of her body, particularly of her breasts. He pretended to tell her everything, but the secret of his sexual fantasies about her he kept to himself. Displaying similar behaviour in his analysis, he pretended to tell the truth; in fact, tried to fool his analyst as he had his mother. In his behaviour with other people he was sincere yet reserved and distrustful so that he never had really close friends. He was a lonesome man.

As soon as he became conscious of the fact that he was 'transferring' his relationship to his mother into his relationship with his analyst, he understood that by doing so he defeated his own purpose, the success of his treatment. From then on he was sincere with his analyst, except at times when other resistances with different backgrounds arose. In other words, through the act of consciousness, i.e., through the perception of unconscious strivings of the id, the ego acquired the faculty to control the repetition of these strivings and to adjust itself to reality—which in this case was represented by the patient's will to recovery.

Not always, as in this example, is a character-trait formed by a compromise between contrasting strivings. There are other formations of character-traits. In this context, however, it is relevant to point out that contrasting strivings frequently remain separate, and alternately find expression. This alternation of feelings permeates also the patient's attitude to his analyst. At times, he is full of love for him, submissive, admires him, at other times he is aggressive, stubborn, defiant, etc. These alternating attitudes, this struggle between masochism and sadism, submission and rebellion, dependence and independence seem to repeat previous states representing a developmental pattern. One needs only to observe the development of children, from infancy to maturity, in order to gain the impression of the constant struggle between the retarding tendencies of the repetition compulsion, crystallized in fixations, dependency on the one hand, and the hunger, avidity for new experiences and impressions for independence, on the other hand, a struggle which finally leads to adaptation to and mastering of reality and instinctual drives. In puberty the struggle between the strivings of the id and the needs of the ego becomes very intense and finally leads to the formation of a normal personality. However, if a disturbance has occurred in the course of this prolonged and complicated development, and the patient is in analysis, the same struggle continues in relation to the analyst in the transference situation, where the course of the development is accelerated and usually brought to an end. In other words, when the patient recognizes the attempts to re-live the past in the present, he usually gives them up or modifies them. In this process the transference, which creates an artificial reality, is unmasked, and this amounts, in a sense, to a re-education. Indeed, from its very beginnings analysis was considered a kind of re-education.

Through transference the patient is re-educated not only in respect to the instincts and surroundings but also in respect to the superego. In order to understand this, we must again turn to the starting point of the analysis. Then the question arises as to why the mere decision to turn for help to an analyst (therapist or priest) creates, in advance, transference. The answer is very simple: in the unconscious id one asks only father or mother for help. The form of the transference is, therefore, predetermined by the patient's relations to his father and mother. The relationship between patient and analyst becomes very similar to that in hypnosis. In obedience to the hypnotist's suggestions the hypnotized person can even have hallucinations, positive as well as negative ones. The influence of the hypnotist is so overwhelming that he may force the hypnotized person to give up temporarily the reality-testing faculty. In the heat of transference the analyst has powers similar to those of the hypnotist, but uses them for opposite purposes: namely, to teach the patient reality testing. Originally, the hypnotist no more than the analyst possesses such power; it is only the patient who has invested him with it.

And how did the patient obtain this power? From his father—through identification with him—would be the answer. This identification led to the differentiation of the superego within the ego. Freud says that the superego is the heir to the Oedipus complex. According to him, the hypnotist is identified with the ego-ideal of the hypnotized person. As later on the term 'ego-ideal' was replaced by the term 'superego', we may say as well that the hypnotist is identified with the superego of the hypnotized. Similarly does the patient in analysis make his analyst identical with his father through the medium of his superego. But since the analyst is perceived as an object of the external world, now equipped with the father's attributes, the patient must have also projected on to him parts of his own superego. This could explain how the analyst obtains the enormous power over the patient. Through analysis of the transference the analyst, however, tries to divest himself of the power granted him by the patient.

There is much more to be said about the parallelism between the state of hypnosis and the psycho-analytical situation. I shall, however, limit myself to the discussion of a few points only.

The following is based on Freud's ideas about hypnosis. He maintains that hypnosis is a group formation of two persons. This group, like any other group, is held together by libidinal ties. In love, these ties are composed of directly sexual instincts and of sexual instincts inhibited in their aims, i.e., desexualized. In hypnosis these ties are only of an aim-inhibited nature. Hypnosis, therefore, corresponds to love with the exclusion of directly sexual instincts. The same humility, the same compliance, the same absence of criticism, the same overestimation in regard to the hypnotist can be observed as in the state of being in love in regard to the loved person. If directly sexual instincts get the upper hand, the group formation is destroyed. The same is true of the psycho-analytic situation as it is likewise a group formation of two. In hypnosis the identification with the hypnotist is a regressive substitute for libidinal ties in the form of desexualized, aim-inhibited sexual attachments to the subject's parents. These ties form, according to Ferenczi, the basis for the transference-readiness or suggestibility. The hypnotist, Freud says, stimulates this readiness by claiming to be in possession of mysterious powers by which he can put the subject to sleep. In fact, as Freud stresses, there is something uncanny about hypnosis and hypnotist. We know from him that the uncanny represents something old and familiar which has been repressed but is on the verge of returning from the unconscious. Upon the hypnotist's order to sleep, the subject withdraws his interest from the outside world and falls asleep. His sleep is, however, a partial one, a dream-like sleep, because the subject, though detached from the external world, nevertheless concentrates his libidinal cathexes on the hypnotist. In this way the hypnotist establishes the *rapport* with the hypnotized person. In the psychoanalytic situation the patient is removed from contact with the external world but remains in contact with his analyst—conditions similar to those in hypnosis.

By putting the subject to sleep, Freud says, 'the hypnotist awakens in the subject a portion of his archaic inheritance which also made him compliant towards his parents and which had experienced an individual re-animation in his relation to his father; what is thus awakened is the idea of a paramount and dangerous personality; towards whom only a passive-masochistic attitude is possible, to whom one's will has to be surrendered—while to be alone with him, "to look him in the face", appears a hazardous enterprise. It is only in some such way as this', Freud adds, 'that we can picture the relation of the individual member of the primal horde to the primal father. . . .'

Hypnosis is thus a precipitate of archaic libidinal ties of mankind in the unconscious id of the present-day individual. Suggestion is a part of hypnosis and helps to establish the rapport (transference) between hypnotist and hypnotized. This archaic relationship seems to be repeated in the psycho-analytic situation. The analyst promises the patient help as if he were in possession of magic powers—and the latter overestimates and believes him. He is taboo to the patient as the primal father is to the primitive individual. The analyst is free and has his own will, while the patient has to submit to the psychoanalytic rules laid down by the analyst. The analyst sits upright, while the patient lies passively on a couch. The analyst is silent most of the time, while the patient tells him everything, gives him his unconscious material, as if performing a sacrificial act. The analyst is omnipotent, he is fearless and can look at the patient, while the patient is afraid of him and is not permitted to see him, like the primitive man who dare not look in the face of the primal father.

As the hypnotist represents the inner and historical reality of the hypnotized, so does the analyst represent the psychological reality of the patient. This relationship between hypnotist and hypnotized leads the latter to replace the external reality by the historical and psychic reality. The ego of the hypnotized person thus makes a regression to a primitive stage of development where indeed the psychic reality replaces the external reality and where the primary process replaces the secondary process.

A similar change occurs in the transference-situation: while the patient is on the couch, his ego becomes temporarily weakened as does the hypnotized person's ego. As soon as the patient complies with the analyst's demand to give up selective, logical thinking and to abandon himself to free associations, the secondary process is supplanted by the primary one; an important function of the ego, reality-testing, is temporarily suspended.

This, however, is valid only for the analytic session itself in which the patient is detached from external reality as is the hypnotized patient in hypnosis. In order to avoid any misunderstanding, it ought to be stressed that in the course of the analysis the patient's ego is strengthened, as the analyst endeavours to make the patient face the external reality and to free him of the dependence upon himself, in so far as he, the analyst, represents the patient's inner reality.

One can imagine what mastery over his narcissism the analyst must have gained not to be intoxicated by the powers granted him by the patient.

The fact that the patient's attitude towards reality is to a certain degree disturbed in neurosis—and in transference—is caused, among other factors, by an excessively strict and critical superego. Through the projection of his superego on the analyst, the patient frees himself in a sense from his superego which is now represented by the analyst. The analyst's superego is supposed to be neutral, usually milder than the patient's own restrictive superego. As the patient identifies at the same time with the analyst, he exchanges, as it were, his own superego—the father's moral standards—for the analyst's. The result of this exchange is that the patient learns not only to cope with the internal reality as represented by instincts and conscience, but also to accept the external world according to its full 'reality-value'; one is almost tempted to say 'at its face value'. The fact that 'reality changes' are accomplished also under the influence of the superego can be understood when we take the following considerations into account. In his *Group Psychology and the Analysis of the Ego* Freud ascribed the reality-testing faculty to the ego-ideal. In *The Ego and the Id* he retracted this statement and ascribed the reality-testing faculty to the ego. In hypnosis this faculty is disturbed by the intervention of the hypnotist who is a representative of the patient's superego (or ego-ideal). It is true that the hypnotized person seems in some way to perceive objects of the external world even in case of negative hallucinations, but this does not alter the fact that the hypnotist can at will suppress the reality-testing faculty of the subject's ego. I once made the statement, and this last fact supports it, that conscious perceptions of the ego must be sanctioned by the superego in order to acquire qualities of full, uncontested reality. This assumption could be helpful in understanding why, in addition to the undoing of repressions, changes in the patient's superego also enhance the reality-testing faculty of the ego.[2]

In conclusion: it seems to me that the tendency to establish identity of perceptions is illustrated in an impressive way by the phenomena of hypnosis and transference. Even the projection of the superego on the analyst proves this thesis. Through this projection the 'father-image' is externalized and then perceived as a quasi-reality; in a sense, the father exists now in the external world (though disguised in the shape of the analyst) where he originally existed.

As long as the father is not recognized in the analyst, the identity of perceptions is latent. Through the analysis of the transference it becomes manifest. Then it diminishes in the same proportion as the repressed becomes conscious. However, it happens that people with successful, solid repressions are well adapted to reality. Their perceptions of actual events are not coloured by repressed experiences, although they may appear emotionally inhibited. On the other hand, this tendency seems to gain control of the perceptive end of the psychic apparatus in dreams, hallucinations and delusions.

Further discussion of this topic would lead to new problems which exceed the scope of this paper.

NOTES

1. In the discussion of this paper Dr. Hartmann and Dr. Lowenstein disagreed with me as to the role of the projection mechanism in the transference situation. They maintained that in transference only the mechanism of displacement is at work. The term 'displacement', we know, means that the psychic stress or affect can be shifted from one element to another *within* the psychic systems. In transference the individual confuses the *mental* image of his father or mother with the real picture of the analyst and behaves as if the analyst were his father or mother. Of course, we recognize in this mechanism a displacement of affects; but, as the external object (the analyst) is treated like a mental image (father or mother), there is no doubt that the mental image is projected on to the analyst. Besides, Freud maintains that processes within the ego can be perceived (with a few exceptions) only with the help of projections.

2. I would like to suggest the following: if hypnosis can really be considered an archaic heritage of mankind and suggestion (or transference) a part of it, then we are justified in assuming that the tendency to establish identical perceptions—i.e. to revive old experiences—can also be inherited. In this case we should have to agree with Freud's hypothesis that not only disposition but also contents can be inherited.

BIBLIOGRAPHY

Ferenczi, S. (1909) 'Introjection und Übertragung', *Jahrbuch für Psychoanalytische und Psychopathologische Forschungen, 1,* 422–457.

Freud, S. *The Interpretation of Dreams.* Authorized Translation by A. A. Brill. London: George Allen & Unwin Ltd. New York: Macmillan Company.

—— 'Fragment of an Analysis of a Case of Hysteria', *Collected Papers,* III, Hogarth Press.

—— 'The Dynamics of the Transference,' *Collected Papers,* II.

—— 'Further Recommendations in the Technique of Psycho-Analysis. Recollection, Repetition and Working Through'. *Collected Papers,* II.

—— 'Beyond the Pleasure Principle,' Int. Psycho-Anal. Library, No. 4.

—— *The Problem of Anxiety.* Translated by Henry A. Bunker. The Psychoanalytic Quarterly Press and W. W. Norton & Co. (Inhibitions, Symptoms and Anxiety). Int. Psycho-Anal. Library, No. 28.

—— *The Future of an Illusion.* Int. Psycho-Anal. Library, No. 15.

—— *The Ego and the Id.* Int. Psycho-Anal. Library, No. 12.

—— *Civilization and its Discontents.* Int. Psycho-Anal. Library, No. 17.

—— The 'Uncanny', *Collected Papers,* IV.

—— *Group Psychology and the Analysis of the Ego.* Int. Psycho-Anal. Library, No. 6.

—— 'A Disturbance of Memory on the Acropolis', *Collected Papers,* V.

—— *An Outline of Psychoanalysis.* Authorized translation by James Strachey. Int. Psycho-Anal. Library, No. 35.

Nunberg, H. 'The Synthetic Function of the Ego', *Practice and Theory of Psychoanalysis.* Nervous and Mental Disease Monographs, also *Int. J. Psycho-Anal.,* **13,** 1931.

—— 'Problems of Therapy', *Practice and Theory of Psychoanalysis.* Nervous and Mental Disease Monographs, also *Int. Z. Psychoanalyse,* **16,** 1928.

—— 'Theory of the Therapeutic Results of Psycho-analysis'. *Practice and Theory of Psychoanalysis.* Nervous and Mental Disease Monographs, also *Int. J. Psycho-Anal.,* **18,** 1937.

—— *Allgemeine Neurosenlehre auf psychoanalytischer Grundlage.* Verlag Hans Huber, Bern-Berlin.

Sterba, R. (1936) 'Zur Theorie der Übertragung', *Imago,* **22.**

15. The Origins of Transference

Melanie Klein

In his *Fragment of an Analysis of a Case of Hysteria*[1] Freud defines the transference situation in the following way:—

> What are transferences? They are new editions or facsimiles of the tendencies and phantasies which are aroused and made conscious during the progress of the analysis; but they have this peculiarity, which is characteristic for their species, that they replace some earlier person by the person of the physician. To put it another way: a whole series of psychological experiences are revived, not as belonging to the past, but as applying to the physician at the present moment.

In some form or other transference operates throughout life and influences all human relations, but here I am only concerned with the manifestations of transference in psycho-analysis. It is characteristic of psycho-analytic procedure that, as it begins to open up roads into the patient's unconscious, his past (in its conscious and unconscious aspects) is gradually being revived. Thereby his urge to transfer his early experiences, object-relations and emotions, is reinforced and they come to focus on the psycho-analyst; this implies that the patient deals with the conflicts and anxieties which have been reactivated, by making use of the same mechanisms and defences as in earlier situations.

It follows that the deeper we are able to penetrate into the unconscious and the further back we can take the analysis, the greater will be our understanding of the transference. Therefore a brief summary of my conclusions about the earliest stages of development is relevant to my topic.

The first form of anxiety is of a persecutory nature. The working of the death instinct within—which according to Freud is directed against the organism—gives rise to the fear of annihilation, and this is the primordial cause of persecutory anxiety. Furthermore, from the beginning of post-natal life (I am not concerned here with pre-natal processes) destructive impulses against the object stir up fear of retaliation. These persecutory feelings from

Reprinted by permission from the *International Journal of Psycho-Analysis* 33 (1952):433–38. Copyright © Institute of Psycho-Analysis.

inner sources are intensified by painful external experiences, for, from the earliest days onwards, frustration and discomfort arouse in the infant the feeling that he is being attacked by hostile forces. Therefore the sensations experienced by the infant at birth and the difficulties of adapting himself to entirely new conditions give rise to persecutory anxiety. The comfort and care given after birth, particularly the first feeding experiences, are left to come from good forces. In speaking of 'forces' I am using a rather adult word for what the young infant dimly conceives of as objects, either good or bad. The infant directs his feelings of gratification and love towards the 'good' breast, and his destructive impulses and feelings of persecution towards what he feels to be frustrating, i.e. the 'bad' breast. At this stage splitting processes are at their height, and love and hatred as well as the good and bad aspects of the breast are largely kept apart from one another. The infant's relative security is based on turning the good object into an ideal one as a protection against the dangerous and persecuting object. These processes— that is to say splitting, denial, omnipotence and idealization—are prevalent during the first three or four months of life (which I termed the 'paranoid-schizoid position' (1946). In these ways at a very early stage persecutory anxiety and its corollary, idealization, fundamentally influence object relations.

The primal processes of projection and introjection, being inextricably linked with the infant's emotions and anxieties, initiate object-relations; by projecting, i.e. deflecting libido and aggression on to the mother's breast, the basis for object-relations is established; by introjecting the object, first of all the breast, relations to internal objects come into being. My use of the term 'object-relations' is based on my contention that the infant has from the beginning of post-natal life a relation to the mother (although focusing primarily on her breast) which is imbued with the fundamental elements of an object-relation, i.e. love, hatred, phantasies, anxieties, and defences.[2]

In my view—as I have explained in detail on other occasions—the introjection of the breast is the beginning of superego formation which extends over years. We have grounds for assuming that from the first feeding experience onwards the infant introjects the breast in its various aspects. The core of the superego is thus the mother's breast, both good and bad. Owing to the simultaneous operation of introjection and projection, relations to external and internal objects interact. The father too, who soon plays a role in the child's life, early on becomes part of the infant's internal world. It is characteristic of the infant's emotional life that there are rapid fluctuations between love and hate; between external and internal situations; between perception of reality and the phantasies relating to it; and, accordingly, an interplay between persecutory anxiety and idealization—both referring to internal and external objects; the idealized object being a corollary of the persecutory, extremely bad one.

The ego's growing capacity for integration and synthesis leads more and more, even during these first few months, to states in which love and hatred, and correspondingly the good and bad aspects of objects, are being synthesized; and this gives rise to the second form of anxiety—depressive anxiety —for the infant's aggressive impulses and desires towards the bad breast (mother) are now felt to be a danger to the good breast (mother) as well. In the second quarter of the first year these emotions are reinforced, because at this stage the infant increasingly perceives and introjects the mother as a person. Depressive anxiety is intensified, for the infant feels he has destroyed or is destroying a whole object by his greed and uncontrollable aggression. Moreover, owing to the growing synthesis of his emotions, he now feels that these destructive impulses are directed against a *loved person*. Similar processes operate in relation to the father and other members of the family. These anxieties and corresponding defences constitute the 'depressive position', which comes to a head about the middle of the first year and whose essence is the anxiety and guilt relating to the destruction and loss of the loved internal and external objects.

It is at this stage, and bound up with the depressive position, that the Oedipus complex sets in. Anxiety and guilt add a powerful impetus towards the beginning of the Oedipus complex. For anxiety and guilt increase the need to externalize (project) bad figures and to internalize (introject) good ones; to attach desires, love, feelings of guilt, and reparative tendencies to some objects, and hate and anxiety to others; to find representatives for internal figures in the external world. It is, however, not only the search for new objects which dominates the infant's needs, but also the drive towards new aims: away from the breast towards the penis, i.e., from oral desires toward genital ones. Many factors contribute to these developments; the forward drive of the libido, the growing integration of the ego, physical and mental skills and progressive adaptation to the external world. These trends are bound up with the process of symbol formation, which enables the infant to transfer not only interest, but also emotions and phantasies, anxiety and guilt, from one object to another.

The processes I have described are linked with another fundamental phenomenon governing mental life. I believe that the pressure exerted by the earliest anxiety situations is one of the factors which bring about the repetition compulsion. I shall return to this hypothesis at a later point.

Some of my conclusions about the earliest stages of infancy are a continuation of Freud's discoveries; on certain points, however, divergencies have arisen, one of which is very relevant to my present topic. I am referring to my contention that object-relations are operative from the beginning of postnatal life.

For many years I have held the view that auto-erotism and narcissism are in the young infant contemporaneous with the first relation to objects— external and internalized. I shall briefly restate my hypothesis: auto-erotism and narcissism include the love for and relation with the internalized good object which in phantasy forms part of the loved body and self. It is to this internalized object that in auto-erotic gratification and narcissistic *states* a withdrawal takes place. Concurrently, from birth onwards, a relation to objects, primarily the mother (her breast) is present. This hypothesis contradicts Freud's concept of auto-erotic and narcissistic *stages* which preclude an object-relation. However, the difference between Freud's view and my own is less wide than appears at first sight, since Freud's statements on this issue are not unequivocal. In various contexts he explicitly and implicitly expressed opinions which suggested a relation to an object, the mother's breast, *preceding* auto-erotism and narcissism. One reference must suffice; in the first of two Encyclopaedia articles,[3] Freud said;

> In the first instance the oral component instinct finds satisfaction by attaching itself to the sating of the desire for nourishment; and its object is the mother's breast. It then detaches itself, becomes independent and at the same time *auto-erotic,* that is, it finds an object in the child's own body.

Freud's use of the term object is here somewhat different from my use of this term, for he is referring to the object of an instinctual aim, while I mean, in addition to this, an object-relation involving the infant's emotions, phantasies, anxieties, and defences. Nevertheless, in the sentence referred to, Freud clearly speaks of a libidinal attachment to an object, the mother's breast, which precedes auto-erotism and narcissism.

In this context I wish to remind you also of Freud's findings about early identifications. In *The Ego and the Id,*[4] speaking of abandoned object cathexes, he said; '. . . the effects of the first identification in earliest childhood will be profound and lasting. This leads us back to the origin of the ego-ideal; . . .' Freud then defines the first and most important identifications which lie hidden behind the ego-ideal as the identification with the father, or with the parents, and places them, as he expresses it, in the 'pre-history of every person'. These formulations come close to what I described as the first introjected objects, for by definition identifications are the result of introjection. From the statement I have just discussed and the passage quoted from the Encyclopaedia article it can be deduced that Freud, although he did not pursue this line of thought further, did assume that in earliest infancy both an object and introjective processes play a part.

That is to say, as regards auto-erotism and narcissism we meet with an inconsistency in Freud's views. Such inconsistencies which exist on a number of points of theory clearly show, I think, that on these particular issues Freud had not yet arrived at a final decision. In respect of the theory of anxiety he stated this explicitly in *Inhibitions, Symptoms and Anxiety*.[5] His realization that much about the early stages of development was still unknown or obscure to him is also exemplified by his speaking of the first years of the girl's life as '. . . lost in a past so dim and shadowy. . . .'[6]

I do not know Anna Freud's view about this aspect of Freud's work. But, as regards the question of auto-erotism and narcissism, she seems only to have taken into account Freud's conclusion that an auto-erotic and a narcissistic stage precede object-relations, and not to have allowed for the other possibilities implied in some of Freud's statements such as the ones I referred to above. This is one of the reasons why the divergence between Anna Freud's conception and my conception of early infancy is far greater than that between Freud's views, taken as a whole, and my views. I am stating this because I believe it is essential to clarify the extent and nature of the differences between the two schools of psycho-analytic thought represented by Anna Freud and myself. Such clarification is required in the interests of psycho-analytic training and also because it could help to open up fruitful discussions between psycho-analysts and thereby contribute to a greater general understanding of the fundamental problems of early infancy.

The hypothesis that a stage extending over several months precedes object-relations implies that—except for the libido attached to the infant's own body—impulses, phantasies, anxieties, and defences either are not present in him, or are not related to an object, that is to say they would operate *in vacuo*. The analysis of very young children has taught me that there is no instinctual urge, no anxiety situation, no mental process which does not involve objects, external or internal; in other words, object-relations are at the *centre* of emotional life. Furthermore, love and hatred, phantasies, anxieties, and defences are also operative from the beginning and are *ab initio* indivisibly linked with object-relations. This insight showed me many phenomena in a new light.

I shall now draw the conclusion on which the present paper rests: I hold that transference originates in the same processes which in the earliest stages determine object-relations. Therefore we have to go back again and again in analysis to the fluctuations between objects, loved and hated, external and internal, which dominate early infancy. We can fully appreciate the interconnection between positive and negative transferences only if we explore the early interplay between love and hate, and the vicious circle of aggression, anxieties, feelings of guilt and increased aggression, as well as the various aspects of objects towards whom these conflicting emotions and anxieties are directed. On the other hand, through exploring these early processes I became convinced that the analysis of the negative transference, which had received relatively little attention[7] in psycho-analytic technique, is a precondition for analysing the deeper layers of the mind. The analysis of the negative as well as of the positive transference and of their interconnection is, as I have held for many years, an indispensable principle for the treatment of all types of patients, children and adults alike. I have substantiated this view in most of my writings from 1927 onwards.

This approach, which in the past made possible the psycho-analysis of very young children, has in recent years proved extremely fruitful for the analysis of schizophrenic patients. Until about 1920 it was assumed that schizophrenic patients were incapable of forming a transference and therefore could not be psycho-analyzed. Since then the psycho-analysis of schizophrenics has been attempted by various techniques. The most radical change of view in this respect, however, has occurred more recently and is closely connected with the greater knowledge of the mechanisms, anxieties, and defences operative in earliest infancy. Since some of these defences, evolved in primal object-relations against both love and hatred, have been discovered, the fact that schizophrenic patients are capable of developing both a positive and a negative transference has been fully understood; this finding is confirmed if we consistently apply in the treatment of schizophrenic patients[8] the principle that it is as necessary to analyse the negative as the positive transference—that in fact the one cannot be analysed without the other.

Retrospectively it can be seen that these considerable advances in technique are supported in psycho-analytic theory by Freud's discovery of the

Life and Death instincts, which has fundamentally added to the understanding of the origin of ambivalence. Because the Life and Death instincts, and therefore love and hatred, are at bottom in the closest interaction, negative and positive transference are basically interlinked.

The understanding of earliest object-relations and the processes they imply has essentially influenced technique from various angles. It has long been known that the psycho-analyst in the transference situation may stand for mother, father, or other people, that he is also at times playing in the patient's mind the part of the superego, at other times that of the id or the ego. Our present knowledge enables us to penetrate to the specific details of the various roles allotted by the patient to the analyst. There are in fact very few people in the young infant's life, but he feels them to be a multitude of objects because they appear to him in different aspects. Accordingly, the analyst may at a given moment represent a part of the self, of the superego or any one of a wide range of internalized figures. Similarly it does not carry us far enough if we realize that the analyst stands for the actual father or mother, unless we understand which aspect of the parents has been revived. The picture of the parents in the patient's mind has in varying degrees undergone distortion through the infantile processes of projection and idealization, and has often retained much of its phantastic nature. Altogether, in the young infant's mind every external experience is interwoven with his phantasies and on the other hand every phantasy contains elements of actual experience, and it is only by analysing the transference situation to its depth that we are able to discover the past both in its realistic and phantastic aspects. It is also the origin of these fluctuations in earliest infancy which accounts for their strength in the transference, and for the swift changes—sometimes even within one session—between father and mother, between omnipotently kind objects and dangerous persecutors, between internal and external figures. Sometimes the analyst appears simultaneously to represent both parents—in that case often in a hostile alliance against the patient, whereby the negative transference acquires great intensity. What has then been revived or has become manifest in the transference is the mixture in the patient's phantasy of the parents as one figure, the 'combined parent figure' as I described it elsewhere.[9] This is one of the phantasy formations characteristic of the earliest stages of the Oedipus complex and which, if maintained in strength, is detrimental both to object-relations and sexual development. The phantasy of the combined parents draws its force from another element of early emotional life—i.e. from the powerful envy associated with frustrated oral desires. Through the analysis of such early situations we learn that in the baby's mind when he is frustrated (or dissatisfied from inner causes) his frustration is coupled with the feeling that another object (soon represented by the father) receives from the mother the coveted gratification and love denied to himself at that moment. Here is one root of the phantasy that the parents are combined in an everlasting mutual gratification of an oral, anal, and genital nature. And this is in my view the prototype of situations of both envy and jealousy.

There is another aspect of the analysis of transference which needs mentioning. We are accustomed to speak of the transference *situation*. But do we always keep in mind the fundamental importance of this concept? It is my experience that in unravelling the details of the transference it is essential to think in terms of *total situations* transferred from the past into the present, as well as of emotions, defences, and object-relations.

For many years—and this is up to a point still true today—transference was understood in terms of direct references to the analyst in the patient's material. My conception of transference as rooted in the earliest stages of development and in deep layers of the unconscious is much wider and entails a technique by which from the whole material presented the *unconscious elements* of the transference are deduced. For instance, reports of patients about their everyday life, relations, and activities not only give an insight into the functioning of the ego, but also reveal—if we explore their unconscious content—the defences against the anxieties stirred up in the transference situation. For the patient is bound to deal with conflicts and anxieties re-experienced towards the analyst by the same methods he used in the past. That is to say, he turns away from the analyst as he attempted to turn away from his primal objects; he tries to split the relation to him, keeping him either as a good or as a bad figure; he deflects some of the feelings and attitudes experienced towards the analyst on to other people in his current life, and this is part of 'acting out'.[10]

In keeping with my subject matter, I have predominantly discussed here the earliest experiences, situations, and emotions from which transference springs. On these foundations, however, are built the later object-relations and the emotional and intellectual developments which necessitate the analyst's attention no less than the earliest ones; that is to say, our field of investigation covers *all* that lies between the current situation and the earliest experiences. In fact it is not possible to find access to earliest emotions and object-relations except by examining their vicissitudes in the light of later developments. It is only by linking again and again (and that means hard and patient work) later experiences with earlier ones and *vice versa,* it is only by consistently exploring their interplay, that present and past can come together in the patient's mind. This is one aspect of the process of integration which, as the analysis progresses, encompasses the whole of the patient's mental life. When anxiety and guilt diminish and love and hate can be better synthesized, splitting processes—a fundamental defence against anxiety— as well as repressions lessen while the ego gains in strength and coherence; the cleavage between the idealized and persecutory objects diminishes; the phantastic aspects of objects lose in strength; all of which implies that unconscious phantasy life—less sharply divided off from the unconscious part of the mind—can be better utilized in ego activities, with a consequent general enrichment of the personality. I am touching here on the *differences* —as contrasted with the similarities—between transference and the first object-relations. These differences are a measure of the curative effect of the analytic procedure.

I suggested above that one of the factors which bring about the repetition compulsion is the pressure exerted by the earliest anxiety situations. When persecutory and depressive anxiety and guilt diminish, there is less urge to repeat fundamental experiences over and over again, and therefore early patterns and modes of feelings are maintained with less tenacity. These fundamental changes come about through the consistent analysis of the transference; they are bound up with a deep-reaching revision of the earliest object-relations and are reflected in the patient's current life as well as in the altered attitudes towards the analyst.

NOTES

1. 1905. Contained in *Collected Papers,* **3,** p. 139.
2. It is an essential feature of this earliest of all object-relations that it is the prototype of a relation between *two* people into which no other object enters. This is of vital importance for later object-relations, though in that exclusive form it possibly does not last longer than a very few months, for the phantasies relating to the father and his penis—phantasies which initiate the early stages of the Oedipus complex—introduce the relation to more than one object. In the analysis of adults and children the patient sometimes comes to experience feelings of blissful happiness through the revival of this early exclusive relation with the mother and her breast. Such experiences often follow the analysis of jealousy and rivalry situations in which a third object, ultimately the father, is involved.
3. 'Psycho-Analysis', 1922. Contained in *Collected Papers,* **5,** p. 119.
4. P. 39. On the same page Freud suggests—still referring to these first identifications—that

they are a direct and immediate identification which takes place earlier than any object cathexis. This suggestion seems to imply that introjection even precedes object-relations.

5. 1926. Chapter 8, p. 96.

6. 1931. 'Female Sexuality'; contained in *Collected Papers*, **5,** p. 254.

7. This was largely due to the undervaluation of the importance of aggression.

8. This technique is illustrated by H. Segal's paper, 'Some Aspects of the Analysis of a Schizophrenic' (*Int. J. Psycho-Anal.,* 31, 1950), and H. Rosenfeld's papers, 'Notes on the Psycho-Analysis of the Super-ego Conflict of an Acute Schizophrenic Patient' (*Int. J. Psycho-Anal.,* **33,** 1952) and 'Transference Phenomena and Transference Analysis in an Acute Catatonic Schizophrenic Patient' (see *Int. J. Psycho-Anal.,* **33,** 1952, 457–464).

9. See *Psycho-Analysis of Children,* particularly Chapters 8 and 11.

10. The patient may at times try to escape from the present into the past rather than realize that his emotions, anxieties, and phantasies are at the time operative in full strength and focused on the analyst. At other times, as we know, the defences are mainly directed against re-experiencing the past in relation to the original objects.

BIBLIOGRAPHY

Freud, Sigmund (1905). 'Fragment of an Analysis of a Case of Hysteria', *Collected Papers,* **3.**

———— (1922). 'Psycho-Analysis', *Collected Papers,* **5.**

———— (1923). *The Ego and the Id.*

———— (1926). *Inhibitions, Symptoms and Anxiety.*

———— (1931). 'Female Sexuality', *Collected Papers* **5.**

Klein, Melanie (1932). *The Psycho-Analysis of Children.* Hogarth Press.

———— (1946). 'Notes on Some Schizoid Mechanisms', *Int. J. Psycho-Anal.,* **27,** also contained in *Developments in Psycho-Analysis,* by Melanie Klein, Paula Heimann, Susan Isaacs, and Joan Riviere. (London: Hogarth Press, 1952).

———— (1948). *Contributions to Psycho-Analysis, 1921–45.* Hogarth Press.

Rosenfeld, Herbert (1952). 'Notes on the Psycho-Analysis of the Super-ego Conflict of an Acute Schizophrenic Patient', *Int. J. Psycho-Anal.,* **33.**

———— (1952). 'Transference Phenomena and Transference Analysis in an Acute Catatonic Schizophrenic Patient', *Int. J. Psycho-Anal.,* **33.**

Segal, Hanna (1950). 'Some Aspects of the Analysis of a Schizophrenic', *Int. J. Psycho-Anal.,* **31.**

16. On Transference

D. W. Winnicott

My contribution to this Symposium on Transference deals with one special aspect of the subject. It concerns the influence on analytical practice of the new understanding of infant care which has, in turn, derived from analytical theory.

There has often, in the history of psycho-analysis, been a delay in the direct application of analytical metapsychology in analytical practice. Freud was able to formulate a theory of the very early stages of the emotional development of the individual at a time when theory was being applied only in the treatment of the well-chosen neurotic case. (I refer to the period of Freud's work between 1905, the *Three Contributions,* and 1914, *Narcissism.*)

For instance, the part of theory that concerns the primary process, primary identification, and primary repression appeared in analytical practice only in the form of a greater respect that analysts had, as compared with others, for the dream and for psychic reality.

As we look back now we may say that cases were well chosen as suitable for analysis if in the very early personal history of the patient there had been good enough infant-care. This good enough adaptation to need at the beginning had enabled the individual's ego to come into being, with the result that the earlier stages of the establishment of the ego could be taken for granted by the analyst. In this way it was possible for analysts to talk and write as if the human infant's first experience was the first feed, and as if the object-relationship between mother and infant that this implied was the first significant relationship. This was satisfactory for the practising analyst, but it could not satisfy the direct observer of infants in the care of their mothers.

At that time theory was groping towards a deeper insight into this matter of the mother with her infant, and indeed the term 'primary identification' implies an environment that is not yet differentiated from that which will be

Reprinted by permission from the *International Journal of Psycho-Analysis* 37 (1956): 386–88. Copyright © Institute of Psycho-Analysis.

the individual. When we see a mother holding an infant soon after birth, or an infant not yet born, at this same time we know that there is another point of view, that of the infant if the infant were already there; and from this point of view the infant is either not yet differentiated out, or else the process of differentiation has started and there is absolute dependence on the immediate environment and its behaviour. It has now become possible to study and use this vital part of old theory in a new and practical way in analytical work, work either with borderline cases or else with the psychotic phases or moments that occur in the course of the analyses of neurotic patients or normal people. This work widens the concept of transference since at the time of the analysis of these phases the ego of the patient cannot be assumed as an established entity, and there can be no transference neurosis for which, surely, there must be an ego, and indeed an intact ego, an ego that is able to maintain defences against anxiety that arises out of instinct the responsibility for which is accepted.

I have referred to the state of affairs that exists when a move is made in the direction of emergence from primary identification. Here at first is absolute dependence. There are two possible kinds of outcome: by the one environmental adaptation to need is good enough, so that there comes into being an ego which, in time, can experience id-impulses; by the other environmental adaptation is not good enough, and so there is no true ego establishment, but instead there develops a pseudo-self which is a collection of innumerable reactions to a succession of failures of adaptation. I would like here to refer to Anna Freud's paper: 'The Widening Scope of Indications for Psycho-Analysis'.[1] The environment, when it successfully adapts at this early stage, is not recognized, or even recorded, so that in the original stage there is no feeling of dependence; whenever the environment fails in its task of making active adaptation, however, it automatically becomes recorded as an impingement, something that interrupts the continuity of being, that very thing which, if not broken up, would have formed itself into the ego of the differentiating human being.

There may be extreme cases in which there is no more than this collection of reactions to environmental failures of adaptation at the critical stage of emergence from primary identification. I am sure this condition is compatible with life, and with physical health. In the cases on which my work is based there has been what I call a true self hidden, protected by a false self. This false self is no doubt an aspect of the true self. It hides and protects it, and it reacts to the adaptation failures and develops a pattern corresponding to the pattern of environmental failure. In this way the true self is not involved in the reacting, and so preserves a continuity of being. This hidden true self suffers an impoverishment, however, that results from lack of experience.

The false self may achieve a deceptive false integrity, that is to say a false ego-strength, gathered from an environmental pattern, and from a good and reliable environment; for it by no means follows that early maternal failure must lead to a general failure of child-care. The false self cannot, however, experience life, and feel real.

In the favourable case the false self develops a fixed maternal attitude towards the true self, and is permanently in a state of holding the true self as a mother holds a baby at the very beginning of differentiation and of emergence from primary identification.

In the work that I am reporting the analyst follows the basic principle of psycho-analysis, that the patient's unconscious leads, and is alone to be pursued. In dealing with a regressive tendency the analyst must be prepared to follow the patient's unconscious process if he is not to issue a directive and so step outside the analyst's role. I have found that it is not necessary to step outside the analyst's role and that it is possible to follow the patient's unconscious lead in this type of case as in the analysis of neurosis. There are differences, however, in the two types of work.

Where there is an intact ego and the analyst can take for granted these earliest details of infant-care, then the setting of the analysis is unimportant relative to the interpretative work. (By setting, I mean the summation of all the details of management.) Even so there is a basic ration of management in ordinary analysis which is more or less accepted by all analysts.

In the work I am describing the setting becomes more important than the interpretation. The emphasis is changed from the one to the other.

The behaviour of the analyst, represented by what I have called the setting, by being good enough in the matter of adaptation to need, is gradually perceived by the patient as something that raises a hope that the true self may at last be able to take the risks involved in starting to experience living.

Eventually the false self hands over to the analyst. This is a time of great dependence, and true risk, and the patient is naturally in a deeply regressed state. (By regression here I mean regression to dependence and to the early developmental processes.) This is also a highly painful state because the patient is aware, as the infant in the original situation is not aware, of the risks entailed. In some cases so much of the personality is involved that the patient must be in care at this stage. The processes are better studied, however, in those cases in which these matters are confined, more or less, to the time of the analytic sessions.

One characteristic of the transference at this stage is the way in which we must allow the patient's past to *be* the present. This idea is contained in Mme. Sechehaye's book and in her title *Symbolic Realization*. Whereas in the transference neurosis the past comes into the consulting room, in this work it is more true to say that the present goes back into the past, and *is* the past. Thus the analyst finds himself confronted with the patient's's primary process in the setting in which it had its original validity.

Good enough adaptation by the analyst produces a result which is exactly that which is sought, namely, a shift in the patient of the main site of operation from a false to a true self. There is now for the first time in the patient's life an opportunity for the development of an ego, for its integration from ego nuclei, for its establishment as a body ego, and also for its repudiation of an external environment with the initiation of a relatedness to objects. For the first time the ego can experience id-impulses, and can feel real in so doing, and also in resting from experiencing. And from here there can at last follow an ordinary analysis of the ego's defences against anxiety.

There builds up an ability of the patient to use the analyst's limited successes in adaptation, so that the ego of the patient becomes able to begin to recall the original failures, all of which were recorded, kept ready. These failures had a disruptive effect at the time, and a treatment of the kind I am describing has gone a long way when the patient is able to take an example of original failure and to be angry about it. Only when the patient reaches this point, however, can there be the beginning of reality-testing. It seems that something like primary repression overtakes these recorded traumata once they have been used.

The way that this change from the experience of being disrupted to the experience of anger comes about is a matter that interests me in a special way, as it is at this point in my work that I found myself surprised. The patient makes use of the analyst's failures. Failures there must be, and indeed there is no attempt to give perfect adaptation; I would say that it is less harmful to make mistakes with these patients than with neurotic patients. The analyst may be surprised as I was to find that while a gross mistake may do but little harm, a very small error of judgement may produce a big effect. The clue is that the analyst's failure is being used and must be treated as a *past* failure, one that the patient can perceive and encompass, and be angry about. The analyst needs to be able to make use of his failures in terms of their meaning for the patients, and he must if possible account for each failure even if this means a study of his unconscious counter-transference.

In these phases of analytic work resistance or that which would be called resistance in work with neurotic patients always indicates that *the analyst has made a mistake,* or in some detail has behaved badly; in fact, the resistance remains until the analyst has found out the mistake and has tried to account for it, and has used it. If he defends himself just here the patient misses the opportunity for being angry about a past failure just where anger was becoming possible for the first time. Here is a great contrast between this work and the analysis of neurotic patients with intact ego. It is here that we can see the sense in the dictum that every failed analysis is a failure not of the patient but of the analyst.

This work is exacting partly because the analyst has to have a sensitivity to the patient's needs and a wish to provide a setting that caters for these needs. The analyst is not, after all, the patient's natural mother.

It is exacting, also, because of the necessity for the analyst to look for his own mistakes whenever resistances appear. Yet it is only by using his own mistakes that he can do the most important part of the treatment in these phases, the part that enables the patient to become angry for the first time about the details of failure of adaptation that (at the time when they happened) produced disruption. It is this part of the work that frees the patient from dependence on the analyst.

In this way the negative transference of 'neurotic' analysis is replaced by objective anger about the analyst's failures, so here again is an important difference between the transference phenomena in the two types of work.

We must not look for an awareness at a deep level of our adaptation successes, since these are not felt as such. Although we cannot work without the theory that we build up in our discussions, undoubtedly this work finds us out if our understanding of our patient's need is a matter of the mind rather than of the psychesoma.

I have discovered in my clinical work that one kind of analysis does not preclude the other. I find myself slipping over from one to the other and back again, according to the trend of the patient's unconscious process. When work of the special kind I have referred to is completed it leads naturally on to ordinary analytic work, the analysis of the depressive position and of the neurotic defences of a patient with an ego, an intact ego, an ego that is able to experience id-impulses and to take the consequences.

What I have described is only the beginning. For me it is the application of the statements I made in my paper 'Primitive Emotional Development' (1945). What needs to be done now is the study in detail of the criteria by which the analyst may know when to work with the change of emphasis, how to see that a need is arising which is of the kind that I have said must be met (at least in a token way) by active adaptation, the analyst keeping the concept of Primary Identification all the time in mind.

NOTES

1. *J. Amer. Psychoanal. Assoc.*, 2, 1954.

17. The Transference Phenomenon in Psychoanalytic Therapy

Janet MacKenzie Rioch

The significance of the transference phenomenon impressed Freud so profoundly that he continued through the years to develop his ideas about it. His classical observations on the patient Dora formed the basis for his first formulations of this concept. He says, "What are transferences? They are the new editions or facsimilies of the tendencies and phantasies which are aroused and made conscious during the progress of the analysis; but they have this peculiarity, which is characteristic for their species, that they replace some earlier person by the person of the physician. To put it another way: a whole series of psychological experiences are revived, not as belonging to the past, but as applying to the person of the physician at the present moment." [1]

According to Freud's view, the process of psychoanalytic cure depends mainly upon the patient's ability to remember that which is forgotten and repressed, and thus to gain conviction that the analytical conclusions arrived at are correct. However, "the unconscious feelings strive to avoid the recognition which the cure demands"; [2] they seek instead, emotional discharge, regardless of the reality of the situation.

Freud believed that these unconscious feelings which the patient strives to hide are made up of that part of the libidinal impulse which has turned away from consciousness and reality, due to the frustration of a desired gratification. Because the attraction of reality has weakened, the libidinal energy is still maintained in a state of regression attached to the original infantile sexual objects, although the reasons for the recoil from reality have disappeared. [3]

Freud states that in the analytic treatment, the analyst pursues this part of the libido to its hiding place, "aiming always at unearthing it, making it accessible to consciousness and at last serviceable to reality." [4] The patient tries to achieve an emotional discharge of this libidinal energy under the

Reprinted by permission from *Psychiatry* 6(1943): 147–56.

pressure of the compulsion to repeat experiences over and over again rather than to become conscious of their origin. He uses the method of transferring to the person of the physician past psychological experiences and reacting to this, at times, with all the power of hallucination.[5] The patient vehemently insists that his impression of the analyst is true for the immediate present, in this way avoiding the recognition of his own unconscious impulses.

Thus, Freud regarded the transference-manifestations as a major problem of the resistance. However, Freud says, "It must not be forgotten that they (the transference-manifestations) and they only, render the invaluable service of making the patient's buried and forgotten love-emotions actual and manifest."[6]

Freud regards the transference-manifestations as having two general aspects—positive and negative. The negative, he at first regarded as having no value in psychoanalytic cure and only something to be "raised"[7] into consciousness to avoid interference with the progress of the analysis. He later[8] accorded it a place of importance in the therapeutic experience. The positive transference he considered to be ultimately sexual in origin, since Freud says, "To begin with, we knew none but sexual objects."[9] However, he divides the positive transference into two components—one, the repressed erotic component, which is used in the service of resistance; the other, the friendly and affectionate component, which, although originally sexual, is the "unobjectionable" aspect of the positive transference, and is that which "brings about the successful result in psycho-analysis, as in all other remedial methods."[10] Freud refers here to the element of suggestion in psychoanalytic therapy, about which I wish to speak in detail a little later on.

At the moment, I should like to state that, although not agreeing with the view of Freud that human behavior depends ultimately on the biological sexual drives, I believe that it would be a mistake to deny the value and importance of his formulations regarding transference phenomena. As I shall indicate shortly, I differ on certain points with Freud, but I do not differ with the formulation that early impressions acquired during childhood are revived in the analytical situation, and are felt as immediate and real—that they form potentially the greatest obstacles to analysis, if unnoticed and, as Freud puts it, the greatest ally of the analysis when understood. I agree that the main work of the analysis consists in analyzing the transference phenomena, although I differ somewhat as to how this results in cure. It is my conviction that the transference is a strictly interpersonal experience. Freud gives the impression that under the stress of the repetition-compulsion the patient is bound to repeat the identical pattern, regardless of the other person. I believe that the personality of the analyst tends to determine the character of the transference illusions, and especially to determine whether the attempt at analysis will result in cure. Horney[11] has shown that there is no valid reason for assuming that the tendency to repeat past experiences again and again has an instinctual basis. The particular character structure of the person requires that he integrate with any given situation according to the necessities of his character structure.

In discussing my own views regarding the transference and its use in therapy, it is necessary to begin at the beginning, and to point out in a very schematic way how a person acquires his particular orientation to himself and the world—which one might call his character structure, and the implications of this in psychoanalytic therapy.

The infant is born without a frame of reference, as far as interpersonal experience goes. He is already acquainted with the feeling of bodily movement—with sucking and swallowing—but, among other things, he has had no knowledge of the existence of another *person* in relationship to himself. Although I do not wish to draw any particular conclusions from this analogy, I want to mention a simple phenomenon, described by Sherif,[12] connected with the problem of the frame of reference. If you have a completely dark room, with no possibility of any light being seen, and you then turn on a small-pin-point of light, which is kept stationary, this light will soon appear to be moving about. I am sure a good many of you have noticed this phenomenon when gazing at a single star. The light seems to move, and it does so, apparently, because there is no reference point in relation to which one can establish it at a fixed place in space. It just wanders around. If, however, one can at the same time see some other fixed object in the room, the light immediately becomes stationary. A reference point has been established, and there is no longer any uncertainty, any vague wandering of the spot of light. It is fixed. The pin-point of light wandering in the dark room is symbolic of the original attitude of the person to himself, undetermined, unstructured, with no reference points.

The new-born infant probably perceives everything in a vague and uncertain way, including himself. Gradually, reference points are established; a connection begins to occur between hunger and breast, between a relief of bladder tension and a wet diaper, between playing with his genitals and a smack on the hand. The physical boundaries and potentialities of the self are explored. One can observe the baby investigating the extent, shape and potentialities of his own body. He finds that he can scream and mother will come, or will not come, that he can hold his breath and everyone will get excited, that he can smile and coo and people will be enchanted, or just the opposite. The nature of the emotional reference points that he determines depends upon the environment. By that still unknown quality called "empathy," he discovers the reference points which help to determine his emotional attitude toward himself. If his mother did not want him, is disgusted with him, treats him with utter disregard, he comes to look upon himself as a thing-to-be-disregarded. With the profound human drive to make this rational, he gradually builds up a system of "reasons why." Underneath all these "reasons" is a basic sense of worthlessness, undetermined and undefined, related directly to the original reference frame. Another child discovers that the state of being regarded is dependent upon specific factors—all is well as long as one does not act spontaneously, as long as one is not a separate person, as long as one is good, as the state of being good is continuously defined by the parents. Under these conditions, and these only, this child can feel a sense of self-regard.

Other people are encountered with the original reference frame in mind. The child tends to carry over into later situations the patterns he first learned to know. The rigidity with which these original patterns are retained depends upon the nature of the child's experience. If this has been of a traumatic character so that spontaneity has been blocked and further emotional development has been inhibited, the original orientation will tend to persist. Discrepancies may be rationalized or repressed. Thus, the original impression of the hostile mother may be retained, while the contact with the new person is rationalized to fit the original reference frame. The new person encountered acts differently, but probably that is just a pose. She is just being nice because she does not know me. If she really knew me, she would act differently. Or, the original impressions are so out of line with the present actuality, that they remain unconscious, but make themselves apparent in inappropriate behavior or attitudes, which remain outside the awareness of the person concerned.

The incongruity of the behavior pattern, or of the attitude, may be a source of astonishment to the other person involved. Sullivan[13] provides insight into the process by the elucidation of what he calls the "parataxic distortions." He points out that in the development of the personality, certain integrative patterns are organized in response to the important persons in the child's past. There is a "self-in-relation-to-A" pattern, or "self-in-relation-to-B" pattern. These patterns of response become familiar and useful. The person learns to get along as a "self-in-relation-to A" or B, C and D, depending on the number of important people to whom he had to adjust in the course of his early development. For example, a young girl, who had a severely dominating mother and a weak, kindly father, learned a pattern of adjustment to her mother which could be briefly described as submissive, mildly rebellious in a secret way, but mostly lacking in spontaneity. Toward the father she developed a loving, but contemptuous attitude. When she encountered other people, regardless of sex, she oriented herself to them partly as the real people they were, and partly as she had learned to respond to her mother and father in her past. She thus was feeling toward the real person involved as if she were dealing with two people at once. However, since it is very necessary for people to behave as rational persons she suppressed the knowledge that some of her reactions were inappropriate to the immediate situation, and wove an intricate mesh of rationalizations, which permitted her to believe that the person with whom she was dealing really was someone either to be feared and submitted to, as her mother, or to be contemptuous of, as her father. The more nearly the real person fitted the original picture of the mother and father, the easier it was for her to maintain that the original "self-in-relation-to A or B" was the real and valid expression of herself.

It happened, however, that this girl had had a kindly nurse who was not a weak person, although occupying an inferior position in the household. During the many hours when she was with this nurse, she was able to experience a great deal of unreserved warmth, and of freedom for self-realization. No demands for emotional conformity were made on her in this relationship. Her own capacities for love and spontaneous activity were able to flourish. Unfortunately, the contact with this nurse was all too brief. But there remained, despite the necessity for the rigid development of the patterns towards the mother and father, a deeply repressed, but still vital experience of self, which most closely approximated the fullest realization of her potentialities. This, which one might call her *real self,* although 'snowed under' and handicapped by all the distortions incurred by her relationship to the parents, was finally able to emerge and become again active in analysis. In the course of this treatment, she learned how much her reactions to people were "transference" reactions, or as Sullivan would say, "parataxic distortions."

I have deliberately tried to schematize this illustration. For instance, when

I speak of the early frame of reference and then just mention the parents, I do not overlook all the other possible reference frames. Also, one has to realize that one pattern connects with another—the whole making a tangled mass that only years of analysis can unscramble. I also have not taken the time to outline the compensatory drives that the neurotic person has to develop in order to handle his life situation. Each compensatory manœuver causes some change in his frame of reference, since the development of a defensive trait in his personality sets off a new set of relationships to those around him. The little child who grows more and more negativistic, because of injuries and frustrations, evokes more and more hostility in his environment. However, and this is important, the basic reactions of hostility on the part of the parents, which originally induced his negativism, are still there. Thus, the pattern does not change much in character—it just gets worse in the same direction. Those persons whose later life experience perpetuate the original frames of reference are more severely injured. A young child, who has a hostile mother, may then have a hostile teacher. If, by good luck, he got a kind teacher and if his own attitude was not already badly warped, so that he did not induce hostility in this kind teacher, he would be introduced into a startlingly new and pleasant frame of reference, and his personality might not suffer too greatly, especially if a kindly aunt or uncle happened to be around. I am sure that if the details of the life histories of healthy people were studied, it would be found that they had had some very satisfactory experiences early enough to establish in them a feeling of validity as persons. The profoundly sick people have been so early injured, in such a rigid and limited frame of reference, that they are not able to make use of kindliness, decency or regard when it does come their way. They meet the world as if it were potentially menacing. They have already developed defensive traits entirely appropriate to their original experience, and then carry them out in completely inappropriate situations, rationalizing the discrepancies, but never daring to believe that people are different to the ones they early learned to distrust and hate. By reason of bitter early experience, they learn never to let their guards down, never to permit intimacy, lest at that moment the death blow would be dealt to their already partly destroyed sense of self-regard. Despairing of real joy in living, they develop secondary neurotic goals which give a pseudo-satisfaction. The secondary gains at first glance might seem to be what the person was really striving for—revenge, power and exclusive possession. Actually, these are but the expressions of the deep injuries sustained by the person. They can not be fundamentally cured until those interpersonal relationships which caused the original injury are brought back to consciousness in the analytical situation. Step by step, each phase of the long period of emotional development is exposed, by no means chronologically; the interconnecting, overlapping reference frames are made conscious; those points at which a distortion of reality, or a repression of part of the self *had* to occur, are uncovered. The reality gradually becomes "undistorted," the self, refound, in the personal relationship between the analyst and the patient. This personal relationship with the analyst is the situation in which the transference distortions can be analyzed.

In Freud's view, the transference was either positive or negative, and was related in a rather isolated way to a particular person in the past. In my view, the transference is the experiencing in the analytic situation the entire pattern of the original reference frames, which included at every moment the relationship of the patient to himself, to the important persons, and to others, as he experienced them at that time, in the light of his interrelationships with the important people.

The therapeutic aim in this process is not to uncover childhood memories which will then lend themselves to analytic interpretation. Here, I think, is an important difference to Freud's view. Fromm[14] has pointed this out in a recent lecture. Psychoanalytic cure is not the amassing of data, either from childhood, or from the study of the present situation. Nor does cure result from a repetition of the original injurious experience in the analytical relationship. What is curative in the process is that in tending to reconstruct with the analyst that atmosphere which obtained in childhood, the patient actually achieves something new. He discovers that part of himself which had to be repressed at the time of the original experience. He can only do this in a interpersonal relationship with the analyst, which is suitable to such a rediscovery. To illustrate this point: if a patient had a hostile parent towards whom he was required to show deference, he would have to repress certain of his own spontaneous feelings. In the analytical situation, he tends to carry over his original frame of reference and again tends to feel himself to be in a similar situation. If the analyst's personality also contains elements of a need for deference, that need will unconsciously be imparted to the patient, who will, therefore, still repress his spontaneity as he did before. True enough, he may act or try to act as if analyzed, since by definition, that is what the analyst is attempting to accomplish. But he will *never* have found his repressed self, because the analytical relationship contains for him elements actually identical with his original situation. Only if the analyst provides a genuinely *new* frame of reference—that is, if he is truly non-hostile, and truly not in need of deference—can this patient discover, and it is a real *discovery,* the repressed elements of his own personality. Thus, the transference phenomenon is used so that the patient will completely reexperience the original frames of reference, and himself within those frames, in a truly different relationship with the analyst, to the end that he can discover the invalidity of his conclusions about himself and others.

I do not mean by this to deny the correctness of Freud's view of transference also acting as a resistance. As a matter of fact, the tendency of the patient to reestablish the original reference frame is precisely because he is afraid to experience the other person in a direct and unreserved way. He has organized his whole system of getting along in the world, bad as that system might be, on the basis of the original distortions of his personality and his subsequent vicissitudes. His capacity for spontaneous feeling and acting has gone into hiding. Now it has to be sought. If some such phrase as the "capacity for self-realization" be substituted in place of Freud's concept of the repressed libidinal impulse, much the same conclusions can be reached about the way in which the transference-manifestations appear in the analysis as resistance. It is just in the safest situation, where the spontaneous feeling might come out of hiding, that the patient develops intense feelings, sometimes of a hallucinatory character, that relate to the most dreaded experiences of the past. It is at this point that the nature and the use by the patient of the transference distortions have to be understood and correctly interpreted by the analyst. It is also here that the personality of the analyst modifies the transference reaction. A patient cannot feel close to a detached or hostile analyst and will therefore never display the full intensity of his transference illusions. The complexity of this process, whereby the transference can be used as the therapeutic instrument and, at the same time, as a resistance may be illustrated by the following example: a patient had developed intense feelings of attachment to a father surrogate in his everyday life. The transference feelings towards this man were of great value in elucidating his original problems with his real father. As the patient became more and more aware of his own personal validity, he found this masochistic attachment to be weakening. This occasioned acute feelings of anxiety, since his sense of independence was not yet fully established. At that point, he developed very disturbing feelings regarding the analyst, believing that she was untrustworthy and hostile, although prior to this, he had succeeded in establishing a realistically positive relationship to her. The feelings of untrustworthiness precisely reproduced an ancient pattern with his mother. He experienced them at this particular point in the analysis in order to retain and to justify his attachment to the father figure, the weakening of which attachment had threatened him so profoundly. The entire pattern was elucidated when it was seen that he was reexperiencing an ancient triangle, in which he was continuously driven to a submissive attachment to a dominating father, due to the utter untrustworthiness of his weak mother. If the transference character of this sudden feeling of untrustworthiness of the analyst had not been clarified, he would have turned again submissively to his father surrogate, which would have further postponed his development of independence. Nevertheless, the development of this transference to the analyst brought to light a new insight.

I wish to make one remark about Freud's view of the so-called narcissistic neuroses. Freud felt that personality disorders called schizophrenia or paranoia cannot be analyzed because the patient is unable to develop a transference to the analyst. It is my view that the real difficulty in treating such disorders is that the relationship is essentially nothing but transference illusions. Such persons hallucinate the original frame of reference to the exclusion of reality. Nowhere in the realm of psychoanalysis can one find more complete proof of the effect of early experience on the person that in attempting to treat these patients. Frieda Fromm-Reichmann[15] has shown in her work with schizophrenics the necessity to realize the intensity of the transference reaction, which have become almost completely real to the patient. And yet, if one knows the correct interpretations, by actually feeling the patient's needs, one can over years of time do the identical thing which is accomplished more quickly and less dramatically with patients suffering a less severe disturbance of their interpersonal relationships.

Another point which I wish to discuss for a moment is the following:

Freud takes the position that all subsequent experience in normal life is merely a repetition of the original one.[16] Thus love is experienced for someone today *in terms* of the love felt for someone in the past. I do not believe this to be exactly true. The child who has not had to repress certain aspects of his personality enters into a new situation dynamically, not just as a repetition of what he felt, say, with his mother, but as an active continuation of it. I believe that there are constitutional differences with respect to the total capacity for emotional experience, just as there are with respect to the total capacity for intellectual experiences. Given this constitutional substrate, the child engages in personal relationships not passively as a lump of clay waiting to be molded, but most dynamically, bringing into play all his emotional potentialities. He may possibly find someone later whose capacity for response is deeper than his mother's. If *he* is capable of that greater depth, he experiences an expansion of himself. Many later in life have met a "great" person and have felt a sense of newness in the relationship which is described to others as "wonderful" and which is regarded with a certain amount of awe. This is not a "transference" experience but represents a dynamic extension of the self to a new horizon.

In considering the process of psychoanalytic cure, Freud very seriously discussed the relationship of analysis to suggestion therapy and hypnosis. He believed as I previously mentioned that part of the positive transference could be made use of in the analysis to bring about the successful result. He says, "In so far we readily admit that the results of psychoanalysis rest upon a basis of suggestion; only by suggestion we must be understood to mean that which we, with Ferenczi, find that it consists of—influence on a person through and by means of the transference-manifestations of which he is capable. The eventual independence of the patient is our ultimate object when we use suggestion to bring him to carry out a mental operation that will necessarily result in a lasting improvement in his mental condition." [17] Freud elsewhere indicates very clearly that in hypnosis, the relationship of the patient to the hypnotist is not worked through, whereas in analysis the transference to the analyst is resolved by bringing it entirely into consciousness. He also says that the patient is protected from the unwitting suggestive influence of the analysts by the awakening of his own unconscious resistances. [18]

I should like to discuss hypnosis a little more in detail and to make a few remarks about its correlation with the transference phenomenon in psychoanalytic therapy.

According to White, [19] the subject under hypnosis is a person striving to act like a hypnotized person as that state is continuously defined by the hypnotist. He also says that the state of being hypnotized is an "altered state of consciousness." However, as Maslow [20] points out, it is not an abnormal state. In everyday life transient manifestations of all the phenomena that occur in hypnosis can be seen. Such examples are cited as the trance-like state a person experiences when completely occupied with an absorbing book. Among the phenomena of the hypnotic state are the amnesia for the trance; the development of certain anaesthesias, such as insensitivity to pain; deafness to sounds other than the hypnotist's voice; greater ability to recall forgotten events; loss of capacity to spontaneously initiate activities; and a much greater suggestibility. This heightened suggestibility in the trance state is the most important phenomenon of hypnosis. Changes in behavior and feeling can be induced, such as painful or pleasant experiences, headaches, nausea, or feelings of well-being. Post-hypnotic behavior can be influenced by suggestion, this being one of the most important aspects of experimental hypnosis for the clarifying of psychopathological problems.

The hypnotic state is induced by a combination of methods which may include relaxation, visual concentration and verbal suggestion. The methods vary with the personality of the experimenter and the subject.

Maslow has pointed out the interpersonal character of hypnosis, which accounts for some of the different conclusions by different experimenters. Roughly, the types of experimenters may be divided into three groups—the dominant type, the friendly or brotherly type, and the cold, detached, scientific type. According to the inner needs of the subject, he will be able to be hypnotized more readily by one type or the other. The brotherly hypnotizer cannot, for instance, hypnotize a subject whose inner need is to be dominated.

Freud[21] believed that the relationship of the subject to the hypnotist was that of an emotional, erotic attachment. He comments on the "uncanny" character of hypnosis and says that "the hypnotist awakens in the subject a portion of his archaic inheritance which had also made him compliant to his parents." What is thus awakened is the concept of "the dreaded primal father," "towards whom only a passive-masochistic attitude is possible, towards whom one's will has to be surrendered."

Ferenczi[22] considered the hypnotic state to be one in which the patient transferred onto the hypnotist his early infantile erotic attachment to the parents with the same tendency to blind belief and to uncritical obedience as obtained then. He calls attention to the paternal or frightening type of hypnosis and the maternal or gentle, stroking type. In both instances the situation tends to favour the "conscious and unconscious imaginary return to childhood."

The only point of disagreement with these views that I have is that one does not need to postulate an *erotic* attachment to the hypnotist or a "transference" of infantile sexual wishes. The sole necessity is a willingness to surrender oneself. The child whose parent wished to control it, by one way or another, is forced to do this, in order to be loved, or at least to be taken care of. The patient transfers this willingness to surrender to the hypnotist.[23]

He will also transfer it to the analyst or to the leader of a group. In any one of these situations the authoritative person, be he hypnotist, analyst or leader, promises by reason of great power or knowledge the assurance of safety, cure or happiness, as the case may be. The patient, or the isolated person, regresses emotionally to a state of helplessness and lack of initiative similar to the child who has been dominated.

If it be asked how in the first place the child is brought into a state of submissiveness, it may be discovered that the original situation of the child had certain aspects which already resemble a hypnotic situation. This depends upon the parents. If they are destructive or authoritarian they can achieve long-lasting results. The child is continuously subjected to being told *how* and *what* he is. Day in and day out, in the limited frame of reference of his home, he is subjected to the repetition, over and over again: "You are a naughty boy." "You are a bad girl." "You are just a nuisance." "You are always giving me trouble." "You are dumb," "you are stupid," "you are a little fool." "You always make mistakes." "You can never do anything right"; or, "that's right; I love you when you are a good boy." "That's the kind of boy I like." "Now you are a nice boy." "Smile sweetly." "Pay attention to mother." "Mother loves a good boy who does what she tells him." "Mother knows best, mother always knows best." "If you would listen to mother, you would get along all right. Just listen to her." "Don't pay attention to those naughty children. Just listen to your mother."

Over and over again, with exhortations to pay attention, to listen, to be good, the child is brought under the spell. "When you get older, never forget what I told you. Always remember what mother says, then you will never get into trouble." These are like post-hypnotic suggestions. "You will never come to a good end. You will always be in trouble." "If you are not good, you will always be unhappy." "If you don't do what I say, you will regret it." "If you do not live up to the right things—again, 'right' as continuously defined by the mother—you will be sorry."

It was called to my attention that the Papago Indians deliberately make use of a certain method of suggestion to influence the child favorably. When the child is falling asleep at night the grandfather sits by him and repeats over and over—"You will be a fast runner. You will be a good hunter." [24]

Hypnotic experiments, according to Hull, [25] indicate that children, on the whole, are more susceptible than adults. Certainly, for many reasons, including that of learning the uses and misuses of language, there is a marked rise of verbal suggestibility up to five years, with a sharp dropping off at around the eighth year. Ferenczi refers to the subsequent effects of threats or orders given in childhood as "having much in common with the post-hypnotic command-automatisms." He points out how the neurotic patient follows out, without being able to explain the motive, a command repressed long ago, just as in hypnosis a post-hypnotic suggestion is carried out for which amnesia has been produced.

It is not my intention in this paper to try to explain the altered state of consciousness which is seen in the hypnotized subject. I have had no personal experience with hypnosis. The reason I refer to hypnosis in discussing the transference is in order to further an understanding of the analytic relationship. The child may be regarded as being in a state of "chronic hypnosis," as I have described, with all sorts of post-hypnotic suggestions thrown in during this period. This entire pattern—this entire early frame of reference —may be "transferred" to the analyst. When this has happened the patient is in a highly suggestible state. Due to a number of intrinsic and extrinsic factors, the analyst is now in the position of a sort of "chronic hypnotist." First, by reason of his position of a doctor he has a certain prestige. Second, the patient *comes* to him, even if expressedly unwillingly; still if there were not something in the patient which was cooperative he would not come at all, or at least he would not stay. The office is relatively quiet, external stimuli relatively reduced. The frame of reference is limited. Many analysts maintain an anonymity about themselves. The attention is focussed on the interpersonal relationship. In this relatively undefined and unstructured field the patient is able to discover his "transference" feelings, since he has few reference points in the analytical situation to go by. This is greatly enhanced by having the patient assume a physical position in the room whereby he does not see the analyst. Thus the ordinary reference points of facial expression and gesture are lacking. True enough, he can look around or get up and walk about. But for considerable periods of time he lies down—itself a symbolically submissive position. He does what is called "free association." This is again giving up—willingly, to be sure—the conscious control of his thoughts. I want to stress the willingness and cooperativeness of all these acts. That is precisely the necessary condition for hypnosis. The lack of immediate reference points permits the eruption into consciousness of the old patterns of feeling. The original frame of reference becomes more and more clearly outlined and felt. The power which the parent originally had to cast the spell is transferred to the analytical situation. Now it is the analyst who is in the position to do the same thing—placed there partly by the nature of the external situation, partly by the patient who comes to be freed from his suffering.

There is no such thing as an impersonal analyst, nor is the idea of the analyst's acting as a mirror anything more than the "neatest trick of the week." Whether intentionally or not, whether conscious of it or not, the analyst does express, day in and day out, subtle or overt evidences of his own personality in relationship to the patient.

The analyst may express explicitly his wish not to be coercive, but if he has an unconscious wish to control the patient, it is impossible for him correctly to analyze and to resolve the transference distortions. The patient is thus not able to become free from his original difficulties and for lack of something better adopts the analyst as a new and less dangerous authority. Then the situation occurs in which it is not "my mother says" or "my father says," but now "my analyst says." The so-called chronic patients who need lifelong support may benefit by such a relationship. I am of the opinion, however, that frequently the long-continued unconscious attachment—by which I do *not* mean genuine affection or regard—is maintained because of a failure on the analyst's part to recognize and resolve the sense of being under a sort of hypnotic spell which originated in childhood.

To develope an adequate therapeutic interpersonal relationship, the analyst must be devoid of those personal traits which tend to unconsciously perpetuate the originally destructive or authoritative situation. In addition to this, he must be able, by reason of his training, to be aware of every evidence of the transference phenomena; and lastly, he must understand the significance of the hypnotic-like situation which analysis helps to reproduce. If, with the best of intentions, he unwittingly makes use of the enormous power with which he is endowed by the patient, he may certainly achieve something that looks like change. His suggestions, exhortations and pronouncements based on the patient's revelation of himself, may certainly make an impression. The analyst may say, "You must not do this just because I say so." That is in itself a sort of post-hypnotic command. The patient then strives to be "an analyzed person acting on his own account"—because he was told to do so. He is still not really acting on his own.

It is my firm conviction that analysis is terminable. A person can continue to grow and expand all his life. The process of analysis, however, as an interpersonal experience, has a definite end. That end is achieved when the patient has rediscovered his own self as an actively and independently functioning entity.

NOTES

1. Freud, Sigmund, *Collected Papers;* London, Hogarth (1933) 3:139.
2. Ibid., 2:321.
3. Ibid., 2:316.
4. Ibid.
5. Ibid., 2:321.
6. Ibid., 3:322.
7. Ibid., 3:319.
8. Freud, Sigmund, *Gesammelte Werke;* London, Imago (1940) 12:223.
9. Freud, *Collected Papers;* 3:139.
10. Ibid.
11. Horney, Karen, *New Ways in Psychoanalysis;* New York, Norton, 1939 (313 pp.).
12. Sherif, Muzafer A. F., *The Psychology of Social Norms;* New York, Harper, 1936 (xii and 210 pp.).
13. Sullivan, Harry Stack, Conceptions of Modern Psychiatry. *Psychiatry* (1940) 3:1–117.
14. Fromm, Erich, Lectures on *Ideas and Ideologies* presented at the New School for Social Research, N.Y.C., 1943.
15. Fromm-Reichmann, Frieda, Transference Problems in Schizophrenics. *Psychoanal. Q.* (1939) 8:412–426.
16. Freud, *Collected Papers;* 3:387.
17. Ibid., 3:319.
18. Freud, *Gesammelte Werke;* 12:226.
19. White, Robert W., A Preface to the Theory of Hypnotism. *J. Abnormal and Social Psychology* (1941) 36:477–505.
20. Maslow, A. H., and Mittelmann, Bela, *Principles of Abnormal Psychology;* New York, Harper, 1941 (x and 638 pp.).
21. Freud, Sigmund, *Group Psychology and the Analysis of the Ego;* London, The International Psycho-Analytical Press, 1922 (134 pp.).
22. Ferenczi, Sandor, *Sex in Psycho-Analysis;* Boston, Badger, 1916 (338 pp.)—in particular, Introjection and Transference.
23. I am indebted to Erich Fromm for suggestions in the following discussion.
24. Underhill, Ruth, *Social Organization of the Papago Indians* [Columbia University Contributions to Anthropology: Vol. 30]; New York, Columbia University Press, 1939 (ix and 280 pp.).
25. Hull, Clark L., *Hypnosis and Suggestibility;* New York, Appleton-Century, 1933 (xii and 416 pp.).

18. Transference Problems in Schizophrenics

Frieda Fromm-Reichmann

Most psychoanalytic authors maintain that schizophrenic patients cannot be treated psychoanalytically because they are too narcissistic to develop with the psychotherapist an interpersonal relationship that is sufficiently reliable and consistent for psychoanalytic work *(1, 12, 13)*. Freud, Fenichel and other authors have recognized that a new technique of approaching patients psychoanalytically must be found if analysts are to work with psychotics *(2, 6, 8, 16, 19, 31–36)*. Among those who have worked successfully in recent years with schizophrenics, Sullivan, Hill, and Karl Menninger and his staff have made various modifications of their analytic approach *(14, 17, 21–25, 28, 29)*.

In our work at the Chestnut Lodge Sanitarium we have found similar changes valuable. The technique we use with psychotics is different from our approach to psychoneurotics *(3, 4, 32, 33)*. This is not a result of the schizophrenic's inability to build up a consistent personal relationship with the therapist but due to his extremely intense and sensitive transference reactions.

Let us see first what the essence of the schizophrenic's transference reactions is and second how we try to meet these reactions.

In order to understand them we must state those parts of our hypothesis about the genesis of these illnesses that are significant for the development of the patient's personal relationships and thus for our therapeutic approach.

We think of a schizophrenic as a person who has had serious traumatic experiences in early infancy at a time when his ego and its ability to examine reality were not yet developed. These early traumatic experiences seem to furnish the psychological basis for the pathogenic influence of the frustrations of later years. At this early time the infant lives grandiosely in a narcissistic world of his own. His needs and desires seem to be taken care of by something vague and indefinite which he does not yet differentiate. As Ferenczi *(7)* noted they are expressed by gestures and movements since

Reprinted by permission from *Psychoanalytic Quarterly* 8, (1939): 412–26.

speech is as yet undeveloped. Frequently the child's desires are fulfilled without any expression of them, a result that seems to him a product of his magical thinking.

Traumatic experiences in this early period of life will damage a personality more seriously than those occurring in later childhood such as are found in the history of psychoneurotics. The infant's mind is more vulnerable the younger and less used it has been; further, the trauma is a blow to the infant's egocentricity. In addition early traumatic experience shortens the only period in life in which an individual ordinarily enjoys the most security, thus endangering the ability to store up as it were a reasonable supply of assurance and self-reliance for the individual's later struggle through life. Thus is such a child sensitized considerably more towards the frustrations of later life than by later traumatic experience. Hence many experiences in later life which would mean little to a 'healthy' person and not much to a psychoneurotic, mean a great deal of pain and suffering to the schizophrenic. His resistance against frustration is easily exhausted.

Once he reaches his limit of endurance, he escapes the unbearable reality of his present life by attempting to reestablish the autistic, delusional world of the infant; but this is impossible because the content of his delusions and hallucinations are naturally colored by the experiences of his whole lifetime *(9–12, 21–25).*

How do these developments influence the patient's attitude towards the analyst and the analyst's approach to him?

Due to the very early damage and the succeeding chain of frustrations which the schizophrenic undergoes before finally giving in to illness, he feels extremely suspicious and distrustful of everyone, particularly of the psychotherapist who approaches him with the intention of intruding into his isolated world and personal life. To him the physician's approach means the threat of being compelled to return to the frustrations of real life and to reveal his inadequacy to meet them, or—still worse—a repetition of the aggressive interference with his initial symptoms and peculiarities which he has encountered in his previous environment.

In spite of his narcissistic retreat, every schizophrenic has some dim notion of the unreality and loneliness of his substitute delusionary world. He longs for human contact and understanding, yet is afraid to admit it to himself or to his therapist for fear of further frustration.

That is why the patient may take weeks and months to test the therapist before being willing to accept him.[1]

However once he has accepted him, his dependence on the therapist is greater and he is more sensitive about it than is the psychoneurotic because of the schizophrenic's deeply rooted insecurity; the narcissistic seemingly self-righteous attitude is but a defense.

Whenever the analyst fails the patient from reasons to be discussed later —one cannot at times avoid failing one's schizophrenic patients—it will be a severe disappointment and a repetition of the chain of frustrations the schizophrenic has previously endured.

To the primitive part of the schizophrenic's mind that does not discriminate between himself and the environment, it may mean the withdrawal of the impersonal supporting forces of his infancy. Severe anxiety will follow this vital deprivation.

In the light of his personal relationship with the analyst it means that the therapist seduced the patient to use him as a bridge over which he might possibly be led from the utter loneliness of his own world to reality and human warmth, only to have him discover that this bridge is not reliable. If so, he will respond helplessly with an outburst of hostility or with renewed withdrawal as may be seen most impressively in catatonic stupor.

One patient responded twice with a catatonic stupor when I had to change the hour of my appointment with her; both times it was immediately dispelled when I came to see her and explained the reasons for the change. This withdrawal during treatment is a way the schizophrenic has of showing resistance and is dynamically comparable to the various devices the psychoneurotic utilizes to show resistance.[2]

The schizophrenic responds to alterations in the analyst's defections and understanding by corresponding stormy and dramatic changes from love to hatred, from willingness to leave his delusional world to resistance and renewed withdrawal.

As understandable as these changes are, they nevertheless may come quite as a surprise to the analyst who frequently has not observed their source. This is quite in contrast to his experience with psychoneurotics whose emotional reactions during an interview he can usually predict. These unpredictable changes seem to be the reason for the conception of the unreliability of the schizophrenic's transference reactions; yet they follow the same dynamic rules as the psychoneurotic's oscillations between positive and negative transference and resistance. *If the schizophrenic's reactions are more stormy and seemingly more unpredictable than those of the psychoneurotic, I believe it to be due to the inevitable errors in the analyst's approach to the schizophrenic, of which he himself may be unaware, rather than to the unreliability of the patient's emotional response.*

Why is it inevitable that the psychoanalyst disappoints his schizophrenic patients time and again?

The schizophrenic withdraws from painful reality and retires to what resembles the early speechless phase of development where consciousness is not yet crystallized. As the expression of his feelings is not hindered by the conventions he has eliminated, so his thinking, feeling, behavior and speech —when present—obey the working rules of the archaic unconscious *(26)*. His thinking is magical and does not follow logical rules. It does not admit a *no,* and likewise no *yes;* there is no recognition of space and time. I, you, and they are interchangeable. Expression is by symbols; often by movements and gestures rather than by words.

As the schizophrenic is suspicious, he will distrust the words of his analyst. He will interpret them and incidental gestures and attitudes of the analyst according to his own delusional experience. The analyst may not even be aware of these involuntary manifestations of his attitudes; yet they mean much to the hypersensitive schizophrenic who uses them as a means of orienting himself to the therapist's personality and intentions towards him.

In other words, the schizophrenic patient and the therapist are people living in different worlds and on different levels of personal development with different means of expressing and of orienting themselves. We know little about the language of the unconscious of the schizophrenic, and our access to it is blocked by the very process of our own adjustment to a world the schizophrenic has relinquished. So we should not be surprised that errors and misunderstandings occur when we undertake to communicate and strive for a rapport with him.

Another source of the schizophrenic's disappointment arises from the following: since the analyst accepts and does not interfere with the behavior of the schizophrenic, his attitude may lead the patient to expect that the analyst will assist in carrying out all the patient's wishes, even though they may not seem to be to his interest, or to the analyst's and the hospital's in their relationship to society. This attitude of acceptance so different from the patient's previous experiences readily fosters the anticipation that the analyst will try to carry out the patient's suggestions and take his part, even against conventional society should occasion arise. Frequently it will be wise for the analyst to agree with the patient's wish to remain unbathed and untidy until he is ready to talk about the reasons for his behavior or to change spontaneously. At other times he will unfortunately be unable to take the patient's part without being able to make the patient understand and accept the reasons for the analyst's position.

For example, I took a catatonic patient who asked for a change of scene one day for lunch to a country inn, another time to a concert, and a third time to an art gallery. After that he asked me to permit him with a nurse to visit his parents in another city. I told him I would have to talk this over with the superintendent and in addition suggested notifying his people. Immediately he became furious and combative because this meant that I was betraying him by consulting with others about what he regarded as a purely personal matter. From his own detached and childlike viewpoint he was right. He had given up his isolation in exchange for my personal interest in him, but he was not yet ready to have other persons admitted to this intimate relationship.

If the analyst is not able to accept the possibility of misunderstanding the reactions of his schizophrenic patient and in turn of being misunderstood by him, it may shake his security with his patient.

The schizophrenic, once he accepts the analyst and wants to rely upon him, will sense the analyst's insecurity. Being helpless and insecure himself —in spite of his pretended grandiose isolation—he will feel utterly defeated by the insecurity of his would-be helper. Such disappointment may furnish reasons for outbursts of hatred and rage that are comparable to the negative transference reactions of psychoneurotics, yet more intense than these since they are not limited by the restrictions of the actual world.

These outbursts are accompanied by anxiety, feelings of guilt, and fear of retaliation which in turn lead to increased hostility. Thus is established a vicious circle: we disappoint the patient; he hates us, is afraid we hate him for his hatred and therefore continues to hate us. If in addition he senses that the analyst is afraid of his aggressiveness, it confirms his fear that he is actually considered to be dangerous and unacceptable, and this augments his hatred.

This establishes that *the schizophrenic is capable of developing strong relationships of love and hatred towards his analyst.*

'After all, one could not be so hostile if it were not for the background of a very close relationship', said one catatonic patient after emerging from an acutely disturbed and combative episode.

In addition, I believe *the schizophrenic develops transference reactions in the narrower sense* which he can differentiate from the actual interpersonal relationship.

A catatonic artist stated the difference between the two kinds of relations while he was still delusional and confused when he said pointing to himself, 'There is the artist, the designer and the drawer', then looking around my office at the desk and finally at me, 'the scientist, the research worker, the psychiatrist. . . . As to these two my fears of changes between treatment and injury do not hold true. Yet, there is also something else between us—and there is fear of injury and treatment—treatment and injury.' Then he implored me: 'Understand! Try to be psychic—that will constitute real communism between us' (here using a political symbol to indicate a personal bond).

Another instructive example was given by an unwanted and neglected middle child of a frigid mother. He fought all his life for the recognition denied him by his family. Ambitious, he had a successful career as a researcher. During the war he was called to a prominent research center some distance from his home. Ten years later, after several frustrating repetitions of his childhood conflicts, he became sick.

The first eighteen months of his analysis were spent in a continuous barrage of hatred and resentment. He would shout: 'You dirty little stinking bitch', or, 'You damned German Jew; go back to your Kaiser!' or, 'I wish you had crashed in that plane you took!'. He threatened to throw all manner of things at me. These stormy outbursts could be heard all over the hospital.

After a year and a half he became less disturbed and began to be on friendly terms with me, accepting willingly some interpretations and suggestions. Asked about his hatred of me, he said, 'Oh, I think I did not actually hate you; underneath I always liked you. But when I had that call to the Institute—do you remember?—I saw what the Germans had done to our men and I hated you as a German for that. Besides, mother, far from being proud of me as you would have expected, hated me for going instead of staying home and supporting her pet, my younger brother. You were mother, and I hated you for that. My sister, although living near the Institute, did not even once come to see me although she had promised to. So you became sister, and I hated you for that. Can you blame me?'

From these examples can one doubt that the schizophrenic demonstrates workable transference reactions?

As the usual psychoanalytic approach is effective only with psychoneurotics, what modifications are necessary in our current technique in order to meet the particular needs of schizophrenics?

Contact with the schizophrenic must begin with a long preparatory period of daily interviews (as in psychoanalysis with children) during which the patient is given the opportunity of becoming acquainted with the analyst, of finding out if the analyst can be of value to him, and of overcoming his suspicion and his anxiety about the friendship and consideration offered to him by the analyst. After that the patient may gain confidence in his physician and at last accept him.

One patient shouted at me every morning for six weeks, 'I am not sick; I don't need any doctor; it's none of your damned business'. At the beginning of the seventh week the patient offered me a dirty crumpled cigarette. I took it and smoked it. The next day he had prepared a seat for me by covering a bench in the yard where I met him with a clean sheet of paper. 'I don't want you to soil your dress', he commented. This marked the beginning of his acceptance of me as a friend and therapist.

Another very suspicious patient after two days of fear and confusion ushering in a real panic became stuporous for a month—mute, resistive to food and retaining excretions. In spite of this rather unpromising picture, I sat with him for an hour every day. The only sign of contact he gave to me or anyone was to indicate by gestures that he wanted me to stay; all that he said on two different days during this period was: 'Don't leave!'.

One morning after this I found him sitting naked and masturbating on the floor of his room which was spotted with urine and sputum, talking for the first time yet so softly that I could not understand him. I stepped closer to him but still could not hear him so I sat down on the floor close to him upon which he turned to me with genuine concern: 'You can't do that for me, you too will get involved'. After he pulled a blanket around himself saying, 'even though I have sunk as low as an animal, I still know how to behave in the presence of a lady'. Then he talked for several hours about his history and his problems.

Finally I offered him a glass of milk. He accepted the offer and I went to get it. When I came back after a few moments his friendliness had changed to hostility and he threw the milk on me. Immediately he became distressed: 'How could I do that to you?' he asked in despair. It seemed as though the few minutes I was out of the room were sufficient time for him to feel that I had abandoned him.

His confidence was regained by my showing that I did not mind the incident. And for eight months of daily interviews he continued to talk. Unfortunately he was then removed from the sanitarium by his relatives.

This also serves to illustrate the difference between the schizophrenic's attitude towards time, and ours. One patient, after I told him I had to leave for a week, expressed it thus: 'Do you know what you are telling me? It may mean a minute and it may mean a month. It may mean nothing; but it may also mean eternity to me.'

Such statements reveal that there is no way to estimate what time means to the patient; hence the inadvisability of trying to judge progress by our standards. These patients simply cannot be hurried and it is worse than futile to try. This holds true in all stages of treatment (15).

This was brought home to me by a catatonic patient who said at the end of five months of what seemed to me an extremely slow movement in the direction of health: 'I ought to tell you that things are going better now; but' —with anxiety in his voice—'everything is moving too rapidly. That ought to make us somewhat sceptical.'

As the treatment continues, the patient is neither asked to lie down nor to give free associations; both requests make no sense to him. He should feel free to sit, lie on the floor, walk around, use any available chair, lie or sit on the couch. Nothing matters except that the analyst permit the patient to feel comfortable and secure enough to give up his defensive narcissistic isolation, and to use the physician for resuming contact with the world.

If the patient feels that an hour of mutual friendly silence serves his purpose, he is welcome to remain silent: 'The happiness to dare to breathe and vegetate and just to be, in the presence of another person who does not interfere', as one of them described it.

The only danger of these friendly silent hours is that the patient may develop more tension in his relationship with the analyst than the patient can stand, thereby arousing great anxiety. It belongs among the analyst's 'artistic' functions, as Hill has called them (14), to sense the time when he should break his patient's friendly silence.

What are the analyst's further functions in therapeutic interviews with the schizophrenic? As Sullivan (24) has stated, he should observe and evaluate all of the patient's words, gestures, changes of attitudes and countenance, as he does the associations of psychoneurotics. Every single production—whether understood by the analyst or not—is important and makes sense to the patient. Hence the analyst should try to understand, and let the patient feel that he tries.[3] He should as a rule not attempt to prove his understanding by giving interpretations because the schizophrenic himself understands the unconscious meaning of his productions better than anyone else.[4] Nor should the analyst ask questions when he does not understand, for he cannot know what trend of thought, far off dream or hallucination he may be interrupting. He gives evidence of understanding, *whenever he does,* by responding cautiously with gestures or actions appropriate to the patient's communication; for example by lighting his cigarette from the patient's cigarette instead of using a match when the patient seems to indicate a wish for closeness and friendship.

'Sometimes little things like a small black ring can do the job', a young catatonic commented after I had substituted a black onyx ring for a silver bracelet I had been wearing. The latter had represented to him part of a dangerous armour of which he was afraid.

What has been said against intruding into the schizophrenic's inner world with superfluous interpretations also holds true for untimely suggestions. Most of them do not mean the same thing to the schizophrenic that they do to the analyst. The schizophrenic who feels comfortable with his analyst will ask for suggestions when he is ready to receive them. So long as he does not, the analyst does better to listen. The following incident will serve as an illustration. A catatonic patient refused to see me. I had disappointed him by responding to his request that someone should spend the whole day with him by promising to make arrangements for a nurse to do so instead of understanding that it was I whom he wanted. For the following three months he threatened me with physical attack when I came to see him daily, and I could talk with him only through the closed door of his room.

Finally he reaccepted me and at the end of a two-and-a-half-hour interview stated very seriously: 'If only you can handle this quite casually and be friendly and leave the young people [the nurses] out of it, I may be able to work things out with you.' The next day in the middle of another hour of confused hallucinatory talking, he went on: 'This is a great surprise to us and we both learned quite a bit. If you could arrange for me to see my friends and to spend more time on an open ward, and if you remain casual we might be able to cooperate.' It is scarcely necessary to say that we acted in accordance with his suggestions.

In contrast to fortunate experiences like these there will remain long stretches on every schizophrenic's lonely road over which the analyst cannot accompany him. Let me repeat that this alone is no reason for being discouraged. *It is certainly not an intellectual comprehension of the schizophrenic but the sympathetic understanding and skillful handling of the patient's and physician's mutual relationship that are the decisive therapeutic factors.*

The schizophrenic's emotional reactions towards the analyst have to be met with extreme care and caution. The love which the sensitive schizophrenic feels as he first emerges, and his cautious acceptance of the analyst's warmth of interest are really most delicate and tender things. If the analyst deals unadroitly with the transference reactions of a psychoneurotic it is bad enough, though as a rule not irreparable; but if he fails with a schizophrenic in meeting positive feeling by pointing it out for instance before the patient indicates that he is ready to discuss it, he may easily freeze to death what has just begun to grow and so destroy any further possibility of therapy.

Here one has to steer between Scylla and Charybdis. If the analyst allows the patient's feelings to grow too strong without providing the relief of talking about them, the patient may become frightened at this new experience and then dangerously hostile toward the analyst.

The patient's hostility should ideally be met without fear and without counterhostility. The form it sometimes takes may make this difficult to do. Let it be remembered, however, that the less fear patients sense in the therapist the less dangerous they are.

One patient explained this to me during the interviews we had in her post-psychotic stage of recovery. 'You remember', she said, 'when you once came to see me and I was in a wet pack and asked you to take me out? You went for a nurse and I felt very resentful because that meant to me that you were afraid to do it yourself and that you actually believed that I was a dangerous person. Somehow you felt that, came back and did it yourself. That did away with my resentment and hostility toward you at once, and from then on I felt I could get well with you because if you were not afraid of me that meant that I was not too dangerous and bad to come back into the real world you represented.'

Sometimes the therapist's frank statement that he wants to be the patient's friend but that he is going to protect himself should he be assaulted may help in coping with the patient's combativeness and relieve the patient's fear of his own aggression.

Some analysts may feel that the atmosphere of complete acceptance and of strict avoidance of any arbitrary denials which we recommend as a basic rule for the treatment of schizophrenics may not accord with our wish to guide them towards reacceptance of reality. We do not believe that is so.

Certain groups of psychoneurotics have to learn by the immediate experience of analytic treatment how to accept the denials life has in store for each of us. *The schizophrenic has above all to be cured of the wounds and frustrations of his life before we can expect him to recover.*

Other analysts may feel that treatment as we have outlined it is not psychoanalysis. The patient is not instructed to lie on a couch, he is not asked to give free associations (although frequently he does), and his productions are seldom interpreted other than by understanding acceptance.

Freud says that every science and therapy which accepts his teachings about the unconscious, about transference and resistance and about infantile sexuality, may be called psychoanalysis. According to this definition we believe we are practising psychoanalysis with our schizophrenic patients.

Whether we call it analysis or not, it is clear that successful treatment does not depend on technical rules of any special psychiatric school but rather on the basic attitude of the individual therapist toward psychotic persons. If he meets them as strange creatures of another world whose productions are nonunderstandable to 'normal' beings, he cannot treat them. If he realizes, however, that the difference between himself and the psychotic is only one of degree and not of kind, he will know better how to meet him. He will be able to identify himself sufficiently with the patient to understand and accept his emotional reactions without becoming involved in them.

SUMMARY

Schizophrenics are capable of developing workable relationships and transference reactions.

Successful psychotherapy with schizophrenics depends upon whether the analyst understands the significance of these transference phenomena and meets them appropriately.

NOTES

1. Years in the case reported by Clara Thompson *(27)*.
2. Edith Weigert-Vowinckel *(30)* observed somewhat similar dynamics in what she calls the 'automatic attitudes' of schizoid neurotics.
3. Diethelm also stresses this viewpoint *(5)*.
4. Laforgue *(18)* attributes the cure of a case of schizophrenia to his interpretative work with the patient. According to my experience I believe it was due to his sensitive emotional approach and not the result of his interpretations.

BIBLIOGRAPHY

1. Abraham, Karl: The Psychosexual Difference between Hysteria and Dementia Praecox, in *Selected Papers*. London: Hogarth Press, 1927.
2. Brill, A. A.: *Schizophrenia and Psychotherapy*. Am. J. of Psych., IX, No. 3, 1929.
3. Bullard, D. M.: *Organization of Psychoanalytic Procedure in the Hospital*. To be published in J. of Nerv. and Ment. Disease.
4. ———*The Application of Psychoanalytic Psychiatry to the Psychoses*. To be published in Psa. Rev.
5. Diethelm, Oskar: *Treatment in Psychiatry*. New York: The Macmillan Co., 1936.
6. Fenichel, Otto: *Outline of Clinical Psychoanalysis*. New York: W. W. Norton Co., 1934.
7. Ferenczi, Sandor: Stages in the Development of the Sense of Reality, in *Contributions to Psychoanalysis*. Boston: Richard G. Badger, 1916.
8. Freud: *On Psychotherapy*. Coll. Papers, I.
9. ———*The Loss of Reality in Neurosis and Psychosis*. Coll. Papers, II.
10. ———*Neurosis and Psychosis*. Coll. Papers, II.
11. ———*Psycho-Analytic Notes upon an Autobiographical Account of a Case of Paranoia (Dementia Paranoides)*. Coll. Papers, III.
12. ———*On Narcissism: An Introduction*. Coll. Papers, IV.
13. ———*A General Introduction to Psychoanalysis*. Lecture XVI. New York: Liveright Publ. Co., 1935.
14. Hill, Lewis B.: *Treatment of the Psychotic Ego*. Read before the Annual Meeting of the Am. Psych. Assn., St. Louis, May 1936.
15. Hinsie, Leland E.: *Treatment of Schizophrenia*. Baltimore: Williams and Wilkins Co.
16. Jelliffe, Smith Ely: *Predementia Praecox*. Am. J. Med. Science, 1907, p. 157.
17. Kamm, Bernhard: *A Technical Problem in the Psychoanalysis of a Schizoid Character*. Bull. of the Menninger Clinic, I, No. 8, 1937.
18. Laforgue, René: *A Contribution to the Study of Schizophrenia*. Int. J. Psa., XVIII, Part 2, 1936.
19. Muller, Max: *Über Heilungsmechanismen in der Schizophrenie*. Berlin: S. Karger.
20. Schilder, Paul: *Entwurf zu einer Psychiatrie auf psychoanalytischer Grundlage*. Int. Psa. Bibliothek, No. XVII, Vienna: Int. Psa. Verlag.
21. Sullivan, Harry Stack: *The Oral Complex*. Psa. Rev., XII, No. 1, 1925.
22. ———*Affective Experience in Early Schizophrenia*. Am. J. of Psych., VI, No. 3, 1927.
23. ———*Research in Schizophrenia*. Am. J. of Psych., IX, No. 3, 1929.
24. ———*The Modified Psychoanalytic Treatment of Schizophrenia*. Am. J. of Psych., XI, No. 3, 1931.
25. ———*Socio-Psychiatric Research. Its Implications for the Schizophrenia Problem and for Mental Hygiene*. Am. J. of Psych., X, No. 6, 1931.
26. Storch, Alfred: *The Primitive Archaic Forms of Inner Experiences and Thought in Schizophrenia*. Nerv. and Ment. Disease Monograph Series No. 36. New York: Nerv. and Ment. Disease Publ. Co.
27. Thompson, Clara: *Development and Awareness of Transference in a Markedly Detached Personality*. Int. J. Psa., Part 3, 1938.
28. Tidd, Charles W.: *Increasing Reality Acceptance by a Schizoid Personality during Analysis*. Bull. of the Menninger Clinic, I, No. 5, 1937.
29. ———*A Note on the Treatment of Schizophrenia. Ibid.*, II, No 3, 1938.

30. Weigert-Vowinckel, Edith: *A Contribution to the Study of Schizophrenia.* Int. J. Psa., XIX, Part 3, 1938.
31. Waelder, Robert: *Schizophrenic and Creative Thinking.* Int. J. Psa., VII, 1926.
32. Weininger, B.: *Psychotherapy During Convalescence from Psychosis.* Psychiatry I, No. 2, 1938.
33. ———*The Importance of Reeducational Therapy in Recovered Psychotic Patients.* To be published.
34. White, William A.: *Study on the Diagnosis and Treatment of Dementia Praecox.* Psa. Rev., VIII, 1917.
35. ———and Jelliffe, Smith Ely: *The Modern Treatment of Nervous and Mental Diseases.* Philadelphia: Lea and Febiger.
36. White, William A.: *Outlines of Psychiatry.* New York: Nervous and Mental Disease Publ. Co.
37. Lewis, Nolan D. C.: *Research in Dementia Praecox.* Scottish Rite of Freemasonry for the Northern Masonic Jurisdiction of the United States of America, 1936.

19. The Psychoanalytic Situation and Transference: Postscript to an Earlier Communication

Leo Stone

In a lecture of May, 1961, subsequently published in expanded form (73), I sought to examine the psychoanalytic situation, the fundamental setting and field of force of our clinical work, in global fashion: historical, descriptive-clinical, and dynamic. In the interval, I have had the stimulating benefit of published reviews and of a variety of other formal and informal responses to the contribution. Furthermore, entirely apart from the question of my own views on the subject, certain intimately related problems have continued to evoke thoughtful contributions. See, for especially relevant examples, the distinguished papers of Gitelson (27), Zetzel (83), and Greenson (34). This long-delayed "postscript" was to give expression to the combined themes of response, comparison, clarification, and further reflection; however, it is clear that these cannot all receive adequate treatment in a single paper of reasonable length. I shall, therefore, emphasize certain selected issues, with the hope that other equally important matters may be dealt with at another time.

There are, in broadest perspective, two general themes in the original communication: a clinical review and point of view, with special attention to the overzealous and indiscriminate applications of the crucial and essential rule of abstinence; and an intimately related hypothesis regarding the underlying dynamics of the psychoanalytic situation as such. In my view of the psychoanalytic situation, transference assumed a pervasive and intrinsic importance, which I should like to review and elaborate somewhat further on this occasion. If my effort toward clarification sometimes broadens, deepens, and complicates matters rather than simplifying them, I offer apology which

Reprinted from the *Journal of the American Psychoanalytic Association* 15 (1967): 3–57, by permission of International Universities Press, Inc.

is not unequivocal; for this vast and relatively bypassed subject deserves reinstatement in its true and legitimately challenging confusedness.

However, before proceeding with this, in view of the fact that the technical aspects of the original book have occasioned the strongest reactions, usually as quite separate from its dynamic hypotheses, I should like to say a few words (in highly condensed fashion) in relation to occasional trends of misunderstanding or misinterpretation, which, it seems to me, would be readily dispelled by careful and nontendentious reading of the original text. For outstanding and central example: the idea that the work proposes the bypassing of the transference neurosis seems inexplicable, in view of its intense concentration on the indispensability of that condition. What is true is that it proposes steps toward the avoidance of spurious iatrogenic regressions, whose tenacity may defeat the purposes for which the neurosis is invoked, i.e., that it be successfully analyzed. Certainly no "do-gooder" utopia, where kindness obviates skill, is suggested. The sophisticated developments of psychoanalytic technique are taken for granted; the decisive importance of interpretation is specifically stated. It is true that this complicated technical subject (53) is not dealt with as such in the book; it is considered only in its total meaning in the dynamic situation. The question of the "scientific attitude," as evoked in this context, seems to me entirely specious. Science finds more decisive representation in the eye and mind of the participant than in a machine-imitating schema of response. The natural-historical method of observation is not outmoded; and it can better take account of inevitable, sometimes necessary or productive human variables, than methods which seek ostentatiously (and unsuccessfully) to eliminate them, or to ignore their inevitable presence. Hippocrates was at least the scientific equal of most modern laboratory technicians. All of this is, of course, without reference to the indisputable fact that the conduct of a psychoanalysis must always place the therapeutic obligation to the patient before all other considerations. The subject of "legitimate gratifications," words which frighten some, if the relevant passages are not carefully read, comprises a tentative effort to codify to the extent possible, and to generalize the importance, of those reservations and exceptions to which Freud called attention from his first mention of the rule of abstinence. His concern about excessive repression was dramatically voiced in the *Outline* (24); but the proposed remedies are somewhat unclear. With regard to a possible psychoanalytic "crypto-radicalism": if my views become more revolutionary, they will be stated as such. At this time, I regret that I cannot offer greater flamboyance. The problems of psychoanalytic technique remain dialectical, the principles of abstinence and firm general structure essential, and yet requiring a certain important and discriminating latitude in modification of the diagrammatic ideal of cognitive and emotional deprivation, lest the latter destroy or vitiate the very ends for which it is employed. There are, of course, other important questions. Some will be touched on, at least implicitly, in the following material.

THE PSYCHOANALYTIC SITUATION AND SPEECH

Can the psychoanalytic situation, as such, and in a general sense, be viewed as other than a special relationship between a patient and his doctor, exchanging, as Freud explains in the *Outline*, full and unreserved communication for full discretion and interpretative skill, based on knowledge of the unconscious?[1] Can it mean something different, or more than this, unconsciously, to all patients?

Others before me have thought that the psychoanalytic situation and process as such have a general unconscious meaning, which reproduces certain fundamental aspects of early development. For example: in 1954, Greenacre (31), and in 1956, Spitz (68), offered concepts of the psychoanalytic situation and of the origins of transference, based largely on the mother-child relationship of the first months of life. Greenacre used the term ''primary transference'' (with two alternatives). Insofar as the concepts of Greenacre and Spitz emphasize the prototypic position of the first months of life, as *reproduced* in the current situation,[2] there are subtle but important differences from the view here presented. Nacht and Viderman (59), in 1960, extended related ideas to their conceptual extreme, requiring metaphysical terminology.[3] One can readily conceptualize the regressive transference drive set up by the situation as having such general *direction* (i.e., toward primitive quasi-union), a reservation which Spitz accepted and specified, in response to Anna Freud. It is indeed the activation of this drive and its opposing cognate which underlies my own construction of the psychoanalytic situation, which is seen primarily as a state of separation, ''deprivation-in-intimacy.''[4]

With the prolonged, sequestered, and strictly abstinent contact of the classical analytic situation, there is inevitably, for the patient, a growing and paradoxical experience of cognitive and emotional deprivation in the personal sphere, the cognitive and emotional modalities in certain respects overlapping or interchangeable, in the same sense that the giving of interpretations may satisfy to varying degree either cognitive or emotional requirements. The patient, we must note, also renounces the important expression of locomotion. If developed beyond a certain conventional communicative degree, even gesture or other bodily expressions tend, by interpretative pressure, to be translated into the mainstream of oral-vocal-auditory language. The suppression of hand activity, considering both its phylogenetic and ontogenetic relation to the mouth (39), exquisitely epitomizes the general burdening of the function of speech, with regard to its latent instinctual components, especially the oral aggressions. I have emphasized that all of the great psychobiological tensions, actual, potential, and emergent, between two persons in a prolonged intimate relationship, are essentially concentrated in, find concrete and demonstrable expression in one great interpersonal vehicle, "the complex psychosomatic activity of speech" (73). It is my conviction that, *without* superfluous deprivations, and whether or not the patient indicates it manifestly, the basic analytic situation is one of great primary austerity for the patient. With Macalpine (55), Lagache (47, 48), and others, I believe that the reaction to this chronic deprivation is the regressive transference neurosis based in its essential outlines on the patient's latent infantile neurosis.

From the objective features of this real and purposive adult relationship, one may derive the inference that "it represents to the unconscious, in its primary and most far-reaching impact, the superimposed series of basic separation experiences in the child's relation to his mother. In this schema, the analyst would represent the mother-of-separation, as differentiated from the traditional physician who, by contrast, represents the mother associated with intimate bodily care. This latent unconscious continuum-polarity facilitates the oscillation from 'psychosomatic' reactions and proximal archaic impulses and fantasies, up to the integration of impulse and fantasy life within the scope of the ego's control and activities" (73, p. 105).

Within this structure, the critical function of speech is seen in a similar perspective, as a continuous telescopic phenomenon ranging from its primitive meanings as physiological contact, resolution of excess or residual primitive oral drive tensions, through the conveyance of expressive, or demanding, or other primitive communications, on up to its role as a securely established autonomous ego function, genuinely communicative in a referential-symbolic sense. To the extent that an important fraction of human impulse life is directed against separation from birth onward, the role of speech which develops rapidly, as the modalities of actual bodily intimacy are disappearing or becoming stringently attenuated (67), has a unique importance as a bridge for the state of bodily separation. In the instinctual contribution to speech, considering it as a phenomenon of organic or maturational "multiple function" (79), the cannibalistic urges loom large; they, and more manifestly, their civilized cognates (to some degree, derivatives?), introjection, and the more complex phenomena of identification, exhibit their functional traces and their continuing potentiality for re-emergence as such, at all times. In such view, the most primitive and summary form of mastery of separation, fantasied oral incorporation, is in a continuous line of development with the highest form of objective dialogue between adults. The demonstrable level of response of the given patient, in this general unconscious setting, will be determined (in ideal principle) by his actually attained level of psychosexual development and ego functioning in its broadest sense, and by his potentiality for regression.

In relation to this view of the psychoanalytic situation, one may reconstruct two essential and original streams of transference, from which the various clinical and demonstrable forms are derived. I have called them (somewhat ineptly): (1) the primal or primordial transference (from now on, primordial)[5] and (2) the mature transference. Both are responses to the fundamental psychobiological fact of separation and eventual separateness.

SEPARATION, THE PRIMORDIAL TRANSFERENCE, AND THE OEDIPUS COMPLEX

The primordial transference as here considered would be literally and essentially derived from the effort to master the series of crucial separations from the mother, beginning with the reactions to birth, as noted by Freud, and, in his own inimitable way, much earlier, by the poet-prophet William Blake (1757–1827).[6] This I mention, in Freud's sense of original traumatic situation (21), and with due cognizance of his and others' disavowal of the fallacious psychological adaptations of the concept, notably in the one-time therapeutic system of Rank. This drive is present thenceforward and participates importantly in all of the detailed complexities of each infantile phase experience, with their inevitable contexts of warmth, pressure, skin, special sense, and speech contacts, in the problems of object relationship, separation and individuation, the multiply determined crises of adolescence, the specific neuroses, and many of the "normal" involvements and solutions of the

conventionally healthy individual. One may assume for it an important participation, even if nonmanifest, in castration anxiety, also in "aphanisis" (42).
The striving, in short, is to establish at least symbolic bodily reunion with
the mother. Further, the striving is to substitute this relationship for the
kaleidoscopic system of relationships which have, in good part and inevitably, replaced it. To the extent that actual and concrete—later, intrapsychic
—barriers prohibit even part or derivative manifestations of this drive, in
relation to the mother, requiring that, in varying modes and degrees, it be
displaced to other individuals, sometimes even there undergoing secondary
repression or otherwise warded off, this is a "transference." In the instance
where the drive actualization remains attached to the person of the actual
mother, it is a primitive symbiotic urge, only a potentiality in relation to
transference. This does of course exist clinically in very sick children (56). It
is rare, in its explicitly primitive modalities, in adults, although not at all
infrequent in its psychological expressions. That such striving may eventuate
in a narcissistic solution (or more primitive regressive state, such as autism
or primary identification) is certainly true; then only fundamental anaclitic
strivings will persist; in psychotic states, even these may disappear. For the
moment, I ask indulgence for the tentative concept that both erotic and
aggressive strivings may, in various ways, express, facilitate, or subserve
this basic organismic striving, apart from the empirical fact that disturbances
in these spheres may be observed to initiate or augment it.[7] One may think
of the original urge as having an undifferentiated or oscillating instinctual
quality, like the bodily approaches described for psychotic children (56); or
it may find more mature expression in the relatively neutralized need for
closeness which causes the normal toddler, at a certain point, to recoil from
his own adventurous achievement (57). While it is a universal ingredient of
human personality, in a tremendous range and variety of expressions, the
quality and quantity of this reaction, apart from innate elements, will be
decisively influenced by earliest vicissitudes, certainly in the neonatal experience with the mother, possibly in the organismic experiences of birth itself
(29, 30). It exhibits itself in the neonate, in a particularly distinctive biological sense, in those requirements for human contact—body warmth, pressure,
skin stimulation, manual manipulation, and allied modalities of closeness—
without which ultimate illness, even death, may result, regardless of how
adequately basic physiological and biochemical needs are met. See Ribble
(65), Spitz (69), and others.   .

The primordial transference only rarely appears as such in our clinical work. When it does appear, it leaves an impression not readily forgotten. This is the case when the underlying (as opposed to symptomatic) transference of the psychotic patient appears, displacing his symptoms, if only transitorily, or at times, in conjunction with them. However, in the usual neuroses or character disorders with which we work, even most so-called "borderlines," this transference is in the sphere of inference, closest to the surface in the separation experience of termination, or in earlier interruptions, or in periods of extreme regression. It may be inferred at times in inveterate avoidance of transference emotion, in extreme and anxious exploitation of the formalized routines of analysis, or in inveterate acting out. What we usually deal with, in the working transference and the transference neurosis, are the phase representations and integrations of this phenomenon, and the larger and more subtle complexes of emotional experience clustering around them. Only a type of psychological need (or rather, demand) which sometimes assumes resemblance to original anaclitic requirements (for example, to exhibit indirectly the wish—rarely, to state it explicitly—that the analyst, in effect, *think* for the patient) would seem not infrequent and often demonstrably allied to the original struggle against separation.

In the great majority of instances, the operational transference will come to display an intimate and critical relationship to the oedipus complex. Here, the primordial transference finds an especially important phase specification. The oedipal transference reiterates, in terms appropriate to the child's state of psychophysiological maturation, the inveteracy, the urge to kill if need be, to cling to the original object as the source of a basic gratification, which comprehends residual elements of past libidinal phases in its organization as such, intimately blended with complex attitudes of object constancy in a larger sense. It is, of course, the infantile prototype of the most general and comprehensive adult solution of the problem of separation, i.e., the institution of marriage. That this usually eventuates in the birth of children tends to close a circle in unconscious fantasy, by way of identification with the children. Obviously, in the healthy parent, this plays a minimal economic role, comparable to that of the residual and repressed incest complex. That the oedipal striving must be given up, in varying degree, in submission to *force majeure,* is a matter of the most far-reaching consequences for either healthy or pathological development. The phrase, "in varying degree," refers to its persistent unconscious fraction, the major energic source of everyday dream and fantasy life, neurosis, or creative achievement. It is also relevant to the general thesis of this paper to suggest that the important position of the oedipus complex in relation to unconscious mental activity, and specifically to that universal proximal derivative of the unconscious, the dream, provides a link between this climactic experience of childhood separation and the most primitive psychophysiological separation. It has been shown that the neurophysiological phenomena which are the objective correlates of dreaming are of strikingly high development in the neonatal period (10). The recently established prevalance of dream erection (11) awakens memories of and further reflections on Ferenczi's *Thalassa,* at least in its ontogenetic aspects (9). At this point, one may well ask: "What of the girl who, development being reasonably favorable, turns to her father with a comparable striving?" If we recognize the important element of biologically determined *faute de mieux* in the girl's psychosexual development (i.e., the castration complex), and the multiple intrinsic and environmental factors usually favoring heterosexual orientation, I would suggest that this represents one of the early focal instances of reality-syntonic transference, which becomes integrated in healthy development. This is the "other side of the coin" from the boy's displacement of unneutralized hostility from his mother, as the first frustrating authority (even in relation to his access to her person), to his father. In optimal instances (again, allowing for inevitable unconscious residues), such reorientations become the dominant conscious and unconscious realities of further development.

This type of reality-syntonic developmental displacement is to be distinguished from the primordial transference problem, which is ubiquitous in the very beginnings of relations to proto-objects, i.e., the question of whether perceptual and linguistic displacement (or deployment) is accompanied by merely "token" displacements of libido and aggression away from the psychic representation of the original object, as opposed to genuine and proportionate shifts of cathexis. In other terms, is the "new object" really a person other than the mother who is loved and hated (to put it oversimply), or is the other person literally a substitute for the original object, a mannikin for that object's psychic representation? In the latter instance, the father is given cognitive status as a father. What is sought and sometimes found in him is a mother. This may be strikingly evident in the oral sphere, and may indeed be maintained for a lifetime. This is true transference (of primordial type), not "transfer" (to borrow the word tentatively from Max Stern [71]), or "normal developmental transference," or "reality-syntonic transference." This deficit of varying degree in instinctual and affective investment of the new and presenting real object, finds its mirror-image problem in the analytic situation, where there is a cognitive lag, which must be repaired by the analyst's interpretative activity, especially in the anticipatory transference interpretation. By this latter activity, recognition of the persisting importance of the original object, rediscovered in the analyst, can be established in consciousness, in relation to his current or developing affective-instinctual importance.

It would be beyond the scope of this paper even to summarize those complicated elements in the mother-infant reciprocal symbiosis which may be thought to exacerbate the primordial transference tendency. One may find invaluable suggestions toward such understanding in the growing literature on early mother-child relationships (or their disruption) (for example: 2, 3, 4, 5, 13, 14, 33, 38, 57, 58, 65, 69, 80, 82). The matter remains complicated; oversimplification is to be avoided. The same is even more true of reconstructions from adult (or even child) analytic work. The analytic work does provide, however imperfectly, a certain access to the residues of *subjective* experience in the period of infancy. Probably the eventual synthesis of the two will permit more dependable clarification. Obviously the relationship to a mother has many facets, even within each developmental phase; each can, to varying degree, introduce further complications, sometimes new solutions; furthermore, the life of an individual, beginning very soon after birth, will include other individuals, conspicuously the father, usually siblings, often adult parental surrogates, who can decisively influence development for good or ill. However, these considerations do not disestablish the general and critical primacy of the original symbiosis with the mother. In relation to the primordial transference striving (in the sense that we have just discussed it), my relevant reconstructive inferences from adult analyses point with general consistency only to the persistence of a variety of anaclitic needs, and diffuse bodily libidinal needs (or rather, demands), accompanied by or permeated with augmented aggressive impulses and fantasies.[8] These, apart from innate infantile disposition, would seem often to be associated with maternal failures in necessary early bodily contacts, gratifications, and stimulations, as described by several authors. It would seem not unlikely that something like the Zeigarnik Effect, stressed by Lagache (47) regarding transference in general, operates from earliest infancy. Thus the mother who responds inadequately, or who interrupts gratification prematurely or traumatically, is sought again and again in others, in the drive to settle "unfinished business." That an opposite or very different tendency may sometimes appear to have prevailed in certain segments of relationship (overstimulation, seduction, satiation, and sudden disappointment, for example), or may be demonstrable in complex spheres of the object relationship (parental possessiveness, undue demands, capricious harshness, failure to meet maturational developmental requirements, or myriad subtle variants) testifies only to the challenging complexity of the problem. Certainly, the phenomenon of regression, on the one hand from the oedipal conflicts, or—possibly more often than realized—from parental failures to meet the complex problems of relatively "neutralized" spheres of development, often contributes importantly to the clinical manifestations. Still, the anterior elements must be conceded at least a logical priority in shaping the child and his contributions to the pattern of later conflict.

In any case, the degree to which there is actual deployment of cathexis from the original object to other environmental objects, including the inanimate, determines (inversely) the power and tenacity of the primordial transference and probably has much to do with the basic predispositions to emotional health and illness, respectively. In other words, if there is true transfer of interest and expectation to the environment, with its growing perceptual (and ultimately linguistic) clarity, it exists for the infant largely in its own right, along with the primary object, the mother, whose unique importance is never entirely lost, in the development of most individuals. That there is also an organismic drive toward the outer environment is most assuredly true; and this provides an important contribution to what I have called the "mature transference," which I shall discuss a little further on. On the basis of resemblances which progress from extreme primitiveness to varying grades of detail, the original object or part objects are sought by the primordial transference, often "found," in other aspects of the environment. It may well be that this urge provides an important dynamic element in primary process and in the mature universal symbolic faculty. In any case, it is the actual power of this regressive drive, fraught at every step with conflict and anxiety, down to the ultimate fear of loss of "self," which can determine (in the light of other factors) whether the transference neurosis, indeed the given oedipus complex itself, or the involvement in life in general, is a play of shadow-shapes, or a system of relatively genuine reactions to real persons, perceived largely in their own right. This latent (dyadic) side of the transference neurosis, its "primordial transference" aspect, I have compared to the "dream screen" of Lewin, which really achieves full ascendancy only in the "blank dream" (49).

It is important to emphasize that the primordial transference includes the actual or potential duality of body and mind within its own scope; and the distinction is of great psychodynamic, sometimes nosologic importance. However well the therapeutic transference (a specification, a derivative of the primordial transference) may have been analyzed, there is, for practical purposes (at least, I have never seen or known an unimpeachable exception), an inevitable residue of longing, of search for the equivalent of an omnipotent, omniscient, all-providing and enveloping parent. The important issue for the individual's health and productiveness is that the critique of accurate perceptions and other autonomous functions be as actively participant as possible, that the social representations of this urge be as constructive and as consistent with successful adaptation as possible. The capacity to translate original bodily strivings into mental representations of relations with an original object, as literal needs are met in other ways, at least opens the endless realm of symbolic activities for possible gratification of the residual and irreducible primordial transference strivings. The anterior requirement, with regard to affirmative viability, is that such strivings, in their literal anaclitic reference, be detached from literal transference surrogates and carried over to functionally appropriate materials, processes, individuals, and transactions, the responsibility for their direction or execution essentially assumed by the individual himself, in early ego identification with the original object. With regard to sexual gratification, the persistent clinging to the primordial object or to literal transference surrogates (in the sense previously specified) leads through the pregenital conflicts to the peak development of the oedipus complex, and (apart from other more specific factors) to its probable failure of satisfactory resolution.

Assuming that sexual interest is genuinely deployed to other objects, even in terms of unconscious representations, to the extent usually achieved, it remains nevertheless an important fact that bodily gratification is sought, usually by both individual and social preference, with another person, who, at least in a generic organic sense, resembles the original incestuous object, most often including cultural-national "kinship." This holds a dual interest: (1) the general acceptance of the principle of symbolic "return" to the original object, if no father (or mother) must be thereby destroyed, or such aggression suggested by close blood kinship; and (2) the paradoxical relation to the centrifugal tendency of the taboo on cannibalism. The latter, of course, with the advance of civilization, finds persistent representation only in symbolic ritual. In relation to the actual eating of flesh, the taboo *tends* to spread, not only to protect human enemies, but to include other animals with whom man may have an "object relationship," conspicuously the dog and horse.

"Vegetarianism," of course, includes all animal life. There is no reason to doubt that the mother is the original object of cannibalistic impulse and fantasy, as she is the first object of the search for genital gratification. In the infantile cannibalistic impulse, the physiological urge of hunger, the drive for summary union, and the prototype of relatively well-defined oral erotic and destructive drives may find conjoint expression. That energies and fantasies derived from this impulse contribute importantly to the phallic organization was an early opinion of Freud (16), which I believe to be profoundly correct. Except where severe pregenital disturbances have infused the phallic impulse as such with impulses (subjectively) dangerous to the object, the latter is not only not menaced with destruction (as in the cannibalistic impulse), but preserved, even enhanced. No doubt the critical difference in the cultural evolution of the two great taboos lies in the problem of the preservation of the object, as opposed to his or her destruction.

The oedipus complex, in a pragmatic analytic sense, retains its position as the "nuclear complex" of the neuroses. For reasons mentioned earlier, it is a climactic organizing experience of early childhood. Apart from its own vicissitudes, it can under favorable circumstances provide certain solutions for pregenital conflicts, or in itself suffer from them, in any case, include them in its structure. Only when the precursor experiences have been of great severity is it a shadowy organically determined new "frame of reference," which hardly has independent and decisive significance of its own. In any case, its attendant phallic conflicts must be resolved in their own right, in the analytic transference. From the analyst (or his current "surrogate" in the outer world), thus from the psychic representation of the parent, the literal (i.e., bodily) sexual wishes must be withdrawn, and genuinely displaced to appropriate objects in the outer world. The fraction of such drive elements which can be transmuted to friendly, tender feeling toward the original object, or to other acceptable (neutralized?) variants, will of course influence the economic problem involved. This genuine displacement is opposed to the sense of "acting out," where other objects are perceptually different substitutes for the primary object (thus for the analyst). This may be thought to follow automatically on the basic process of coming to terms with ("accepting") the childhood incestuous wish and its parricidal connotations. Such assumption does not do justice to the dynamic problems implicit in tenaciously persistent wishes. To the extent that these wishes are to be genuinely disavowed or modified, rather than displaced, a further important step is necessary: the thorough analysis of the functional meaning of the persistent wishes and the special etiologic factors entering into their tenacity, as reflected in the transference neurosis. Thus, I cannot subscribe, in principle, to the literal accuracy of the concept phrased by Wilhelm Reich (64), "transference of the transference," as the final requirement for dissolution of the erotic analytic transference, even though the clinical discussion, which is its context, is useful. This expression would imply that the object representation which largely determines the distinctive erotic interest in the analyst can remain essentially the same, so long as the actual object changes. While a semantic issue may be involved to some degree, it is one which impinges importantly on conceptual clarity. I have often wondered what would have happened if an old popular song had remained current in the days when psychoanalysis became an important element in popular culture. The first line was—"I want a girl just like the girl that married dear old dad." The man who sang it in the dormitory shower would surely have suffered psychological lynching. Yet the truth is that the fortunate "average man," who as, even in his unconscious, yielded his sexual claim to his mother to his father's prerogative, can, if he very much admires his mother's physical and mental traits, seek someone like her. The neurotic cannot do this, and may indeed fail in his sexual striving (in its broadest sense), even when the subject is disguised by the outer appearance of remote race or culture.

SOME INTERCURRENT RESERVATIONS

I am aware that such definite conceptualization of one basic element in the phenomenon of transference may be, indeed should be, subject to the reservations appropriately attaching themselves to any very clear-cut ideas about remote and obscure areas of observation and inference. On the other hand, I do believe that this view is not only relatively simple and well-defined, but consistent with the clinical concept of transference, its clinical derivation and its generally accepted place in the psychoanalytic process. Furthermore, it does encompass an important and intrinsic purpose of the psychoanalytic process, however imperfectly achieved. Such concepts are, however, always subject to further reflection, study, and—if need be—revision. This is also relevant to the general problem of transference versus therapeutic (or working) alliance. Whereas the "positive" transference was often in the past confused grossly and amiably with affirmative elements in the adult personal relationship or the therapeutic alliance, the tendency of recent years has been to make the distinction increasingly clear-cut (see, for example, 12, 34, 72,

83). Here, too, the sharp distinction is clinically very useful, and represents an important advance over the loose and blurred terminology of the past. The view of the transference as distinct from the "real relationship," I have stated more than once (72, 73). However, the clear-cut, rigidly established distinction does not necessarily encompass all details of the reality. It is ineluctably true that certain real relationships or real personalities facilitate the development of transference in certain patients; others impede it; or the emergent transference is differently "slanted" in different instances. I have stressed the element of variable but necessary "resemblance" to the original object (72, 73), in the emergence of the transference response. This does not refer to "pure" (i.e., latent) transference, as it may be demonstrable in dreams, with or without therapy, or indeed autoplastically, in neurosis, for here the object is an old intrapsychic representation; rather it refers to that clinical transference which surges through defenses toward a real object, of distinctive character, under special conditions, i.e., the analyst. It is also true that the therapeutic alliance includes certain elements of transference, as described earlier. Among these are the "mature transference," which (when genuine) is largely ego syntonic. The patient's character, even, to some degree, those epiphenomena deriving from cultural and family standards and values, cannot be dissociated from the mode of emergence, the expression, and the fate of the clinical transference. The degree of conscious acceptance, and thus the general economic distribution, of erotic or aggressive strivings will have much to do with such considerations. Or, the obstinate insistence on the carrying out, or at least the indefinite maintenance, of erotic impulse and fantasy will probably be more often a function of widespread character traits than of the strength of the particular transference urge under consideration, as isolated from such interrelationship. Nor can such *quantitative* manifest reactions be separated easily and immediately from the qualities and traits of the analyst—his youth, quick-wittedness, and physical attractiveness (or otherwise)—for single simple example. In the well-defined, relatively accessible forms of neurotic character, the adult ego-syntonic system of object relations is often dominated by the unresolved oedipus complex, not seldom in manifestly nonerotic contexts, such as occupation. It is true that in such instances the connections with the incest complex of childhood can often be re-established, that this theme will appear in the clinical transference, and that the germane character traits are not beyond reasonable modification. However, it is to be expected that the pregenital and other factors which have contributed to creating a neurotic character instead of a neurosis will have a widespread and tenacious place in the adult personality with whom one must deal in the analysis, regarding his transference, among other analytic problems. This is, of course, particularly relevant to the problem of "acting out."

The "nonneurotic" character, with a neurosis, is a compound of "transfers" (distinguished from "transferences" in the sense mentioned early in the paper) of ego-syntonic integrating identifications (beginning with the earliest identifications in the ego, but including the important institution of the superego), clustered about and pervading the biologically determined maturational-developmental tendencies of the ego and the drives, in a relatively stable dynamic and economic interrelationship. His "transferences," the conflictual (unneutralized?) elements in his basic object relations, forced to operate through or across the (weakened) repression barrier, find expression in his neurosis. This would be assumed to include in a central position, in one form or another, the elements of the irredentist unregenerate oedipus complex. The thrust of the dynamic wish would be (again, in "overclear" statement): "I want my mother sexually. Not just another desirable woman whom I can love, not even a woman just like my mother. *Only* my Mother! Therefore I want to kill my father!" The further step in this idealized conception of transference is that any woman who excites desire is "perceived" unconsciously as the patient's mother, any real (or fantasied) male rival, as his father, with a possible variety of predictable consequences. Clearly, the nonneurotic portion of the patient's personality has evolved in relation to the same critical early family objects as the neurotic elements, and has the same biological core. It is unlikely, therefore, that they are permanently and rigidly disconnected from one another, except where (in principle) isolated traumatic elements have been consigned to repression. The neurotic character may, not infrequently, in the course of improvement, develop a neurosis. But even the individual "nonneurotic" character is in (less obvious) continuum with his neurosis, with his "transferences." The spontaneous onsets, fluctuations, or remissions of neuroses (and more subtle spontaneous alterations of character) are germane to this continuum. The affirmative aspect of this connectedness has been emphasized by Loewald (50). If one keeps in mind the reservations mentioned earlier about clarity of conceptualization, the explanatory discussion of Kohut (44), and Kohut and Seitz (45), with accompanying diagram (45, p. 136), is a very useful contribution to the understanding of this complicated problem. Both Loewald and Kohut make important, although different use of one of Freud's three conceptions of

transference, i.e., the "transference" from the unconscious to the preconscious (15, pp. 562–564).

FURTHER COMMENTS ON PRIMORDIAL TRANSFERENCE

To the extent that the primordial transference includes, at least potentially, a
largely psychological ("mental") component, the concept "transference of
the transference" would be applicable to this component. For it does appear
that certain aspects of the search for the omnipotent and omniscient caretaking parent are, for practical purposes, inextinguishable. As suggested earlier,
there are indeed important qualitative and quantitative distinctions in the
mode of persistence of such strivings. However, even to the extent that they
are detached from the analyst and carried into some reasonably appropriate
expression in everyday life, they retain at least a subtle quality which con-
travenes reality, one which derives from earliest infancy, and remains—to
this extent—a transference. "Santa Claus" lives on, where one might least
expect to meet him, whether as a donor of miracle drugs or of far more
complex panaceas.

   If one assigns to this parasymbiotic transference drive a true primordial
origin, it is necessary to take cognizance of certain important concepts
dealing with the earliest period of life. If we assume a powerful original
organismic drive toward an original "object," a "striving" to nullify separation from the beginning, how does this square with concepts such as
"primary narcissism," or the "objectless phase," or "the primal psychophysiological self" (41)? (We note in passing that there are those who do not
accept these as usually construed. See Balint [1], for example, or Fairbairn
[6, 75], or—conspicuously—Melanie Klein and her students [43, 66]).
These are states, variously defined or conceived, which apply to the earliest
neonatal period, in which mental life, to state it oversimply, exists only as
potential, in physiological processes. Since there is (we postulate) no clear
awareness of a self separate from the mother, there can be no "mentally"
represented or experienced drive to obliterate the separation (referring to a
self and object, conceived of as separate, in a continuing sense). There are,
of course, discharge phenomena, the precursors of purposive activity; and
there are urgent physiological needs, directed toward fulfillment or relief,
rather than toward an object as such. However, in relation to these physiological needs as archaic precursors of object relationships, it must be noted that
in all, except respiration and spontaneous sphincter relief (even in these

instances, not without exception or reservation), the need fulfillment must be mediated by the primordial object (or her surrogate). There is also, of course, the uniquely important requirement for "holding" (82), in a literal expression, from the outset. (The maternal partner in human symbiosis here supplies what the neonate cannot seek by "clinging"? See Bowlby [4, 5], Murphy [58].) In that sense, from the very beginning, there must be experience of physiological ebb and flow of tension (even if restricted to the coenesthetic), connected with a peripheral sensory registration, which is the protophase of the recognition of separation from the object (or nonpresence of the object) as a painful experience, her presence or apposition the converse. That the general context may be one in which the sense of unity is preponderant, or, more accurately, that there is no general awareness of "separateness" as such, means that the drive for union does not exist in a general psychological sense. It is, so to speak, satisfied. That object constancy, with its cognate "longing," is a later and quite different experience from the urgencies of primitive need fulfillment is true; however, regardless of what may be added by maturational and developmental considerations, instinctual and perceptual, there is no reason to assume other than a core of developmental continuity from the earliest needs and their fulfillment to the later state, and indeed some continuing degree of contingency based on them. There is a very rough parallel in the way certain analytic patients, before a firm relationship with the analyst is established, signal certain primitive experiences and tendencies in special reactions to the end of the hour, to the nonvisibility of the analyst, to interruption of their associations, to failure of the analyst to talk, and similar matters. We must note that in the basic formation of the ego itself, there is evidence of primitive reactions to separations (20, p. 29), in the form of very early identifications, based on caretaking functions (38). Certainly in the very development of autonomous ego functions, not only the matter of specific training, but the quality and quantity of the mother's investment in them, have a decisive role in the character of their development. And in the case of object constancy, in its connotation of libidinal cathexis (37, p. 173), where no need whatsoever (emotional or otherwise) is met for prolonged periods, the importance of the object is, to put it mildly, liable to deteriorate, or to suffer complicating aggressive change. Probably the characteristic features of the later developing relation to the object (love and the wish for love), as separable if not always separated from demonstrable primitive need fulfillment, have a special relationship to those "ancillary" aspects of neonatal nurture, mentioned earlier, whose lack has been shown to be an actual threat to life in some instances, not to speak of sound emotional development. So that from the first, regardless of the assumed state of libidinal (and aggressive) economy, or the assumed state of psychological nondifferentiation between self and potential object, there are critical precursive phenomena, objectively observable, and probably proto-typic subjective experiences of separation, which are the forerunners of all subsequent experiences of the kind. One may generalize to the effect that, with maturation and development, secondary identification, and the various other processes of "internalization" in its broadest sense, the problem of separation and its mastery becomes correspondingly more complex, and changes with the successive phases of life, but never entirely disappears.

In the view of the psychoanalytic situation described earlier, the latent mobilization of experiences of separation stimulated by the situational struc-ture awakens the driving primordial urge to undo or to master the painful separations which it represents, usually embodied in the various forms of clinical transference with which we are familiar. One legitimate gratification which tends to mitigate superfluous transference regression is the transmis-sion of understanding. And this leads us to a consideration of what I have called the "mature transference."

THE MATURE TRANSFERENCE

It is sometimes thought that by the "mature transference" I mean, in effect, the "therapeutic alliance," or a group of mature ego functions which enter into such alliance. Now, there is some blurring and overlapping at the conceptual edges in both instances; but the concept as such is largely distinct from either one, as it is from the primitive transferences, which we have been discussing. Whether the concept is thought by others to comprehend a demonstrable actuality is a further question; this question, of course, can only follow on conceptual clarity. What I have in mind is a nonrational urge, not directly dependent on the perception of immediate clinical purposes, a true "transference" in the sense that it is displaced (in currently relevant form) from the parent of early childhood to the analyst. Its content is not anti-sensual, but largely nonsensual (sometimes transitional, as in the child's pleasure in so-called "dirty words") (8) and encompasses a special and not minuscule sphere of the object relationship: the wish to understand, and to be understood; the wish to be given understanding, i.e., teaching, specifically by the parent (or later surrogate); the wish to be taught "controls" in a nonpunitive way, corresponding to the growing perception of hazard and conflict; and very likely the implicit wish to be provided with and taught channels of substitutive drive discharge. With this, there may well be a wish, corresponding to that element in Loewald's description of therapeutic process (50), to be seen in terms of one's developmental potentialities by the analyst. No doubt, the list could be extended into many subtleties, details, and variations. However, one should not omit to specify that, in its peak development, it would include the wish for increasingly accurate interpretations and the wish to facilitate such interpretations by providing adequate material; ultimately, of course, by identification, to participate in, or even be the author of, the interpretations.[9] The childhood system of wishes which underlies the transference is a correlate of biological maturation, and the latent (i.e., teachable) autonomous ego functions, appearing with it (36). However, there is a drivelike quality in the particular phenomena, which disqualifies any conception of the urge as identical with the functions. No one who has ever watched a child importune a parent with questions, or experiment with new words, or solicit her interest in a new game, or demand storytelling or reading, can doubt this. That this finds powerful support and integration in the ego identification with a loved parent is undoubtedly true, just as it is true of the identification with an analyst toward whom a positive relationship has been established. That "functional pleasure" participates, certain specific ego energies perhaps, very likely the ego's own urge to extend its hegemony in the personality (79), I do not doubt. However, I stress the drive element, even the special phase configurations and colorations, and with it the importance of object relations, libidinal and aggressive, for a specific reason. For just as the primordial transference seeks to undo separation, in a sense to obviate object relationships as we know them, the "mature transference" tends toward separation and individuation (57), and increasing contact with the environment, optimally with a largely affirmative (increasingly neutralized) relationship toward the original object, toward whom (or her surrogates) a different system of demands is now increasingly directed. The further consideration which has led me to emphasize the drivelike element in these attitudes as integrated phenomena, as examples of "multiple function" rather than as the discrete exercise of function or functions, is the conviction that there is a continuing dynamic relation of relative interchangeability between the two series, at least based on the response to gratification a significant zone of complicated energic overlap, possibly including the phenomenon of neutralization. That the empirical "interchangeability" is not unlimited goes without saying, but this in no way diminishes its decisive importance. In my previous communication, I mentioned that the excessive transference neurosis regression, which can so seriously vitiate the affirmative psychoanalytic process, finds a prototype in the regressive behavior and demands of certain children, who do not receive their fair share of teaching, "attention," play, nonseductive affectionate demonstration, nonexploitative interest in development, and similar matters, from their parents. In the psychoanalytic situation, both the gratifications offered by the analyst and the freedom of expression by the patient are much more severely limited, and concentrated, practically entirely (in the everyday demonstrable sense), in the sphere of speech; on the analyst's side, further, in the transmission of understanding.

Whereas the primordial transference exploits the primitive aspects of speech, the mature transference urges seek the heightened mastery of the outer and inner environment, a mastery to which the mature elements in speech contribute importantly. I have elsewhere stressed that the most clearcut genetic prototype for the free association-interpretation dialogue is indeed in the original learning and teaching of speech, the dialogue between child and mother. It is interesting to note that just as the profundities of understanding between people often include—"in the service of the ego"—transitory introjections and identifications, the very word "communication," representing the central ego function of speech, is intimately related etymologically, even in certain actual usages, to the word chosen for that major religious sacrament which is the physical ingestion of the body and blood of the Deity. Perhaps this is just another suggestion that the oldest of individual problems does, after all, continue to seek its solution, in its own terms, if only in a minimal sense, and in channels so remote as to be unrecognizable.

The mature transference is a dynamic and integral part of the "therapeutic alliance," along with the tender aspects of the erotic transference, even more attenuated (and more dependable) "friendly feeling" of adult type, and the ego identification with the analyst. Indispensable, of course, are the genuine adult need for help, the crystallizing rational and intuitive appraisal of the analyst, the adult sense of confidence in him, and innumerable other nuances of adult thought and feeling. With these, giving a driving momentum and power to the analytic process, but always, by its very nature, a potential source of resistance, and always requiring analysis, is the primordial transference and its various appearances in the specific therapeutic transference. That it is, if well managed, not only a reflection of the repetition compulsion in its baleful sense, but a living presentation from the id, seeking new solutions, "trying again," so to speak, to find a place in the patient's conscious and effective life, has important affirmative potentialities. This has been specifically emphasized by Nunberg (60), Lagache (47, 48), and Loewald (50), among others. Loewald (50) has recently elaborated very effectively the idea of "ghosts" seeking to become "ancestors," based on an early figure of speech of Freud (15, p. 553n.). The mature transference, in its own infantile right, provides some of the unique quality of propulsive force, which comes from the world of feeling, rather than the world of thought. If one views it in a purely figurative sense, that fraction of the mature transference which derives from "conversion" is somewhat like the propulsive fraction of the wind in a boat sailing close-hauled to windward; the strong headwind, ultimate source of both resistance and propulsion, is the primordial transference. This view, however, should not displace the original and independent, if cognate, origin of the mature transference. To adhere to the figure of speech, a favorable tide or current would also be required! It is not that the mature transference is in itself entirely exempt from analytic clarification and interpretation. For one thing, in common with other childhood spheres of experience, there may have been traumas in this sphere, punishments, serious defects or lacks of parental communication, listening, attention, or interest. In general, this is probably far more important than has hitherto appeared in our prevalent paradigmatic approach to adult analysis, even taking into account the considerable changes due to the growing interest in ego psychology. "Learning" in the analysis can, of course, be a troublesome intellectualizing resistance. Furthermore, both the patient's communications and his reception and utilization of interpretations may exhibit only too clearly, as sometimes in the case of other ego mechanisms, their origin in and tenacious relation to instinctual or anaclitic dynamisms; greediness for the analyst to talk (rarely the opposite), uncritical acceptance (or rejection!) of interpretations, parroting without actual assimilation, fluent, "rich," endlessly detailed associations without spontaneous reflection or integration, direct demands for solution of moral and practical problems entirely within the patient's own intellectual scope, and a variety of others. It may not always be easy to discriminate between the utilization of speech by an essentially instinctual demand, and an intellectual or linguistic trait, or habit, determined by specific factors in their own developmental sphere. However, the underlying essentially genuine dynamism which I have been discussing remains largely of a character favorable to the purposes and processes of analysis, as it was to the original processes of maturational development, communication, and benign separation. I agree with Lagache (47, 48) on the desirability of separating the current unqualified usage, "positive" and "negative" transference, as based on the patient's immediate state of feeling, from a classification based on the essential effect on analytic process. In the latter sense, the mature transference is, in general, a "positive transference." [10]

ARCHAIC FORERUNNERS OF TRANSFERENCE

The clinical fact of the interaction of drive, defense, and autonomous ego (sometimes superego) (22, 60), in matters of perception, is indisputable, easily demonstrable in everyday life, where people so often "see what they want to see," occasionally even "what they *must* see," sometimes with strange combinations of both! [11] This tendency has an archaic *Anlage*. Very early in the history of specific interpersonal reactions is the three-month smiling response to any bearer of a moving face, without regard to individual traits (69). It may be quite reasonably assumed that this requires some degree of psychic organization, at least the existence of memory of gratification, and the capacity to associate this with an object in the outer world. What is striking is the rudimentary nature of the perceptual stimulus (two eyes, nose, forehead, and motion straight on), and the corresponding interchangeability of the objects (or object precursors). This is, in other words, a primitive "transference" response of a sort, a "prototransference"; at the very least, it is an *Anlage* of the capacity for displacement and generalization based on rudimentary (but nevertheless indispensable) resemblance, in this instance, limited to a "sign Gestalt," which will later appear in the transference phenomenon of adult life. [12] It is reasonable to assume that the question of sheer clarity, i.e., neurophysiological efficiency of perception, is fundamental in the (perceptual) aspect of the phenomenon. However, the response is definitely to a sign Gestalt associated with the bearer of security or gratification. It is not, therefore, beyond our consideration that neurophysiological immaturity and relative strength of drive are synergistic in this phenomenon, the prototype of much later, much more complex situations, where the "balance of power" between perceptual functions, defense, drive, and internalized prohibitions or demands may also modify perception, or interpretation of perception, toward the heightened importance of the "common denominator." Only a few months after the smiling response (between six and eight months), the variously adverse reaction to unfamiliar persons appears. Again, since this is a sharp change in behavior, we may assume that it is, at least in great part, dependent on a sharply accelerated maturation of perceptual capacity. It may well be that the memory traces are richer in detail, and "unfamiliar" is correspondingly more nearly accurate. However, one must observe that even though the mother (or her surrogate) is uniquely favored, there is still some degree of displacement from the original nurturing or caretaking person to others in the immediate environment, and that the common features now have an important added dimension of "resemblance," the common denominator of "familiarity." Further, the distinctly negative reaction ("stranger anxiety") obviously includes something more than mere categorization as nonfamiliar. The stranger is bad, frightening, at least, in some way, distressing. Spitz explains this essentially on the basis of the child's recognition that the stranger is not his mother, that his mother "has left him." However, it is well to recall the view of Freud that the infant tends to externalize the source of his pains, discomforts, tensions. In the light of an established "good object" and a related coterie of "familiars," is it not likely that the unhappy stranger is the logical object for investment with hostility and fear, derived from the infant's own inner tensions and his inevitable negative experiences with the intimates, whom he is beginning to love? Xenophobia of varying degree is, of course, a reaction which is never entirely lost in adult life; and Freud (19) makes explicit reference to the proximity of the concept "stranger" and "enemy" in relation to the paranoid mechanism. Possibly, in the Kleinian system (43, 66), this phenomenon would be assigned to the "depressive position," the "nonmother" evoking the anxiety (or guilt) that the mother has been destroyed? Obviously, the question of what constitutes resemblance, of what is adequate for symbolism, condensation, and displacement, changes with the growing accuracy of perception and the richness of its associative background, with the increasing importance of reality testing, and of impulse control, which develop *pari passu* with general ego development, and the growing ascendancy of the "secondary process." With this development, the conditions facilitating transference evolve in rough correspondence, gradually including considerations of greater functional significance. (See Jacobson's discussion of this complicated evolution, in a different context [41].) There are individuals to whom complex human character traits or functions seem all but inextricably linked to physique. However, in line with maturation of discernment and the capacity for thinking in nonconcrete terms, the functional aspects of parents, and the traits which accompany or influence parental functions, usually become increasingly important: the nurturing or caretaking, and the inevitable disciplinary functions, in their satisfactory or unsatisfactory role in the child's life. In any case, to most adults, the transference "tag" of the parental-like function is at once a stable, dependable, nonseductive reality, and at the same time, a stimulus, through deep archaic reverberation, of the anaclitic, and still more profound symbiotic, elements in the struggle against separation, which find representation in the various shades of the therapeutic transference. Furthermore, to the extent that this is integrated in the adult reality of the analytic situation, i.e., the analyst's physicianly commitment, no violence need be done to the patient's sense of reality or emotional requirement, currently or in the future prospect. Basically determined by the genetic aspects of the pathology, the economic balance of the two streams of transference will nonetheless be influenced, as it was in the original states of separation, by the nuances of attitude of the analyst, i.e, by whether the successive "weanings" to understanding are truly "weanings to" (i.e., to other "food") in the original sense, or whether the emphasis of the term is, as it is largely used nowadays, essentially in the sphere of deprivation, of giving up something.

COMMENTS ON THE TRANSFERENCE NEUROSIS AND TRANSFERENCE INTERPRETATION

A few remarks about clinical considerations in the transference neurosis, and the problem of transference interpretation, may be offered at this point. The whole situational structure of analysis (in contrast with other personal relationships), its dialogue of free association and interpretation, and its deprivations as to most ordinary cognitive and emotional interpersonal strivings tend toward the separation of discrete transferences from their synthesis with one another and with defenses, in character or symptoms, and with deepening regression, toward the re-enactment of the essentials of the infantile neurosis, in the transference neurosis. In other relationships, the "give-and-take" aspects—gratifying, aggressive, punitive or otherwise actively responsive, and the open mobility of search for alternative or greater satisfaction—exert a profound dynamic and economic influence, so that only extraordinary situations, or transferences of pathological character, or both, occasion comparable regression.[13]

It is a curious fact that whereas the dynamic meaning and importance of the transference neurosis have been well established since Freud gave this phenomenon a central position in his clinical thinking, the clinical reference, when the term is used, remains variable and somewhat ambiguous. For example, Greenson, in his excellent recent paper (34), speaks of it as appearing "when the analyst and the analysis become the central concern in the patient's life." I do not wish to repeat in detail my own previous remarks in this connection (73). However, I think that it is worthwhile to specify certain aspects of Greenson's definition, for the term "central" is somewhat ambiguous, as to its specific reference. Certainly the term would apply to the symbolic position of the analyst in relation to the patient's experiencing ego (70), and the symbolically decisive position which he correspondingly assumes in relation to the other important figures in the patient's current life. However, while the analysis is in any case, and for multiple reasons, exceedingly important to the seriously involved patient, there is a free observing portion of his ego, also involved, but not in the same sense as that involved in the transference regression and revived infantile conflicts. And there is, of course, always the integrated adult personality, however diluted it may seem at times, to whom the analysis is one of many important realistic life activities. I think it is rare then, although it certainly does occur, that the analysis actually exceeds in importance the other major concerns, attachments, and responsibilities of the patient's life; nor do I think it desirable that this should occur. On the other hand, if construed with proper attention to the economic considerations as mentioned, the concept is important, both theoretically and clinically. In the theoretical direction, I refer to the assumption that there is a continuing system of object relationships and conflict situations, most important in unconscious representations, but participating to some degree in all others, deriving in a successive series of transferences from the experiences of separation from the original object, the mother. In this sense, the analyst is indeed, to a uniquely important portion of the patient's personality, the portion that "never grew up," a central figure. In the clinical sense, I refer to the importance of the transference neurosis as outlining for us the essential and central analytic task, providing by its very currency and demonstrability a relatively secure cognitive base for our work. By its inclusion of the patient's essential psychopathological processes and tendencies, in their original functional connections, it offers, in its resolution or marked reduction, the most formidable lever for analytic cure. However, the transference neurosis must be seen in its interweaving with the patient's extra-analytic system of personal contacts. The relationship to the analyst may indeed influence the course of relationships to others, in the same sense that the clinical neurosis did, except that the former is alloplastic, relatively exposed, and subject to constant interpretation. It is also an important fact that, except in those rare instances where the original dyadic relationship appears to return, the analyst, even in the strictly transference sphere, cannot be assigned all the transference roles simultaneously. Other actors are required. He may at times oscillate with confusing rapidity between the status of mother and father, but he is usually predominantly in one of these roles for long periods, someone else representing the other. Furthermore, apart from "acting out," complicated and mutually inconsistent attitudes, anterior to awareness and verbalization, may require the seeking of other transference objects: husband or wife, friend, another analyst, and so forth. Children, even the patient's own children, may be invested with early strivings of the patient, displaced from the analysis, to permit the emergence or maintenance of another system of strivings. Physicians, of course, may find in their patients their own strivings, mobilized by the analysis, even experience the impulses which they would wish to call forth in the analyst. The range is extensive, varied, and complicated, requiring constant alertness. Transference interpretation therefore often has a necessarily paradoxical inclusiveness, which is an important reality of technique. There is another aspect, and that is the dynamic and economic impact of the intimate and actual *dramatis personae* of the transference neurosis on the progress of the analysis as such, and on the patient's motivations, as well as his real life avenues for recovery. For the persons in his milieu may fulfill their "positive" or "negative" roles in transference only too well, in the sense that an analyst motivated by a "blind" countertransference may do the same. Apart from their roles in the transference drama, which may facilitate or impede interpretative effectiveness, they can provide the substantial and dependable real life gratifications which ultimately facilitate the analysis of the residual analytic transferences; or their capacities or attitudes may occasion overload of the anaclitic and instinctual needs in the transference, which renders the same process far more difficult. In the most unhappy instances, there can be a serious undercutting of the motivations for basic change.

There is also the fundamental question of the role of the transference interpretation. At the Marienbad Symposium (76) most of Strachey's colleagues appeared to accept the essential import of his contribution (74, 76), and thus the unique significance of the transference interpretation, despite the various reservations as to details and emphases on other important aspects of the therapeutic process. Nevertheless, there are still many who, if not in doubt regarding the great value of transference interpretations are inclined to doubt their uniqueness, and to stress the importance of economic considerations in determining the choice as to whether transference or extratransference interpretations may be indicated. Now, apart from the realistic considerations mentioned in the preceding passage (in a sense, the necessarily "distributed" character of a variable fraction of transference interpretation), there is the fact that the extra-analytic life of the patient often provides indispensable data for the understanding of detailed complexities of his psychic functioning, because of the sheer variety of its references, some of which cannot be reproduced in the relationship to the analyst. For example, there is no repartee (in the ordinary sense) in the analysis. The way the patient handles the dialogue with an angry employer may be importantly revealing. The same may be true of the quality of his reaction to a real danger of dismissal. There are not only the realities, but the "formal" aspects of his responses. These expressions of his personality remain important, even though his "acting out" of the transference (assuming this was the case) may have been even more important, and, of course, requiring transference interpretation. Furthermore, they remain useful, if discriminatingly and conservatively treated, even if they are inevitably always subject to that epistemological reservation, which haunts so much of analytic data. Of course, the "positive" transference has a role in the utilization of such interpretations: it is what enables the patient to listen to them and take them seriously!

In an operational sense, it would seem that extratransference interpretations cannot be set aside, or underestimated in importance. But the unique effectiveness of transference interpretations is not thereby disestablished. No other interpretation is free, within reason, of the doubt introduced by not really knowing the "other person's" participation in love, or quarrel, or criticism, or whatever the issue. And no other situation provides for the patient the combined sense of cognitive acquisition, with the experience of complete personal tolerance and acceptance, that is implicit in an interpretation made by an individual who is an object of the emotions, drives, or even defenses, which are active at the time. There is no doubt that such interpretations must not only (in common with all others) include personal tact, but must be offered with special care as to their intellectual reasonableness, in relation to the immediate context, lest they defeat their essential purpose. It is not too often likely that a patient who has just been jilted in a long-standing love affair, and is suffering exceedingly, will find useful an immediate interpretation that his suffering is due to the fact that the analyst does not reciprocate his love, even though a dynamism in this general sphere may be ultimately demonstrable, and acceptable to the patient. On the other hand, once the transference neurosis is established, with accompanying subtle (sometimes gross) colorations of the patient's life, then more far-reaching often anticipatory, transference interpretations are indeed indicated; for, if all of the patient's libido and aggression is not, in fact, invested in the analyst, he has at least an unconscious role in all important emotional transactions; and, if the assumption is correct that the regressive drive, mobilized by the analytic situation, is in the direction of restoration of a single all-encompassing relationship, specified pragmatically in the individual case by the actually attained level of development, then there is indeed a dynamic factor at work, importantly meriting interpretation as such, to the extent that available material supports it. This would be the immediate clinical application of the material regarding the ''cognitive lag,'' mentioned earlier.

TRANSFERENCE OBJECT AND OBJECT REPRESENTATION

In considering more broadly the function of the transference in the psychoanalytic process, one is confronted by the apparently naïve, but nonetheless important question of the role of the actual (current) object as compared with that of the object representation of the original personage in the past.[14] We recall Freud's paradoxical, somewhat gloomy, but portentous concluding passage in ''The Dynamics of Transference'' (17): ''This struggle between the doctor and the patient, between intellect and instinctual life, between understanding and seeking to act, is played out almost exclusively in the phenomena of transference. It is on that field that the victory must be won—the victory whose expression is the permanent cure of the neurosis. It cannot be disputed that controlling the phenomena of transference presents the psycho-analyst with the greatest difficulties. But it should not be forgotten that it is precisely they that do us the inestimable service of making the patient's hidden and forgotten erotic impulses immediate and manifest. For when all is said and done, it is impossible to destroy anyone *in absentia* or *in effigie*'' (108).

Both object and representation are made necessary by the basic phenomenon of original separation. Indeed, the existence of an image of the object, which persists in the absence of that object, is one of the important beginnings of psychic life in general, certainly an indispensable prerequisite for object relationship, as generally construed. Whether this is viewed as (or at times demonstrably is) an unstable introject, which is always subject to alternative projection, or an intrapsychic object representation clearly distin-guished from the self representation, or a firm identification in the superego, or in the ego itself, these phenomena are in various ways components of the system of mastery of the fact of separation, or separateness, from the origi-nally absolutely necessary anaclitic or (in the very earliest period) symbiotic "object." In the light of clinical observation, it would appear to be the relatively stable (parental) object representation, at times drawing to varying degree on the more archaic phenomena,[15] at moments, even in nonpsychotic patients, overwhelmed by them, sometimes a restoration from oedipal iden-tification, which provides the preponderant basis for most demonstrable analytic transferences, in neurotic patients. The transference is effectively established when this representation invests the analyst to a degree—depend-ing on intensity of drive and mode of ego participation—which ranges all the way from wishing and striving to remake the analyst, to biased judgments and misinterpretations of data, finally to actual perceptual distortions.[16]

However richly and vividly the old object representation as such may be invested, however rigidly established the libidinal or aggressive cathexis of the image may be, this as such can become the actual and exclusive focus of full instinctual discharge, or of complicated and intense instinct-defense solutions, only in states of extreme pathological severity. This is consistent with the usual and general energy-sparing quality of strictly intrapsychic processes. For the vast majority of persons, viable to any degree, including those with severe neuroses, character distortions, addictions, and certain psychoses, the striving is toward the living and actual object, even at the cost of intense suffering. In a sense, this returns us to the beginnings, to the state in which the psychological "object-to-be" (if you prefer) has a critical importance never again to be duplicated, except in certain acute life emergen-cies, even if the object is not firmly perceived as such, in the sense of later object relations. And it does seem that trace impressions from the earliest contacts in the service of life preservation, plus the associated instinctual gratifications, and innumerable secondarily associated sensory impressions, are activated by the specific inborn urges of sexual maturation. These propel the individual to renew many of the earliest modes of actual bodily contact, in connection with seeking for specific instinctual gratification. Or, to look away from clear-cut instinctual matters to the more remote elaborations of human contact: few regard loneliness as other than a source of suffering, even when self-imposed, as an apparent matter of choice; and the forcible imposition of "solitary confinement" is surely one of the most cruel of punishments.

I mention these few generalities because I think that they have some important implications. No reaction to another individual is all transference, just as surely as no relationship is entirely free of it. There is not only the general maturational-developmental drive toward the outer world, but the seeking for a variety of need and pleasure satisfactions, learned or stimulated in relation to the primordial object, but necessarily and inevitably transferred from this object to generically related things and persons in the expanding environment. These may be used or enjoyed without penalty, if the distinction between the original and the new is profoundly and genuinely established (with due respect for the quantitative "relativism" of such concepts). The range of such inevitable displacements ("transfers") is endless in all spheres —sexual, aggressive, aesthetic, utilitarian, intellectual. More immediately relevant, in the lives of those whose development has been relatively healthy, are those individuals whose vocations provide similarities or parallels, however rarefied, to the caretaking functions of the original parents: teachers, physicians, clergymen, political rulers, occasionally others. Again it must be noted that such persons perform real functions, that the adult individual's interest in them, his specific need for them, often greatly outweighs similar reactions to parents, who retain their unique place for a complex and variable combination of other reasons. For such surrogate parents perform for the adult what his parents largely performed for him in earliest years; and the psychological comparison is with an old object representation, or with an early identification, to which such latter-day parent surrogates may indeed add important layers or elaborations. It is on the basis of such functional resemblances that persons in these roles have a unique transference valence. The analyst is first perceived as a real object, who awakens hope of help, and who offers it, on the basis of his therapeutic competence. This operates in the patient's experience at all levels of integration, from that of actual and immediate perception, evaluation, and response, to the activation of original parental object representations and their cathexes. That the analyst becomes invested with such representations, in forms ranging from wishes or demands to functional or even perceptual misidentifications, comprises the broad range of phenomena which we know as the therapeutic transference. Thus, the complicated structural phenomena of conflict are activated in relation to a real object, and such activation is uniquely dependent on the participation of this object, in a situation whose realities revive, with their affirmative associations, the memories of old and painful frustrations. In this situation, the continuing and prolonged contact, under strictly controlled conditions, is an important real factor, which has been elaborated previously. Without these actualities, dream life, or—in instances of greater energic imbalance between impulses and defense—neurosis, will be the spontaneous solutions, while everyday "give-and-take" object relations are, at least on the surface, maintained as such. Occasionally, neurotic behavior, where "transferences" dominate the everyday relationships, will supervene.

Interpretation, recollection or reconstruction, and, of course, working through, are essential for the establishment of effective insight, but they cannot operate mutatively if applied only to memories in the strict sense, whether of highly cathected events or persons. For it is the thrust of wish or impulse, or the elaboration of germane dynamic fantasies, and the corresponding defensive structures and their inadequacies, associated with such memories, which give rise to neurosis. It is a parallel thrust which creates the transference neurosis. Where memories are clear and vivid, through recall, or accepted as much through reconstruction, and associated with variable, optional, and adaptive, rather than rigidly "structuralized" response patterns, the analytic work has been done.

This view does place somewhat heavier than usual emphasis on the horizontal coordinate of operations, the conscious and unconscious relation to the analyst as a living and actual object, who becomes invested with the imagery, traits, and functions of critical objects of the past. The relationship is to be understood in its dynamic, economic, and adaptive meanings, in its current "structuralized" tenacity, the real and unreal carefully separated from one another. The process of subjective memory or of reconstruction, the indispensable genetic dimension, is, in this sense, invoked toward the decisive and specific autobiographic understanding of the living version of old conflict, rather than with the assumption that the interpretative reduction of the transference neurosis to gross mnemic elements is, in itself and automatically, mutative. At least, this view of the problem would seem appropriate to most chronic neuroses embedded in germane character structures of some complexity. That neurotic symptoms connected with isolated traumatic events, covered by amnesia, may, at times, disappear on restoration of memories with adequate affective discharge, regardless of technical method, is of course indisputably true, even though the details of process, including the role of transference, are probably not yet adequately understood. Psychoanalysis was born in the observation of this type of process. Indeed, for some time, the role of the transference, in the early writings of both Freud and Ferenczi, seemed weighted somewhat in the direction of its resistance functions (i.e., as directed against recall), although its affirmative functions were soon adequately appreciated, and placed in the dialectical position, which has obtained to the present day. This last is well illustrated by the quotation from Freud, in the beginning of this section.

THE INTERPLAY OF PAST AND PRESENT, AND THE ROLE OF ILLUSION

However, even if it is insufficient for exclusive reliance, in relation to the complicated neurotic problems we are largely called on to treat, it would be fallacious to assign to the recall and reconstruction of the past an exclusively explanatory value (in the intellectual sense), important though that function be, and difficult as its full-blown emotional correlate may be to come by. There is no doubt that, even in complicated neuroses, with equivalently complicated transference neuroses, the genuinely experienced linking of the past and present can have, at times, a certain uniquely specific dynamic effect of its own, a type of telescoping or merging of common elements in experience, which must be connected with the meaninglessness of time in unconscious life, as against its stern authority in the life of consciousness and adaptation to everyday reality. Contributing decisively to such experience, to whatever degree it occurs, is of course the vivid currency of the transference neurosis, and central in this, the reincarnation of old objects in an actual person, the analyst.

Thus, an allied problem in the general sphere of transference is the fascinating and often enigmatic interplay of past and present. If one wishes to view this interplay in terms of a stereotyped formulation, the matter can remain relatively uncomplicated—as a formulation! Unfortunately, this is too often the case. The phenonemon, however, retains some important obscurities, which I cannot thoroughly dispel, but to which I would like to call attention. To concentrate on the dimension of time, I omit references to the many complicated and intermediate aspects of technique, however essential. For example, we can assume that the transference neurosis re-enacts the essential conflicts of the infantile neurosis in a current setting. If a reasonable degree of awareness of transference is established, the next problem is the genetic reduction of the neurosis to its elements in the past, through analysis of the transference resistance and allied intrapsychic resistances, ultimately genetic interpretations, recollections and reconstructions, and working through. As the transference is related to its genetic origins, the analyst thereby emerges in his true, i.e., real, identity to the patient; the transference is putatively "resolved." To the extent that one follows the traditional view that all resistances, including the transference itself, are ultimately directed against the restoration of early memories as such, this is a convincing formulation. Indeed, in its own right, it has a certain tightly logical quality. However, we know that all this is not so readily accomplished, apart from the special intrapsychic considerations described by Freud in "Analysis Terminable and Interminable" (23). Although in a favorable case, much of the cognitive interpretative work can be accomplished, there remains the fact that cognition alone, in its bare sense, does not necessarily lead to the subsidence of powerful dynamisms, to the withdrawal of "cathexes" from important real objects. For, as mentioned a short while ago, the analyst is a real and living object, apart from the representations with which the transference invests him, and which are interpretable as such. There is, not seldom, a confusing interrelation and commingling of the emergent responses due to an old seeking, and those directed toward a new individual in his own right. Both are important; furthermore, there are large and important zones of overlapping. Apart from such considerations, even the explicitly incestuous transference is currently experienced (at least in good part) by a full-grown adult (like the original Oedipus), instead of a totally and actually helpless child. To be sure, the latter state is reflected subjectively in the emergent transference elements of instinctual striving; but it is subject to analysis, and the residue is something significantly, if not totally, different. It is these residual sexual wishes, presumably directed toward the person of the analyst *as such,* which must be displaced to others. If, as generally agreed, the revival of infantile fantasies and strivings in the biologically mature adolescent (41) presents a new and special problem, one must assume distinctiveness of experience for the adult, although it is true that in the majority of instances, adequate solution is favored by the adult state. There is, in any case, a residual real relationship between persons who have worked together in a prolonged, arduous, and intimate relationship, which, strictly speaking, is not a transference; but there may be mutual coloration, blending, and some confusion between the two spheres of feeling. The general tendency is, I believe, to ignore this dual aspect; in continuing professional relationships, probably both components are gratified to some degree. Above all, there is the ubiquitous power of the residual primordial transference, the urge to cling to an omnipotent parent, to resist the displacement of its "sublimated" anaclitic aspects, even if the various representations of the wishes for bodily intimacy have been thoroughly analyzed and successfully displaced. The outcome is largely the "transference of the transference" mentioned earlier, in a different context. For everyday reality can provide no actual answer to such cravings. In this connection, note Freud's genial envy of Pfister (25). If the man of faith finds this gratification in revealed religion, others in a wide range of secular beliefs and "leaders," the modern rational and skeptical intellectual is less fortunate in this respect. Presumably free, he is prone to invest even intellectual disciplines or their proponents with inappropriate expectations and partisan passions. I have mentioned elsewhere that our own field does not provide exception to this tendency (73).

Of unequivocal importance, and I think largely overlooked, is the sheer fact of current continued physical proximity, as a dynamic and economic factor of great importance in itself, in the prolongation of transference effects. The flood of neurophysiological stimuli occasioned by the analyst's presence causes an entirely different intrapsychic situation from that prevailing in his absence, regardless of how one conceptualizes the difference. Thus, the gradual "weaning" to independence, via reduction of hours, is very useful in many instances; in some, it may be that the dissolution of the transference (in a practical sense), if well analyzed, occurs, as Macalpine (55) suggests, only after regular visits cease. There are a certain number of patients who will never show a terminal phase (or incipient adaptation to the idea of termination as a reality), without relatively arbitrary setting of a termination date. Even though it has been tendentiously misunderstood in one or two instances, I shall reiterate my suggestion (73), as worthy of trial, that a predismissal period of varying duration, following what would ordinarily be regarded as termination, be devoted to vis-à-vis interviews, at reduced frequency, dealing in integrated fashion with whatever preoccupations the patient is impelled to bring to such valedictory. The vis-à-vis element adds the further advantage of testing tenacious transference images against the actuality.

The urge toward actual instinctual gratifications and allied satisfactions, the need to be rid of burdens of time and expense, the sheer urge toward independent functioning, often participate importantly in the dynamics of ultimately successful separation. Certainly, the analyst's own nonarrogant but firm inaccessibility to residual transference wishes of the patient (however expressed), coupled with the conscious and unconscious wish to set him free for development of his individual potentialities, also contribute to this important development.

Apart from and anterior to the indubitably important ancillary elements in the dissolution of clinical transference, mediated in the sphere of reality, the restoration of the past in gross mnemic units, whether by recollection or reconstruction, finds specifying and augmenting support toward effectiveness in the increasingly detailed technical exploitation of the transference neurosis, in the sense of the analysis of the dynamic nuances which it presents. In other words, if the exposure of a man's oedipus complex, or indeed his passive homosexual solution of its vicissitudes, is an important step in the analytic work, the further understanding of the determinants of the pathological augmenting elements in the incestuous fixation, or the specific determinants of the choice of solution in the crosscurrents of the childhood setting, is most liable to be accessible in a useful way in the details of the transference neurosis, where they lend themselves to reconstruction, which is often far more useful than the gross units of spontaneous recollection. In proceeding to such further analysis, such concepts as the universality of the oedipus complex, or intrinsic bisexuality, become only the more helpful, rather than suffering degradation to the position of stereotypic impediments. Such processes, in common with respect for the realities of the analytic (and extra-analytic) setting, serve not only to faciliate the genuine recollection and reconstruction of the past, but to provide a context in which recall and reconstruction can more often "cast the balance," i.e., provide that mutative or at least catalytic element in insight which is distinctively psychoanalytic. Whether or not it serves to resolve the transference neurosis entirely, it contributes something not be dispensed with, toward its adequate understanding and resolution.

Other views of the role of transference in therapeutic change have grown up, often in direct relationship and adjacency to the original schema, sometimes deviating rather widely from it. I shall not review these, at this time. Horney (40), for example, omitting all detailed considerations, presents a view whose logic is, in a sense, antithetical to that of the classical view. While not discarding the etiological importance of the early past, the principal emphasis is on the transference as a current interpersonal relationship, involving the patient's adult character, whose pathological devices are to be exposed and resolved or changed, as such. The prompt resort to interpretation of the past by the analyst is viewed as a facilitation of the patient's resistance to facing the current confrontations and a tendency to leave the essential dynamic issue unaltered. I think it is a commonplace of intelligent conservative analytic technique to be aware of such resistance flights into the past, and to incorporate that awareness in the interpretative schema. It is furthermore quite usually agreed that the analysis of current dynamisms (including first, the resistances) takes precedence over genetic reduction. However, unless the current conflict can *only* be met in direct confrontation, i.e., unless evasion is the only neurotic reality, we assume that, ultimately, the genetic analysis of this conflict—in our immediate reference, the transference neurosis—will accomplish a type of understanding not otherwise available, which facilitates the stripping of transference illusion away from the person of the analyst. By this we mean, apart from the obscure dynamism implicit in the subjective time dimension, an explanatory source beyond the general and rational, and the referents established by scientific observation, in the sense that it rests on exquisitely personal subjective experience. This can of course be integrated with current experience along the lines which are part of standard technique. It is also difficult to gainsay the assumption that, in general, the alterative power of original experience is greater to the extent that it has occurred in an early developmental, i.e., formative period, and that the data recalled or reconstructed (under proper technical conditions, including proper evaluation and critique) may be assumed to have created the special potentialities for the current experience under consideration. Now this genetic reconstruction, like the evolution of the manifest transference in the first place, requires the benign ego splitting emphasized by Sterba (70); for the psychological realities connected with the past and present, respectively, are far from naturally congruent. It is indeed on this basis, although it presents its own problems of energic distribution, that the logic of our view rests. Nevertheless, even though the concept of a "transference" (Horney did minimize the importance of the term, as such) dealt with essentially in current terms, in relation to current realities, is perplexing, and from our point of view *a priori* fallacious, there is a certain stark hard-headed (even if wrong-headed) consistency in the view that the individual must necessarily work out his problems with the other individual with whom he is actually involved, in the situation which creates the confrontation, without distraction by the "past." At least, it places in bolder relief certain problems of our own assumptions.[17]

To come closer to the continuing mainstream of psychoanalytic thought, let us look at the concept of the transference interpretation, and its implications, to whatever degree it is regarded as specifically "mutative," whether in more general usage, or in the specific sense postulated by Strachey a few decades ago (74, 76). Strachey's view lends itself readily to examination because it is so clear-cut. I wish to make it clear that I do not regard the mechanisms described by Strachey as the central and inclusive mechanisms of therapeutic change, or even, in the form described, as necessarily constituting the comprehensive actualities of mutative effect in transference interpretation. However, I do not doubt the importance of superego modification in analysis and its role in facilitating or permitting necessary processes of modification in the ego; nor do I question the uniqueness of impact of the transference interpretation. In common with most of his colleagues at the Marienbad Symposium, I find much that is phenomenologically valid in Strachey's contribution, the introjective details at least interesting, and the explanatory effort in itself worthwhile. The introjective processes may indeed play a variable role in the impact of interpretation, as in other special spheres of communication, in the complex sense mentioned earlier. At the very least, Strachey's view may be taken as a tangible and clear-cut construct of a phenomenon which presents paradigmatically certain problems of the "past and present." These are present, however they are viewed, or included implicitly in other explanatory efforts even if no more spectacularly than in terms of the benignly tolerant "psychoanalytic atmosphere." (See, for example, Bibring [76], even if in a different context of explanation, and with important reservations; or Nunberg's reference [60] to the projection of the patient's superego on the analyst, and modification of his superego through identification with the analyst.)

It appears to me that the "transference interpretation" as elaborated by Strachey, or as used in the current psychoanalytic vernacular, refers not so much to the genetic interpretation of the current transference attitude, as it means a concise direct statement to the patient of an attitude toward the analyst which is at the moment active, but unconscious or, possibly more often, preconscious. It is indeed specified by Strachey that genetic material may follow promptly; and Glover (28, p. 121) specifies that the interpretation is incomplete, until the genetic aspect is included. Strachey's original reference was to hostility. Let us say the interpretation is: "You wish to kill me." From the impact of such interpretation, there ensues, putatively, a series of changes in the superego, in which introjections of the analyst as a good (i.e., nonaggressive) object are gradually substituted for the archaic fantasy objects. The whole process takes origin by virtue of the analyst's power "(his strictly limited power) as auxiliary superego."

Whether or not one views the impact of such interpretation in this or another framework (note Bibring's and Fenichel's comments at the Symposium [76]), there is no doubt of its important effect (when it is correct and well timed). The same is, of course, to some extent true of the analyst's genuine acceptance of the patient's conscious aggressions, especially (in apparent paradox) when these do not have to do with such gross matters as killing, rape, devouring, or attacks of equivalent primitiveness. For, given a reasonably mature patient, both analyst and patient readily take distance from such impulses or fantasies. This is not always true of personal criticisms or derogations, snidely contemptuous comparisons, for example, especially if they find some resonance in vulnerable aspects of the analyst's self-image. Analysts vary as much in their capacities to handle such aggressions as they do in their interpretative skills, and they are not one whit less important! That the impact of interpretation of an impulse or wish, which has not been clearly in awareness, is greater than the acceptance of conscious verbal aggressions is, however, true. The experience is unique, and includes factors beyond the exchange of archaic for good object, especially where the wish or impulse has been genuinely unconscious. Apart from the surprise of discovery, there is (for single example) the provision of words for the hitherto wordless, permitting the decisive intrapsychic "transference" to the preconscious, with its important general implications. With those which are generally accepted, I would submit my personal conviction that this important process bears some obscure relation to the very origins of speech, i.e., the biological translation from the instinctual contributions to these origins, specifically the cannibalistic aggressions.

In any case, to return to the central question: how can we—or can we— in the light of our present psychology and metapsychology, understand such effects? We expect the patient to maintain a clear picture of who the analyst really is. According to Strachey, the ego of the patient, at the moment of emergence of the aggression, perceives the differences between the analyst and the archaic fantasy object. But is he not aware of this difference, as a *condition* of the emergence? Presumably the superego reaction to the "wish to kill" is either archaic in a pregenital sense, or derived from the oedipus complex, in either case, from a remote situation, in the remote past. The analyst is a professional person, engaged and remunerated by the patient to help him, largely by understanding him, and, in turn, by giving him that understanding. It is at the analyst's behest and under his explicit guarantees that the patient follows the basic rule and accepts the regressive transference fantasies which are mobilized by the analytic situation. To phrase it as a naïve bystander might: "What then is so remarkable about his (the analyst's) being tolerant? He is supposed to be! Besides, it's only talk." (This last is, of course, the condition which makes the whole transaction possible for both patient and analyst.) How then does the analyst's attitude influence that of the fierce internalized parent image of the past, reacting punitively or vengefully to the child's murderous wishes? Strachey warns against the analyst playing the good parent lest he become confused with the opposite (i.e., the good archaic) fantasy object. It is imperative that the patient's sense of reality not be strained in either direction, lest the analyst be introjected as a good or bad fantasy object. But even if this pitfall is avoided, there remains, and all the more vividly thereby, the problem of the noncomparable objects. (Actually, and from my point of view, paradoxically, Strachey makes a special issue of just this difference; indeed, it is the implicit cornerstone assumption of his essential argument.) I am not speaking of the genetic interpretation as such, which may follow on the other, or the spontaneous recovery of genetic material, facilitated by the transference interpretation, for these, at least in principle, disestablish (or at least, diminish or modify) the hostility, by creating awareness of its past origins, thus, its probable current inappropriateness. This is a different effect, close to the original schema; in schematic-cognitive principle, it remains unquestionably clear.

But let us return to the more direct transaction between analyst and patient. A unique aspect of the technical work of analysis is the involvement of the analyst's whole personality. In short, to be totally "objective" would require a sort of de-personalization. The patient knows that some things must hurt at times. So it is, by greatly oversimplified analogy, as if one were an orthopedist, and told a child to exercise his sick muscles by kicking one in the shins, and then, to his surprise, did not become angry, when the instructions were followed with wholehearted enthusiasm. "Look, he really meant it!" But this would be in the sphere of the integrated real relationship. What about the less readily demonstrable provinces of the mind? Does something of the sort described by Strachey occur, despite the noncongruent contexts involved? Within the regressed sphere of transference illusion, which does not, however, encompass the entire functioning ego, a transaction at least analogous to that described by Strachey may well occur. But this requires that another latent transference illusion be unconsciously available, also investing the analyst, albeit tacitly, as background for the immediate aggressive fantasy, given a sense of body, vividness, and reality by his living presence, i.e., the representation of a good object, not essentially a fantasy object, from an equivalent past. It is then as if the analyst were a good mother (or a good father) saying: "You wish to kill me, but I still accept you and wish to help you!" For we may assume that all, except those whose early vicissitudes have been at the remote pole of severity, have preserved images of (actual) good objects; and that these, perhaps augmented in some by wistful fantasy *(faute de mieux)*, may well include the capacity to love (a child) in the face of destructive aggression. Apart from idealized fantasy objects (in the archaic Kleinian sense), this wish and corresponding fantasy would seem to be clinically demonstrable in many patients. But what of the observing portion of the ego? It is there to join with the actual (i.e., "nontransference") analyst in understanding all this, in placing it where it belongs, in the genetic past. Can important structural changes, as opposed to purely transference effects, occur without its participation? I do not believe so. If I must speculate (and I can do little more), I would say that it participates in, at least acquiesces to, the powerful force of illusion. However, if I may, for a moment, talk with tongue in cheek, yet gravely, it does this from a somewhat less naïve and "involved" point of view than its other functional portion, in the same sense that it acquiesces, at least temporarily, to the vagaries of the creative imagination, or other productive inconsistencies of human psychic life. It is as if there is an awareness that what is being tested in the present is veritably "what might have been," and that furthermore if the analyst, as a person, has met the acid test of unconscious probing, he may indeed, all the more convincingly, wear the robes of a good and "timeless" unconscious image from the past, to give them life and meaning (a "taste of blood") (15, 50), in the sphere of illusion, while structures within the psyche undergo some degree of modification on that basis.

In Winnicott's admirable contribution on "Transitional Objects and Transitional Phenomena" (80), he places strong emphasis on the role of illusion, deriving from the child's omnipotent reactions to good mothering, and the subsequent enduring and pervasive role of illusion in human mental life. It is the inevitable ("normal") breaches of this perfection of maternal response which establish the primordia of the experience of separation, but which may contribute nonetheless, if in a different sense, to the illusory feeling of omnipotence, as a larval organismic striving for mastery of separation, and thus to the genesis of the primordial transference. The "transitional object" is, in itself, an important transference object, with unique features which derive from its usually being inanimate (albeit usually invested with suggestive body qualities, such as odor). And there is, of course, an important element of illusion, in the sense of conjuror's magic, in the psychoanalytic transference, mediated by the subordination (or to varying degree, the acquiescence) of adult mental functions. The patient does, after all, "invoke" mother or father, in the person of the analyst, as Aladdin invoked the genie. The living presence of the analyst perhaps obviates the lamp-rubbing! One might say that the observing portion of the ego, identified with the adult, the analyst, takes a tolerant attitude toward the childlike portion's experimentation with its hitherto unconscious images similar to that which the sensible parent takes toward the child's dependence on his "transitional object." I have, in my earlier communication (73), mentioned the quality of "serious play-acting" which is implicit in the psychoanalytic situation and process. This refers to that tacit agreement between the analyst and the persistently adult portion of the patient's ego, to take seriously those emotions and fantasies which the patient will experience in the unfolding of his transference neurosis. If one includes in this the mutative interplay between present transference and past experience, the role of illusion extends further, i.e., into the deeper intrapsychic processes of the patient himself.

However, I believe that there are other considerations and phenomena which support and give greater validity and power to this illusory process. For just as the child is assisted by the transitional object in his gradual progression to an object relationship which will provide what he (in an "average expectable" sense) will require,[18] the transitional but living analytic illusion, in much more complex fashion, readies him for reasonably available real relationships, with a revised organization of internal images. The analyst, outsider and "hired hand" though he be at the outset, does perform a therapeutic function, which, in its best development, calls on sound and benevolent parental identifications. This is a part of the ongoing process between patient and analyst, integrated in the current realities of the situation. One may be certain that the patient tests these, and that on the outcome of such testing depend many critical nuances of the therapeutic alliance. While both adult patient and analyst are relatively firm psychic compounds in reality, there is an ineluctable difference between the psychic and concrete, which with the "timelessness of the unconscious" permits images, fantasies, impulses, identifications, to live, in effect, in individual psychic actuality, not just as analytic potentialities, like the elements of chemical compounds, but concurrently with their existence in adult integrations. Thus, Glover's remark in the Marienbad Symposium regarding the *"attitude* [his italics], the true unconscious attitude of the analyst to his patients'' (76) may be invested with further meaning. The patient's real wishes and his transference alike seek out this remote sphere of feeling, impinge on it, and react to it. In the sense that this includes somehow the attitudes and wishes of a genuinely benign parent,[19] apart from the literal instrumentalities of professional function, the patient finds an answering reverberation to his transference testing, which, in psychic reality, supports his operational illusion.

All of this is not irrelevant to recent attempts to construe or interpret the psychoanalytic situation itself, and transference as implicit in it, in terms of very early and general infantile experience; in other words, to view the situation in terms of a spectrum range between its adult actualities and purposes, and the perennial, if only partial wish, to restore the infant's relationship to his first and most important object. In any such effort, there is, I would think, the implicit assumption that whatever the form of the manifest clinical transference, it is a variant, a specification, of a phenomenon latent and implicit in the situational structure, which tends to deviate from the forms of the ubiquitous "give-and-take" transference of everyday life. The latter tend by the very fact of mobile seeking and elicitation of responses to maintain a relatively fixed and integrated level, barring unusual pathology, or unusual frustration, or both.

Whatever the developmental phase or level of integration which finds expression in the transference, there are at least unconscious reverberations, between the two persons involved, which include self and object images (or their earliest precursors in physiological experience) ranging from the anaclitic or symbiotic beginnings, to the integrated elaborated representations of adult years. These thus play a role in the realities of the relationship, in transference, and in their interaction. Whereas in my original presentation, my stress was on the technical modification of the analytic attitude and general responses, in the direction of more discriminatingly selective implementation of the essential rule of abstinence, I have, on this occasion, sought to examine further, under the pressure of my own perplexities, some unclear elements in the participation of clinical transference in the therapeutic process. Such reflections, insofar as they may deal with processes which largely remain unconscious, do not thereby diminish in any sense the importance of the manifest technical exchanges between patient and analyst, which are indeed also the principal carriers of the nonmanifest. However, they draw further attention to the necessary and productive, if sometimes silent, role of illusion in the psychoanalytic process. Paradoxically, at the same time, the importance of the analyst as a real object is heightened, in the sense of that vague but certainly critical sphere, the participation of what the analyst really is, in the depths of his unconscious life, in the contrapuntal course of the development and involution of transference illusion. I hope that, if I have not brought notable clarification to these subjects, I have at least excited renewed interest in their intellectual challenges.

SUMMARY

The paper, a delayed "postscript" to an earlier communication, *The Psychoanalytic Situation: An Examination of Its Development and Essential Nature,* seeks to reiterate, in some instances amplify, toward further clarification, certain underlying dynamic constructs of the original work, with special reference to the pervasive functions of transference. There are further comments, in good part of clinical nature, on the transference neurosis and transference interpretation. In the interest of space economy, at this time, there is minimal condensed response to selected criticisms or misunderstandings of the clinical implications of the earlier work. The subject of comparison and possible integration with germane contributions of recent years is largely deferred. In the sense of "further reflection" by the author, two subjects are discussed: (1) transference object and object representation, and (2) the interplay of past and present, and the role of illusion.

NOTES

1. See page 173 of the *Outline* (24) for the paragraph which defines the analytic situation. The sentence given is a paraphrased excerpt.
2. (a) Greenacre (31): "I have already indicated that I believe the matrix of this is a veritable matrix; i.e., comes largely from the original mother-infant quasi-union of the first months of life. This I consider the basic transference; or one might call it the primary transference, or some part of primitive social instinct" (p. 672). It is possible, of course, that I read this brief introductory passage too literally. There is a partial reiteration, of slightly different elaboration, on p. 674. Most of the paper is devoted to other considerations.

    (b) Spitz (68): "It is not the objectless phase which returns in the transference of the patient. It is the analytical setting which reproduces many of the elements of this phase.

Through this reproduction the analytical setting pulls, funnel-like, the patient's transference in the direction of the objectless phase'' (p. 383).

3. "But the analytic situation as a whole goes beyond the elementary dynamic of transference, perhaps to include the original, primitive experience of Being and to express its essence. From this point of view it is legitimate to describe the analytic situation as an ontological experience" (p. 386).

4. In the views quoted, sometimes in more remotely related instances, it is difficult to be certain how much the differences are verbal, or to what degree there are real differences in fundamental premises. If I seem to stickle on this question, it is because: (a) the idea of separation as an excitant of transference phenomena is of fundamental importance in my views; and this has not always been understood, even by intellectually sympathetic readers. (b) Great as is my emphasis on the *unconscious* meaning and power of the analytic situation, I do not believe that its concrete and manifest realities actually reproduce early situations to the degree that is sometimes thought. There are certain resemblances, and there is the tremendous power of transference illusion; to these there may be added important supporting elements from the analyst's emotional participation. This question reappears in the final section of the paper.

5. In using this term, I should note that the meaning intended is quite different from that of Ferenczi, who, in his pioneer paper of 1909, used the term "primordial transferences" for the first object love and the first object hate, as transferred from autoerotic feelings (7).

6. "Infant Sorrow," in *Songs of Experience.*

7. The justification for asking this indulgence lies in the empirically established importance of this striving, normal or pathological, and its obvious connections with either or both of the great instinctual drives, from the beginning of life to its end, including the "fear of death" itself. It has an old position in psychoanalytic thought. (See Freud, 16, p. 224.) Throughout this paper, I deal with "separation" in its broadest and most inclusive sense. It seems inescapable that the growing interest in the role of separation in development (57), in separation anxiety (4), in possible specific instinctual components in attachment phenomena (4), and the question of the primary or secondary character of the latter phenomena (4, 5, 58) will ultimately occasion a general re-examination of the theory of drives and of anxiety.

8. The complexities of instinct and anxiety theory do not lend themselves to facile disposition. However, a clinical impression derived from reflection on total experience over many years is probably not without *some* significance. With regard to female patients in whom *unconscious* homosexual urges are singularly tenacious and pervasive, the background of one form or another of severe maternal deprivation, in some instances with noteworthy harshness, in others, quite subtle, has been conspicuous (regardless of other factors). To my surprise, this brought with it the afterreflection that the same was true of males with inveterate incestuous fixations to the mother (again apart from other complicated considerations). Assuming that one does not set aside such impression (for any of myriad methodological reasons), there are many possible inferences. My own, which seems to accumulate supporting rationale and observations through the years, is in the following direction: that, apart from its instinctual sources, the aggression aroused by such relationships can take the form of "irredentist" insistent and coercive tenacity, the urge to force or extort what has not been given, and to punish the object for the delinquency at the same time. In the instances under consideration, such impulses can be fused with the erotic impulses and thus contribute to the "fixation." It has long been my conviction that a miniature of the same phenomenon is intrinsic in the structure of the "normal" phase and oedipus complex. Note the infancy history of Sophocles' Oedipus!

9. This explicit apposition of the role of technique and of "mature transference" wish is, I

think, appropriate and useful in further diminishing the (apparent) gap between the two essential and interacting systems of psychoanalytic process, the emotional and the cognitive.

10. Again, we are considering "transference" as not identical with, although importantly related to, "therapeutic alliance." The question is whether "positive" or "negative" are to be derived from the current descriptive quality of the infantile elements in the personal relationship or from the dynamic effect on the analytic process (47, 48). It would be better that the former be stated in frankly descriptive terms, i.e., hostile or erotic, with specifying variants. The primordial transference is intrinsically and inevitably ambivalent. It is a truism that an erotic transference can conceal severe hostilities, and, even when "pure," can occasion obstinate resistances; a hostile transference (even assuming its genuineness), if accepted and verbalized, in the context of an active "mature transference," may be compatible with excellent analytic progress. Note Kris's incidental remark in describing the "good analytic hour" (46, p. 447).

11. In the justly treasured and richly meaningful story of Andersen, "The Emperor's New Clothes" (a story which Freud [15] has examined, from a different point of view), the people only pretend to see the clothes of the naked king. In our time, which has seen repeatedly the spectacular rise and fall of political tyrants, it would seem that actual perception of the ruler's virtues and capacities (his "clothes") has often undergone radical change, in susceptible personalities, with the fling in either direction of the hero's fortunes.

12. In these and subsequent remarks (regarding the "eight-month anxiety"), I take considerable interpretative liberty with the work of Spitz, and his co-workers, omitting all observational and conceptual refinements so carefully presented in Spitz's recent book (69). Needless to say, I am greatly indebted to these remarkable contributions.

13. There is a problem connected with the central importance of the transference neurosis in current clinical psychoanalytic thought, which would really merit a separate communication in its own right. However, it can be mentioned at this point. It is, in fact, a specification of a problem dealt with by Freud in "Analysis Terminable and Interminable" (23), and especially relevant to the importance of the present and living object in the analytic process. I refer to individuals who have had apparently satisfactory analyses, yet suffer severe relapses, sometimes after a latent period of some years. Particularly in mind are those whose secondary symptoms are of great severity, of a type apparently unsuspected—or at least not clearly discerned—in the original analytic experience. In my own observation of a few such instances, I have every reason to infer that the deepest problems of object relationship and the associated erotic-aggressive phase problems did not enter actively into the transference neurosis in the original analysis. To put it more accurately: those severe transference problems which seemed nuclear in the severe secondary illness were apparently not emotionally active in the first analysis, except possibly in "acting out," to whose more profound motivations access was not obtained. Interpretable "material" was not lacking in these instances, in the first analysis; what later erupted in the form of severe illness was not unfamiliar to the patient in verbal-intellectual terms. I am forced to assume that the personality guarded itself tenaciously against the emotional re-emergence in the transference of what had been sequestered in early childhood, "grown around" so to speak, in a sort of epi-personality (albeit, in some cases, forceful and effective). The catastrophic aspect lies in the fact that, in such instances, the vicissitudes of "real life," sometimes combined with the end results of cumulative neurotic behavior or "acting out," do produce the demands, disappointments, threats, and the extreme anxious-hostile responses in the patient which were automatically and primitively feared and avoided in the therapeutic situation. As always, it is difficult to specify the balance between pathology and technique, in every case. By technique, I mean, of course, the question of interpretations which were clearly indi-

cated. Certainly, one must join in Freud's (remarkably tolerant) pessimism (23) regarding any effort to elicit by personal activity the latent transference conflict. One inevitably thinks of some connection with Winnicott's concept of true and false selves (81) in certain cases; this connection may well exist. However, I cannot at this point, verify the very early reconstructive elements, nor the technical phenomena, which he specifies (except, of course, the need to make adaptations in severely regressed patients), at least as major generalizations about these cases.

14. This is, of course, a complicated matter, both metapsychologically and empirically. I am aware that all psychological transactions, cathexis, for example, are held to refer necessarily to a representation rather than to the actual object in the outer world. Furthermore, the analyst himself, as himself, gives rise to an internalized representation, which presumably becomes increasingly clear and important, in comparison with the parent image which invests his own, in the transference, as the analysis progresses. In this passage, I am, as stated, interested essentially in the dynamic function of the analyst as a currently real and living object in the revival and solution of problems in the remote past. I suppose that one can view his role as mediated by his intrapsychic representation in the patient, the representation as continuously receiving ''nutriment'' through the influx of perceptual data, because of his living presence. (See Gaarder [26] in this connection, also Rapaport [63].) However, Freud did not often make an issue of the distinction, and Hartmann could oppose ''one's own person'' to ''object representation'' on the same page on which he suggests the usefulness of referring to representations in both instances (37, p. 127). I mention this only because of my inference, no doubt subjectively colored, and possibly quite unjustified, that there is a persistent interest in the distinctive meaning of the ''self'' and the ''object''— psychologically—apart from, and in addition to, their representations. At any rate, that is my own tendency. Also, at this moment, my interest is essentially empirical and clinical, with constructs invoked only as immediately necessary. With regard to the early object whose representation is preserved in the unconscious, there can be no doubt of its exclusively psychological nature. However, the relation between such representations and the internalized perceptual experience of later transference objects is indeed complicated. (See, for example, the problems implicitly posed in this sphere by Pfeffer's study [61].) The question of the original roles of physical and psychological traits of the object, respectively, and their relation to one another, in forming persistent ''representations,'' is equally complex, and, further, probably varies considerably with the individuals under consideration.

15. In the view of Melanie Klein (43), not only do the origins of transference lie in the earliest neonatal period, with its complicated system of internal and external objects, commingling of real and fantasy elements, projection and introjection, and other germane mechanisms, but these must be dealt with in the analytic transference. (Mrs. Klein does, however, also emphasize the importance of later developments, and their integration with the phenomena of the very earliest period.) While one sees these phenomena at times, and one can keep an open mind about their genetic position in others, I cannot verify their frequent appearance or accessibility in the transference of most adult patients.

16. In relation to one of the patients mentioned by Nunberg (60), the author uses the term ''transference readiness'' to specify reactions in which the patient *wishes* that he were like her father, and is constantly displeased with his failure to be like him, as opposed to the situation in which the patient reacts as though the analyst *were* the patient's father. I understand the effort toward semantic-conceptual clarity regarding the term ''transference.'' However, I am not convinced that the adjacent concept ''readiness'' fulfills such criterion. Is the difference really not in the sphere of certain qualities of the ego in its response to

warded-off impulse and fantasy, or, as mentioned earlier, in the economic sphere, the "balance of power"? Is this type of "transference-ready" patient ever going to have a transference, in the sense of transference illusion, or is this her particular and painful mode of expressing her transference?

17. In a relatively recent paper by Szasz (77), exceedingly ingenious in its dialectic, although (to me) not persuasive in its interpretation of certain important facts of process and scientific history, the defense elements in the concept of transference, on the *analyst's* side, beginning (in the author's view) with its very discovery, are stressed, although the brilliance and indispensability of the discovery are acknowledged. While it is true that a real relationship can mistakenly be viewed as transference, this problem has been under active scrutiny and discussion for some time. The possibility of such error in no way diminishes the critical importance of the transference. Its opposite counterpart remains the more frequent and serious problem. Szasz does not, in this paper, propose a new system of technique, only the overriding importance of certain personal qualities in the analyst, a requirement with which very few would disagree.

18. Pollock (62) has employed a similar analogy.

19. Some germane considerations deserve brief mention here. The first is the hazard of sentimentalizing this concept, or further, of contributing to a "mystique" regarding unconscious curative powers. No one can cure with the adequate unconscious attitude alone. The patient requires the pabulum of good technical method, just as certainly as a child needs certain concrete ministrations—even from the best parent in the world! Second: just as surely as it is true that the practice of analysis is a remarkably exacting profession in many ways (35), so is it probably true that an appropriate unconscious attitude toward patients is not the exclusive property of an anointed few. It exists, at least potentially, in most reasonably decent people. What is intended in this passage is to postulate an important process which occurs in analyses. It is, of course, true that some individuals may fail in this respect, as in others; or any of us may fail or be inadequate, with certain patients, sometimes without being aware of the lack or failure. The general problem lies more in having analyzed thoroughly the distortions in this all-important sphere of one's unconscious life, and in the continuing analysis of the specific "countertransference neurosis" (78) with each patient. Beyond this, there is the ability to accept without conflict a benevolent disposition toward one's patient, with the concomitant ability to distinguish between such genuine disposition, as implemented by the technically correct instrumentalities of psychoanalytic procedure, and an attitude which presses for extra-analytic expression, which tends toward "spoiling," overindulgence, overanxious concern, and other obviously distorting modalities of expression. One can reasonably assert that the latter is not the expression of an uncomplicated benevolent attitude, in a well-schooled analyst, any more than it is in an intelligent parent.

BIBLIOGRAPHY

1. Balint, M. Early developmental states of the ego: primary object-love (1937). *Primary Love and Psycho-analytic Technique.* London: Tavistock Publications, 1965, pp. 74–90.

2. Benedek, T. Adaptation to reality in early infancy. *Psychoanal. Quart.,* 7:200–215, 1938.

3. Benedek, T. The psychosomatic implications of the primary unit: mother-child. *Amer. J. Orthopsychiat.,* 19:642–654, 1949.

4. Bowlby, J. Separation anxiety. *Int. J. Psycho-Anal.,* 41:89–113, 1960.

5. Bowlby, J. Note on Dr. Lois Murphy's paper (with reply by Dr. Murphy). *Int. J. Psycho-Anal.*, 45:44–48, 1964.

6. Fairbairn, W. R. D. Synopsis of an object-relations theory of the personality. *Int. J. Psycho-Anal.*, 44:224–225, 1963.

7. Ferenczi, S. Introjection and transference (1909). *Sex in Psychoanalysis.* New York: Basic Books, 1950, pp. 35–93.

8. Ferenczi, S. On obscene words (1911). *Sex in Psychoanalysis.* New York: Basic Books, 1950, pp. 132–153.

9. Ferenczi, S. *Thalassa: A Theory of Genitality* (1923). Albany: The Psychoanalytic Quarterly, Inc., 1938.

10. Fisher, C. Psychoanalytic implications of recent research on sleep and dreaming. *J. Amer. Psychoanal. Assn.*, 13:197–303, 1965.

11. Fisher, C. Dreaming and sexuality. In *Psychoanalysis—A General Psychology,* ed. R. M. Loewenstein, L. M. Newman, M. Schur, A. J. Solnit. New York: International Universities Press, 1966, pp. 537–569.

12. Freud, A. The widening scope of indications for psychoanalysis: discussion. *J. Amer. Psychoanal. Assn.*, 2:607–620, 1954.

13. Freud, A. *Normality and Pathology in Childhood: Assessments of Development.* New York: International Universities Press, 1965.

14. Freud, A. & Burlingham, D. *Infants without Families.* New York: International Universities Press, 1944.

15. Freud, S. The interpretation of dreams (1900). *Standard Edition,* 4 & 5. London: Hogarth Press, 1953.

16. Freud, S. Three essays on the theory of sexuality (1905). *Standard Edition,* 7:125–243. London: Hogarth Press, 1953.

17. Freud, S. The dynamics of transference (1912). *Standard Edition,* 12:97–108. London: Hogarth Press, 1958.

18. Freud, S. Some character-types met with in psycho-analytic work (1916). *Standard Edition,* 14:309–333. London: Hogarth Press, 1957.

19. Freud S. Some neurotic mechanisms in jealousy, paranoia and homosexuality (1922). *Standard Edition,* 18:221–232. London: Hogarth Press, 1955.

20. Freud, S. The ego and the id (1923), *Standard Edition,* 19:3–66. London: Hogarth Press, 1961.

21. Freud, S. Inhibitions, symptoms and anxiety (1926). *Standard Edition,* 20:77–174. London: Hogarth Press, 1959.

22. Freud, S. A disturbance of memory on the Acropolis (1936). *Standard Edition,* 22:239–248. London: Hogarth Press, 1964.

23. Freud, S. Analysis terminable and interminable (1937), *Standard Edition,* 23:211–253. London: Hogarth Press, 1964.

24. Freud, S. An outline of psychoanalysis (1940). *Standard Edition,* 23:141–207. London: Hogarth Press, 1964.

25. Freud, S. & Pfister, O. *Psychoanalysis and Faith: The Letters of Sigmund Freud and Oskar Pfister* (1909–1939), ed. H. Meng & E. L. Freud. New York: Basic Books, 1963, pp. 39–40, 63.

26. Gaarder, K. The internalized representation of the object in the presence and in the absence of the object. *Int. J. Psycho-Anal.*, 46:297–302, 1965.

27. Gitelson, M. The curative factors in psycho-analysis: 1. The first phase of psychoanalysis. *Int. J. Psycho-Anal.*, 43:194–205, 234, 1962.

28. Glover E. *The Technique of Psycho-Analysis*. New York: International Universities Press, 1955.

29. Greenacre, P. The predisposition to anxiety, (1941). In *Trauma, Growth, and Personality*. New York: Norton, 1952, pp. 27–82.

30. Greenacre, P. The biological economy of birth (1945). In *Trauma, Growth and Personality*. New York: Norton, 1952, pp. 3–26.

31. Greenacre, P. The role of transference: practical considerations in relation to psychoanalytic therapy. *J. Amer. Psychoanal. Assn.*, 2:671:684, 1954.

32. Greenacre, P. On focal symbiosis. In *Dynamic Psychopathology in Childhood*, ed. L. Jessner & E. Pavenstedt. New York: Grune & Stratton, 1959, pp. 243–256.

33. Greenacre, P. Considerations regarding the parent-infant relationship. *Int. J. Psycho-Anal.*, 41:571–584, 1960.

34. Greenson, R. R. The working alliance and the transference neurosis. *Psychoanal. Quart.*, 34:155–181, 1965.

35. Greenson, R. R. That "impossible" profession. *J. Amer. Psychoanal. Assn.*, 14:9–27, 1966.

36. Hartmann, H. *Ego Psychology and the Problem of Adaptation* (1939). New York: International Universities Press, 1958.

37. Hartmann, H. *Essays on Ego Psychology*. New York: International Universities Press, 1964.

38. Hendrick, I. Early development of the ego: identification in infancy. *Psychoanal. Quart.*, 20:44–61, 1951.

39. Hoffer, W. Mouth, hand and ego-integration. *The Psychoanalytic Study of the Child, 3/4:49–56*. New York: International Universities Press, 1949.

40. Horney, K. *New Ways in Psychoanalysis*. New York: Norton: 1939.

41. Jacobson, E. *The Self and the Object World*. New York: International Universities Press, 1964.

42. Jones, E. Fear, guilt, and hate (1929). *Papers on Psycho-Analysis*. Baltimore: Williams & Wilkins, 5th ed., 1949, pp. 304–324.

43. Klein, M. The origins of transference. *Int. J. Psycho-Anal.*, 33:433–438, 1952.

44. Kohut, H. Introspection, empathy, and psychoanalysis: an examination of the relationship between mode of observation and theory. *J. Amer. Psychoanal. Assn.*, 7:459–483, 1959.

45. Kohut, H. & Seitz, P. F. D. Concepts and theories of psychoanalysis. In *Concepts of Personality*, ed. J. M. Wepman & R. W. Heine. Chicago: Aldine, 1963, pp. 113–141.

46. Kris, E. On some vicissitudes of insight in psycho-analysis. *Int. J. Psycho-Anal.*, 37:445–455, 1956.

47. Lagache, D. Some aspects of transference, *Int. J. Psycho-Anal.*, 34:1–10, 1953.

48. Lagache, D. La doctrine Freudienne et la théorie du transfert. *Acta Psychother.*, 2:228–249, 1954.

49. Lewin, B. D. Sleep, the mouth and the dream screen. *Psychoanal. Quart.*, 15:419–434, 1946.

50. Loewald, H. W. On the therapeutic action of psycho-analysis. *Int. J. Psycho-Anal.*, 41:1–18, 1960.

51. Loewald, H. W. The superego and the ego-ideal: II. Superego and time. *Int. J. Psycho-Anal.*, 43:264–268, 1962.

52. Loewald, H. W. Internalization, separation, mourning, and the superego. *Psychoanal. Quart.*, 31:483–504. 1962.

53. Loewenstein, R. M. Some thoughts on interpretation in the theory and practice of psycho-

analysis. *The Psychoanalytic Study of the Child*, 12:127–150. New York: International Universities Press, 1957.

54. Loewenstein, R. M. Some considerations on free association. *J. Amer. Psychoanal. Assn.*, 11:451–473, 1963.

55. Macalpine, I. The development of the transference. *Psychoanal. Quart.*, 19:501–539, 1950.

56. Mahler, M. S. On childhood psychosis and schizophrenia: autistic and symbiotic infantile psychoses. *The Psychoanalytic Study of the Child*, 7:286–305. New York: International Universities Press, 1952.

57. Mahler, M. S. On the significance of the normal separation-individuation phase, with reference to research in symbiotic child psychosis. In *Drives, Affects, Behavior*, ed. M. Schur. New York: International Universities Press, 1965, 2:161–169.

58. Murphy, L. B. Some aspects of the first relationship, *Int. J. Psycho-Anal.*, 45:31–43, 1964.

59. Nacht, S. & Viderman, S. The pre-object universe in the transference situation. *Int. J. Psycho-Anal.*, 41:385–388, 1960.

60. Nunberg, H. Transference and reality. *Int. J. Psycho-Anal.*, 32:1–9, 1951.

61. Pfeffer, A. Z. The meaning of the analyst after analysis: a contribution to the theory of therapeutic results. *J. Amer. Psychoanal. Assn.*, 11:229–244, 1963.

62. Pollock, G. H. On symbiosis and symbiotic neurosis. *Int. J. Psycho-Anal.*, 45:1–30, 1964.

63. Rapaport, D. The theory of ego autonomy: a generalization. *Bull. Menninger Clin.*, 22:13–35, 1958.

64. Reich, W. *Character-Analysis* (1933). New York: Orgone Institute Press, 1945, pp. 134–136.

65. Ribble, M. A. *The Rights of Infants*. New York: Columbia University Press, 1944.

66. Segal, H. *Introduction to the Work of Melanie Klein*. New York: Basic Books, 1964.

67. Sharpe, E. F. Psycho-physical problems revealed in language: an examination of metaphor. *Int. J. Psycho-Anal.*, 21:201–213, 1940.

68. Spitz, R. A. Transference: the analytical setting and its prototype. *Int. J. Psycho-Anal.*, 37:380–385, 1956.

69. Spitz, R. A. & Cobliner, W. G. *The First Year of Life: A Psychoanalytic Study of Normal and Deviant Development of Object Relations*. New York: International Universities Press, 1965.

70. Sterba, R. The fate of the ego in analytic therapy. *Int. J. Psycho-Anal.*, 15:117–126, 1934.

71. Stern, M. M. The ego aspect of transference. *Int. J. Psycho-Anal.*, 38:1–12, 1957.

72. Stone L. The widening scope of indications for psychoanalysis. *J. Amer. Psychoanal. Assn.*, 2:567–594, 1954.

73. Stone, L. *The Psychoanalytic Situation: An Examination of Its Development and Essential Nature*. New York: International Universities Press, 1961.

74. Strachey, J. The nature of the therapeutic action of psycho-analysis. *Int. J. Psycho-Anal.*, 15:127–159, 1934.

75. Sullivan, C. T. Freud and Fairbairn: two theories of ego-psychology. *Doylestown Foundation Papers*. Doylestown: Doylestown Foundation, 1963.

76. Symposium on the Theory of the Therapeutic Results of Psycho-Analysis (E. Glover, O. Fenichel, J. Strachey, E. Bergler, H. Nunberg, E. Bibring), *Int. J. Psycho-Anal.*, 18:125–189, 1937.

77. Szasz, T. S. The concept of transference, *Int. J. Psycho-Anal.*, 44:432–443, 1963.

78. Tower, L. E. Countertransference. *J. Amer. Psychoanal. Assn.*, 4:224–255, 1956.

79. Waelder, R. The principle of multiple function (1930). *Psychoanal. Quart.*, 5:45–62, 1936.

80. Winnicott, D. W. Transitional objects and transitional phenomena. *Int. J. Psycho-Anal.*, 34:89–97, 1953.
81. Winnicott, D. W. On transference, *Int. J. Psycho-Anal.*, 37:386–388, 1956.
82. Winnicott, D. W. The theory of the parent-infant relationship. *Int. J. Psycho-Anal.*, 41:585–595, 1960.
83. Zetzel, E. R. The theory of therapy in relation to a developmental model of the psychic apparatus. *Int. J. Psycho-Anal.*, 46:39–52, 1965.

20. Notes on Transference: Universal Phenomenon and Hardest Part of Analysis

Brian Bird

As an introduction I would like to make a few general remarks about transference as I see it. Transference, in my view, is a very special mental quality that has never been satisfactorily explained. I am not satisfied, for instance, either with what has been written about it or with its use in analysis. To me, our knowledge seems slight, and our use limited. This view, admittedly extreme, is possible only because transference is such a very remarkable phenomenon, with a great and largely undeveloped potential. I am particularly taken with the as yet unexplored idea that transference is a universal mental function which may well be the basis of all human relationships. I even suspect it of being one of the mind's main agencies for giving birth to new ideas, and new life to old ones. In these several respects, transference would seem to me to assume characteristics of a major ego function.

I tend to go along with those who consider transference unique as it occurs in the analytic situation, and with those who hold that the analysis and resolution of a transference neurosis is the only avenue to the farthest reaches of the mind. It is also my belief that transference, in one form or another, is always present, active, and significant in the analytic situation. From this it should follow that rarely is there a need to give up on the transference or to doubt that everything that goes on in analysis has a transference meaning. I would also be inclined to agree with those, perhaps few in number, who harbor the idea that analysts themselves regularly develop transference reactions to their patients, including periods of transference neurosis, and that these transference reactions play an essential role in the analytic process.

Finally, I want to point out that this paper is not a comprehensive study of transference. Nor is it a review paper, for, with the exception of a few references to some of Freud's writings, there is little or no mention of what

Reprinted from the *Journal of the American Psychoanalytic Association* 20 (1972): 267–301, by permission of International Universities Press, Inc.

has been written on the subject by others. As to how transference works, it seems likely there are more questions than answers. Therefore, I hope it will be understood that what I say is for question-raising, and anything sounding like an answer should be especially questioned.

SOME VIEWS ON FREUD AND TRANSFERENCE

As a prefatory remark about Freud and transference, the observation can be offered that Freud wrote only briefly about transference and did so, in the main, before 1917. Another observation which can rarely be made about Freud's works, and which everyone may not agree with, is that, with one or two exceptions, what he did write on transference did not reach the high level of analytical thought which has come to be regarded as standard for him. Some indication of what his contributions consist of is given by the editors of the Standard Edition, who list them in several places. One of the longer lists, in a footnote on page 431 of Volume 16, includes six references: "Studies on Hysteria" with Breuer (1895), the Dora paper (1905), "The Dynamics of Transference" (1912), "Observations on Transference-Love" (1915), the chapter on transference in the Introductory Lectures (1917), and "Analysis Terminable and Interminable" (1937). Although the editors in no sense suggest that these six papers include everything Freud wrote on the subject, it does seem evident that, considering the essential importance of transference to analysis, he wrote little. Moreover, the three papers in which transference is the specific theme, "The Dynamics of Transference," "Transference-Love," and the transference chapter in the Introductory Lectures, come across as perhaps his least significant contributions.

Freud's first direct mention of transference occurs in "Studies on Hysteria" (1895). His first significant reference to it, however, did not appear until five years later when, in a letter to Fliess on April 16, 1900, he said (Freud, 1887–1902) he was "beginning to see that the apparent endlessness of the treatment is something of an inherent feature and is connected with the transference" (p. 317). In a footnote to this letter the editors state that, "This is the first insight into the role of transference in psycho-analytic therapy."

Despite these early references, it seems correct to say that yet another five years was to go by before the phenomenon of transference was actually introduced. Even then the introduction was far from prominent, for it was tacked on like an afterthought as a four-page portion of a postscript to what was perhaps Freud's most fascinating case history to date, the case of Dora (1905, pp. 116–120).

Using data from Dora's three-month-long, unexpectedly terminated analysis, and especially from her dramatic transference reactions which had taken him quite unawares, Freud now gave to transference its first distinct psychological entity and for the first time indicated its essential role in the analytic process. His account, although in general more than adequate—in fact elegant and remarkably "finished"—was brief, almost laconic, and perhaps not an entirely worthy introduction to such a truly great discovery. What was uniquely great was his recognizing the usefulness of transference. In his analysis of Dora he had noted not only that transference feelings existed and were powerful, but, much to his dismay, he had realized what a serious, perhaps even insurmountable, obstacle they could be. Then, in what seems like a creative leap, Freud made the almost unbelievable discovery that transference was in fact the key to analysis, that by properly taking the patient's transference into account, an entirely new, essential, and immensely effective heuristic and therapeutic force was added to the analytic method.

The impact on analysis of this startling discovery was actually much greater and much more significant than most people seem to appreciate. Although the role of transference as the *sine qua non* of analysis was and is widely accepted, and was so stated by Freud from the first, it has almost never been acclaimed for having brought about an entire change in the nature of analysis. The introduction of free association to analysis, a much lesser change, received and still receives much more recognition.

One of the reasons for the relatively unheralded entry of transference into analysis may have been the circumstances of its discovery. Although Freud's new ideas were recorded as if they arose as a sudden inspiration during the Dora analysis, they may in fact have developed somewhat later. In the paper's prefatory remarks, for instance, Freud (p. 13) said he had not discussed transference with Dora at all, and in the postscript (p. 119), he said he had been unaware of her transference feelings. Also pointing to a later discovery date is the extraordinary delay in the paper's publication. According to the editors' note (p. 4), the paper had been completed and accepted for publication by late January 1901, but this date was then actually set back more than four and a half years until October 1905. The editors add: "We have no information as to how it happened that Freud . . . deferred publication." In my opinion, his reason may have been that only during those four and a half years, as a consequence of his own self-analysis, did he come to an understanding of the significance of the transference. Only then may it have been possible for him to turn again to the Dora case, to apply to it what he had learned in himself, to write his beautiful essay as part of the postscript, and at last to release the paper for publication.

Freud's self-analysis has been considered from many angles, but not significantly, as far as I know, from the standpoint of transference. Opponents of the idea that there is such a thing as definite self-analysis, some of whom say it is impossible, generally object on grounds that without an analyst there can be no transference neurosis. Freud clearly demonstrated, I think, the situation that may be necessary to fill this need: self-analysis may require at least a half-way satisfactory transference object. In Freud's case, the main transference object at this time seems to have been Fliess, who filled the role rather well. As with any analyst, his "real" impact on Freud was slight. He was essentially a neutral figure, relatively anonymous and physically separate. All of this, plus Fliess's own reciprocal transference reactions, made it possible for Freud to endow Fliess with whatever qualities and whatever feelings were essential to the development of Freud's transference, and, it should be added, his transference neurosis. In the end, of course, the transference was in part resolved. Freud's eventual awakening to the realization of the presence within him of such strange and powerful psychological forces must have come as a stupendous disillusionment, directed not only toward Fliess but toward himself, and yet his subsequent working out of some of these transference attachments must have been both an intellectual triumph and an immensely healing and releasing process.

It was this event, the development, the discovery, and then the resolution within himself of the complexities of the transference neurosis, that constituted the actual center of his self-analysis, and it was this event that was the beginning of analysis as we know it.

In the years following this revolutionary discovery, the central role of transference in analysis gained remarkably wide acceptance, and it has easily held this central position ever since. What the substance of this central position consists of, however, is something of a mystery, for, in my opinion, nothing about analysis is less well known than how individual analysts actually use transference in their day-to-day work with patients. At a guess, because each analyst's concept of transference derives variably but significantly from his own inner experience, transference probably means many different things to different analysts.

In the same individually determined way, even Freud's own pupils must have differed on this issue, not only from him but from each other. Although some of their differences may have been slight, others may have contributed significantly to later analytic developments. A question could be raised, for instance, whether differences in handling the transference which at first were the property of one analyst gradually developed into formal clinical methods used by many, and whether these clinical methods, after having been conceptualized, served as the beginning of various divergent schools of analysis. Such an occurrence, consistent with my belief that analytic ideas do arise in this way, primarily out of transference experiences in the analytic situation, would lead to the question whether the history of the ideological differences among various schools might be found to be more consistently traceable to idiosyncratic differences in what was actually said and done in response to transference reactions than to any other factor. Whatever the case, many differences and divergencies did occur among the early analysts, and all of them, I suspect, had to do in some major way with differences in the handling of the transference.

Strangely, Freud himself seems to have taken little part in influencing this rapid and divergent period of growth. Usually accused of being too dominating in such matters, Freud seems to have done just the opposite during the development of this most critical aspect of analysis, the process itself, and, for reasons unknown, detached himself from it.

What was needed, one might be inclined to say, was not leadership in the form of domination, but leadership in trying to provide what was lacking, and to me is still lacking, namely, an analytical rationale for transference phenomena. The question must be asked, of course, whether in fact this would have been a good thing at that particular time in psychoanalytic history. Perhaps not. The exercise of closure, which Freud's structuring might have amounted to, although adding to understanding and stability at a certain theoretical level, could at another level, as such closures have often done, have placed many obstacles in the way of further analytical developments. Thus, his leaving the matter of transference wide open, even though it led to confusion and uncertainty, may have been just as well.

In many ways the closest Freud ever came to establishing a formal analytical rationale for transference was his first attempt, in the postscript to the case of hysteria (1905). These few pages are, in my opinion, among the most important of all Freud's writings, outweighing by far the paper to which they are appended. Yet, I suspect, the case of Dora has always been taught as an entity rather than, as I would have it, ancillary to the essay on transference. In that essay Freud was clear: his ideas revealed tremendous insights and promised more to come. Imagine his being able to say at this early time that during analysis no new symptoms are formed, and that, instead, the powers of the neurosis are occupied in creating a new edition of the same disease. Just think of the analytic implications of his saying that this "new edition" consists of a special class of mental structures, for the most part unconscious, having the peculiar characteristic of being able to replace earlier persons with the person of the analyst, and in this fashion applying all components of the original neurosis to the person of the analyst at the present time. Surely as profound a statement as any he ever made.

Then he goes on to say that there is no way to avoid transference, that this "latest creation of the desire must be combated like all the earlier ones" (p. 116), and that, although this is by far the hardest part of analysis, only after the transference has been resolved can a patient arrive at a sense of conviction of the validity of the connections which have been constructed during analysis.

He concludes by saying: "In psycho-analysis . . . all the patient's tendencies, including hostile ones, are aroused; they are then turned to account for the purposes of the analysis by being made conscious, and in this way the transference is constantly being destroyed. Transference, which seems ordained to be the greatest obstacle to psycho-analysis, becomes its most powerful ally . . ." (p. 117).

These remarkable observations, written in declarative style, with no hint of vacillation, vagueness, or ambivalence, convey a sense of deep conviction that could arise, one feels, only from Freud's own hard-won inner experience. Nowhere is there a suggestion that transference is a mere technical matter. Far from it. Here, in these few lines, Freud announces that he has come upon a new and exciting kind of mental function, or, as I believe, a new and exciting kind of ego function.

Very quickly, however, Freud's conviction seems to have failed him. Nothing he wrote afterward about transference was at this level, and most of his later references were a retreat from it. For instance, he never did develop the promising idea that the mind constantly creates new editions of the original neurosis and includes in them an ever-changing series of persons. Instead, he tended to become less specific, even referring to transference at times in broad terms as if it were no more than rapport between patient and analyst, or as if it were an interpersonal or psycho-social relationship, concepts which, of course, a great many analysts have since adopted, but which were not part of Freud's original ideas.

Perhaps his most persistent deviation was an on-and-off tendency to regard transference merely as a technical matter, often writing of it as an asset to analysis when positive and a liability when negative.

Significantly, because it indicated that an active struggle was still going on within him, Freud occasionally expressed once again, even though briefly, his earlier insights, particularly his idea that transference is an essential although unexplored part of mental life. An example of this appears in his otherwise quite indifferent account of transference in "An Autobiographical Study" (1925). Transference, he says, "is a universal phenomenon of the human mind . . . and in fact dominates the whole of each person's relations to his human environment" (p. 42). In these few words Freud again made the point, and in declarative fashion, that transference is a mental structure of the greatest magnitude. But he never really followed it up.

Rather extensive evidence of his departure from the original concept and of his continuing struggle with that concept is seen most clearly, I believe, in one of his last and one of his greatest works, "Analysis Terminable and Interminable" (1937). To my narrowly focused eyes, "Analysis Terminable and Interminable" is much more than a courageous, brilliant, and pessimistic appraisal of the difficulties and limitations of analysis. Although transference is little mentioned in the paper, a great deal about it comes through, some quite directly, some by easy inference. When looked at in this way, two themes stand out: Freud's personal frustrations with the enigmas of transference, and his tacit placing of transference in the very center of success and failure in analysis, both as a therapy and as a developing science. What also comes through, to me, is the perplexing realization of how far Freud had, by now, seemingly moved away from his original concepts. Or had he?

It is utterly perplexing, for instance, in reading his otherwise brilliant discussion of the ending of an analysis, to find that he makes no mention of what he had said so compellingly in this connection 30 years earlier: that for analysis to be effective, there must be a transference neurosis and that this neurosis must be resolved in the analytic situation.

His 1937 discussion of the negative side of transference is equally perplexing. Referring (pp. 221–222) to what is assumed to be Ferenczi's late-developing antagonism and to Ferenczi's rebuke that the negative transference should have been analyzed, Freud explains the situation rather lamely, it seems to me, by saying that even if such negative feelings had been detected in latent form, it was doubtful that the analyst had the power to activate them short of some unfriendly piece of behavior in reality on the analyst's part. Further on (p. 223), he also raises the question whether it is wise to stir up a pathogenic conflict which is not betraying itself. Contrast these views with his 1905 statement: "In psycho-analysis . . . all the patient's tendencies, including hostile ones, are aroused . . ." And in the next sentence, "Transference, which seems ordained to be the greatest obstacle to psycho-analysis, becomes its most powerful ally . . ." (p. 117). Here, it seems to me, Freud is saying that transference is precisely the power which is able to arouse "all the patient's tendencies," even latent ones, even ones which do not betray themselves, and that this arousal is not a matter of being wise or unwise but of being essential.

Other evidence of his strange and at least partial removal of transference from analysis appears where he says: ". . . we can only achieve our therapeutic purpose by increasing the power of analysis to come to the assistance of the ego. Hypnotic influence seemed to be an excellent instrument . . . but the reasons for our having to abandon it are well known. No substitute for hypnosis has yet been found" (1937, p. 230). As I read it, this statement seems to be a paradox. What about transference? Is not transference this very power, the power Freud now says we have not yet found? Indeed, what better definition of transference could there be than to say, using Freud's words, that when properly taken into account, transference increases, in the most exquisite way, "the power of analysis to come to the assistance of the ego"? Is this not precisely what transference does? Is this not what Freud had earlier said its function was?

Again, toward the end of the paper (p. 247), in an otherwise masterful discussion of difficulties contributed by the individuality of the analyst, he fails almost completely to direct these difficulties to their most obvious source, the countertransference.

This fluid, inconstant, and ever-shifting state of Freud's views on transference may be explained, I believe, by the fact that for so much of his life he was himself deeply engaged in transference situations with many different persons. It should not be forgotten that Freud's discoveries were made primarily on himself. His primary sources were his own transference experiences. This, I suspect, was the principal executive agent of Freud's genius: his great capacity to become deeply involved in and to resolve myriad transference feelings, and then to derive from such experiences the basic principles governing them. One has to wonder, of course, whether this creative process was in any way unique with Freud. Perhaps not. Perhaps all great discoveries, or at least all "creative leaps," are made, via the transference, within the discoverer's own person. Perhaps all monumental breachings of the confines of the known depend not only upon the basic givens of genius but upon a capacity for greatly heightened cathexis of certain ego apparatuses, a development which, in turn, may require the kind of power generated by the ego only in a transference situation.

In this connection I would like to mention Isaac Newton, whose revolutionary discoveries were so far-reaching and so immense as to place him among the greatest geniuses of all time. My sketchy knowledge suggests that the circumstances of Newton's staggering creative breakthroughs might be profitably studied from the standpoint of transference and of transference's possible role in hypercathecting Newton's tremendously rich and expanded inner resources. The circumstances I refer to were unusual. In his third and fourth years at Cambridge as a bright but not remarkable student, he worked with and was encouraged by a gifted mathematician who was one of the few who recognized Newton as being something special. In 1665 the Great Plague forced the University to close for 18 months, and the students were dispersed. Newton went to his mother's house in the small village of his birth and he stayed there almost the entire time, completely cut off from all colleagues and practically isolated from the world. There, according to Andrade (1954), at the age of 23 and 24, alone with his mother and his thoughts, "the young Newton mastered the basic laws of mechanics; convinced himself that they applied to heavenly as well as to earthly bodies and discovered the fundamental law of gravitational attraction: invented the methods of the infinitesimal calculus: and was well on his way to his great optical discoveries" (p. 50). Other developments in Newton's long life might also be studied from the point of view of transference and creative productivity. Of particular interest are the intense and often stormy relations with his colleagues and the great impact these changing friendships and enmities may have had on his creativity.

In the case of Freud, the perplexing attitudes he took toward transference, his vacillations, contradictions, and omissions, his great insight and his apparent obtuseness, may all have reflected changes and phases of what was then going on in him with respect to the level and quality of his transference attachments to people, and his attempts to resolve and understand those attachments. In this respect, it might be scientifically rewarding to study

Freud's personal data, particularly his letters, for evidence of transference reactions in his relations with various persons, and, taking the study a step further, for evidence of causal connections between the content or nature of these relationships and the particular analytic developments he was working on at the time.

Although the constant activity of Freud's great transference capacity was essential to his genius, it may also have been the very thing that prevented him from giving to transference itself the highly cathected and creative attention he gave, with such success, to many other subjects; and, because he did not, transference never attained a cohesive and stable analytic entity.

TRANSFERENCE: THE HARDEST PART OF ANALYSIS

Without being entirely aware of doing so, most of us have tended to follow and to extend Freud's somewhat meandering transference path. And, like Freud, we have moved steadily away from his original concepts.

How far we may have moved is uncertain, but a milestone of sorts, indicating how far we may have gone by 1952, is recorded in Orr's paper "Transference and Countertransference: A Historical Survey" (1954). Orr sums it up this way: "Most, if not all, recent psychoanalytic articles concerned with technique agree that handling of the transference continues to be the *sine qua non* of the treatment." But things were changing. "Increasingly," Orr says, ". . . 'handling' is taken to mean 'manipulation' in one form or another, and with the intensity of the transference or the depth of the therapeutic regression the points at issue." And although Orr could say that "the development, interpretation and resolution of the transference neurosis in the analytic relationship is still the hallmark of psychoanalysis for perhaps a majority of analysts today," he added the qualification that "for a considerable minority this is by no means the case, or at least not without considerable attenuation and modification" (p. 646).

By 1952, therefore, it seems possible that a great many analysts may have already given up on rigorous concepts of the transference neurosis and on a rigorous handling of it. The extent of this giving up, I think, is not surprising. Freud himself seems to have anticipated it even from the beginning, for in his 1905 paper, on page 116, he says: "This [the transference] happens . . . to be by far the hardest part of the whole task." Then he adds this most remarkable sentence: "It is easy to learn how to interpret dreams, to extract from the patient's associations his unconscious thoughts and memories and to practice similar explanatory arts . . .'' This short statement, I believe, was intended to be a warning: the transference, Freud implies, is so hard to work with that we will be tempted to attenuate, modify, or even omit it. But if we do this, the warning goes on, analysis will be reduced to an explanatory art.[1]

The general sense of this warning seems clear, but Freud's stated reason why transference is so hard to work with scarcely matches the seriousness of the warning. "Transference,'' he says, ". . . has to be detected almost without assistance and with only the slightest clues . . .'' Is this all there is to it? Or is Freud's warning in response to yet another reason? Is he saying, as I think likely, how very hard it is *on the analyst* to work effectively with the transference neurosis? We forget sometimes that a neurosis is based upon conflict and that what is specific about a transference neurosis is the active involvement of the analyst in the central crunch of this conflict. The wear and tear of this abrasive experience can be considerable and must surely be one of the major reasons some analysts pull away from the transference neurosis and away from analysis itself. Yet if analysis is to proceed successfully, if a transference neurosis is to develop and be analyzed, the analyst cannot pull away, cannot merely sit back, observe, interpret, and "practise similar explanatory arts.'' In addition, via the influence of the analytic situation, the patient must be enabled to include the analyst in his neurosis, or, as it were, to share his neurosis with the analyst. Only in this way, it seems, can the patient effectively reawaken the early stages of his neurosis, only in this way can its latent parts and forces be rendered sufficiently identifiable and functional to be available for analysis.

Accomplishing this is not easy. By the time a patient comes to analysis, his neurosis has moved a long way from where it began. Not only will it have gone through many changes and phases but, in all likelihood, it will have established itself as a rather fixed, walled-off, and independent institution. As a consequence, the drives and defenses originally involved in creating the neurosis may now act mainly within the confines of this neurotic institution and may no longer respond readily to extraneurotic influences. The only force powerful enough to bring the constituents of this encapsulated structure back into the main stream of the patient's mental functioning seems to be the transference neurosis. Bringing this about, calling as it does for the active inclusion of the analyst in the patient's neurosis, is probably, as perhaps Freud meant, the hardest part of analysis; but, as he also may have meant, it is what analysis is all about, it is what the analytic situation is set up to do, and it is why definitive analytic work leans so heavily upon the analyst's skilled fortitude.

Admittedly, many potential dangers attend the analyst's becoming involved in the patient's neurosis. The commonest would seem to be the analyst's unawareness of his own reciprocal transference reactions. A more subtle danger threatens when the analyst, although understanding his own transference, gains his insights so exclusively from this inner source that he pays little or no attention to the possible inapplicability of these insights to the patient's current transference developments. Although these and other problems with the analyst's transference involvement are obviously serious, the alternatives are not particularly inviting, for I have yet been unable to find evidence that a "safe" analysis, in which such dangers do not arise, has much chance of reaching the patient where he need to be reached.

In view of how hard the whole thing is, can it be too speculative to believe that Freud's 1905 prediction may have come true, that, as an act of self-defense, handling of the transference has been steadily attenuated until analysis has finally become, in a great many hands at least, an explanatory art?

TRANSFERENCE AND TRANSFERENCE NEUROSIS

Although things may not have gone quite this far, I do believe they have reached a point where most analysts nowadays work only with transference feelings. They either ignore the transference neurosis or believe, as anyone has a right to, that there are no significant differences between a transference neurosis and other transference reactions, that transference is simply transference. For myself, I believe just the opposite: there are differences, and they are significant. And I feel sure that if we could only learn more, a great deal more, about both transference and transference neurosis, life would be easier for the analyst and analysis would be better for the patient.

For me, the transference neurosis is essential to the analytic situation. Not the whole of it by any means, or even the most of it, but essential. Sharing a place with the transference neurosis are at least two other kinds of relationships: one based on ordinary transference feelings and the other on reality considerations—those of a patient to his doctor. These three share the time, as it were. All are important, all overlap, but each is specific. Each comes and goes, appearing and disappearing in response to a seemingly endless number of influences. The easiest relationship to maintain and to work with, and the one most generally used in analysis, is characterized by the patient's almost constant attribution of transference feelings to the person of the analyst. The most difficult relationship to establish and to work with, the one most easily lost hold of, the one that is essential if definitive analytic work is to be done, is the transference neurosis. The one most likely to interfere with the others, and often the hardest to exclude, is the reality relationship.

In my view, as I have said, a transference neurosis differs fundamentally from those transference feelings which a patient experiences and expresses during much of the analytic time. When I think of transference, I think of feelings, of reactions, and of a repetition of past events; but when I think of transference neurosis, I think literally of a neurosis. A transference neurosis is merely a new edition of the patient's original neurosis, but with me in it. This new edition is created, for reasons I wish I knew more about and in ways that are quite perplexing, by the patient's shifting certain elements *of his neurosis* onto me. In this way he replaces *in his neurosis* mental representations of a past person, say his father, with mental representations of me. Although this maneuver would make it seem that the patient now regards me as his father, the actual situation is somewhat different. Because the maneuver is basically intrapsychic and deals with specific elements of his neurosis, I come to represent, not his father, but an aspect of his neurosis which, although contributed to by early, primarily oedipal experiences with his father, is now an intrapsychic structure of its own.

As I see it, this is quite different from what happens in a simple transference reaction. In a transference reaction, the patient displaces certain cathexes from early memories of his father to me, as if in the present. This is transference in its universal sense; it is the means of displacing feelings and attachments from one object to another, and of repeating the past in the present. In this process the two separate identities—the father and I—are merged, but the patient's own identity and my identity remain clear and separate. This is not the case with a transference neurosis. There the patient includes me somehow in the structure, or past structure, of his neurosis. As a result of the process the identity difference between him and me is lost, and for the moment and for the particular area affected by the transference neurosis, I come to represent *the patient himself*. More specifically, I come to represent come complex of the patient's neurosis or some element of his ego, superego, drives, defenses, etc., which has become part of his neurosis.

I do not, however, represent as such actual persons from the past, except in the form in which they have been incorporated into the patient's neurotic organization.

May I present an example of what I mean?

For the first two years of a young man's analysis, he became increasingly affected by one of his most crippling characteristics: an inability to get things done. Although generally stiff, rigid, and inhibited, there was more than this to his inability to act. Faced with a situation in which he should take specific action, he would balk and withhold such action in a procrastinating, stubborn, helpless, and often harmful way. Historically, throughout the patient's childhood, this characteristic led his mother into endless nagging at him to get things done, and, when nagging did no good, in her frustration she wound up doing them for him. It was not surprising, I think, that in analysis I came to play the same role and that eventually my interpretations came to be regarded either as nagging or as my doing his work for him. Although the patient easily recognized the similarity of this to what had gone on in childhood, disappointingly he gained nothing analytically useful from it.

One reason he did not, which took me quite a while to discover, was that the *act* of interpretation itself had become deeply involved in the transference. With this change, the *content* lost its importance, and instead he reacted to almost everything I said, interpretation or not, as if I were nagging him or doing something for him. But there was more to it than this. Upon realizing that such a shift had taken place, I became much less interpretive, in fact much more quiet all around. Surprisingly, the patient responded to my substantial quietness as if it did not exist. He went right on talking about one situation after the other in which he had failed to act, and went right on feeling that I was nagging and acting for him, although now I rarely even commented on what he reported.

This peculiar behavior, I suspected, indicated that still another shift had occurred. This was no longer a simple transference reaction, and I no longer represented a mother-object. This was a transference neurosis. In it his representation of me, now internalized, stood for certain elements of his neurosis, particularly, it seemed, elements of his ego and superego. In effect, the conflict was now remarkably self-contained; he was now nagging himself and doing things for himself. Upon noting this shift, I did my best to explain it to the patient and to speculate on what was revealed by it. What seemed most apparent was that in this way he was revealing a significant capacity to take over his own affairs and to be effective in getting things done, and that indeed the very strength of this drive might be a central factor causing his ego in his neurosis to react against it.

The patient responded to this formulation with a sense of its aptness. He began to appreciate the internal, personal, and conflicting nature of his neurosis and to accept some responsibility himself for his troublesome behavior. He also recalled periods of time when he had in fact been active and aggressive and had had no difficulty getting things done.

Following these inner discoveries, but only then, we were able to explore with meaning some of the origins of his problems as they concerned his relations with his mother.

In this particular instance, interpreting the transference neurosis in this specific way made a significant difference, a difference which effectively made this phase of the patient's analysis more than "an explanatory art." Very often, of course, this difference may not matter. The target, after all, is immense, and in whatever form an interpretation is made, if it is aimed generally in the right direction, it may have an impact. But when the difference does matter, as it commonly does, it may matter very much.

It is also true, of course, that the transference neurosis is not always available to work with. Being an on-and-off thing, as I believe it to be, there may be long periods when it is not in evidence. This means that the bulk of the bread-and-butter work of analysis is carried on largely in a transference relationship that is broader and less specific than a transference neurosis. Interpretations and constructions based on material evoked by these day-to-day transference reactions enable the patient's neurosis to unfold, and his character structure to come into clearer view. When the process goes further, as it may, the infantile neurosis may be retrieved from limbo and some of its vicissitudes may be traced. Doing this much is a great deal, but, much as it may seem it will not reach all the way to the center of the patient.

This can happen, in my experience, only if the persistent and effective handling of the daily transference reactions, along with everything else it does, sets the stage for the appearance of episodes of transference neurosis. These may be short or long, clamorous or silent, but, in whatever way they appear, they will provide an opportunity to carry analysis the further step that does promise to reach the patient as nothing else can. It is this further step, however, which, because it is the hardest part of analysis, may never be taken.

Adding to whatever else makes this further step hard, are difficulties caused by transference itself: transference and transference neurosis are both subject to such serious limitations, interferences, and distortions that they may be very slow to develop, or they develop in such ways that long periods of analysis must go by before they reach a useful and workable state. Some of these interferences are iatrogenic, some seem to be a specific feature of the kind of disorder affecting the patient, and some may be inherent limitations in the phenomenon of transference itself. What I propose to do for the remainder of the paper is to comment on some of these interferences and limitations.

THE IMPACT OF REALITY ON TRANSFERENCE

"Reality" is a difficult word to use to everyone's satisfaction or even to one's own satisfaction. In this instance I use it rather arbitrarily to designate the direct, here-and-now impact of the analyst upon the patient. Reality, in this sense, contrasts with the impact the analyst has through his representation in the patient's fantasy life, neurosis, and transference. Since both kinds of impact seem always to coexist and since the former—the analyst's real impact—may be the worst enemy of the transference, the matter of their differentiation is possibly the most challenging aspect of analysis.

The analytic situation, which is set up to shut out ordinary reality intrusions, cannot and possibly should not exclude them all. In the beginning months, for instance, reality inevitably has the upper hand. The analyst, the office, the procedure, are all overwhelmingly real. Everything is strange, frightening and exciting, gratifying and frustrating. Until the patient can test it and orient himself to it, the impact of this reality is usually so great that even an ordinary useful transference relationship cannot be expected to develop.

Perhaps the most confusing aspect of this beginning period is the frequent appearance in it of what I regard as a false transference relationship. With great intensity and clarity, the patient may reveal, through transference-like references about the analyst, some of the deepest secrets not only of his neurosis but of its genesis. This pseudotransference, too good to be true, is almost sure to be nothing more than the patient's attempt to deal with the new situation: as completely as he can, he goes through, in respect to the person of the analyst, the entire spectrum of his various patterns of behavior. If, as it is easy to do, the analyst overlooks the likelihood that the patient's relationship with him at this time is real and that almost everything said about it is best related to this reality, analysis may get off to a very bad start. And if, as is even easier to do, the analyst interprets the genetic meanings of the openly exposed material, a good transference relationship may be seriously delayed and a workable transference neurosis may never appear. Even after initial reality has had time to fade, reality may continue to intrude in ways that are very hard to detect and that are very troublesome.

One of the most serious problems of analysis is the very substantial help which the patient receives directly from the analyst and the analytic situation. For many a patient, the analyst in the analytic situation is in fact the most stable, reasonable, wise, and understanding person he has ever met, and the setting in which they meet may actually be the most honest, open, direct and regular relationship he has ever experienced. Added to this is the considerable helpfulness to him of being able to clarify his life story, confess his guilt, express his ambitions, and explore his confusions. Further real help comes from the learning-about-life accruing from the analyst's skilled questions, observations, and interpretations. Taken altogether, the total *real* value to the patient of the analytic situation can easily be immense. The trouble with this kind of help is that if it goes on and on, it may have such a real, direct, and continuing impact upon the patient that he can never get deeply enough involved in transference situations to allow him to resolve or even to become acquainted with his most crippling internal difficulties. The trouble in a sense is that the direct nonanalytical helpfulness of the analytic situation is far too good! The trouble also is that we as analysts apparently cannot resist the seductiveness of being directly helpful, and this, when combined with the compelling assumption that helpfulness is bound to be good, permits us to credit patient improvement to "analysis" when more properly it should often be recognized as being the result of the patient's using us, and the analytic situation, as model, preceptor, and supporter in dealing practically with his immediate problems.

Gross examples of this kind of reality-caused problem are common: a neurotically inept medical student who was able to stay in school for four years and graduate only because of the literal day-by-day support he took from visits to his analyst; a man with an unstable hold on his business whose analysis became little more than a source of real support needed to keep his business intact; and a woman whose analysis was almost completely absorbed in using it to keep a teetering marriage from collapsing. In none of these patients did any significant transference relationship develop. Instead, they clung to their actual dependence upon the analyst and the analytic situation. Because this problem so often goes unrecognized, and because even when recognized it is not sufficiently dealt with, this kind of usefulness may be one of the major reasons why analysis fails.

Perhaps I should mention one more difficult-to-handle intrusion of reality into the analysis. This is the definitive and final interruption of the transference neurosis caused by the reality of termination. Here, in a sense, the situation is reversed and the intrusion is analytically desirable, since ideally the impact of the reality of impending and certain termination is used to facilitate the resolution of the transference. As with the resolution of earlier episodes of transference neurosis, this final one is brought about principally by the analyst's interpretations and reconstructions. As these take effect, the transference neurosis and, hopefully, along with it the original neurosis is resolved. This final resolution, however, which is much more comprehensive, is usually very difficult and may not come about at all without the help of the reality of termination. Accordingly, any attenuation of the ending, such as tapering off or casual or tentative stopping, should be expected to stand in the way of an effective resolution of the transference. Yet, it seems to me, this is what most commonly happens to an ending, and because of this a great many patients may lose the potentially great benefit of a thorough resolution and are forever after left suspended in the net of unresolved transference.

Yet, slurring over a rigorous termination seems understandable. As difficult as transference neurosis may be on the analyst at other times, this ending period, if rigorously carried out, simply has to be the period of his greatest emotional strain. There can surely be no more likely time for an analyst to surrender his analytic position and, responding to his own transference, become personally involved with his patient than during the process of separating from a long and self-restrained relationship. Accordingly, it may be better to slur over the ending lightly than to mishandle it in an attempt to be rigorous.

SOME SPECIAL TRANSFERENCE DIFFICULTIES IN THE CASE OF NEGATIVE, DESTRUCTIVE TENDENCIES

Various other difficulties with transference, both in its development and in its analysis, occur, as we all know, in respect to the nature of different forms of illness, e.g., acting out, psychosis, character disorders, etc.[2] But rather than discuss particular situations such as these, I would like to consider a different kind of difficulty, one which I think casts a very dark shadow on all transference manifestations and which may therefore be a severely limiting factor in analytic work generally.

This limiting factor, which may be universal, is the apparent inability of transference to reproduce with any verity the full range of man's negative, destructive tendencies. In contrast to libidinal drives, even the mildest and commonest negative ones seem to run into a good deal of trouble finding their way into the transference, ending up at best as wishes, feelings, and fantasies, while the more robust varieties, those involving literal destructive acts, seem to stand little chance of entering the transference at all.

The question why this limitation exists is not easy to answer. One suggestion, speculative to be sure, but nonetheless seeming to be worth serious consideration, is that negative, destructive tendencies are derivatives of a "death instinct" and as such are bound, not by ordinary principles of mental functioning, but by whatever principles do govern this elusive concept. Unfortunately, I believe, little study is being devoted to clarifying this important issue. Most analysts seem to have turned their back on the death instinct and on Freud's attempts to explore it. Many of us, with some logic, explain away our disinterest on grounds that the death instinct is a biological and not a psychological concept and therefore is not within our province.

Another somewhat less logical but perhaps more significant reason for our shying away from the death instinct is that analysts seem to shy away from everything touching on violence, destruction, and death. In our developmental theory, for instance, we prefer to regard the concepts of "killing of the parents" and "sexual union with the parents" as more or less antithetical equals, each suffering much the same fate at the instance of the ego's resolution of the Oedipus complex. In this way we are able to gloss over the differences between the two concepts and to avoid facing the apparent fact that, while the ego's oedipal impact does make it possible later on in life for sexual union to be normally carried out with a substitute for the parents, it does not make it possible for killing to be carried out normally at all. That there is no norm for whatever the killing drive consists of is not an insignificant matter. Most of us, of course, try to get around this difficulty by means of the somewhat fuzzy assumption that oedipal events do convert the killing drive into a much nicer one called aggression, which we regard as normal. Our accepting this rather broad assumption makes it easy to ignore the possibility that man's tendency to kill may not be basically changed by oedipal events, and to ignore the likelihood that whatever control the ego does have over violent tendencies is somewhat tenuous. Perhaps the most surprising thing we ignore is the overwhelming evidence of how uncertain the ego's control is, viz., the tremendous outbursts of violence that surround us in our daily life.

Even our analytic language, which leans heavily on euphemisms, seems designed to ignore the reality of destruction. We tend to use words like "negative," "aggressive," and "hostile" in describing patient behavior that may have caused actual damage. Or we speak of angry feelings, murder fantasies, castration wishes, and death wishes in respect to a patient's determined attempt to cause harm. To me, this language always seems at least once removed from what we are actually dealing with, or should be dealing with.

The inappropriateness of our language came home to me one day with a patient who, as we say so nicely, liked to "castrate" men. While listening to her describe some extreme behavior of this kind, I suddenly asked myself the question, What would I call this behavior outside of analysis? The answer was easy. I would call it vicious and destructive. So I told the patient what I had been thinking. She was shocked by these terms, but she admitted that the euphemisms we usually used had made it very easy for her to ignore the literal harm caused by her behavior.

In addition to failing to recognize a patient's violent intentions and actions for what they are, analysts sometimes further obscure the situation by regularly discouraging a patient from allowing his anger to deepen to the stage where its basic violent quality is unmistakable. Some of us sense a patient's "negative feelings" or "hostility" so accurately, and draw his attention to it so quickly, that nothing but superficial use can be made of it. Or when angry accusations do come from the patient, we nip them off too prematurely and may even couch our interpretations in just the right way to clear ourselves of the accusations.

Similarly, when a patient behaves violently in his daily life and reports this to us, we tend to get uneasy, and, although we may not tell him to stop, we may directly warn him of the consequences, or in our interpretations may feel compelled to add a subtle warning or in some way to introduce a suppressive note.

Why, one has to wonder, is this suppression needed? Is it because we all sense the limited extent to which actual destructive tendencies can enter into the transference neurosis, and thus the limited extent of their analyzability? Is this incapacity perhaps what we refer to when we say, as we commonly do, in the case of incompletely analyzed patients, that certain key aspects of their neurosis simply did not arise in the transference?

Was this, I wonder, the particular concept of transference which Freud had gradually come around to and which was responsible, especially in "Analysis Terminable and Interminable," for his becoming so cautious and pessimistic about the mobilization and analysis of negative elements? Is this why he said of Ferenczi that even if latent negative feelings could have been aroused, it would probably not have been wise to do so? Should we, therefore, if we are to follow the line Freud seems to have taken, consider discarding altogether his 1905 statement, "In psychoanalysis . . . all the patient's tendencies, including hostile ones, are aroused; they are then turned to account for the purposes of the analysis by being made conscious, and in this way the transference is constantly being destroyed" (p. 117)? Or should we, while acknowledging the known and suspected limitations, nevertheless continue to search for evidence of significant negative representation in the transference? And, in doing this, should we perhaps concern ourselves not merely with watered-down versions of violence, such as aggressiveness, negative feelings, hostility, anger, etc., but with harmful actions, particularly actions directed against the analyst?

Tentatively I would like to suggest what may be a rather common but generally unacknowledged way in which patients attempt to cause the analyst harm, and perhaps succeed at it more often than we think. This is to convert some element of the analytic situation into a weapon to use against the analyst. That a patient does use his analysis to attack and to injure others, especially his family, is well known. That he would try to injure the analyst by the same means should not be surprising. He has to use what is available to him, and the various elements of the analytic situation are about all he has.

Most suited to be used as weapons, I should think, are a patient's resistances. Almost any aspect of analysis can be used as a resistance, and almost any resistance carried a step further can be used as a more or less effective weapon. This further step is usually taken only after analysis is well along, and consists of the patient's clinging so determinedly to some form of behavior that it threatens to engulf and destroy the entire analysis. Although the resulting stalemate is terribly frustrating to the analyst, the patient himself is often unperturbed by it, even when it means that month after month, year after year, he shows no improvement. Typically, the resistance seems more directed against the fact of analysis than against any specific part of it and may strikingly lessen or disappear if the analyst, in despair, announces a termination date.

The best known and most talked-of resistance of this kind is the so-called negative therapeutic reaction. Such reactions, of course, have been written about by many authors, and there is probably little to add to what has been said about them. Except one thing! Rarely have these very serious, very difficult, and very puzzling reactions been regarded as an attack upon the analyst. Yet, in addition to whatever else they may mean, this is precisely what many, or even most, of them may be. Why they are not readily seen in this way is something of a mystery. Every analyst, I suspect, would be willing to regard these reactions as deadly serious and as imposing severe limitations on the outcome of even the best analyses. No one, it seems, is unaware that most analytic patients at some point in their analysis, in varying degrees and in various ways, take an unconscious but implacable stand against analytic advance, that some patients regularly and silently undo each step of progress, and that some even seem absolutely bent on destroying the analysis and with it their chance for various life successes. The self-destructive aims in such behavior are usually obvious, and it may even be obvious that along with this behavior the patient is trying, often unconsciously, to hurt the analyst.

This much seems clear. But it is probably rare for us as analysts to set our euphemisms aside and to suspect these stalemates, these therapeutically negative events, of being not merely hostile fantasies, wishes, or reactions, but very real destructive acts, actual attempts to injure us, the analyst. Is this not indeed probably the only way a patient can envision actually doing us serious harm? By and large, an analyst is immune to a patient's simple slings and arrows; they are chaff which the analyst blows away without being damaged. The patient's coming late, his delayed fee payments, his withholding of material, his carping criticisms, his open anger, his demands, his teasing, his acting out, even his outright quitting, are all, at most, irritating or unpleasant. But this other thing is different. The patient's largely unconscious determination to make the analysis go nowhere, his slow, often silent, and secret undermining of the analyst's every more, is not merely irritating, it hits the analyst in the very center of his functional life, and it may cause harm.

Peculiarly, although often sensing frustration, many of us do not suspect such resistances of being a personal attack. Perhaps, if we did, we would be in a better position to deal with them. That is to say, when, as I believe happens, resistances are used to attack the analyst, it would seem to follow that, in order to discover the neurotic meaning of these resistances, we must first discover and analyze their current "transference" use. Doing this would seem to begin by confronting the patient with what he is doing. I choose the word "confront" in place of "interpret" for the same reason that I prefer "destructive" and "harmful" to "hostile" and "negative," viz., to move from the concept of wish to the concept of deed, from hostile feelings to hostile acts. In my experience, resolving this destructive situation depends upon speaking of it directly, even assertively, in terms of action.

The patient's initial reaction to this confrontation depends upon many variables. A common reaction is a verbal attack in return, an attack which, perhaps for the first time, contains an injurious intent that is unmistakable to both patient and analyst. Sometimes the reaction is dramatic. One patient responded by telling me, with some wonderment in his voice, that for several weeks he had been carrying a gun in his car. Whatever the response, it will no doubt be a welcome relief, for the patient as well as for the analyst, from what has probably been a monotonous, many-months-long stalemate.

Significant success, however, can be counted only if the response leads to some rather detailed "chapter and verse" discoveries as to how and why the patient's malicious intent against the analyst was actually developed and carried out. This might include gaining some idea of how much the patient's attack was simply a matter of transference, how much it was caused by the analysis mobilizing his destructive impulses, and, finally, how much it was a retaliation for attacks made on him by the analyst.

Although it is tempting to attribute all occurrences of patient malice to transference, the opposite consideration is not without appeal. Is it possible that the ego's internalization of hostile-aggressive drive elements and their per se inclusion in intrapsychic structure is so limited that in the analytic situation they are represented more as a reality than as a transference fantasy?

With regard to the effect of the analytic process upon the patient's negative posture, it is again tempting to make an assumption, viz., the situation should improve as analysis goes along. It may, however, be just the reverse. The analysis of neurotic libidinal elements may gradually bring about, through a defusion-like process, a freeing of hostile-aggressive elements, which may then be increasingly applied to the analyst and to the analysis itself.

In regard to the third factor, how much the patient's destructive action is a retaliation, there surely must be many points of view. Ideally, it could be said, the analyst should do nothing hostile toward the patient. He should not make hostile remarks, should not phrase his interpretations as attacks, should not be silently hostile, and so on. Perhaps we can all agree on a policy of this sort, even while also agreeing that many of us do not always live up to it. Some of us, at least some of the time, do speak caustically, sarcastically, and accusingly, do put ridicule in our voice, and sullenness in our silence. Personally, I would be inclined to say that I am not too concerned about these overt, individually characteristic hostile acts. What concerns me more about the analyst is something different. To me, the analytic setting, in which the analyst remains constant as an objective, detached, uninvolved interpreter of the patient's productions, is almost sure to bring about a silent but significant build-up of the analyst's own unconscious negative-destructive impulses. As this goes on, the analyst can rarely avoid putting some of these impulses into action, and, like the patient, the analyst, being unable to represent these negative feelings fully in his own transference, will be forced to put them into action and will do so in about the only way available to him: by using elements of the analytic situation as a weapon. What I come to, then, is the proposition that a stalemate in the analysis, an implacable resistance, an unchanging negative therapeutic reaction—anything of this kind should be suspected of consisting of a silent, secret, but actual destructive act engaged in by *both* patient and analyst.

In this respect I would refer again to Freud's comments about Ferenczi in ''Analysis Terminable and Interminable,'' where he implied that the patient's negative feelings for the analyst could have been mobilized only by an unfriendly act on the part of the analyst, the inference being, I believe, that the analyst should not say anything to the patient which might be regarded as unfriendly. My suspicion here is that we tend to lean too far backward on this issue, so far backward that our not confronting the patient becomes in itself not merely an unfriendly act but a destructive one. By not confronting the patient with the actuality of the patient's secret, silent obstruction of analytic progress, the analyst himself silently introduces even greater obstructions.

I suppose what I am saying is that, to me, analysis, especially as it concerns negative destructive elements, is not merely an intellectual or an emotional experience; rather, it is as well a conflict, a conflict starting out within the patient's neurosis as an intrapsychic event and gradually becoming a conflict within the analytic situation. Only then, only when the analytic situation becomes, in a sense, an adversary situation, should we expect the kind of transference neurosis to develop that can admit to it a representation of destructive impulses strong enough and faithful enough to permit this aspect of the patient's neurosis to be effectively analyzed.

I do not mean by this that analysts should fight with their patients. Nor do I mean that an adversary situation per se is good. What I do mean is something rather different. I am referring specifically to the patient's intrapsychic neurotic life. In it, expectably, are many destructive elements. These elements, as I think many of us would assume, do not remain or perhaps do not even exist in isolation. They are engaged with other destructive elements, either as protagonist or antagonist or as both, to form an organized intrapsychic conflict. This organized conflict, which might be regarded more accurately as an adversary situation, seems to constitute a unitary neurotic structure and, as such, I believe, seems to stand a chance of finding representation in the transference neurosis. If it does, it should be expected to appear there as an adversary situation between patient and analyst. This is what I mean when I say that perhaps only when the analytic situation becomes an adversary situation should we suspect that a transference neurosis adequate enough to represent destructive impulses has developed.

In order for such a transference neurosis to come about, the analyst, through the analytic process, must somehow enable the patient to extend his intrapsychic conflicts to include the analyst. Whereupon the analyst becomes protagonist and the patient antagonist, or vice versa, in a real conflict within the analysis. In this way, through the patient's attributing one of the two or more adversary positions to the analyst, and through the patient's then being able to espouse more single-mindedly the opposing position, the patient's negative-hostile-destructive forces are likely to achieve a more personal, current, powerful, and real quality, a quality that hopefully makes them amenable to analysis.

In order for this to happen, I am tempted to believe, the analyst's own transference involvement is necessary. For one thing, his own transference may be the factor that enables him to accept an adversary role in the patient's neurosis. For another, it may be that only through the analyst's insight into his own "destructive" transference involvement can he understand and analyze the patient's destructive forces. The first thing he will be able to understand, I should think, is that the patient's literal attacks upon him, the patient's literal attempts to destroy the analyst, probably represent in the transference neurosis the patient's own intrapsychic destructive struggles, the patient's own attempts to destroy certain aspects of himself, and his own equally destructive attempts to preserve himself and instead to destroy others.

The analyst, at this point of his understanding, will recognize most clearly that the patient's internal destructive forces are organized as an intrapsychic adversary situation, an organization which, with some success and some failure, and perhaps at great expense, has prevented these destructive forces from completely annihilating either himself or others.

To say that the development and analysis of a transference neurosis of this kind is the hardest part of analysis seems believable. For it to happen at all, I feel sure, requires major contributions from both analyst and patient. From the analyst it requires great perseverance, and, despite how tangled and acerbic and hopeless the analysis may seem to get, it requires rather strict adherence to the principles of the analytic method. There is nothing the analyst can do to deliberately create an adversary situation. He can only not stand in the patient's way. It is the patient's business to bring his adversary situation in to the analysis. This is what is required of him—that he do what, hopefully, the analytic situation permits him naturally to do.

When the transference neurosis does develop, neither patient nor analyst may realize for awhile that it has. What they will realize, very likely, is only that the analysis has been caught up in a stalemate, a negative therapeutic reaction, a strong immovable resistance, or in some other seemingly impossible negative struggle between patient and analyst. Hopefully, this struggle will eventually be recognized as a transference neurosis, as a re-enactment in the transference of various destructive elements of the patient's neurosis, a re-enactment in which unconscious destructive acts of the analyst are likely to be involved.

This dark and ominous time, when both patient and analyst are about ready to call it quits, is, according to my thesis, perhaps the only kind of transference in which the patient's most deeply destructive impulses may be analyzable. If, as is sometimes possible, the analyst is able to work his way through this tremendously difficult, anger-laden impasse, the most effective, enduring analytical progress may be made.

CLOSING REMARKS: NOTES ON TRANSFERENCE AS AN EGO FUNCTION

The foregoing, on one score at least, brings me around to the paper's introduction and impels me to close the paper by commenting again on two ideas I opened with: the notion that an analyst's transference reactions are essential to the analyzing process, and the notion that transference is an ego function. Boiled down, these two ideas seem but one: if the analyst's transference is essential to the analyzing process, it could hardly be thought of as anything other than an ego function; and, conversely, if transference is an ego function, the analyst's transference would have to be seen as essential to his analyzing activity.

As to the nature of transference, there has never been much popular support for its designation as a regular function of the ego. This turn of affairs is somewhat surprising in view of Freud's early comments, especially in the Dora case (1905), where his description of transference was of a kind that could be reasonably attributed only to the ego. Perhaps failure to make this attribution is a consequence of our rather complete dependence upon transference in conducting clinical analysis. This dependence understandably may have established transference so securely as a technique that the analyst has seldom given himself the opportunity to wonder about its nature as a phenomenon, or about which agency of the mind it works with or belongs to. When these questions do come to mind, however, it is extremely difficult, for me at least, to escape the idea that transference must be regarded as one of the ego's principal structures, a very special, very powerful, and possibly even a very basic ego apparatus. Most remarkable is the closeness of its relationship to the drives. This closeness, amounting almost to an alliance with the drives, may make it possible, although seemingly paradoxical, to think of transference as being the ego's main antirepressive device. Such antirepressive action, so clearly exemplified by the usefulness of transference in analysis, may be seen as the power which in a general sense endows the ego with its crucial capacity to evoke, maintain, and put to use the past-in-the present. It may also be this antirepressive force that enables transference to activate and expedite other parts of the ego, particularly, it would seem, the ego's conflict-free givens and its differentiating, synthesizing, and creative capacities.

If this is correct, if transference is indeed to be regarded as a significant ego function, a number of inferences are rather obvious. One is that analysis does not "cause" transference. Yet, although not caused by analysis, transference as it occurs in analysis does seem unique. What is unique, however, may not be transference itself but rather the effect upon transference of the unique conditions of the analytic situation. These conditions may affect most strongly such things as the choice of content of transference reactions, the intensity of these reactions, their exclusiveness, and their sharp focus on the person of the analyst. Although, as a result of these conditions, transference developments in analysis may differ from those occurring elsewhere, this does not mean that in analysis transference as a function is any different.

Another rather obvious inference, following from the first, is that transference can never be resolved. The content may be, but not the function. Through analysis, the symptomatic, neurotic, and historical complexes which have been brought into the transference may be resolved, but not the function itself. The function of transference, like other functions of the ego, may be affected by analysis in many ways, but it never goes away.

Still another inference is a general one concerning transference and the analyst. If transference is to be regarded as an ever active ego function, then the analyst's transference goes on all the time too, just like the patient's, and despite what he might wish to think, his transference has not been resolved in his own analysis. Admittedly the impact of the analytic situation upon the analyst is vastly different from what it is upon the patient, but many aspects of that situation do favor development in the analyst of transference reactions involving his patient. This does not mean, however, that it would be correct to believe the analyst should attempt to inhibit his transference function, much less disavow it. Yet, what the analyst should do about his own transference is a question that has never been significantly pondered over. Aside from my belief that the analyst's transference is remarkably useful in the process of analyzing and may even be essential for certain aspects of analysis, what can be said?

Would it be wrong, I wonder, to propose that this ego function be dealt with in the same way the analyst deals with his other ego functions? Just as the analyst must consciously regulate his responses to other functions in order to create and sustain the analytic situation, should he not also regulate his responses to his transference activity? This does not mean, I should think, that the analyst must decide either whether or when a transference reaction to his patient exists. Such an attempt is beside the point on at least two counts. For one thing, significant transference reactions are usually not conscious; and, for another, transference activity in some form is always going on.

In view of these considerations, the simplest position for the analyst to take, and the one most likely to be helpful, may be to assume that *all* feelings and reactions of the analyst concerning the patient are *prima-facie* evidence of the analyst's transference. Under this arrangement every feeling of warmth, pity, sadness, anger, hope, excitement, even interest; every feeling of coldness, indifference, disinterest, boredom, impatience, discouragement; and every absence of feeling, should be assumed to contain significant elements of the analyst's transference as focused on the patient. This would mean, essentially, that everything arising in the analyst about his patient is assumed to be part of the substance of analysis, that nothing represents merely the analyst's "real" reaction to his patient, and that especially when something seems most real it can be counted on to contain important aspects of the analyst's transference.

Were the analyst to take this rather imperative view of his own transference potential, he might be much more likely to remain abreast of the personal, neurotic meanings of the myriad but often subtle reactions and attitudes he develops toward his patient. This in turn might make it possible for him at least to keep his transference out of the patient's way and hopefully to use it to further the analysis.

The final inference I want to draw from all this is perhaps the most promising. This is that transference, if it indeed belongs to the family of ego functions, can be counted on to possess many of this family's characteristics. Thus, presently existing knowledge about the ego should provide many ready-made leads as to the nature of transference. The ego's ways of reality testing, for instance, its responses to internal and external stimuli, its uses of defense mechanisms, may all reveal much about the basic phenomenology of transference. Similarly, much may be surmised about transference's functional vicissitudes by assuming that transference suffers the same general developmental and neurotic deficiencies, distortions, limitations, and fixations to which various other functions of the ego are susceptible. A particularly important study would seem to be the special strengths of transference functioning, especially its way of joining with other agencies to serve and facilitate the individual's idiosyncratic interests and developments. Such a study, for instance, might center on the ego's object relations with reference to the question of whether transference is the ego function mainly responsible for their development.

Viewing transference in this way as an ego function means, of course, relinquishing certain elements of our existing viewpoints. One prominent feature of these existing viewpoints, no matter what form they take, is how hard they are to define or even to elicit. Another is how unquestioning we seem to be about the viewpoints we grew up with, how easily we assume transference to be but a therapeutically helpful given, an isolated psychological event having little to do with other psychological events, and, except in the analytic situation, to be lacking useful purpose. Assigned, without even wondering why, to neither ego nor id, it is usually dropped somewhere in between. Labeled but rarely described, it is most commonly called a projection or a repetition of the past, neither of them labels of great distinction.

Nevertheless, no matter how inadequate the form in which transference presently exists, it is a form that is deeply entrenched and that does not beg for change. Accordingly, wresting transference from its syntonic limbo is not likely to be easy and may be impossible; but doing so, bringing it out into open view where it can be contemplated as a major member of the ego family, is to me an utterly fascinating prospect, one that permits me to see transference not only as the best tool clinical analysis has, but possibly the best tool the ego has. It well may be, as Freud suggested, the basis of all human relationships and, as I have suggested, may be involved in all the ego's differentiating, integrative, and creative capacities. It is these aspects of transference that offer the most exciting questions, and it is with these questions that I wish to close my paper.

NOTES

1. Ten years later in "Transference-Love" (1915) Freud again makes the same point: ". . . the only really serious difficulties he [the analyst] has to meet lie in the management of the transference" (p. 159).
2. In two papers (Bird, 1954 and 1957) I have described some of the transference difficulties met with in a specific, narcissistic form of acting out.

REFERENCES

Andrade, E., *Sir Isaac Newton*. New York: Doubleday, 1954.
Bird, B. (1954), Symposium on antisocial acting out. Amer. J. Orthopsychiat., 24:685–698.
———(1957), A specific peculiarity of acting out. J. Amer. Psychoanal. Assn., 5:630–647.
Freud, S. [1887–1902], *The Origins of Psycho-Analysis*. Letter 133. New York: Basic Books, 1954.
———(1905), Fragment of an analysis of a case of hysteria. *Standard Edition*, 7:3–122. London: Hogarth Press, 1953.
———(1912), The dynamics of transference. *Standard Edition*, 12:99–108. London: Hogarth Press, 1958.
———(1915), Observations on transference-love. *Standard Edition*, 12:158–171. London: Hogarth Press, 1958.
———(1917), Introductory lectures on psycho-analysis. *Standard Edition*, 16:431–447. London: Hogarth Press, 1963.
———(1925), An autobiographical study. *Standard Edition*, 20:3–74. London: Hogarth Press, 1959.

——(1937), Analysis terminable and interminable. *Standard Edition*, 23:211–253. London: Hogarth Press, 1964.

Freud, S. & Breuer, J. (1895), Studies on Hysteria, *Standard Edition*, 2. London: Hogarth Press, 1955.

Orr, D. (1954), Transference and countertransference: a historical survey, J. Amer. Psychoanal. Assn., 2:621–670.

21. The Analysis of the Transference

Merton M. Gill

The analysis of the transference is generally acknowledged to be the central feature of analytic technique. Freud regarded transference and resistance as facts of observations, not as conceptual inventions. He wrote: ". . . the theory of psychoanalysis is an attempt to account for two striking and unexpected facts of observation which emerge whenever an attempt is made to trace the symptoms of a neurotic back to their sources in his past life: the facts of transference and of resistance . . . anyone who takes up other sides of the problem while avoiding these two hypotheses will hardly escape a charge of misappropriation of property by attempted impersonation, if he persists in calling himself a psychoanalyst" (1914a, p. 16). Rapaport (1967) argued, in his posthumously published paper on the methodology of psychoanalysis, that transference and resistance inevitably follow from the fact that the analytic situation is interpersonal.

Despite this general agreement on the centrality of transference and resistance in technique, it is my impression, from my experience as a student and practitioner, from talking to students and colleagues, and from reading the literature, that the analysis of the transference is not pursued as systematically and comprehensively as I think it could be and should be. The relative privacy in which psychoanalysts work makes it impossible for me to state this view as anything more than my impression. On the assumption that even if I am wrong it will be useful to review issues in the analysis of the transference and to state a number of reasons that an important aspect of the analysis of the transference, namely, resistance to the awareness of the transference, is especially often slighted in analytic practice, I am in this paper going to spell out these issues and reasons.

I must first distinguish clearly between two types of interpretation of the transference. The one is an interpretation of resistance to the awareness of transference. The other is an interpretation of resistance to the resolution of

Reprinted from the *Journal of the American Psychoanalytic Association* 27, suppl. (1979): 263–88, by permission of International Universities Press, Inc.

transference. The distinction has been best spelled out in out literature by Greenson (1967) and Stone (1967). The first kind of resistance may be called defense transference. Although that term is mainly employed to refer to a phase of analysis characterized by a general resistance to the transference of wishes, it can also be used for a more isolated instance of transference of defense. The second kind of resistance is usually called transference resistance. With some oversimplification, one might say that in resistance to the awareness of transference, the transference is what is resisted, whereas in resistance to the resolution of transference, the transference is what does the resisting.

Another more descriptive way of stating this distinction between resistance to the awareness of transference and resistance to the resolution of transference is between implicit or indirect references to the transference and explicit or direct references to the transference. The interpretation of resistance to awareness of the transference is intended to make the implicit transference explicit, while the interpretation of resistance to the resolution of transference is intended to make the patient realize that the already explicit transference does indeed include a determinant from the past.

It is also important to distinguish between the general concept of an interpretation of resistance to the resolution of transference and a particular variety of such an interpretation, namely, a genetic transference interpretation —that is, an interpretation of how an attitude in the present is an inappropriate carry-over from the past. While there is a tendency among analysts to deal with explicit references to the transference primarily by a genetic transference interpretation, there are other ways of working toward a resolution of the transference. This paper will argue that not only is not enough emphasis being given to interpretation of the transference in the here and now, that is, to the interpretation of implicit manifestations of the transference, but also that interpretations intended to resolve the transference as manifested in explicit references to the transference should be primarily in the here and now, rather than genetic transference interpretations.

A patient's statement that he feels the analyst is harsh, for example, is, at least to begin with, likely best dealt with not by interpreting that this is a displacement from the patient's feeling that his father was harsh but by an elucidation of some other aspect of this here-and-now attitude, such as what has gone on in the analytic situation that seems to the patient to justify his feeling or what was the anxiety that made it so difficult for him to express his feelings. How the patient experiences the actual situation is an example of the role of the actual situation in a manifestation of transference, which will be one of my major points.

Of course, both interpretations of the transference in the here and now and genetic transference interpretations are valid and constitute a sequence. We presume that a resistance to the transference ultimately rests on the displacement onto the analyst of attitudes from the past.

Transference interpretations in the here and now and genetic transference interpretations are of course exemplified in Freud's writings and are in the repertoire of every analyst, but they are not distinguished sharply enough.

Because Freud's case histories focus much more on the yield of analysis than on the details of the process, they are readily but perhaps incorrectly construed as emphasizing work outside the transference much more than work with the transference, and, even within the transference, emphasizing genetic transference interpretations much more than work with the transference in the here and now (see Muslin and Gill, 1978). The example of Freud's case reports may have played a role in what I consider a common maldistribution of emphasis in these two respects—not enough on the transference and, within the transference, not enough on the here and now.

Before I turn to the issues in the analysis of the transference, I will only mention what is a primary reason for a failure to deal adequately with the transference. It is that work with the transference is that aspect of analysis which involves both analyst and patient in the most affect-laden and potentially disturbing interactions. Both participants in the analytic situation are motivated to avoid these interactions. Flight away from the transference and to the past can be a relief to both patient and analyst.

I divide my discussion into five parts: (1) the principle that the transference should be encouraged to expand as much as possible within the analytic situation because the analytic work is best done within the transference; (2) the interpretation of disguised allusions to the transference as a main technique for encouraging the expansion of the transference within the analytic situation; (3) the principle that all transference has a connection with something in the present actual analytic situation; (4) how the connection between transference and the actual analytic situation is used in interpreting resistance to the awareness of transference; and (5) the resolution of transference within the here and now and the role of genetic transference interpretation.

THE PRINCIPLE OF ENCOURAGING THE TRANSFERENCE TO EXPAND WITHIN THE ANALYTIC SITUATION

The importance of transference interpretations will surely be agreed to by all analysts, the greater effectiveness of transference interpretations than interpretations outside the transference will be agreed to by many, but what of the relative roles of interpretation of the transference and interpretation outside the transference?

Freud can be read either as saying that the analysis of the transference is auxiliary to the analysis of the neurosis or that the analysis of the transference is equivalent to the analysis of the neurosis. The first position is stated in his saying (1913, p. 144) that the disturbance of the transference has to be overcome by the analysis of transference resistance in order to get on with the work of analyzing the neurosis. It is also implied in his reiteration that the ultimate task of analysis is to remember the past, to fill in the gaps in memory. The second position is stated in his saying that the victory must be won on the field of the transference (1912, p. 108) and that the mastery of the transference neurosis "coincides with getting rid of the illness which was originally brought to the treatment" (1917, p. 444). In this second view, he says that after the resistances are overcome, memories appear relatively without difficulty (1914b, p. 155).

These two different positions also find expression in the two very different ways in which Freud speaks of the transference. In "Dynamics of Transference," he refers to the transference, on the one hand, as *"the most powerful resistance* to the treatment" (1912, p. 101) but, on the other hand, as doing us "the inestimable service of making the patient's . . . impulses immediate and manifest. For when all is said and done, it is impossible to destroy anyone *in absentia* or *in effigie"* (1912, p. 108).

I believe it can be demonstrated that his principal emphasis falls on the second position. He wrote once, in summary: "Thus our therapeutic work falls into two phases. In the first, all the libido is forced from the symptoms into the transference and concentrated there; in the second, the struggle is waged around this new object and the libido is liberated from it" (1917, p. 455).

The detailed demonstration that he advocated that the transference should be encouraged to expand as much as possible within the analytic situation lies in clarifying that resistance is primarily expressed by repetition, that repetition takes place both within and outside the analytic situation, but that the analyst seeks to deal with it primarily within the analytic situation, that repetition can be not only in the motor sphere (acting) but also in the psychical sphere, and that the psychical sphere is not confined to remembering but includes the present, too.

Freud's emphasis that the purpose of resistance is to prevent remembering can obscure his point that resistance shows itself primarily by repetition, whether inside or outside the analytic situation: "The greater the resistance, the more extensively will acting out (repetition) replace remembering" (1914b, p. 151). Similarly in "The Dynamics of Transference" Freud said that the main reason that the transference is so well suited to serve the resistance is that the unconscious impulses "do not want to be remembered . . . but endeavour to reproduce themselves . . ." (1912, p. 108). The transference is a resistance primarily insofar as it is a repetition.

The point can be restated in terms of the relation between transference and resistance. The resistance expresses itself in repetition, that is, in transference both inside and outside the analytic situation. To deal with the transference, therefore, is equivalent to dealing with the resistance. Freud emphasized transference within the analytic situation so strongly that it has come to mean only repetition within the analytic situation, even though, conceptually speaking, repetition outside the analytic situation is transference too, and Freud once used the term that way: "We soon perceive that the transference is itself only a piece of repetition, and that the repetition is a transference of the forgotten past not only on to the doctor but also on to all the other aspects of the current situation. We . . . find . . . the compulsion to repeat, which now replaces the impulsion to remember, not only in his personal attitude to his doctor but also in every other activity and relationship which may occupy his life at the time . . ." (1914b, p. 151).

It is important to realize that the expansion of the repetition inside the analytic situation, whether or not in a reciprocal relationship to repetition outside the analytic situation, is the avenue to control the repetition: "The main instrument . . . for curbing the patient's compulsion to repeat and for turning it into a motive for remembering lies in the handling of the transference. We render the compulsion harmless, and indeed useful, by giving it the right to assert itself in a definite field" (1914b, p. 154).

Kanzer has discussed this issue well in his paper on "The Motor Sphere of the Transference" (1966). He writes of a "double-pronged stick-and-carrot" technique by which the transference is fostered within the analytic situation and discouraged outside the analytic situation. The "stick" is the principle of abstinence as exemplified in the admonition against making important decisions during treatment, and the "carrot" is the opportunity afforded the transference to expand within the treatment "in almost complete freedom" as in a "playground" (Freud, 1914b, p. 154). As Freud put it: "Provided only that the patient shows compliance enough to respect the necessary conditions of the analysis, we regularly succeed in giving all the symptoms of the illness a new transference meaning and in replacing his ordinary neurosis by a 'transference neurosis' of which he can be cured by the therapeutic work" (1914b, p. 154).

The reason it is desirable for the transference to be expressed within the treatment is that there, it "is at every point accessible to our intervention" (1914b, p. 154). In a later statement he made the same point this way: "We have followed this new edition [the transference-neurosis] of the old disorder from its start, we have observed its origin and growth, and we are especially well able to find our way about in it since, as its object, we are situated at its very center" (1917, p. 444). It is not that the transference is forced into the treatment, but that it is spontaneously but implicitly present and is encouraged to expand there and become explicit.

Freud emphasized *acting* in the transference so strongly that one can overlook that repetition in the transference does not necessarily mean it is *enacted*. Repetition need not go as far as motor behavior. It can also be expressed in attitudes, feelings, and intentions, and, indeed, the repetition often does take such form rather than motor action. Such repetition is in the psychical rather than the motor sphere. The importance of making this clear is that Freud can be mistakenly read to mean that repetition in the psychical sphere can only mean remembering the past, as when he writes that the analyst "is prepared for a perpetual struggle with his patient to keep in the psychical sphere all the impulses which the patient would like to direct into the motor sphere; and he celebrates it as a triumph for the treatment if he can bring it about that something the patient wishes to discharge in action is disposed of through the work of remembering" (1914b, p. 153).

It is true that the analyst's effort is to convert acting in the motor sphere into awareness in the psychical sphere, but transference may be in the psychical sphere to begin with, albeit disguised. The psychical sphere includes awareness in the transference as well as remembering.

One of the objections one hears, from both analysts and patients, to a heavy emphasis on interpretation of associations about the patient's real life primarily in terms of the transference is that it means the analyst is disregarding the importance of what goes on in the patient's real life. The criticism is not justified. To emphasize the transference meaning is not to deny or belittle other meanings, but to focus on the one of several meanings of the content that is the most important for the analytic process, for the reasons I have just summarized.

Another way in which interpretations of resistance to the transference can be, or at least appear to the patient to be, a belittling of the importance of the patient's outside life is to make the interpretation as though the outside behavior is primarily an acting out of the transference. The patient may undertake *some* actions in the outside world as an expression of and resistance to the transference, that is, acting out. But the interpretation of associations about actions in the outside world as having implications for the transference need mean only that the choice of outside action to figure in the associations is codetermined by the need to express a transference indirectly. It is because of the resistance to awareness of the transference that the transference has to be disguised. When the disguise is unmasked by interpretation, it becomes clear that, despite the inevitable differences between the outside situations and the transference situation, the content is the same for the purpose of the analytic work. Therefore the analysis of the transference and the analysis of the neurosis coincide.

I stress this point particularly because some critics of earlier versions of this paper argued that I was advocating the analysis of the transference for its own sake rather than in the effort to overcome the neurosis. As I cited above, Freud wrote that the mastering of the transference neurosis "coincides with getting rid of the illness which was originally brought to the treatment" (1917, p. 444).

HOW THE TRANSFERENCE IS ENCOURAGED TO EXPAND WITHIN THE ANALYTIC SITUATION

The analytic situation itself fosters the development of attitudes with primary determinants in the past, i.e., transferences. The analyst's reserve provides the patient with few and equivocal cues. The purpose of the analytic situation fosters the development of strong emotional responses, and the very fact that the patient has a neurosis means, as Freud said, that ". . . it is a perfectly normal and intelligible thing that the libidinal cathexis [we would now add negative feelings] of someone who is partly unsatisfied, a cathexis which is held ready in anticipation, should be directed as well to the figure of the doctor'' (1912, p. 100).

While the analytic setup itself fosters the expansion of the transference within the analytic situation, the interpretation of resistance to the awareness of transference will further this expansion.

There are important resistances on the part of both patient and analyst to awareness of the transference. On the patient's part, this is because of the difficulty in recognizing erotic and hostile impulses toward the very person to whom they have to be disclosed. On the analyst's part, this is because the patient is likely to attribute the very attitudes to him which are most likely to cause him discomfort. The attitudes the patient believes the analyst has toward him are often the ones the patient is least likely to voice, in a general sense because of a feeling that it is impertinent for him to concern himself with the analyst's feelings, and in a more specific sense because the attitudes the patient ascribes to the analyst are often attitudes the patient feels the analyst will not like and be uncomfortable about having ascribed to him. It is for this reason that the analyst must be especially alert to the attitudes the patient believes he has, not only to the attitudes the patient does have toward him. If the analyst is able to see himself as a participant in an interaction, as I shall discuss below, he will become much more attuned to this important area of transference, which might otherwise escape him.

The investigation of the attitudes ascribed to the analyst makes easier the subsequent investigation of the intrinsic factors in the patient that played a role in such ascription. For example, the exposure of the fact that the patient ascribes sexual interest in him to the analyst, and genetically to the parent, makes easier the subsequent exploration of the patient's sexual wish toward the analyst, and genetically the parent.

The resistances to the awareness of these attitudes is responsible for their appearing in various disguises in the patient's manifest associations and for the analyst's reluctance to unmask the disguise. The most commonly recognized disguise is by displacement, but identification is an equally important one. In displacement, the patient's attitudes are narrated as being toward a third party. In identification, the patient attributes to himself attitudes he believes the analyst has toward him.

To encourage the expansion of the transference within the analytic situation, the disguises in which the transference appears have to be interpreted. In the case of displacement the interpretation will be of allusions to the transference in associations not manifestly about the transference. This is a kind of interpretation every analyst often makes. In the case of identification, the analyst interprets the attitude the patient ascribes to himself as an identification with an attitude he attributes to the analyst. Lipton (1977b) has recently described this form of disguised allusion to the transference with illuminating illustrations.

Many analysts believe that transference manifestations are infrequent and sporadic at the beginning of an analysis and that the patient's associations are not dominated by the transference unless a transference neurosis has developed. Other analysts believe that the patient's associations have transference meanings from the beginning and throughout. That is my opinion, and I think those who believe otherwise are failing to recognize the pervasiveness of indirect allusions to the transference—that is, what I am calling the resistance to the awareness of the transference.

In his autobiography, Freud wrote: "The patient remains under the influence of the analytic situation even though he is not directing his mental activities on to a particular subject. We shall be justified in assuming that nothing will occur to him that has not some reference to that situation" (1925, pp. 40–41). Since associations are obviously often not directly about the analytic situation, the interpretation of Freud's remark rests on what he meant by the "analytic situation."

I believe Freud's meaning can be clarified by reference to a statement he made in "The Interpretation of Dreams." He said that when the patient is told to say whatever comes into his mind, his associations become directed by the "purposive ideas inherent in the treatment" and that there are two such inherent purposive themes, one relating to the illness and the other— concerning which, Freud said, the patient has "no suspicion"—relating to the analyst (1900, pp. 531–532). If the patient has "no suspicion" of the theme relating to the analyst, the clear implication is that the theme appears only in disguise in the patient's associations. My interpretation is that Freud's remark not only specifies the themes inherent in the patient's associations, but also means that the associations are simultaneously directed by these two purposive ideas, not sometimes by one and sometimes by the other.

One important reason that the early and continuing presence of the transference is not always recognized is that it is considered to be absent in the patient who is talking freely and apparently without resistance. As Muslin and I pointed out in a paper on the early interpretation of transference (Gill and Muslin, 1976), resistance to the transference is probably present from the beginning, even if the patient is talking apparently freely. The patient may well be talking about issues not manifestly about the transference which are nevertheless also allusions to the transference. But the analyst has to be alert to the pervasiveness of such allusions to discern them.

The analyst should proceed on the working assumption, then, that the patient's associations have transference implications pervasively. This assumption is not to be confused with denial or neglect of the current aspects of the analytic situation. It is theoretically always possible to give precedence to a transference interpretation if one can only discern it through its disguise by resistance. This is not to dispute the desirability of learning as much as one can about the patient, if only to be in a position to make more correct interpretations of the transference. One therefore does not interfere with an apparently free flow of associations, especially early, unless the transference threatens the analytic situation to the point where its interpretation is mandatory rather than optional.

With the recognition that even the apparently freely associating patient may also be showing resistance to awareness of the transference, the formulation that one should not interfere as long as useful information is being gathered should replace Freud's dictum that the transference should not be interpreted until it becomes a resistance (1913, p. 139).

CONNECTION OF ALL TRANSFERENCE MANIFESTATIONS WITH SOMETHING IN THE ACTUAL ANALYTIC SITUATION

As a prelude to a further discussion of the interpretive technique for expansion of the transference within the analytic situation, I will argue that every transference has some connection to some aspect of the current analytic situation. Of course all the determinants of a transference are current in the sense that the past can exert an influence only insofar as it exists in the present. What I am distinguishing is the current reality of the analytic situation, that is, what actually goes on between patient and analyst in the present, from how the patient is currently constituted as a result of his past.

All analysts would doubtless agree that there are both current and transferential determinants of the analytic situation, and probably no analyst would argue that a transference idea can be expressed without contamination, as it were, that is, without any connection to anything current in the patient-analyst relationship. Nevertheless, I believe the implications of this fact for technique are often neglected in practice. I will deal with them as my next point. Here I want only to argue for the connection.

Several authors (e.g., Kohut, 1959, Loewald, 1960) have pointed out that Freud's early use of the term transference in "The Interpretation of Dreams," in a connection not immediately recognizable as related to the present-day use of the term, reveals the fallacy of considering that transference can be expressed free of any connection to the present. That early use was to refer to the fact that an unconscious idea cannot be expressed as such, but only as it becomes connected to a preconscious or conscious content. In the phenomenon with which Freud was then concerned, the dream, transference took place from an unconscious wish to a day residue. In "The Interpretation of Dreams" Freud used the term transference both for the general rule that an unconscious content is expressible only as it becomes transferred to a preconscious or conscious content and for the specific application of this rule to a transference to the analyst. Just as the day residue is the point of attachment of the dream wish, so must there be an analytic-situation residue, though Freud did not use that term, as the point of attachment of the transference.

Analysts have always limited their behavior, both in variety and intensity, to increase the extent to which the patient's behavior is determined by his idiosyncratic interpretation of the analyst's behavior. In fact, analysts unfortunately sometimes limit their behavior so much, as compared with Freud's practice, that they even conceptualize the entire relationship with the patient a matter of technique, with no nontechnical personal relation, as Lipton (1977a) has pointed out.

But no matter how far the analyst attempts to carry this limitation of his behavior, the very existence of the analytic situation provides the patient with innumerable cues which inevitably become his rationale for his transference responses. In other words, the current situation cannot be made to disappear —that is, the analytic situation is real. It is easy to forget this truism in one's zeal to diminish the role of the current situation in determining the patient's responses. One can try to keep past and present determinants relatively perceptible from one another, but one cannot obtain either in "pure culture." As Freud wrote: "I insist on this procedure [the couch], however, for its purpose and result are to prevent the transference from mingling with the patient's associations imperceptibly, to isolate the transference and to allow it to come forward in due course sharply defined as a resistance" (1913, p. 134). Even "isolate" is too strong a word in the light of the inevitable intertwining of the transference with the current situation.

If the analyst remains under the illusion that the current cues he provides to the patient can be reduced to the vanishing point, he may be led into a silent withdrawal, which is not too distant from the caricature of an analyst as someone who does indeed refuse to have any personal relationship with the patient. What happens then is that silence has become a technique rather than merely an indication that the analyst is listening. The patient's responses under such conditions can be mistaken for uncontaminated transference when they are in fact transference adaptations to the actuality of the silence.

The recognition that all transference must have some relation to the actual analytic situation, from which it takes its point of departure, as it were, has a crucial implication for the technique of interpreting resistance to the awareness of transference, to which I turn now.

THE ROLE OF THE ACTUAL SITUATION IN INTERPRETING RESISTANCE TO THE AWARENESS OF TRANSFERENCE

If the analyst becomes persuaded of the centrality of transference and the importance of encouraging the transference to expand within the analytic situation, he has to find the presenting and plausible interpretations of resistance to the awareness of transference he should make. Here, his most reliable guide is the cues offered by what is actually going on in the analytic situation: on the one hand, the events of the situation, such as change in time of session, or an interpretation made by the analyst, and, on the other hand, how the patient is experiencing the situation as reflected in explicit remarks about it, however fleeting these may be. This is the primary yield for technique of the recognition that any transference must have a link to the actuality of the analytic situation, as I argued above. The cue points to the nature of the transference, just as the day residue for a dream may be a quick pointer to the latent dream thoughts. Attention to the current stimulus for a transference elaboration will keep the analyst from making mechanical transference interpretations, in which he interprets that there are allusions to the transference in associations not manifestly about the transference, but without offering any plausible basis for the interpretation. Attention to the current stimulus also offers some degree of protection against the analyst's inevitable tendency to project his own views onto the patient, either because of countertransference or because of a preconceived theoretical bias about the content and hierarchical relationships in psychodynamics.

The analyst may be very surprised at what in his behavior the patient finds important or unimportant, for the patient's responses will be idiosyncratically determined by the transference. The patient's response may seem to be something the patient as well as the analyst consider trivial, because, as in displacement to a trivial aspect of the day residue of a dream, displacement can better serve resistance when it is to something trivial. Because it is connected to conflict-laden material, the stimulus to the transference may be difficult to find. It may be quickly disavowed, so that its presence in awareness is only transitory. With the discovery of the disavowal, the patient may also gain insight into how it repeats a disavowal earlier in his life. In his search for the present stimuli which the patient is responding to transferentially, the analyst must therefore remain alert to both fleeting and apparently trivial manifest references to himself as well as to the events of the analytic situation.

If the analyst interprets the patient's attitudes in a spirit of seeing their possible plausibility in the light of what information the patient does have, rather than in the spirit of either affirming or denying the patient's views, the way is open for their further expression and elucidation. The analyst will be respecting the patient's effort to be plausible and realistic, rather than seeing him as manufacturing his transference attitudes out of whole cloth.

I believe it is so important to make a transference interpretation plausible to the patient in terms of a current stimulus that, if the analyst is persuaded that the manifest content has an important implication for the transference but he is unable to see a current stimulus for the attitude, he should explicitly say so if he decides to make the transference interpretation anyway. The patient himself may then be able to say what the current stimulus is.

It is sometimes argued that the analyst's attention to his own behavior as a precipitant for the transference will increase the patient's resistance to recognizing the transference. I believe, on the contrary, that, because of the inevitable interrelationship of the current and transferential determinants, it is only through interpretation that they *can* be disentangled.

It is also argued that one must wait until the transference has reached optimal intensity before it can be advantageously interpreted. It is true that too hasty an interpretation of the transference can serve a defensive function for the analyst and deny him the information he needs to make a more appropriate transference interpretation. But it is also true that delay in interpreting runs the risk of allowing an unmanageable transference to develop. It is also true that deliberate delay can be a manipulation in the service of abreaction rather than analysis and, like silence, can lead to a response to the actual situation which is mistaken for uncontaminated transference. Obviously important issues of timing are involved. I believe an important clue to when a transference interpretation is apt and which one to make lies in whether the interpretation can be made plausibly in terms of the determinant I am stressing, namely, something in the current analytic situation.

A critic of an earlier version of this paper understood me to be saying that all the analyst need do is to interpret the allusion to the transference, but that I did not see that interpretation of why the transference had to be expressed by allusion rather than directly is also necessary. Of course I agree, and meant to imply this as well as other aspects of the transference attitude in saying that when the analyst approaches the transference in the spirit of seeing how it appears plausibly realistic to the patient, it paves the way toward its further elucidation and expression.

THE RELATIVE ROLES OF RESOLUTION OF THE TRANSFERENCE WITHIN THE ANALYTIC SITUATION AND BY GENETIC TRANSFERENCE INTERPRETATION

Freud's emphasis on remembering as the goal of the analytic work implies that remembering is the principal avenue to the resolution of the transference. But his delineation of the successive steps in the development of analytic technique (1920, p. 18) makes clear that he saw this development as a change from an effort to reach memories directly to the utilization of the transference as the necessary intermediary to reaching the memories.

In contrast to remembering as the way the transference is resolved, Freud also described resistance as being primarily overcome in the transference, with remembering following relatively easily thereafter: "From the repetitive reactions which are exhibited in the transference we are led along the familiar paths to the awakening of the memories, which appear without difficulty, as it were, after the resistance has been overcome" (1914b, pp. 154–155); and "This revision of the process of repression can be accomplished only in part in connection with the memory traces of the process which led to repression. The *decisive* part of the work is achieved by creating in the patient's relation to the doctor—in the 'transference'—new editions of the old conflicts. . . . Thus the transference becomes the battlefield on which all the mutually struggling forces should meet one another" (1917, p. 454; emphasis added). This is indeed the primary insight Strachey (1934) clarified in his seminal paper on the therapeutic action of psychoanalysis.

There are two main ways in which resolution of the transference can take place through work with the transference in the here and now. The first lies in the clarification of what are the cues in the current situation which are the patient's point of departure for a transference elaboration. The exposure of the current point of departure at once raises the question of whether it is adequate to the conclusion drawn from it. The relating of the transference to a current stimulus is, after all, part of the patient's effort to make the transference attitude plausibly determined by the present. The reserve and ambiguity of the analyst's behavior is what increases the ranges of apparently plausible conclusions the patient may draw. If an examination of the basis for the conclusion makes clear that the actual situation to which the patient responds is subject to other meanings than the one the patient has reached, he will more readily consider his pre-existing bias, that is, his transference.

Another critic of an earlier version of this paper suggested that, in speaking of the current relationship and the relation between the patient's conclusions and the information on which they seem plausibly based, I am implying some absolute conception of what is real in the analytic situation, of which the analyst is the final arbiter. That is not the case. My writing that what the patient must come to see is that the information he has is subject to other possible interpretations implies the very contrary to an absolute conception of reality. In fact, analyst and patient engage in a dialogue in a spirit of attempting to arrive at a consensus about reality, not about some fictitious absolute reality.

The second way in which resolution of the transference can take place within the work with the transference in the here and now is that in the very interpretation of the transference the patient has a new experience. He is being treated differently from how he expected to be. Analysts seem reluctant to emphasize this new experience, as though it endangers the role of insight and argues for interpersonal influence as the significant factor in change. Strachey's emphasis on the new experience in the mutative transference interpretation has unfortunately been overshadowed by his views on introjection, which have been mistaken to advocate manipulating the transference. Strachey meant introjection of the more benign superego of the analyst only as a temporary step on the road toward insight. Not only is the new experience not to be confused with the interpersonal influence of a transference gratification, but the new experience occurs together with insight into both the patient's biased expectation and the new experience. As Strachey points out, what is unique about the transference interpretation is that insight and the new experience take place in relation to the very person who was expected to behave differently, and it is this which gives the work in the transference its immediacy and effectiveness. While Freud did stress the affective immediacy of the transference, he did not make the new experience explicit.

It is important to recognize that transference interpretation is not a matter of experience, in contrast to insight, but a joining of the two together. Both are needed to bring about and maintain the desired changes in the patient. It is also important to recognize that no new techniques of intervention are required to provide the new experience. It is an inevitable accompaniment of interpretation of the transference in the here and now. It is often overlooked that, although Strachey said that only transference interpretations were mutative, he also said with approval that most interpretations are outside the transference.

In a further explication of Strachey's paper and entirely consistent with Strachey's position, Rosenfeld (1972) has pointed out that clarification of material outside the transference is often necessary to know what is the appropriate transference interpretation, and that both genetic transference interpretations and extratransference interpretations play an important role in working through. Strachey said relatively little about working through, but surely nothing against the need for it, and he explicitly recognized a role for recovery of the past in the resolution of the transference.

My own position is to emphasize the role of the analysis of the transference in the here and now, both in interpreting resistance to the awareness of transference and in working toward its resolution by relating it to the actuality of the situation. I agree that extratransference and genetic transference interpretations and, of course, working through are important too. The matter is one of emphasis. I believe interpretation of resistance to awareness of the transference should figure in the majority of sessions, and that if this is done by relating the transference to the actual analytic situation, the very same interpretation is a beginning of work to the resolution of the transference. To justify this view more persuasively would require detailed case material.

It may be considered that I am siding with the Kleinians who, many analysts feel, are in error in giving the analysis of the transference too great if not even an exclusive role in the analytic process. It is true that Kleinians emphasize the analysis of the transference more, in their writings at least, than do the general run of analysts. Indeed, Anna Freud's (1968) complaint that the concept of transference has become overexpanded seems to be directed against the Kleinians. One of the reasons the Kleinians consider themselves the true followers of Freud in technique is precisely because of the emphasis they put on the analysis of the transference. Hanna Segal (1967, pp. 173–174), for example, writes as follows: "To say that all communications are seen as communications about the patient's phantasy as well as current external life is equivalent to saying that all communications contain something relevant to the transference situation. In Kleinian technique, the interpretation of the transference is often more central than in the classical technique."

Despite their disclaimers to the contrary, my reading of Kleinian case material leads me to agree with what I believe is the general view that Kleinian transference interpretations often deal with so-called deep and genetic material without adequate connection to the current features of the present analytic situation and thus differ sharply from the kind of transference interpretation I am advocating.

The insistence on exclusive attention to any particular aspect of the analytic process, like the analysis of the transference in the here and now, can become a fetish. I do not say that other kinds of interpretation should not be made, but I feel the emphasis on transference interpretations within the analytic situation needs to be increased or at the very least reaffirmed, and that we need more clarification and specification of just when other kinds of interpretations are in order.

Of course it is sometimes tactless to make a transference interpretation. Surely two reasons which would be included in a specification of the reasons for not making a particular transference interpretation, even if one seems apparent to the analyst, would be preoccupation with an important extratransference event and an inadequate degree of rapport, to use Freud's term, to sustain the sense of criticism, humiliation, or other painful feeling the particular interpretation might engender, even though the analyst had no intention of evoking such a response. The issue may well be, however, not of whether or not an interpretation of resistance to the transference should be made, but whether the therapist can find that transference interpretation which in the light of the total situation, both transferential and current, the patient is able to hear and benefit from primarily as the analyst intends it.

Transference interpretations, like extratransference interpretations, indeed like any behavior on the analyst's part, can have an effect on the transference, which in turn needs to be examined if the result of an analysis is to depend as little as possible on unanalyzed transference. The result of any analysis depends on the analysis of the transference, persisting effects of unanalyzed transference, and the new experience which I have emphasized as the unique merit of transference interpretation in the here and now. It is especially important to remember this lest one's zeal to ferret out the transference itself become an unrecognized and objectionable actual behavior on the analyst's part, with its own repercussions on the transference.

The emphasis I am placing on the analysis of resistance to the transference could easily be misunderstood as implying that it is always easy to recognize the transference as disguised by resistance or that analysis would proceed without a hitch if only such interpretations were made. I mean to imply neither, but rather that the analytic process will have the best chance of success if correct interpretation of resistance to the transference and work with the transference in the here and now are the core of the analytic work.

I close with a statement of a conviction designed to set this paper into a broader perspective to psychoanalytic theory and research. The points I have made are not new. They are present in varying degrees of clarity and emphasis throughout our literature. But like so many other aspects of psycho-analytic theory and practice, they fade in and out of prominence and are rediscovered again and again, possibly occasionally with some modest con-ceptual advance, but often with a newness attributable only to ignorance of past contributions. There are doubtless many reasons for this phenomenon. But not the least, in my opinion, is the almost total absence of systematic and controlled research in the psychoanalytic situation. I mean such research in contrast to the customary clinical research. I believe that only with such systematic and controlled research will analytic findings become solid and secure knowledge instead of being subject to erosion again and again by waves of fashion and what Ernst Lewy (1941) long ago called the "return of the repression" to designate the retreat by psychoanalysts from insight they had once reached.

SUMMARY

Let me summarize. I distinguish between two major different relationships between transference and resistance. One is resistance to awareness of the transference and the other is resistance to resolution of the transference.

I argue that the bulk of the analytic work should take place in the transference in the here and now. I detailed Freud's view that the transference should be encouraged to expand within the analytic situation. I suggested that the main technique for doing so, in addition to the analytic setup itself, is the interpretation of resistance to the awareness of transference by searching for the allusions to the transference in the associations not manifestly about the transference; that in making such interpretations one is guided by the connection to the actual analytic situation which every transference includes; that the major work in resolving the transference takes place in the here and now, both by way of examining the relation between the transference and the actuality of the analytic situation from which it takes its point of departure and the new experience which the analysis of the transference inevitably includes; and that, while genetic transference interpretations play a role in resolving the transference, genetic material is likely to appear spontaneously and with relative ease after the resistances have been overcome in the transference in the here and now. Working through remains important, and it, too, takes place primarily in the transference in the here and now.

REFERERENCES

Freud, A. (1968), Acting out. *Writings,* 7:94–109. New York: International Universities Press, 1971.

Freud, S. (1900), The interpretation of dreams. *Standard Edition,* 5.

———— (1912), The dynamics of transference. *Standard Edition,* 12:99–108.

———— (1913), On beginning the treatment (Further recommendations in the technique of psychoanalysis, I). *Standard Edition,* 12:123–144.

———— (1914a), On the history of the psycho-analytic movement. *Standard Edition,* 14:7–66.

———— (1914b), Remembering, repeating, and working through (Further recommendations on the technique of psycho-analysis, II). *Standard Edition,* 12:147–156.

———— (1917), Introductory lectures on psycho-analysis. *Standard Edition,* 16.

———— (1920), Beyond the pleasure principle. *Standard Edition,* 18:7–64.

———— (1925), An autobiographical study. *Standard Edition,* 20:7–74, London: Hogarth Press, 1959.

Gill, M. & Muslin, H. (1976), Early interpetation of transference. *J. Amer. Psychoanal. Assn.,* 24:779–794.

Greenson, R. (1967), *The Technique and Practice of Psychoanalysis.* New York: International Universities Press.

Kanzer, M. (1966), The motor sphere of the transference. *Psychoanal. Quart.,* 35:522–539.

Kohut, H. (1959), Introspection, empathy, and psychoanalysis. In *The Search for the Self.* New York: International Universities Press, 1978, pp. 205–232.

Lewy, E. (1941), The return of the repression. *Bull, Menninger Clinic,* 5:47–55.

Lipton, S. (1977a), The advantages of Freud's technique as shown by his analysis of the Rat Man. *Internat. J. Psycho-Anal.,* 58:255–274.

———— (1977b), Clinical observations on resistance to the transference. *Internat. J. Psycho-Anal.,* 58:463–472.

Loewald, H. (1960), On the therapeutic action of psychoanalysis. *Internat. J. Psycho-Anal.,* 41:16–33.

Muslin, H. & Gill, M. (1978), Transference in the Dora case. *J. Amer. Psychoanal. Assn.,* 26:311–328.

Rapaport, D. (1967), The scientific methodology of psychoanalysis, In *Collected Papers*, ed. M. M. Gill. New York: Basic Books, 1967, pp. 165–220.

Rosenfeld, H. (1972), A critical appreciation of James Strachey's paper on the nature of the therapeutic action of psychoanalysis. *Internat. J. Psycho-Anal.*, 53:455–462.

Segal, H. (1967), Melanie Klein's technique. In *Psychoanalytic Techniques*, ed. B. Wolman. New York: Basic Books, pp. 168–190.

Stone, L. (1967), The psychoanalytic situation and transference. *J. Amer. Psychoanal. Assn.*, 15:3–57.

Strachey, J. (1934), The nature of the therapeutic action of psychoanalysis. Reprinted in *Internat. J. Psycho-Anal.* (1969), 50:275–292.

22. The Unobjectionable Part of the Transference

Martin H. Stein

To introduce this subject I shall begin with Freud's (1912) statement about transference resistance:

Thus the solution of the puzzle is that transference to the doctor is suitable for resistance to the treatment only in so far as it is a negative transference or a positive transference of repressed erotic impulses. If we 'remove' the transference by making it conscious, we are detaching only those two components of the emotional act from the person of the doctor; the other component, which is admissible to consciousness and unobjectionable, persists and is the vehicle of success in psychoanalysis exactly as it is in other methods of treatment [p. 105].

The "negative transference" and "positive transference of repressed erotic impulses" have generally been accepted as sources of resistance, although we have come to recognize that "removing" them by making them conscious is much more difficult than it sounds. But most of us have no doubts about the necessity of resolving them to a considerable extent, even if we are not so optimistic about being able to "remove" them. How often we do all we can in this respect is open to question.

I shall direct my attention here to what Freud called "the other component, which is admissible to consciousness and unobjectionable, persists and is the vehicle of success in psychoanalysis. . . ." On the face of it, it is reasonable enough to assume that there is some factor that allows the patient to begin work and to continue to cooperate in the process of analysis, and that this factor bears some relation to the positive transference, without, however, being very clearly based on "repressed erotic impulses."

Inevitably, this brings us to question how we are first to cultivate this component, which is essential for the success of the analysis; what is to be done with it as the analysis draws to a close; and how we may recognize and understand the origins, development, and meanings of this useful, even

Reprinted from the *Journal of the American Psychoanalytic Association* 29 (1981): 869–92, by permission of International Universities Press, Inc.

essential component. The answer to the latter question, as we shall see, is by no means clear. This positive component has by no means been neglected in the literature and in clinical work, but we may question whether it has been subjected to the same degree of analytic scrutiny as have other elements of the transference. It has been exploited most obviously by those who developed the concept of the ''alliance'' between patient and analyst, for example, Greenson (1967, the working alliance) and Zetzel (1970, the therapeutic alliance). Greenson emphasized that the working alliance is indeed part of the transference, at the same time contrasting it with the full-blown transference neurosis (p. 209); he sees them as parallel antithetical forces in the analysis. Elsewhere, he refers to ''transference reactions, a working alliance and [the] real relationship'' (p. 223).

Greenson and Zetzel are by no means alone or even in a minority in considering some concept such as the working alliance integral to our understanding of the therapeutic process in analysis. There are many variants: Erikson's (1959) ''basic trust,'' numerous references to ''rapport,'' and the like. One way or another they all seem to be related to Freud's ''unobjectionable'' component, although we may conclude that their true sources are far more ancient.

For better or worse, the terms working alliance and therapeutic alliance have entered into the common parlance of psychoanalysis and perhaps even more intrusively into the variants of psychoanalysis classed as psychotherapy. It is generally stated that an adequate alliance is a necessary prerequisite for successful therapy, a claim which on the face of it might seem incontrovertible. Of course, the patient must be willing to do his best to conform to the behavioral demands of the treatment, to come to the analyst's office with some regularity, to talk as honestly as he can, to pay his bills and generally to demonstrate that he and the analyst have some goals in common. If, on the other hand, he behaves in such a way as to make the analysis impossible, we could claim that an adequate alliance was never established or, if it were, not maintained. But if all goes swimmingly, we might congratulate ourselves on the maintenance of a good working alliance.

I share with Brenner (1979), Curtis (1979), and others a serious concern about the usefulness of the concept and, even more, about its capacity to be misleading by encouraging the blurring of important transference elements and impeding our search for the nature of the ''unobjectionable'' component to which Freud referred.

Let me illustrate this by reference to a special group of patients. These are typically young intelligent adults who enter analysis rather readily and take to the process with considerable skill and apparent ease. They tend to be highly articulate, and their lives are well organized, or at least not chaotic. They have varying degrees of anxiety, uncomfortable but not disorganizing, and there are generally a few neurotic symptoms with phobic and obsessional features, usually moderate in severity. They have decent, if not ideal, relations with their families, are capable of close friendship, and do work that is productive. They are generally self-supporting, if not quite on a level one would expect on the basis of their general intellectual level and training. They are, by and large, likable, attractive people, cultivated and often gifted.

Their reaction to the analytic process is quite characteristic. They find it interesting, even gratifying; they associate well, bring in dreams which are capable of being interpreted in a surprisingly large number of instances; they respond to most interpretations thoughtfully, often raising objections that reflect a healthy skepticism. They appear, above all, to be highly rational, demonstrating excellent judgment about most matters. Their friends regard them as not only normal, but as givers of good advice. In their manifest expressions and daily behavior, they are, if anything, a bit too reasonable. Acting out, when it occurs, is rarely impulsive or particularly destructive.

Their expressions of transference are again characteristic. Being knowledgeable, they accept the inevitability of attraction to their analysts, even the likelihood that it may take sexual forms, particularly when expressed in dreams. Very often they will reveal this attraction through clever teasing and a kind of innocent flirtation, all the while reminding themselves and the analyst that it can go no further. It is almost as if they were saying, "If only you were young and handsome or a woman instead of a man, etc., etc., I could fall in love with you! Even though sometimes you make the most appallingly stupid remarks, I do like and respect you." And so they go on expressing their transference feelings, predominantly positive, respectful, and sometimes affectionate, employing the very effective devices of teasing and irony. Flashes of anger do occur, but they seem as a rule to be self-limited and only rarely deeply disturbing, with one exception which I shall come to later.

Such patients often dispose of their neurotic symptoms within a few months of beginning analysis, and they go on analyzing just as eagerly as before. Resistance is expressed with silences, usually not very prolonged; by complaints, not very bitter; or by acting out, not particularly disruptive. One condition, however, does not change. These attractive people may be married or single, living with a lover or alone, but they are not in love and doubt the capacity for passionate sexuality. They may be affectionate, but sexual intensity seems strangely lacking in these otherwise sensitive and often loving individuals.

The issue is this: their most passionate feelings, previously inhibited, find their goal in the transference. They fall in love, after a fashion, with the older man or woman analyst, but do so in a way which can be readily concealed by what looks like the "unobjectionable" component of the trans-ference and is manifested by their devotion to analysis or to what some would call "the working alliance." It seems a device for reliving and at the same time concealing the intense, infantile oedipal conflict. It is not expressed in obviously seductive forms. The analyst is indeed seduced, not in becoming a lover, but rather into a kind of pleasant appreciative parent surrogate, charmed by intelligence, warmth, and humor, concerned about his patient's welfare, and perhaps failing to notice and deal with the underlying sexuality and hatred that are so effectively disguised.

These are "good patients" who are cooperative, interesting and very adept at the analytic process. They demonstrate very little evidence of severe pathology; their conflicts appear to be centered about the resolution of the oedipal phase; but they are not limited to these conflicts by any means, nor would we expect them to be. Ego and superego functions are highly devel-oped, with perhaps a too skillful use of the synthetic function and too unsparing a tendency to self-criticism which, again, is expressed through irony rather than obvious self-flagellation. They have generally been healthy babies and attractive children, precocious above all. In adolescence they may have been troubled and rebellious, most often, however, giving the impres-sion of unusual adaptability during that protean phase.

These do not, alas, constitute the majority of patients we see in practice, but they are by no means so rare as some would claim. Current emphasis on "narcissistic" and "borderline" character disorders has had the effect of diverting attention from just those patients who have the most to gain from analysis and from whom we have the most to learn.

In them, at any rate, the transference neurosis is very highly developed, taking on distinctly oedipal forms: it is powerfully defended by these pa-tients, who demonstrate the characteristics of brilliant, charming, and preco-cious children, who on a superficial level appear very mature. The main current of their sexuality becomes directed into the analysis, turning the process into a kind of exciting, yet innocent, liaison. When this transference neurosis is brought to these patients' attention, that is, interpreted for what it is, the reaction is likely to be dramatic: most often they become anxious and depressed, experience great difficulty in associating, stop remembering dreams, and may be inclined to engage in acting out. This seems to be the one area of interpretation that produces a distinct reaction of anger and some distress. The analysis is no longer such an unalloyed pleasure, and one almost regrets having introduced the subject. After all, the machine had been running so smoothly!

In completing my somewhat idealized description of this group of patients, I must remind myself and you that there is considerable variation among them. Some have rather worse family histories, but seem to have been protected during childhood by one or more loving and admired adults; some appear to have been endowed, genetically or otherwise, to deal with traumatic situations better than most; and not all of them get on with their families quite so decently.

What they do have in common is their high intelligence combined with considerable cultural breadth, a highly developed ego and superego organization, the use of sophisticated and effective defenses, a history of having established a well-developed oedipal organization, and difficulty in achieving resolution of the conflicts arising out of that phase.

This type of transference neurosis is certain to evoke complicated reactions in the analyst, stimulating his own transference neurosis or, as it is more usually described, his countertransference. One has a tendency to fall into a comfortable situation dominated by mutual teasing, appreciation, and intellectual competition. It is likely, therefore, that such patients will evoke on the part of the analyst what corresponds to the "unobjectionable" component of the transference. He finds himself regarding the patient as if he or she were a favorite child, going out of his way to be kindly and protective, taking considerable pride in the patient's accomplishments, and so on.

Even though such attitudes are kept strictly within the bounds of analytic propriety (these patients, for one thing, are too sensible to allow otherwise), their subtle effects may nevertheless be hostile to the analytic process, perpetuating infantile patterns on the part of the analysand, and making it very difficult for both parties to bring about a proper termination. In this respect the analysis of the "good" patient offers difficulties which, while they are certainly less disturbing than those presented by other, more troublesome patients, are just as important to resolve by an unflagging attention to the transference resistance concealed by such attractive gifts.

The emphasis I place on the role in the resistance of such traits as rationality, intelligence, and the capacity for cooperative effort should not be construed as a denigration of their vital part in making analysis at all possible, and in advancing the process. It hardly needs to be said that they are integral components of any sort of mature, not to say civilized, behavior. Nevertheless, it may be necessary to remind ourselves from time to time that even the most essential and finely constructed instruments are double-edged; these aspects of character are no exceptions. We are simply less likely to recognize their function not only in resolving, but in maintaining neurosis; and they may operate by seducing the analyst into the self-satisfying belief that he has accomplished far more than is in fact the case. Sadly, therefore, we must confront and analyze unsparingly those traits we are most likely to admire.

I shall mention only briefly my view that the same principles and problems would apply if the structure of the neurosis had been more firmly rooted in preoedipal than in oedipal conflict. The difficulties would simply have been more severe for both analyst and patient.

Solving the problem of analyzing the transference neurosis, necessary for more than purely abstract reasons, would have been impossible, I should judge, had we adhered literally to Freud's (1913) principles. In that statement he had not only described this unobjectionable part of the transference, but went further: *"So long as the patient's communications and ideas run on without any obstruction, the theme of transference should be left untouched"* (p. 139). Once again, this dictum can be evoked to support the concept of a working alliance and, while not quoted by Kohut (1971), may well have contributed to his specific advice to delay interpreting positive, idealizing statements made by the narcissistic analysand.

If we examine Freud's statement more closely, we are struck by a number of difficulties. First, what is meant by "admissible to consciousness"? In 1912, it implied that this transference component was part of the system Pcs-Cs. Since during this same period interpretation consisted in essence of making conscious that which had been unconscious, it would in any case have been irrelevant, if not conceptually impossible, to do more than draw the patient's attention ("hypercathexis") to it; but there could be no question of unconscious elements playing an important role.

In the case of the patients I have described, many derivatives of oedipal fantasies may be largely within awareness. Nonerotic or de-erotized admiration and affection may be conscious from the first, and their role in the analytic process may be quite clear. What is generally obscure is the role of this positive, overtly nonerotic transference in maintaining a powerful resistance, not only to the resolution of inhibitions, but also to the analytic exploration of hidden springs of defiance and revenge. What looks accessible to consciousness may be so only in part; what seems free of suppressed erotic impulses may be by no means so in fact; and what seems altogether unobjectionable may after a time constitute the most difficult aspect of the transference neurosis. What appears on the surface to be so very positive may also bee a screen for stubborn aggressive elements, in that respect a persistent obstacle to analytic resolution.

To return now to Freud's 1912 formulation, we need to be reminded that he never regarded consciousness as a simple matter, but always conceived of it as fluid and uncertain of definition. This is evident in Chapter VII of *The Interpretation of Dreams* and is elaborated in his brilliant little paper, "A Note upon the 'Mystic Writing-Pad' '' (1925) in which he presents a view of consciousness as not simply a passive receptor, but rather as being dependent on an active function:

This agrees with a notion which I have long had about the method by which the perceptual apparatus of our mind functions, but which I have hitherto kept to myself. My theory was that cathectic innervations are sent out and withdrawn in rapid periodic impulses from within into the completely pervious system *Pcpt.-Cs.* So long as that system is cathected in this manner, it receives perceptions (which are accompanied by consciousness) and passes the excitation on to the unconscious mnemic systems; but as soon as the cathexis is withdrawn, consciousness is extinguished and the functioning of the system comes to a standstill. It is as though the unconscious stretches out feelers, through the medium of the system *Pcpt.-Cs.* towards the external world and hastily withdraws them as soon as they have sampled the excitations coming from it.

He might have been describing a kind of psychic radar, an ingenious device by which the mind tests external reality.[1] In any case, a careful reading of his work from the *Project* (1895) to the *New Introductory Lectures* (1933) gives no comfort to those who would see a simple definition of what was meant by "admissible to consciousness." How accessible, how fleeting, under what conditions, are all open questions, the answers to which are not determined in any simple way.

By 1937, when Freud published "Analysis Terminable and Interminable," it was evident how much his views had developed. He no longer insisted on the existence of a relatively simple nonerotic or de-erotized conscious positive transference which required no analysis. Now, with some regret, he emphasized the presence of conflictual elements which were inaccessible to analysis not because they were conscious and "unobjectionable," but because they were latent or inactive during the period of the treatment. They could, in fact, be very objectionable indeed. Not the least of these conflicts were those centered on the transference which, unanalyzed, could so often predispose to future difficulties.

These latent conflicts, he decided, could not be brought into the analysis by the analyst, either by verbal intrusions or by active manipulation, maneuvers he regarded as both ineffective and potentially damaging. Yet in the same paper he stated what appears to be a contradiction, in his disavowal of the principle of "letting sleeping dogs lie." He went further: "Analytic experience has taught us that the better is always the enemy of the good and that in every phase of the patient's recovery we have to fight against his inertia, which is ready to be content with an incomplete solution" (Freud, 1937, p. 231).

It is difficult to define precisely what would justify us in regarding a conflict as inactive or latent and therefore inaccessible to analysis. Undoubtedly some conflicts are so heavily defended during the period of analysis that even as we suspect their presence, we are baffled in our efforts to uncover them, much less to analyze them. We may become aware of them only when the patient returns to us for further help or when he enters analysis with a colleague and lets us know of his decision. It is possible to achieve some comfort by convincing ourselves that conditions had not been propitious, for example, that the patient was a candidate in training, was caught in a difficult marriage or in some other situation that favored stubborn resistances. No doubt this is often the case—I have used the excuse myself—but still, was that the only reason? Could we and should we have done more?

The analyst, by his very presence and his willingness to listen, sets up a relationship described by Bird (1972) as a "false" transference, to become in effect "the worst enemy of the transference." I agree with his assessment of the complications inherent in this necessary early development of the analytic situation, but I am not inclined to consider it "false," but rather very much a part of the transference. For one thing, it is often manifested before the first visit, sometimes even in transparent dreams, and as such it reflects the wishes and fantasies of the patient rather than his recognition of the reality of the situation.

It would be wise, therefore, to question ourselves as to the nature of this response, to ask which conflicts are being expressed and concealed by it, and to what extent it is dependent on the reality of the analytic situation. The patient's conviction that the person he consults is benign, wise, and helpful is, we hope, justified by the reality. Yet we know well enough that a patient may experience extreme distrust of an analyst who is in fact perfectly trustworthy; and conversely he may place his implicit confidence in one who deserves it not at all. The personal successes of so many charlatans in the mental health field is evidence enough.

This positive response to the analyst corresponds in part at least to Freud's unobjectionable component, and in its more developed phases it may be called the working alliance. But in spite of the fact that it is necessary and useful for initiating and maintaining the analysis, we are hardly justified in concluding that it is altogether accessible to consciousness, nor that it is by its nature unobjectionable. In fact, it carries a particularly heavy load of unconscious conflict, much of which has to be repressed in order for the treatment to begin, and its long-term effects are often highly objectionable. Eventually, therefore, we need to understand this phenomenon as thoroughly as any other we encounter in analysis. If we accept that sooner or later it must be interpreted, we accept also that we must study it in detail. But how?

It is instructive to listen carefully to a patient's first impressions of us. They may consist of apparently diverse observations about the furniture of the office, of personal idiosyncracies, and the like. At the same time there appears to be a neglect of such matters as whether or not we are relaxed and confident, youthful or aged in appearance and manner, and other factors we regard as far more significant.

This is not to say that these latter details are not perceived and stored in memory, quite the contrary. But they are often repressed and subject to distortion, to appear later in the analysis in various forms. Often the patient will question, for example, whether I wear glasses, although he has seen me a hundred times or more, never without them; or he will be wildly wrong in estimating my age, or suddenly become aware of a picture that has been facing the couch for years. Such familiar phenomena may, with some effort, be understood and analyzed; it is my belief that they contain the clues that can help us solve the mystery of the unobjectionable element.

The patient's reactions to and impressions of the analyst are built up of many determinants. They are first and most profoundly the needs and desires he brings to the analysis, the unconscious wishes that seek to be gratified.

Superimposed on these are his early impressions of the analyst, derived from a host of perceptions, for example, the mode of referral, the initial telephone call, early impressions of appearance and manner, discussions of indications and conditions for the analysis, including hours and fees. An entry into a new world, it often takes on an overwhelming quality—far too much to be dealt with in a few sessions. Inevitably its effects are manifested throughout the course of even a very long analysis, often in forms that make their sources difficult to detect. Yet here is the material of much of the transference, especially of the unobjectionable component.

This aspect is not so willingly scrutinized with the same intensity with which we approach other phenomena. The reasons are, upon examination, not so obscure. For one thing, the trusting, positive attitude of the analysand does allow the analysis to continue, and it is comfortable for both parties— unless the analyst forces himself to put aside that comfort. Second, it seems to be free of conflict. Third, it seems to make sense, to be entirely rational, that one person should admire and trust another who is so worthy of it. And finally, we are influenced by the dictum that we analyze the transference only when it serves the resistance, advice that would be easy to follow if we could always be sure when that took place. I suspect that such ready prescience is a very rare gift. If we resist the temptation to take the positive transference for granted, therefore, we must find some way of analyzing a component which on the surface looks unanalyzable.

In 1955 Lewin wrote "Dream Psychology and the Analytic Situation," a work which has been insufficiently recognized for its theoretical and technical importance. It described the analyst as fulfilling a double role, first as one who encourages the patient to allow himself to regress, to suspend criticism, to associate freely, to put himself into his past, to allow himself to feel relatively helpless and to restrain his impulses toward physical movement, although not to speech. Lewin pointed out the analogy with hypnosis, with the analyst as inducer of quasi-sleep and dreaming states, in which the wish to analyze is substituted for the wish to sleep.

The encouragement of regression is fundamental to the analytic process, but it is by no means the analyst's only function, a fact that seems to be ignored in many therapeutic innovations. The analyst must also become the one who rouses the "dreaming patient, who interprets, who encourages and guides the process of self-observation. By this token, he is the one who awakens, who insists on the substitution of secondary for primary process, of higher ego functions for more archaic ones. Inevitably he becomes the transference representative of that agency most often responsible for insomnia, the conscience.

I would venture that the loving, conscious, unobjectionable part of the transference is directed toward the analyst as the one who soothes, who induces sleep and allows the patient to feel less frightened, for he is "in good hands"; but not for a long time can this love be directed toward the one who accomplishes the awakening. It is possible, of course, to conduct a long treatment while maintaining one's role as the inducer of sleep and dreams, to accomplish a good deal in the way of symptom relief, and thus be rewarded by expressions of gratitude. Whether, without fulfilling one's role as awakener, one may be rewarded by having accomplished effective analysis is another matter. I would say not (Stein, 1965, 1966, 1973).

To employ Lewin's striking metaphor, I suggest that we experiment in treating the patient's demands on the analyst as if these were derivative of unconscious wishes expressed in a dream, and that we consider the various perceptions which are stored and used from time to time as if they were the memories and day residue employed by the dream work. By this device we may treat the patient's overtly expressed attitudes as if they corresponded to a manifest dream. We make the assumption that there are unconscious wishes that seek gratification, that such wishes are subject to conflict and must attain expression in disguised forms. In order to achieve expression, memory traces of percepts, including day residues, are used both to afford a vehicle for the wish fulfillment and to disguise, so far as necessary, their true purpose. Thus these wishes are allowed to reach consciousness in some form in spite of disapproval by other agencies—e.g., by evading the (preconscious) censorship according to the model described in The Interpretation of Dreams (Freud, 1900), or the (largely unconscious) repressive functions of the ego and superego according to the later structural model.

The patient's wishes and fantasies may be worked over further, brought into more rational, logical, organized form by a process analogous to secondary revision; in the topographic model this is a function of the preconscious system; in the structural model it would be considered a manifestation of the synthetic function of the ego. The description of secondary revision, described by Freud in 1900, may be regarded as one of the earliest precursors of the structural model of the ego.

Let us pursue further the analogies between this aspect of transference and the secondary revision of dreams. Freud (1900) wrote: "As a result of its efforts, the dream loses its appearance of absurdity and disconnectedness and approximates to the model of an intelligible experience'' (p. 490). The connection of secondary revision with daydreams may also be extended to the transference; how much of the patient's attitudes are based on fantasies of what the ideal patient-analyst relationship should be? A respectful, filial attitude, an eager pupil-teacher reenactment, an innocent liaison with no threat of consummation? All of these are so appropriate, so sensible, so truly helpful to the analysis that we tend to forget how much of the wildly irrational, erotic, and hostile they may conceal. By this process certain aspects of this analysis are thus ''molded'' into kind of a daydream (p. 492).

In what is admittedly a highly simplified fashion, we might consider the case of these patients who treat their analysts as if they were kindly, intelligent, benign, well-trained and disciplined, very interested and even fond of them, but not a danger in any erotic sense. It seems a reasonable enough description of the actual situation so long as one does not examine its unconscious components.

Rather than taking this at face value as an intelligent patient's evaluation of the reality of the analytic situation, accepting gratefully a fine working alliance or an unobjectionable component, if instead we insist upon the arduous and possibly disagreeable task of analyzing beliefs and attitudes, we find something very different, far more conflicted, complex, and not altogether benign. The patient has been a model analysand, working hard, associating well, bringing gifts of associations and dreams. For example, she may be charming without being erotically seductive, and faithful to the point of causing concern on the part of both of us. It seems to be entirely rational, justified by the reality of the situation. It is, of course, much too good to be true, for it is not accompanied by progress in the most urgent therapeutic goals, for example, that of achieving a gratifying sexual life and an ultimately satisfying career. There are also likely to be curious distortions and self-deceptions displayed, for example, when a patient talks of herself as obnoxious and without friends, statements that are manifestly false whatever their unconscious truth. And young women patients particularly complain of the usual distortions of body image so common in them, of being fat and ugly, all the while being quite aware of the contrary. They may be fishing for compliments, but that is not all. These analyses, smooth as they seem to be most of the time, do not altogether result in untroubled ''sleep.'' Sometimes without understanding why, patients become frightened, agitated, and depressed, as if repressed impulses had broken through, rather like a bad dream.

We might now try the experiment of treating this material as if it were a manifest dream, consisting of a childlike, innocent, and highly educational liaison under the name of analysis. The underlying wishes that have emerged contain erotic fantasies about the parents, combined usually with violent impulses to destroy them both. Behind the well-behaved and rational person may be the image of a lustful, destroying angel, who would kill without mercy in a kind of oedipal rage. In order to allow these wishes to achieve any kind of expression, they must be made more acceptable for the patient by allowing her to assume such desires without penalty and whose weakness is such that she need not fear actually destroying the beloved parents. Or they may be expressed more openly by an ironic stance, which allows them to be proclaimed, only to be disowned.

The use of memory traces may again be compared to how they are dealt with in the dream work. The patient may recall being a great favorite of many older people and always having been a teacher's pet at school, always loved; these generally appear to be accurate. They often recall at least one and perhaps more screen memories which include some early sexual experience with a parent, fantasies which may have been related to horseplay with siblings and even more to medical procedures later in childhood. Most of the childhood memories reported in the analysis are generally quite plausible and subject to relatively little obvious distortion, except for the inevitable effects of the passage of time. There is little of the bizarre and strange about them, reflecting both the powerful reality sense of these patients and the fairly highly organized structure of their intelligent and well-disciplined families.

Whatever is observed in the analytic environment, the patient uses as a day residue, as material to carry fantasies. Yet the whole is likely to be so sensible, so rationalized, so free of manifest erotic or violent elements, that we may assume that a powerful synthesizing ego function is at work, rather like a very effective secondary revision of an otherwise bizarre and disturbing dream, with few breakthroughs of incongruous ideation and affect.

This process, again by analogy, "protects sleep," that is, it helps the ego to maintain a comfortable regressive state of affairs in analysis, in which the patient is apparently a sensible, conscious, and sophisticated adult and at the same time an erotically excited, vengeful child. To "awaken" her, that is, to interpret, would be to lead her to recognize her unconscious wishes for what they are, to help her deal with her repressive and ironic defenses which have allowed the neurosis to continue and the analysis to go on without much real impact on the most important problem. To continue in a sleeplike state, on the other hand, permits her to act both roles and to continue to play out the surprising contradictions in her personality.

So long as we suppose that interpretation "removes" the transference, as Freud suggested in 1912 (p. 105), we should be hesitant to bring it to consciousness before it has produced a resistance—assuming we are so prescient as to be able to detect the moment at which that latter event occurs. But we are not sure any more that transference is so easily "removed" by interpretation. It seems certain that Freud no longer believed this when he wrote "Analysis Terminable and Interminable."

How and when to interpret phenomena such as these constitutes a real enough dilemma. Kohut (1971), for example, approaching his patients with a theory which emphasizes a developmental view and puts aside conflictual considerations, would "accept," possibly for a long period, even the most highly idealized expressions of admiration for himself. And he warns against "premature interpretation" of such positive expressions, especially in the cases he classifies as narcissistic character disorders.

Many years earlier Phyllis Greenacre (1954), employing a somewhat different point of view, cautioned against early transference interpretations with narcissistic patients who are prone to acting out, since such interventions might well result in at least temporary impairment of certain defensive controls and result in episodes of destructive behavior. She made it clear that she was discussing a limited group of patients and her remarks were not confined to the "unobjectionable" component. She was at the same time very much concerned with the development of fixed over-idealizing attitudes toward the analyst and the problems engendered by these.

Without question it is rarely if ever advisable to interpret the patient's friendly, cooperative attitudes during the early part of analysis. It is not merely likely to be inadvisable; it is worse than that, because during the first few weeks or months we could not possibly understand the unconscious components of this phenomenon. Early interpretations might hit close to mark, out of luck or intuition, but during the phase when we hardly know the patient it would be foolhardy to venture definite statements of meaning.

We need not interpret early, therefore, and could not if we would. But there is a vast difference in accepting a phenomenon as reality-based, conflict-free, representing only itself, and, on the other hand, treating it more properly as a surface manifestation of a complex set of opposing forces, most of which operate outside of conscious awareness, and which require explanation sooner or later in the course of analysis.

The questions we encounter are like those that are addressed to a particularly well-defended dream which has taken on a superficially reasonable form. A good example would be Freud's "Dream of the Botanical Monograph." It is brief enough to repeat: "I had written a monograph on a certain plant. The book lay before me and I was at the moment turning over a folded coloured plate. Bound up in each copy there was a dried specimen of the plant, as though it had been taken from a herbarium" (1900, p. 169). It would have been easy to jump to the conclusion, by no means incorrect, that the dream expressed the wish that the yet incomplete monograph which was intended to make his reputation was already published and on display. How reasonable and easy to understand! Freud was, fortunately, not so easily satisfied. He discovered, in his analysis of the dream, references to matters ranging from his experiments with cocaine back to infantile sexual investigations to which he understandably only alluded.

Similarly, if the patient imagines that his analyst is a fine and helpful person, he is expressing a wish, which on the face of it is perfectly reasonable. He is, we hope, correct in his expectations. We are certainly not obliged to contradict him, any more than we contradict the statements of a manifest dream. But we are obliged to ask ourselves questions, not only about the origins of this wish, which may impress us as both obvious and universal, but also about a complex of different wishes and defensive operations which may lie concealed beneath this understandable and benign phenomenon. To what extent is it seductive? To what degree masochistic and tricky? Is it possible that the patient harbors a deeply passive wish which says in effect, "You are so great, my fate lies in your hands; do your best and I shall yet defeat you"?

These inquiries need not be spoken out loud, but neither need they be entirely a secret from the patient. The latter, when deeply engaged in the analytic process, is likely to be especially sensitive to nuances in the analyst's state of mind, especially with respect to emotionally charged attitudes, a phenomeon commonly observed in children and present to a disconcerting degree in certain paranoid individuals. In the analysis of neurotic patients it varies with the state of regression encouraged by use of the couch and of free association.

Complex as it is, there is nothing necessarily mysterious about it. While the patient does not during the session itself see the analyst's facial expression, he is generally keenly aware of his minimal responses, his tone of voice, movements, and the like. Furthermore, he has the opportunity to pick up clues from the latter's expression at the beginning and end of the session. That he may draw some quite inaccurate conclusions is to be expected, and these misinterpretations themselves become material for the analysis. A patient senses pretty quickly and often accurately, for example, whether the analyst responds to expressions of appreciation by a warm glow of satisfaction or by a questioning attitude, the latter signifying a willingness to wait until the phenomenon can be understood in depth.

Whether the analyst reacts by "acceptance" or by questioning makes considerable difference in the future course of the treatment. What has often been taken for granted as an "empathic" approach tends to reduce emphasis on the importance of questioning, treating the patient's appreciation, for example, as if it were simply genuine, taking it at face value, justifying this by the need to establish the kind of transference situation that is believed essential for the progress of the treatment.

Such an approach has its own appeal; it appears to be humane, understanding, and protective; it is often regarded as a manifestation of a loving attitude on the part of the analyst, which is perfectly appropriate—a counterpart, it would seem, of the unobjectionable component on the part of the patient. Nevertheless, we must raise questions whether its usefulness may not ultimately be outweighed by its cost.

The failure to maintain a questioning attitude, an active curiosity about the unconscious dynamics and meaning of this type of response, is likely to favor the persistence of troublesome misunderstanding as to the true nature of the transference. This may in turn lead to serious errors in attempts to understand the sources of the patient's difficulties. It is a mistake, therefore, to place too great an emphasis on an introspective-empathic response at the expense of thoughtful questioning and evaluation of all types of data obtained by observation of the analytic situation. One of the risks of the former approach is that patient and analyst may find themselves existing in a state of mutual narcissistic regression, a kind of near-erotic mutual sleep. This can be a very gratifying experience for both; its prototype was the sleep therapy employed by the Greeks at Epidaurus and Pergamum, which provided symptomatic relief. We need not decry it, so long as it is recognized.

Analysis, however, requires regular "arousal" in Bertram Lewin's sense, accomplished by the analyst's activity, by questioning and interpretation, which may be explicit and verbalized or silent, expressed by less intrusive means, e.g., by gesture, look and tone. Only in this way are we likely to achieve some understanding of the function and the origins of the "unobjectionable'' component as well as the other factors in the transference with which it is likely to be joined.

It would be desirable at this point to establish some hypotheses to account for the origins of this phenomenon of transference. This is not so easily accomplished, and must wait for further exploration. Up to now, our efforts have been partial at best, and for the most part have failed to take into account such factors as genetic endowment, at the one extreme, and late childhood, adolescent, and adult experiences at the other. Its genetic sources have been sought for largely in the experiences of early childhood, the neonatal and preverbal phases by choice, concentrating especially on mother-child exchanges. It would be rash to deny the importance of early mothering in this regard, but it is difficult to be persuaded by those who would make it the one crucial determinant, as if good mothering were not only the earliest, but also the only essential genetic factor in the capacity to develop this aspect of transference.

It is a too-simple if appealing explanation, and too dependent upon treating the manifest phenomenon as the whole article, as if the patient's trust and cooperation were a direct reflection of the trust and cooperation he learned at his mother's breast, and on the other hand, as if it reflected the need to replace a disappointing ''unempathic'' mother by a new and more reliable object—or ''selfobject,'' to employ Kohut's (1971) term.

Primordial explanations are understandably popular. Those historical events which are most deeply buried in the distant past are the most difficult to evaluate and thus the more apt for myth-making. Even the most meticulous hypotheses about the psychic development of preverbal children require inferences based on giant steps which become even larger when we attempt to extend them into explanations of behavior and symptoms in adults. It is undeniable that very early experiences contribute significantly to the nature and severity of adult psychopathology, and the more we know about them the better. But to know them is not nearly enough. It is essential that we undertake the arduous task of tracing the effects of such experiences through later childhood, adolescence, and adult life, thus establishing the coherent chain of historical events which is indispensable for a soundly based sense of conviction. It is only by accomplishing this that we may be able to prevent psychological explanations from deteriorating into a series of appealing fantasies, a kind of pseudo history based on presumed prehistoric events, which tends to operate as a defense against the discovery of something close to the genuine article.

Gill (1979) has described some of the difficulties in the tendency to interpret transference by a too-ready resort to early genetic factors rather than by recognizing the immediate context of the analytic situation. We need not go all the way with him in his emphasis on the "here and now" in the analysis of the transference, to recognize the relevance of his argument.

SUMMARY

Even those aspects of transference which initially favor the analytic process and seem to have the least connection with resistance do become integral parts of the transference neurosis and contribute massively to some of the most subtle difficulties in the process, especially in its resolution. These phenomena are, by their very appearance of rationality and cooperation, all the more difficult to bring under analytic scrutiny. They operate as resistances not only to the analysis of preoedipal conflicts, but even more effectively in the case of neurotic disorders centered on inadequate resolution of oedipal conflicts, i.e., in the so-called classical neurosis, "the case of the ideal analytic patient."

I suggest, therefore, that the appearance of the "unobjectionable component" be regarded not only as a welcome manifestation of certain conflict-free psychic elements, but also as the manifest resultant of a complex web of unconscious conflicts which must be, and are capable of being, sought for and described. Further, that their analysis may be facilitated by the use of a process analogous to that employed in the analysis of dreams, particularly with respect to secondary revision.

Finally, I have emphasized that these aspects of transference, which we are tempted to explain, and in effect dismiss, by reductionist references to early development, be regarded rather as the complex resultant of a prolonged historical experience, and that they be so interpreted.

NOTES

1. It is intriguing to note how many modern technological advances in the field of communication, for example, radar, sonar, digital computers, correspond to the images Freud used as models for the psychic apparatus in 1900.

REFERENCES

Bird, B. (1972). Notes on transference: universal phenomenon and hardest part of analysis. *J. Amer. Psychoanal. Assn.*, 20:267–301.

Brenner, C. (1979). Working alliance, therapeutic alliance, and transference. *J. Amer. Psychoanal. Assn.*, 27:137–158.

Curtis, H. C. (1979). The concept of therapeutic alliance: implications for the "widening, scope." *J. Amer. Psychoanal. Assn.*, 27:159–192.

Erikson, E. H. (1959). *Identity and the Life Cycle. Psychol. Issues,* Monogr. 1. New York: International Universities Press.

Freud, S. (1895). Project for a scientific psychology. *Standard Edition,* 1.

––––––– (1900). The interpetation of dreams. *Standard Edition,* 4 & 5.

––––––– (1912). The dynamics of transference. *Standard Edition,* 12.

––––––– (1913). On beginning the treatment (Further recommendations on the technique of psycho-analysis. *Standard Edition,* 12.

––––––– (1925). A note upon the 'mystic writing-pad.' *Standard Edition,* 19.

––––––– (1933). New introductory lectures on psychoanalysis. *Standard Edition,* 22.

––––––– (1937). Analysis terminable and interminable. *Standard Edition,* 23.

Gill, M. M. (1979). The analysis of the transference. *J. Amer. Psychoanal. Assn.*, 27:263–288.

Greenacre, P. (1954). The role of transference. In *Emotional Growth.* New York: International Universities Press, 1971, pp. 627–640.

Greenson, R. R. (1967). *The Technique and Practice of Psychoanalysis.* New York: International Universities Press.

Kohut, H. (1971). *The Analysis of the Self.* New York: International Universities Press.

––––––– (1977). *The Restoration of the Self.* New York: International Universities Press.

Lewin, B. D. (1955). Dream psychology and the analytic situation. *Psychoanal. Q.*, 24:169–199.

Stein, M. H. (1965). States of consciousness in the analytic situation. In *Drives, Affects, Behavior,* 2, ed. M. Schur. New York: International Universities Press.

––––––– (1966). Self Observation, Reality and the Superego. *Psychoanalysis—A General Psychology: Essays in Honor of Heinz Hartmann,* ed. R. M. Loewenstein, L. M. Newman, M. Schur, & A. J. Solnit. New York: International Universities Press.

––––––– (1973). Acting out as a character trait. *Psychoanal. Study Child,* 28:347–364.

Zetzel. E. (1970). *The Capacity for Emotional Growth.* New York: International Universities Press.

23. The Interpretation of Transference and the Conditions for Loving

Roy Schafer

The progress of the discipline of psychoanalysis is expressed perhaps most obviously in its theory of transference and the therapeutic effects of the interpretation of transference. The theory of transference rests on assumptions concerning repetition and regression or the influence of the past on the present; the roles of activity, passivity, and defensive measures; and the content of unconscious fantasy and conflict. The theory of the therapeutic effects of interpretation rests on these same assumptions and on others concerning the nature of insight, the role of the therapeutic relationship, the accessibility of unconscious fantasy and conflict to conscious influence, and the balance in the psychoanalytic process between, on the one hand, reliving and re-experiencing of the past and, on the other, new experience.

Clearly, the topic is vast, and one cannot hope to do justice in any single discussion to all the valuable contributions to the extensive literature on it; nor can one cover all that is widely understood and accepted in ordinary good practice. In this paper I shall limit myself to re-examining some of the assumptions I just mentioned, doing so from the standpoint of the revised mode of psychoanalytic conceptualization I call action language. Insofar as I have presented the premises and rules of this "new language for psychoanalysis" elsewhere at some length (Schafer, 1976), I shall not dwell on them here.

In particular, I shall attempt to clarify the relationship between relived experience and new experience within the interpreted transferences, for the question of what in these transferences is real, artificial, and mere stereotyped repetition has not yet been satisfactorily settled. I shall point out how Freud was indecisive in this respect. In order to trace Freud's thinking on this topic, and also to anchor the discussion in the psychoanalytic situation, I shall take up what Freud called the conditions for loving as well as his direct remarks

Reprinted from the *Journal of the American Psychoanalytic Association* 25 (1977): 335–62, by permission of International Universities Press, Inc.

on transference; I shall also introduce a clinical example as a concrete reference point for some of the theoretical considerations to follow. For present purposes, I consider it unnecessary to take up the problematic distinction between transference and transference neurosis; I shall simply refer to those major transference phenomena that call for interpretation.

On the assumption that it is arbitrary to separate consideration of transference from consideration of its interpretation, much of the following exposition will deal with certain aspects of the logic of interpretation and the question how it is possible for the act of interpretation to break into the closed circle of unconscious fantasy and make possible significant new experience. To this end it will be useful to discuss briefly fresh metaphor as a step toward new experience, unconscious "certainty," and the contribution made to insight through the coordination of the terms in which the past and present are to be understood. Despite their brevity, these discussions should enhance our understanding of the interpretation of transference and the conditions for loving.

FREUD ON THE CONDITIONS FOR LOVING AND TRANSFERENCE

Freud's views on the matters under discussion may be best approached through his introduction of the idea of conditions for loving in the course of discussing the analysis of transferences. For example, Freud says in this context that ". . . each individual . . . has acquired a specific method of his own in his conduct of his erotic life—that is, in the preconditions to falling in love which he lays down, in the instincts he satisfies and the aims he sets himself in the course of it" (1912b, p. 99). In another place, Freud is advising the analyst to adopt a special attitude toward erotic transferences; this is the attitude that combines attentiveness, neutrality, nongratification, and insistence on analyzing the erotic feelings as "unreal" but necessary features of the treatment. He goes on to describe the consequence of maintaining this attitude in the following words: "The patient, whose sexual repression is of course not yet removed but merely pushed into the background, will then feel safe enough to allow all her preconditions for loving, all the phantasies springing from her sexual desires, all the detailed characteristics of her state of being in love, to come to light; and from these she will herself open up the way to the infantile roots of her love" (1915, p. 166). And in a number of papers dating from about the same time, that is between 1910 and 1922, he describes particular conditions for loving. Among these are the man's condition that the woman he loves sexually must somehow be degraded or in need of rescue or that there be an injured third party in the interpersonal configuration (1910, 1912a); also, in the instance of male homosexuality, in addition to the partner's possessing a penis, there is the condition that the young man who is loved be the same age that the lover was when he developed his now dominant identification with his mother (1922).

Freud described many such conditions throughout his writings. Although he was obviously intent on particularizing the conditions for loving, nothing stands in the way of our including under that designation the general or universal conditions for loving on which we now put so much emphasis, especially in our analysis of the preoedipal phase of development and their sequelae. Freud set forth a general outline of development (e.g., in the "Three Essays on the Theory of Sexuality" [1905]) that easily accomodates this general extension of the idea of conditions for loving.

I have been using Riviere's translation "conditions for loving" in preference to Strachey's "preconditions for loving" for two reasons. The first is that Freud's word for it was *Liebesbedingungen,* not *Liebesvorbedingungen.* My second and more important reason is to minimize the suggestion that Freud was here referring to causes of loving. The word conditions does have a causal ring. Nevertheless, although Freud was somewhat ambiguous in this respect—he did distinguish these "conditions" from "behavior in love"—one may assert that, logically, the points he made are descriptive in character rather than causal. That is to say, far from being about the causal conditions of loving, they describe actions: what one does in loving or how one does it, and these, in turn, include the people one chooses to love and the conduct one exhibits in loving them. Viewed in context, to "lay down" a condition, as Freud put it, can only mean to love in one way rather than another or to choose in accordance with certain rules rather than others. It is the clarification of these rules and choices, or the analytic translation of these regulated and consistent actions, that establishes the infantile prototypes or "roots" of loving.

It should go without saying that one must always take into account the darker side of loving—its fearful, mistrustful, hateful features; for my purposes, however, I shall speak mainly of the positive side of transference love.

But now, in order to understand Freud's account of loving, one must move on to his views on transference repetitions. When Freud discussed the transference love that brings to light these conditions for loving he seemed to be groping his way toward an adequately complex conception of it. Sometimes he says it is mere repetition. For example, ". . . the transference itself is only a piece of repetition" (1914, p. 151). And he says this of transference: ". . . while the patient experiences it as something real and contemporary, we have to do our therapeutic work on it, which consists in a large measure in tracing it back to the past" (1914, p. 152). But then, in the same paper of 1914, when speaking of the transference neurosis specifically, he modifies his account: "The transference thus creates an intermediate region between illness and real life, through which the transition from the one to the other is made. The new condition has taken over all the features of the illness; but it represents an artificial illness which is at every point accessible to our intervention. It is a piece of real experience, but one which has been made possible by especially favourable conditions, and it is of a provisional nature" (p. 154).

Another of Freud's suggestions that transference refers to more than repetition of the past is this description of the analysand: ". . . he repeats everything that has already made its way from the sources of the repressed into his manifest personality—his inhibitions and unserviceable attitudes and his pathological character-traits" (1914, p. 151). A year later, Freud adds this important point: "It is true that the [transference-] love consists of new editions of old traits and that it repeats infantile reactions. But this is the essential character of every state of being in love. There is no such state which does not reproduce infantile prototypes" (1915, p. 168). And he emphasizes that this transference love is genuine even though it is greatly intensified by resistance, more unrealistic than normal love in its disregard for consequences and its idealizing features, more clearly dependent on its infantile prototypes, and so the less free, adaptable, or modifiable of the two.

Thus, in Freud's view, the differences between transference love and normal loving are quantitative rather than "essential," and the repetitiveness of transference love pertains to features of current life as well as to the repressed past. And yet, only a few years later, Freud shifts the emphasis back to the earlier type of formulation when he says this of the analysand: "He is obliged to *repeat* the repressed material as a contemporary experience instead of, as the physician would prefer to see, *remembering* it as something belonging to the past. These reproductions, which emerge with such unwished-for exactitude, always have as their subject some portion of infantile sexual life. . . . what appears to be reality is in fact only a reflection of a forgotten past" (1920, pp. 18–19).

These shifts of emphasis indicate that Freud had not thought through something essential. He was in effect juxtaposing and accepting two views of the matter without integrating them. On the one hand, transference love is sheerly repetitive, merely a new edition of the old, artificial and regressive (in its ego aspects particularly) and to be dealt with chiefly by translating it back into its infantile terms. (From this side flows the continuing emphasis in the psychoanalytic literature on reliving, re-experiencing, and re-creating the past.) On the other hand, transference is a piece of real life that is adapted to the analytic purpose, a transitional state of a provisional character that is a means to a rational end and as genuine as normal love. (From this side flows the emphasis in our literature on the healing powers inherent in the therapeutic relationship itself, especially with respect to early privations and deprivations). We are not in a position to disagree entirely with either conception of transference, transference neurosis, and transference-laden therapeutic effects. The problem is, how to integrate the two.[1] In tackling this problem, I shall be drawing especially on the classical discussions of transference and interpretation presented by Strachey (1934), Kris (1956), Rycroft (1958), Loewald (1960, 1971), and Stone (1961, 1967). More recently published papers by Blum (1971), Gray (1973), Leavy (1973), and Schimek (1975) present orientations that are relevant or similar to the one that follows here. But first a clinical example to serve as a point of clinical reference for the theoretical analysis to be undertaken.

A CLINICAL EXAMPLE

A young man in analysis had been realizing in an ever more agitated fashion how disturbed and confined he had always felt in connection with certain characteristic features of his father's conduct. His father followed the strict policy of always behaving sensibly, responsibly, gently, and kindly; the man thus fit the familiar pattern of reaction formation against anal-sadistic and phallic-sadistic modes of action. As is usually the case with marked reactive practices of this sort, these modes of action were cruel in their effects, for they stimulated the son to think himself especially unworthy and unable to love, and so, in keeping with Freud's generalization, "to doubt every lesser thing as well." But, as is also usually the case in such family contexts, the boy himself became more and more disposed to act sadistically, especially in the wishful fantasies he unconsciously elaborated.

One main reason for this development was, of course, that he identified himself unconsciously with his father as a sadistic figure. Another reason was that he angrily regarded his father as castrating in several ways: for one thing, he saw his "blameless" father as setting a standard of controlled manhood he could never hope to meet; also, he experienced a seduction into loving this paragon in what was for him a passive-feminine manner; additionally, he came to view the masculine sexual role as one that was intolerably dirty, exhibitionistic, selfish, and rapacious, and so felt cut off from ordinary sexual activity; and to top it off, in a reaction against his painfully guilty, doubt-ridden daily activities, he virtually ceased working and was forfeiting his young manhood in this respect, too. Understandably, he had presented himself for analysis as a dispirited, cynical, indecisive, apathetic, melancholy person. Consciously, he professed only love and esteem for his father, while attacking unmercifully the rigid postures of tolerance and forbearance adopted by his humanistically oriented friends.

Before going any further, I should clarify a number of features of my exposition of this bit of analysis. First, when I say "his father," I am referring to the father imago, which I take to have been only partly faithful to the father more objectively considered. It was an imago maintained mostly unconsciously and built up during different phases of psychosexual development. Second, this imago had been defined principally through close inspection of his various father-transferences and my countertransference reactions to them. Third, it had been possible to define these transferences at all clearly only by sorting them out from an array of mother-transferences, each with its own developmental and attitudinal complexities. Fourth, the relevant analytic data included the usual wide range of phenomena: they extended from bodily fantasies and enactments, such as constipation, masturbation, and archaic ideas of retribution and damage, to sober attempts to remember, reconstruct, and organize just how events, long remembered in a neurotic way, had actually transpired. Finally, my explanatory account, since it is not a complete synopsis and analysis of the analysis itself, can give only a limited picture of the multiple meanings of those details I do mention.

Returning now to the young man: One day when he was well into the treatment, he experienced one of his most anguished yet liberated and liberating moments during the analysis. He was recounting once again, but more insightfully than ever before, a scene that served as a prototype of his childhood relation with his father. In this scene, his father had forbidden him to do something because it would have upset his mother. Thereupon the boy had stormed off to his room. His father had followed him and taken a long time, patiently and calmly, to explain and to justify his having issued the prohibition. It seemed that this father had determined, for his own neurotic reasons, to get his young son to agree that issuing the prohibition had been the right, kind, rational thing for him to have done. But the son, already going round in a vicious circle, had reacted to these acts of coercion and seduction even more angrily, erotically, and guiltily. It had been, as he now portrayed it in some detail, slow torture under paralyzing conditions. At this point, the analysand half sat forward on the couch, clutched the empty air in front of him, wept miserably, and pleaded—to himself, his father, me, the gods above—"What could I tell him? What could I say to him?" *Then,* as a boy, he had been inarticulate. *Now,* as an advanced analysand, he had answers to these questions and could see how impossible it would have been to think them or utter them in that situation.

As he now viewed the matter, he had found his father wanting in the capacity to tolerate or contain his enraged mode of reacting. In Winnicott's terms, this father had not provided him with the safety of a holding relationship in which he could remain, as long as need be, the frustrated, angry child and not lose his father in the process. His father had characteristically abandoned him at those moments of experienced need for a father that are so important in a child's development.

The son had experienced these abandonments all the more painfully in the context of his mother's failings as a mother. In his presentation of her, she was a pleasant but ineffectual woman who required constant support and protection from her husband and children; left to her own resources she would soon react anxiously and depressively herself. It seemed that reacting that way had been, among other things, her way of controlling the family. Thus the mother imago was that of the inadequate holding mother of infancy and childhood. Not only had this figure deprived her son of his developmentally necessary early experiences of distress-in-safety; additionally, she had enforced, unconsciously, that terrible reversal of generations in which the child must hold the mother. It was this reconstructed relationship that had been established as the original context of his reacting depressively and his turning desperately to his apparently motherly father to get the parental holding he urgently wished for. But, in our reconstruction, his father, too, had failed him in this respect. In relation to these parental imagos the son had established a mistrustful, despairing, and hateful outlook on himself and others.

This analytically established picture of a boyhood illustrates how a familiar condition for loving was not met: the condition of the convincing, sustained readiness of those who are loved to contain one's more or less projective assaults on them, to tolerate the role of bad breast or phallus, arbitrary authority or villain of some other kind, and to endure being abandoned.

Ideally, the analyst provides this containing, tolerating, and enduring within the transference relation. The analyst even fosters these crises through interpretation of the defensive measures by which the analysand forestalls making this crucial test of the relationship. And the analyst passes the test, not through ordinary loving-kindness, but by standing fast as the interpreting analyst, recognizing the assault frankly, allowing it to be developed and sustained in the light of its developmental importance, and helping the analysand to endure it through understanding it more fully in all its crucial contemporary as well as infantile significance. Having met this condition for loving, the analyst is loved gratefully as a good mother, father, breast, womb, phallus, friend, and analyst. Not all at once, of course, not once and for all, and not altogether, for this is only part of the work.

To mention one additional and essential factor: In achieving this experience within the transference relationship, the analysand engages in less "splitting of ambivalence" and idealizing, and so begins to view the analyst, and each parent, more objectively, openly, and sturdily as a whole figure. A whole figure is one that is "good but also bad," to use Jacobson's (1964) phrase for it, which is to say a stable one that can be loved and hated. Being better loved, the analyst is more freely attacked. The analysand now tolerates his or her experiencing of relationships ambivalently, thereby demonstrating that new and more inclusive conditions for loving have been developed. This development bears as much on loving oneself as on loving others. That is to say, tolerating the ambivalent mode is, correlatively, a condition of healthy "narcissism" and "object love": the one implies the other rather than being at its expense, as Freud assumed, or, as Kohut (1971) assumes, an independent line of development.

In his analysis, the young man of my example had reached his climactic questions and this turning point—a turning point that had a tragic quality in its being simultaneously terrible, wonderful, and irreversible—through the sustained analysis of his transferences. As one might expect, he had, among other things, been construing my consistently trying to understand him neutrally or impartially as a replication of his father's guilt-inducing and castrating actions, and he had been dealing with my interventions accordingly. That is to say, either he had been attacking me scornfully and vituperatively, as he had been doing to his tolerant friends, or he had been acting despondently, ruminatively, and inertly, sometimes concealing the latter by forcing himself to act jovially and zestfully, as he had been doing for his father. All of which I had been pointing out on numerous occasions and in various ways. It should be added that in part he was still enacting this father-transference when he clutched the air in his agitated way, for by that gesture at that moment he was shaking, perhaps choking and silencing, me as well as his father, and he was reaching out to both of us to be held in the right way at last. But consciously and genuinely, the accent had by now shifted to his hitherto idealized father, and he was on new ground, for he had slowly seen the point of these transference interpretations as his various ways of resisting had been taken up. Now, at last, he had integrated hitherto unintegrated bodily, emotional, and verbal constituents of experience. His conditions for loving had been significantly modified.

THE INTERPRETATION OF TRANSFERENCE REPETITIONS

That the transference repetitions are unvarying cannot, of course, be true in any ordinary descriptive sense. *They appear as unvarying only upon interpretation.* It is interpretation that redescribes actions in the. terms of one or another transference theme. For example, the dominant transference theme during one phase of the analysis of the young man of my clinical example was unacknowledged rebellion against his father's coercion; in this connection, the analysand's acting raucously, impulsively, negligently, selfishly, unproductively, and hurtfully to women all counted as repetitive instances of rebelliousness against the father—*but only through redescription.* And that line of interpretation was only one of the strategies of redescription I followed during the analysis as I tried to work out the multiple meanings and life-historical background of the analysand's transferences. Freud's designation of transferences as 'new editions'' does, after all, contain the word 'new,'' thereby recognizing that there are other, common-sense descriptions of the transference actions in question.

This redescription according to transference themes must be characterized as a simplification of what is said to be going on. It is an act of subtraction, abstraction, or analysis of form, depending on how one wants to view it. It simplifies the inevitable though variously presented dramas of life: the individuating baby with its bodily modes of comprehension and experience, and the changing, conflictual, irrational relations of family members during one's psychosexual development. Interpretive simplification in terms of these dramas makes for that one kind of intelligibility so distinctively psychoanalytic and unquestionably essential to the analytic work. Far from being simpleminded, it is, when rightly applied, a sophisticated and imaginative model of understanding. Simplifying in this way does not destroy some absolute truth; rather, it develops the psychoanalytically necessary version of the truth. Although it is reductive, it is not crude or unthinking reductionism; in fact, sooner or later, in and out of the transferences, it is the source of new complexities.

As the analysand manifests transferences and finds them redescribed as such by the analyst's interpretations, he or she goes on to enact them in ways that are progressively more concentrated and transparent, relative to these interpretations. The reasons for this change are many; they range from the analysand's identifying with the analyst to the implicit and effective reassurance provided by the analyst's conduct that it is safe, even if painful, to change in this way; it is a change that brings one subjectively closer to the fantasized paternal phallus and maternal breast, face, womb, and "wound." In this connection, the analyst must, of course, sort out genuine change from the analysand's perseveratively resisting through compliantly delivering what seems to be expected; while this sorting out is no easy task, it can usually be performed well enough to allow the analysis to develop further. The analyst performs this task through transference interpretations of the resisting itself; for example, he or she may interpret the overly compliant analysand's resisting as a matter of taking the part of a good, castrated boy-girl or latency child acting now on behalf of the father-analyst by dwelling on the theme of transference.

Increasingly, the analytic relationship is installed as the framework and the reference point for everything of which special note is taken; for example, it is the reference point for the topics introduced and avoided, together with their timing and their emotional qualities, and for overt behavior in and out of the hours. The analysis of transferences promotes two developments: first, especially during the hours themselves, the world most real and of most concern is the analytic relation itself, and second, that world is of most interest and value when it can be interpreted as the analysand's own construction. That is to say, the analysis becomes primarily the contemplation of the fantasized or invented aspects of the relationship. This is so even when the analysand has temporarily succeeded in forcing or seducing the analyst into actualizing some assigned countertransference role in the relationship.

The analysand invents many versions of the analytic relationship in the transference fantasies. Sooner or later, however, all these versions are redescribed through interpretation as sheerly repetitive. It is this way of analyzing transferences that seems to warrant calling them "artificial" and "new editions." But these designations are tied to the interpretive method being used, and one would be wrong to attribute an "as if" character to the development of the transference neurosis. Nor would one be correct in saying that the relaxation of defense against the transference involvement brings the analysis closer to the truth, for the defensive features are themselves parts of the truth or part of the transferences, too. Rather, the change that takes place is an altered version of reality based on another way of apprehending self and others in relationship. There are only *ways* of apprehending reality, there being no single, authoritative, context-free reality to use as a criterion or to be held fast no matter what one is aiming to understand. As Grossman (1967) pointed out, the introspectible world reflects the purposes for which one is introspecting. Although the version enacted in the transference neurosis includes many infantile, irrational features, it is as real as any other version.

To return now to the analysand's getting to be increasingly preoccupied with the fantasized transference relationship: this preoccupation establishes a special atmosphere of solitude in the analytic setting. Paradoxically, this solitude plays an essential role in the fullest possible expansion of the analysand's conditions for loving. The paradox is perhaps best described in Winnicott's phrase, "being alone together" (1958; see also Green's recent development of the idea of "absence" in the analytic relationship, 1975, esp. p. 12). The solitude captures that tension generated in the psychoanalytic situation that Freud devised: it is both the foundation and the summit of the analytic relationship, for if two people can be alone together, they are in the best position to develop freely the emotional and cognitive possibilities of the relationship. It takes in the deprivation in the two-person relationship described so well by Stone (1961, 1967). And it includes the solitariness so vividly presented by Thomas Mann in "Death in Venice": speaking of the solitary person, Mann writes:

A solitary, unused to speaking of what he sees and feels, has mental experiences which are at once more intense and less articulate than those of a gregarious man. They are sluggish, yet more wayward, and never without a melancholy tinge. Sights and impressions which others brush aside with a glance, a light comment, a smile, occupy him more than their due; they sink silently in, they take on meaning, they become experience, emotion, adventure. Solitude gives birth to the original in us, to beauty unfamiliar and perilous—to poetry. But also, it gives birth to the opposite: to the perverse, the illicit, the absurd [1913, p. 26].

"Being alone together" adds this to the accounts of Stone and Mann: that a shared reality is developed in which new transference interpretations, jointly developed, stated by the analyst, and uniquely modified by the analysand, become the basis of enriched, intensified modes of constituting experience in the life of the analysand. These constitutive modes, too, will be redescribed as repetition so far as that seems possible and useful.

The major transference phenomena represent the achievement of such simplified, focused ways of defining and acting within the analytic relationship that there can be no mistaking their meanings or avoiding their emotional manifestations or implications. The mode of experiencing is clear, compact, intensified. Here, as Freud emphasized, is the ground for conviction: nothing important is being dealt with *"in absentia* or *in effigie"* (1912b, p. 108).

UNCONSCIOUS CERTAINTY

The idea of ground for conviction implies, not doubt, but convictions or certainties unconsciously maintained by the analysand. These are the convictions—e.g., that the analyst is indeed persecutory—that stand in the way of transference interpretations' being taken for what they are rather than as further evidence in support of the convictions themselves. It is essential to hold a correct view of the status unconsciously accorded these convictions by the analysand. They are far from being merely anxiously and rigidly held positions, though they are these too.

In this regard, one may bring into consideration an adaptation of Wittgenstein's discussions in On Certainty (1969). The transference interpretation is an attempt to correct certain beliefs about self and others that the analysand has been holding fast against all evidence. The analysand has been holding these beliefs so fast that he or she gives every appearance of using them as methodological principles or principles of knowing. This is to say that, for the analysand, these beliefs must be taken as true if he or she is to be able to make judgments of claims about anything else, for nothing else is more certain than they are. They serve as tests of what is true.[2] One such belief might be, "I am worthless." That it is held fast is made evident by how the believer will judge anyone who thinks otherwise to be a fool, a dupe, a manipulator, or another worthless person who cannot know any better.

Thus the person in question will reinterpret all contrary evidence in the light of this belief rather than begin to question the belief itself. One's entire idea of reality and of one's relation to it is at stake. In this context, for the analyst to respond in kind by agreeing or disagreeing with the belief would be to discredit himself or herself as a person and analyst. Further, as Strachey (1934) has pointed out, the analyst would be providing a good magical introject to counter a bad one, and in doing so would be making a poor move in the game of analysis. The transference interpretation is a good move in a game different from the analysand's. This is a game or a set of practices into which the analysand must be initiated and ultimately become an expert. But it is, in Wittgenstein's sense, only a game, that is to say, an approach to reality that consistently uses one language or one set of rules or practices, thereby making a more adaptive reality in which a certain mode of experiencing is extended in scope, intensified, and made amenable to further transformation. To call it a game is, of course, not to say that it is frivolous, merely pretense, or a nonanalytic social psychological phenomenon.

In making transference interpretations, the analyst attempts to throw into question these certainties or beliefs unconsciously held fast. The analyst as analyst takes nothing presented by the analysand for granted. It is inherent in the analytic attitude that it is only by finding other ways to understand what the analysand holds to be both unquestionably true and damaging that it will ever be possible to develop and carry through an analysis. In saying why they are treated as certainties and how that came to be so, in pointing out the analysand's uses of these convictions and their consequences, and, above all, in showing how they shape what is painful, pleasurable, and limiting in the analytic relationship, the analyst tries to help the analysand become more genuinely a co-worker in the analysis.

But for the analysand, this attempt on the analyst's part represents for a long time an assault on his or her idea of reality. As such, it is to be resisted strenuously, even if subtly. It is not only the specific sense of the interpretation that is threatening; it is also the interpretation's throwing into question the analysand's entire mode of making sense. Here the analyst counts on the analysand's having been making more than one kind of sense of the events of his or her life, that is, of having multiple, *conflicting* conceptions of what is real or true, based on other infantile psychosexual convictions as well as more or less rational, communally shared conceptions of the real and the true. Were the analysand to be maintaining only one, self-enclosed, set of convictions, he or she could never consider the interpretation as such. If, for example, persecution were the issue, then every interpretation of persecutory fantasy would be experienced merely as further persecution. And we do know that every analytic process goes through phases during which each intervention is regarded as a seduction, a castration, etc., according to the unconsciously maintained certainty that is dominant at the time. At least for the time being, though perhaps forever, the analysand's interpretive circle is closed—or appears to be.

Yet, given a reasonably well-chosen analysand, the reductive transference interpretations do seem to make a difference, and so one must pursue the question of how the ground for conviction referred to by Freud does develop during the analysis. Perhaps the old relationships that serve as prototypes in the transference interpretations were not identical with all that is now being lived, interpreted, and believed in as transference. Perhaps *in principle* they could not be identical. If this were so, the reductive formulation of manifest transference interpretation may obscure the importance of other factors that play an important part in the changes that are observed. In this regard it is worth considering whether new experience, far from being only a consequence of transference interpretation, is somehow inherent in the developing repetitive transferences themselves.

METAPHOR AND NEW EXPERIENCE

In taking up these questions, we are entering an area of life in which things are also other than themselves, where meaning is multifaceted, and where the line between the old and the new is blurred. It should, I think, help develop an answer to these questions to consider briefly some interrelated aspects of the psychology of metaphor. In the psychology of metaphor we shall find a useful analogy to the psychology of transference interpretations. My focus will be on newly encountered good metaphors, those in response to which we say "That's it exactly!" or "That really captures it!" or "That says it all!"

Some literary and linguistic analysts (see e.g., Lewis, 1936; Snell, 1953), and also people in everyday life, believe that there are experiences that can only be expressed metaphorically. And it is for this achievement that these metaphors, which may be entire poems as well as lines or even words, are so highly valued. But how can this be so? Just what is the "it" that the metaphor "is" or "captures" or "says"? If this "it" or this "experience" can only be rendered metaphorically, then we can know it only as such, that is, as the metaphor itself. In this I agree with the position put forward by T. S. Eliot (1933) and D. W. Harding (1963) in their discussions of poetry. For in these instances we are granting that there is no known and logically independent version of the experience that can serve to validate the metaphor. Whatever the metaphor makes available to us depends on it and so cannot be used to prove its correctness.

It seems justified to conclude that the metaphor is a new experience rather than a mere paraphrase of an already fully constituted experience. The metaphor creates an experience that one has never had before. It is an experience one has not realized by oneself. The metaphor does, of course, suggest certain constituent experiences of which one may have been more or less dimly aware.[3] One may say, therefore, that the metaphor speaks for these constituents, on the existence of which much of its appeal depends. But in its organizing and implicitly rendering these constituents in its new way, it is a creation rather than a mere paraphrase or new edition. Paraphrases and new editions never speak as forcefully as good new metaphors, nor could they facilitate further new experience. One analytically familiar feature of these creations is that they make it safe and pleasing to experience something that otherwise would be considered too threatening and so would be kept in fragmented obscurity through defensive measures.[4]

Thus, when one says, "That's it exactly!" one is implicitly recognizing and announcing that one has found and accepted a new mode of experiencing one's self and one's world, which is to say, asserting a transformation of one's own subjectivity. Something is now said to be true, and in a sense it is true, but it is true for the first time. Nothing just like it can ever happen again, for the second time cannot be the same as the first. One can't step into the same river twice. A revelatory metaphor re-encountered or repeated later may lose some of its force; alternatively, it may gain in significance; but it cannot remain exactly the same metaphor or mobilize an experience identical with the first. The point applies as well to new metaphors that are similar to familiar ones; they have to be judged or experienced through their conventionalized predecessors, as through methods of knowing or already proved instruments of perceiving. The audience and the performer, who may be one person, have not stood still.

INTERPRETATION AND NEW EXPERIENCE

What I have said about the psychology of metaphor is analogous to the transformational aspects of developed transferences and the steadfast interpretations that both facilitate and organize them as transferences. Allowing that these transferences and "remembered" experiences come into existence over a period of time, nothing that is identical with them has ever before been enacted, and nothing identical with them will ever be enacted again. They are creations that may be fully achieved only under specific analytic conditions. For example, at the time of his childhood scene with his father, the young man of my clinical example could not have had the specific experience I recounted. Strictly speaking, he was not reliving that moment. As a boy, he must have experienced some of the main precursors and constituents of his present mode of experience, but he could not have done so in the present articulated and integrated manner. That present manner was the basis of his anguished outcry. Words like re-creating, re-experiencing and reliving simply do not do justice to the phenomena. In the way he was doing it, he was living that moment for the first time.

In making this claim, I an not contradicting some of our well-established ideas about interpretation and insight. I am not, for example, disputing the point that insight refers to more than the recovery of lost memories, and takes in, as well, a new grasp of the significance and interrelations of events one has always remembered. It is in the latter connection that the analysand will say, as Freud pointed out, "As a matter of fact I've always known it; only I've never thought of it" (1914, p. 148). In fact, it is to develop that point further to say that the young child simply does not have the means of fully defining what we later regard as its own life experiences. It takes an adult to do that, especially with the help of an analyst. It was, after all, Freud's analysis of adults that made it possible to define infantile psychosexuality. In this respect, but without disrespect, child analysis always retains a quality of applied psychoanalysis. The adult definition of infantile psychosexuality is "artificial" in the same way that the interpreted transference neurosis is: both are ways of describing as true something that was not true in quite that way at the time of its greatest developmental significance. This apparent paradox about "remembering" as a form of creating goes a long way, I think, toward saying what it is that is distinctive about psychoanalytic interpretation.

In steadfastly and perspicaciously making transference interpretations, the analyst helps constitute new modes of experience and new experiences. This newness characterizes the experience of analytic transferences themselves. Unlike extra-analytic transferences, they can no longer be sheerly repetitive or merely new editions. Instead, they become repetitive new editions understood as such because defined as such by the simplifying and steadfast transference interpretations. Instead of responding to the analysand in kind, which would actualize the repetition, the analyst makes an interpretation. This interpretation does not necessarily or regularly match something the analysand already knows or has experienced unconsciously. Although the analysand does often seem to have already represented some things unconsciously in the very terms of the interpretation, equally often he or she does not seem to have done so at all. To think otherwise about this would be, in effect, to claim that, unconsciously, every analysand is Freud or a fully insightful Freudian analyst. And that claim is absurd.

It would be closer to the truth to say this: Unconsciously, the analysand already knows or has experienced fragmentary, amorphous, uncoordinated constituents of many of the transference interpretations. Alternatively, one may say that, implicitly, the analysand has been insisting on some as yet unspecified certainties and, in keeping with this, following some set of as yet unspecified rules in his or her actions; these the transference interpretations now organize explicitly. Each transference interpretation thus refers to many things that have already been defined by the analysand, and it does so in a way that transforms them. That's why one may call it interpretation; otherwise it would be mere repeating or sterile paraphrasing. Interpretation is a creative redescription that implicitly has the structure of a simile. It says, "This is like that." Each interpretation does, therefore, add new actions to the life the analysand has already lived.

Technically, redescription in the terms of transference-repetition is necessary. This is so because, up to the time of interpretation and working through, the analysand has been, in one sense, unable and, in another sense, unconsciously and desperately unwilling, to conduct his or her life differently. In and of themselves, the repetitions cannot alter the symptoms, the subjective distress, the wasting of one's possibilities; rather, they can only perpetuate a static situation by repeatedly confirming its necessity. They prove once again the unconsciously maintained, damaging certainties. But once they get to be viewed as historically grounded actions and subjectively defined situations, as they do upon being interpreted and worked through, they appear as having always been, in crucial respects, inventions of the analysand's making and, so, as his or her responsibility. In being seen as versions of one's past life, they may be changed in significant and beneficial ways. Less and less are they presented as purely inevitable happenings, as a fixed fate or as the well-established way of the world. Here we encounter a second paradox that goes to the heart of psychoanalytic interpretation, namely, that responsible, insightful change is possible through psychoanalysis just because, as a child, the analysand mistakenly assumed and then denied responsibility for much that he or she encountered in the early formative environment and during maturation.

COORDINATING PAST AND PRESENT EXPERIENCE

One major point remains to be made about the logic of viewing transference interpretations as simplifying yet innovative redescriptions. This point is that the interpretations bring about a coordination of the terms in which to state both the analysand's current problems and their life-historical background. The analysand's symptoms and distress are described as actions and modes of action, with due regard for the principle of multiple function or multiple meaning; in coordination with that description, the decisive developmental situations and conflicts are stated as actions and modes of action. Continuity is established between the childhood constructions of relationships and self and the present constructions of these. Interpretation of transferences shows how both are part of the same set of practices, that is, how they follow the same set of rules. Past and present are coordinated to show continuity rather than arranged in a definite causal sequence.

In the same way, the *form* of analytic behavior and the *content* of associations are given coordinate descriptions, say, as being defiant, devouring, or reparative. Or, in the case of depression, the depressive symptoms, the depressive analytic transference, the themes of present and past loss, destructiveness and helplessness, all will be redescribed under the aspect of one continuously developing self-presentation. And this coordination will be worked out in that hermeneutically circular fashion in which the analyst defines both the facts to be explained and the explanations to be applied to these facts. In the end, as is well known, both the paramount issues of the analysis and the leading explanatory account of them are likely to be significantly different from the provisional versions of them used at the beginning of the analysis.

This is the sophisticated cognitive simplification that promotes the convincing development and recognition of transference and the emotional experiencing of the past *as it is now remembered*. The coordination of terms is the only way to break into the vicious circle of the neurotic disturbance and reduce its unconsciously self-confirming character. New meaning is established by steadfast interpretation of transferences and the conditions for loving of which they are enactments.

That this kind of analytic work is not simply intellectual is shown by the analytic example presented above: that analysand was now operating according to rules which, through previous transference interpretations and coordination of terms, had changed. The changed rules were implicit in this hitherto-avoided experiencing of the past. It was not re-experiencing, or not mainly that: in it special way, it was experiencing that past for the first time.

CONCLUSION

In conclusion I should like to mention two implications of the foregoing remarks.

1. The transference phenomena that finally constitute the transference neurosis are to be taken as regressive in only some of their aspects. This is so because, viewed as achievements of the analysis, they have never existed before as such; rather, they constitute a creation achieved through a novel relationship into which one has entered by conscious and rational design. The analytic definition of the conditions for loving has never been arrived at before; they have never been so simplified, organized, intensified, and transparent as they get to be in the analytically circumscribed and identified transference neurosis. It seems a more adequate or balanced view of transference phenomena to regard them as multidirectional in meaning rather than as simply regressive or repetitive. This would be to look at them in a way that is analogous to the way we look at creative works of art. We would see the transferences as creating the past in the present, in a special analytic way and under favorable conditions. Essentially, they represent movement forward, not backward.

2. It is wrong to think that interpretation deals only in what is concealed or disguised or, what is its correlate, that "the unconscious" is omniscient. In particular, it cannot be the case that "the unconscious" knows all about transference and repetition. By establishing new connections, comprehensive contexts, and coordinated perspectives on familiar actions, interpretation creates new meanings or new actions. Not everything that has not yet been organized has been actively kept apart by defensive measures; not everything

that has not yet been recognized has been denied. This point is obvious, really, but it is often obscured by formulations, some of Freud's among them, which suggest that interpretation is just uncovering. (See in this connection, Fingarette, 1963).

I mentioned earlier that Freud was groping in these connections. I would now suggest that he had to grope owing to his having drawn a sizeable number of distinctions too sharply; past and present, old and new, genuine and artificial, repetition and creation, the subjective world and the objective world, dream and reality, solitude and intimacy, and union and separation. He also distinguished too sharply between the psychoanalytic method and its results, and between psychoanalytic description and explanation. Each of these pairs we may now view differently on the strength of Freud's discoveries as well as advances made by others in psychoanalytic theory and the general theory of knowledge. We may view them, that is to say, as features of action or experience rather than as mutually exclusive types of action or experience. And we may realize that they are such features only as described or redescribed and organized by an observer following a plan. For us today, these distinctions are simultaneously more uncertain and less conducive to needless uncertainty than they were for Freud in his day.[5]

NOTES

1. It has been suggested—correctly, I think,—that Freud's stress on repetition was in part a response to real and threatened public disapproval of the erotic transferences that female analysands developed in relation to their male analysts (Charles Rycroft, personal communication).
2. I am indebted to Tom Morawetz of Yale University for letting me see his work in progress on Wittgenstein's On Certainty.
3. As Ella Freeman Sharpe (1940), among others, has argued, metaphor is derived from and touches on certain unconsciously elaborated, wishful psychological events and fantasies.
4. My formulation of this point does not fundamentally clash with the established psychoanalytic proposition that art is a means of mastering emotions through some relaxation and realignment of defense that permits expression and gratification of instinctual drives in relative safety. It is just that I am no longer viewing emotion as an inherently autonomous and quantitative entity or process of discharge that must be mastered by the psychic functions we ascribe to the ego structure. In the terms of action language (Schafer, 1976, esp. Part IV), it would be preferable to say, with regard to mastery, that it is the person enacting emotional experience in a manner that he or she now views as less threatening because it implies less in the way of drastic action, both in what is privately or unconsciously imagined and in what is publicly performed. In this view, far from being encountered passively and only then dealt with as happenings, affects are features of actions or personal agency.

5. I wish to thank Cecily de Monchaux, Sara van den Berg and Merton M. Gill for their helpful comments on earlier versions of this paper.

REFERENCES

Blum, H. P. (1971), On the conception and development of the transference neurosis. *J. Amer. Psychoanal. Assn.*, 19:41–53.

Eliot, T. S. (1933), *The Use of Poetry and the Use of Criticism*. New York: Barnes & Noble, 1970.

Fingarette, H. (1963), *The Self in Transformation*. New York: Basic Books.

Freud, S. (1905), Three essays on the theory of sexuality. *Standard Edition*, 7:125–243. London: Hogarth Press, 1953.

———— (1910), A special type of choice of object made by men. *Standard Edition*, 11:163–176. London: Hogarth Press, 1957.

———— (1912a), On the universal tendency to debasement in the sphere of love. *Standard Edition*, 11:177–190. London: Hogarth Press, 1957.

———— (1912b), The dynamics of transference. *Standard Edition*, 12:97–108. London: Hogarth Press, 1958.

———— (1914), Remembering, repeating and working-through. *Standard Edition*, 12:145–156. London: Hogarth Press, 1958.

———— (1915), Observations on transference-love. *Standard Edition*, 12:157–171. London: Hogarth Press, 1958.

———— (1920), Beyond the pleasure principle. *Standard Edition*, 18:1–64. London: Hogarth Press, 1955.

———— (1922), Some neurotic mechanisms in jealousy, paranoia and homosexuality. *Standard Edition*, 18:221–232. London: Hogarth Press, 1955.

Gray, P. (1973), Psychoanalytic technique and the ego's capacity for viewing intrapsychic activity. *J. Amer. Psychoanal. Assn.*, 21:474–494.

Green, A. (1975), The analyst, symbolization and absence in the analytic setting (on changes in analytic practice and analytic experience). *Internat. J. Psycho-Anal.*, 56:1–22.

Grossman, W. I. (1967), Reflections on the relationships of introspection and psycho-analysis. *Internat. J. Psycho-Anal.*, 48:16–31.

Harding, D. W. (1963), *Experience into Words: Essays on Poetry*. London: Chatto and Windus.

Jacobson, E. (1964), *The Self and the Object World*. New York: International Universities Press.

Kohut, H. (1971), *The Analysis of the Self*. New York: International Universities Press.

Kris, E. (1956), The recovery of childhood memories in psychoanalysis. *The Psychoanalytic Study of the Child*, 11:54–88. New York: International Universities Press.

Leavy, S. (1973), Psychoanalytic interpretation. *The Psychoanalytic Study of the Child*, 28:305–330. New Haven: Yale University Press.

Lewis, C. S. (1936), *The Allegory of Love: A Study in Medieval Tradition*. Oxford: Clarendon Press.

Loewald, H. (1960), On the therapeutic action of psycho-analysis. *Internat. J. Psycho-Anal.*, 41:16–33.

———— (1971), The transference neurosis: Comments on the concept and the phenomenon. *J. Amer. Psychoanal. Assn.*, 19:54–66.

Mann, T. (1913), Death in Venice. In *Stories of a Lifetime*, Vol. 2. London: Secker & Warburg, 1961.

Rycroft, C. (1958), An enquiry into the function of words in the psycho-analytical situation. *Internat. J. Psycho-Anal.*, 39:408–415.

Schafer, R. (1976), *A New Language for Psychoanalysis.* New Haven and London: Yale University Press.

Schimek, J. (1975), The interpretations of the past: Childhood trauma, psychical reality, and historical truth. *J. Amer. Psychoanal. Assn.*, 23:845–865.

Sharpe, E. F. (1940), Psycho-physical processes revealed in language: An examination of metaphor. *Internat. J. Psycho-Anal.*, 21:201–213.

Snell, B. (1953), *The Discovery of the Mind: The Greek Origins of European Thought.* Oxford: Blackwell.

Stone, L. (1961), *The Psychoanalytic Situation.* New York: International Universities Press.

——— (1967), The psychoanalytic situation and transference: Postscript to an earlier communication. *J. Amer. Psychoanal. Assn.*, 15:3–58.

Strachey, J. (1934), The nature of the therapeutic action of psycho-analysis. *Internat. J. Psycho-Anal.*, 15:127–159.

Winnicott, D. W. (1958), The capacity to be alone. *Internat. J. Psycho-Anal.*, 39:416–420.

Wittgenstein, L. (1969), *On Certainty.* New York: Harper.

24. The Transference Neurosis: Comments on the Concept and the Phenomenon

Hans W. Loewald

An unusually gifted and inhibited young man of 19, an only child, ill at ease and intense, came for analysis because of grave concerns about his prolific sexual fantasies (mainly heterosexual), fears of homosexuality (no overt activity ever, as far as I know), absence of heterosexual involvement, and restriction of his social life. It soon became apparent that his relationship to me, from the very beginning, tended to be a duplicate of his relationship to his father which seemed to be a kind of slavish adoration, imitation, and submissive love, with some evidence of rebellion against that position, deep resentment, and of attempts to extricate himself from it. The patient's love for his father seemed as excessive as his hatred and contempt for his mother, who was described as an impulse-ridden, chaotic woman with a host of fads, superstitions, and prejudices.. This was in contrast to the father, who was pictured as a passionately rational, rigidly balanced, hard-working man, successful in his work, studious, and retiring. The mother appeared to be slavishly devoted to her husband, looking up to him with childlike respect and admiration, but making great demands on his composure and forbearance by her irrational, anxiety-ridden attitudes toward the family and views on life —the very opposite to his.

Here seems to be an example of a very rapidly-developing transference neurosis. Although many other currents, of course, were present, the patient was in an ambivalent love relationship with his father, showing a mixture of attempted identification with an ideal and a feminine, masochistically oriented object relationship with him, which had the earmarks of an unconscious identification with his mother. This constellation was quickly transferred to me. One aspect of the prominence and compulsive nature of heterosexual fantasies was that they represented a defensive struggle against succumbing to this libidinal position, although elements of a positive oedipal position

Reprinted from the *Journal of the American Psychoanalytic Association* 19 (1971):54–66, by permission of International Universities Press, Inc.

were by no means absent. I shall not go into the details of the case or describe the course of the analysis. I have greatly oversimplified things in this brief sketch and have concentrated on some salient features which made their appearance very early in the analysis, through his verbal accounts as well as in the form of verbalized and unverbalized transference manifestations. The patient had, from the beginning, considerable awareness of his behavior and feelings toward me and was quickly able to grasp some of their historical determinants.

One might raise the question whether one should speak here of a transference *neurosis*, inasmuch as the transference was so immediate and massive. But the patient had a remarkable capacity for gaining or regaining perspective on himself, for self-observation and reflection. He showed what Freud and Ferenczi have called a passion for transference—then considered characteristic for hysteria—together with a capacity for insight. Granted that there were many preoedipal problems, it is fair to say that he had reached the oedipal phase, however slanted and distorted, but had not passed beyond it in many crucial aspects. In fact, no significant progress appeared to have occurred in his psychosexual development since the oedipal period. There was evidence of only superficial repression of his Oedipus complex during the latency period. A fairly straight line seemed to lead from the oedipal period to the time he came for treatment, without any significant modification. He still was in the oedipal period, as documented by the nature of his transference and by many details of his extensive fantasy life. His intellectual development, however, had proceeded well, and this not merely in the area of his special field of interest, but in many areas, including his ability to apply his intelligence and powers of observation to his own psychic life. He had many obsessive-compulsive character traits. One is tempted to say that the development of certain ego functions had outstripped, probably since early childhood, the development of his instinctual-emotional life, in the sense in which Freud has spoken of it in "The Predisposition to Obsessional Neurosis" (1913, p. 325).

The transference clearly had a primitive quality, perhaps not unlike that of children who are seen prior to the latency period. It was soon apparent that the transference, while desirable in the interest of maintaining rapport with this isolated patient who only too easily retreated from contact with people, worked as a powerful resistance, in the sense of his tending to repeat the neurotic entanglement en bloc in the analysis. Having become reasonably certain of the patient's capacity for reflection, for taking distance from himself, I began cautiously, but very early, to interpret in genetic terms certain of his transference manifestations, and, from the beginning, to engage and utilize his interest in and capacity for self-understanding. Such a course, that is, to make early transference interpretations, seemed possible also just because of the massive transference which, combined with his vivid descriptions of childhood and current events, made important features of the transference situation much more transparent than they often are at such an early stage of an analysis. Furthermore, in the face of a quickly developing transference neurosis—in contrast to a slow, gradual development of it which would need to be facilitated and promoted—resistance analysis, in terms of slow, painstaking work on complex character defenses, was not called for at this time. The major resistance, in this respect not unlike many hysteria cases, was the transference itself. Thus it needed analytic work from the start. To avoid misunderstanding, I should underline that the patient talked freely about his past and current life, perhaps even somewhat compulsively, so that in terms of time spent on it my interpretive activity was minimal.

I have chosen this case to introduce the subject, not as a typical example of a transference neurosis, or to demonstrate that there is such a thing, but in order to give a clinical illustration that would point to the difficulties and complexities of the issue. These difficulties stem, at least in part, from the problems inherent in the modern concept of neurosis. What are the distinguishing features of neurosis compared with borderline cases, character disorders, and psychosis; and to what extent do we still understand neurosis as a distinct, circumscribed illness in an otherwise relatively healthy individual, or at any rate in an individual who is impaired mainly by this circumscribed illness? An illness, furthermore, which would be comparable to an acute physical illness which has become chronic and requires an acute exacerbation in order to be treated successfully? Do character neuroses fit such a comparison, and if not, should they be classified as neuroses? There is also the fact that a neurosis with a more or less distinct symptomatology (such as conversion symptoms, phobias or obsessive-compulsive symptoms) for which the patient seeks help, usually if not always, on closer observation, shows a degree of character pathology, i.e., traits of a character neurosis.

My concern in this case was the danger of an early stalemate or disruption of the analysis because of the massive transference which would tend in the direction of a mere transference repetition. But does transference neurosis not mean repetition of the infantile neurosis, reactivation of it, with the assumption that in the course of the analysis a new and healthier outcome can be achieved? What kind of repetition? In his paper, "Remembering, Repeating and Working Through," Freud (1914) distinguishes between reproduction by action and reproduction in the psychic field. Reproduction or, if I may be permitted this substitution, repetition in the psychic field by remembering, reflecting, and working-through is the therapeutic path of analysis. This path cannot be taken unless the infantile neurosis is reactivated in the transference, as transference neurosis. Intellectual insight is not enough; fruitful and effective self-understanding cannot be achieved unless the significant experiences and inner conflicts which led to the neurosis become alive again in the present and regain a measure of immediacy and urgency in the transference neurosis. On the other hand, reliving of the infantile neurosis, per se, is fruitless. Many patients in various disguised, or not so disguised, ways relive or continue their infantile neuroses in their everyday lives before they ever come to analysis. But they don't know it. If repression and other defenses are successful enough and not too crippling, the need for treatment does not arise, at least not on the grounds of feeling significantly handicapped or sick. This is often a problem with people who start analysis for professional reasons, such as psychoanalytic candidates, psychiatric residents, psychologists, and others. Their childhood neurosis often has—for purposes of everyday life—been successfully repressed. Ego restrictions and unresolved conflicts become apparent and troublesome mainly in their professional work.

We are here in the area of character problems and problems of character analysis, and it is in this area, it seems to me, that the question frequently arises: where is the transference neurosis? This often is a question not only with the so-called normal patient, but with the many patients who come for analysis because of character difficulties, general feelings of inadequacy or unhappiness, slow-burning depression, marital difficulties, or work problems. In contrast to the old-fashioned symptom-neurosis, one might say that their neurosis is spread over much of the whole personality. No well-defined symptomatology, no well-defined infantile neurosis, and thus no transference neurosis, in that sense, can be detected. Of course, these patients too, show transference manifestations of various kinds of intensities, but these tend to remain diffuse, seemingly disconnected and sporadic; to arrive at the delineation of a neurosis as a more or less coherent, sequential, circumscribed development seems difficult or impossible. In fact, it sometimes seems that trying to do that forces the material into uncongenial channels.

Perhaps we need far more observation and research on the differences in the infantile antecedents which in one case make for a character neurosis and in another for what presents as a symptom neurosis. I do not, however, wish to imply that clear dividing lines can be drawn here. Our progressive understanding of neurosis has led us to recognize character problems in "symptom neurosis" which earlier were not recognized or not subjected to analytic work. In the course of character-analytic work, "new" symptoms may make their appearance; somatic ailments, as for instance, headaches, backaches, sore throats, colds, disturbances of the digestive system, may reveal themselves as equivalents of neurotic symptoms.

From clinical impressions I would venture to suggest that differences in parental attitudes and child-rearing have something to do with differences in neurotic development, at least in certain cases. I am reasonably convinced that such factors, rather than, or in addition to, innate disposition, play, in a number of cases, a far greater role than was recognized in the analytic work of earlier days. In a large number of families, many problems of psycho-sexual development and growing-up tend to be pushed under the rug, so to speak, often because of the parents' own personality restrictions and uncertainties, their tendencies to evade direct confrontations, prohibitions, and injunctions, but no less to evade the more open, unabashed expression of their own love-hate involvement with their children and of their own emotional-instinctual needs and urges. Such trends, tending to diffuse, repress, and suppress clear-cut feelings toward their children as well as in their children, may have some bearing on the diffusion and spread of neurosis over the total personality development, resulting in what we call character neurosis. Defenses would become more insidious in proportion to the insidiousness and blunting of instinctual life and affect-expression. In such measure as there is less unhampered and unself-conscious communication, negative and positive, with one's children, there is perhaps less "trauma" but also less bliss and joy in childhood, and more of a climate favoring a general formation of character, which in its very structure is more defensive, cautious, and often bland and colorless. The occasions for symptom formation would be lessened.

The analytic situation, to the extent to which the analyst, owing to the requirements of noninvolvement, tends to suppress his own instinctual-affective currents instead of being cognizant of them and 'sublimating' them, is apt to play into such character defenses and reinforce them. Because of the emotional tensions inherent in the analytic process in combination with the requirement for noninvolvement, the analytic situation lends itself only too easily to a perpetuation or reinforcement of this type of defensive character. It has impressed me that people with outspoken symptomatology, whether hysterical or obsessive-compulsive, often seem able to function outside the area invaded by their symptoms more fully and whole-heartedly than many of the less obviously sick character problems we see in analysis today.

There are those who tend to think that the concept of transference neurosis is no longer useful, and that searching for or trying to promote the transference neurosis leads too often only to frustration and skepticism on the part of candidates and others who attempt to find it in their patients. In addition to what I have described, many character disorders and borderline cases are genetically to be derived not so much, certainly not so exclusively, from an infantile neurosis originating in the cluster of oedipal problems, but from deficiencies and deformations of ego development antedating the oedipal period and the development of an infantile neurosis in the classical sense, based, as the latter are, on problems of relatively advanced ego development.

While this is true, perhaps our modern emphasis on ego problems and functions and on ego analysis carries with it the danger of concentrating too heavily on autonomous ego functioning, and of losing sight of the instinctual-affective, experiential roots and determinants of ego development, thus neglecting the infantile neurosis and its object-related instinctual nature. Emphasis on the autonomy of the ego did not intend to lead to a relative neglect of the transference neurosis, but may nevertheless have done so.

As I see it, the concept of transference neurosis has not lost its value. But it is true that the picture and consequently our concept of neurosis have changed so as to include most prominently what we call character neurosis, a form of neurosis which is more formless and more hidden; and the same can be said for the transference neurosis. Furthermore, the prominence of preoedipal problems and of deviations and distortions of ego formation at early stages in many patients seen nowadays, tends to obscure the clear delineation of a transference neurosis. As distinguished from the character neuroses, here the specifically neurotogenic problems of the oedipal period are intertwined with early developmental problems and colored by them. The latter, arising in a period of development prior to the relatively unblurred differentiation between self and object world, would make for complex constellations of relatedness in the analytic setting (primitive identifications, projective and introjective processes) which are different from classical transference phenomena.

Let me now come back briefly to what I consider the important and enduring aspect of the concept of transference neurosis: it defines the analytic process as an active, preconscious-conscious repetition of early pathogenic experiences and their intrapsychic pathological vicissitudes, in the interest and as a method of mastering and resolving them in new ways. Freud, again in "Remembering, Repeating and Working Through," says that it is mainly the handling of the transference which is the means by which we can tame and master the compulsion to repeat and transform it into a motive for remembering. What has to be done is to give "all the symptoms of the illness a new transference meaning" and to replace the patient's "ordinary neurosis by a 'transference neurosis' of which he can be cured by the therapeutic work" (1914, p. 154). If we do not cling to the word "symptoms," but include the wider areas of character and of ego pathology, this still stands today as the procedure at which we aim. In this sense transference neurosis is not so much an entity to be found in the patient, but an operational concept. We may regard it as denoting the retransformation of a psychic illness which originated in pathogenic interactions with the important persons in the child's environment, into an interactional process with a new person, the analyst, in which the pathological infantile interactions and their intrapsychic consequences may become transparent and accessible to change by virtue of the analyst's objectivity and of the emergence of novel interaction-possibilities. The illness, which had become an autonomous process and an automatic response regardless of environmental changes and reactions and even attracting and provoking pathogenic reactions similar to the original ones, becomes alive again and clarified as originating in pathogenic interactions with the environment. Our therapeutic work has its limitations insofar as the original illness is not a response to environmental influences but is due to innate deficiencies; and to the extent to which the intrapsychic consequences of pathological interactions may be irreversible. The latter is more likely, the earlier the pathological interactions took place.

Understood in this light, the transference neurosis is indeed a creature of the analytic situation and not simply a repeat performance or continuation of the old illness, as seemed to be the case with the patient described in the beginning of this presentation. The patient's initial behavior was automatic, as it would be with any other person in his environment who fit certain paternal characteristics. His transference was immediate and was a resistance; his transference neurosis, which is not to be confused with resistance, was still to develop. The difference between such transference manifestations and transference neurosis or transference illness, then, would be that the former are essentially automatic responses, signs and symptoms of the old illness; whereas the transference neurosis is a creation of the analytic work done by analyst and patient, in which the old illness loses its autonomous and automatic character and becomes reactivated and comprehensible as a live responsive process and, as such, changing and changeable. New and different transference manifestations arise as signs of this new process. As promoted by the analyst, the transference neurosis is curative; as taking place in the patient, it is a healing process. What makes it into an illness different from the infantile and from the presenting one is that the forces operative in the latter are given different responses or no responses feeding the old processes. The more complex, diffuse, and hidden the old neurotic processes are, as in character neurosis, the more complex, diffuse, and hidden is the transference neurosis. The latter is not and could not be more obvious and tangible as a delimited process than the illness which brought the patient to the analyst.

"The transference," Freud continues in the same paper, "thus creates an intermediate region between illness and real life through which the transition from the one to the other is made. The new condition has taken over all the features of the illness; but it represents an artificial illness which is at every point accessible to our intervention. It is a piece of real experience, but one which has been made possible by especially favorable conditions . . ." (1914, p. 154). The intermediate region between (old) illness and real life is the transference neurosis. It is a "piece of real experience" made possible by our presence and our interventions, just as the infantile neurosis was "a piece of real experience," "made possible" by the presence and the pathogenic interventions of the original environment.

It is not Freud's opinion that this new artificial disease, the transference neurosis, is an artifact unilaterally created by the analyst. It is brought about by man's libidinal nature, by the fact that the patient will, if he is not too "narcissistic," form an attachment to the analyst, repeating the characteristics of his attachments and responses to the original love objects—as ambivalent as they are likely to have been—and by the analyst's different responses. What the analyst promotes in the handling of the transference is not so much the attachment to the analyst but the patient's awareness of his attachment (and defenses against it), of the nature of this attachment, of its historical determination; and the analyst does this by his empathic and interpretive responses and by abstaining from repeating the pathogenic responses of the past. Giving a new meaning, a transference meaning to the illness, does not signify that a new meaning is invented, not does it merely signify that the old meaning is newly revealed to the patient, but that a meaning is created, by the interactions between patient and analyst, which has new dynamic tensions and engenders new, healthier motivations of its own.

The transference neurosis, in this sense, is the patient's love life—the source and crux of his psychic development—as relived in relation to a potentially new love object, the analyst, who renounces libidinal-aggressive involvement for the sake of understanding and achieving higher psychic organization. From the point of view of the analyst, this means neither indifference nor absence of love-hate, but persistent renunciation of involvement, a constant activity of uninvolving which tends to impel the patient to understand himself in his involvement instead of concentrating exclusively, albeit unconsciously, on the object. The resolution of the transference neurosis consists in achieving such higher psychic organization which gradually replaces the transference illness, and by virtue of which object-involvement on a more mature level becomes possible.

In many respects, similar developments, under favorable conditions, take place in the healthy transition from the oedipal phase to the latency period, and again in the transition from adolescence to adulthood. Spontaneous, "nonartificial" incestuous involvements are partially relinquished and transformed so that individuation and new involvement can proceed. This is facilitated and promoted by parental instinctual disengagement.

Looking at it from another angle, perhaps one might think of the concept, transference neurosis, as an ideal construct. The ideal construct structures, and thus always oversimplifies, a complex aggregation of events, brings some order into an at first chaotic constellation and sequence of events; it functions as an organizing principle which is gradually distilled out of the events when investigated in a certain perspective; it is neither arbitrarily imposed on them nor can it be found in them as an entity in pure culture.

On the other hand, let us also not forget the experiential meaning of such words as neurosis, illness, etc. It cannot be too unusual for patients—I certainly remember it from the time I was a patient on the couch—to experience, at least at times, being in analysis as an illness, insofar as it is a regressive and unsettling experience, not dissimilar to the passions and conflicts stirred up anew in the state of being in love which, from the point of view of the ordinary order and emotional tenor and discipline of life, feels like an illness, with all its deliciousness and pain.

The main enduring view of the concept of transference neurosis, then, to my mind, lies in its defining the nature, scope, and point of impact of psychoanalysis as mental therapy. The issue is that the patient's illness, neurosis, maladjustment, character disorder, regarded as originating in his life experiences from early on, is drawn into a new context, the analytic relationship developing between patient and analyst. In this new context the crucial pathogenic experiences, and the patient's ways of assimilating them, of defending against them, and of letting himself be defeated by them, gain new intensity and urgency. This makes them available for fresh psychic work. Insofar as the pathogenic experiences and pathological ways of coping with them are still active, in the sense in which a volcano is said to be still active, the "passion for transference"—as in the case I described—amounts to no more than a continuation of an acute automatic process transported into the new setting of the analytic situation which then creates the potential for the development of a transference neurosis. In many other cases, processes which had become subterranean or slowed to a standstill or frozen are apt to become more active again in the analytic situation, and all the defensive forces of the patient tend to be mobilized against such reactivation. Here, for long periods of time the prominent task will have to be the analytic work on the defenses in the form of demonstrating them as resistances in the transference setting, i.e., of giving them a transference meaning. In the first type, schematically speaking, resistance against the analytic development of a transference neurosis consists in the direct, unmediated transferred instinctual currents (and of primitive blocks, rather than complex defenses, against them). It is resistance against that aspect of the analytic work which has to do with renewed psychic organization. In the second type, resistance is directed against that disorganization (regression if you will) which is required to make reorganization possible.

Needless to say, almost any actual treatment situation will show both phases or aspects in different combinations, with one or the other predominating at different periods of treatment or depending on the nature of the case. Depending on how far the treatment can be truly psychoanalytic in scope, with the goal of significant psychic reorganization as distinguished from the various superficial, if often at least temporarily helpful rearrangements and readjustments, the point of impact is the transference, and the process of treatment and of change consists in a creative repetition of the disease as transference neurosis. The field of origin and initial action of pathogenic events is the field of interaction between the child and his human environment. The intrapsychic process we call illness, by entering and then being actively engaged in, the new interactional context of the analytic field of forces, becomes transformed into the transference neurosis. The transference neurosis represents "an intermediate region between illness and real life" as well as a transitional stage between disease process and healing process.

Much takes place in psychoanalytic treatment which does not reach such depth or which is preparatory to reaching it and has only delayed and indirect effects. A decisive engagement, such as is represented by a fully developed transference neurosis, may never or not distinctly come to pass in an analysis. Yet the repercussions of what has occurred may turn out to be deeper and more far-reaching than anticipated. A struggle may be won or lost far from the battlefield and by roundabout ways. Significant movements in the process of the transference illness or significant advances toward its resolution may go unnoticed by patient and analyst or may not be available for even disguised communication. The transference neurosis is by no means in all instances or at all times clearly visible and may even be largely a silent process without necessarily losing its impact. Some patients, throughout the analysis, maintain a distance from open emotional involvement with the analyst, and the analytic work may mostly take place at a considerable remove from the transference arena itself. This may but does not necessarily mean that these patients remain isolated from affect and that their gains in self-understanding and self-mastery and release are shallow. But it does probably indicate that such patients have to maintain a kind of narcissistic screen behind which significant inner reorganization may take place, as though the poignant interactions and strong passions of the transference neurosis have to be filtered through this protective screen in order to be bearable and useful.

REFERENCES

Freud, S. (1913), The predisposition to obsessional neurosis. *Standard Edition*, 12:311–326. London: Hogarth Press.
——— (1914), Remembering, repeating and working through. *Standard Edition*, 12:145–156. London: Hogarth Press.

25. Transference Interpretations *Only?*

Nathan Leites

In the following pages I shall be examining Anglo-American psycho-analytic literature (excluding Kleinian) from the late forties to the present. Often I shall express assertions about transference as if I held them, where the context will, I hope, show that they are ideas I describe and discuss. Where I speculate about motives which make for or against the acceptance of a hypothesis, it is, of course, understood that they are not pertinent for assessing its truth or falsity.

The subject with which I shall be concerned is the relationship between interpreting transference on the one hand and interpreting the patient's past and present life outside of the hour on the other hand. That is, I shall not deal with another relationship, which Greenson (1972) and Greenson & Wexler (1969, 1970) have clarified in recent years: the relation between those reactions of the patient to the analyst which are transference and those which are not.

Not being a clinician, I do not attempt to give answers to the questions I raise, or to have a stand on the hypotheses I articulate. But, as the reader will easily see, my prejudices are with Anna Freud, Phyllis Greenacre and Leo Stone rather than with Brian Bird and Paul Gray. That is, while transference interpretation is indeed crucial, non-transference interpretation, it seems to me, may also be of strong importance. However, those whose sympathies are contrary to mine might still be able to disregard my partisan inflections and agree, in whole or in part, with my structuring of the problem. The purpose of this paper is not to judge, but to undertake an operation without which any judgement may be vitiated: to articulate what has unduly been taken for granted—with the accompanying illusion that it had been fully discussed. Capital changes, I shall submit, have occurred—for better or worse—with little confrontation between the hypotheses discarded and those replacing them—both remaining largely unstated even if universally under-

Reprinted by permission from the *International Journal of Psycho-Analysis* 58 (1977):275–87. Copyright © Institute of Psycho-Analysis.

stood. Enhancement of explicitness over previous discussions seems to me a necessary condition for the re-examination of presently-held beliefs. I hope that it also will be useful for further improvement of technique.

TRANSFERENCE AT ALL TIMES

In the classical conception of transference the patient was really concerned with the major persons in his childhood when addressing the analyst. More recently, the patient has come to be viewed as apt to be unconsciously engaged with the analyst while ostensibly absorbed in somebody else. To be sure, it may then be taken for granted that the analyst, in turn, stands for say, a parent. But usually that point is not stressed, and the reaction which is interpreted is not one where the patient does displace towards the analyst, but rather away from him. Formerly, the perceptiveness of the analyst was to reveal the parent behind himself; now he may discover himself behind the parent or spouse. A typical contemporary case is a patient with 'a disposition to pick quarrels with her husband because of his silences'; a conduct which 'diverted a problem from the couch, where she did not verbalize her complaints about the analyst's silence'. The analyst may thus always be present though never in the patient's conscious mind: 'The quarrels with the husband became . . . the sole preoccupation of the patient and the sole content of the analytic sessions' (Kanzer, 1961, pp. 338–9). Thus they were filled with what I propose to call reactions of disguised transference.

That no standard word already exists for this well-known, and, of course, important relationship, indicates how little awareness there has been that 'transference' has, to a substantial extent, reversed its direction. That is, it travels no more only from parent to analyst, but also from the analyst to a person of the patient's past or present. The very magnitude of the shift— putting the analyst where the parent was—seems to have militated against lucidity about it. Sandler and his colleagues recall:

In *The Ego and the Mechanisms of Defence* (1936) Anna Freud had distinguished different types of transference phenomena according to the degree of their complexity. These are: (1) *transference of libidinal impulses,* in which . . . wishes attached to infantile objects . . . attempt to break through towards . . . the analyst; (2) *transference of defence,* in which former defensive measures . . . are repeated; and (3) *acting in the transference,* in which the transference . . . spills over into the patient's . . . life (Sandler *et al.,* 1969, p. 638).

No notice is taken of the fact that the displacement in (3) is not the same as in (1) and (2). It is rare to see Ekstein (1960), reporting upon a patient whose 'association about . . . [an] aunt could be considered a displacement from the analyst,' not call this, as everybody else does, just 'transference' but 'displaced transference' (p. 513). Awareness of the difference on which I am focusing is more muted when Giovacchini (1965) speaks of the 'multiple "transference reactions" that are part of the patient's . . . life' (p. 294): his quotation marks, unexplained, are all that stand between displacing towards the analyst and away from him. The same difference seems obscured when Giovacchini (1965) goes on to note that 'transference reactions . . . converge around the analyst'.

'He reminisced about the sudden death of his father,' recalls Kanzer (1952), re-examining the Rat Man. 'His parent had passed away as the young man lay resting for an hour.' That this memory—there is no suggestion that it is not close to what had happened—came to the patient when he lay resting for an hour in his analyst's presence suggests to Kanzer something unlikely to have occurred to the original analyst of the case: 'death wishes toward Freud?' (Kanzer, 1952, p. 185). Instead of the analyst standing for the parent, as was first thought to be the usual, it is the parent who hides the analyst: 'reverse transference,' in a forgotten coinage of Fenichel's. 'The patient who . . . dwells on a parent . . . who did not understand him,' observes Kanzer (1961) a decade later, 'invites . . . examination of the analyst's current empathy with him' (p. 329). So far from the (perceived) reality of the patient's childhood determining his conception of the analyst, it is the reality of the analyst which fashions the patient's beliefs about his early years; or at least determines which among those he will bring up in the hour. In therapy with Mack Brunswick, the Wolf Man dreams of *his mother* taking holy pictures down from a wall and throwing them to the floor so that they break and fall into bits. The next day he dreams with pleasure of the famous tree, the intertwining of whose branches he admires. This sequence, one may now suggest, expresses 'the wish and the belief that *Mack Brunswick* is powerful enough . . . to rid him of his entanglement with *Freud and his colleagues*'; for one now returns to Rank's contention that the six wolves in the great dream represent six photographs of analysts hung up in Freud's consulting room (Offenkrantz & Tobin, 1973, pp. 76–7; my italics). 'Near the end of the analysis, the patient dreamed of *mother* having a penis and grafting it on to her by intercourse.' The patient penetrates to a deeper layer? Perhaps, but all we are told is that 'this was to be *the analyst's* final "gift" . . .' (Ross, 1973, p. 341; my italics).

In classical transference—displacement from childhood persons to the analyst—the idea of sexual relations with mother evoked more anxiety than that of intercourse with the analyst. In more recent times, the opposite seems implied.

A variety of aspects of the analytic situation foster, as has often been pointed out, 'feelings of safety' (Greenacre, 1966, p. 195). 'Patients are often allowed . . . to experience impulses toward the analyst,' Gray (1973) recalls, 'by virtue of the physically restraining aspect of the couch—both the instruction to remain upon it and the immobility of the position' (p. 485). There is also the patient's 'conviction that the analyst will not get . . . involved by the patient's . . . impulses' (Loewenstein, 1963, p. 466). On the other hand, there persists in the patient 'the fierce parent image of the past, reacting punitively or vengefully to the child's murderous wishes' (Stone, 1967, p. 50). Thus the classical position, which these passages recall, is still presented.

In contrast, more recently it is asserted that the analyst appears to the patient as the most dangerous object of all.

Impulses towards persons with whom the patient is intensely and conflict-ingly involved in life will, it is implied, provoke less anxiety in the hour than those directed towards the analyst. These other persons are—unlike the analyst—absent from the hour; never mind that they may become present shortly! 'The displacement from me to his wife,' reports Gray (1973) about a patient whose fear of his aggression was severe, 'failed to achieve any . . . expression of aggression even at a safer location.' For 'in the presence of the analyst, even in the displacement . . . aggression . . . became unsafe' (pp. 482–3). 'Whenever I made an interpretation of her death wishes toward *me,*' reports Giovacchini (1963) 'she became extremely anxious.' Thereupon, 'as is so often the case,' 'her associations . . . indicated . . . similar feelings towards her *husband and oldest daughter*': a change of target 'helping her to avoid the intense feeling . . . she was . . . experiencing' (p. 144; my italics).

In one affirmation (usually implied), both the analyst and the major persons of childhood are equally unsafe for the patient '. . . Severe hurts in . . . relationships [in life] were acceptable,' Jacobson (1973) reports about a patient, 'as long as they helped avoid . . . the relationship with the analyst,' since the latter 'threatened . . . repetition of childhood humiliations and disappointments' (p. 405).

In a contrasting (also usually implied) assertion, which furnishes the basis for 'reverse transference', within the hour the now distant parents are less formidable than the present analyst; the unconscious has ceased to be timeless. 'He mentioned on several occasions,' Rappaport (1959) remarks about a patient, 'that his father has a foreign accent, but I had to remind him that I, too, had a foreign accent.' There is now nothing unexpected in 'a patient's producing an openly incestuous dream when faced with . . . sexual attraction to the analyst' (Glenn, 1969, p. 360).

To be sure, it is, in Stone's (1967) words, 'a commonplace of . . . conservative analytic technique to be aware of . . . flights into the past' (p. 46)—flights perhaps not only from the analyst, but also from current life. But the trend discussed here goes farther: affirming the *likelihood,* if not more, that when the patient talks about a parent, it is the analyst who is, deeper down, on his mind.

If the word 'transference' designates both displacement towards the analyst and away from him, it becomes possible to assert that '*everything* that goes on in analysis has a transference meaning' (Bird, 1972, p. 267; my italics).

With regard to a patient in whose dreams 'events were always at a distance,' it will now be said that 'this mirrored her relationship with me' (Stewart, 1973, pp. 345–6). This excludes the inverse possibility: that the reaction to the analyst mirrored a pervasive stance established before the analysis and, until this moment, unchanged by it.

The contention that there is nothing but transference in the hour is usually advanced with the implication—rarely more—that observation shows this to be the case. In a few instances, an argument is adumbrated.

Thus, one may (again, of course, implicitly) conclude from the fact that there is transference to there being nothing but it. 'He has to remember,' Heimann (1956) remarks about the analyst in a manner that does not seem distinctively Kleinian, 'that all the patient says and does is taking place in the transference situation' (p. 307): one that apparently renders all that occurs in it of the same consistency.

Or one may infer that all in the hour is transference from the fact that the patient is talking *to* the analyst. 'The patient tells a dream,' Heimann explains, 'not just because it just happened to come into his mind,' i.e., for instance, not because in the analytic situation there is an *Auftreib* (Freud) of unconscious feelings directed towards his early persons, feelings expressed in the dream. Rather, 'it came into his mind because to tell it to his analyst is a suitable way of expressing his impulses toward him' (Heimann, 1956, pp. 305–6). Similarly, according to Kanzer, 'the very communication [to the analyst] of an episode from . . . [the patient's current] life . . . hints at the possibility . . . [of] transference implications' (Kanzer, 1966, p. 536): and such a 'hint' easily becomes a presumption, if not a certainty.

Again, that the patient be exclusively preoccupied with the analyst may seem an expected counterpart to the fact that the analyst is wholly orientated towards the patient. 'His communications,' observed Rycroft (1958) about the patient, 'tend to be concerned, consciously or unconsciously, with the analyst, just as those of the analyst tend [sic] to be concerned with the patient' (p. 410): the patient's spontaneity and the analyst's professional intent will have the same result.

In these various affirmations, the omnipresence of the transference is the situation's doing. But it may be the analyst's: 'The analyst by confrontation and interpretation,' advances Giovacchini (1965), 'introduces a . . . frame of reference causing unconscious determinants to become associated with himself' (p. 294).

Whatever the reason, if the patient's past or his present life appear in the hour, it is not because of the charges attached to them; for in the hour these are drained or dwarfed by the attraction to the analyst. If the patient is concerned with the non-hour in the hour, it is in the service of his hour with his analyst. A patient recalled that his wife, the day before, had become 'explosively irritable' at him, that then 'some anger welled up in himself,' but that he 'had controlled his outward response.' All this, we are told, is due not only or also to the charge of that experience persisting in the hour, but solely to the patient's 'fear of having and revealing such feelings (anger) in my presence'; a fear because of which 'he was required . . . to recapitulate an emotion-controlling sequence' (Gray, 1973, pp. 482–3). Such are the perceptions stemming from what Kanzer (1952) two decades earlier called 'a full appreciation of the extent to which memories constitute . . . reflections of attitudes in the present' (p. 189). In the earlier belief, the patient repeated so as not to remember in the hour; now he remembers so as not to repeat there.

Similarly, if the patient imports into the analysis some stance which has been habitual with him from before, this again is not due to the persistence within the hour of a play of forces reigning outside of it: the trait in question, once it has entered the hour, is merely used by the patient to react to the analyst.

One may now discover transference aspects even in a patient's highly charged and presumably correct memory of an event in his pre-analytic life. The Rat Man during his student days, after his father's death, developed the habit of interrupting his studies *between twelve and one* at night, of opening the door as if someone were standing outside, of taking out his penis and looking at it in *the mirror;* all of which Freud related to the patient's feelings towards his father. But Kanzer, already in the early fifties, discerns transference 'implications' in the one-hour interval during which the patient alternated between 'conforming to and defying . . . the fundamental rule'. (Far from 'the father's ghost . . . [having] settled itself on . . . the analyst,' as the author comments in a classical vein, the analyst's reality penetrates into what existed before him.) Similarly, the pre-analytic 'struggle to control exhibitionism' becomes 'the urge to confess to the therapist, with ultimate sexual aims,' and: 'mirror = analyst?' (Kanzer, 1952, p. 188).

It needs catastrophe to break the reign of transference; happiness will apparently not do. 'Certain contemporary events . . . such as the loss or serious threat of loss of a loved one . . . are' [i.e. should be—N. L.], Gray observes, 'recognized' by the analyst 'as realities "outside" '; that is, 'the resulting emotional task of the patient' does here, and only here, 'extend inside his analytic hours' (Gray, 1973, p. 486).

If *all* in the hour is transference, then at least *much* in the patient's life outside the hour also has that character. Moving in the direction of 'saying' that 'all acting out' does have 'a relation to the transference,' Greenacre (1968) asserts that all acting out 'must be viewed as having at least an implicit relation' of that kind (p. 216). Thereupon, as is usually the case, the law thus advanced is added to the meaning of a pre-existing term (in this case, 'acting out'), without the resulting change of definition being declared. 'In the present context,' observes Brenner (1969), 'the term "acting out" is being used in a . . . limited . . . sense.' For 'it now refers to those situations in which, without the patient being aware of it, his behavior . . . outside the analytic hour expresses . . . the transference, i.e. is motivated by thoughts and feelings about his analyst' (Brenner, 1969, p. 338). (Notice the 'i.e.': in conformity with the tendency noted above, what I called 'disguised' transference has become *the* 'transference'.) Here it is implied that the more recent meaning of 'acting out' is narrower than the early one adopted by Freud which Brenner paraphrases thus: 'patients . . . motivated to action in their . . . lives by wishes and conflicts . . . stirred up by *analysis*' [my italics]. However, proposing to illustrate this original meaning, Brenner turns out to be exemplifying what he asserts to be the present one: the patient 'may . . . embark on a . . . love affair, change his career, . . . decide to marry, for reasons . . . largely unconscious . . . which have to do primarily with wishes concerning his *analyst* and his conflicts about those wishes' [my italics]. Indeed, what now is 'stirred up by analysis' other than reactions towards the analyst?

The accent on disguised transference and the contention that in a patient all is transference, have two obvious appeals. The patient is concerned with nobody but the analyst who has, in the patient's mind, blotted out all past and present outside of the hour. But only the analyst, with his skill and courage, can perceive his own hidden dominance.

STRACHEY'S LAW

With a frequency and emphasis appropriate to the importance of the contention, one hears and reads that the reliving of infantile reactions 'in the *transference*' is a necessary condition for therapeutic effect. It is then implied that only *transference interpretations* contribute directly to that effect (whether or not non-transference interpretations foster transference reactions, which can then become the target of effective interpretations). That implication is, however, rarely made explicit. Indeed, the whole subject of the respective roles of transference and non-transference interpretations is little dealt with in so many words. There is not even a standard term for non(extra)-transference interpretations, also known as interpretations of content.

One is tempted to deny such near-silence on a crucial matter. '[The] unique role given to the transference in the psychoanalytic process to the exclusion of all other avenues of communication,' observes Anna Freud in the later sixties, 'is, to date, one of the points of controversy in the analytic world' (A. Freud, 1969, pp. 147–8). This suggests not only disagreement, but also much printed discussion of it. However, there is, in Anna Freud's own writings, unless I am in error, no place at which she has dealt with this matter in any other way than in passing; nor could anybody, I surmise, cite even a small collection of references in which the 'controversy' would be conducted. Strachey's article of 1934 having been republished in the journal of its original appearance 35 years later acknowledged, to be sure, its importance. But this unusual way of honouring it would hardly have been chosen, had its overwhelming acceptance in the meantime not been accompanied by near-silence in print. Yet according to Menninger & Holzman in the early seventies, there had been 'a running debate between . . . proponents of transference interpretation and proponents of content interpretation' extending over 'decades' (Menninger & Holzman, 1973, p. 138).

To give but a few instances of the actual situation as far as I have been able to perceive it, when in the mid fifties Zetzel reports on a discussion of 'the traditional psychoanalytic technique and its variations,' she allots one line to the mere mention, within parentheses, of a disagreement between Greenacre and Waelder on nothing less than the question whether 'the analysis of the transference situation' is 'the main core of analysis' or not (Zetzel, 1953, p. 533); and, to my knowledge, the remarks of the two contestants have never been published. Dealing with 'the psychoanalytic situation' in a book in the early sixties, Stone (1961) does not focus on the matter. When, late in the decade, he adds a lengthy 'postscript' (Stone, 1967), he does, however, allot two pages to what he himself calls a 'fundamental' question. His introductory lines seem to support my contention that there has been no debate. 'At the Marienbad Symposium' [1937], Stone observes—recalling a crucial event, almost never remembered, 30 years after its occurrence— '*most* of Strachey's colleagues appeared to accept . . . the unique significance of the transference interpretation . . . Nevertheless, there are still *many* who . . . are inclined to doubt . . . [that] uniqueness' (Stone, 1967, pp. 34–5; my italics). This seems to suggest—correctly—that 'many' for several decades formed a silent opposition to an orthodoxy which, in its turn, soon renounced expressing its view in public print. One of the 'technical precepts' to which Brenner addresses himself in the late sixties is the thesis that 'every interpretation must be a transference interpretation, if it is to be effective' (Brenner, 1969, p. 347). Not only does he give to this point but one page of his twenty, he also calls it a 'dictum': it is spoken rather than written. I have chosen the two analysts quoted both because of the relative elaborateness of treatment they accord to our question and because of their prominence. Characteristically, both of them oppose the 'dictum' in question. Its adherents, prevailing in oral communications, have had less of a need to write since the later thirties. Still, Tower may recall 'the universally accepted dictum'—once more that significant word—'that true insight is achieved in the analysis of transferences only' (Tower, 1956, p. 236), which furnished 'a . . . raison d'être' for her own subject, countertransference.

One may prefer affirming the dominance of the transference rather than of the interpretations bearing on it. '[Analytic] work,' Heimann (1956) recalls, 'proceeds through the medium of the patient's emotional relations with his analyst' (p. 303).

Or one may enunciate a mere primacy of transference interpretations— 'the *paramount* role . . . [of] the analysis of transference' (Loewenstein,

1954, p. 190; my italics). This only few would contest. But then one may convey that in fact *only* transference interpretations are effective by neglecting to stake out the implicitly-admitted domain of their rivals. Observing that 'the analyst seeks to . . . [inform the patient] of details and relations within . . . his . . . mental activity which . . . he is unable to perceive or communicate himself,' Rycroft affirms that 'the analyst is able to do this, *largely though not entirely,* because . . . [the patient's] communications *tend* to be concerned, consciously or unconsciously, with the analyst (Rycroft, 1958, p. 410; my italics): he does not further discuss the residual domain indicated by the words I have emphasized.

Or the dictum may be merely an implicit premise of one's reasoning: taken for granted rather than proclaimed. Observing, with regard to patients given to severe regressive states, that 'special care must be taken . . . to bear in mind . . . the fragmentizing effect . . . especially of *genetic* interpretations,' Frosch specifies that 'such *genetic transference* interpretations are . . . made very cautiously early in the treatment of such patients, if at all' (Frosch, 1967, pp. 619–20; my italics).

Alternatively, the affirmation that only 'transference interpretations' are effective may be strengthened by discreetly extending the meaning of the crucial term, clear though it may appear at the outset. 'It often happens,' observes Strachey (1934), 'that when one is *ostensibly* giving an extra-transference interpretation, one is *implicitly* giving a transference one' (p. 290; my italics). As he does not indicate the observations which would decide whether this is the case or not, the statement that only (explicit or implicit) transference interpretations are effective becomes harder to disprove. Saying to the patient, 'You see in your *employer* a replica of your *nurse,*' Kanzer observes, 'the analyst makes clear that *he himself* is neither the nurse nor the employer'; by what is ostensibly a non-transference interpretation, 'he disentangles himself from both components of the transference' (Kanzer, 1953, p. 152; my italics). So why not count this as a 'transference interpretation'?

In the heyday of its proclamation, the mid thirties, the assertion of benefits accruing from transference interpretation was accompanied by denials that advantages might be derived from non-transference interpretations, and even by warnings of the damage they might cause—unless 'they can be made to act as "feeders" for the transference' (Strachey, 1934, p. 290). Since then, this negative complement to the dictum has almost disappeared from print. 'The analyst plays into . . . resistance by directing interpretations extra-analytically *[sic]* rather than to the transference *per se*': who might be the author of this statement appearing in the later sixties? Gitelson, but in a posthumously-published spoken 'aphorism' (Gitelson, 1967, p. 266).

The reticence with which the claim made for transference interpretations has come to be advanced has allowed an extreme variant to progress silently at the expense of a moderate one. When Strachey (1934) put forward his striking contention that only transference interpretations are 'mutative', he added that the breakthroughs operated by them had to be prepared and exploited by numerous 'extra-transference' interpretations (cf. p. 290), in spite of their weakness and dangers (pp. 288–90), Now that derogation of non-transference interpretations has largely ceased, it also appears to me more often implied that non-transference interpretations best be avoided altogether.

A parallel development has perhaps been the slow decline of a classical contention: that analysis begins with a phase in which the analyst's silence and non-transference interpretations foster the arrival of a second phase in which the charges both of the past and of present life have been sharply reduced in favour of the analyst, so that only transference interpretations become appropriate; and will then cure. As time has passed, less seems to be made of the difference between what happens in 'transference neurosis' and non-'transference-neurotic' transference situations (here, too, a standard word appears to be lacking).

The 'dictum' is usually denied in as muted a fashion as it is affirmed. It is exceedingly rare to read a judgement as clear and decisive as that of Menninger & Holzman (1973) who 'dismiss in a sentence' the rival claims made for interpreting resistance, transference, and content: 'all three are necessary' (p. 138).

Even when made openly, a denial of the dictum can still be mitigated. When Stone declares that 'extratransference interpretations cannot be . . . underestimated', he qualifies this commendation not only by a 'it would seem that', but also by making it clear from the start that this is the case 'in an *operational* sense' (Stone, 1967, p. 35; my italics): perhaps transference interpretations retain the privilege of effectiveness in a *theoretical* sense? In another manner, the gravity of denying the dictum is reduced by underestimating what it claims and how widely it is held. '*Some* analysts contend,' Roland observes, 'that *once the transference neurosis is established,* the relevant context *(for dream interpretation)* is always related to the transference neurosis.' It is merely this which, as 'our experience indicates,' is 'very often', but 'definitely not always the case' (Roland, 1971, p. 432; my italics).

Or lack of emphasis may mitigate the denial: that 'interpretations other than those directly and demonstrably impinging on the transference can be . . . effective' is asserted by Stone in a footnote (1961, p. 141). Alternatively, the denial of the dictum may be merely implicit. Thus, according to Anna Freud, 'fixations to repressed traumatic events are loosened with the trauma being brought back to consciousness *in memory,* or relived and interpreted in the transference' (A. Freud, 1965, p. 226; my italics). Those 'resistances [which] stem on the one hand from the ego's attempt to maintain the status quo of defense . . . [and] on the other hand from the id's . . . clinging to distorted forms of satisfaction,' she observes, 'prove to be, when interpreted, *next to the transference,* the best . . . material on the way to analytic cures' (A. Freud, 1969, p. 136; my italics). 'Under . . . [the] heading' that 'there is a hierarchy of interpretations' Loewenstein places '*the choice* between . . . interpretations of transference as opposed to that part of the material which is not included in the patient's relations to the analyst' (Loewenstein, 1951, pp. 6–7; my italics).

Denial may be both implicit and sharp when the equality of transference and non-transference interpretations is bluntly asserted—with regard to some aspect other than effectiveness. 'The interpreting of transference reactions,' it 'seems' to Fenichel in the early forties, 'presents no special problems: everything that has been said about interpretation in general holds true for analysis of the transference' (Fenichel, 1941, p. 73). It was left to Payne to be more explicit: she includes Fenichel among those who 'hold the view that the analysis of instinct derivatives and the defences against them is as important as direct transference interpretations' (Payne, 1946, p. 14). (Once more, there is a saving thought: might these rivals not be 'indirect' transference interpretations?) 'There will, of course, be phantasies in every analysis about the analyst's feelings toward the patient,' observes Little (1951), adding: 'they have to be interpreted *like any other* phantasies' (pp. 38–9; my italics).

Perhaps feeling on firm ground both in past doctrine and current practice, those who deny that transference interpretations only are effective offer few reasons. But there are some. 'The extra-analytic life of the patient,' Stone (1967) advances, includes reactions 'some of which cannot be reproduced in the relationship to the analyst.' For instance, 'there is no repartee . . . in the analysis' (p. 35). Also, the patient's 'reaction to a real danger of dismissal' by an employer may differ from his response to what he in part knows to be the unreal danger of the analyst's abrupt termination of the therapy (ibid.).

As to derivations of the claim that only transference interpretations *are* effective, one which is all too obvious is, perhaps for that reason, rarely adduced: if all reactions of the patient in the hour are transference ones, the 'dictum' follows easily. 'His communications,' Rycroft observes about the patient, 'tend to be concerned, consciously or unconsciously, with the analyst. . . . The analyst's communications to the patient tend, *therefore,* to be concerned with his feelings and ideas about the analyst' (Rycroft, 1958, p. 410; my italics). 'Since all analytic "material" may be construed as [why not: *is?*—N. L.] related to the . . . transference,' argues Stone in a footnote, ' "non-transference" interpretations are . . . derivative extensions *[sic]* of transference interpretations' (Stone, 1961, p. 141)—transference-interpretations-only follows from all-is-transference.

That 'interpretation . . . cannot operate mutatively if applied only to memories,' even of 'highly cathected events or persons' follows for Stone also from an implied assertion of the isomorphy between aetiology and therapy: as 'it is the thrust of . . . impulse . . . and the corresponding defensive structure . . . which give rise to neurosis,' so 'it is a parallel thrust which creates the transference neurosis' through the interpretation of which 'mutation' occurs (Stone, 1967, pp. 40–41).

In another derivation, equally rare, the singular force of transference interpretation is due to the fact that the person who makes it is also the one to whom the reaction interpreted is addressed; that, in Strachey's (1934) less general formulation, 'the giver of the interpretation and the object of the id-impulse interpreted are one and the same person' (p. 290). For this fosters (or even is a necessary condition of) the patient's adopting aspects of the analyst's attitude towards him: a mechanism of cure (ibid.). 'No other situation,' observes Stone, provides for the patient the combined sense of cognitive acquisition . . . [and] acceptance that is implicit in an interpretation made by an individual who is . . . [also the] object of the . . . [patient's] drives . . . [and] defenses' (Stone, 1967, p. 35).

Further, 'no other interpretation is free, within reason, of the doubt introduced by not . . . knowing the 'other person's' [in the patient's past or present life] participation in . . . whatever the issue' (ibid.). 'The analyst can never be as certain of his assessments [of the patient's outside life],' observe

Greenson & Wexler (1969), 'as he is in regard to the relationship . . . between himself and the patient' (p. 34) which procures for transference interpretations a higher chance of being both correct and demonstrable. 'On reviewing the case histories of my [largely psychotic] patients of recent years,' reports Boyer (1971), 'I find I have been confronting them more and more with their . . . distortions of events in the consultation room and less with external events'; for 'where the events are known *to the analyst,*' he 'can then remind the patient of what actually transpired' (p. 71; my italics).

In addition, in the case of transference interpretations, the events interpreted are also better known *to the patient* than those of his past or even of his current life. 'Owing to the fact that the object of the id-impulse is not . . . present,' Strachey (1934) points out, 'it is less easy for the patient, in the case of an extra-transference interpretation, to become . . . aware of the distinction between the real object and the phantasy object' (p. 289). In comparing the pertinence for analysis of the patient's reactions to his current 'objects' as against those he develops towards his analyst, it may indeed be taken for granted that insight into the latter is easier to come by than into the former. 'Following the sessions in which I told him about my move [to another city],' Weiss reports about a patient, 'he gets his girlfriend to act out his grief and despair and his wish to cling to me'; then 'he looks at her with disdain and disgust.' While 'this pattern of . . . projecting his . . . feelings had been repeated many times before,' it 'could not be analysed': 'in the context of the transference neurosis' (Weiss, 1972, p. 509). It is implied— and only that—that had he reacted in similar fashion to being forced to leave an employer to whom he was attached, the chance of insight would have been smaller.

Mainly, however, the claim that only transference interpretations are effective is derived through these propositions: an interpretation is effective only

(*a*) if the reaction interpreted has an *intensity* exceeding a certain (unspecified) level;

(*b*) if that reaction, rather than being remembered (with whatever intensity), occurs *very near* the moment at which it is being interpreted (and, as I have already noted, is directed toward a person *present;* as it so happens, the interpreter himself).

As to (*b*), it follows that only transference interpretations can be effective. If 'in response to transference interpretations repetition gives way to modification,' it is, Heimann explains, 'because the transference interpretation enables the patient's ego to perceive . . . its impulses . . . makes them conscious *at the moment* when they are . . . roused in a direct . . . *immediate relationship with their object.*' For 'immediacy . . . engenders conviction' (Heimann, 1956, p. 305; my italics)—a formulation which perhaps covers both the statement that immediacy *fosters* conviction (uncontroversial, but insufficient to establish the claim for which the point is adduced) and the contention that there is *no* conviction *without* immediacy: sufficient for the conclusion sought, but less convincing than the first variant. 'By being concerned . . . with . . . "outside" reality,' notes Gray (1973), 'a defense against something immediate would be provided' (pp. 480–481).

As to the relationship between the intensity of a reaction and the effectiveness of interpreting it (see (*a*) above), it is advanced that, during the hour, reactions to what is outside it (the patient's past, current, and future life) do not reach the critical level of intensity, unless they are disguised transference reactions or have already been connected with undisguised ones. But transference reactions are apt to qualify.

For, at the moment of interpretation, they and only they are about the present. 'Extra-transference interpretations are far less likely [than transference ones] to be given at the point of urgency,' Strachey explains, 'since the object of the id-impulse which is brought into consciousness . . . is not . . . present.' That is, as these interpretations are 'concerned with impulses . . . distant . . . in time,' these impulses 'are . . . likely to be devoid of . . . energy' (Strachey, 1934, p. 289).

Thus 'the analyst is not . . . primarily to interpret something that happened in the past; it is happening now' (Heimann, 1956, p. 307). 'The reality,' recalls Little (1957), 'that is present . . . in every analysis is the analyst himself' (p. 251).

Before him, life pales. 'As is usual with patients who lose loved objects during analysis,' one may report about one who lost both parents early in his treatment, 'he showed practically no grief or mourning . . . at the time, since, *as we would expect,* the analyst *immediately* replaces the lost parent,' —in this case parents. However, 'I felt the mourning would be activated . . . during . . . termination' (Weiss, 1972, p. 507; my italics), with the aid of the patient's reacting strongly, of course, to the loss of his analyst.

A rare acknowledgement of life being highly charged even during analysis may be facilitated by the consequences being a transference interpretation after all. 'I did not interpret the dream to him in terms of his feelings about

his wife,' Klauber reports, 'as I considered that her failure to accept their
. . . child rendered his feelings of rejection by her too painful for my
intervention.' It was for this reason that 'I related my interpretation . . . to
the transference. I suggested that the dream referred to his . . . having missed
sessions owing to his trip and to his jealousy over what other patients I might
have been seeing in his hours' (Klauber, 1967, p. 426).

But it is unusual to find the affirmation that life becomes insignificant in
the hour clearly denied. 'I think it is rare,' observes Stone in this rare vein,
'that the analysis . . . exceeds in importance the other major concerns . . .
of the patients' life' ('nor do I think it desirable,' he adds, 'that this should
occur'). That is, 'except in . . . rare instances . . . the analyst cannot be
assigned all . . . transference roles'. More particularly, 'he is usually predominantly in one of these roles [those of mother or father] for long periods,'
while 'somebody else [is] representing the other' (Stone, 1967, pp. 33–4).

As the hour drains the charge of current life, so it does that of the past.
Or, as we have already seen, the mere passage of time is now believed to
reduce even crucial early charges. Even in analysis, 'conflicts of the remote
past' remain 'concerned with dead circumstances and mummified personalities' (Strachey, 1934, p. 277). 'Impulses . . . distant . . . in time . . . are
. . . likely to be devoid of energy' (Strachey, 1934, p. 289) and remain that
way, the analytic situation notwithstanding. When 'the patient is . . . looking
back . . . at what he once felt with his parents,' Heimann (1956) reports
from her experience, he does so 'coolly and intellectually' (p. 307). Wallerstein (1967) records:

The central event of . . . [a] patient's growing up concerned the father's abrupt
disappearance from her life when she was seven. For some time he had been engaged
in . . . sexual play in front of and with his three children. . . . Apparently one of the
servants got wind of the patient's involvement in these episodes, and this led to the
patient being forced to divulge it all to her mother. The patient did not remember
seeing her father after that. . . . Only after several years of analysis upon insistent
direct questioning did the patient find out from her mother that the father had been
'put on a boat to Australia.' . . . [Now when] these memories returned [they were]
devoid of affect. . . . On the other hand, whenever I would be gone . . . even if only
for a few days, she would be seized by an intense fear that I would disappear. . . .
(pp. 570–571)

In such circumstances—and it is more and more implied that they predominate—'the . . . transference interpretation . . . has the . . . advantage,'
in Heimann's (1970) words, 'that it bridges the actual ego with its *lost* past'

(p. 146; my italics). But we hear less and less how the arousal of feelings towards the present—the analyst—led to the emergence of repressed early affects—that reappearance which used to heal. Now their recovery 'in the transference' may suffice.

The contrary configuration—'she could experience with full force . . . her affect in relation to her mother (though not to me)' (Klauber, 1967, p. 431)—is rarely mentioned and apt to be forgotten when one goes 'theoretical'.

Thus the earlier belief in the power of the analytic situation to conjure up the past in strength has by now, to a substantial extent, been tacitly abandoned. It is rare to continue declaring that 'in the psychoanalytic situation . . . [the] backward look becomes very vivid,' that 'the "I" of . . . [the] present moment . . . is then replaced by the I of a dozen years ago, or a score' [notice the modesty of the amounts—N.L.] (Menninger & Holzman, 1973, pp. 71–2). Rather, what used to be a central tenet may now be discreetly expressed when the emphasis is on the opposite. 'During unhappy love affairs and during . . . mourning,' explains Anna Freud, 'insufficient libido is available' not only 'to cathect . . . the analyst'—first thought—but also 'to flow back to "the past" ' (A. Freud, 1958, pp. 146–7). If it still does, just one part of the analytic situation—naturally, the analyst as target of the patient's feelings—may be singled out as responsible for the event. Thus, there is, Stone advances, paraphrasing Loewenstein, '[a] heightened subjective reality with which a memory . . . [becomes] invested, *in being communicated to the analyst*' (Stone, 1961, p. 97; my italics). Or the resurrection of memory by the analytic situation may be but a transition precisely to transference. 'The analyst's request for free association,' observes Nunberg in the early fifties—still stressing a factor which came to be rarely mentioned when transference had become 'the driving force acting throughout the . . . analytic process' (Veszy-Wagner, 1961, p. 33)—'stimulates reproduction of old memories' which, in turn, 'stirs up emotions which once accompanied them.' However, 'these emotions' do not with interpretation, permit the beginning of insight as the next step. What follows is, rather, that they 'try to attach themselves to the only real object available, the psychoanalyst' (Nunberg, 1951, p. 4).

If the past succeeds in this attempt, it becomes capable of being resurrected, through the mediation of the present: the analyst. 'There are moments in the analysis,' Heimann (1956) observes, 'when the patient recovers his . . . original objects. He then dwells on memories . . . , speaks with deep

. . . concern about them. . . . [His] original objects . . . are . . . present, they are felt as . . . [a] part of . . . his present life.' A crucial aspect of the analytic process, other than transference? No, for it is 'transference interpretations [which] have led to contact with the object from whom . . . conflicts had been transferred' (Heimann, 1956, p. 309); the object with whom no direct contact is possible. That this is so may be taken for granted, occasionally even by an analyst who demurs from that thesis when it confronts him explicitly. Thus, for Anna Freud (1958), the 'elusive mood swings of adolescence . . . , unlike the affective states of infancy and early childhood, seem disinclined to re-emerge . . .'—in analysis? No, 'in connection with the person of the analyst' (A. Freud, 1958, p. 143): they just cannot emerge without that connexion.

At the very least, it will take 'unusual events in the patient's life,' such as 'bereavement or threat of bereavement' to make him 'not take the detour via the transference,' but rather directly 'arrive at . . . contact with his original objects' (Heimann, 1956, p. 310): what used to be the normal power of the analytic situation has now become the privilege of catastrophe (even that extremity, as we have seen earlier, may not suffice to break through the wall which the analyst interposes). Short of disaster, the transfer of the forgotten past not on to the analyst, but on to all other domains of the present, is as incapable of procuring access to crucial memories as the transference on to the analyst is continuously adequate for this effect.

Does this belief—as well as the others discussed previously—command practice as much as it expresses conviction? Discussing ' "positive transference" . . . in the sense of that . . . which carries the whole process of an analysis,' Loewald (1960) notes that it 'tends to be discredited in modern analytic writing and teaching, although not in treatment itself' (p. 32). Perhaps such a divergence is not limited to this particular aspect of a subject to which so much contained passion is attached.

Were there less of that, more attention and even assent might have been accorded to those who, while of course 'not in doubt regarding the great value of transference interpretations,' still, with Stone (1967), 'are inclined to doubt their uniqueness' (pp. 34–5). The distinctive point here does not seem to be, as Stone suggests, 'the importance' accorded to 'economic considerations in determining . . . whether transference or extra-transference interpretations . . . [are] indicated' (p. 35). Rather, it is the abandonment of the certainty (portrayed above) that such considerations will *always* be in favour of a transference interpretation; i.e. that the charge of a transference reaction is *always* higher than that of one not directly involving the analyst (for what, after all, in analysis is not connected with him obliquely?). *'Many times'* —thus Greenacre formulates what is uncontroversial—in the transference 'memories' are 'not merely . . . talked about with a *partial* reliving' but rather 'being . . . experienced with . . . *full* . . . resonance'; which 'probably' makes transference, *then*, 'the most convincing medium of . . . interpretation' (Greenacre,1954, p. 674; my italics). There are, however, it is thus implied, also moments in analyses—absent in some, rare in others, perhaps frequent in a few—when the unmediated 'reliving' of crucial memories furnishes more 'resonance' for an interpretation than the patient's reactions to the analyst. On the other hand, of course, and still in Greenacre's words, 'the person of the analyst may assume even greater significance than that of reality relationships of past or present' (Greenacre, 1959, p. 489). In this case, one will interpret the transference—not because of the absolute weakness of everything else (as advocates of transference-interpretations-only are apt to imply), but rather because of the even higher force of the patient's reactions to the analyst. The situation just described is *frequent* enough. It is not, for all that, *constant* in analysis, as it indeed would be if it followed from the mere fact that, for the patient, there is only one human presence: the analyst.

ACKNOWLEDGEMENTS

Micheline Guiton allowed me to consult an unpublished manuscript on the treatment of the matters discussed above in French psychoanalysis; Ralph Greenson and Robert Stoller helpfully reviewed an earlier draft; Louise Strouse suggested changes in formulations.

REFERENCES

Bird, B. (1972). Notes on transference: universal phenomenon and hardest part of analysis. *J. Am. Psychoanal. Assn.* **20**, 267–301.

Boyer, L. B. (1971). Psychoanalytic technique in the treatment of certain characterological and schizophrenic disorders. *Int. J. Psycho-Anal.* **52**, 67–85.

Brenner, C. (1969). Some comments on technical precepts in psycho-analysis. *J. Am Psychoanal. Assn.* **17**, 333–352.

Ekstein, R. (1960). A historical survey on the teaching of psycho-analytic technique. *J. Am. Psychoanal. Assn.* **8**, 500–516.

Fenichel, O. (1941). *Problems of Psychoanalytic Technique*. New York: Psychoanalytic Quarterly Inc.

Freud, A. (1958). Adolescence. In *Research at the Hampstead Child Therapy Clinic and Other Papers.* New York: International Universities Press, 1969.

Freud, A. (1965). *Normality and Pathology in Childhood.* London: Hogarth Press.

Freud, A. (1969). Difficulties in the path of psychoanalysis. In *Problems of Psychoanalytic Technique and Theory.* London: Hogarth Press, 1972.

Frosch, J. (1967). Severe regressive states during analysis: introduction. *J. Am. Psychoanal. Assn.* **15,** 491–507, 619–620.

Giovacchini, P. (1963). Somatic symptoms and the transference neurosis. *Int. J. Psycho-Anal.* **44,** 143–150.

Giovacchini, P. (1965). Transference, therapy and synthesis. *Int. J. Psycho-Anal.* **46,** 287–296.

Gitelson, M. (1967). Analytic aphorisms. *Psychoanal. Q.* **36,** 260–270.

Glenn, J. (1969). Testicular and scrotal masturbation. *Int. J. Psycho-Anal.* **50,** 353–362.

Gray, P.(1973). Psychoanalytic technique and the ego's capacity for viewing intrapsychic activity. *J. Am. Psychoanal. Assn.* **21,** 474–494.

Greenacre, P.(1954). The role of transference: practical considerations in relation to psychoanalytic therapy. *J. Am. Psychoanal. Assn.* **2,** 671–684.

Greenacre, P. (1959). Certain technical problems in the transference relationship. *J. Am. Psychoanal. Assn.* **7,** 484–502.

Greenacre, P. (1966). Problems of overidealization of the analyst and of analysis: their manifestations in the transference and countertransference relationship. *Psychoanal. Study Child* **21.**

Greenacre, P. (1968). The psychoanalytic process, transference, and acting out. *Int. J. Psycho-Anal.* **49,** 211–218.

Greenson, R. R. (1972). Beyond transference and interpretation. *Int. J. Psycho-Anal.* **53,** 213–217.

Greenson, R. R. & Wexler, M. (1969). The nontransference relationship in the psychoanalytic situation. *Int. J. Psycho-Anal.* **50,** 27–39.

Greenson, R. R. & Wexler, M. (1970). Discussion of 'The non-transference relationship in the psychoanalytic situation.' *Int. J. Psycho-Anal* **51,** 143–145, 147–150.

Heimann, P. (1956). Dynamics of transference interpretations. *Int. J. Psycho-Anal.* **37,** 303–310.

Heimann, P. (1970). Opening remarks to a discussion of 'The non-transference relationship in the psychoanalytic situation.' *Int. J. Psycho-Anal.* **51,** 145–147.

Jacobson, J. G. (1973). Reliving the past, perceptual experience and the reality-testing functions of the ego. *Int. J. Psycho-Anal.* **54,** 399–413.

Kanzer, M. (1952). The transference neurosis of the Rat Man. *Psychoanal. Q.* **21,** 181–189.

Kanzer, M. (1953). Past and present in the transference. *J. Am. Psychoanal. Assn.* **1,** 144–154.

Kanzer, M. (1961). Verbal and nonverbal aspects of free association. *Psychoanal. Q.* **30,** 327–350.

Kanzer, M. (1966). The motor sphere of the transference. *Psychoanal. Q.* **35,** 522–539.

Klauber, J. (1967). On the significance of reporting dreams in psychoanalysis. *Int. J. Psycho-Anal.* **48,** 424–432.

Little, M. (1951). Countertransference and the patient's response to it. *Int. J. Psycho-Anal.* **32,** 32–40.

Little, M. (1957). 'R'—the analyst's total response to his patient's needs. *Int. J. Psycho-Anal.* **38,** 240–254.

Loewald, H. D. (1960). On the therapeutic action of psychoanalysis. *Int. J. Psycho-Anal.* **41,** 16–33.

Loewenstein, R. M. (1951). The problem of interpretation. *Psychoanal. Q.* **20,** 1–14.

Loewenstein, R. M. (1954). Some remarks on defences, autonomous ego and psychoanalytic technique. *Int. J. Psycho-Anal.* **35,** 188–193.

Loewenstein, R. M. (1963). Some considerations on free association. *J. Am. Psychoanal. Assn.* **11,** 451–473.

Menninger, K. A. & Holzman, P. S. (1973). *Theory of Psychoanalytic Technique.* New York. Basic Books.

Nunberg, H. (1951). Transference and reality. *Int. J. Psycho-Anal.* **32,** 1–9.

Offenkrantz, W. & Tobin, A. (1973). Problems of the therapeutic alliance: Freud and the Wolf Man. *Int. J. Psycho-Anal.* **54,** 75–78.

Payne, S. (1946). Notes on the development of theory and practice in psychoanalytic technique. *Int. J. Psycho-Anal.* **27,** 12–19.

Rappaport, E. A. (1959). The first dream in an erotized transference. *Int. J. Psycho-Anal.* **40,** 240–245.

Roland, A. (1971). The context and unique function of dreams in psychoanalytic therapy: clinical approach. *Int. J. Psycho-Anal.* **52,** 431–439.

Ross, M. (1973). Some clinical and theoretical aspects of working through. *Int. J. Psycho-Anal.* **54,** 331–343.

Rycroft, C. (1958). An enquiry into the function of words in the psychoanalytical situation. *Int. J. Psycho-Anal.* **39,** 408–415.

Sandler, J., Holder, A., Kawenoka, M., Kennedy, H. E. & Neurath, L. (1969). Notes on some theoretical and clinical aspects of transference. *Int. J. Psycho-Anal.* **50,** 633–645.

Stewart, H. (1973). The experiencing of the dream and the transference. *Int. J. Psycho-Anal.* **54,** 345–347.

Stone, L. (1961). *The Psychoanalytic Situation.* New York: International Universities Press.

Stone, L. (1967). The psychoanalytic situation and transference: postscript to an earlier communication. *J. Am. Psychoanal. Ass.* **15,** 3–58.

Strachey, J. (1934). The nature of the therapeutic action of psychoanalysis. [Reprinted] *Int. J. Psycho-Anal.* **50** (1969), 275–292.

Tower, L. (1956). Countertransference. *J. Am. Psychoanal. Assn.* **4,** 224–255.

Veszy-Wagner, L. (1961). The analytic screen: an instrument or an impediment in the psychoanalytic technique. *Int. J. Psycho-Anal.* **42,** 32–42.

Wallerstein, R. S. (1967). Reconstruction and mastery in the transference psychosis. *J. Am. Psychoanal. Assn.* **15,** 551–583.

Weiss, S. S. (1972). Some thoughts and clinical vignettes on translocation of an analytic practice. *Int. J. Psycho-Anal.* **53,** 505–513.

Zetzel, E. (reporter) (1953). Panel on 'The traditional psychoanalytic technique and its variations.' *J. Am. Psychoanal. Assn.* **1,** 526–537.

26. The Psychoanalytic Treatment of Narcissistic Personality Disorders: Outline of a Systematic Approach

Heinz Kohut

INTRODUCTORY CONSIDERATIONS

The classification of the transferencelike structures mobilized during the analysis of narcissistic personalities presented here is based on previous conceptualizations (Kohut, 1966) of which only the following brief summary can be given. It was suggested that the child's original narcissistic balance, the perfection of his primary narcissism, is disturbed by the unavoidable shortcomings of maternal care, but that the child attempts to save the original experience of perfection by assigning it on the one hand to a grandiose and exhibitionistic image of the self: the *grandiose self*, and, on the other hand, to an admired you: the *idealized parent imago*. The central mechanisms which these two basic narcissistic configurations employ in order to preserve a part of the original experience are, of course, antithetical. Yet they coexist from the beginning and their individual and largely independent lines of development are open to separate scrutiny. At this moment it can only be pointed out that, under optimum developmental conditions, the exhibitionism and grandiosity of the archaic grandiose self are gradually tamed, and that the whole structure ultimately becomes integrated into the adult personality and supplies the instinctual fuel for our ego-syntonic ambitions and purposes, for the enjoyment of our activities, and for important aspects of our self-esteem. And, under similarly favorable circumstances, the idealized parent imago, too, becomes integrated into the adult personality. Introjected as our idealized superego, it becomes an important component of our psychic organization by holding up to us the guiding leadership of its ideals. If the child, however, suffers severe narcissistic traumata, then the grandiose self does not merge into the relevant ego content but is retained in its unaltered form

Reprinted from the *Psychoanalytic Study of the Child* 23 (1968):86–113, by permission of International Universities Press, Inc.

and strives for the fulfillment of its archaic aims. And if the child experiences traumatic disappointments in the admired adult, then the idealized parent imago, too, is retained in its unaltered form, is not transformed into tension-regulating psychic structure but remains an archaic, transitional object that is required for the maintenance of narcissistic homeostasis.

Severe regressions, whether occurring spontaneously or during therapy, may lead to the activation of unstable, prepsychological fragments of the mind-body-self and its functions which belong to the stage of *autoerotism* (cf. Nagera, 1964). The pathognomonically specific, transferencelike, thera-peutically salutary conditions, however, on which I am focusing, are based on the activation of psychologically elaborated, cohesive configurations which enter into stable amalgamations with the *narcissistically* perceived psychic representation of the analyst. The relative stability of this narcissistic trans-ference-amalgamation, however, is the prerequisite for the performance of the analytic task in the pathogenic narcissistic areas of the personality.

THE NARCISSISTIC TRANSFERENCES

I shall now examine the two narcissistic transferences delimited in accord-ance with the previously given conceptualizations: the therapeutic activation of the idealized parent imago for which the term *idealizing transference* will be employed and the activation of the grandiose self which will be called the *mirror transference*.

Therapeutic Activation of the Idealized Parent Imago: The Idealizing Transference

The *idealizing transference* is the therapeutic revival of the early state in which the psyche saves a part of the lost experience of global narcissistic perfection by assigning it to an archaic (transitional) object, the idealized parent imago. Since all bliss and power now reside in the idealized object, the child feels empty and powerless when he is separated from it and he attempts, therefore, to maintain a continuous union with it.

Idealization, whether it is directed at a dimly perceived archaic mother-breast or at the clearly recognized oedipal parent, belongs genetically and dynamically in a narcissistic context. The idealizing cathexes, however, although retaining their narcissistic character, become increasingly neutral-ized and aim-inhibited. It is especially in the most advanced stages of their early development that the idealizations (which now coexist with powerful object-instinctual cathexes) exert their strongest and most important influence on the phase-appropriate internalization processes. At the end of the oedipal period, for example, the internalization of object-cathected aspects of the parental imago accounts for the contents (i.e., the commands and prohibitions) and functions (i.e., praise, scolding, punishment) of the superego; the internalization of the narcissistic aspects, however, for the exalted position of these contents and functions. It is from the narcissistic instinctual component of their cathexes that the aura of absolute perfection of the values and standards of the superego and of the omniscience and might of the whole structure are derived. That stream of narcissism, however, which is subsumed under the term idealized parent imago remains vulnerable throughout its whole early development, i.e., from the stage of the incipient, archaic idealized object (which is still almost merged with the self) to the time of the massive reinternalization of the idealized aspect of the imago of the oedipal parent (who is already firmly established as separate from the self). The period of greatest vulnerability ends when an idealized nuclear superego has been formed, since the capacity for the idealization of his central values and standards which the child thus acquires exerts a lasting beneficial influence on the psychic economy in the narcissistic sectors of the personality.

The beginning of latency, however, may be considered as still belonging to the oedipal phase. It constitutes the last of the several periods of greatest danger in early childhood during which the psyche is especially susceptible to traumatization because after a spurt of development a new balance of psychological forces is only insecurely established. If we apply this *principle of the vulnerability of new structures* to the superego at the beginning of latency and, in particular, to the newly established idealization of its values and standards and of its rewarding and punishing functions, it will not surprise us to learn from clinical experience that a severe disappointment in the idealized oedipal object, even at the beginning of latency, may yet undo a precariously established idealization of the superego, may recathect the imago of the idealized object, and thus lead to a renewed insistence on finding an external object of perfection.

Under optimal circumstances the child experiences gradual disappointment in the idealized object—or, expressed differently: the child's evaluation of the idealized object becomes increasingly realistic—which leads to a withdrawal of the narcissistic idealizing cathexes from the object imago and to their gradual (or more massive but phase-appropriate) internalization, i.e., to the acquisition of permanent psychological structures which continue, endopsychically, the functions which had previously been fulfilled by the idealized object. If the child's relationship to the idealized object is, however, severely disturbed, e.g., if he suffers a traumatic (intense and sudden, or not phase-appropriate) disappointment in it, then the child does not acquire the needed internal structure, but his psyche remains fixated on an archaic object imago, and the personality will later, and throughout life, be dependent on certain objects in what seems to be an intense form of object hunger. The intensity of the search for and of the dependency on these objects is due to the fact that they are striven for as a substitute for missing segments of the psychic structure. These objects are not loved for their attributes, and their actions are only dimly recognized; they are needed in order to replace the functions of a segment of the mental apparatus which had not been established in childhood.

The structural defects which are the result of early disturbances in the relationship with the idealized object cannot be discussed within the confines of this essay. The following clinical illustration will instead focus on the effect of later traumatic disappointments, up to and including early latency.

Mr. A., a tall, asthenic man in his late twenties, was a chemist in a pharmaceutical firm. Although he entered analysis with the complaint that he felt sexually stimulated by men, it soon became apparent that his homosexual preoccupations constituted only one of the several indications of an underlying broad personality defect. More important were periods of feeling depressed (with an associated drop in his work capacity); and, as a trigger to the preceding disturbance, a specific vulnerability of his self-esteem, manifested by his sensitivity to criticism, or simply to the absence of praise, from the people whom he experienced as his elders or superiors. Thus, although he was a man of considerable intelligence who performed his tasks with skill and creative ability, he was forever in search of approval: from the head of the research laboratory where he was employed, from a number of senior colleagues, and from the fathers of the girls whom he dated. He was sensitively aware of these men and of their opinion of him. So long as he felt that they approved of him, he experienced himself as whole, acceptable, and capable; and was then indeed able to do well in his work and to be creative and successful. At slight signs of disapproval of him, however, or of lack of understanding for him, he would become depressed, would tend to become first enraged and then cold, haughty, and isolated, and his creativeness deteriorated.

The cohesive transference permitted the gradual reconstruction of a certain genetically decisive pattern. Repeatedly, throughout his childhood, the patient had felt abruptly disappointed in the power of his father just when he had (re-)established him as a figure of protective strength and efficiency. As is frequent, the first memories which the patient supplied subsequent to the transference activations of the crucial pattern referred to a comparatively late period. The family had come to the United States when the patient was nine and the father, who had been prosperous in Europe, was unable to repeat his earlier successes in this country. Time and again, however, the father shared his newest plans with his son and stirred the child's fantasies and expectations; but time and again he sold out in panic when the occurrence of unforeseen events and his lack of familiarity with the American scene combined to block his purposes. Although these memories had always been conscious, the patient had not previously appreciated the intensity of the contrast between the phase of great trust in the father, who was most confidence-inspiring while he was forging his plans, and the subsequent disappointment.

Most prominent among the patient's relevant recollections of earlier occurrences of the idealization-disappointment sequence were those of two events which affected the family fortunes decisively when the patient was six and eight years old respectively. The father who, during the patient's early childhood, had been a virile and handsome man had owned a small but flourishing industry. Judging by many indications and memories, father and son had been very close emotionally and the son had admired his father greatly. Suddenly, when the patient was six, German armies invaded the country, and the family, which was Jewish, fled. Although the father had initially reacted with helplessness and panic, he had later been able to re-establish his business, though on a much reduced scale, but, as a consequence of the German invasion of the country to which they had escaped (the patient was eight at that time), everything was again lost and the family had to flee once more.

The patient's memories implicated the beginning of latency as the period when the structural defect was incurred. There is no doubt, however, that earlier experiences, related to his pathological mother, had sensitized him and accounted for the severity of the later acquired structural defect.

Described in metapsychological terms, his defect was the insufficient idealization of the superego and, concomitantly, a recathexis of the idealized parent imago of the late preoedipal and the oedipal stages. The symptomatic result of this defect was circumscribed yet profound. Since the patient had suffered a traumatic disappointment in the narcissistically invested aspects of the father imago, his superego did not possess the requisite exalted status and was thus unable to raise the patient's self-esteem. In view of the fact, however, that the patient had not felt equally deprived of those aspects of the father imago that were invested with object-instinctual cathexes, his superego was relatively intact with regard to those of its contents and functions that were built up as the heir to the object-instinctual dimensions of the oedipal father relationship. His nuclear goals and standards were indeed those of his cultural background transmitted by his father; what he lacked was the ability to feel more than a fleeting sense of satisfaction when living up to his standards or reaching his goals. Only through the confirmatory approval of external admired figures was he able to obtain a sense of heightened self-esteem. In the transference he seemed thus insatiable in two demands that he directed toward the idealized analyst: that the analyst share the patient's values, goals, and standards (and thus imbue them with significance through their idealization); and that the analyst confirm through the expression of a warm glow of pleasure and participation that the patient had lived up to his values and standards and had successfully worked toward a goal. Without the analyst's expression of his empathic comprehension of these needs, the patient's values and goals seemed trite and uninspiring to him and his successes were meaningless and left him feeling depressed and empty.

The Genesis of the Pathogenic Fixation on the Idealized Parent Imago

As can be regularly ascertained, the essential genetic trauma is grounded in the parents' own narcissistic fixations, and the parents' narcissistic needs contribute decisively to the child's remaining enmeshed within the narcissistic web of the parents' personality until, for example, the sudden recognition of the shortcomings of the parent, or the child's sudden desperate recognition of how far out of step his own emotional development has become, confronts him with the insuperable task of achieving the wholesale internalization of a chronic narcissistic relationship. The complexity of the pathogenic interplay between parent and child, and the varieties of its forms, defy a comprehensive description. Yet in a properly conducted analysis, the crucial pattern will often emerge with great clarity.

Mr. B., for example, established a narcissistic transference in which the analyst's presence increased and solidified his self-esteem and thus, secondarily, improved his ego functioning and efficiency.[1] To any impending disruption of this beneficial deployment of narcissistic cathexes, he responded with rage, and with a decathexis of the narcissistically invested analyst, and a hypercathexis of his grandiose self, manifested by cold and imperious behavior. But, finally (after the analyst had gone away, for example), he reached a comparatively stable balance: he withdrew to lonely intellectual activities which, although pursued with less creativity than before, provided him with a sense of self-sufficiency. In his words, he "rowed out alone to the middle of the lake and looked at the moon." When, however, the possibility of re-establishing the relationship to the narcissistically invested object offered itself, he reacted with the same rage that he had experienced when the transference—to use his own significant analogy—had become "unplugged." At first I thought that the reaction was nonspecific, consisting of yet unexpressed rage about the analyst's leaving, and of anger at having to give up a new-found protective balance. These explanations were, however, incomplete since the patient was in fact by his reactions describing an important sequence of early events. The patient's mother had been intensely enmeshed with him, and had supervised and controlled him in a most stringent fashion. His exact feeding time, for example, and in later childhood, his eating time, was determined by a mechanical timer—reminiscent of the devices which Schreber's father employed with his children (Niederland, 1959)—and thus the child felt that he had no mind of his own and that his mother was continuing to perform his mental functions long beyond the time when such maternal activities, carried out empathically, are indeed phase-appropriate and required. Under the impact of the anxious recognition of the inappropriateness of this relationship, he would in later childhood withdraw to his room to think his own thoughts, uninfluenced by her interference. When he had just begun to achieve some reliance on this minimum of autonomous functioning, his mother had a buzzer installed. From then on, she would interrupt his attempts of internal separation from her whenever he wanted to be alone. The buzzer summoned him more compellingly (because the mechanical device was experienced as akin to an endopsychic communication) than would have her voice or knocking. No wonder, then, that he reacted with rage to the return of the analyst after he had "rowed to the center of the lake to look at the moon."

The Process of Working Through and Some Other Clinical Problems in the Idealizing Transference

Little need be said concerning the beginning of the analysis. Although there may be severe resistances, especially those motivated by apprehensions about the extinction of individuality due to the wish to merge into the idealized object, the pathognomonic regression will establish itself spontaneously if the analyst does not interfere by premature transference interpretations. The working-through phase of the analysis can, however, begin only after the pathognomonic idealizing transference has been firmly established. It is set into motion by the fact that the instinctual equilibrium which the analysand aims to maintain is sooner or later disturbed. In the undisturbed transference the patient feels powerful, good, and capable. Anything, however, that deprives him of the idealized analyst creates a disturbance of his self-esteem: he feels powerless and worthless, and if his ego is not assisted by interpretations concerning the loss of the idealized parent imago, the patient may turn to archaic precursors of the idealized parent imago or may abandon it altogether and regress further to reactively mobilized archaic stages of the grandiose self. The retreat to archaic idealizations may manifest itself in the form of vague, impersonal, trancelike religious feelings; the hypercathexis of archaic forms of the grandiose self and of the (autoerotic) body self will produce the syndrome of emotional coldness, tendency toward affectation in speech and behavior, shame propensity, and hypochondria.

Although such temporary cathectic shifts toward the archaic stages of the idealized parent imago and of the grandiose self are common occurrences in the analysis of narcissistic personalities, they may be precipitated by seemingly minute narcissistic injuries the discovery of which may put the analyst's empathy and clinical acumen to a severe test.

The essence, however, of the curative process in the idealizing transference can be epitomized in a few comparatively simple principles. A working-through process is set in motion in which the repressed narcissistic strivings with which the archaic object is invested are admitted into consciousness. Although the ego and superego resistances with which we are familiar from the analysis of the transference neuroses also do occur here, and although there are in addition specific ego resistances (motivated by anxiety concerning hypomanic overstimulation) which oppose the mobilization of the idealizing cathexes, the major part of the working-through process concerns the loss of the narcissistically experienced object. If the repeated interpretations of the meaning of separations from the analyst on the level of the idealizing narcissistic libido are given with correct empathy for the analysand's feelings —in particular for what appears to be his lack of emotions, i.e., his coldness and retreat, e.g., in response to separations—then there will gradually emerge a host of meaningful memories which concern the dynamic prototypes of the present experience. The patient will recall lonely hours during his childhood in which he attempted to overcome a feeling a fragmentation, hypochondria, and deadness which was due to the separation from the idealized parent. And he will remember, and gratefully understand, how he tried to substitute for the idealized parent imago and its functions by creating erotized replacements and through the frantic hypercathexis of the grandiose self: how he rubbed his face against the rough floor in the basement, looked at the mother's photograph, went through her drawers and smelled her underwear; and how he turned to the performance of grandiose athletic feats in which flying fantasies were being enacted by the child, in order to reassure himself. Adult analogues in the analysis (during the weekend, for example) are intense voyeuristic preoccupations, the impulse to shoplift, and recklessly speedy drives in the car. Childhood memories and deepening understanding of the analogous transference experiences converge in giving assistance to the patient's ego, and the formerly automatic reactions become gradually more aim-inhibited.

The ego acquires increasing tolerance for the analyst's absence and for the analyst's occasional failure to achieve a correct empathic understanding. The patient learns that the idealizing libido need not be immediately withdrawn from the idealized imago and that the painful and dangerous regressive shifts of the narcissistic cathexes can be prevented. Concomitant with the increase of the ability to maintain a part of the idealizing investment despite the separation, there is also an enhancement of internalization, i.e., the analysand's psychic organization acquires the capacity to perform some of the functions previously performed by the idealized object.

Therapeutic Activation of the Grandiose Self:
The Mirror Transference

Analogous to the idealized object in the idealizing transference, it is the grandiose self which is reactivated in the transferencelike condition referred to as the *mirror transference.*

The mirror transference constitutes the therapeutic revival of the developmental stage in which the child attempts to retain a part of the original, all-embracing narcissism by concentrating perfection and power upon a grandiose self and by assigning all imperfections to the outside.

The mirror transference occurs in three forms which relate to specific stages of development of the grandiose self:

1. An archaic form in which the self-experience of the analysand includes the analyst; it will be referred to as *merger through the extension of the grandiose self.*
2. A less archaic form in which the patient assumes that the analyst is like him or that the analyst's psychological makeup is similar to his; it will be called the *alter-ego transference* or *twinship.*
3. A still less archaic form in which the analyst is experienced as a separate person who, however, has significance to the patient only within the framework of the needs generated by his therapeutically reactivated grandiose self. Here the term *mirror transference* is most accurate and will again by employed. In this narrower sense the mirror transference is the reinstatement of the phase in which the gleam in the mother's eye, which mirrors the child's exhibitionistic display, and other forms of maternal participation in the child's narcissistic enjoyment confirm the child's self-esteem and, by a gradually increasing selectivity of these responses, begin to channel it into realistic directions. If the development of the grandiose self is traumatically disturbed, however, then this psychic structure may become cut off from further integrative participation in the development of the personality. Insecurely repressed in an archaic form, it is, on the one hand, removed from further external influence; yet, on the other hand, continues to disturb realistic adaptation by its recurrent intrusions into the ego. In the mirror transference, however, it may become cohesively remobilized, and a new road to its gradual modification is opened.

The central activity in the clinical process during the mirror transference concerns the raising to consciousness of the patient's infantile fantasies of exhibitionistic grandeur. In view of the strong resistances which oppose this process and the intensive efforts required in overcoming them, it may at times be disappointing for the analyst to behold the apparently trivial fantasy which the patient has ultimately brought into the light of day.

True, at times even the content of the fantasy permits an empathic understanding of the shame and hypochondria, and of the anxiety which the patient experiences: shame, because the revelation is at times still accompanied by the discharge of unneutralized exhibitionistic libido; and anxiety because the grandiosity isolates the analysand and threatens him with permanent object loss.

Patient C., for example, told the following dream during a period when he was looking forward to being publicly honored: "The question was raised of finding a successor for me. I thought: How about God?" The dream was partly the result of the attempt to soften the grandiosity through humor; yet it aroused excitement and anxiety, and led, against renewed resistances, to the recall of childhood fantasies in which he had felt that he was God.

In many instances, however, the nuclear grandiosity is only hinted at. Patient D., for example, recalled with intense shame and resistance that as a child he used to imagine that he was running the streetcars in the city. The fantasy appeared harmless enough; but the shame and resistance became more understandable when the patient explained that he was operating the streetcars via a "thought control" which emanated from his head, above the clouds.

Although the content of the grandiose fantasy cannot be further discussed here, it is important to clarify the role of the mirror transference which enables its emergence. As indicated before, the patient's major resistances are motivated by his attempt to escape from the uneasy elation alternating with fear of permanent object loss, painful self-consciousness, shame-tension, and hypochondria which is due to the dedifferentiating intrusions of grandiose fantasies and narcissistic-exhibitionistic libido into the ego. The transference, however, functions as a specific therapeutic buffer. In the mirror transference, in the narrower sense, the patient is able to mobilize his grandiose fantasies and exhibitionism on the basis of the hope that the therapist's empathic participation and emotional response will not allow the narcissistic tensions to reach excessively painful or dangerous levels. In the twinship and the merger, the analogous protection is provided by the long-term deployment of the narcissistic cathexes upon the therapist, who now is the carrier of the patient's infantile greatness and exhibitionism.

Later, especially with the aid of the very last clinical example referred to in this presentation, some of the specific, concrete clinical steps by which the mobilized infantile narcissistic demands gradually become tamed and neutralized will be demonstrated. Here, however, the general significance of the mirror transference in the context of therapy will be examined.

The rational aims of therapy could not, by themselves, persuade the vulnerable ego of the narcissistically fixated analysand to forego denial and acting out and to face and to examine the needs and claims of the archaic grandiose self. In order to actuate, and to maintain in motion, the painful process which leads to the confrontation of the grandiose fantasies with a realistic conception of the self, and to the realization that life offers only limited possibilities for the gratification of the narcissistic-exhibitionistic wishes, a mirror transference must be established. If it does not develop, the patient's grandiosity remains concentrated upon the grandiose self, the ego's defensive position remains rigid, and ego expansion cannot take place.

The mirror transference rests on the therapeutic reactivation of the grandiose self. That the analyst can be enlisted in the support of this structure is an expression of the fact that the formation of a cohesive grandiose self was indeed achieved during childhood; the listening, perceiving, and echoing-mirroring presence of the analyst now reinforces the psychological forces which maintain the cohesiveness of the self-image, archaic and (by adult standards) unrealistic though it may be. Analogous to the therapeutically invaluable, controlled, temporary swings toward the disintegration of the idealizing parent imago when the idealizing transference is disturbed, we may encounter as a consequence of a disturbance of the mirror transference the temporary fragmentation of the narcissistically cathected, cohesive (body-mind) self and a temporary concentration of the narcissistic cathexes on isolated body parts, isolated mental functions, and isolated actions, which are then experienced as dangerously disconnected from a crumbling self. As is the case in the idealizing transference, these temporary disturbances of the transference equilibrium occupy in the analysis of narcissistic personalities a central position of strategic importance which corresponds to the place of the structural conflict in the ordinary transference neuroses; and their analysis tends to elicit the deepest insights and leads to the most solid accretions of psychic structure.

The following constitutes an especially instructive illustration of such a temporary regressive fragmentation of the therapeutically activated grandiose self.

Mr. E. was a graduate student whose psychopathology and personality structure will not be discussed except to say that he sought relief from painful narcissistic tension states by a number of perverse means in which the inconstancy of his objects and sexual goals were indicative of the fact that he could trust no source of satisfaction. This brief report concerns a weekend during an early phase of the long analysis when the patient was already beginning to realize that separations from the analyst[2] upset his psychic equilibrium, but when he did not yet understand the specific nature of the support which the analysis provided. During earlier weekend separations a vaguely perceived inner threat had driven him to dangerous voyeuristic activities in public toilets during which he achieved a feeling of merger with the man at whom he gazed. This time, however, he was able, through an act of artistic sublimation, not only to spare himself the aforementioned cruder means of protection against the threatened dissolution of the self, but also to explain the nature of the reassurance he was receiving from the analyst. During this weekend, the patient painted a picture of the analyst. The key to the understanding of this artistic production lay in the fact that in it the analyst had neither eyes nor nose—the place of these sensory organs was taken by the analysand. On the basis of this evidence and of additional corroborative material, the conclusion could be reached that a decisive support to the maintenance of the patient's narcissistically cathected self-image was supplied by the analyst's perception of him. The patient felt whole when he thought that he was acceptingly looked at by an object that substituted for an insufficiently developed endopsychic function: the analyst provided a replacement for the lacking narcissistic cathexis of the self.

Some General Therapeutic Considerations Concerning the Mirror Transference

The analysand's demands for attention, admiration, and for a variety of other forms of mirroring and echoing responses to the mobilized grandiose self, which fill the mirror transference in the narrow sense of this term, do not usually constitute great cognitive problems for the analyst, although he may have to mobilize much subtle understanding to keep pace with the patient's defensive denials of his demands or with the retreat from them when the immediate empathic response to them is not forthcoming. Here it is of decisive importance that the analyst comprehend and acknowledge the phase-appropriateness of the demands of the grandiose self and that he grasp the fact that for a long time it is a mistake to emphasize to the patient that his demands are unrealistic. If the analyst demonstrates to the patient that the narcissistic needs are appropriate within the context of the total early phase that is being revived in the transference and that they have to be expressed, then the patient will gradually reveal the urges and fantasies of the grandiose self, and the slow process is thus initiated that leads to the integration of the grandiose self into the realistic structure of the ego and to an adaptively useful transformation of its energies.

The empathic comprehension of the reactivation of the earlier developmental stages (the alter-ego transference or twinship; the merger with the analyst through the extension of the grandiose self) is, however, not achieved easily. It is, for example, usually difficult for the analyst to hold fast to the realization that the meagerness of object-related imagery with regard to current and past figures as well as with regard to the analyst himself is the appropriate manifestation of an archaic narcissistic relationship. A frequent misunderstanding of the mirror transference in general and of the therapeutic activation of the most archaic stages of the grandiose self in particular thus consists in its being mistaken for the outgrowth of a widespread resistance against the establishment of an object-instinctual transference. And many analyses of narcissistic personality disorders are either short-circuited at this point (leading to a brief analysis of subsidiary sectors of the personality in which ordinary transferences do occur while the principal disturbance, which is narcissistic, remains untouched) or are forced into a mistaken and unprofitable direction against diffuse, nonspecific, and chronic ego resistances of the analysand.

If the establishment of a mirror transference is, however, not prevented, the gradual mobilization of the repressed grandiose self will take place and a number of specific, pathognomonic, and therapeutically valuable resistances will be set in motion. The principal end of the working-through processes in the idealizing transference is the internalization of the idealized object which leads to the strengthening of the matrix of the ego and to the strengthening of the patient's ideals; the principal end of the working-through processes in the mirror transference is the transformation of the grandiose self which results in a firming of the ego's potential for action (through the increasing realism of the ambitions of the personality) and in increasingly realistic self-esteem.

An important question posed by the analysis of narcissistic personalities, especially in the area of the grandiose self, concerns the degree of therapeutic activity which needs to be employed by the analyst. In applying Aichhorn's technique with juvenile delinquents (1936), for example, the analyst offers himself actively to the patient as a replica of his grandiose self, in a relationship which resembles the twinship (or alter-ego) variant of a mirror transference (see also A. Freud's illuminating summary [1951]). A delinquent's capacity to attach himself to the analyst in admiration indicates, however, that an idealized parent imago and the deep wish to form an idealizing transference are (preconsciously) present, but, in consequence of early dis-appointments, they are denied and hidden. It was Aichhorn's special under-standing for the delinquent that led him to offer himself first as a mirror image of the delinquent's grandiose self. He was thus able to initiate a veiled mobilization of idealizing cathexes toward an idealized object without yet disturbing the necessary protection of the defensively created grandiose self and its activities. Once a bond is established, however, a gradual shift from the omnipotence of the grandiose self to the more deeply longed-for omnipo-tence of an idealized object (and the requisite therapeutic dependence on it) can be achieved.

In the analytic treatment of the ordinary cases of narcissistic personality disturbance, however, the active encouragement of idealization is not desir-able. It leads to the establishment of a tenacious transference bondage, bringing about the formation of a cover of massive identification and hamper-ing the gradual alteration of the existing narcissistic structures. But a sponta-neously occurring therapeutic mobilization of the idealized parent imago or of the grandiose self is indeed to be welcomed and must not be interfered with.

There are two antithetical pitfalls concerning the form of the interpreta-tions which focus on the narcissistic transferences: the analyst's readiness to moralize about the patient's narcissism and his tendency toward abstractness of the relevant interpretations.

The triad of value judgments, moralizing, and therapeutic activism in which the analyst steps beyond the basic analytic attitude to become the patient's leader and teacher is most likely to occur when the psychopathology under scrutiny is not understood metapsychologically. Under these circum-stances the analyst can hardly be blamed when he tends to abandon the ineffective analytic armamentarium and instead offers himself to the patient as an object to identify with in order to achieve therapeutic changes. If lack of success in areas that are not yet understood metapsychologically is toler-ated, however, without the abandonment of analytic means, then the occur-rence of new analytic insights is not prevented and scientific progress can be made.

Where metapsychological understanding is not entirely lacking but is incomplete, analysts tend to supplement their interpretations with suggestive pressure and the weight of the personality of the therapist becomes of greater importance. There are thus certain analysts who are said to be exceptionally gifted in the analysis of "borderline" cases, and anecdotes about their therapeutic activities become widely known in analytic circles. But just as the surgeon, in the heroic era of surgery, was a charismatically gifted individual who performed great feats of courage and skill, while the modern surgeon tends to be a calm, well-trained craftsman, so also with the analyst. As our knowledge about the narcissistic disorders increases, their treatment becomes the work of analysts who do not employ any special charisma of their personalities but restrict themselves to the use of the tools that provide rational success: interpretations and reconstructions. There are, of course, moments when a forceful statement is indicated as a final move in persuading the patient that the gratifications obtained from the unmodified narcissistic fantasies are spurious. A skillful analyst of an older generation, for example, as asserted by local psychoanalytic lore, would make his point at a strategic juncture by silently handing over a crown and scepter to his unsuspecting analysand instead of confronting him with yet another verbal interpretation. In general, however, the psychoanalytic process is most enhanced if we trust the spontaneous synthetic functions of the patient's ego to integrate the narcissistic configurations gradually, in an atmosphere of analytic-empathic acceptance, instead of driving the analysand toward an imitation of the analyst's scornful rejection of the analysand's lack of realism.

The second danger, namely, that interpretations regarding the narcissistic transference might become too abstract, can be much diminished if we avoid falling victim to the widespread confusion between object relations and object love. We must bear in mind that our interpretations about the idealizing transference and the mirror transference are statements about an intense object relationship, despite the fact that the object is invested with narcissistic cathexes, and that we are explaining to the analysand how his very narcissism leads him to a heightened sensitivity about certain specific aspects and actions of the object, the analyst, whom he experiences in a narcissistic mode.

If the analyst's interpretations are noncondemnatory; if he can clarify to the patient in concrete terms the significance and the meaning of his (often acted-out) messages, of his seemingly irrational hypersensitivity, and of the back-and-forth flow of the cathexis of the narcissistic positions; and especially, if he can demonstrate to the patient that these archaic attitudes are comprehensible, adaptive, and valuable within the context of the total state of personality development of which they form a part—then the mature segment of the ego will not turn away from the grandiosity of the archaic self or from the awesome features of the overestimated, narcissistically experienced object. Over and over again, in small, psychologically manageable portions, the ego will deal with the disappointment at having to recognize that the claims of the grandiose self are unrealistic. And, in response to this experience, it will either mournfully withdraw a part of the narcissistic investment from the archaic image of the self, or it will, with the aid of newly acquired structure, neutralize the associated narcissistic energies or channel them into aim-inhibited pursuits. And over and over again, in small, psychologically manageable portions, the ego will deal with the disappointment at having to recognize that the idealized object is unavailable or imperfect. And, in response to this experience, it will withdraw a part of the idealizing investment from the object and strengthen the corresponding internal structures. In short, if the ego learns first to accept the presence of the mobilized narcissistic structures, it will gradually integrate them into its own realm, and the analyst will witness the establishment of ego dominance and ego autonomy in the narcissistic sector of the personality.

REACTIONS OF THE ANALYST

Reactions of the Analyst during the Mobilization of the Patient's Idealized Parent Imago in the Idealizing Transference

Some time ago I was consulted by a colleague concerning a stalemate which seemed to have been present from the beginning of the analysis and to have persisted through two years of work. Since the patient, a shallow, promiscuous woman, showed a serious disturbance of her ability to establish meaningful object relationships and presented a history of severe childhood traumata, I tended initially to agree with the analyst that the extent of the narcissistic fixations prevented the establishment of that minimum of transferences without which analysis cannot proceed. Still, I asked the analyst for an account of the early sessions, with particular attention to activities on his part which the patient might have experienced as a rebuff. Among the earliest transference manifestations several dreams of this Catholic patient had contained the figure of an inspired, idealistic priest. While these early dreams had remained uninterpreted, the analyst remembered—clearly against resistance—that he had subsequently indicated that he was not a Catholic. He had justified this move by her supposed need to be acquainted with a minimum of the actual situation since in his view the patient's hold on reality was tenuous. This event must have been very significant for the patient. We later understood that, as an initial, tentative transference step, she had reinstated an attitude of idealizing religious devotion from the beginning of adolescence, an attitude which in turn had been the revival of awe and admiration from childhood. These earliest idealizations, as we could conclude later, had been a refuge from bizarre tensions and fantasies caused by traumatic stimulations and frustrations from the side of her pathological parents. The analyst's misguided remark, however, that he was not a Catholic—i.e., not an idealized good and healthy version of the patient—constituted a rebuff for her and led to the stalemate, which the analyst, with the aid of a number of consultations concerning this patient and his response to her, was later largely able to break.

I am focusing neither on the transference nor on the effect of the analyst's mistake on the analysis, but on the elucidation of a countertransference symptom. A combination of circumstances, among them the fact that I observed other, similar incidents, allows me to offer the following explanation with a high degree of conviction. An analytically unwarranted rejection of a patient's idealizing attitudes is usually motivated by a defensive fending off of narcissistic tensions, experienced as embarrassment and leading even to hypochondriacal preoccupations, which are generated in the analyst when repressed fantasies of his grandiose self become stimulated by the patient's idealization.

Are these reactions of the analyst in the main motivated by current stress, or are they related to the dangerous mobilization of specific repressed unconscious constellations?

In a letter to Binswanger, Freud (1913) expressed himself as follows about the problem of countertransference: "What is given to the patient," Freud said, must be "consciously allotted, and then more or less of it as the need may arise. Occasionally a great deal. . . ." And later Freud set down the crucial maxim: "To give someone too little because one loves him too much is being unjust to the patient and a technical error."

If a patient's incestuous object-libidinal demands elicit an intense unconscious response in the analyst, he may become overly technical vis-à-vis the patient's wishes or will not even recognize them—at any rate, his ego will not have the freedom to choose the response required by the analysis. A parallel situation may arise in the analysis of a narcissistic personality disturbance when the remobilization of the idealized parent imago prompts the analysand to see the analyst as the embodiment of idealized perfection. If the analyst has not come to terms with his own grandiose self, he may respond to the idealization with an intense stimulation of his unconscious grandiose fantasies and an intensification of defenses which bring about his rejection of the patient's idealizing transference. If the analyst's defensive attitude becomes chronic, the establishment of a workable idealizing transference is interfered with and the analytic process is blocked.

It makes little difference whether the rejection of the patient's idealization is blunt, which is rare; or subtle (as in the instance reported), which is common; or, which is most frequent, almost concealed by correct, but prematurely given, genetic or dynamic interpretations (such as the analyst's quickly calling the patient's attention to idealized figures in his past or pointing out hostile impulses which supposedly underlie the idealizing ones). The rejection may express itself through no more than a slight overobjectivity of the analyst's attitude; or it may reveal itself in the tendency to disparage the narcissistic idealization in a humorous and kindly way. And finally, it is even deleterious to emphasize the patient's assets at a time when he attempts the idealizing expansion of the ingrained narcissistic positions and feels insignificant by comparison with the therapist—appealing though it might seem when the analyst expresses respect for his patient. In short, during those phases of the analysis of narcissistic personalities when an idealizing transference begins to germinate, there is only one correct analytic attitude: to accept the admiration.

Reactions of the Analyst during the Therapeutic Mobilization of the Patient's Grandiose Self in the Mirror Transference

The mirror transference occurs in different forms which expose the analyst to different emotional tasks. In the mirror transference in the narrower sense the patient reacts to the ebb and flow of the analyst's empathy with, and response to, his narcissistic needs, and the presence of the analyst is thus acknowledged. Even these circumstances, however, may elicit reactions in the analyst which interfere with the therapeutic reactivation of the grandiose self since the analyst's own narcissistic needs may make him intolerant of a situation in which he is reduced to the role of mirror for the patient's infantile narcissism. In the twinship (alter-ego) and merger varieties of the remobilization of the grandiose self, however, the analyst is deprived of even the minimum of narcissistic gratification: the patient's acknowledgment of his separate existence. While in the mirror transference the analyst may become incapable of comprehending the patient's narcissistic needs and of responding to them, the most common dangers in the twinship or merger are his boredom, his lack of emotional involvement with the patient, and his precarious maintenance of attention. A theoretical discussion of these failures must, however, be omitted here. On the one hand, it would require an examination of the psychology of attention in the absence of stimulation by object cathexes; on the other hand, one would have to study certain aspects of the vulnerability of empathy in analysts which are genetically related to the fact that a specific empathic sensitivity, acquired in an early narcissistic relationship, often contributes decisively to the motivation for becoming an analyst. Instead of a theoretical discussion, however, the attempt will be made to illuminate the subject matter with the aid of a clinical example.

Miss F., age twenty-five, had sought analysis because of diffuse dissatisfactions. Despite the fact that she was active in her profession and had numerous social contacts, she was not intimate with anyone, and felt different from other people and isolated. She had a series of love relationships but had rejected marriage because she knew that such a step would be a sham. She was subject to sudden changes in her mood with an associated uncertainty about the reality of her feelings and thoughts. In metapsychological terms the disturbance was due to a faulty integration of the grandiose self which led to swings between states of anxious excitement and elation over a secret "preciousness" which made her vastly better than anyone else (during times when the ego came close to giving way to the hypercathected grandiose self) and states of emotional depletion (when the ego used all its strength to wall itself off from the unrealistic, grandiose substructure). Genetically, the fact that the mother had been depressed during several periods early in the child's life had prevented the gradual integration of the narcissistic-exhibitionistic cathexes of the grandiose self. During decisive periods of her childhood the girl's presence and activities had not called forth maternal pleasure and approval. On the contrary, whenever she tried to speak about herself, the mother deflected, imperceptibly, the focus of attention to her own depressive self-preoccupations, and thus the child was deprived of that optimal maternal acceptance which transforms crude exhibitionism and grandiosity into adaptably useful self-esteem and self-enjoyment.

During extended phases of the analysis, beginning at a time when I did not yet understand the patient's psychopathology, the following progression of events frequently occurred during analytic sessions. The patient would arrive in a friendly mood, settle down quietly, and begin to communicate her thoughts and feelings: about current topics; the transference; and insights concerning the connection between present and past, and between transferences upon the analyst and analogous strivings toward others. In brief, the first part of the sessions had the appearance of a well-moving self-analysis when the analyst is, indeed, little else than an interested observer who holds himself in readiness for the next wave of resistances. The stage in question lasted much longer, however, than the periods of self-analysis encountered in other analyses. I noted, furthermore, that I was not able to maintain the attitude of interested attention which normally establishes itself effortlessly and spontaneously when one listens to an analysand's work of free associations during periods of relatively unimpeded self-analysis. And, finally, after a prolonged period of ignorance and misunderstanding during which I was inclined to argue with the patient about the correctness of my interpretations and to suspect the presence of stubborn, hidden resistances, I came to the crucial recognition that the patient demanded a specific response to her communications, and that she completely rejected any other. Unlike the analysand during periods of genuine self-analysis, the patient could not tolerate the analyst's silence, but, at approximately the mid-point of the sessions, she would suddenly get violently angry at me for being silent. (The archaic nature of her need, it may be added, was betrayed by the suddenness with which it appeared—like the sudden transition from satiation to hunger or from hunger to satiation in very young children.) I gradually learned, however, that she would immediately become calm and content when I, at these moments, simply summarized or repeated what she had in essence already said (such as, "You are again struggling to free yourself from becoming embroiled in your mother's suspiciousness against men." Or, "You have worked your way through to the understanding that the fantasies about the visiting Englishman are reflections of fantasies about me"). But if I went beyond what the patient herself had already said or discovered, even by a single step only (such as: "The fantasies about the visiting foreigner are reflections of fantasies about me and, in addition, I think that they are a revival of the dangerous stimulation to which you felt exposed by your father's fantasy-stories about you"), she would again get violently angry (regardless of the fact that what I had added might be known to her, too) and would furiously accuse me, in a tense, highpitched voice, of undermining her, that with my remark I had destroyed everything she had built up, and that I was wrecking the analysis.

Certain convictions can only be acquired firsthand and I am thus not able to demonstrate in detail the correctness of the following conclusions. During this phase of the analysis the patient had begun to remobilize an archaic, intensely cathected image of the self which had heretofore been kept in repression. Concomitant with the remobilization of the grandiose self, on which she had remained fixated, there also arose the renewed need for an archaic object that would be nothing more than the embodiment of a psychological function which the patient's psyche could not yet perform for itself: to respond empathically to her narcissistic display and to provide her with narcissistic sustenance through approval, mirroring, and echoing. The patient thus attempted, with the aid of my confirming, mirroring presence, to integrate a hypercathected archaic self into the rest of her personality. This process began at this stage with a cautious reinstatement of a sense of the reality of her thoughts and feelings; it later moved gradually toward the transformation of her intense exhibitionistic needs into an ego-syntonic sense of her own value and an enjoyment of her activities.

Due to the fact that I was at that time not sufficiently alert to the pitfalls of such transference demands, many of my interventions interfered with the work of structure formation. But I know that the obstacles that opposed my understanding lay not only in the cognitive area; and I can affirm, without transgressing the rules of decorum and without indulging in the kind of immodest self-revelation which ultimately hides more than it admits, that there were specific hindrances in my own personality which stood in my way. There was a residual insistence, related to deep and old fixation points, on seeing myself in the narcissistic center of the stage; and, although I had of course for a long time struggled with the relevant childhood delusions and thought that I had, on the whole, achieved dominance over them, I was not up to the extreme demands posed by the conceptually unaided confrontation with the reactivated grandiose self of my patient. Thus I refused to entertain the possibility that I was not an object for the patient, not an amalgam with the patient's childhood loves and hatreds, but only, as I reluctantly came to see, an impersonal function, without significance except insofar as it related to the kingdom of her own remobilized narcissistic grandeur and exhibitionism. For a long time I insisted, therefore, that the patient's reproaches related to specific transference fantasies and wishes on the oedipal level—but I could make no headway in this direction. It was ultimately, I believe, the high-pitched tone of her voice which expressed such utter conviction of being right—the conviction of a very young child; a pent-up, heretofore unexpressed conviction—which led me on the right track. I recognized that, whenever I did more (or less) than to provide simple approval or confirmation in response to the patient's reports of her own discoveries, I became for her the depressive mother who deflected the narcissistic cathexes from the child upon herself, or who did not provide the needed narcissistic echo.

The clinical situation described in the foregoing pages and, especially, the analyst's therapeutic responses to it require further elucidation.

At first hearing I might seem to be stating that, in instances of this type, the analyst must indulge a transference wish of the analysand; specifically, that the patient had not received the necessary emotional echo or approval from the depressive mother, and that the analyst must now give it to her in order to provide a "corrective emotional experience" (Alexander, French, et al., 1946).

There are indeed patients for whom this type of indulgence is not only a temporary tactical requirement during certain stressful phases of analysis but who cannot ever undertake the steps which lead to that increased ego dominance over the childhood wish which is the specific aim of psychoanalytic work. And there is, furthermore, no doubt that, occasionally, the indulgence of an important childhood wish—especially if it is provided with an air of conviction and in a therapeutic atmosphere that carries a quasi-religious, magical connotation of the efficacy of love—can have lasting beneficial effects with regard to the relief of symptoms and behavioral change in the patient.

The analytic process in analyzable cases, however, as in the one described in the present clinical vignette, develops in a different way. Although, for tactical reasons, the analyst might in such instances transitorily have to provide what one might call a *reluctant compliance with the childhood wish*, the true analytic aim is not indulgence but mastery based on insight, achieved in a setting of (tolerable) analytic abstinence. The recognition of the specific childhood demand was only the beginning of the working-through process concerning the grandiose self. It was followed by the recall of clusters of analogous memories concerning her mother's entering a phase of depressive self-preoccupation during later periods of the patient's life. Finally, a central set of poignant memories, upon which a series of earlier and later ones seemed to be telescoped, referred specifically to episodes when she came home from kindergarten and early elementary school. At such times she would rush home as fast as she could, joyfully anticipating telling her mother about her successes in school. She recalled then how her mother opened the door, but, instead of the mother's face lighting up, her expression remained blank; and how, when the patient began talking about school and play and about her achievements and successes of the preceding hours, the mother appeared to listen and participate, but imperceptibly the topic of the conversation shifted and the mother began to talk about herself, her headache and her tiredness and her other physical self-preoccupations. All that the patient could directly recall about her own reactions was that she felt suddenly drained of energy and empty; she was for a long time unable to remember feeling any rage at her mother on such occasions. It was only after a prolonged period of working through that she could gradually establish connections between the rage which she experienced against me, when I did not understand her demands, and feelings she had experienced as a child.

This phase was then followed by a slow, shame-provoking, and anxious revelation of her persistent infantile grandiosity and exhibitionism; the working through accomplished during this period led ultimately to increased ego dominance over the old grandiosity and exhibitionism, and thus to greater self-confidence and to other favorable transformations of her narcissism in this segment of her personality.

CONCLUDING REMARKS

The foregoing examination must, in its entirety, be considered a summarizing preview of a broader study; no retrospective survey of the findings and opinions that have been presented will, therefore, be given. It must be stressed, however, that there are some important aspects of the subject matter which either could only be mentioned briefly or had to be disregarded altogether.

Thus, as mentioned initially, it was necessary to omit almost all references to the work of others, such as, for example, the significant contributions by H. Hartmann (1953), K. R. Eissler (1953), E. Jacobson (1964), and A. Reich (1960); furthermore, it was not possible to compare the approach toward our subject matter taken in the present study with that chosen by such important authors as Federn (1952) on the one hand and Mahler (1952) on the other; and, finally, still within the same context, it was not possible to discuss the work of Melanie Klein and her school which often appears to be concerned with disorders that are related to those scrutinized in this essay.

No attempt was made to define and delimit the area of psychopathology with which this study is dealing; the question of the appropriateness of the use of the term transference in the present context could not be taken up; the discussion of the role of aggression had to be bypassed; the recurrent traumatic states in which the focus of the analysis shifts temporarily to the near-exclusive consideration of the overburdenedness of the psyche could not be illuminated; many other difficulties, therapeutic limitations and failures were not considered; and, most regrettably, it was not possible to demonstrate the specific wholesome changes that occur as a result of the transformation of the narcissistic structures and of their energies. In all: it was the aim of this contribution to give the outline of a systematic approach to the psychoanalytic treatment of narcissistic personalities; a thorough scrutiny of the subject could not be undertaken.

NOTES

1. The episode described here concerns a patient who was treated by a colleague (a woman) in regular consultation with the author.
2. This analysis was carried out by a senior student at the Chicago Institute for Psychoanalysis under regular supervision by the author.

BIBLIOGRAPHY

Aichhorn, A. (1936), The Narcissistic Transference of the "Juvenile Impostor." In *Delinquency and Child Guidance*, ed. O. Fleischmann, P. Kramer, & H. Ross. New York: International Universities Press, 1964, pp. 174–191.

Alexander, F., French, T. M., et al. (1946), *Psychoanalytic Therapy: Principles and Application*. New York: Ronald Press.

Eissler, K. R. (1953), Notes upon the Emotionality of a Schizophrenic Patient and Its Relation to Problems of Technique. *Psychoanal. Study Child*, 8:199–251.

Federn, P. (1952), *Ego Psychology and the Psychoses*, ed. E. Weiss, New York: Basic Books.

Freud, A. (1951), Obituary: August Aichhorn. *Int. J. Psycho-Anal.*, 32:51–56.

Freud, S. (1913), Letter to Ludwig Binswanger of February 20, 1913. In Binswanger, L. *Erinnerungen an Sigmund Freud*. Bern: Francke Verlag, 1956, p. 65.

Hartmann, H. (1953), Contribution to the Metapsychology of Schizophrenia. *Psychoanal. Study Child*, 8:177–198.

Jacobson, E. (1964), *The Self and the Object World*. New York: International Universities Press.

Kohut, H. (1966), Forms and Transformation of Narcissism. *J. Amer. Psychoanal. Assn.*, 14:243–272.

Mahler, M. S. (1952), On Child Psychosis and Schizophrenia: Autistic and Symbiotic Infantile Psychoses. *Psychoanal. Study Child*, 7:286–305.

Nagera, H. (1964), Autoerotism, Autoerotic Activities, and Ego Development. *Psychoanal. Study Child*, 19:240–255.

Niederland, W. G. (1959), Schreber: Father and Son. *Psychoanal. Q.*, 28:151–169.

Reich, A. (1960), Pathologic Forms of Self-esteem Regulation. *Psychoanal. Study Child*, 15:215–232.

27. Presence of the Analyst

Jacques Lacan

So that I would not always have to be looking for a box of matches, someone gave me a very large box, as you can see. On it is written the following motto: *the art of listening is almost as important as that of saying the right thing.* This apportions our tasks. Let us hope that we will measure up to them.

Today I shall be dealing with the transference, or rather I shall approach the question, in the hope of giving you some idea of the concept, as I promised I would do in my second talk.

1

The transference is usually represented as an affect. A rather vague distinction is then made between a positive and a negative transference. It is generally assumed, not without some foundation, that the positive transference is love—though it must be said that, in the way it is used here, this term is employed in a very approximate way.

At a very early stage, Freud posed the question of the authenticity of love as it occurs in the transference. To come to the point, it is usually maintained that in these circumstances it is a sort of false love, a shadow of love. But Freud himself did not weigh down the scales in this direction—far from it. Not least among the consequences of the experience of the transference was that it led Freud to take the question of what is called true love, *eine echte Liebe,* further perhaps than it had ever been taken.

In the case of the negative transference, commentators are more prudent, more restrained, in the way they refer to it, and it is never identified with hate. They usually employ the term ambivalence, a term which, even more than the first, conceals things very well, confused things that are not always handled in a satisfactory way.

It would be truer to say that the positive transference is when you have a soft spot for the individual concerned, the analyst in this instance, and the negative transference is when you have to keep your eye on him.

There is another use of the term transference that is worth pointing out, as when one says that it structures all the particular relations with that other who is the analyst, and that the value of all the thoughts that gravitate around this relation must be connoted by a sign of particular reserve. Hence the expression—which is always added as a kind of afterthought or parenthesis, as if to convey some kind of suspicion, when used about the behaviour of a subject—*he is in full transference*. This presupposes that his entire mode of apperception has been restructured around the dominant centre of the transference.

I will not go any further because this double semantic mapping seems to me to be adequate for the moment.

We cannot, of course, remain satisfied with this, since our aim is to approach the concept of the transference.

This concept is determined by the function it has in a particular praxis. This concept directs the way in which patients are treated. Conversely, the way in which they are treated governs the concept.

It might seem to settle the question at the outset if we could decide whether or not the transference is bound up with analytic practice, whether it is a product, not to say an artefact, of analytic practice. Ida Macalpine, one of the many authors who have been led to express their opinions on the transference, has carried as far as possible the attempt to articulate the transference in this direction. Whatever her merits—she is a very stubborn person—let me say at once that I cannot, in any sense, accept this extreme position.

In any case, approaching the question in this way does not settle it. Even if we must regard the transference as a product of the analytic situation, we may say that this situation cannot create the phenomenon in its entirety, and that, in order to produce it, there must be, outside the analytic situation, possibilities already present to which it will give their perhaps unique composition.

This in no way excludes the possibility, where no analyst is in view, that there may be, properly speaking, transference effects that may be structured exactly like the gamut of transference phenomena in analysis. It is simply that, in discovering these effects, analysis will make it possible to give them an experimental model that need not necessarily be at all different from the model I shall call the natural one. So to bring out the transference in analysis, where it acquires its structural foundations, may very well be the only way of introducing the universality of the application of this concept. It should be enough, then, to open up this package in the sphere of analysis and, more especially, of the *doxa* that goes with it.

This, after all, is a truism. Nevertheless, it is a rough indication worth making as a start.

2

The aim of this introduction is to remind you that if we are to approach the fundamentals of psycho-analysis we must introduce a certain coherence into the major concepts on which it is based. Such a coherence is already to be found in the way I have approached the concept of the unconscious—which, you will remember, I was unable to separate from the presence of the analyst.

Presence of the analyst—a fine phrase that should not be reduced to the tear-jerking sermonizing, the serous inflation, the rather sticky caress to be found in a book that has appeared under this title.

The presence of the analyst is itself a manifestation of the unconscious, so that when it is manifested nowadays in certain encounters, as a refusal of the unconscious—this is a tendency, readily admitted, in some people's thinking —this very fact must be integrated into the concept of the unconscious. You have rapid access here to the formulation, which I have placed in the forefront, of a movement of the subject that opens up only to close again in a certain temporal pulsation—a pulsation I regard as being more radical than the insertion in the signifier that no doubt motivates it, but is not primary to it at the level of essence, since I have been driven to speak of essence.

I have shown, in a maieutic, eristic way, that one should see in the unconscious the effects of speech on the subject—in so far as these effects are so radically primary that they are properly what determine the status of the subject as subject. This proposition was intended to restore the Freudian unconscious to its true place. Certainly, the unconscious has always been present, it existed and acted before Freud, but it is important to stress that all the acceptations given, before Freud, to this function of the unconscious have absolutely nothing to do with the Freudian unconscious.

The primal unconscious, the unconscious as archaic function, the unconscious as veiled presence of a thought to be placed at the level of being before it is revealed, the metaphysical unconscious of Edward von Hartmann —whatever reference Freud makes to it in an *ad hominem* argument—above all the unconscious as instinct—all this has nothing to do with the Freudian unconscious, nothing at all, whatever its analytic vocabulary, its inflections, its deviations may be—nothing at all to do with our experience. I will ask analysts a straight question: *have you ever, for a single moment, the feeling that you are handling the clay of instinct?*

In my Rome report,[1] I proceeded to a new alliance with the meaning of the Freudian discovery. The unconscious is the sum of the effects of speech on a subject, at the level at which the subject constitutes himself out of the effects of the signifier. This makes it clear that, in the term *subject*—this is why I referred it back to its origin—I am not designating the living substratum needed by this phenomenon of the subject, nor any sort of substance, nor any being possessing knowledge in his *pathos,* his suffering, whether primal or secondary, nor even some incarnated logos, but the Cartesian subject, who appears at the moment when doubt is recognized as certainty— except that, through my approach, the bases of this subject prove to be wide, but, at the same time much more amenable to the certainty that eludes it. This is what the unconscious is.

There is a link between this field and the moment, Freud's moment, when it is revealed. It is this link I express when I compare it with the approach of a Newton, an Einstein, a Planck, an a-cosmological approach, in the sense that all these fields are characterized by tracing in the real a new furrow in relation to the knowledge that might from all eternity be attributed to God.

Paradoxically, the difference which will most surely guarantee the survival of Freud's field is that the Freudian field is a field which, of its nature, is lost. It is here that the presence of the psycho-analyst, as witness of this loss, is irreducible.

At this level, we can get nothing more out of it—for it is a dead loss, with no gain to show, except perhaps its resumption in the function of pulsation. The loss is necessarily produced in a shaded area—which is designated by the oblique stroke with which I divide the formulae which unfold, in linear form, opposite each of the terms, unconscious, repetition, transference. This area of loss even involves, as far as these facts of analytic practice are concerned, a certain deepening of obscurantism, very characteristic of the condition of man in our times of supposed information—obscurantism which, without really knowing why, I can well believe will be regarded as incredible in the future. What I mean by obscurantism is, in particular, the function assumed by psycho-analysis in the propagation of a style that calls itself the *American way of life,* in so far as it is characterized by the revival of notions long since refuted in the field of psycho-analysis, such as the predominance of the functions of the ego.

In this sense, then, the presence of the psycho-analyst, seen in the very same perspective in which the vanity of his discourse appears, must be included in the concept of the unconscious. Psycho-analysts of today, we must take account of this slag in our operations, as we must of the *caput mortuum* of the discovery of the unconscious. It justifies the maintenance, within analysis, of a conflict situation, necessary to the very existence of analysis.

If it is true that psycho-analysis rests on a fundamental conflict, on an initial, radical drama as far as everything that might be included under the heading psychical is concerned, the innovation to which I refer, and which is called *recall of the field and function of speech and language in psycho-analytic experience,* does not claim to exhaust the possibilities of the unconscious, since it is, itself, an intervention in the conflict. This recall has an immediate implication in that it has itself a transferential effect. In any case, this is recognized by the fact that my seminar has been criticized precisely for playing, in relation to my audience, a function regarded by the orthodoxy of the psycho-analytic association as dangerous, for intervening in the transference. Now, far from denying it, I would regard this effect as radical, as constituting, indeed, this renewal of the alliance with Freud's discovery. This indicates that the cause of the unconscious—and you see that the word cause is to be taken here in its ambiguity, a cause to be sustained, but also a function of the cause at the level of the unconscious—this cause must be conceived as, fundamentally, a lost cause. And it is the only chance one has of winning it.

That is why, in the misunderstood concept of repetition, I stress the importance of the ever avoided encounter, of the missed opportunity. The function of missing lies at the centre of analytic repetition. The appointment is always missed—this is what constitutes, in comparison with *tuché,* the vanity of repetition, its constitutive occultation.

The concept of repetition brings me to the following dilemma—either I assume quite simply my implication as analyst in the eristic character of the discord of any description of my experience, or I polish up the concept at the level of something that would be impossible to objectify, if not at the level of a transcendental analysis of cause.

Cause might be formulated on the basis of the classical formula of the *ablata causa tollitur effectus*—I would have only to stress the singular of the protasis, *ablata causa*, by putting the terms of the apodosis in the plural *tolluntur effectus*—which would mean that *the effects are successful only in the absence of cause*. All the effects are subjected to the pressure of a transfactual, causal order which demands to join in their dance, but, if they held their hands tightly, as in the song, they would prevent the cause intruding in their round.

At this point, I should define unconscious cause, neither as an existent, nor as a οὐχ ὄυ, a non-existent—as, I believe Henri Ey does, a non-existent of possibility. It is a μὴ ὄυ of the prohibition that brings to being an existent in spite of its non-advent; it is a function of the impossible on which a certainty is based.

3

This brings us to the function of the transference. For this indeterminate of pure being that has no point of access to determination, this primary position of the unconscious that is articulated as constituted by the indetermination of the subject—it is to this that the transference gives us access, in an enigmatic way. It is a Gordian knot that leads us to the following conclusion—the subject is looking for his certainty. And the certainty of the analyst himself concerning the unconscious cannot be derived from the concept of the transference.

It is striking, therefore, to observe the multiplicity, the plurality, the plurivalence even, of the conceptions of the transference that have been formulated in analysis. I do not claim to be able to provide you with an exhaustive account of them. I shall simply try to guide you through the paths of a chosen exploration.

At its emergence in the writings and teachings of Freud, a sliding-away (*glissement*), which we cannot impute to him, lies in wait for us—this consists in seeing in the concept of the transference no more than the concept of repetition itself. Let us not forget that when Freud presents it to us, he says—*what cannot be remembered is repeated in behaviour*. This behaviour, in order to reveal what it repeats, is handed over to the analyst's reconstruction.

One may go so far as to believe that the opacity of the trauma—as it was then maintained in its initial function by Freud's thought, that is to say, in my terms, its resistance to signification—is then specifically held responsible for the limits of remembering. And, after all, it is hardly surprising, given my own theorization, that I should see this as a highly significant moment in the transfer of powers from the subject to the Other, what I call the capital Other (*le grand Autre*), the locus of speech and, potentially, the locus of truth.

Is this the point at which the concept of the transference appears? It would seem so, and one often goes no further. But let us look at it more closely. In Freud, this moment is not simply the moment-limit that seems to correspond to what I designated as the moment of the closing up of the unconscious, a temporal pulsation that makes it disappear at a certain point of its statement (*énoncé*). When Freud introduces the function of the transference, he is careful to mark this moment as the cause of what we call the transference. The Other, latent or not, is, even beforehand, present in the subjective revelation. It is already there, when something has begun to yield itself from the unconscious.

The analyst's interpretation merely reflects the fact that the unconscious, if it is what I say it is, namely, a play of the signifier, has already in its formations—dreams, slips of tongue or pen, witticisms or symptoms—proceeded by interpretation. The Other, the capital Other, is already there in every opening, however fleeting it may be, of the unconscious.

What Freud shows us, from the outset, is that the transference is essentially resistant, *Übertragungswiderstand*. The transference is the means by which the communication of the unconscious is interrupted, by which the unconscious closes up again. Far from being the handing over of powers to the unconscious, the transference is, on the contrary, its closing up.

This is essential in noting the paradox that is expressed quite commonly in the fact—which may even be found in Freud's writings—that the analyst must await the transference before beginning to give his interpretation.

I want to stress this question because it is the dividing line between the correct and incorrect conception of the transference.

In analytic practice, there are many ways of conceiving the transference. They are not necessarily mutually exclusive. They may be defined at different levels. For example, although the conceptions of the relation of the subject to one or other of those agencies which, in the second stage of his *Topography,* Freud was able to define as the ego-ideal or the super-ego, are partial, this is often simply to give a lateralized view of what is essentially the relation with the capital Other.

But there are other divergences that are irreducible. There is a conception which, wherever it is formulated, can only contaminate practice—I am referring to the conception which would have the analysis of the transference proceed on the basis of an alliance with the healthy part of the subject's ego, and consists in appealing to his common sense, by way of pointing out to him the illusory character of certain of his actions in his relation with the analyst. This is a thesis that subverts what it is all about, namely the bringing to awareness of this split in the subject, realized here, in fact, in presence. To appeal to some healthy part of the subject thought to be there in the real, capable of judging with the analyst what is happening in the transference, is to misunderstand that it is precisely this part that is concerned in the transference, that it is this part that closes the door, or the window, or the shutters, or whatever—and that the beauty with whom one wishes to speak is there, behind, only too willing to open the shutters again. That is why it is at this moment that interpretation becomes decisive, for it is to the beauty one must speak.

I can do no more than suggest here the reversion involved in this schema in relation to the model one has of it in one's head. I say somewhere that *the unconscious is the discourse of the Other.* Now, the discourse of the Other that is to be realized, that of the unconscious, is not beyond the closure, it is *outside.* It is this discourse, which, through the mouth of the analyst, calls for the reopening of the shutter.

Nevertheless, there is a paradox in designating this movement of closure as the initial moment when the interpretation may assume its full force. And here is revealed the permanent conceptual crisis that exists in analysis concerning the way in which the function of the transference should be conceived.

The contradiction of its function, which causes it to be apprehended as the point of impact of the force of the interpretation by the very fact that, in relation to the unconscious, it is a moment of closure—this is why we must treat it as what it is, namely, a knot. Whether or not we treat it as a Gordian knot remains to be seen. It is a knot, and it prompts us to account for it—as I have been doing for several years—by considerations of topology. It will not be thought unnecessary, I hope, to remind you of these.

4

There is a crisis in analysis and, to show that there is nothing biased in this, I would support my view by citing a recent article that demonstrates this in the most striking way—and it is the work of no mediocre mind. It is a closely argued, very engaging article by Thomas S. Szasz—who hails from Syracuse, which fact, unfortunately, does not make him any more closely related to Archimedes, for this Syracuse is in New York State—which appeared in the latest number of *The International Journal of Psycho-Analysis.*

The author was inspired to write this article by an idea in keeping with the line of investigation that inspired his earlier article, a truly moving search for the authenticity of the analytic way.

It is quite striking that an author, who is indeed one of the most highly regarded in his circle, which is specifically that of American psycho-analysis, should regard the transference as nothing more than a defence on the part of the psycho-analyst, and should arrive at the following conclusion—*the transference is the pivot on which the entire structure of psycho-analytic treatment rests.* This is a concept that he calls *inspired*—I am always suspicious of *faux amis* in English vocabulary, so I have tried to tread warily when translating it. This *inspired,* it seemed to me, did not mean *inspiré,* but something like *officieux. It is an inspired and indispensable concept*—I quote —*yet it harbours the seeds, not only of its own destruction, but of the destruction of psycho-analysis itself. Why? Because it tends to place the person of the analyst beyond the reality testing of patients, colleagues, and self. This hazard must be frankly recognized. Neither professionalization, nor the 'raising of standards,' nor coerced training analyses can protect us from this danger.* And here the confusion arises—*only the integrity of the analyst and of the analytic situation can safeguard from extinction the unique dialogue between analysand and analyst.*

This blind alley that Szasz has created for himself is, for him, necessitated by the very fact that he can conceive of the analysis of the transference only in terms of an assent obtained from the healthy part of the ego, that part which is capable of judging reality and of separating it from illusion.

His article begins thus, quite logically—*Transference is similar to such concepts as delusion, illusion, and phantasy.* Once the presence of the transference has been established, it is a question of agreement between the analysand and the analyst, except that here the analyst is a judge against whom there is neither appeal nor recourse; we are led to call any analysis of the transference a field of pure, uncontrolled hazard.

I have taken this article only as an extreme case, but a very revealing one, so as to encourage us to restore here a determination that should bring into play another order—that of truth. Truth is based only on the fact that speech, even when it consists of lies, appeals to it and gives rise to it. This dimension is always absent from the logical positivism that happens to dominate Szasz's analysis of the concept of transference.

My own conception of the dynamics of the unconscious has been called an intellectualization—on the grounds that I based the function of the signifier in the forefront. Is it not apparent that it is in this operational mode—in which everything makes light of the confrontation between a reality and a connotation of illusion attributed to the phenomenon of the transference—that this supposed intellectualization really resides?

Far from us having to consider two subjects, in a dual position, to discuss an objectivity that appears to have been posited there as the gravitational effect of a compression in behaviour, we must bring out the domain of possible deception. When I introduced you to the subject of Cartesian certainty as the necessary starting-point of all our speculations as to what the unconscious reveals, I pointed out the role of essential balancer played in Descartes by the Other which, it is said, must on no account be deceptive. In analysis, the danger is that this Other will be deceived. This is not the only dimension to be apprehended in the transference. But one has to admit that if there is one domain in which, in discourse, deception has some chance of success, it is certainly love that provides its model. What better way of assuring oneself, on the point on which one is mistaken, than to persuade the other of the truth of what one says! Is not this a fundamental structure of the dimension of love that the transference gives us the opportunity of depicting? In persuading the other that he has that which may complement us, we assure ourselves of being able to continue to misunderstand precisely what we lack. The circle of deception, in so far as it highlights the dimension of love at the point named—this will serve us as an exemplary door to demonstrate the trick next time.

But this is not all I have to show you, for it is not what radically causes the closure involved in the transference. What causes it, and this will be the other side of our examination of the concepts of the transference, is—to come back to the question mark inscribed in the left part, the shaded, reserved part—what I have designated by the *objet a*.

QUESTIONS AND ANSWERS

F. Wahl: *To what theory of knowledge, in the system of existing theories, might what you said in the first half of the lecture be related?*

Lacan: Since I am saying that it is the novelty of the Freudian field to provide us in experience with something that is fundamentally apprehended like that, it is hardly surprising if you cannot find a model for it in Plotinus.

Having said this, I know that, despite my refusal to follow Miller's first question on the subject of an ontology of the unconscious, I nevertheless gave you a little rope with some very precise references. I spoke of the ὄν, of the οὐχ. With the ὄν, I was referring specifically to the formulation of it given by Henri Ey, of whom it cannot be said that he is the best qualified person to speak of the unconscious—he manages to situate the unconscious somewhere in his theory of consciousness. I spoke of the μὴὄν, of the prohibition, of the says-no. This does not go very far as a strictly metaphysical indication, and I do not think that here I am transgressing the boundaries that I have laid down for myself. All the same, it does structure in a perfectly transmissible way the points on which your question bears. In the unconscious there is a corpus of knowledge (*un savoir*), which must in no way be conceived as knowledge to be completed, to be closed.

ὄν, οὐχ ὄν, μὴ ὄν—to use these terms is still to over-substantify the unconscious. This is why I have carefully avoided them. What there is beyond, what a little while ago I called the beauty behind the shutters, this is what is in question and which I have not touched on today. It is a question of mapping out how something of the subject is, behind the screen, magnetized, magnetized to the profound degree of dissociation, of split. This is the key-point at which we must see the Gordian knot.

P. Kaufmann: *What relation is there between what you have designated as slag and what you earlier spoke of as remainder?*

Lacan: In human destiny, the remainder is always fruitful. The slag is the extinguished remainder. Here, the term slag is used in an entirely negative way. It refers to that true regression that may occur on the plane of the theory of psychological knowledge, in so far as the analyst finds himself placed in a field in which he has no other course but to flee. He then seeks for assurances in theories that operate in the direction of an orthopaedic, conformist therapeutics, providing access for the subject to the most mythical conception of *happiness* [English in the original—Tr.]. Together with an uncritical manipulation of evolutionism, this is what sets the tone of our era. By slag, I mean here the analysts themselves, nothing more—whilst the discovery of the unconscious is still young, and it is an unprecedented opportunity for subversion.

NOTES

1. 'Fonction et champ de la parole et du language en psychanalyse,' *Écrits,* Paris, Ed. du Seuil, 1966; 'The Function and Field of Speech and Language in Psycho-Analysis,' *Écrits: a selction,* trans. Alan Sheridan, London, Tavistock Publications, 1977.

28. An Ego Psychology–Object Relations Theory Approach to the Transference

Otto F. Kernberg

AN OVERVIEW OF MY APPROACH

Having spelled out my general theoretical and technical approach in earlier work (Kernberg, 1975, 1976, 1980, 1984), and having illustrated it with extended clinical material more recently (1986a, 1986b, 1987), I will limit myself here to providing the briefest outline of that approach, to be followed by a description of its clinical aspects as applied to the management of the transference.

My ego psychology–object relations theory is anchored in the theoretical and clinical contributions of Jacobson (1964, 1967, 1971) and Mahler (1971, 1972; Mahler and Furer, 1968; Mahler, et al., 1975). I have also been influenced by Erikson (1951, 1956, 1959), Melanie Klein (1945, 1946, 1952a, 1957), Fairbairn (1954), Winnicott (1958, 1965), and Sandler (Sandler and Rosenblatt, 1962; Sandler and Sandler, 1978).

My theory of motivation adheres closely to Freud's dual drive theory, but considers drives indissolubly linked to object relations; I also consider the separation of source, pressure, aim, and object of drives, as in traditional metapsychology, artificial. I think that libidinal and aggressive drive derivatives are invested in object relations from the very onset of the symbiotic phase, that the ideational and affective representations of drives are originally undifferentiated from each other, and that affect states representing the most primitive manifestations of drives are essential links of self- and object representations from their origins on.

My theoretical formulation proposes that affects are the primary motivational system and, internalized or fixated as the frame of internalized object relations, are gradually organized into libidinal and aggressive drives as hierarchically supraordinate motivational systems. This concept distinguishes my position from the theories of motivation of the major contributors I have

Reprinted by permission from the *Psychoanalytic Quarterly* 56(1987): 197–221.

listed, but the emphasis on the central clinical position of affects is common to all of us. In my view, affects are constitutionally determined and developmentally activated primary motivators. I believe that after they have been integrated into the drives, they become the signals of drive activation.

Also in agreement with the authors I have mentioned, I believe that the internalizations of object relations are originally dyadic, and that self- and object representations established under the impact of various affect states are the building blocks of what eventually constitutes the id, the ego, and the superego.

In agreement with Jacobson and Mahler, I have proposed a developmental model for the conceptualization of the structural characteristics of psychotic, borderline, and neurotic psychopathology, and stressed differences in the structural characteristics of these three levels of emotional illness.

I have considered the ego, superego, and id the underlying structural organization of the classical psychoneuroses and neurotic characters and stressed that at this level the vicissitudes of impulse-defense configurations are predominantly expressed as conflicts involving the three psychic agencies and external reality. The oedipus complex is the dominant conflictual constellation that reflects the culmination of the development of sexual and aggressive drives in the context of the representational world of early childhood and is crucially involved in the consolidation of the superego.

Patients with neurotic personality organization present well-integrated superego, ego, and id structures; within the psychoanalytic situation, the analysis of resistances brings about the activation, in the transference, first, of relatively global characteristics of these structures, and later, the internalized object relations of which they are composed. The analysis of drive derivatives occurs in the context of the analysis of the relation of the patient's infantile self to significant parental objects as projected onto the analyst.

The borderline personality organization, in contrast, shows a predominance of preoedipal conflicts and psychic representations of preoedipal conflicts condensed with representations of the oedipal phase. Conflicts are not predominantly repressed and therefore unconsciously dynamic. Rather, they are expressed in mutually dissociated ego states reflecting the defense of primitive dissociation or splitting. The activation of primitive object relations that predate the consolidation of ego, superego, and id is manifest in the transference as apparently chaotic affect states, which have to be analyzed in sequential steps (Kernberg, 1984). In summary, I wish only to stress that the approach to the interpretation of the primitive transferences of borderline patients suggested in my earlier work may bring about a transformation of part object relations into total object relations, of primitive transferences (largely reflecting stages of development that predate object constancy) into the advanced transferences of the oedipal phase.

Within my ego psychology–object relations theory framework, unconscious intrapsychic conflicts are always between (a) certain units of self- and object representations under the impact of a particular drive derivative (clinically, a certain affect disposition reflecting the instinctual side of the conflict) and (b) contradictory or opposing units of self- and object representations and their respective affect dispositions reflecting the defensive structure. Unconscious intrapsychic conflicts are never simply between impulse and defense; rather, the drive derivative finds expression through a certain internalized object relation, and the defense, too, is reflected by a certain internalized object relation.

At severe levels of psychopathology, splitting mechanisms stabilize such dynamic structures within an ego-id matrix and permit the contradictory aspects of these conflicts to remain—at least partially—conscious, in the form of primitive transferences. In contrast, patients with neurotic personality organization present impulse-defense configurations that contain specific unconscious wishes reflecting sexual and aggressive drive derivatives embedded in unconscious fantasies relating to the oedipal objects. Here, we find relatively less distortion both of the self-representations relating to these objects and of the representations of the oedipal objects themselves. Therefore the difference between past pathogenic experiences and their transformation into currently structured unconscious dispositions is not as great as is found in the primitive transferences in patients with borderline personality organization.

My emphasis is on the internalized object relation rather than on the impulse-defense configuration per se: the unconscious, wishful fantasy expresses such an object relation. The two ways in which, according to Freud (1915), unconscious wishes may become conscious (in the form of ideational representatives and as affects) are, in my view, evident in the relation between a self-representation and an object representation under the impact of a certain affect. Glover (1955), when he pointed to the need to identify both libidinal drive derivatives and ego- and superego-derived identifications in the transference, was, I believe, pointing in the same direction. If the transference neurosis is expressed in (a) instinctual impulses expressed as affects and (b) identifications reflecting internalized object relations, then the object relations frame of reference I propose may be considered a direct clinical application of the metapsychological concept of the dynamic unconscious and the conditions under which it appears in consciousness.

The analysis of the transference is a central concern in my general technical approach. Transference analysis consists in the analysis of the reactivation in the here-and-now of past internalized object relations. The analysis of past internalized object relations in the transference constitutes, at the same time, the analysis of the constituent structures of ego, superego, and id and their intra- and interstructural conflicts. In contrast to the culturalists or interpersonal object relations theoreticians, such as Sullivan (1953, 1962) and Guntrip (1961, 1968, 1971), and to Kohut's (1971, 1977) self psychology, I conceive of internalized object relations as not reflecting actual object relations from the past. Rather, they reflect a combination of realistic and fantasied—and often highly distorted—internalizations of such past object relations and defenses against them under the effects of activation and projection of instinctual drive derivatives. In other words, there is a dynamic tension between the here-and-now, which reflects intrapsychic structure, and the there-and-then unconscious genetic determinants derived from the "actual" past, the patient's developmental history.

I assume that in all cases the transference is dynamically unconscious in the sense that, either because of repression or of splitting, the patient unconsciously distorts the current experience because of his fixation to pathogenic conflicts with a significant internalized object of the past. The major task is to bring the unconscious transference meanings in the here-and-now into full consciousness by means of interpretation. This is the first stage in analyzing the relation between the unconscious present and the unconscious past.

Rather than making a direct connection between currently conscious or preconscious experiences in relation to the therapist and the conscious past, or to an assumed unconscious past (as I believe self psychologists tend to do), I expect the patient's free associations to the uncovered unconscious transference meanings in the here-and-now to lead us into the unconscious past. I therefore suggest reconstructions to the patient in tentative and open-ended formulations that should permit him to proceed in any one of several directions.

My theoretical framework is expressed clinically in the way I listen to patients. My only expectation is that the patient's free associations will lead to the emergence in the transference of past internalized object relations superimposed on the actual interactions of patient and analyst.

I wish to stress again that I leave the question of assumed genetic origins in the process of uncovering the unconscious meaning in the here-and-now as open-ended as I can. Although it is true that the nature of the activated object relation itself points to its probable genetic and developmental origins, I think it premature to pin down this hypothetical origin before the patient's free associations and exploration of unconscious meanings of his behavior in the here-and-now have given access to new evidence. I am always acutely aware of the danger that any preconceived notions the analyst has may close this investigative field prematurely. A theoretical frame that locates dominant conflicts of the patient in a predetermined area or time seems to me to constitute an important limitation to the analyst's and the patient's freedom to explore the origins of the unconscious present in the unconscious past.

The Kleinian tendency to relate primitive defensive operations and object relations to the first year of life (Klein, 1945, 1946, 1952b, 1957), or Kohut's assumption that an ever-present fragility of the self is the primary determinant (Reed, 1986), or, for that matter, to consistently search for the oedipal determinants or for pathology of separation-individuation, etc., brings about an unwarranted narrowing of the interpretive frame and limits the analyst's capacity for discovering and investigating the unknown.

CHANNELS OF COMMUNICATION OF THE TRANSFERENCE

The unconscious object relations that superimpose themselves on the actual one—the patient and the analyst working together within the jointly agreed upon boundaries of the psychoanalytic situation—might be either a variety of unconscious object relations in conflict with each other or a defensively functioning object relation activated against an underlying, contrasting one with impulsive functions. These unconscious object relations may emerge through various "channels." With patients presenting neurotic personality organization, and in the advanced stages of treatment of patients with more severe character pathology and borderline pathology, they emerge mostly from the patient's free associations.

Let me illustrate with a clinical vignette. Ms. A, an architect in her early thirties, consulted me because of chronic interpersonal difficulties in her work and a severe depression related to the breakup of an extramarital relationship with a senior business associate she described as being sadistic. Diagnostic evaluation revealed a hysterical personality with strong masochistic features. A happy early childhood relation with her father had turned into bitter struggles with him during her adolescence, in the context of his having severe marital difficulties. Ms. A saw her mother as an innocent victim. A sexually intolerant, suppressive atmosphere in the home had become internalized in Ms. A's own rigid repression of all sexual impulses until only a few years before starting her analysis: she was frigid with her husband and was able to achieve orgasm only in extramarital affairs.

A few weeks after beginning her analysis, her mood improved, and she now conveyed the impression of a nice, "innocent," submissive little girl who seemed eager to please the analyst. She was obviously trying hard to say whatever came into her mind, and the dominant content of her early free associations related to her work, particularly to her bosses, who seemed to her narrow-minded, biased, uninformed professionals, lacking an original, creative approach to design. She was so obviously dismissive of her bosses that she herself raised the question during a session whether she might be risking losing her job. She had, indeed, lost a job with another firm in the not so distant past because of her interpersonal difficulties.

When I said I was puzzled by the cheerful way in which she expressed her concerns over the prospect of being thrown out, she acknowledged a "daredevil" attitude in herself, adding that this might indeed be dangerous but it was gratifyingly exciting, too. Further associations revealed her fantasies of meeting her boss, who would sternly notify her that she would have to leave, and whom she would then let know by means of subtle insinuations that she was interested in him as a man. This, in her fantasy, might lead to a sexual relation with him at the very time he was dismissing her from the business. It was exciting to be sexually involved with a man who had thrown her out.

I think this vignette illustrates the early emergence of a "nice little girl" attitude in the transference as a defense against the underlying temptation of a pseudorebellious, provocatively aggressive attitude toward a male authority aimed at bringing about an underlying, desired self-punitive sexual relation (presumably, with a sadistic father image). The fact that the apparently positive early transference relationship permitted the emergence of the underlying negative transference dispositions in the content of the patient's free associations, rather than directly in the transference relationship itself, actually gave us a lead time to elaborate this unconscious conflict before its full actualization in the transference. The focus on the contents of free association, on the communication of Ms. A's subjective experience, was the predominant communicative channel through which the unconscious pathogenic object relation emerged in the transference.

In patients with severe character pathology and borderline personality organization, the emergence of dominant unconscious object relations in the transference typically occurs by means of another channel, namely, nonverbal communication. This does not mean that what is verbally communicated through free association in these cases is not relevant or important, but rather that the nonverbal communication acquires economic (that is, affective) predominance in conveying information to the analyst.

A postgraduate college student in his late twenties, Mr. B. came for consultation because of chronic difficulties in relationships with women, uncertainty about his professional interests and future, and deep passivity in his work and daily life. Mr. B, in his early analytic sessions, dwelt on detailed descriptions of the altercations he was having with his present woman friend. My efforts to clarify further what the issues were in what appeared to me confusing descriptions of these arguments elicited ironic comments from him that I was slow and pedestrian and did not grasp the subtlety of what he was telling me. He also expected me to approve immediately the statement he had made and the actions he had taken regarding his woman friend. I asked why he felt the need for me to immediately support his actions or agree with his evaluation of her. He now angrily accused me of not being sympathetic to him and of being the traditional, poker-faced psychoanalyst.

Soon Mr. B also began to complain that I was not providing him with any new understanding that would permit him to deal more effectively with his woman friend. But when, after getting a better feeling for what was actually going on in their interactions, I did question his interpretations of her behavior and also wondered about the reasons for some of his behaviors, he accused me of taking her part, of being unfairly biased against him, and, in fact, of making his relations with her worse by undermining his own sense of security. He also offered me various psychoanalytic theories to account for his woman friend's sadistic behavior toward him. He pointed out to me that he himself was obviously a masochistic character and, with growing anger, that I was not doing my job—I was not relating what was happening to him now with his childhood experiences.

Although my initial diagnosis of Mr. B had been severe character pathology with paranoid, narcissistic, and infantile features—and I was prepared for stormy transference developments—I was taken aback by the intensity of his complaints and accusations, and I became increasingly cautious in making any comments to him. He immediately perceived my cautiousness and accused me angrily of treating him like a ''sickie,'' rather than being direct with him. I then focused on his difficulty in accepting anything I said that was different from his own thinking, pointing to the internal conflict he experienced in his relationship with me: he very much wanted me to help him and to be on his side while, at the same time, he experienced everything that came from me as either hostile and damaging or absurd and worthless. Mr. B agreed (for the first time) with my assessment of the situation. He said that he found himself very much in need of help and faced with an incompetent and hostile analyst. I then asked whether he was indeed convinced that this was a reality because, if it was, it would naturally lead him to ask why he had selected me as his therapist, and he was not raising that question. He immediately accused me of trying to throw him out. I told him I was trying to understand how he felt and not necessarily confirming his views of me.

He then reviewed the circumstances that had led him to consult with me and to select me as an analyst after several unhappy experiences with other psychotherapists. In the course of this review, it emerged that Mr. B had been very pleased when I accepted him as a patient, but had also felt very unhappy about what he experienced as the enormous difference in our status. He talked about how painful it was to him to have to consult professionals he considered representative of the most conservative psychiatric and psychoanalytic establishment. Because I had been highly recommended to him, he had consulted me, but now he was wondering whether a brief psychotherapy with a therapist from one of the "antipsychiatry" schools might help him much more. I suggested that it might be preferable for him to perceive me as incompetent and hostile if this permitted him to preserve his own self-esteem, although this perception of me was also frustrating his wish to be helped. In other words, I began to interpret the acting out of needs to devalue and disparage me that reflected dissociated envy of me.

I believe that this case illustrates how, from the beginning of the treatment, the principal channel of communication for unconscious object relations activated in the transference was reflected in the patient's attitude toward me rather than in the content of free associations per se. Certainly the content of his verbal communication was important in clarifying what went on in the relationship with me, but the nature of Mr. B's behavior was the dominant focus of communication.

On the surface, he was devaluing me as an admired yet enviously resented parental authority, with himself a grandiose and sadistic child. At a deeper level, he was enacting unconsciously the relationship of a frustrated and enraged child with a much needed parental image; but he also deeply resented that parental figure because he perceived it as controlling and devaluating. This view of the parental object triggered intense rage, expressed in the wish to devalue and destroy the object while, at a still deeper level, he unconsciously hoped that it might survive. In fact, it took many weeks to unravel these unconscious meanings in the here-and-now. Months later, we learned that this object relation reflected an unconscious relationship with Mr. B's mother and that his repeated failure in relationships with women followed a strikingly similar pattern to the one described in his relationship with me. All these women and I myself represented mother in this transference enactment.

There is still a third channel of communication, which might be considered an outgrowth of the second one, except that here the nonverbal communication is expressed in the apparent absence of any specific object relation in the transference. Under these circumstances, over a period of many months or even years, there is minimal transference regression and an almost total absence of manifest aggression or of libidinal investment in the transference, an indication of the patient's incapacity to depend upon the analyst.

I have stressed elsewhere (Kernberg, 1984) that such patients present subtle, pervasive, and highly effective transference resistances against being dependent on the analyst and against the related regression in the transference in general, a condition that might be described as a "closure of the analytic space." To put it more concretely, an absence of emotional depth, of emotional reality, and of fantasy in the analytic encounter becomes the dominant resistance in the treatment.

I described elsewhere (Kernberg, 1986b) an artist in his late twenties who consulted because of his dissatisfaction with his bisexual style of life and his growing sexual inhibition. This man's personality had strong narcissistic features and an "as if" quality. His mother had died when he was nine years old, and an older sister had taken over her household duties while his father took over many of the mother's functions. The description of both parents was vague and contradictory. The patient conveyed a quality of unreality about his entire history. He had an adequate surface social adaptation, but there was something artificial in his appearance. He was one of those patients whose "perfect free association" effectively mimics an authentic analytic process. There was something mechanical about him, and I found it extremely difficult to link this impression to any concrete manifestations in the transference. He showed similar lack of involvement with his woman friend, toward whom, in spite of good reasons to the contrary, he showed absolutely no signs of jealousy.

By the third year of his analysis, although I was able to maintain my interest in him, I felt that I was being seduced into a strange inactivity and tolerance of this situation, as if I were watching a theatrical display that had no depth and presented itself as from a film screen. It was as if the patient could neither acknowledge me as a person different from himself yet available to him, nor acknowledge his own presence in the room beyond that of recorder of external reality. I finally decided to focus on the nature and the symptoms of his consistent unavailability to me and my unavailability to him as he conveyed it in his attitude in the hours. I used the technique I have described elsewhere (Kernberg, 1984) of imagining how a "normal" patient might behave in a particular hour in order to sharpen my focus on the concrete manifestations of the artificiality in this man's relation with me.

The effect of my focus on this "absence" in the transference was striking: the patient began to experience anxiety in the sessions. Over a period of several weeks, his anxiety increased, and his associations changed significantly. He developed an intense fear of me, with an image of me as somebody totally unreal, who presented the façade of a friendly psychoanalyst that covered an underlying frightening empty space. He was alone in the middle of a devastating experience of himself as damaged, disintegrating, incapable of being either boy or girl. It was as if only dead objects surrounded him.

In the course of a few weeks this man changed from an almost inanimate robot to what can best be described as an abandoned, terrified child. Activated in the transference was an intense primitive object relation and, as part of my countertransference reaction, a concordant identification (Racker, 1957) with that self-representation. Following this episode, an intensely ambivalent relation to a powerful father emerged in the transference, with projection onto me of the image of a sadistic, controlling, savage father who would be disgusted by the patient's sexual fantasies and wishes. In short, for the first time it was as if elements that had previously been presented in a flat mosaic of past experiences now acquired depth in the transference. This case, I believe, dramatically illustrates the predominance of the "third channel" of the constant yet latent "space" of the analytic encounter.

TRANSFERENCE, UNCONSCIOUS PRESENT, AND
UNCONSCIOUS PAST

I have stressed that it is crucial to first uncover the unconscious meanings of the transference in the here-and-now and to make fully conscious the expression of this object relation in the transference before attempting reconstructions of the past. In the course of this process, the previously unacknowledged, denied, repressed, projected, or dissociated object relation may now be fully acknowledged and become ego-dystonic. This is where the analytic questions can be raised: what are the genetic determinants of the presently activated unconscious intrapsychic conflict, and how are these interpreted to the patient?

Our first case, Ms. A, provided dynamic information that would seem quite naturally to reflect a masochistic transformation of a positive oedipal relationship. As is characteristic of better functioning patients, the links between the consciously known history from the past and the unconscious activation of repressed object relations in the here-and-now were apparently direct. I nevertheless avoided any reference to her relationship with her father until the patient herself, wondering about her need to first transform a good relationship with a man into a bad one in order to then sexualize it, started to associate about her adolescent interactions with her father.

With Mr. B, the postgraduate college student, a very chaotic and complex acting out in the transference could not be linked directly with any known aspects of the patient's past: the information he had conveyed about his past was itself so contradictory and chaotic that it would have been difficult to accept any of its aspects at face value. It took a long time to clarify the unconscious meanings in the here-and-now; only when that had been accomplished could I begin to raise the question of what should be explored in terms of genetic and developmental antecedents.

The dynamics of Mr. B's desperate search for dependency upon a dangerously and cruelly controlling object might lead theoreticians of different persuasions to different conclusions: (a) a Mahlerian might conclude that it related to the rapprochement subphase of separation-individuation; (b) a Kleinian might relate it to an envied good (and/or bad) breast; (c) a traditional ego psychologist might think in terms of the guilt-determined anal regression from a positive oedipal conflict. But because I had no information about what developmental stage this conflict had originated in, or regressed to, I avoided speculating about it before the unconscious here-and-now developments had become completely conscious and ego-dystonic.

In the case of the artist, the danger of premature genetic reconstructions is really highlighted. Here, even at the time of a breakthrough from a long analytic stalemate, I refrained from linking the activated primitive object relation with any aspect of the past before further evidence emerged in the transference, in the patient's free associations, in short, in the emergence of new and unexpected material.

In summary then, I attempt to carry out, first, "atemporal" constructions of the unconscious meanings in the here-and-now, and only later, when the conditions warrant it, cautiously to transform such constructions into reconstructions of the unconscious past. Similarly, I try to avoid the genetic fallacy of equating the most primitive with the earliest, as well as any mechanical linkage of certain types of psychopathology with fixed stages of development.

My three cases also illustrate another aspect of my technique: namely, the importance of carefully exploring the developments in the patient's experience both outside the analytic hours and in the analytic relationship itself. With Ms. A, I spent considerable time exploring the relationship with her colleagues and superiors at work before attempting to link that material to the relationship with me: and that, in spite of my very early observation of her "nice little girl" attitude in the analytic hours.

My first efforts with Mr. B were genuinely focused upon the clarification of the chaotic relationship with his woman friend. Only when, in the course of the paralysis of all my efforts to help him gain further understanding, it became obvious that the transference issues had acquired highest interpretive priority, did I focus consistently on his relationship with me. I had to wait a long time before I could link the relationship with his woman friend and the relationship with me.

In the third case, of course, a long history of failure of efforts to explore both the patient's extra-analytic and his analytic relationships led to the diagnosis of what I have referred to as the closure of the analytic space with this patient. In general terms, economic criteria (that is, the search for areas of dominant affective activation, whether conscious or unconscious) should dictate whether the focus of intervention is predominantly on an interaction with the patient in the hour, or in the patient's external reality (Kernberg, 1984).

It must be apparent by now that while I strongly emphasize the analysis of the unconscious meanings of the transference in the here-and-now, I do not neglect the importance of the analysis of genetic antecedents, the there-and-then. In my emphasis on the here-and-now, I am in agreement with Gill's proposals. I do believe, however, that, by overextending the concept of the transference as "an amalgam of past and present," Gill (1982, p. 177) blurs the differentiation of what is inappropriate in the here-and-now and needs to be explained by its origin elsewhere.

I think it is an error to include the actual aspects of the analyst's behavior that trigger and/or serve to rationalize the patient's transference as part of the transference itself. For the analyst to phobically avoid acknowledging the reality of an aspect of his behavior noticed by the patient, and which triggers a certain reaction by the patient, is a technical error; even further, the analyst's failure to be aware of what in his own behavior may have unconsciously triggered aspects of the transference is also an error of technique. I think it is a distortion of the classical concept of transference to assume that the analyst's realistic contributions to the interaction with a patient should be ignored or denied; to do so is to misuse the concept of transference as a distortion of actual reality because it implies that the analyst is perfectly adjusted and one hundred percent normal. As I pointed out in earlier work (Kernberg, 1984),

Patients rapidly become expert in detecting the analyst's personality characteristics, and transference reactions often first emerge in this context. But to conclude that all transference reactions are at bottom, at least in part, unconscious or conscious reactions to the reality of the analyst is to misunderstand the nature of the transference. The transference is the inappropriate aspect of the patient's reaction to the analyst. The analysis of the transference may begin by the analyst's "leaving open" the reality of the patient's observations and exploring why particular observations are important at any particular time.

If the analyst is aware of realistic features of his personality and is able to accept them without narcissistic defensiveness or denial, his emotional attitude will permit him to convey to the patient: "So, if you are responding to something in me, how do we understand the intensity of your reaction?" But the analyst's character pathology may be such that the patient's transference reaction to him results in the erosion of technical neutrality. When the analyst is incapable of discriminating between the patient's realistic and unrealistic perceptions of him, countertransference is operating. (p. 266)

In my view, what is enacted in the transference is never a simple repetition of the patient's actual past experiences. I agree with Melanie Klein's (1952b)

proposal that the transference derives from a combination of real and fantasied experiences of the past, and defenses against both. This is another way of stating that the relations between psychic reality and objective reality always remain ambiguous: the more severe the patient's psychopathology and the more distorted his intrapsychic structural organization, the more indirect is the relation between present structure, genetic reconstruction, and developmental origins. But to conclude that reconstruction of the past is impossible because it is difficult, and to use the difficulty of connecting past with present to question the possibility of uncovering the past is really an evasion and is unwarranted.

COUNTERTRANSFERENCE, EMPATHY, MEMORY, AND DESIRE

My views of countertransference have been spelled out in earlier work (Kernberg, 1975, 1984). Here, in summary, I want to stress the advantage of a "global" concept of countertransference, which includes, in addition to the analyst's unconscious reactions to the patient or to the transference (in other words, the analyst's transferences), (a) the analyst's realistic reaction to the reality of the patient's life, (b) the analyst's realistic reaction to his own life as it may become affected by the patient, and (c) the analyst's realistic reaction to the transference. For practical purposes, all these components—but not the analyst's realistic emotional reaction to the patient's transference—should remain rather subdued under ordinary psychoanalytic circumstances.

Obviously, if the analyst has retained severe nonanalyzed character pathology or if an unfortunate mutual "resonance" exists between the patient's and the analyst's character pathology, the analyst's transferences to the patient may be accentuated. The greater the patient's psychopathology and the more severely regressive the transference, the more intense the therapist's realistic emotional responses to the patient. It is this area of the realistic responses to the patient and their links with the analyst's deeper transference dispositions that presents both potential dangers for countertransference acting out and potential assets in the form of clinical material to be explored by the analyst and integrated in his understanding of the transference.

I assume that Racker's (1957) concepts of concordant and complementary identifications in the countertransference are well known by now. Their respective functions in increasing empathy with a patient's central subjective experience (in concordant identification) and in maintaining empathy with what the patient is dissociating or projecting (in complementary identification) are also well known. In my view, complementary identification in the countertransference is of particular importance in the analysis of patients with severe character pathology and regressive transference developments. By means of unconscious defensive operations, particularly projective identification, patients are able, through subtle behavioral communications, to induce emotional attitudes in the analyst that reflect aspects of the patient's own dissociated self-representations or object representations.

The psychoanalyst's introspective analysis of his complementary countertransference reaction thus permits him to diagnose projected aspects of the patient's activated internalized object relations, particularly those communicated nonverbally and by alteration in the "analytic space"—the habitual, silent relationship between patient and analyst. Under optimal circumstances, the analyst's understanding of his own affective pressure that derives from the patient's unconscious communications in the transference may lead to a fuller understanding of the object relation activated in the transference.

My attitude regarding the activation in the analyst of intense emotional dispositions toward the patient, particularly at times of transference regression, is to tolerate my own feelings and fantasies about the patient, with the clear understanding that I attempt to use them to better understand what is going on in the transference. I remain consistently alert to the need to protect the patient from any temptation I might have to act on these feelings or to communicate them to him or her. Absolute noncommunication of countertransference reactions to the patient is the counterpart of the analyst's freedom to work with them and use them in his interpretations.

A related issue is to determine the nature of what is projected onto the analyst and activated in the countertransference. In essence, patients may project a self-representation while they enact the object representation of a determined object relation activated in the transference, or, vice versa, they may project an object representation while enacting the corresponding self-representation. These projections tend to be relatively stable in patients with neurotic personality organization, but are unstable and rapidly alternating in patients with severe character pathology and borderline personality organization.

For example, the architect, Ms. A, unconsciously tried to ingratiate herself with me as an object representation of her father in order to protect herself against her own impulses to defy me as a father and to seduce me into an aggressive—and sexualized—counterattack. There was a relatively stable activation of several self-representations under the impact of different affective states in the patient, and a relatively stable projection onto me of object representations unconsciously representing father under different affective states. In other words, we did not "exchange personalities."

But Mr. B showed a rapid and almost chaotic alternation of self- and object representations in his identifications and in his projections onto me, reflecting different affective states as well. For example, at one point, he would project onto me a withholding, indifferent, and rejecting parental image, perceiving me as dominant, self-centered, unable to tolerate any view different from my own, and ready to angrily dismiss the patient (my child) who dared to think differently. Only minutes before or after such an experience, Mr. B would identify himself with the image of such a parental figure, and dismiss me (his child), declaring that he had just decided to stop his analysis because he could not tolerate such a totally misguided and obstinate analyst. His attitude implied that such a sudden termination of his relationship with me would come most naturally, and without any risk of missing me. In other words, there was a rapid exchange between us of the roles of the sadistic, neglecting parent and the neglected, mistreated child.

I think it is of crucial importance that the analyst tolerate the rapidly alternating, at times completely contradictory, emotional experiences that signal the activation of complementary self- and object representations of a primitive internalized object relation. The analyst's capacity to tolerate such rapid changes in his emotional responses to the patient without denial or acting out includes several preconditions.

First, the analyst must maintain strict boundaries in the analytic situation of space, time, privacy outside the treatment hours, and a sense of his own physical security during the sessions.

Second, the analyst must be able to tolerate, as part of his empathic response to the patient, the activation of primitively aggressive, sexual, and dependent affect states in himself. Thus, for example, the analyst must accept his own aggression in the countertransference (Winnicott, 1949), such as the gratifying experience of sadistic control; this experience may be much more of a problem for the analyst than tolerating, for example, developmentally more advanced levels of sexual arousal.

Third, it is important that the analyst maintain sufficient confidence in his creativity as part of his analytic work so that he may tolerate the patient's need to destroy his efforts without a reactive counterattack, devaluation of the patient, or withdrawal from him. Only if the analyst can feel comfortable with his own aggression will he be able to interpret aggression in the patient without fearing that this is an attack on the patient, or without submitting to the patient's accusation that he is being attacked (a manifestation of the patient's intolerance of his own aggression).

The impression I have gained from studying the clinical material presented by self psychologists is that they implicitly or explicitly accept the view that the analyst's interpretation of aggression in the patient corresponds to an attack on the patient, as if all aggression were "bad." Obviously, such a view of the analyst cannot but reinforce the patient's own conviction that aggression is bad and that he must defend himself against this "accusation" by whatever means at his disposal.

As I have stressed in earlier work (Kernberg, 1975), empathy must therefore include not only concordant identification with the patient's ego-syntonic, central subjective experience, but also complementary identification with the dissociated, repressed, or projected aspects of the patient's self-concept or his object representations.

Wilfred Bion, in a paper he called "Notes on Memory and Desires" (1967), stressed the importance of facing the patient's material in each session without preconceived notions about the patient's dynamics ("memory") and without any particular wishes regarding the patient's material, functioning, and experience, as well as any wishes not related to the patient at all ("desire"). Insofar as this contribution, in my view, marks an indirect criticism of the formulations of interpretations prevalent in the Kleinian school, and a plea for complete openness to new material with a minimum of analytic preconceptions, his point is well taken. I think, however, that Bion neglected the importance of the analyst's long-range experience with the patient's material, the understanding of an analytic process that develops over a period of weeks and months, an understanding that may become a frame of reference to be used by the analyst without his becoming enslaved by it.

My point is that the analyst needs to maintain a sense of the continuity of the analytic process and, particularly, a view of the patient, his behavior, and his reality that transcends the subjective view of the patient at any particular moment, in any particular hour, as well as the patient's own "myths" or preconceived organization of his own past. Such a frame of reference ("memory") is the counterpart to the analyst's tolerating periods of nonunderstanding, in the course of which he may expect new knowledge to emerge eventually. Similarly, regarding the analyst's "desire," the tolerance of impulses, wishes, and fears about the patient that evolve throughout time may provide the analyst with important information that may enter his awareness in the sessions, again, without necessarily enslaving him.

While much of what I have said may apply to psychoanalytic psychotherapy with nonanalyzable borderline and narcissistic patients, my intention has been to spell out my basic approach to the transference in the context of standard psychoanalysis with a broad spectrum of patients. It has been my experience that when I apply this approach to patients with neurotic personality organization (Kernberg, 1987), it differs little from a traditional ego psychology approach or from other object relations theories. In contrast, the differences between my approach and that of self psychology are obviously profound and global. In my work with regressed patients, however, important differences between my approach and traditional ego psychology, the British object relations schools, and the culturalists' object relations techniques in this country seem to emerge.

REFERENCES

Bion, W. R. (1967). Notes on memory and desires. *Psychoanal. Forum,* 2:272–273, 279–280.

Erikson, E. H. (1951). Growth and crises of the healthy personality. In *Identity and the Life Cycle. Selected Papers.* New York: International Universities Press, 1959, pp. 50–100.

—— (1956). The problem of ego identity. *J. Amer. Psychoanal. Assn.,* 4:56–121.

—— (1959). *Identity and the Life Cycle. Selected Papers.* New York: International Universities Press.

Fairbairn, W. R. D. (1954). *An Object-Relations Theory of the Personality.* New York: Basic Books.

Freud, S. (1915). The unconscious. *Standard Edition,* 14.

Gill, M. M. (1982). *Analysis of Transference, Vol. 1. Theory and Technique. Psychol. Issues,* Monogr. 53. New York: International Universities Press.

Glover, E. (1955). *The Technique of Psychoanalysis.* New York: International Universities Press.

Guntrip, H. J. S. (1961). *Personality Structure and Human Interaction. The Developing Synthesis of Psychodynamic Theory.* New York: International Universities Press

—— (1968). *Schizoid Phenomena, Object Relations and the Self.* New York: International Universities Press.

—— (1971). *Psychoanalytic Theory, Therapy, and the Self.* New York: Basic Books.

Jacobson, E. (1964). *The Self and the Object World.* New York: International Universities Press.

—— (1967). *Psychotic Conflict and Reality.* New York: International Universities Press.

—— (1971). *Depression. Comparative Studies of Normal, Neurotic, and Psychotic Conditions.* New York: International Universities Press.

Kernberg, O. F. (1975). *Borderline Conditions and Pathological Narcissism.* New York: Aronson.

——— (1976). *Object Relations Theory and Clinical Psychoanalysis*. New York: Aronson.

——— (1980). *Internal World and External Reality. Object Relations Theory Applied*. New York: Aronson.

——— (1984). *Severe Personality Disorders: Psychotherapeutic Strategies*. New Haven/London: Yale University Press.

——— (1986a). Identification and its vicissitudes as observed in psychosis. *Int. J. Psychoanal.*, 67:147–159.

——— (1986b). "Mythological encounters" in the psychoanalytic situation. *Proceedings of the First Delphi Int. Psychoanal. Symposium*.

——— (1987). Projection and projective identification: developmental and clinical aspects. *J. Amer. Psychoanal. Assn.* 35:795–820.

Klein, M. (1945). The oedipus complex in the light of early anxieties. In *Contributions to Psycho-Analysis, 1921–1945*. London: Hogarth, 1948, pp. 339–390.

——— (1946). Notes on some schizoid mechanisms. In *Developments in Psycho-Analysis*, ed. J. Riviere. London: Hogarth, 1952, pp. 292–320.

——— (1952a). Some theoretical conclusions regarding the emotional life of the infant. In *Developments in Psycho-Analysis*, ed. J. Riviere. London: Hogarth, pp. 198–236.

——— (1952b). The origins of transference. *Int. J. Psychoanal.*, 33:433–438.

——— (1957). *Envy and Gratitude. A Study of Unconscious Sources*. New York: Basic Books.

Kohut, H. (1971). *The Analysis of the Self. A Systematic Approach to the Psychoanalytic Treatment of Narcissistic Personality Disorders*. New York: International Universities Press

——— (1977). *The Restoration of the Self*. New York: International Universities Press.

Mahler, M. S. (1971). A study of the separation-individuation process and its possible application to borderline phenomena in the psychoanalytic situation. *Psychoanal. Study Child*, 26:403–424.

——— (1972). On the first three subphases of the separation-individuation process. *Int. J. Psychoanal.*, 53:333–338.

——— & Furer, M. (1968). *On Human Symbiosis and the Vicissitudes of Individuation. Vol. 1. Infantile Psychosis*. New York: International Universities Press.

———, Pine, F. & Bergman, A. (1975). *The Psychological Birth of the Human Infant. Symbiosis and Individuation*. New York: Basic Books.

Racker, H. (1957). The meanings and uses of countertransference. *Psychoanal. Q.*, 26:303–357.

Reed, G. S. (1986). Exegesis of self-psychology and classical psychoanalysis. *J. Amer. Psychoanal. Assn.*

Sandler, J. & Rosenblatt, B. (1962). The concept of the representational world. *Psychoanal. Study Child*, 17:128–145.

——— & Sandler, A. (1978). On the development of object relationships and affects. *Int. J. Psychoanal.*, 59:285–296.

Sullivan, H. S. (1953). *The Interpersonal Theory of Psychiatry*. New York: Norton.

——— (1962). *Schizophrenia as a Human Process*. New York: Norton.

Winnicott, D. W. (1949). Hate in the countertransference. In *Collected Papers. Through Paediatrics to Psychoanalysis*. New York: Basic Books, 1958, pp. 194–203.

——— (1958). *Collected Papers. Through Paediatrics to Psycho-Analysis*. New York: Basic Books.

——— (1965). *The Maturational Processes and the Facilitating Environment. Studies in the Theory of Emotional Development*. New York: International Universities Press.

29. Changes in Psychoanalytic Ideas: Transference Interpretation

Arnold M. Cooper

Interpretation of the transference is central to all psychoanalytic models. Definitions of transference and transference interpretation have changed greatly during the past half-century, influenced by major movements in philosophy, advances in psychoanalytic research and theory, and changes in our understanding of Freud. This paper suggests that historical, relatively simple, concepts of the transference as the reproduction in the present of significant relationships from the past do not adequately meet current clinical and theoretical demands. Modernist views of the transference emphasize as additional sources of transference responses, the role of the analytic background of safety, the constant modification of unconscious fantasy and internal representations, and the interactive nature of transference responses, with important interpersonal and intersubjective components. It is suggested that the evolving modernist views of transference and transference interpretation permit a fuller accounting for transference phenomena and open the way for better informed interventions. A brief discussion of the issue of psychological "truth" and "distortion" as applied to transference phenomena is presented. The themes are illustrated with clinical vignettes.

Psychoanalysts, since the earliest days of the *Studies on Hysteria* (Breuer and Freud, 1893–1905), have always given special attention to the transference and to the interpretation of transference, believing it to be central in our theory and technique. While there has never been a lack of interest in transference interpretation, it has recently become a particular focus of study and discussion. It is not clear why this is so, and the reasons may vary in different parts of the international psychoanalytic community. In America, at least, Gill's (1982) recent, and somewhat radical presentation of transference interpretation has surely helped to grab our attention. I believe another reason for our intensified interest in transference interpretation is the opportunity it provides for discussion of the full panoply of diverse analytic theories and techniques that today compete for our attention and allegiance. In this respect

Reprinted from the *Journal of the American Psychoanalytic Association* 35 (1987): 77–98, by permission of International Universities Press, Inc.

transference interpretation seems to have replaced self-psychology as the encompassing topic that allows analysts of varied persuasions to discuss almost every aspect of psychoanalysis.

Despite the diversity of analytic views that abound today, analysts seem to agree on the centrality of the transference and its interpretation in analytic process and cure, differing only in whether transference is everything or almost everything. This somewhat unusual degree of agreement may be aided by our inability to give a clear definition of what transference is.

CURRENT VIEWS OF THE TRANSFERENCE AND ITS INTERPRETATION

Laplanche and Pontalis (1973), in their dictionary, write, with some sense of despair, "The reason it is so difficult to propose a definition of transference is that for many authors the notion has taken on a very broad extension, even coming to connote all the phenomena which constitute the patient's relationship with the psychoanalyst. As a result the concept is burdened down more than any other with each analyst's particular views on the treatment—on its objective, dynamics, tactics, scope, etc. The question of the transference is thus beset by a whole series of difficulties which have been the subject of debate in classical psychoanalysis" (p. 456).

Sandler (1983) has discussed how the terms transference and transference resistance as well as other terms have undergone profound changes in meaning as new discoveries and new trends in psychoanalytic technique assumed ascendency. He said, ". . . major changes in technical emphasis brought about the extension of the transference concept, which now has dimensions of meaning which differ from the official definition of the term" (p. 10). I am not sure there has ever been a simple official definition of the term. While a certain flexibility of definition makes conversation possible in a field of diverse views, that we may never be clear on what any two people mean when they use the term is a significant handicap to our discourse.

With this in mind we might review one of Freud's last comments on transference. In *An Outline of Psycho-Analysis* (1940), published posthumously, he wrote of the analytic situation:

The most remarkable thing is this. The patient is not satisfied with regarding the analyst in the light of reality as a helper and advisor who, moreover, is remunerated for the trouble he takes and who would himself be content with some such role as that of a guide on a difficult mountain climb. On the contrary, the patient sees in him the return, the reincarnation, of some important figure out of his childhood or past, and consequently transfers on to him feelings and reactions which undoubtedly applied to this prototype. This fact of transference soon proves to be a factor of undreamt-of importance, on the one hand an instrument of irreplaceable value and on the other hand a source of serious dangers. . . . The analyst may shamefacedly admit to himself that he set out on a difficult undertaking without any suspicion of the extraordinary powers that would be at his command. . . .

Another advantage of transference, too, is that in it the patient produces before us with plastic clarity an important part of his life-story, of which he would otherwise have probably given us only an insufficient account. He acts it before us, as it were, instead of reporting it to us [pp. 174–176].

Freud saw the transference interpretation as a method of strengthening the ego against past unconscious wishes and conflicts.

It is the analyst's task constantly to tear the patient out of his menacing illusion and to show him again and again that what he takes to be new real life is a reflection of the past. And lest he should fall into a state in which he is inaccessible to all evidence, the analyst takes care that neither the love nor the hostility reach an extreme height. This is effected by preparing him in good time for these possibilities and by not overlooking the first signs of them. Careful handling of the transference on these lines is as a rule richly rewarded. If we succeed, as we usually can, in enlightening the patient on the true nature of the phenomena of the transference, we thus shall have struck a powerful weapon out of the hand of his resistance and shall have converted dangers into gains. For a patient never forgets again what he has experienced in the form of transference; it carries a greater force of conviction than anything he can acquire in other ways [p. 177].

While Freud, at one or another time entertained almost all possible views of the transference, I believe these statements at the end of his career give a clear sense of where he stood. He believed that the transference represents a *true* reconstruction of the past, a vivid reliving of earlier desires and fears that distort the patient's capacity to perceive the "true nature" of the present reality. The analyst is a wise guide who already knows the path, and the task of the transference interpretation is cognitive "enlightenment" that carries the emotional conviction of lived experience, while preventing excessive emotional regression.

Although it is a vast oversimplification and the division is not sharp, I shall suggest that there have been two major ideas about the transference and its interpretation during the history of psychoanalysis. One is explicit in Freud, as I quoted him earlier; the other is implicit. The first idea, close to Freud, is that the transference is an enactment of an earlier relationship, and the task of transference interpretation is to gain insight into the ways that the early infantile relationships are distorting or disturbing the relationship to the analyst, a relationship which is, in turn, a model for the patient's life relationships. I shall refer to this as the *historical* model of transference, implying both that it is older and that it is based on an idea of the centrality of history. The second view regards the transference as a new experience rather than an enactment of an old one. The purpose of transference interpretation is to bring to consciousness all aspects of this new experience including its colorings from the past. I shall refer to this as the *modernist* model of the transference, implying both that it is newer, in fact still at an early stage of evolution, and that it is based on an idea of the immediacy of experience. I would like to distinguish this discussion of models of transference and transference interpretation from the debate on the "here-and-now" interpretation that Gill has brought to the fore. Gill is primarily interested in issues of technique, and both models that I will discuss lend themselves to interpretive work in the here-and-now. These two models are not entirely mutually exclusive, but they do imply significant differences in basic assumptions and in treatment goals. Although the historical view is clearer and prettier, I believe that the modernist version of transference interpretation is more interesting and more promising.

In the first, historical, view, the importance of transference interpretation lies in the opportunity it provides in the transference neurosis for the patient to reexperience and undo the partially encapsulated, one might say "toxic," neurosogenic early history. In the second, modernist, view, the purpose of transference interpretation is to help the patient see, in the intensity of the transference, the aims, character, and mode of his current wishes and expectations as influenced by the past.

The historical view is more likely to regard the infantile neurosis as a "fact" of central importance for the analytic work, to be uncovered and undone. The modernist view regards the infantile neurosis, if acknowledged at all, as an unprivileged set of current fantasies rather than historical fact. From this modernist perspective, the transference resistance *is* the core of the analysis, to be worked through primarily because of the rigidity it imposes on the patient, not because of an important secret that it conceals.

Similarly, it is a corollary of the historical conception to view the transference neurosis as a distinct phenomenon that develops during the analysis as a consequence of the expression of resistance to drive-derived aims that are aroused toward the analyst. Those holding the modernist view, much more influenced by object-relational ideas of development, are likely to blur the idea of a specific transference neurosis in favor of viewing all transference responses as reflecting shifting self-and object representations as they are affected by the changing analytic relationship, and significant transferences may be available for interpretation very early in the analysis. There is no doubt that the modernist view also reflects the scarcity of the once classical neurotic patient.

The historical view is more likely to see the analyst as a more or less neutral screen upon which drive-derived needs will enact themselves. He is observer and interpreter, not coparticipant in the process of change. The person of the analyst is of lesser importance. Those taking the modernist view hold that the analyst is an active participant, a regulator of the analytic process, whose personal characteristics powerfully influence the content and shape of the transference behaviors, and who will himself be changed in the course of the treatment.

The historical view emphasizes the content and precision of the transference interpretation, especially as it reconstructs the past. The modernist view, at least in some hands, is likely to deemphasize reconstructive content and see the transference interpretation as one aspect of the interpersonal relationship in the present, acting as a new emotional and behavioral regulator, when past relationships have been inadequate or absent. Incidentally, this concept of a relationship as an organismic regulator is consonant with current research on grieving men and motherless mice and monkeys, in all of whom a missing relationship creates vast neuroendocrine and emotional consequences.

ORIGINS OF NEWER CONCEPTS OF
TRANSFERENCE INTERPRETATION

The increasing influence of the modernist version of transference and its interpretation represents an adaptation to several long-term philosophical, scientific, and cultural shifts we can now recognize. This changing view of transference is also the most visible emblem of the deep changes in psychoanalytic theory that are now quietly taking place, and of the theoretical pluralism that is so prevalent today (Cooper, 1985).

One of these long-term changes in the climate in which psychoanalysis dwells results from a large philosophical debate concerning the nature of history, veridicality, and narrative. Kermode (1985) has written of the change during this century in our modes of understanding and interpreting the past and the present: "Once upon a time it seemed obvious that you could best understand how things are by asking how they got to be that way. Now attention [is] directed to how things are in all their immediate complexity. There is a switch, to use the linguists' expressions, from the diachronic to the synchronic view. Diachrony, roughly speaking, studies things in their coming to be as they are; synchrony concerns itself with things as they are and ignores the question how they got that way" (p. 3). This distinction, put forth by de Saussure (1915), has achieved philosophical dominance today and is the clear source of the hermeneutic view so prevalent in psychoanalysis, proposed by Ricoeur (1970). From here it is a short distance to Schafer (1981), or Gill (1982), or Spence (1982), who in varying ways adopt the synchronic view. In this view, the analytic task is interpretation, *with* the patient, of the events of the analytic situation—usually broadly labeled transference—with a construction rather than a reconstruction of the past. In effect, while there is a past of "there and then" it is knowable only through the filter of the present, of "here and now." There is no other past than the one we construct, and there is no way of understanding the past except through its relation to the present.

I would emphasize that psychoanalysis, like history but unlike fiction, does have anchoring points. History's anchoring points are the evidences that events did occur. There was a Roman empire, it did have dates, actual persons lived and died. These "facts" place a limit on the narratives and interpretations that may seriously be entertained. Psychoanalysis is anchored in its scientific base in developmental psychology and in the biology of attachment and affects. Biology confers regularities and limits on possible histories, and our constructions of the past must accord with this scientific knowledge. Constructions of childhood that are incompatible with what we know of developmental possibilities may open our eyes to new concepts of development, but more likely they alert us to maimed childhoods that have led our patients to unusual narrative constructions in the effort to maintain self-esteem and internal coherence. A second, far less secure, anchor is the enormous amount of convergent data that accumulate during the course of an analysis, which are likely to give the analyst the impression that he is reconstructing rather than constructing the figures and the circumstances of his patient's past. While a diachronic view may no longer suffice, it may also not be fully dispensable if our patients' histories are to maintain psychoanalytic coherence, rooted in bodily experience, and the loving, hating and terrifying affects accompanying the fantastic world of infantile psychic reality. Not all analysts are yet as ready as Spence, for example, to give up all claim to the truth value or explanatory power of the understanding of the past, even if it is limited to knowing past constructions of the past. Nevertheless, the change in philosophical outlook during our century is profound and contributes to our changing view of the analytic process as exemplified in the transference and its interpretation.

Approaching the same issue from an entirely different vantage point, Emde (1981), speaking for the "baby-watchers" and discussing changing models of infancy and early development, details a second source of the major change of climate to which I refer. He writes, "The models suggest that what we reconstruct, and what may be extraordinarily helpful to the patient in 'making a biography,' may never have happened. The human being, infant and child, is understood to be fundamentally active in constructing his experience. Reality is neither given nor necessarily registered in an unmodifiable form. Perhaps it makes sense for the psychoanalyst to place renewed emphasis on recent and current experience—first, as a context for interpreting early experience and second, because it contains within it the ingredients for potential amelioration. . . . Psychoanalysts are specialists in dealing with the intrapsychic world and in particular with the dynamic unconscious. But we need to pay attention not only to the intrapsychic realm, conflict-laden and conflict-free, but also to the interpersonal realm" (pp. 217–218). He concludes, ". . . we have probably placed far too much emphasis on early experience itself as opposed to the process by which it is modified or made use of by subsequent experience" (p. 219).

This view of psychic development, discarding the timeless unconscious and so powerfully at odds with the views that were held by psychoanalysts during the time when most of our ideas of transference interpretation were formed, clearly suggests the modernist model of transference interpretation.

A change in the cultural environment of psychoanalysis provides a third source for the changing model of transference interpretation. Valenstein (personal communication) describes oscillations in psychoanalytic outlook between an emphasis on cognition at one end, and on affect at the other. One might see these as differences between old-fashioned scientific and romantic world views. Surely the period of ego psychology, perhaps reflected in the English translation of Freud, and certainly reflected in the effort to insist on the libidinal energetic point of view, represented the attempt to see psychoanalysis as Freud usually did, as an objective science in the nineteenth-century style, with hypotheses created out of naïve observation. It accorded with that view to see the transference as an objective reflection of history.

We are currently in one of our more romantic periods. It is consonant with that view to see transference as an activity—stormy, romantic, active, affective—a kind of adventure from which the two individuals emerge changed and renewed. In this romantic view, interpretations of the transference are intended to remove obstacles interfering with the heightening and intimacy of the experience, with the implication that self-knowledge and change will result from the encounter. As romantic figures, the patient and analyst set forth on a quest into the unknown, and whether or not one of them returns with a Holy Grail, they return with many new stories to tell and a new life experience—the analysis. Gardner's (1983) book, *Self Inquiry,* epitomizes this romantic view of analyst and patient as a poet-pair engaged in mutual self-inquiry. It is clear that many analysts would rather be artists than scientists. By contrast, the older, cognitive view of the transference is of an intellectual journey, emotionally loaded of course, but basically a trip back in history, seeking truth and insight.

Finally, our newer ideas of transference interpretation come from the rereading and reinterpreting of Freud that necessarily accompany the changes in outlook that I have been describing. Corresponding to the swings of analytic culture between classical and romantic, there were swings in psychoanalytic technique from Freud's actual technique, as reconstructed from his notes and the reports of his patients, to the so-called "classical" technique that held sway after Freud's death, and again to the currently changing technical scene. Lipton (1977) has insisted that in the 1940's and 1950's the so-called "classical" technique replaced Freud's own more personal and relaxed technique, probably in reaction to Alexander's suggestion of the corrective emotional experience. It was Lipton's view that the misnamed "classical" technique, in contrast to Freud's, emphasized rules for the analyst's behavior and sacrificed the purpose of the analysis. Eissler's 1953 description of analysis as an activity that ideally uses only interpretation became the paradigm for "classical" analysis. It was, Lipton says, a serious and severe distortion of the mature analytic technique developed by Freud. Freud regarded the analyst's personal behaviors, the personality of the analyst, and the living conditions of the patient as nontechnical parts of every analysis, as exemplified for Lipton in the case of the Rat Man. The so-called "classical" (and in his view non-Freudian) technique attempted to include every aspect of the analytic situation as a part of technique and led to the model of the silent, restrained psychoanalyst. Lipton's argument is persuasive.

These two different models of technique have obvious implications concerning the transference and its interpretation. Unless we believe in an extreme version of the historical model, we must expect that the silent, restrained, nonparticipatory psychoanalyst will elicit different responses from his patient than will the vivid, less-hidden, more responsive analyst. The range of personal behaviors available to the analyst before we need be concerned that the analyst is engaging in activities that are excessively self-revelatory or that force the patient into a social relationship is probably much broader than we thought a few years ago. But we also know that almost any behavior of the analyst, including restraint or silence, immediately influences the patient's responses. In these newer views of the analytic situation it is not easy to know what in the transference are iatrogenic consequences of analyst behaviors rather than intrapsychically derived patient behaviors.

It is evident today that psychoanalysts, under the sway of their theories and personalities, differ greatly concerning matters to which they are sensitive, and, of course, we can interpret only the transferences we perceive. Despite this limitation, a review of the literature reveals, along with the usual rigidities, a laudable tendency to describe one's experience as fully as possible, without heed to how it contradicts belief, often blurring over when experience and theory do not match. However, we have always been better at what we do than at what we say we do. This is exemplified in Heimann's (1956) paper. Speaking from a modified Kleinian perspective, and holding the historical theory of transference interpretation, Heimann managed 30 years ago to describe vividly and to support passionately much of what today is under discussion as the modernist version. That her positions were contradictory bothered her not at all. While many of us prefer to think we are following our theories, like all good scientists, good psychoanalysts, beginning with Freud, have always seen and responded to far more than our theories admit. When we have seen too much, we change our theories.

I have spoken of long-term trends in philosophy, child development, cultural attitudes, and psychoanalytic techniques that have influenced the development of psychoanalysis during the last half of this century. I will not discuss here how these trends, as well as our ever-increasing knowledge and our increasing distance from Freud's authority, have led to specific theoretical developments (Cooper, 1984, 1985), many of them inferred in the newer transference model. Our current pluralistic theoretical world, in which almost all analysts are working, wittingly or not, with individual amalgams of Freud's drive theory, ego psychology, interpersonal Sullivanian psychoanalysis, object-relations theory, Bowlbyan or Mahlerian attachment theory, and usually smuggled-in versions of self-psychology, lies at the base of the newer ideas and disagreements concerning transference interpretation.

Although the historical definitions of transference and transference interpretation have the merit of seeming precision and limited scope, they are based on a psychoanalytic theory that no longer stands alone and has lost ground to competing theories. Of necessity, the historical definition is being replaced, or at least subsumed, by modernist conceptions that are more attuned to the theories that abound today.

In this hodge-podge setting, it might help us both in our thinking about transference interpretations and in our understanding of the theories we hold, if we discuss a few of the sharper alternatives that are now available, indeed, confront the psychoanalyst. I shall present a brief vignette to illustrate some of the issues. It will become apparent that in my conception of the modernist view, we have not abandoned the historical perspective; rather, it has become a component part of a larger, more complex conception.

CLINICAL VIGNETTE

A woman in the second year of analysis says, "This treatment is all flattened out. It's like everything else in my life. It goes on, but nothing comes of it, certainly nothing good." Suddenly the patient begins sobbing uncontrollably and says, "You never give up on me. You keep thinking there's hope." And then, after a pause, for the first time in her adult life, she vividly and movingly recalls the detailed circumstances of her father's leaving her mother and herself when she was five years old.

Let me begin by pointing to the obvious. I made *no* interpretation and yet a long-repressed memory emerged to consciousness with full affective coloring. Why did this happen? The feeling that nothing was happening was frequent during the treatment, often felt by me as well as by the patient, as I was the target of her projections. These complaints were usually accompanied by her insisting that she could not understand why I bothered to treat her when surely I had more worthwhile patients. I had made many interpretations relating these feelings about the two of us to her feelings about a father who had abandoned her, and she had regularly responded with polite boredom.

There were a number of converging reasons for a new memory to emerge at this point in the analysis: she wanted to be sure that I would remain hopeful and not give up on her; she was giving me a gift for showing an interest in her; furthermore, my interest in her confirmed her self-pitying view that her parents had *never* been interested; she felt guilty for obstructing my efforts, etc. More than anything else, though, she was responding to mounting anxiety over an impending disruption of our appointments. Whereas in the past such anxiety regularly led to depressive anger, a sense of rejection, and impending panic, this time, in response to a new and growing conviction that I would not abandon her, this new memory allowed her to emphasize the difference between her father and me, thus partially relieving her anxiety. The earlier transference interpretations relating to her disappointing father, combined with the actual safety and reliability of the relationship with me in the analytic setting, had eventually led to a changing perception of me that could no longer be denied by the patient. This created a changing intrapsychic balance.

Under these new circumstances, inner conscience increasingly became the ally of the analyst, as the patient began to experience the growing discrepancy between her developmentally derived internalized expectations of me and the predictable actuality of that relationship. In effect, the voice of conscience, ever on the attack, found a newly accessible failing and said, "Feel guilty for not letting him help you and for insisting on continuing your masochistic disappointments." The new memory enabled her to make a new compromise: "Even though I admit that my analyst is different from my father, my father *was* just as bad as I claimed, and I'll now prove it. I also feel safe enough now to revive those old and terrible memories." Later in the treatment, she will even remember good times with her father.

In one important aspect, the analytic situation acts as a Proustian madeleine. It awakens sweet resonances of the sense of childhood security and safety, whether actual or fantasied, and thus allows the release of memories, even painful memories. This portion of the transference is usually interpretable only in retrospect.

At the risk of further complicating this little vignette, I will try to summarize what I have described. A recovered memory, an important event marking a change in the analytic atmosphere, was the result of a number of interacting factors. (1) There was a background of specific old-fashioned transference interpretations—in effect, "you think I am your father, but I am not." Many of these interpretations related to the missing memories. (2) These interpretations were made in the here-and-now—when the patient felt angry and rejected, I talked about how she was actually making a statement about me —that I am, in her opinion, just like her father, and I encouraged her to talk about how I was like him, or why she was now frightened of me or angry at me. (3) While the analyst was, of course, often the object of projections of representations of the past, I played an equally important role as the necessary background of safety for the patient's experimentation with new self- and object representations. Projections onto the analyst may occur during this experimentation, but those experiments are going on everywhere in the patient's life, and the analyst may not always be the center of interest. (4) A change in intrapsychic balance occurred, with the need for new compromises, because of increasing unconscious cognitive dissonance and new alignments of guilty feeling. A mismatch of internal representations and new perceptions is never tolerable, and in neurosis we rearrange our perceptions to suit our rigidly held internal expectations. The persistence, constancy, and facilitating qualities of the analytic environment, including the transference interpretations, provide not only a background of safety, but lead to a new psychic reality of greater tolerance for shameful and frightening unconscious fantasies. Paradoxically, they also create increasing guilt over maintaining old grievances in a new environment. (5) This led to a need for a new adaptation to an old danger—the impending disruption of the sessions—because the old adaptation had become too conflictual. Inner conscience would no longer permit simple enactments of the old fantasy of abandonment. (6) Finally, the outcome of all these ingredients was the need for a new intrapsychic compromise formation. To achieve this, a memory was recaptured (incidentally, confirmed by her mother). The memory, whether created or recaptured, was important in helping the patient to organize a new transference relationship with the analyst, more clearly distinguishing him from the damaging remembered father, and in helping her to restore a more satisfactory arrangement with her altered superego. She could begin to accept her anger at the father of childhood without quite so much need to justify and enact it in the present.

The historical view of the transference interpretation—the analyst as abandoning father—has played a part in this transference reorganization, but only one part. The modernist version of the transference interpretations urges us toward a richer and more inclusive understanding of the transference events. The patient is changing, indeed, in response to the analyst's transference interpretations; but she is changing in the course of a *relationship* with the analyst. In this relationship, transference interpretation has played a vital role not only in helping her to gain insight, but also in helping her to regulate her feelings and her relationship with me, as well as mine with her. Her expectations of me have changed. We have attained better empathic contact.

It is here that what I referred to earlier as the "romantic" and intersubjective emphasis of the modernist view becomes apparent, in the effort of two people to connect affectively.

When we speak of transference interpretations, it is probably wise to include also those that are silent—the many interpretations we entertain but never utter to the patient. These silent transference interpretations—hypotheses about what is happening in the analysis—are crucial for the analyst's conduct of the treatment, influencing the way he listens and intervenes, and leading to many subsidiary interpretations. These unspoken interpretations deserve to be considered in any narrative of the analytic process, even though they may achieve utterance only later in the analysis. Their absence is at least one reason why recorded analyses often sound stilted.

The modernist view also stresses the open-endedness of the analytic situation. The new experiences of the interpretations and the facilitating environment of the analytic setting force significant alterations of internal representations, structures, and conflicts. This changing intrapsychic balance leads not only to alterations in the transference, but, far more important from the patient's point of view, it leads to changes in extratransference relationships as well. These changes outside the analysis may then facilitate new experiences in the analysis. In fact, one of the significant elements in the background of our vignette was the patient's greatly improved relationship with her husband. Psychoanalysis is not a closed system of an intrapsychic world impinging on a single target.

DISCUSSION

I would like to stress two of the points that have already been implied in what has been said. The first pertains to the relative roles of intrapsychic and interpersonal perspectives. Since Freud's discovery of psychic reality, it has been part of the historical conception to focus primarily on the intrapsychic life of the patient, the psyche being conceived largely as driven toward objects, rather than formed and constantly reforming in relation to objects. Analysts holding this view (Curtis, 1980) of course acknowledge the interpersonal aspect, but they are likely to see it as a part of the surround rather than a part of the core of analytic work. They believe that the intrapsychic realm is the only one to which analytic expertise applies, and that any emphasis on the interpersonal is liable to lead to dilution of analytic work, excessive intrusion of the analyst into the patient's life, or a shallow corrective emotional experience.

All these dangers are real, and have occurred in the history of psychoanalysis, but I believe, with Gill and Emde recently and Sullivan long ago, that we cannot fully interpret transference resistances without acknowledging their interpersonal quality. There has been a mistaken tendency to equate psychic reality with the intrapsychic, and to neglect the contribution of interpersonal interaction to the creation of new psychic reality.

Freud (1905), in the postscript to the Dora case, made this point when he wrote, "I ought to have listened to the warning myself. 'Now,' I ought to have said to her, 'it is from Herr K. that you have made a transference on to me. Have you noticed anything that leads you to suspect me of evil intentions similar (whether openly or in some sublimated form) to Herr K.'s? Or have you been struck by anything about me or got to know anything about me which has caught your fancy, as happened previously with Herr K.?' Her attention would then have been turned to some detail in our relations, or in my person or circumstances, behind which there lay concealed something analogous but immeasurably more important concerning Herr K." (p. 118). While Freud was interested in the hidden motive, he recognized that the route to it was through the interpersonal connection. Although he spoke of the transference from Herr K. onto himself, he implied that it could not have occurred unless the patient had seen something about him that made such a concordance of perception possible. Schwaber (1983) has emphasized this point. Of course, the patient needs to match the interpersonal world to his intrapsychic world, and to achieve this he or she uses all available data, no matter how one-sidedly perceived—the analyst's silences or his talkativeness, attitudes, tastes in art, manner of dress, speech habits, etc. The analyst who cannot tolerate this close scrutiny himself and denies the veracity of his foibles that are included in the patient's transference is unable fully to interpret the transference and is encouraging deceit in the analytic relationship. At the same time, the analyst must be able to discover how his foibles and failures are being used in the service of the patient's neurosis, as well as to distinguish the *mis*perceptions that patients create to suit their needs. Otherwise, indeed, the patient's neurotic defenses are strengthened.

This touches on the issue of "distortion" in the patient's communications to the analyst. Schwaber (1983) and Gill (1982), from somewhat different perspectives, have both suggested that the analyst is in no better position to know the patient's "truth" or the correctness of his perceptions than is the patient. They maintain that both parties' views of the transference are valid, and it is a failure of logic to think of transference interpretations as "correcting" distortions. Schafer (1985) criticizes Gill's view as removing the gradients of expertise, of need for help, of closeness to conflict, etc., that characterize the different responsibilities of therapist and patient in the analytic situation. I would go further and suggest that the concept of defense, central to the idea of transference resistance, carries with it the clear implication that the patient, in the neurotic areas of his psychic functioning, has to some degree unconsciously constricted, distorted, and rigidified his perceptual, affective, and cognitive capacities. We know that all historians are biased, and we have every reason to be alert to the unconscious sources of bias in the histories constructed by our patients.

It behooves the analyst to know not only the content of his patient's narrative, but the needs that compel its construction, the elements that must be a part of any human history that are missing in the particular history, and the effect of the shared experience of analyst and patient in creating new histories, often quite different from each of them. When the patient in our vignette said everything is flattened out, it would not be unreasonable for the analyst to suspect that exactly the opposite was the case. The purpose of the analyst's alertness to distortion is not to correct his patient, but to allow him to understand the needs that are dictating the patient's construction.

I shall give another vignette to illustrate my view of the problem. A woman in her last months of analysis said, "I never wanted to say thank you to my mother. That would have meant to be chained to her. . . . It's terrible, but to feel free I had never to be spontaneous with my mother." I said, "It's been very difficult for you here to feel that you could be entirely spontaneous and trust me not to make you feel guilty or dependent." The patient became silent for a time and went on, "It makes me very angry to hear you say that I didn't trust you. It isn't that I didn't trust you, it was that whatever you said invoked in me a reaction like my mother had said it. As a child I was always uniform, balanced, defended. If I thought I mistrusted you how could I keep coming here? If I kissed my mother goodbye before going to school and at the same time thought that I wanted her to be dead, I'd be terribly guilty. It's hard to accept that you could allow me to have both feelings toward you."

The patient felt accused over the matter of trust, explaining that it had nothing to do with the analyst, but was a reaction to her mother. She sharply differentiated (some would say split) between the analyst she trusts enough to keep coming, and the analyst-mother whom she mistrusts. One of the aims

of interpretation is to develop the capacity to bring these different representations closer together with less anxiety and guilt.

This dialogue had been preceded by years of work on both her feelings
about the analyst and about her mother. Initially, her mother was simply
absent from her childhood description, dismissed as a bland, not very intelligent woman, who played no part in her upbringing; in fact, the patient from
earliest years recalled that she was the one who took care of her incompetent
mother, and she had no memories of ever being cared for. From the analyst's
perspective, it is essential both to understand what the patient believes and to
hypothesize about how that belief came about. We know that childhood
could not have been as the patient recalled it; her mother did care for her as a
little girl, even though the patient is also telling us that she felt inadequately
cared for. It wounds her narcissism to have to admit that she was not always
the independent oedipal victor she later became. Distortions of history have
been elaborated, and the analyst will try to understand the psychological
circumstances, intrapsychic and interpersonal, that led this woman to erase
any evidences of infantile helplessness, to eradicate her mother's essential
caretaking, and to adopt her thinly disguised hostile attitude toward a fantasied helpless mother. The analytic aim is not to contradict the patient's view;
rather it is to be alert to predictable reactions that will arise in the transference
with the patient who holds such beliefs (e.g., her fear of attachment and
dependency, her mistrust of the analyst's capacity to tolerate her murderous
competitiveness) and to be ready to assist the patient in her struggle to come
to grips with internalized versions of her mother and herself that she has not
been able to entertain consciously. For example, during years of analysis,
this woman insisted that everything I did was guided entirely by my need to
obey the rules of my profession, and had nothing to do with her personally.
She also maintained she did not in any way know me or anything about me.
These beliefs can be clearly regarded as transference distortions by means of
which the patient attempted to maintain her original repression of both her
attachment to her deeply depressed and disappointing mother, and of her
mother's interest in her child, however faulty that interest was. In fact, when
she was ready to know what she knew, she knew an enormous amount, both
about me and about her mother. Until then, as far as she was concerned, it
was an honest statement. The concept of distortion neither demeans the
patient nor implies a single correct truth.

CONCLUSION

The transference and its interpretation are at the center of all considerations of analytic theory and technique. Freud, throughout his life, seemed astonished by the power of transference, and we are no less so. The concept was relatively simple when we understood persons as in the grip of their drives, and the purpose of the analysis was the expansion of consciousness. Today, the idea of transference has become so complex that we are no longer sure what in the analysis is not transference, and if it is not, what it is. Our loss of innocence is part of a large change in world view concerning history and truth. Major philosophical, scientific, and cultural movements, as well as our own researches, have led to a new and desirable situation of theoretical pluralism in psychoanalysis, although at the price of the loss of a great overarching theory. As a result, our once straightforward historical understanding of transference interpretation has yielded to a more polymorphous and confusing, but more interesting modernist view. This modernist view has raised our awareness of elements of the transference that were previously neglected, and it has opened the way for experimentation and reconsideration of many old problems.

REFERENCES

Breuer, J. & Freud, S. (1893–1905). Studies on hysteria. *Standard Edition,* 2.
Cooper, A. M. (1984). Psychoanalytic inquiry and new knowledge. In *Reflections on Self Psychology,* ed. J. D. Lichtenberg & S. Kaplan. Hillsdale, N.J.: Analytic Press, pp. 19–34.
——— (1985). Psychoanalysis at one hundred: beginnings of maturity. *J. Amer. Psychoanal. Assn.,* 32:245–267.
Curtis, H. C. (1980). The concept of therapeutic alliance: implications for the "widening scope." In *Psychoanalytic Explorations of Technique,* ed. H. Blum. New York: International Universities Press, 1980, pp. 159–192.
Eissler, K. R. (1953). The effect of the structure of the ego on psychoanalytic technique. *J. Amer. Psychoanal. Assn.,* 1:104–143.
Emde, R. (1981). Changing models of infancy and the nature of early development: remodeling the foundation. *J. Amer. Psychoanal. Assn.,* 29:179–220.
Freud, S. (1905). Fragment of an analysis of a case of hysteria. *Standard Edition,* 7.
——— (1940). An outline of psycho-analysis. *Standard Edition,* 23.
Gardner, R. M. (1983). *Self Inquiry.* New York: Little, Brown.
Gill, M. (1982). *Analysis of Transference. Vol. 1, Theory and Technique. Psychol. Issues,* Monogr. 53. New York: International Universities Press.
Heimann, P. (1956). Dynamics of transference interpretation. *Int. J. Psychoanal.,* 37:303–310.
Kermode, F. (1985). Freud and interpretation. *Int. Rev. Psychoanal.,* 12:3–12.
Laplanche, J. & Pontalis, J.-B. (1973). *The Language of Psychoanalysis.* New York: Norton.

Lipton, S. (1977). The advantages of Freud's technique as shown in his analysis of the Rat Man. *Int. J. Psychoanal.*, 58:255–274.

Ricoeur, P. (1970). *Freud and Philosophy, an Essay on Interpretation.* New Haven: Yale University Press.

Sandler, J. (1983). Reflections on some relations between psychoanalytic concept and psychoanalytic practice. *Int. J. Psychoanal.*, 64:1–11.

Saussure, F. De (1915). *Course in General Linguistics*, trans. W. Baskin. London: Collins, 1974.

Schafer, R. (1981). *Narrative Actions in Psychoanalysis.* Worcester, Mass.: Clark University Press.

————— (1985). Wild analysis. *J. Amer. Psychoanal. Assn.*, 33:275–299.

Schwaber, E. (1983). Psychoanalytic listening and psychic reality. *Int. Rev. Psychoanal.*, 10:379–392.

Spence, D. P. (1982). *Narrative Truth and Historical Truth.* New York: Norton.

Name Index

Italic numbers indicate references.

Abraham, K., 21, 191, 196, 202, 213, *218,*
219, 278
Aichhorn, A., 5, 94–109, 468, 469, *479*
Alexander, F., 6, *13,* 56, 145, *149,* 195,
197, *219,* 477, *479*
Andrade, E., 339, *360*
Arlow, J. A., 172, *186*

Balint, M., 142, *148,* 295, *326*
Benedek, T., *326*
Bergler, E., *329*
Bergman, A., 492, *510*
Bernfeld, S., 62
Bernheim, H., 189, 190, 202, 215, 218
Bibring, E., 137, *148,* 172, *186,* 316, 317,
329
Bibring-Lehner, G., 5, 6, 115–22
Bion, W. R., 508, *509*
Bird, B., 10, 331–60, *360,* 389, *400,* 438,
452
Blake, W., 284
Bleuler, E., 33
Blum, H. P., 405, *421*
Bowlby, J., 296, *326, 327*
Boyer, L. B., 447, *452*
Brenner, C., 7, 172–86, *186,* 383, *400,*
440, 442, *452*
Breuer, J., *220,* 332, *361,* 511 *527*
Brill, A. A., *278*
Bullard, D. M., *278*

Charcot, J.-M., 215
Cobliner, W. G., 285, *329*
Cooper, A. M., 13, 511–27, *527*
Curtis, H. C., 383, *400,* 523, *527*

Dalbiez, R., 193, *219*
Deutsch, H., *170*
Diethelm, O., *278*

Eissler, K. R., 478, *479, 527*
Ekstein, R., 435, *452*
Eliot, T. S., 415, *421*
Emde, R., 517, *527*
Erikson, E. H., 383, *400,* 492, *509*

Fairbairn, W. R. D., 295, *327, 329,* 492,
509
Federn, P., 226, 478, *479*
Fenichel, O., 139, *148,* 153, 166, 169, *170,*
188, 195, 196, 205, 212, *218,* 267, *278,*
317, *329,* 436, 445, *452*
Ferenczi, S., 3, 15–26, 33, 68, 72, 74, *170,*
190, 195, 201, 202, 203, 205, *218,* 219,
235, 261, 262, 264, *266,* 267, *278,* 287,
327, 337, 351, 354
Fingarette, H., 420, *421*
Fisher, C., *327*
French, T. M., *13, 219,* 477, *479*
Freud, A., 5–6, 110–14, 137, *148,* 195,
196, 201, *219,* 240, 247, *327,* 377, *380,*
435, 441, 445, 450, 451, *453,* 468, *479*
Freud, S., 1, 3–4, 9, *13,* 15–16, 17, 18,
20, 21, 22, 25, 26, 28–47, 50, 52, 54,
55, 72, 80, 84–85, 91–92, 143, *148,* 151,
153, 164, 166, 168, *170,* 185, *186,* 189,
190, 191, 192, 195, 196, 197, 198, 201,
202, 208, 210, 213, 215, *218,* 219, *220,*
223, 226, 229, 231, 232, 233, *235,* 236,
239, 240, 241, *245,* 246, 252, 253, 260,
261, 262, *266,* 267, *278,* 281, 291, 300,
302, 303, 307, 312, *327, 329,* 332, 333,
335, 336, 337, 338, 340, 351, 354, 357,
360, 361, 362, 365, 366, 367, 368, 370,
371, 372, 375, *380,* 382, 387, 388, 389,
392, 395, 396, *400,* 402, 403, 404, 412,
416, *421,* 424, 426, 429, 430, *433,* 472,
479, 494, *509,* 511, 512, 513, 524, *527*
Friedman, L., 182, *186*

Subject Index

Abreaction, in psychoanalysis, 72–73
Acting out, transference and, 91, 113, 195, 196, 229, 440
Affective suggestion, 192
Aggression, transference interpretation of, 316–17
Alter-ego transference. *See* Mirror transference
Ambivalence, of neurotics, 34
"Analysis Terminable and Interminable" (Freud), 143, 312, 351, 354, 388, 395
Analyst
 arousal of patient by, 397–98
 as auxiliary superego, 56, 59–61, 64–65, 203
 changing analysts, 116, 117–18, 122, 156
 characteristics of, and transference, 18–19
 empathetic approach, 397
 Freud's concept of, 167–68
 frustration/gratification by, 169, 173
 functions of, 126, 391–92
 humanness in therapy, 169, 174, 175, 185
 improvement of patient and, 24–25
 induction of transference neurosis, 167
 methods of, 166–68
 in patient's dreams, 17–18
 personality and transference, 504
 physical proximity and, 313
 presence of, and transference, 482–85
 representation of, 18
 rigidity of, 175, 176
 rule of abstinence, 168, 183
 safeguarding transference, 168
 sex of, and transference, 6, 19
 varieties of transference, 19–20, 53
 views of, 169
 in working alliance, 166–69
Analytic situation, working alliance and, 165–66
Anxiety
 depressive, 238
 persecutory, 236–37
Anxiety neurosis, 20
Authority figures, transference and, 97

Auto-eroticism, in infant, 239–40
Autosuggestion, 190, 191

Borderline personalities, 469, 493, 497
Brief psychotherapy, 129–30, 200

Character neurosis, 428
Character-traits, formation of, 229–30
Child rearing, neurosis and, 427
Children
 induction of submissiveness in, 262–63
 interpretation and, 200
 prerequisites to transference development, 201
 suggestibility of, 263–64
 superego of, 58
 See also Infant
Classical analytic patient, 162–64
Complementary identifications, in countertransference, 505–6
Confidentiality, analysis and, 132–33
Consciousness, reality testing and, 388
Countertransference, 94, 147–48, 358–59, 386, 445, 472
 case examples, 506–7
 complementary identification in, 505–6
 global concept of, 505
 mechanisms in, 212
 object relations view, 505–9
 projections of patient and, 506, 522
 requirements of analyst, 507–9
"Current Concepts of Transference" (Zetzel), 150

Day residue, 394
Death instinct, 147, 195, 236
 destructive tendencies and, 349
Deep interpretation, 70–71, 139
Defense transference, 111, 363
Delinquent child
 actions of analyst vs. educator, 97–98
 attitude toward authority and, 97
 basis for, 96
 categories of delinquents, 96–97

About the Editor

AARON H. ESMAN, M.D., is an internationally known psychoanalyst and psychiatrist with a long career as a clinician and a teacher. After many years as chief psychiatrist and director of training at the Jewish Board of Family and Children's Services in New York, he is now professor of clinical psychiatry and director of adolescent services at the New York Hospital–Cornell Medical Center. He is also a member of the faculty of the New York Psychoanalytic Institute.